A FIRST LOOK AT
COMMUNICATION
THEORY

A FIRST LOOK AT
COMMUNICATION
THEORY

FOURTH EDITION

EM GRIFFIN
Wheaton College

Special Consultant: Glen McClish
San Diego State University

Boston Burr Ridge, IL Dubuque, IA Madison, WI New York San Francisco St. Louis
Bangkok Bogotá Caracas Lisbon London Madrid
Mexico City Milan New Delhi Seoul Singapore Sydney Taipei Toronto

ACI -9004

McGraw-Hill Higher Education

A Division of The **McGraw-Hill** *Companies*

Editorial director: *Phillip A. Butcher*
Sponsoring editor: *Marjorie Byers*
Developmental editor: *Jennie Katsaros*
Marketing manager: *Kelly M. May*
Senior project manager: *Gladys True*
Senior production supervisor: *Heather D. Burbridge*
Freelance design coordinator: *Mary Christianson*
Photo research coordinator: *Sharon Miller*
Supplement coordinator: *Craig Leonard*
Compositor: *ElectraGraphics, Inc.*
Typeface: *10/12 Palatino*
Printer: *Quebecor Printing Book Group/Fairfield*

Library of Congress Cataloging-in-Publication Data

Griffin, Emory A.
  A first look at communication theory / Em Griffin; special
consultant, Glen McClish.
    p.   cm.
  Includes bibliographical references (p.) and index.
  ISBN 0-07-229153-2
  1. Communication—Philosophy.   I. McClish, Glen Arthur.
II. Title.
P90.G725   2000
303.2'01—dc21   99–27152
                                      CIP

http://www.mhhe.com

ABOUT THE AUTHOR

Em Griffin is Professor of Communication at Wheaton College in Illinois, where he has taught for the past twenty-nine years and has been chosen Teacher of the Year. He received his bachelor's degree in political science from the University of Michigan, and his M.A. and Ph.D. in Communication from Northwestern University. His research interest centers on the development of close friendships.

Professor Griffin is the author of three applied communication books: *The Mind Changers* analyzes practical techniques of persuasion; *Getting Together* offers research-based suggestions for effective group leadership; and *Making Friends* describes the way that quality interpersonal communication can build close relationships. He also speaks and leads workshops on these topics in the United States, Singapore, and the Philippines. Professor Griffin's wife, Jean, is an artist. They have two married, adult children, Jim and Sharon, and two grandchildren, Alison and Kyle.

PREFACE FOR INSTRUCTORS

A First Look is written for students who have no background in communication theory. It's designed for undergraduates enrolled in entry-level courses. In the past, many departments reserved systematic coverage of communication theory for a capstone course or senior seminar, so communication theory texts were addressed to a sophisticated audience. Now the trend in the field is to offer a broad introduction to theory relatively early in a student's program. *A First Look* is written for that beginning student.

Balance as a Guide in Theory Selection   The aim of this book is to present thirty-two specific theories in a way that makes them both interesting and understandable. By the time readers complete the book they should have a working knowledge of theories that explain a wide range of communication phenomena. My ultimate goal is to help students see the relationship between different theoretical positions, and the final chapter offers an integrative synthesis. But before students can integrate the leading theoretical ideas in our field, they need to have a clear understanding of what the theories are. The bulk of the book provides that raw material.

With the help of journal and yearbook editors, and feedback from over 100 communication theory professors, I've selected a wide range of theories that reflect this diversity within the discipline. Some theories are proven candidates for a Communication Theory Hall of Fame. For example, Aristotle's analysis of logical, emotional, and ethical appeals continues to set the agenda for many public-speaking courses. Mead's symbolic interactionism is formative for interpretive theorists who are dealing with language, thought, self-concept, or the effect of society upon the individual. The axioms of Watzlawick's interactional view continue to be debated by interpersonal scholars, and no student of mediated communication should be ignorant of McLuhan's radical claim of technological determinism. I include these theories for their historical and foundational significance.

It would be shortsighted, however, to limit the selection to the classics of communication. Some of the discipline's most creative approaches have only recently emerged. For example, Leslie Baxter and Barbara Montgomery's theory of relational dialectics offers insight into the ongoing tensions inherent in personal relationships. Byron Reeves and Clifford Nass' bold media equation is just beginning to be seriously discussed within the communication discipline. And Gerry Philipsen's speech codes theory upgrades the ethnography of communication from a methodology to a theory that can be used to explain, predict, and control discourse about discourse. I've also included cutting-edge theories generated by communication scholars who currently test and hone their ideas at conventions, workshops, and seminars sponsored by ICA, NCA, and other communication associations.

Organizational Plan of the Book   Each chapter introduces a single theory in about ten pages. I've found that most undergraduates think in terms of discrete packets of information, so the coverage-in-depth approach gives them a chance to focus their thoughts while reading a single assignment. In this way, students can gain a true understanding of important theories rather than acquire only a vague familiarity with a confusing jumble of related ideas. The one-chapter–one-theory arrangement also gives teachers the opportunity to drop theories or rearrange the order of presentation without tearing apart the fabric of the text.

The opening chapter lays the groundwork for understanding the difference between objective and interpretive theories. Chapter 2 presents two sets of criteria for determining a good theory. I apply these standards to Bormann's symbolic convergence theory because he has dual scientific and rhetorical agendas. Then in the successive thirty-one self-contained chapters, I present the other theories featured in the book. Each theory is discussed within the context of a communication topic: interpersonal messages, cognitive processing, relationship development, relationship maintenance, influence, group decision making, organizational communication, public rhetoric, media and culture, media effects, intercultural communication, gender and communication. These communication context sections usually contain two or three theories. Each section has a brief introduction that outlines the crucial issues that the theorists address and places the subsequent chapters within that context. The placement of theories in familiar categories helps students recognize that theories are answers to questions they've been asking all along. The final chapter cuts across these contextual categories and integrates theories by the choices and commitments their authors have made.

Because all theory and practice have value implications, I've interspersed eleven one- to two-page Ethical Reflections throughout the text. Consistent with the focus of this text, each ethical principle is the central tenet of a specific ethical theory. I also raise ethical questions throughout the text. Other disciplines may ignore these thorny issues, but to discuss communication as a process that is untouched by questions of good and bad, right and wrong, virtue and vice would be to disregard an ongoing concern in our field.

Features of Each Chapter   Most people think in pictures. Students will have a rough time understanding a theory unless they apply its explanations and interpretations to concrete situations. The typical chapter uses an extended example to illustrate the "truth" a theory proposes. I encourage readers to try out ideas by visualizing a first meeting of freshman roommates, responding to conflict in a dysfunctional family, trying to persuade other students to support a zero tolerance policy on driving after drinking, considering whether they might really treat their computer as if it were another person, and many more. I also use the films *Nell, Roger & Me, When Harry Met Sally, Children of a Lesser God,* and Toni Morrison's book *Beloved* to illustrate principles of the theories. Finally, I bring my own life to the pages with extended examples from my role as a voluntary mediator, my service on the international board of a third-world development organization, and my membership on a search committee with the responsibility of selecting new faculty members for our college communication department. The case study in each chapter follows the pedagogical principle of explaining what students don't yet know in terms of ideas and images already within their experience.

Some theories are tightly linked with an extensive research project. For example, cultivation theory is supported by Gerbner's repeated surveys of societal fear cultivated by violence on television. Philipsen's speech codes theory began with a three-year ethnographic study of what it means to speak like a man in Teamsterville. And Delia's constructivist research continues to be dependent on Crockett's Role Category Questionnaire. When such exemplars exist, I describe the research in detail so that students can learn from and appreciate the benefits of grounding theory in systematic observation. Thus, readers of *A First Look* are led through a variety of research designs and data analyses.

Students will encounter the names of Baxter, Berger, Burke, Burgoon, Deetz, Fisher, Gudykunst, Kramarae, Pacanowsky, Pearce, Philipsen, Ting-Toomey, Wood, and many others in later communication courses. I therefore make a concerted effort to link theory and theorist. By pairing a particular theory with its originator, I try to promote both recall and respect for a given scholar's effort.

The text of each chapter concludes with a section that critiques the theory. This represents a hard look at the ideas presented in light of the criteria for a good theory outlined in Chapter 2. I usually provide a brief summary of the theory's strengths and then turn to the weaknesses, unanswered questions, and possible errors that still remain. I try to stimulate a "That makes sense, and yet I wonder . . . " response among students.

I include a short list of thought questions after the text of each chapter. Labeled "Questions to Sharpen Your Focus," these probes encourage students to make connections between ideas in the chapter and also to apply the theory to their everyday communication experience. The words printed in italics also remind students of the key terms of a given theory.

Every chapter ends with a short list of annotated readings entitled "A Second Look." The heading refers to resources for students who are interested in a theory and want to go further than a ten-page introduction allows. The top item is the resource I recommend as the starting point for further study. The other listings identify places to look for material about each of the major issues raised in the chapter. The format is designed to offer practical encouragement and guidance for further study without overwhelming the novice with multiple citations. The sources of quotations and citations of evidence are listed in a "Notes" section at the end of the book.

I believe you and your students will get a good chuckle out of the cartoons I've selected, but their main function is to illustrate significant points in the text. I committed to use "Calvin and Hobbes," "The Far Side," "Dilbert," "Cathy," and quality art from the pages of *The New Yorker* and *Punch* magazines. Perceptive cartoonists are modern-day prophets—their humor serves the educational process well when it slips through mental barriers or attitudinal defenses that didactic prose can't penetrate.

While no author considers his or her style ponderous or dull, I believe I've presented the theories in a clear and lively fashion. Accuracy alone does not communicate. I've tried to remain faithful to the vocabulary each theorist uses so that the student can consider the theory in the author's own terms, but I also translate technical language into more familiar words. Students and reviewers cite readability and interest as particular strengths of the text. I encourage you to sample a chapter dealing with a theory you regard as difficult so that you can decide for yourself.

New Features in the Fourth Edition   Although I've retained the features that students appreciated in earlier editions of the text—writing style, short chapters, extended examples, cartoons—I've made several changes in response to suggestions culled from those who teach communication theory. There was general agreement that the number of theories should not increase, that theories dropped should be ones students already know or will get in other courses, and that new chapters should introduce theories constructed by scholars within the communication discipline. So I've dropped five theories and added the following four:

David Buller and Judee Burgoon's interpersonal deception theory

Scott Poole's adaptive structuration theory

Byron Reeves and Clifford Nass' media equation

Sandra Harding and Julia Wood's standpoint theory

Perhaps less obvious to someone merely browsing through the table of contents, I've significantly revised and updated the seven chapters that present coordinated management of meaning, uncertainty reduction, the interactional view, elaboration likelihood model, semiotics, cultural studies, agenda-setting, and face-negotiation. In almost all of the other chapters, I've added a new section, a current example, or more recent citations in the Second Look annotated bibliography.

If you are disappointed that I no longer include a theory that is one of your favorites, you can find that chapter in the archives section of the web site I've created for teachers and students who use the book:

www.afirstlook.com

You may continue to assign it for your class, and while at the site, you and your students might browse through a series of aids that support the text and can enrich your course.

From my perspective, the most significant change in the book is the new introductory chapter, "Mapping the Territory," which introduces seven traditions within the field of communication theory. Based on the overall conception of Robert Craig, University of Colorado communication professor and the first editor of *Communication Theory*, the chapter locates seven distinct theoretical traditions within our discipline. I then offer a definition of communication that captures the practical focus of that tradition, and present an example of an early scholar who operated from that theoretical stance. At the end of the chapter I present a map showing the relationship between the seven traditions on an objective-interpretive continuum, an epistemological distinction I now carry throughout the book.

As for students, perhaps the new feature they will appreciate most is the Glossary found in Appendix A. I've made an effort to define terms in a way consistent with how they are used in the text. When a term is associated with a particular theory, that linkage is spelled out.

Finally, those who have used previous editions of the text will note that I've folded the verbal and nonverbal message sections into the rest of the book. Information theory and meaning of meaning are now presented as pioneer work within two distinct traditions in the "Mapping the Territory" chapter. Symbolic interactionism and coordinated management of meaning are now more appropriately slotted as theories of interpersonal messages. They are joined by the expectancy violations model, a theory that is no longer restricted to nonverbal behavior. And a rewritten semiotics chapter is now located in the media and culture section, a place where it probably should have been from the start. With the exception of Chapters 1–3 and the final integrative chapter, the whole book is now organized around contexts in which given theories are typically applied.

Acknowledgments Glen McClish, now Chair of the Department of Rhetoric and Writing Studies at San Diego State University, is the person who has provided the greatest scholarly wisdom, suggested revisions, editorial assistance, cartoon ideas, and motivational encouragement for this edition of *A First Look*. Teachers who are familiar with his instructor's manual for the 3rd edition will understand just how fortunate I am to have his almost daily assistance. Glen's notes on each theory prepared them to walk into the classroom with far more understanding than they would have had otherwise. He has served me the same way, and fortunately for all of us, has again written the instructors manual that accompanies this 4th edition. Glen was instrumental in the revision of the chapter on Barthes' semiotics, was highly involved in the rest of the media and culture section, and has made significant contributions to the public rhetoric and integrative section as well. He offered insightful critiques and edits for my treatment of every other theory in the book. As stated on the title page, he is indeed a very special consultant.

I am pleased to acknowledge the wisdom and counsel of many other generous people who have helped me complete this project. I'm particularly grateful for ten advisors and friends who repeatedly answered questions, offered suggestions, combed through drafts of chapters, and encouraged me when I got bogged down. They are:

Glenn Sparks, Purdue University, who contributed the Coke commercial analysis for the opening chapter, is my ongoing advisor for media effects, and is a close friend.

Marty Medhurst, Texas A & M, who also wrote a Coke commercial critique for Chapter 1 and has continually enriched my understanding of rhetoric.

Bob Craig, University of Colorado, who even though he knew my use of his "Communication Theory as a Field" would greatly truncate his sophisticated analysis, graciously gave me access to his work prior to publication and spent hours discussing definitions of communication, characteristics of traditions, and where different theories might fit.

Larry Frey, Loyola University of Chicago, who had a strong influence on the introductory framework in Chapters 1 and 2 and on the group decision-making section.

Linda Putnam, Texas A & M, who graciously invested many hours at the start of this project so that I might gain an understanding of organizational communication.

Cliff Christians, University of Illinois, who over two decades has helped me appreciate the breadth and depth of communication ethics.

Brant Burleson, Purdue University, who led me through a vast quantity of constructivist research and made me aware of cutting-edge developments in our field.

Ron Adler, Santa Barbara City College, whose fingerprints are all over the symbolic interaction chapter, and who graciously regards me as a kindred spirit in our love of movies and our approach to writing.

James Anderson, University of Utah, who helped me construct and apply the objective-interpretive continuum that is the backbone of the integrative chapters.

Chris Pieper, Communications Director for the Center for Public Policy Priorities in Austin, Texas, who was instrumental in my understanding and chapter revision of Hall's cultural studies.

The unselfish assistance of these ten scholars gives fresh meaning to the term collegiality. If any of the portions of the text referred to above are less than helpful or in error, it's undoubtedly because I didn't sufficiently heed the advice and counsel of these tremendously forthcoming colleagues.

Since the inception of *A First Look*, McGraw-Hill has enlisted the aid of communication scholars to review each edition of the text. The extensive and helpful comments of six reviewers of the 3rd edition provided excellent suggestions on how to proceed in this current effort. I am thankful to Raymond Buchanan, Pepperdine University; Holly Bognar, University of Akron; Marshall Scott Poole, Texas A&M University; Francine Marrus, Clemson University; Lenore Langsdorf, Southern Illinois University, Carbondale; and Linda Lederman, Rutgers University.

I asked research assistant Paige Garber to conduct forty phone interviews with communication theory instructors who were "field testing" the 3rd edition in their classes. I am grateful to the following teachers who volunteered their time and candid assessments to ensure that this edition would be responsive to instructor needs: Sam Andrews, Texas Southern University; Chuck Aust, Kennesaw State University; Virginia Bachelor, SUNY Brockport; Catherine Becker, Radford University; Judy Bowker, Oregon State University; Katherine Carter, University of Nebraska; Susan Collie, Winona State University; Cecil Cramer, Liberty Baptist College; Jim Detwiler, Cornerstone College; Randy Dillon, Southwest Missouri State University; Robert Dawson, DePauw University; Gene Ellis, Elizabethtown College; Jane Elmes-Crahall, Wilkes University; Kory Floyd, University of Arizona; Brian Furio, York College; Ed Funkhauser, North Carolina State University; Dennis Grady, Eastern Michigan University; Wade Kenny, University of Dayton; Kerry Kuhlman, Geneva College; Charles Lester, Palm Beach Atlantic College; Russell Lowery-Hart, St. Edwards University; John Ludlum, Otterbein College; Debra Mazloff, University of St. Thomas; Darrell Mullins, Salisbury State University; Charles Petri, SUNY Buffalo; Linda Pledger, University of Arkansas, Little Rock; Fred Powell, SUNY Brockport; Linnea Ratcliff, Truman State University; Diana Rehlim, St. John's University; David Robinson, Youngstown State University; Mary Rohlfing, Boise State University; Cindy Roper, Abilene Christian College; James Rosene, University of Southern Alabama; Wallace Schmidt, Rollins College; Denise Solomon, University of Wisconsin, Madison; Rick Street, Texas A&M University; Teresa Thompson, University of Dayton; Michael Vickery, Alma College; Enid Waldhart, University of Kentucky; Eric Watts, Wake Forest University; Ron Whitt, Wayne State College; Shirley Williams-Kirksey, Clark Atlanta University; and Margaret Zulick, Wake Forest University. I am thankful to Paige for the professionalism she brought to this interviewing task. The results she compiled have spurred many of the changes outlined in the previous section.

Many professors and students at Wheaton College helped shape the final product. My Communication department colleagues—Gary Larson, Lynn Cooper, Ken Chase, and Ed Hollatz—were always willing to drop what they were doing to discuss an idea, suggest a resource, or review a chapter. Teaching assistant Glynka FritzMiller steeped herself in the forerunners of standpoint epistemology, early critical theorists, and the methodology of performance studies artists. Performance artist Ashley Olsen also contributed her insights. Former editor Carol Freeze Berry kept me from making errors that slipped by in previous editions. And computer artist Matt Fairfield created most of the new figures for this edition. See Figures 3.3, 10.2, and 30.3 for examples of his fine work. One other Wheaton connection provided invaluable assistance on the preparation of the manuscript. Russ Proctor of Northern Kentucky University, who married a former Wheaton communication major and who is a leading expert on the use of feature films to illustrate communication principles, shared his knowledge to help create the list of movies presented in Appendix D.

My relationship with the professionals at McGraw-Hill has been highly satisfactory. Publisher Phil Butcher, sponsoring editor Marge Byers, and developmental editor Jennie Katsaros share my vision of a text accessible to students with no prior knowledge of communication theory, and they continually encourage me to reach out to this reader. With their encouragement and backing, I am conducting video interviews with a dozen theorists featured in the book. A tape should be available by the fall term of 2000.

A special thanks goes to project manager Gladys True and designer Mary Christianson for their incredible flexibility and responsiveness to my requests. I have never been inclined to do things "by the book," and Gladys has appeared unflappable throughout my almost daily phone calls asking for special consideration or a variance on normal procedures. I picture myself as the "high maintenance" person in the cartoon on page 147 and Gladys as the partner who "can fix anything." Other authors are envious when they hear of my experience.

Without the care, commitment, friendship, organizational ability, and editing skill of Robyn Gibson, this edition would still be "in press." Robyn was a student in my communication theory class who showed a keen grasp of the material and a clear style of writing. When I discovered she was also the student supervisor of the writing center at the college, I asked her to work with me. After graduation she stayed in the area for an additional six months until the book was completed. Robyn vetted every word sent to the publisher. She also helped revise the face-negotiation chapter when the deadline loomed and handled much of the painstaking work of putting together the glossary and index. Robyn considers this edition a joint venture; I refer to it as "our book."

Finally, I want to gratefully recognize the continued encouragement, understanding, and loving support of my wife, Jean—not just on this project but throughout thirty-nine years of marriage. Her love, sense of humor, and parallel passion to create art have made it possible for me to throw myself into this project.

Em Griffin

CONTENTS

PART ONE

Overview

INTRODUCTION

This is a book about theories—communication theories. After that statement you may already be stifling a yawn. Many college students, after all, regard theory as obscure, dull, and irrelevant.

People outside the classroom are even less charitable. An aircraft mechanic once chided a professor: "You academic types are all alike. Your heads are crammed so full of theory you wouldn't know which end of a socket wrench to grab. Any plane you touched would crash and burn. All *Ph.D.* stands for is 'piled higher and deeper.' "

The mechanic may be right. It's ironic, however, that in order to criticize the study of theory, he used his own implicit theory of scholastic ineptness. Whether or not we recognize our ideas and assumptions as theories, we can't avoid using them in our daily lives.

The creators of theories examined in this book disagree with the mechanic's view of theory as being trivial and useless. Along with Kurt Lewin, one of the founders of modern social psychology, they believe that there is nothing as practical as a good theory. Perhaps an example from a theory you already know will back up this claim.

Theories Make Life Better. Consider the following situation. Jan is watching the late-night news on a local TV station and is anxious to hear the weather forecast. She's getting married the next day and has planned an outdoor garden reception. On the chance that it might rain, she has lined up a banquet room at a restaurant as a backup. But she must let the manager of the restaurant know by midnight whether or not she'll use the room. What's it to be? Inside or outside?

A smiling meteorologist tells her to expect a sunny day tomorrow with a high in the mid-eighties, but with a slight chance of thundershowers. Jan is encouraged, but over the years she has grown skeptical of anything the weather forecasters have to say. She thinks they should spend less time looking at their instruments and more time looking out the window. At this point she wants more clues about the next day's weather, so she switches to the cable weather channel to listen to a more detailed weather report.

The cable channel's meteorologist points to a current weather map. The predominant feature on the map is a grey, saw-toothed crescent 200 miles to the northwest. The forecaster refers to it as a "fast-moving cold front backed by a high-pressure system." Jan is tempted to tune out the technical jargon, but with only an hour left to call in her decision to the restaurant manager, she listens intently to the meteorologist's explanation of the cold frontal weather system.

As the meteorologist continues the forecast for the following evening, Jan notes that the jagged line has passed over to the southeast. Having followed the words closely, she sighs with relief, cancels the banquet room, and tells her fiancé that any rain will be over by noon. It may be a bit breezy at the reception, with the temperature dropping into the seventies, but no one should get wet.

Jan made her decision solely on the basis of theory. There was no actual buzz saw ripping its way toward her hometown. The map was simply a model of the weather occurring over thousands of square miles. She placed her confidence in a well-tested theory regarding the movement of air. There's

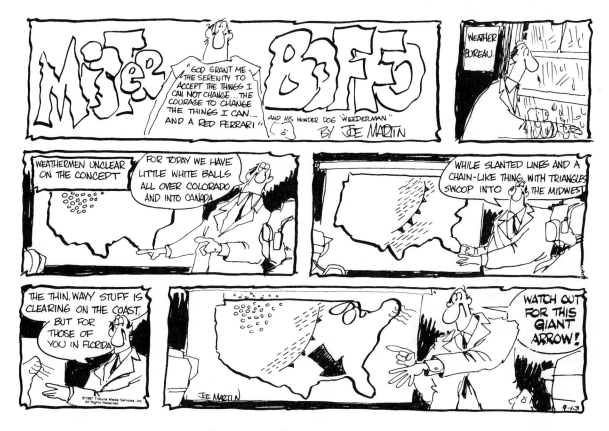

Cartoon reprinted by permission of Joe Martin.

about a 90 percent chance she's made the right decision.

Only since World War I have the weatherwise thought in terms of air masses with sharp leading edges. Before that, everyone had assumed that cold and warm air blended together like water from two faucets mixing in a basin. During the war, a perceptive man named Vilhelm Bjerknes suggested that instead of merging, distinct masses of air collide like armies along a battlefront, with the weaker mass retreating before the greater force. At that moment, weather forecasting took a giant step toward becoming a science.

A working knowledge of cold fronts can ensure that Jan and her guests stay dry at the wedding reception. But weather theory doesn't offer Jan much wisdom on how to develop a solid relationship with her husband. However, a number of communication theories covered in this book could be helpful to Jan once the honeymoon is over.

For example, symbolic interactionism describes how Jan's reaction to her husband will operate as a self-fulfilling prophecy that affects his self-image. When their family system is lopsided because of power struggles, the interactional view offers advice on how to reestablish the equilibrium by reframing the situation. Uncertainty reduction theory claims that the more Jan discovers about her spouse, the more comfortable she'll be with not knowing everything he thinks or does throughout the day. Relational dialectics theory highlights the ongoing tension the couple will feel trying to balance their twin desires for intimacy and independence. Finally, Deborah Tannen's theory of gender differences in communication style confirms that communication patterns in their marriage will be normal, if not entirely satisfying. (Jan hopes she's marrying a "big ear" who will listen sympathetically in times of trouble, but her husband may feel compelled to give advice on how to fix the problem.) While air mass theory might help Jan have a good wedding, communication theory could help her have a better marriage.

A Guide to the Communication Scene. Theories are maps of reality. The truth they depict may be objective facts "out there" or subjective meanings inside our heads. Either way, we need to have theory to guide us through unfamiliar territory. In that sense, this book of theories is like a scenic atlas that pulls together thirty-two must-see locations. It's the kind of travel guide that presents a close-up view of each site. After using the atlas to briefly visit a number of places, you might want to pursue a more in-depth study of a particular theory. But the first step is simply to see and appreciate the view.

This atlas of theories charts the key features of the communication process. The chapters in Part I introduce you to the nature and scope of the field. These chapters are like a satellite photo of the earth—they give you a panoramic view of the communication process.

Following the introductory chapters, we examine the actual turf. Each chapter presents a single theory to help you focus on individual theories one at a time.

The chapters are organized into four major parts: interpersonal communication, group and public communication, mass communication, and cultural context. The theories are categorized according to the primary context in which they operate. Since theories are tentative answers to questions that occur to people

as they mull over specific communication situations, it makes sense to group them according to the different communication settings that prompt the initial questions.

The collection of theories on interpersonal communication considers one-on-one interaction. The next part deals with face-to-face involvement in group and public settings. The part on mass communication pulls together theories that explore the effects of electronic and print media. The final part focuses on culture, a communication context so pervasive that we often fail to realize its impact.

This organizational plan is like having four separately indexed file cabinets. Although there is no natural progression from one part to another, the plan provides a convenient way to classify and retrieve the thirty-two theories. The scheme also lends itself to further division into common topical concerns. For example, the interpersonal part splits into sections on interpersonal messages, cognitive processing, relationship development, relationship maintenance, and influence.

Since communication isn't a value-free activity, I've added sections on ethical reflections in Parts II through V. Many of the thirty-two communication theories I present have ethical implications. To deal with human intercourse as a mechanical process separate from values would be like discussing sex using ground rules that prohibit any reference to love. In line with the text's focus on theory, I present brief sketches of at least two ethical positions under each communication context. The theorists I've selected not only present distinct views on *how* we should communicate in that context, they also offer diverse reasons *why* we should care to act morally in the first place.

The final chapter compares and contrasts theories according to their basic assumptions. Theories about communication share some common features, but there are also important distinctions that need to be acknowledged. Once you understand the theories, you'll be able to make connections and spot the differences.

Hints for Reading. The book usually introduces more than one theory within a topic area. For example, the section on interpersonal messages presents four distinct views of how our words and actions work in shaping our relationships. Don't assume that one has to be true and the others false. Rather, they all help explain the communication process. Just as there is more than one effective way to deliver a speech, so every communication issue has multiple interpretations. Each may be legitimate.

You'll also find a consistent effort to link each theory with its author. It takes both wisdom and courage to successfully plant a theoretical flag. In a process similar to the childhood game king-of-the-hill, as soon as a theorist builds a theory of communication, critics try to pull it down. That's okay, because truth is discerned by survival in the rough-and-tumble world of competitive ideas. But the survivors deserve to have their names associated with their creations.

There is a second reason for tying a theory to its author. Many of you will do further study in communication, and a mastery of names like Deetz, Burgoon, Delia, Berger, Fisher, and Burke will allow you to enter into the dialogue without being at a disadvantage. Ignoring the names of theorists could prove to be false economy in the long run.

Don't discount the importance of the questions at the end of each chapter. They are there to help you sharpen your focus on key points of the theory. The questions can be answered by pulling together information from the text and, in some cases, from the text of your life. The italicized words in the questions highlight terms that you'll need to know in order to understand the theory.

I've included cartoons for your learning and pleasure. A cartoonist can illustrate a feature of the theory in a way more memorable than a few extra paragraphs. In addition to enjoying their humor, you can use the cartoons as minitests of comprehension. If you can't figure out why a particular cartoon appears where it does, consider the possibility that you don't completely understand the theory, and make a renewed effort to grasp the theorist's idea.

Some students are afraid to try. Like travelers whose eyes glaze over at the sight of a road map, they have a phobia about theories that seek to explain human intentions and behavior. I sympathize with their qualms and misgivings, but the theories in this book haven't dehydrated my life or made it more confusing. On the contrary, they add clarity and provide a sense of competence as I communicate with others. I hope they do that for you as well. I've created a Web site that might help make it happen as you read about each theory: www.afirstlook.com

CHAPTER 1

Talk About Theory

I met Glenn Sparks and Marty Medhurst my first year teaching at Wheaton College. Glenn and Marty were friends who signed up for my undergraduate persuasion course. As students, both men were interested in the broadcast media. After graduating from Wheaton, both went on to earn master's degrees at Northern Illinois University. Each then earned a doctorate at separate universities, and both are now nationally recognized communication scholars. Glenn is on the faculty at Purdue University; Marty is at Texas A & M University.

Despite their similar backgrounds and interests, Glenn and Marty are radically different in their approaches to communication. Glenn calls himself a behavioral scientist while Marty refers to himself as a rhetorician. Glenn's training was in empirical research; Marty was schooled in the humanities. Glenn conducts experiments; Marty interprets text.

Glenn and Marty represent two distinct perspectives within the field of communication theory. Ernest Bormann, a theorist at the University of Minnesota, refers to communication theory as an "umbrella term for all careful, systematic and self-conscious discussion and analysis of communication phenomena."[1] I like this definition because it's broad enough to include the different kinds of work that both Glenn and Marty do, and it also covers the diverse theories presented in this book.

To understand the theories ahead, you need to first grasp the crucial differences between the objective and interpretive approaches to communication. As a way to introduce the distinctions, I asked Glenn and Marty to bring their scholarship to bear on a contemporary communication phenomenon—a television commercial.

SCIENCE OR INTERPRETATION: TWO VIEWS OF A SWIMMING ELEPHANT

In the competitive soft drink market, Diet Coke vies with Diet Pepsi for audience attention. In an earlier edition of this text, Glenn and Marty analyzed a Diet Pepsi commercial that used supermodel Cindy Crawford to hold viewer interest. For this edition I've chosen a Diet Coke ad that features an equally arresting model—a swimming elephant. Under the title, "Diet Coke's Refreshment Packed in Swimming Trunks," *Advertising Age* columnist Bob Garfield sets the scene:

> The spot opens with an underwater camera, panning left from the tendrils of some marine plant to an enormous, shadowy figure swimming awkwardly toward the lens, Is it an octopus? Is it a manatee? Is it Aunt Bernice?
>
> Oh, dear me, it's an elephant. A swimming elephant. . . .
>
> The elephant is swimming through a lagoon toward a brightly colored raft, where a slim and beautiful woman is drinking Diet Coke from the new contour bottle. The lady, who has an ice bucket full of Diet Cokes on her raft, returns to her paperback, oblivious to the approaching company. . . .
>
> The floating sun goddess is neither the subject of the elephant's affections, nor the reason for the 200-meter pachyderm crawl. What he's after is the soda pop. Reaching with his prehensile trunk, he pilfers one from the ice bucket, leaving on the raft in exchange four damp peanuts.[2]

Glenn: An Objective Perspective

As a behavioral scientist, I want to understand the causes of human behavior. As my understanding increases, I'll be able to offer explanations of why people act the way they do. I'll also be able to predict people's behavior before it occurs.

My particular area of interest is media effects. I would like to discover how mass media messages *affect* people's thoughts, values, feelings, attitudes, and behavior. So my approach to the Diet Coke ad is to ask, "What can I learn about the effects of advertising from this commercial?"

The answer to this question can never be found by simply discussing the words and pictures that appear on the screen. It's true that an in-depth analysis might reveal all sorts of interesting things about the content of the ad. And I could even speculate about how the commercial will affect the viewers. But my scientific instincts would not be satisfied with mere speculation.

After identifying a particular feature of the ad that might affect people, most scientists would like to develop a *theory* that explains the effect. For example, I might think that the image of a swimming elephant is so rare that it will be particularly powerful in holding the attention of viewers. Given that most people have a positive emotional reaction to elephants, I could also predict that this increased audience attention will result in people wanting to buy Diet Coke. My theory would present a rationale for why we pay attention to unusual things and why positive feelings should result in wanting to buy the advertised product.

Constructing a theory is not enough, however. Along with other scientists, I want an objective test of media theories to find out if they are valid. Perhaps I could run a study to see if the ad is, in fact, a more powerful attention-getter than other ads that don't feature bizarre sights like swimming elephants. After people watch the ad, I'd check which brand of soft drink they preferred.

Testing the audience is a crucial scientific enterprise. I might think I know the meaning that the audience will assign to the ad, or how the ad will affect them—but until I actually measure its impact, I can't be sure.

As a media effects researcher, I want to go beyond this single commercial. I'm interested in gathering support for general principles that apply across *many* advertisements. I might hypothesize that "increased attention to objects that cause pleasant feelings will result in greater persuasion." By testing principles such as this, our knowledge of communication processes can accumulate and progress over time.

Marty: An Interpretive Perspective

This ad is best understood as an allegory. An allegory is a symbolic story in which there is both a surface (or manifest) meaning and a deeper (or latent) meaning.

On the surface, this ad seems pretty simple: an elephant swims across part of the ocean to snatch a bottle of Diet Coke from a bathing beauty who is perched on an isolated floating raft. The elephant's journey is set to the tune of an old-fashioned sounding song that asks:

Is it love? Yes my dear.
Is it love that draws me near?
Is it love that brings me back into your arms?

The elephant seems at home in the water—almost as though he is dancing along with the music. He single-mindedly makes his way to the raft, deposits four peanuts, snatches a bottle of Diet Coke, then swims away to the sounds of "Is it Love?" As we watch the elephant swim away, a voice-over says, "The irresistible taste of Diet Coke." The Diet Coke logo then appears on the screen with the slogan, "This is refreshment."

But there is more to this ad than immediately meets the eye. It is significant that of the nineteen separate shots that make up the ad, the elephant appears in fourteen of them—far more than the bathing beauty or the bottle of Diet Coke. This is a crucial interpretive key, for it indicates the significance that the makers of the ad attach to the elephant.

I believe this ad is an allegory about what all "elephants" (i.e., overweight people) need to do if they want to attract the attention (or perhaps even love) of a beautiful woman:

First, overweight people must earnestly want that which they do not have. This is symbolized by the effort the elephant makes to swim across a large body of water to obtain what he wants. The water stands between the elephant and the object of his desire. Reaching the object requires swimming—a form of exercise without which the object cannot be obtained.

Second, when the elephant reaches the raft he immediately turns in his peanuts—a high-fat food item—in exchange for the Diet Coke. Clearly this symbolizes a need for a change in one's eating habits before one can attain the desired object. It is also a none-too-subtle allusion to the low cost of Diet Coke (mere peanuts).

CALVIN AND HOBBES © 1986 Watterson. Reprinted with permission of Universal Press Syndicate. All rights reserved.

Finally, it is not until after the elephant has exercised, changed his eating habits, and made off with the Diet Coke that the bathing beauty even notices his existence. The implication of the visual text seems clear: If overweight people want beautiful people to notice them, they had better change their behaviors—and what better way to start that change than by drinking Diet Coke.

Although both of these scholars focus on the unique image of a swimming elephant, Glenn's objective approach and Marty's interpretive approach to communication study clearly differ in starting point, method, and conclusion. Glenn is a *scientist* who works hard to be *objective.* Throughout these introductory chapters I will use those terms interchangeably. Marty is a *rhetorical critic* who does *interpretive* study. Here the labels get tricky.

While it's true that all rhetorical critics do interpretive analysis, not all interpretive scholars are rhetoricians. Most (including Marty) are *humanists,* but a growing number of postmodern communication theorists reject that tradition. These scholars refer to themselves with a bewildering variety of brand names: hermeneuticists, poststructuralists, deconstructivists, phenomenologists, cultural studies researchers, and social action theorists, as well as combinations of these terms. Writing from this postmodernist perspective, University of Utah theorist James Anderson observes:

> With this very large number of interpretive communities, names are contentious, border patrol is hopeless and crossovers continuous. Members, however, often see real differences.[3]

All of these scholars from Marty on down do *interpretive* analysis—scholarship concerned with meaning—yet there's no common term like scientist that includes them all. So from this point on I'll use the designation *interpretive scholars* or the noun forms *interpretivists* or *interpreters* to refer to the entire group, and only use *rhetorician, humanist, critic,* or *postmodernist* when I'm singling out that particular subgroup.

The separate worldviews of interpretive scholars and scientists reflect contrasting assumptions about ways of arriving at knowledge, the core of human nature, questions of value, the very purpose of theory, and methods of research. The rest of this chapter sketches these differences.

WAYS OF KNOWING: DISCOVERING THE TRUTH VERSUS CREATING MULTIPLE REALITIES

How do we know what we know, if we know it at all? This is the central question addressed by a branch of philosophy known as *epistemology*. You may have been in school for a dozen-plus years, read assignments, written papers, and taken tests without ever delving into the issue, "What is truth?" With or without in-depth study of the issue, however, we all inevitably make assumptions about the nature of knowledge.

Scientists assume that Truth is singular. There's one reality "out there" waiting to be discovered through the five senses of sight, sound, touch, taste, and smell. Since the raw sense data of the world are accessible to any competent observer, seeing is believing. Of course, no one person can know it all, but individual researchers pool their findings and build a collective body of knowledge about how the world operates. Scientists consider good theories to be mirrors of nature. They are confident that once a valid principle is discovered, it will continue to be recognized as true as long as the conditions remain relatively the same.

Interpretive scholars seek truth as well, but they are much more tentative about the possibility of revealing objective reality. They believe, in fact, that truth is largely subjective; meaning is highly interpretive. Rhetorical critics like Marty are not relativists, arbitrarily assigning meaning on a whim. They do maintain, however, that we can never entirely separate the knower from the known. Convinced that meaning is in the mind rather than the verbal sign, all interpretive scholars are comfortable with the notion that a text may have multiple meanings. Rhetorical critics are successful when they convince others to share their interpretation of the way a text works. As Anderson notes, "truth is a struggle, not a status."[4]

HUMAN NATURE: DETERMINISM VERSUS FREE WILL

One of the great debates throughout history revolves around the question of human choice. Hard-line determinists claim that every move we make is the result of heredity ("biology is destiny") and environment ("pleasure stamps in, pain stamps out"). On the other hand, free will purists insist that every human act is ultimately voluntary ("I am the master of my fate; I am the captain of my soul"[5]). Although few communication theorists are comfortable with either extreme, most tend to cluster into one of these two camps. Scientists stress the forces that shape human behavior; interpretive scholars focus on conscious choices made by individuals.

The difference between these two views of choice inevitably creeps into the language people use to explain their actions. Individuals who feel like puppets

DILBERT reprinted by permission of United Features Syndicate, Inc.

on strings say, "I *had* to . . . ," while people who feel they pull their own strings say, "I *decided* to . . ." The first group speaks in a passive voice: "I was distracted from studying by the argument at the next table." The second group speaks in an active voice: "I stopped studying to listen to the argument at the next table."

In the same way, the language of scholarship often reflects theorists' views of human nature. Behavioral scientists usually describe human conduct as occurring *because of* forces outside the individual's awareness. The explanation tends not to appeal to mental reasoning or any kind of inner life, seeing behavior instead as a result of stimulus-response bonds. As Glenn suggested, people *will* watch a swimming elephant.

In contrast, interpretive scholars tend to use phrases such as *in order to* or *so that*, since they attribute behavior to conscious intent. Their choice of words suggests that people are *free agents*, that they could decide to respond differently under an identical set of circumstances. For example, Marty would hold that an obese viewer could identify with the elephant's quest on one occasion, yet scoff at the fantasy the next time around. The consistent interpretivist wouldn't ask *why* the viewer chose a given response. As Anderson explains, "True choice demands to be its own cause and its own explanation."[6]

Human choice is therefore problematic for the behavioral scientist because as individual freedom goes up, predictability of behavior goes down. Conversely, the roots of humanism are threatened by a highly restricted view of human freedom. In an impassioned plea, British author C. S. Lewis exposes the paradox of stripping away people's freedom and yet expecting them to exercise responsible choice:

> In a sort of ghastly simplicity we remove the organ and expect of them virtue and enterprise. We laugh at honor and are shocked to find traitors in our midst. We castrate and bid the geldings be fruitful.[7]

Lewis assumes that significant decisions are value laden, and most interpretive scholars would agree. Notice how Marty's explanation of the elephant's swim engages the moral life of the viewer. The story is a mini morality play—physical fitness is a virtue.

WHAT DO WE VALUE MOST? OBJECTIVITY VERSUS EMANCIPATION

When we talk about *values* we are discussing questions of relative worth. Values are the traffic lights of our lives, priorities that guide what we think, feel, and do. The professional values of communication theorists reflect the commitments they've made concerning knowledge and human nature. Since most social scientists regard Truth as singular, they place a high value on objectivity. Because humanists and others in the interpretive camp believe that the ability to choose is what separates humanity from the rest of creation, they value scholarship that expands the range of free choice.

As a behavioral scientist, Glenn works hard to maintain his objectivity. He is a man with strong moral and spiritual convictions, but he doesn't want his personal values to distort human reality or confuse what *is* with what he thinks *ought to be*. Glenn is particularly upset when he hears about researchers who fudge the findings of a study to shore up a questionable hypothesis. He shares the academic goal of Harvard sociologist George Homans to let the evidence speak for itself: "When nature, however stretched out on the rack, still has a chance to say 'no'—then the subject is science."[8]

Marty is aware of his own ideology and is not afraid to bring his values to bear upon a communication text under scrutiny. By revealing the psychological appeals built into the swimming elephant spot, Marty provides people with the resources to resist the commercial message. Critical interpreters value socially relevant research that seeks to liberate people from oppression of any sort— economic, political, religious, emotional, and so on. They decry the detached stance of scientists who refuse to take responsibility for the results of their work. Whatever the pursuit—a Manhattan Project to split the atom or a Genome Project to map human genes—critical interpreters insist that knowledge is never neutral.

THE PURPOSE OF THEORY: UNIVERSAL LAWS VERSUS RULES FOR INTERPRETATION

Even if Glenn and Marty could agree on the nature of knowledge, the extent of human autonomy, and the ultimate value of scholarship, their words would still sound strange to each other because they use distinct vocabularies to accomplish different goals. As a behavioral scientist, Glenn is working to pin down universal laws of human behavior that cover a variety of situations. As a rhetorical critic, Marty strives to articulate unique acts of interpretation.

If these two scholars were engaged in fashion design rather than research design, Glenn would probably find or tailor a coat suitable for many occasions that covers everybody well—one size fits all. Marty might apply principles of fashion design to style a coat that makes a statement for a single client—a one-of-a-kind, custom creation. Glenn constructs and tests. Marty interprets and applies.

Theory testing is the basic activity of the behavioral scientist. Glenn starts with a hunch about how the world works, and then crafts a tightly worded hypothesis that temporarily commits him to a specific prediction. As an empiricist, he can never completely "prove" that he has made the right gamble; he can only show in test after test that his behavioral bet pays off. Prediction and control are the name of the game.

The interpretive scholar explores the web of meaning that constitutes human existence. When Marty creates scholarship, he isn't trying to *prove* theory. However, he could *use* rhetorical theory to interpret the written, spoken, and nonverbal texts of people's lives. Robert Ivie, former editor of the *Quarterly Journal of Speech*, suggests that rhetorical critics ought to use theory this way:

We cannot conduct *rhetorical* criticism of social reality without benefit of a guiding rhetorical theory that tells us generally what to look for in social practice, what to make of it, and whether to consider it significant.[9]

RESEARCH METHODS: EXPERIMENTS, SURVEYS, TEXTUAL ANALYSIS, ETHNOGRAPHY

Whether the quest is for prediction and control, or for interpretation and understanding, theorists know that the task demands research. A leading textbook on communication inquiry presents four primary techniques for the study of communication.[10] Experiments and survey research offer quantitative ways for the scientist to test theory. Textual analysis and ethnography provide qualitative tools that aid the interpretive scholar's search for meaning. I'll briefly describe the distinct features of each method. After working through the differences, take a look at Figure 1.1, which gives you questions to ask as you read about a study of communication that uses one of these four methods.

1. Experiments

Working on the assumption that human behavior is not random, an experimenter tries to establish a cause-and-effect sequence by systematically manipulating one variable (the independent variable) in a tightly controlled situation to learn its effects on another variable (the dependent variable). For example, Glenn suggested showing the Diet Coke commercial to a panel of soft drink consumers to determine whether attention to an engaging visual stimulus of a swimming elephant would affect response to the advertiser's product. For purposes of comparison, he could show a less novel ad for Diet Coke to a similar group. To make certain that he had successfully manipulated the independent variable of attention, he might use lab equipment to monitor eye blinks, pupil dilation, and the direction of gaze of each subject.

After the ads were shown, Glenn would then measure each group's expressed desire for Diet Coke—on attitude scales, through competitive taste tests with Diet Pepsi, or by actual consumer behavior in the store. If viewers captivated by the sight of a swimming elephant responded more favorably to the sponsor's product than subjects who were exposed to a more mundane appeal, the centrality of attention to the persuasion process would gain support.

2. Surveys

Using questionnaires or conducting interviews, survey researchers rely on self-report data to discover what people think, feel, or intend to do. Coca-Cola committed a classic market blunder in 1985 by altering its basic formula to take away the familiar bite and make the soda sweeter. The company introduced the change after conducting one hundred thousand taste tests with non-Coke drinkers, but they neglected to check with their loyal customers. Sales plum-

EXPERIMENTAL RESEARCH

How precise are the hypotheses? Is each a clearly worded, simple, single cause-effect prediction?

Are the hypotheses interesting or are they self-evident?

Were subjects randomly assigned to the experimental groups? Did everyone studied in the experiment have an equal chance of being assigned to the different experimental conditions?

Was the manipulation of the independent variable "life-like" enough to allow the researcher to generalize the findings beyond the confines of this particular experiment?

Were important extraneous variables that may confound the findings controlled for? Might the findings be due to other events that occurred between the time the subjects experienced the independent variable and when they were measured on the dependent variable?

SURVEY QUESTIONNAIRE AND INTERVIEW RESEARCH

Is there a response bias in the sample? Could there be differences between those who participated and those who did not? Was the response rate sufficient for the purposes of the research?

Was the choice of a questionnaire or an interview appropriate for answering the research question posed?

Were the questions worded clearly and leading questions avoided?

Were respondents guaranteed anonymity?

Did the interviewers receive sufficient training? Did they probe effectively?

TEXTUAL ANALYSIS: RHETORICAL CRITICISM

Were the most appropriate texts selected for analysis?

Is the researcher sure that the texts selected are complete and accurate? What might be left out of these texts, and how might any omissions affect the results?

What type of rhetorical criticism was it: historical, Neo-Aristotelian, generic feminist, metaphoric, narrative, dramatistic, fantasy theme analysis?

Did the critic produce a compelling argument about the meaning of the text?

In the final analysis, did the essay produce a richer understanding of human persuasion?

ETHNOGRAPHIC RESEARCH

What justified observation or interviews as the appropriate methods to use? Were the observations conducted on-site, where people are communicating naturally?

Did the observers exhaustively record all the communication behavior related to the research questions?

Are the findings described in sufficiently rich and vivid detail (a "thick description") so the reader may visualize the communication behavior observed and the context in which it occurred?

What assurances are provided that inferences are grounded in the data, not imposed or biased by the researcher's a priori assumptions?

Do the article's findings "put you in the respondents' shoes," so that you now have a better sense of how people in the group being studied act, think, speak and/or react to others?

FIGURE 1.1 Twenty Questions to Guide Evaluation of Four Research Methods
(Selected from Frey, Botan, Friedman, and Kreps, *Interpreting Communication Research: A Case Study Approach.*)

meted until public outcry forced the company to restore the original taste. Marketed today as "Classic Coke," the name reminds us not to automatically assume that we know how people will react. They may not be charmed by a swimming elephant. If we want to know, we need to ask.

Survey methodology also helps scientists validate theory. For example, a researcher might question a representative sample of shoppers who purchased six-packs of cola the week following the ad's blanket buy on television. A positive correlation between vivid recall of the ad and a report of an uncharacteristic choice of Diet Coke over other no-calorie soft drinks would give credence to theories of influence that focus on attention. Of course, there's no guarantee that these purchases weren't affected by prime shelf display or discount pricing. It's difficult to support cause-and-effect relationships from correlational data. Yet, unlike a highly controlled laboratory experiment, a well-planned survey gives the social scientist a chance to get inside the heads of people in a "real-life" situation. There's less rigor than in an experiment, but more vigor.

3. Textual Analysis

The aim of textual research is to describe and interpret the characteristics of a message. You may have noticed from Marty's analysis of the Diet Coke ad that the word *text* is not limited to written materials. Communication theorists use this term to refer to any intentional symbolic expression—verbal or nonverbal. Marty's critique is a contemporary example of the oldest tradition in communication research—the intensive study of a single message grounded in a humanistic perspective. Rhetorical criticism is the most common form of textual analysis.

An increasing number of interpretive scholars aren't content merely to interpret the intended meanings of a text. They want to expose and publicly resist the ideology that permeates the accepted wisdom of society. These critical scholars reject any notion of permanent truth or meaning. To traditional thinkers, their activity looks like a few angry children in kindergarten knocking over other kids' blocks, but they are intentionally using theory to carve out a space where people without power can be heard.

Lana Rakow, a feminist scholar in the Communication Department at the University of North Dakota, would have us consider the plight of women watching almost any female model in a television commercial. Female viewers can't escape the portrayal of unattainable thinness as the erotic ideal, and they are continually invited to see their body as "the object of men's fetishistic gaze."[11]

For Rakow and other theorists critical of the "culture industries," advertising is the linchpin of oppression that needs to be resisted by those who are aware that television imposes meaning on the viewer. Their form of textual analysis isn't a detached and impartial enterprise; it is a powerful tool in the service of a reformist agenda.

Although Marty's reading of the Diet Coke commercial may not appear particularly radical, it includes a significant—if implicit—social critique. Highlighting our culture's obsession with thinness, he suggests that the ad plays to viewer anxiety over excess pounds through association with the rotund pachyderm. In fact, Marty's claim that the ad targeted weight-conscious viewers was sufficiently subversive to incur the disapproval of Coca-Cola. The company expressed its displeasure with his analysis by denying me permission to run photos from the ad in this book. Diet Coke may be sugar-free, but the decision to prohibit publication illustrates the interpreter's claim that knowledge is never value-free.

4. Ethnography

In the 1990 Academy Award–winning film *Dances with Wolves,* Kevin Costner plays John Dunbar, a nineteenth-century Army lieutenant alone on the Dakota plains.[12] Amidst some anxiety and with great tentativeness, Dunbar sets out to understand the ways of the Sioux tribe camped a short distance away. He watches carefully, listens attentively, appreciates greatly, and slowly begins to participate in the tribal rituals. He also takes extensive notes. That's ethnography!

Princeton anthropologist Clifford Geertz says that ethnography is "not an experimental science in search of law, but an interpretive [approach] in search of meaning."[13] As a sensitive observer of the human scene, Geertz is loath to impose his way of thinking onto a society's construction of reality. He wants his theory of communication grounded in the meanings that people within a culture share. Getting it right means seeing it from their point of view.

Most people have long regarded advertising as a world unto itself. A communication researcher could view the Diet Coke commercial as an artifact of this particular subculture and seek to understand the web of meaning surrounding the creation of this and other television spots. An ethnographer would look for the rites, ceremonies, rituals, myths, legends, stories, and folklore that reflect the shared meanings and values of the advertising industry. Perhaps you could find an ad agency that would welcome you as an intern willing to assume a participant-observer role.

LOOKING BACK, LOOKING AHEAD

In this chapter I've introduced five crucial differences between objective and interpretive theories of communication. Using Glenn and Marty as representative theorists, I outlined their separate answers to questions of how we gain knowledge, how free we are to act, and what values should guide our study. Finally, I've shown that scientists and interpreters have different reasons for studying theory, which in turn influence the research methods they use.

A basic grasp of these distinctions will help you understand where like-minded thinkers are going and why they've chosen a particular path to get there. While some communication theorists have a foot in both camps, I find it helpful at the outset to view most of the theories in this book as originating in either an objective or interpretive worldview.

In Chapter 2, "Weighing the Words," I introduce widely accepted standards that you can use to evaluate the worth of each theory. Since objective and interpretive theories of communication differ markedly, I offer two separate sets of criteria. Yet surprisingly, by the end of the chapter you may conclude that objective and interpretive theories have numerous points of contact.

QUESTIONS TO SHARPEN YOUR FOCUS

1. Compare Glenn Sparks and Marty Medhurst's approaches to the Diet Coke commercial. Which analysis makes the most sense to you? Why?

2. How do *scientists* and *interpretive scholars* differ in their answers to the question, "What is truth?" Which perspective do you find more satisfying?

3. Think of the communication classes you've taken. Did an objective or interpretive perspective undergird each course? Was this due to the subject matter or to the professor's orientation to the discipline?

4. How would a *rhetorician* view *experiments, surveys, textual analysis,* and *ethnography* as research methods? How do *empiricists* regard the same methodologies?

A SECOND LOOK

Recommended resource: James A. Anderson, *Communication Theory: Epistemological Foundations,* Guilford, New York, 1996.

Introduction to theory: Ernest Bormann, *Communication Theory,* Sheffield, Salem, Wisc., 1989, pp. 105–256.

Contemporary scientific scholarship: Charles Berger and Steven Chaffee, *Handbook of Communication Science,* Sage, Newbury Park, Calif., 1987.

Contemporary rhetorical scholarship: Sonja Foss, Karen Foss, and Robert Trapp, *Contemporary Perspectives on Rhetoric,* 2d ed., Waveland, Prospect Heights, Ill., 1991.

Defense of empirical scholarship: Robert Bostrom and Lewis Donohew, "The Case for Empiricism: Clarifying Fundamental Issues in Communication Theory," *Communication Monographs,* Vol. 59, 1992, pp. 109–129.

Defense of interpretive scholarship: Arthur Bochner, "Perspectives on Inquiry II: Theories and Stories," in *Handbook of Interpersonal Communication,* 2d ed., Mark Knapp and Gerald Miller (eds.), Sage, Thousand Oaks, Calif., 1994, pp. 21–41.

Scientific research: Glenn Sparks, Cheri Sparks, and Kirsten Gray, "Media Impact on Fright Reactions and Belief in UFOs: The Potential Role of Mental Imagery," *Communication Research,* Vol. 22, 1995, pp. 3–23.

Rhetorical analysis: Martin J. Medhurst, "The Rhetorical Structure of Oliver Stone's JFK," *Critical Studies in Mass Communication,* Vol. 10, 1993, pp. 128–143.

Critical approach to theory: Stanley Deetz, *Democracy in an Age of Corporate Colonization,* State University of New York, Albany, 1992, "The Role of Communication Studies," pp. 65–90.

Research methods: Lawrence R. Frey, Carl H. Botan, Paul G. Friedman, and Gary L. Kreps, *Investigating Communication: An Introduction to Research Methods,* Prentice Hall, Englewood Cliffs, N.J., 1991.

Communication Encyclopedia: International Encyclopedia of Communications, Vols. 1–4, Oxford University Press, New York, 1989.

CHAPTER 2

Weighing the Words

of Ernest Bormann's Symbolic Convergence Theory

In Chapter 1 we looked at two distinct approaches to communication theory—objective and interpretive. Because the work of social scientists and interpreters is so different, they often have trouble understanding and valuing their counterparts' scholarship. This workplace tension parallels the struggle between ranchers and farmers in Rodgers and Hammerstein's Broadway musical *Oklahoma!* One song calls for understanding and cooperation:

> The farmer and the cowman should be friends,
> Oh, the farmer and the cowman should be friends,
>   One man likes to push a plough,
>   The other likes to chase a cow,
> But that's no reason why they cain't be friends.[1]

The problem, of course, is that farmers and ranchers want to push a plough or chase a cow over the same piece of land. Daily disputes over fences, water, and government grants make friendship tough. The same can be said of the turf wars that are common between objective and interpretive scholars. Differences in ways of knowing, views of human nature, values, goals of theory building, and methods of research seem to ensure tension and misunderstanding.

Friendly attitudes between empiricists and critical interpreters are particularly hard to come by when each group insists on applying its own standards of judgment to the work of the other group. As a first-time reader of communication theory, you could easily get sucked in to making the same mistake. If you've had training in the scientific method and judge the value of every communication theory by whether or not it predicts human behavior, you'll automatically reject 50 percent of the theories presented in this book. On the other hand, if you've been steeped in the humanities and expect every theory to help unmask the meaning of a text, you'll easily dismiss the other half.

Regardless of which approach you favor, not all objective or interpretive communication theories are equally good. For each type, some are better than others. Like moviegoers watching one of Clint Eastwood's early westerns, you'll want a way to separate the good, the bad, and the ugly. Since I've included theories originating in both the social sciences and the humanities, you need to have two separate lenses through which to view their respective claims. This chapter offers that pair of bifocals. I hope by the time you finish you'll be on friendly terms with the separate criteria that behavioral scientists and a wide range of interpretive scholars use to weigh the works and words of their colleagues.

A TEST CASE: ERNEST BORMANN'S SYMBOLIC CONVERGENCE THEORY

University of Minnesota professor Ernest Bormann developed a theory of communication that is unusual in that it has both interpretive and objective roots. The project started as a method of rhetorical criticism, a long-honored tradition in humanistic study. Bormann called his method *fantasy theme analysis,* and he used it to study a type of communication that takes place in small groups.

Bormann soon discovered a link between the dramatic imagery members use when they talk to each other and the degree of group consciousness and solidarity. In standard social science fashion, he defined his terms and then crafted a cause-and-effect hypothesis, which he now believes holds for all groups, regardless of where they meet, who they are, or why they get together. Simply stated, Bormann's symbolic convergence theory maintains that "the sharing of group fantasies creates symbolic convergence."[2]

Some people restrict the term *fantasy* to children's literature, sexual desire, or things "not true." Bormann, however, uses the word to refer to "the creative and imaginative interpretation of events that fulfills a psychological or rhetorical need."[3] In a small group setting, this definition includes any reference to events in the group's past, speculation about what might happen in the future, and any talk about the world outside the group. The term does not cover comments about actions taking place "here and now" within the group. Fantasies are expressed in the form of stories, jokes, metaphors, and other imaginative language that interprets or places a "spin" on familiar events. Voiced fantasies become vehicles to share common experiences and invest them with an emotional tone.

Picture a group of cattlemen having a regular Saturday morning breakfast in a Great Falls, Montana, cafe. One rancher tells a story about a man carrying a briefcase who knocked on his door: "Hello, Mr. Clayton Rogers," the stranger says. "I'm from the federal government and I'm here to help you."

Whether or not the event really happened is not the issue. Symbolic convergence theory is concerned with the group's response. Does the punch line fall flat, or is it greeted with a burst of derisive laughter? Do others lose their self-consciousness and vie to tell their own tales of bureaucratic interference? Bormann says that we can spot a *fantasy chain reaction* by increased energy within the group, an upbeat tempo in the conversation, and especially through a common response to the imagery.

Most fantasies don't chain out; they fall on deaf ears. But when one catches fire within the group, the same *fantasy theme* runs throughout the multiple narratives—à la *Seinfeld*. Perhaps at the Saturday breakfast the hero of every man's account is a crafty rancher, while the villain of each story is a bumbling federal agent. Or maybe each image reflects a collective suspicion of a Washington conspiracy to take away grazing rights. Whatever the theme, Bormann believes that by sharing common fantasies, a collection of individuals is transformed into a cohesive group. He calls the process *symbolic convergence.*

Through symbolic convergence, individuals build a sense of community or a group consciousness. References to *I*, *me*, and *mine* give way to pronouns that assume a joint venture—*we*, *us*, and *ours*. Groups draw even closer when they share a cluster of fantasy themes. Along with a distrust of Washington, the Saturday morning breakfast group might express disdain for "interfering gun-control lobbyists" and "tree-hugging environmentalists." They may also talk nostalgically about the "Old West," where rugged individuals took care of their own problems. When the same set of integrated fantasy themes is voiced repeatedly across many groups, Bormann describes people's view of social reality as a *rhetorical vision.*

The concept of rhetorical vision moves symbolic convergence theory beyond its original small group context. A coherent rhetorical vision can be spread and reinforced through recurring media messages. Often an entire master script is triggered by a single code word, slogan, or nonverbal symbol. For example, the mere mention of "Waco," "Ruby Ridge," or the "Endangered Species Act" may evoke the ranchers' collective hostility toward the federal government on any Saturday morning. Bormann is convinced that symbolic convergence explains the meeting-of-minds and sense of communion taking place among the men at that breakfast table in a Montana cafe.

Now that you have a thumbnail sketch of fantasy themes and symbolic convergence, let's take a look at the distinct criteria that objective or interpretive scholars use to judge the quality of Bormann's theory. We'll start with the wisdom of science.

WHAT MAKES AN OBJECTIVE THEORY GOOD?

Symbolic convergence theory is credible because it fulfills what a leading text on social research methods calls the "twin objectives of scientific knowledge." The theory explains the past and present, and it predicts the future. Scientists of all kinds agree on three other criteria for a good theory as well—simplicity, testability, and usefulness. The rest of this section takes a closer look at these five requirements.

Scientific Standard 1: Explanation of the Data

A good objective theory explains an event or behavior. British philosopher Karl Popper writes that "Theories are nets cast to catch what we call the world."[4] Scientific philosopher Abraham Kaplan says that theory is a way of making sense out of a disturbing situation.[5] A good objective theory brings clarity to an otherwise jumbled situation; it draws order out of chaos.

Group discussions are often chaotic. Even though a leader urges members to "speak one at a time" and "stick to the point," participants will often interrupt each other and go off on verbal tangents. According to symbolic convergence theory, graphic digressions and boisterous talk aren't signs of a flawed process. Rather, they are evidence that the group is coming together. As Bormann says, "The explanatory power of the fantasy chain analysis lies in its ability to account for the development, evolution, and decay of dramas that catch up groups of people and change behavior."[6]

A good theory synthesizes the data, focuses our attention on what's crucial, and helps us ignore that which makes little difference. Bormann's theory organizes these verbal inputs into a coherent whole. His focus on the cohesive effect of chained fantasy goes beyond the raw data. It explains what's happening.

A good theory also explains *why*. When Willie Sutton was asked why he robbed banks, the Depression-era bandit replied, " 'Cuz that's where they keep the money." It's a great line, but as a theory of motivation, it lacks explanatory power. There's nothing in the words that casts light on the internal processes or environmental forces that led Sutton to crack a safe while others tried to crack the stock market.

Symbolic convergence explains the process as well as the result. Bormann suggests that group members often voice fantasies as a way to relieve tensions within the group.[7] The atmosphere may be charged with interpersonal conflict, the group as a whole might be frustrated by its inability to come up with a good solution, or perhaps individuals import their own brand of stress as each walks in the door. Whatever the reason, a joke, story, or vivid analogy provides welcome relief. Most members really don't care how fantasy chains work; they're just thankful to have a pleasant diversion. In like manner, you can be a skillful public speaker without understanding why the audience likes what you say. But when you take a course in communication *theory*, you've lost your amateur status. The reason *why* something happens becomes as important as the fact that it does.

Scientific Standard 2: Prediction of Future Events

A good objective theory predicts what will happen. Prediction is possible only when dealing with things we can see, hear, touch, smell, and taste again and again. As we notice things happening over and over in the same way, we begin to speak of universal laws. In the realm of the physical sciences, we are seldom embarrassed. Objects don't have a choice about how to behave.

The social sciences are another matter. While theories about human behavior often cast their predictions in cause-and-effect terms, a certain humility on the part of the theorist is advisable. Even the best theory may only be able to talk in terms of probability and tendencies—not absolute certainty. That's the kind of soft predictive power Bormann claims for symbolic convergence theory.

Bormann believes that rhetorical visions contain motives that prompt or impel true believers to act out a fantasy. Consider what we now know about Timothy McVeigh, the man who was convicted of bombing the federal building in

Oklahoma City. McVeigh's antigovernment passions were reinforced by militia group members convinced that they must prepare for inevitable armed conflict with federal agents. McVeigh was also an avid reader of *The Turner Diaries*,[8] a hate novel that glorifies white supremacist violence against minority groups and the federal government. According to symbolic convergence theory, when we spot people who are steeped in fantasies that exalt violence, we can anticipate the act itself.[9] Knowing who, when, and where is much less certain.

Bormann has had little success predicting when a fantasy will capture a group's imagination. Members with rhetorical skill seem to have a better chance of providing the spark, but there's no guarantee that their words will ignite others. Even when a skillful imagemaker sparks a fantasy chain, he or she has little control over where the conversation will go. Fantasy chains seem to have a life of their own. You can see why most social scientists want more predictive power than Bormann's theory offers.

Scientific Standard 3: Relative Simplicity

A good objective theory is as simple as possible. A few decades ago a cartoonist named Rube Goldberg made people laugh by sketching plans for complicated machines that performed simple tasks. His "better mousetrap" went through a sequence of fifteen mechanical steps that were triggered by turning a crank and ended with a bird cage dropping over a cheese-eating mouse.

Goldberg's designs were funny because the machines were so needlessly complex. That can happen with scientific explanations as well; it's easy to get caught up in the grandeur of a theoretical construction. "Why say it simply when you can say it elaborately?" Yet the rule of parsimony states that given

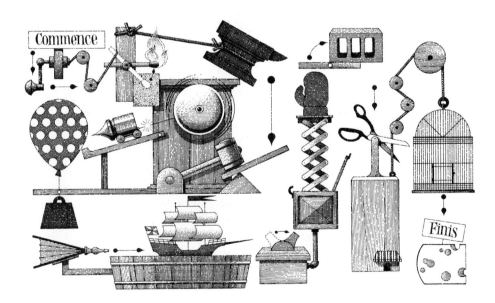

two plausible explanations for the same event, we should accept the simpler version.

College professors often criticize others for offering simple solutions to complex questions. It's a jungle out there, and we're quick to pounce on those who reduce the world's complexity to a simplistic "me Tarzan, you Jane." But every so often a few explorers will cut through the underbrush and clear a straight path to a truth, which they announce in simple, direct, concise terms. Consider Bormann's summary statement, cited earlier: "The sharing of group fantasies creates symbolic convergence."[10] Simplicity is a virtue of his theory.

Scientific Standard 4: Hypotheses That Can Be Tested

A good objective theory is testable. If a prediction is wrong, there ought to be a way to demonstrate the error. Karl Popper called this requirement "falsifiability" and saw it as the defining feature of scientific theory.[11] Some theories are so broad or sloppily stated that it's impossible to imagine empirical results that could disprove their hypotheses. But if there is no way to prove a theory false, then the claim that it's true seems hollow. A boyhood example may help illustrate this point.

When I was 12 years old, I had a friend named Mike. We spent many hours shooting baskets in his driveway. The backboard was mounted on an old-fashioned, single-car garage whose double doors opened outward like the doors on a cabinet. In order to avoid crashing into them on a drive for a lay-up, we'd open the doors during play. But since the doors would only swing through a 90-degree arc, they extended about four feet onto the court along the baseline.

One day Mike announced that he'd developed a "never-miss" shot. He took the ball at the top of the free-throw circle, drove toward the basket, then cut to the right corner. When he got to the baseline, he took a fade-away jump shot, blindly arching the ball over the top of the big door. I was greatly impressed as the ball swished through the net. When he boasted that he never missed, I challenged him to do it again—which he did. But a third attempt was an air ball—it completely missed the rim.

Before I could make the kind of bratty comment junior high boys make, he quickly told me that the attempt had not been his never-miss shot. He claimed to have slipped as he cut to the right, and therefore jumped from the wrong place. Grabbing the ball, he drove behind the door and again launched a blind arching shot. Swish. *That*, he assured me, was his never-miss shot.

I knew something was wrong. I soon figured out that any missed attempt was, by definition, not the fabled never-miss shot. When the ball went in, however, Mike heralded the success as added evidence of 100 percent accuracy. I now know that I could have called his bluff by removing the net from the basket so that he couldn't hear whether the shot went through. This would have forced him to declare from behind the door whether or not the attempt was of the never-miss variety. But as long as I played by his rules, there was no way to disprove his claim. Unfortunately, some theories are stated in a similar fashion. They are presented in a way that makes it impossible to prove them false. They shy away from the put-up-or-shut-up standard—they aren't testable.

Symbolic convergence theory is vulnerable at this point. Since Bormann claims that shared fantasies create cohesive groups, an empirical researcher's first task is to measure these variables separately. This is not as easy as it sounds. Because most groups already have a history, it's difficult to know whether a fantasy chain is a trigger for new solidarity among members or merely a reflection of a group consciousness that's already in place. Indeed, leading advocates of the theory seem to confound the two variables, often treating the presence of a fantasy chain as proof of group cohesiveness. Note, for example, how the two concepts merge in the following passage: "For a fantasy theme to chain out, a saga to exist, a symbolic cue to convey meaning, or a rhetorical vision to evolve, there must be a shared group consciousness within a rhetorical community."[12] You can see why many outside observers consider symbolic convergence theory a never-miss shot—it's not falsifiable.

Scientific Standard 5: Practical Utility

A good objective theory is useful. Since a fundamental goal of any science is increased control, scientific theories should offer practical help. Symbolic convergence theory does this well. Bormann and his followers have used fantasy theme analysis to advise small groups, improve organizational communication, conduct market research, and assess public opinion. To illustrate the pragmatic value of the methodology, John Cragan (Illinois State University) and Donald Shields (Indiana State University) require students in their applied research classes to analyze the way that high school seniors talk about college.

Symbolic convergence theory claims that most rhetorical visions employ one of three competing master analogues—a righteous vision, a social vision, or a pragmatic vision. That's what Cragan's and Shields' students typically find.[13] Potential applicants who embrace a *righteous* vision are interested in a school's academic excellence, the reputation of its faculty, and special programs that it offers. Those who adopt a *social* vision see college as a way to get away from home, meet new friends, and join others in a variety of social activities. High school seniors who buy into a *pragmatic* vision want a marketable degree that will help them get a good job. Knowledge of these distinct visions could help admissions officers develop a strategy to appeal to graduates who would most appreciate the character of their campus.

In the introduction to this book I cited Lewin's claim that there is nothing as practical as a good theory. This final standard of utility suggests that scientific theories that aren't practical aren't good. As you read about theorists who work from an objective perspective, let usefulness be a crucial test of each theory. If a theory offers helpful advice, act on it; if it offers no pragmatic insight for your life, discard it. There is one caution, however. Most of us can be a bit lazy or shortsighted. We have a tendency to consider as unimportant anything that's hard to grasp or can't be applied to our lives right now. Before dismissing a theory as irrelevant, make certain you understand it and consider how others have made use of its advice. I'll try to do my part by presenting each theory as clearly as possible and suggesting possible applications.

WHAT MAKES AN INTERPRETIVE THEORY GOOD?

Unlike scientists, humanists don't have an agreed-on five-point set of criteria for evaluating their theories. But even though there is no universally approved model for interpretive theories, humanists and other interpreters repeatedly urge that theories should accomplish some or all of the following functions: create understanding, identify values, inspire aesthetic appreciation, stimulate agreement, and reform society. The rest of this chapter examines these oft-mentioned ideals.

Interpretive Standard 1: New Understanding of People

Interpretive scholarship is good when it offers fresh insight into the human condition. Working out of a humanistic tradition, rhetorical critics seek to gain new understanding by analyzing the activity that they regard as uniquely human—symbolic interaction. Suppose that an interpretive scholar wanted to study communication of politicians whose reputations are on the line. He or she would start by selecting one or more texts—Richard Nixon's "Checkers" speech, Ted Kennedy's explanation of the Chappiquiddick tragedy, transcripts of presidential news conferences and White House communiqués on the Clinton/Lewinsky affair, or any other text that could shed light on political crisis communication.

After verifying that the electronic or print record was accurate, the critic would do a "close reading" of the text. This is a fine-tooth-comb analysis of words, images, and ideas. The critic would also examine the historical *context* that influenced the creation of the message and the way the audience interpreted it.

When rhetorical theory is good, it helps the critic understand the text. For example, the neo-Aristotelian classification of logical, emotional, and ethical appeals might help the critic account for the dramatic political impact of Nixon's last-ditch television address. A Burkean analysis of Kennedy's account of Mary Jo Kopechne's drowning offers insight as to why the Senator placed so much emphasis on the scene of the accident. Or Michael Pacanowsky's cultural approach to organizations could suggest that Clinton's responses to the press are a product of a White House culture that has its own rites, rituals, and myths. You'll read about these theories in the pages to come. If they help you make sense out of complex communication, then they fulfill the first interpretive standard for a good theory.

Some critics fear that by relying on rhetorical theory, we will read our preconceived ideas into the text rather than letting the words speak for themselves.

They suggest there are times when we should "just say no" to theory. But Bormann notes that rhetorical theory works best when it suggests universal patterns of symbol-using: "A powerful explanatory structure is what makes a work of humanistic scholarship live on through time."[14]

Bormann's call for a powerful explanatory structure in humanistic theory is akin to the behavioral scientist's insistence that theory explains why people do what they do. But the two notions are slightly different. Science wants an objective explanation; humanism desires subjective understanding. Klaus Krippendorff of the Annenberg School of Communication at the University of Pennsylvania urges us to recognize that we are both the cause and the consequence of what we observe. His *self-referential imperative* for building theory states: "Include yourself as a constituent of your own construction."[15]

To the extent that Krippendorff's imperative means abandoning a detached and dispassionate stance, Bormann's fantasy theme analysis is self-referential. In his preface to *The Force of Fantasy*, the theorist describes the personal thrill of discovery and creation:

> Mulling over the materials for my book in the history of religious and reform speaking at the same time as I was caught up in these exciting new developments in small group communication resulted in one of those exhilarating moments of illumination when it seemed clear to me that the force of fantasy is just as strong in mass communication as it is in small group interaction. Merging the discoveries in group fantasies with recent developments in rhetorical criticism provided me with my critical method—the fantasy theme analysis of rhetorical visions.[16]

This is not the account of a detached observer. However, inasmuch as the self-referential imperative calls for explicit recognition that scholars affect and are affected by the communication they study, fantasy theme analysis remains a spectator sport.

Interpretive Standard 2: Clarification of Values

A good interpretive theory brings people's values into the open. The theorist readily acknowledges his or her own ethical stance and actively seeks to unmask the ideology behind the message under scrutiny. Since fantasy theme analysis is based on the assumption that meaning, emotion, and motive for action are manifest in the content of a message, value clarification is a particular strength of symbolic convergence theory.

Not all interpretivists occupy the same moral ground, but there are core values most of them share. For example, humanists usually place a high premium on individual liberty. Krippendorff wants to make sure that scholars' drive for personal freedom extends to the people they study. His *ethical imperative* directs the theorist to "Grant others that occur in your construction the same autonomy you practice constructing them."[17] When theorists follow this rule, monologue gives way to dialogue.

Many interpretive scholars value equality as highly as they do freedom.

This commitment leads to a continual examination of the power relationships inherent in all communication. Critical theorists, in particular, insist that scholars can no longer remain ethically detached from the people they are studying or from the political and economic implications of their work. "There is no safe harbor in which researchers can avoid the power structure."[18]

As for symbolic convergence theory, Bormann's method of analyzing group fantasies seems to be ethically neutral. However, his commentary on nineteenth-century romantic pragmatism suggests that he is a man who applauds restoring the American dream of freedom, equal opportunity, hard work, and moral decency.[19] His readers would probably conclude that he'd be more in sympathy with the rhetorical vision of the African-American Million Man March on Washington to pledge self-reliance than with the Rambo fantasies of the white Montana militia.

Interpretive Standard 3: Aesthetic Appeal

Good interpretive scholarship doesn't just consider issues of artistry and aesthetics—it embodies them. Art looks at old material in a new way. The *form* of a communication theory can capture the imagination of a reader just as much as the content. According to University of Washington professor Barbara Warnick, a rhetorical critic can fill one or more of four roles—artist, analyst, audience, and advocate.[20] As an artist, the critic's job is to spark appreciation.

Symbolic convergence writing sometimes fails the test of artistry. Readers of one journal article have to plough through a ponderous sentence that runs over two hundred words![21] Yet if Bormann and his followers don't write with the lucidity or wit of an essayist for the *Atlantic* or the *New Yorker,* they aren't afraid to support their key ideas with the words of people who do. For example, Bormann underscores the importance of fantasy with Robert Frost's observation that "society can never think things out; it has to see them acted out by actors."[22]

Even when symbolic convergence prose seems heavy going, I'm intrigued by the descriptions of fantasy themes that emerge from Harley-Davidson bikers, unwed mothers, and from *The Big Book* of Alcoholics Anonymous. An analysis of AA literature reveals a rhetorical vision that is best characterized as "Fetching Good Out of Evil," a felicitous expression introduced by Bormann.[23] It only takes a few such apt turns of phrase to heighten the aesthetic appeal of the theory.

Interpretive Standard 4: A Community of Agreement

We can identify a good interpretive theory by the amount of support it generates within a community of like-minded scholars. Interpretation of meaning is subjective, but whether or not the interpreter's case is reasonable is decided ultimately by others in the field. Their acceptance or rejection is an objective fact that helps verify or vilify the theorists' judgment.

John Stewart is the editor of *Bridges, Not Walls*—a collection of humanistic articles on interpersonal communication. As the book has progressed through seven editions, Stewart's judgment to keep, drop, or add each new theoretical work was made possible by the fact that humanistic scholarship is "not a solitary enterprise carried out in a vacuum." It is instead, he says, "the effort of a community of scholars who routinely subject their findings to the scrutiny of editors, referees, and readers."[24]

A rhetorical theory can't meet the community of agreement standard unless it becomes the subject of widespread analysis. Sometimes rhetoricians address their critical arguments only to an audience of "true believers" who are already committed to the author's approach. Former NCA president David Zarefsky warns that rhetorical validity can be established only when a work is debated in the broad marketplace of ideas. For this rhetorical critic from Northwestern University, sound arguments differ from unsound ones in that

> sound arguments are addressed to the general audience of critical readers, not just to the adherents of a particular "school" or perspective. . . . They open their own reasoning process to scrutiny.[25]

When it comes to widespread scrutiny, Bormann has done it right. He's published his ideas in major journals that are open to rhetorical scholarship—the *Quarterly Journal of Speech, Communication Theory,* and *Journal of Communication* among them. While not all communication scholars find value in his theory, the majority do. When confronted by critics, Bormann has responded publicly and convincingly.[26]

Fantasy theme analysis has become a standard method of symbolic study. Based on the human nature assumption that people are symbol-users in general and storytellers in particular, the approach squares neatly with several other theories in this book.[27] As you can see, the community of agreement that supports Bormann's theory is both wide and articulate.

Interpretive Standard 5: Reform of Society

A good interpretive theory often generates change. Contrary to the notion that we can dismiss social philosophy as "mere rhetoric," the critical interpreter is a reformer who can have an impact on society. Kenneth Gergen, a Swarthmore College social psychologist, states that theory has

> the capacity to challenge the guiding assumptions of the culture, to raise fundamental questions regarding contemporary social life, to foster reconsideration of that which is "taken for granted," and thereby to generate fresh alternatives for social action.[28]

Fantasy theme analysis reliably documents rhetorical visions that contain motives to go public, gain converts, and use the mass media to spread their truth. Yet symbolic convergence theory itself has no reform agenda for society. Scholars trying to identify fantasy chains would rather probe than preach.

Bormann is trying to achieve a more modest change. As I stressed in Chapter 1, social scientists and humanists in our discipline have typically gone their separate ways. Bormann would like it otherwise. He's crafted a theory that understands fantasy theme analysis as "a liberal and humanizing art, a scholarly endeavor which aims to illuminate the human condition."[29] Definitely humanistic. But his claim that sharing fantasies (whatever they are) tends to draw people together (whoever they are) makes symbolic convergence theory a general theory of communication. Definitely scientific. Inasmuch as Bormann's joint venture between interpretive and objective study is a model that encourages rhetoricians and empiricists to work in harmony, it meets the reform agenda criterion.

BALANCING THE SCALE: SIMILAR WEIGHTS AND MEASURES

Figure 2.1 summarizes the standards that I suggest you use as you evaluate a communication theory. You'll find that I often refer to these requirements in the critique sections at the end of each chapter. As you might expect, the thirty-two theories presented in this book stack up rather well against these criteria (otherwise I wouldn't have picked them in the first place). But constructing theory is difficult, and most theories have an Achilles' heel that makes them vulnerable to criticism. All of the theorists you'll read about readily admit a need for fine tuning, and some even call for major overhauls.

Throughout this chapter I have urged using separate measures for weighing the merits of objective and interpretive theories. Yet a side-by-side comparison of the two lists in Figure 2.1 suggests that the standards used by scientists and interpretive scholars may not be as different as first thought. Consider the parallels at each of the five points:

1. *Explanation* tries to answer the question, Why? So does *understanding*.

2. *Prediction* and *value clarification* both look to the future. The first suggests what *will* happen; the second, what *ought* to happen.

3. For many students of theory, *simplicity* has *aesthetic appeal*.

Scientific Theory	Interpretive Theory
Explanation of Data	Understanding of People
Prediction of Future	Clarification of Values
Relative Simplicity	Aesthetic Appeal
Testable Hypotheses	Community of Agreement
Practical Utility	Reform of Society

FIGURE 2.1   Summary of Criteria for Evaluating Communication Theory

   4. *Testing hypotheses* is a way of achieving a *community of agreement.*

   5. A theory that actually *reforms* part of the world is certainly *practical.*

For teachers and students of communication, the parallels cited above suggest that scientists and interpreters should be friends. In fact, many communication theorists are grounded somewhere in between these two positions. So in Chapter 3, "Mapping the Territory," I describe and locate seven traditions that make up the field of communication theory and plot their relative affinity for objective or interpretive thinking.

QUESTIONS TO SHARPEN YOUR FOCUS

1. Ernest Bormann's *symbolic convergence theory* has both *objective* and *interpretive* features. Does it seem to be a better scientific or interpretive theory? Why?

2. How can we call a scientific theory good if it is *capable of being proved wrong?*

3. How can we decide when a *rhetorical critic* provides a *reasonable interpretation?*

4. Any theory involves some trade-offs; no theory can meet every standard of quality equally well. Of the ten criteria discussed, which is most important to you? Which one is least important?

A SECOND LOOK

Scientific approach: Steven Chaffee and Charles Berger, "What Communication Scientists Do," in *Handbook of Communication Science,* Charles Berger and Steven Chaffee (eds.), Sage, Newbury Park, Calif., 1987, pp. 99–122.

Scientific evaluation: Steven Chaffee, "Thinking About Theory" and Michael Beatty, "Thinking Quantitatively," in *An Integrated Approach to Communication Theory and Research,* Michael Salwen and Don Stacks (eds.), Lawrence Erlbaum Associates, Mahwah, N.J., 1996, pp. 15–32 and 33–43.

Interpretive approach: Thomas B. Farrell, "Beyond Science: Humanities Contributions to Communication Theory," in *Handbook of Communication Science,* Charles Berger and Steven Chaffee (eds.), Sage, Newbury Park, Calif., 1987, pp. 123–139.

Interpretive evaluation: Klaus Krippendorff, "On the Ethics of Constructing Communication," in *Rethinking Communication,* Vol. 1, Brenda Dervin, Lawrence Grossberg, Barbara O'Keefe, and Ellen Wartella (eds.), Sage, Newbury Park, Calif., 1989, pp. 66–96.

Recommended resource: Ernest Bormann, "Symbolic Convergence Theory: A Communication Formulation," *Journal of Communication,* Vol. 35, No. 4, 1985, pp. 128–138.

Interpretive analysis: Ernest Bormann, "Fantasy Theme Analysis and Rhetorical Theory," in *The Rhetoric of Western Thought,* 5th ed., James Golden, Goodwin Berquist, and William Coleman (eds.), Kendall/Hunt, Dubuque, Iowa, 1992, pp. 365–384.

Empirical research: Ernest Bormann, Roxann Knutson, and Karen Musolf, "Why Do People Share Fantasies? An Empirical Investigation of a Basic Tenet of the Symbolic Convergence Communication Theory," *Communication Studies,* Vol. 48, 1997, pp. 254–276.

Applied research: John Cragan and Donald Shields, *Symbolic Theories in Applied Communication Research: Bormann, Burke, and Fisher,* Hampton, Cresskill, N.J., 1995, chapters 2 and 6.

Critique and response: Ernest Bormann, John Cragan, and Donald Shields, "In Defense of Symbolic Convergence Theory: A Look at The Theory and its Criticisms After Two Decades," *Communication Theory,* Vol. 4, 1994, pp. 259–294.

CHAPTER 3

Mapping the Territory

(Seven Traditions in the Field of Communication Theory)

In their hit single, "The Things We Do For Love," the British rock group 10cc declares, "Communication is the problem to the answer."[1] Since the lyrics that follow don't explain this cryptic statement, listeners are free to interpret *communication* in different ways. *First Look* readers face the same ambiguity. Up to this point I have resisted defining the term *communication,* and I've yet to stake out the boundaries that mark the field of communication theory. That's because scholars hold widely divergent views as to what communication is, and it's hard to map the territory when surveyors don't agree on the size, shape, or exact location of the field. In that sense, there's little discipline in our discipline.

University of Colorado communication professor Robert Craig agrees that the terrain is confusing if we insist on looking for some kind of grand theoretical overview that brings all communication study into focus—a top-down, satellite picture of the communication landscape. Craig suggests, however, that communication theory is a coherent field when we understand communication as a practical discipline.[2] He's convinced we should begin our search for different types of theory on the ground where real people grapple with everyday problems and practices of communication. Craig explains that "all communication theories are relevant to a common practical lifeworld in which *communication* is already a richly meaningful term."[3] From this bottom-up perspective, communication theory is not the language of a land with no inhabitants. Rather it is the systematic and thoughtful response of communication scholars to questions posed as humans interact with each other—the best thinking within a practical discipline.

Craig thinks it's reasonable to talk about a *field of communication theory* if we take a collective look at the actual approaches that researchers have used to study communication problems and practices. He identifies seven established traditions of communication theory that include most, if not all, of what theorists have done. These already established traditions offer "distinct, alternative vocabularies" that describe different "ways of conceptualizing communication problems and practices."[4] This means that scholars within a given tradition talk comfortably with each other, but often take potshots at those who work in other camps. As Craig suggests, we shouldn't try to smooth over these between-group battles. Theorists argue because they have something important to argue about.

In the rest of the chapter I'll outline the seven traditions that Craig describes. Taken together, they provide a helpful survey of the field of communication theory. The classification will also help you understand why some theories share common ground, while others are effectively fenced off from each other by conflicting goals and assumptions. As I introduce each tradition, I'll highlight how its advocates tend to define communication, suggest a practical communication problem that this kind of theory addresses, and describe an early theorist or school of theorists who helped set the agenda for those who followed.[5]

THE SOCIO-PSYCHOLOGICAL TRADITION
Communication as Interpersonal Influence

The socio-psychological tradition epitomizes the scientific or objective perspective described in Chapter 2. Scholars in this tradition believe there are communication truths that can be discovered by careful, systematic observation. They look for cause-and-effect relationships that will predict when a communication behavior will succeed, and when it will fail. When they find such causal links, they are well on the way to answering the ever-present question of persuasion practitioners: "What can I do to get them to change?"

When researchers search for universal laws of communication, they try to focus on what *is* without being biased by their personal view of what *ought to be*. As empiricists, they heed the warning of the skeptical newspaper editor: "You think your mother loves you? Check it out—at least two sources." For communication theorists in the socio-psychological tradition, checking it out usually means designing and running a series of controlled experiments.

Psychologist Carl Hovland was one of the "founding fathers" of experimental research on the effects of communication.[6] Hovland headed up a group of thirty researchers at Yale University who sought to lay a "groundwork of empirical propositions concerning the relationships between communication stimuli, audience predisposition, and opinion change," and to provide "an initial framework for subsequent theory building."[7]

Working within a framework of *"who* says *what* to *whom* and with what *effect,"* the Yale Attitude Studies explored three separate causes of persuasive variation:

Who—source of the message (expertise, trustworthiness)

What—content of the message (fear appeals, order of arguments)

Whom—audience characteristics (personality, susceptibility to influence)

The main *effect* they measured was opinion change as revealed by attitude scales given before and after the message. Although the Yale researchers plowed new ground in many areas, their work on source credibility attracted the most interest.

Hovland and his colleagues discovered that a message from a high-credibility source produced large shifts of opinion compared to the same message coming from a low-credibility source. For example, an article on cures for the common cold carried more weight when it was attributed to a doctor writing in *The New England Journal of Medicine* than to a staff reporter from *Life* magazine. Once this overall effect was firmly established, they began to test specific variables one by one.

The Yale researchers found two types of credibility—*expertness* and *character*. Experts were those who seemed to know what they were talking about; audiences judged character on the basis of perceived sincerity. Expertness turned out to be more important than character in boosting opinion change, but the persuasive effects didn't last. Within a few weeks the difference between high and low credible sources disappeared. Hovland and his colleagues called this the "sleeper effect" and ran further experiments to figure out why it happened and ways to overcome it. They discovered that, over time, people forget where they heard or read about an idea, and that by reestablishing a link between the source and the message, credibility would still make a significant difference. Beyond the specific findings, the Yale Attitude Studies are significant to the socio-psychological tradition of communication theory because the researchers didn't accept any claim on faith. They systematically checked it out.

THE CYBERNETIC TRADITION
Communication as Information Processing

MIT scientist Norbert Wiener coined the word *cybernetics* to describe the field of artificial intelligence.[8] The term is a transliteration of the Greek word for "steersman" or "governor," and pictures the way feedback makes information processing possible in our heads and on our laptop computers. During World War II, Wiener developed an antiaircraft firing system that adjusted future trajectory by taking into account the results of past performance. His concept of feedback anchored the cybernetic tradition that regards communication as the link connecting the separate parts of any system, such as a computer system, a family system, an organizational system, or a media system.

The idea of communication as information processing was firmly established by Claude Shannon, a Bell Telephone Company research scientist who developed a mathematical theory of signal transmission. His goal was to get maximum line capacity with minimum distortion. Shannon showed little interest in the meaning of a message or its effect on the listener. His theory merely aimed at solving the technical problems of high-fidelity transfer of sound.

Since Bell Laboratories paid the bill for Shannon's research, it seems only fair to use a telephone call you might make to explain his model shown in Figure 3.1. Shannon would see you as the information source. You speak your message into the telephone mouthpiece, which transmits a signal through the telephone-wire channel. The received signal picks up static noise along the way, and this altered signal is reconverted to sound by the receiver in the earpiece

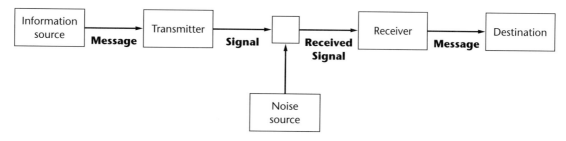

FIGURE 3.1   Shannon and Weaver's Model of Communication
(Adapted from Shannon and Weaver, *The Mathematical Theory of Communication.*)

at the destination. Information loss occurs every step of the way so that the message received differs from the one you sent. The ultimate aim of information theory is to maximize the amount of information the system can carry.

Most of us are comfortable with the notion that information is simply "stuff that matters or anything that makes a difference."[9] For Shannon, however, *information* refers to the reduction of uncertainty. The amount of information a message contains is measured by how much it combats chaos. If you phone home and tell your family that you've just accepted a public relations internship in Chicago for the summer, you've conveyed lots of information because your message reduces a great amount of your folks' uncertainty about your immediate future. The less predictable the message, the more information it carries. There are many fine things that can be said over a communication channel that don't qualify as information. Perhaps your phone call is merely an "I just called to say I love you" reminder. If the person on the other end has no doubt of your love, the words are warm ritual rather than information. When the destination party already knows what's coming, information is zero.

Noise is the enemy of information because it cuts into the information-carrying capacity of the channel between the transmitter and receiver. Shannon describes the relationship with a simple equation:[10]

$$\text{Channel Capacity} = \text{Information} + \text{Noise}$$

Every channel has an upper limit on the information it can carry. Even if you resort to a fast-talking monologue, a three-minute telephone call restricts you to using a maximum of 600 words. But noise on the line, surrounding distractions, and static in the mind of your listener all suggest that you should devote a portion of the channel capacity to repeating key ideas that might otherwise be lost. Without a great amount of reiteration, restatement, and redundancy, a noisy channel is quickly overloaded. On the other hand, needless duplication is boring for the listener and wastes channel capacity. Shannon regards communication as the applied science of maintaining an optimal balance between predictability and uncertainty. His theory of signal transmission is an engineer's response to everyday problems of system glitches, overloads, and breakdowns.

"Our biggest problem around here is lack of information. Of course, I have nothing to base that on."

Reproduced by permission of Punch.

Shannon's diagram of information flow appears in almost every communication textbook, which is likely due to the fact that it was paired with an interpretive essay by Warren Weaver that applied the concept of information loss to interpersonal communication. Feedback was not an inherent feature of Shannon and Weaver's information model; it took other theorists in the cybernetic tradition to introduce concepts of interactivity, power imbalances, and emotional response into communication systems.

THE RHETORICAL TRADITION
Communication as Artful Public Address

Greco-Roman rhetoric was the main source of wisdom about communication well into the twentieth century. In the fourth century B.C., Demosthenes raged against the sea with pebbles in his mouth in order to improve his articulation when he spoke in the Athenian assembly. A few hundred years later, the Roman statesman Cicero refined and applied a system for discovering the key issue in any legal case. In 1963 Martin Luther King, Jr., crafted his moving "I Have A Dream" speech using such stylistic devices as visual depiction, repetition, alliteration, and metaphor. These three men, and thousands like them, perpetuated the Greco-Roman tradition of oratory that began with the Sophists in the ancient city-states of the Mediterranean, and still continues today. Whether talking to a crowd, a legislative assembly, a jury, or a single judge, orators seek practical advice on how to best present their case.

There are a half-dozen features that characterize this influential tradition of rhetorical communication:

- A conviction that speech distinguishes humans from other animals. Of oral communication, Cicero asks: "What other power could have been strong enough either to gather scattered humanity into one place, or to lead it out of its brutish existence in the wilderness up to our present condition of citizens, or, after the establishment of social communities, to give shape to laws, tribunals, and civic rights?"[11]

- A confidence that public address delivered in a democratic forum is a more effective way to solve political problems than rule by decree or resorting to force. Within this tradition, the phrase "mere rhetoric" is a contradiction of terms.

- A setting where a single speaker attempts to influence an audience of many listeners through explicitly persuasive discourse. Public speaking is essentially one-way communication.

- Oratorical training as the cornerstone of a leader's education. Speakers learn to develop strong arguments and powerful voices that carry to the edge of a crowd without electronic amplification.

- An emphasis on the power and beauty of language to move people emotionally and stir them to action. Rhetoric is more art than science.

- Oral public persuasion as the province of males. Until the 1800s, women had virtually no opportunity to have their voices heard. So a key feature of the women's movement in America has been the struggle for the right to speak in public.

Within the rhetorical tradition, there has been an ongoing tension between the relative value of study and practice in the development of effective public speakers. Some speech coaches believe there is no substitute for honing skills before an audience. "Practice makes perfect," they say. Other teachers insist that practice merely makes permanent. If speakers don't learn from the systematic advice of Aristotle (see Chapter 20) and others in the Greco-Roman tradition, they are doomed to repeat the same mistakes whenever they speak. The fact that this debate continues suggests that both factors play an important role in artful public address.

THE SEMIOTIC TRADITION
Communication as the Process of Sharing Meaning Through Signs

Semiotics is the study of signs. A *sign* is anything that can stand for something else. High body temperature is a <u>sign</u> of infection. Birds flying south <u>signal</u> the coming of winter. An expensive car <u>signifies</u> wealth. An arrow <u>designates</u> which direction to go.

Words are also signs, but of a special kind. They are *symbols*. Unlike the examples cited above, most symbols have no natural connection with the things they describe. There's nothing in the sound of the word *kiss* or anything visual in the letters *h-u-g* that signifies an embrace. One could just as easily coin the term *snarf* or *clag* to symbolize a close encounter of the romantic kind. The same thing is true for nonverbal symbols like winks or waves.

Cambridge University literary critic I. A. Richards was one of the first in the semiotic tradition to systematically describe how words work. According to Richards, words are arbitrary symbols that have no inherent meaning. Like chameleons that take on the coloration of their environment, words take on the meaning of the context in which they are used. He therefore railed against the semantic trap which he labeled "the proper meaning superstition"—the mistaken belief that words have a precise definition. For Richards and other semiologists, meanings don't reside in words or other symbols; meanings reside in people.

Together with his British colleague, C. K. Ogden, Richards created his semantic triangle to show the indirect relationship between symbols and their supposed referents. Figure 3.2 illustrates the iffy link between the word *dog* and the actual hound that may consume the majority of your groceries.

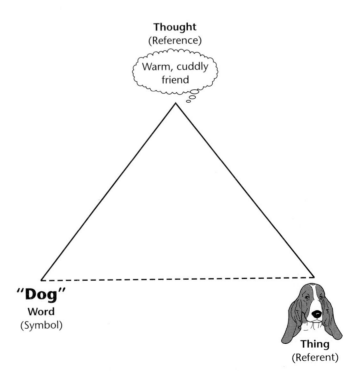

FIGURE 3.2   Richards' Semantic Triangle
(Adapted from Ogden and Richards, *The Meaning of Meaning*.)

The top of the triangle shows some thoughts that you might have when observing the Hush Puppy pictured at the lower right. Once you perceive the actual animal, thoughts of warmth and faithful friendship fill your mind. Since there is a direct or causal relationship between the referent and the reference, Richards connected the two with a solid line.

Your thoughts are also directly linked with the dog symbol at the lower left of the triangle. Based on childhood language learning, using the word *dog* to symbolize your thoughts is quite natural. Richards diagrammed this causal relationship with a solid line as well.

But the connection between the word *dog* and the actual animal is tenuous at best. Richards represented it with a dotted line. Two people could use that identical word to stand for completely different beasts. When you say *dog,* you might mean a slow-moving, gentle pet who is very fond of children. When I use the word I might mean a carnivorous canine who bites anyone—and is very fond of children. (Note the slippery use of the term *fond* in this example.) Unless we both understand that ambiguity is an inevitable condition of language, you and I are liable to carry on a conversation about dogs without ever realizing we're talking about two very different breeds.

Although Richards and Ferdinand de Saussure (the man who coined the term *semiology*) were fascinated with language, many researchers in the semiotic tradition focus on nonverbal emblems and pictorial images. For example, the French semiologist Roland Barthes analyzed the emotional and ideological meanings created by print and broadcast media (see Chapter 24). But whether the signs are a few pictures or thousands of words, scholars in this tradition are concerned with the way signs mediate meaning, and how they might be used to avoid misunderstanding rather than create it.

THE SOCIO-CULTURAL TRADITION
Communication as the Creation and Enactment of Social Reality

The socio-cultural tradition is based on the premise that, as people talk, they produce and reproduce culture. Most of us assume that words reflect what actually exists. However, theorists in this tradition suggest that the process often works the other way around. Our view of reality is strongly shaped by the language we've used since we were infants.

We've already seen that the semiotic tradition holds that most words have no necessary or logical connection with the ideas they represent. For example, the link between black marks on a page that spell **g-r-e-e-n** and the color of the lawn in front of the library is merely a convention among English-speaking people. Although socio-cultural theorists agree that the term *green* is arbitrary, they also claim that the ability to <u>see</u> green as a distinct color depends on having a specific word to label the 510–560 nanometer band of the electromagnetic wave spectrum.[12] English offers such a word, but many Native American languages don't. Within these cultures, yellow is described as merging directly into blue. We might be tempted to label these speakers "color blind," yet they

Reprinted with permission of Kaiser Aluminum &
Chemical Corporation from COMMUNICATION:
THE TRANSFER OF MEANING by Don Fabun.
Copyright © 1968, Kaiser Aluminum & Chemical
Corporation.

really aren't. Linguists in the socio-cultural tradition would say that these language users inhabit a different world.

University of Chicago linguist Edward Sapir and his student Benjamin Lee Whorf were pioneers in the socio-cultural tradition. The Sapir–Whorf hypothesis of linguistic relativity states that the structure of a culture's language shapes what people think and do.[13] "The 'real world' is to a large extent unconsciously built upon the language habits of the group."[14] Their theory of linguistic relativity counters the assumptions that all languages are similar and that words merely act as neutral vehicles to carry meaning.

Consider the second-person singular pronoun that English speakers use to address another person. No matter what the relationship, Americans use the word *you*. German speakers are forced to label the relationship as either formal (*Sie*) or familiar (*du*). They even have a ceremony (*Bruderschaft*) to celebrate a shift in relationship from *Sie* to *du*. Japanese vocabulary compels a speaker to recognize many more relational distinctions. That language offers ten alternatives—all translated "you" in English—yet only one term is proper in any given relationship, depending on the gender, age, and status of the speaker.

While most observers assume that English, German, and Japanese vocabularies *reflect* cultural differences in relationship patterns, the Sapir–Whorf hypothesis suggests that it works the other way around as well. Language actually structures our perception of reality. As children learn to talk, they also learn what to look for. Most of the world goes unnoticed because it is literally *unremarkable.*

Contemporary socio-cultural theorists claim that it is through the process of communication that "reality is produced, maintained, repaired, and transformed."[15] Or stated in the active voice, *persons-in-conversation co-construct their own social worlds.*[16] When these perceptual worlds collide, the socio-cultural tradition offers help in bridging the culture gap that exists between "us" and "them."

THE CRITICAL TRADITION
Communication as a Reflective Challenge of Unjust Discourse

The term *critical theory* comes from the work of a group of German scholars known as the "Frankfurt School" because they were part of the independent Institute for Social Research at Frankfurt University. Originally set up to test the ideas of Karl Marx, the Frankfurt School rejected the economic determinism of orthodox Marxism, yet carried on the Marxist tradition of critiquing society.

The leading figures of the Frankfurt School—Max Horkheimer, Theodor Adorno, and Herbert Marcuse—were convinced that "all previous history has been characterized by an unjust distribution of suffering."[17] They spotted this same pattern of inequality in modern western democracies where the "haves" continued to exploit the "have nots." Frankfurt School researchers offered thoughtful analyses of discrepancies between the liberal values of freedom and equality that leaders proclaimed, and the unjust concentrations and abuses of power that made these values a myth. These critiques offered no apology for their negative tone or pessimistic conclusions. As Marcuse noted, "Critical theory preserves obstinacy as a genuine quality of philosophical thought."[18] When Hitler came to power in Germany, that obstinacy forced the Frankfurt School into exile—first to Switzerland, then to the United States.

What types of communication research and practice are critical theorists <u>against</u>? Although there is no single set of abuses that all denounce, critical theorists consistently challenge three features of contemporary society:

1. *The control of language to perpetuate power imbalances.* Critical theorists condemn any use of words that inhibits emancipation. For example, feminist scholars point out that women tend to be a muted group because men are the gatekeepers of language. The resultant public discourse is shot through with metaphors drawn from war and sports—masculine arenas with their own in-group lingo. This concept of muted groups is not new. Marcuse claimed that "the avenues of entrance are closed to the meaning of words and ideas other than the established one—established by the publicity of the powers that be, and verified in their practices."[19]

2. *The role of mass media in dulling sensitivity to repression.* Marx claimed that religion was the opiate of the masses, distracting working-class audiences from their "real" interests. Critical theorists see the "culture industries" of television, film, CDs, and print media as taking over that role. Adorno was hopeful that people might rise in protest once they realized their unjust repression. Yet he noted that "with populations becoming increasingly subject to the power of mass communications, the pre-formation of people's minds has increased to a degree that scarcely allows room for an awareness of it on the part of the people themselves."[20] Marcuse was even more pessimistic about social change coming from the average citizen who is numbed by the mass media. He claimed that hope for change in society comes from "the outcasts and outsiders, the exploited and persecuted of other races and other colors, the unemployed and the unemployable."[21]

3. *Blind reliance on the scientific method and uncritical acceptance of empirical findings.* Horkheimer claimed that "it is naïve and bigoted to think and speak only in the language of science."[22] <u>Naïve</u> because science is not the value-free pursuit of knowledge that it claims to be. <u>Bigoted</u> because survey researchers assume that a sample of public opinion is a true slice of reality. Adorno contends that "the cross-section of attitudes represents, not an approximation to the truth, but a cross-section of social illusion."[23] These theorists are particularly critical of leaders in government, business, and education who use the empirical trappings of social science to validate an unjust status quo—to "bless the mess" which obviously favors them.

Critical theorists are less specific about what they are <u>for</u>. Their essays are filled with calls for liberation, emancipation, transformation, and consciousness raising, but they are often vague on how to achieve these worthy goals. They do, however, share a common ethical agenda that considers solidarity with suffering human beings as our minimal moral responsibility. That's why Adorno declared, "To write poetry after Auschwitz is barbaric."[24] Most critical theorists hope to move beyond feelings of sympathy and stimulate a more demanding ethical conduct which Craig calls *praxis*. He defines the word as "theoretically reflective social action,"[25] and many of the thinkers featured in "Ethical Reflections" throughout the book are energized by that same goal.

THE PHENOMENOLOGICAL TRADITION
Communication as the Experience of Self and Others Through Dialogue

Although *phenomenology* is an imposing philosophical term, it basically refers to the intentional analysis of everyday life from the standpoint of the person who is living it. Thus the phenomenological tradition places great emphasis on people's interpretation of their own subjective experience. An individual's story becomes more important—and more authoritative—than any research hypothesis or communication axiom. As psychologist Carl Rogers asserts, "Neither the Bible nor the prophets—neither Freud nor research—neither the revelations of God nor man—can take precedence over my own direct experience."[26]

The problem, of course, is that no two people have the same life story. Since we cannot experience another person's experience, we tend to talk past each other and then lament, "Nobody understands what it's like to be me." Can two people get beyond surface impressions and connect at a deeper level? Based on years of nondirective counseling experience, Carl Rogers was confident that personal and relational growth is indeed possible.

Rogers believed that his clients' health improved when his communication created a safe environment for them to talk. He described three necessary and sufficient conditions for personality and relationship change. If clients perceived a counselor's (1) congruence, (2) unconditional positive regard, and (3) empathic understanding, they could and would get better.[27]

Congruence is the match or fit between an individual's inner feelings and outer display. The congruent counselor is genuine, real, integrated, whole, transparent. The noncongruent person tries to impress, plays a role, puts up a front, hides behind a facade. "In my relationship with persons," Rogers wrote, "I've found that it does not help, in the long run, to act as though I was something I was not."[28]

Unconditional positive regard is an attitude of acceptance that isn't contingent on performance. Rogers asked, "Can I let myself experience positive attitudes toward this other person—attitudes of warmth, caring, liking, interest, and respect?"[29] When the answer was "Yes," both he and his clients matured as human beings. They also liked each other.

Empathic understanding is the caring skill of temporarily laying aside our views and values and of entering into another's world without prejudice. It is an active process of seeking to hear the other's thoughts, feelings, tones, and meanings as if they were our own. Rogers thought it was a waste of time to be suspicious or to wonder, "What does she really mean?" He believed that we help people most when we accept what they say at face value. We should assume that they describe their world as it really appears to them.

Although Rogers' necessary and sufficient conditions emerged in a therapeutic setting, he was certain that they were equally important in all interpersonal relationships. Jewish philosopher and theologian Martin Buber reached a similar conclusion. He held out the possibility of authentic human relationships through dialogue—an intentional process in which the only agenda both parties have is to understand what it's like to be the other. The ideas of Rogers, Buber, and others in the phenomenological tradition have permeated the textbooks and teaching of interpersonal communication.

FENCING THE FIELD OF COMMUNICATION THEORY

The seven traditions I've described have deep roots in the field of communication theory. Of course, theorists, researchers, and practitioners working within a given tradition often hear criticism that their particular approach has no legitimacy. In addition to whatever arguments they might muster to defend their choice, they can also claim "squatters' rights" because scholars who went before already established the right to occupy that portion of land. Taking the real estate metaphor seriously, in Figure 3.3 I've charted the seven traditions as bounded parcels of land that collectively make up the larger field of study. A few explanations are in order.

First, the seven charted traditions might not cover every approach to communication theory. Craig considers the possibility that a feminist, aesthetic, economic, spiritual, or media tradition should also be included.[30] He ultimately

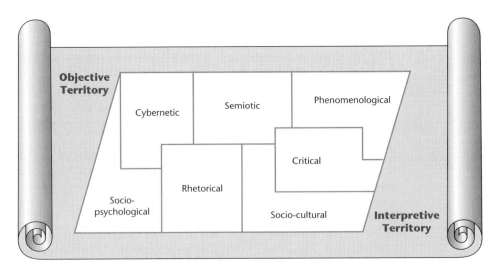

FIGURE 3.3   A Survey Map of Traditions in the Field of Communication Theory

decides that these approaches can best be located among the seven traditions already named, but his openness to new candidates suggests that the map of the field may need to expand.

Second, hybrids are possible across traditions. You've seen throughout the chapter that each tradition has its own way of defining communication and its own distinct vocabulary. So it's fair to think of the lines on the map that divide the individual parcels as fences built to keep out strange ideas. Scholars are an independent bunch, however. They climb fences, read journals, and fly to far-away conferences. This cross-pollination sometimes results in theory grounded in two or three traditions. I make an effort in Appendix C to assign each theory to a single tradition, but a third of them straddle a fence.

Finally, it's important to realize that the location of each tradition on the map is far from random. My rationale for placing them where they are is the distinction between *objective* and *interpretive* theories outlined in the previous chapters. Using criteria presented in Chapters 1 and 2, the socio-psychological tradition is most objective, so it occupies the far left position on the map. Moving from left to right, the traditions become more interpretive and less objective. The phenomenological tradition seems the most interpretive, so it occupies the position farthest to the right. The order of presentation in this chapter followed the same progression—a gradual shift from objective to interpretive concerns. Scholars working in adjacent traditions usually have an easier time appreciating each other's work. On the map they share a common border; professionally they are closer together in their basic assumptions.

This framework of seven traditions can help make sense out of the great diversity in the field of communication theory. As you read about a theory in the media effects section, remember that it may have the same ancestry as a theory you studied earlier in the relationship development section. I'll draw connections along the way and systematically sort the theories by tradition after you've had a chance to understand them. Hopefully by then you'll want to take issue with the 10cc lyric, "Communication is the problem to the answer." In their own way, each of these seven different traditions of communication theory tells us how communication can be the answer to the problem.

QUESTIONS TO SHARPEN YOUR FOCUS

1. Considering the difference between *objective* and *interpretive* theory, can you make a case that the *rhetorical* tradition is less objective than the *semiotic* one, or the *socio-cultural* tradition more interpretive than the *critical* one?

2. The lyrics of "The Things We Do For Love" describe romance as an emotional roller-coaster. If true, which of the seven highlighted *definitions of communication* offer the most promise of helping you achieve a stable relationship?

3. Craig characterizes communication as a *practical discipline*. What kind of communication problems would the *socio-psychological* tradition help resolve? The *cybernetic* tradition? The *phenomenological* tradition?

4. The map in Figure 3.3 represents seven traditions in the field of communication theory. In which region do you feel most at home? What other areas would you like to explore? Where would you be uncomfortable? Why?

A SECOND LOOK

Recommended resource: Robert T. Craig, "Communication Theory as a Field," *Communication Theory,* Vol. 9, 1999, pp. 119–161.

Communication as a practical discipline: Robert T. Craig, "Communication as a Practical Discipline," in *Rethinking Communication,* Vol. 1, Brenda Dervin, Lawrence Grossberg, Barbara O'Keefe, and Ellen Wartella (eds.), Sage, Newbury Park, Calif., 1989, pp. 97–122.

Socio-psychological tradition: Carl Hovland, Irving Janis, and Harold Kelley, *Communication and Persuasion,* Yale University, New Haven, Conn., 1953, pp. 1–55.

Cybernetic tradition: Norbert Wiener, *The Human Use of Human Beings,* Avon, New York, 1967, pp. 23–100.

Rhetorical tradition: Thomas M. Conley, *Rhetoric in the European Tradition,* Longman, New York, 1990, pp. 1–52.

Semiotic tradition: C. K. Ogden and I. A. Richards, *The Meaning of Meaning,* Harcourt, Brace & World, New York, 1946, pp. 1–23.

Phenomenological tradition: Carl Rogers, "The Characteristics of a Helping Relationship," *On Becoming a Person,* 1961, pp. 39–58.

Socio-cultural tradition: Benjamin Lee Whorf, "The Relation of Habitual Thought and Behaviour to Language," in *Language, Culture, and Personality: Essays in Memory of Edward Sapir,* University of Utah, Salt Lake City, 1941, pp. 123–149.

Critical tradition: Raymond Morrow with David Brown, *Critical Theory and Methodology,* Sage, Thousand Oaks, Calif., 1994, pp. 3–34, 85–112.

PART TWO

Interpersonal Communication

INTERPERSONAL MESSAGES

Literary critic I. A. Richards recognized the power of visual association in the way we think. He described thinking as the process of sorting experience into various categories.[1] The metaphor of sorting through mental memories like a batch of photos resonates with my own cognitive experience, because like many people, I tend to think in pictures. For example, when I hear the word *risk* I imagine skydivers plunging toward the earth, commodity traders betting their bankroll on the future price of soybeans, or a shy college student confessing old fears to a new friend.

The human inclination to think pictorially has a bearing on how we study interpersonal messages. I could define interpersonal communication as *the process of creating unique shared meaning,* but the impact of this statement depends on the images it calls to mind. Many people imagine some kind of game and various communication scholars refer to *language games, rules of the game, game-like behavior,* and even *game theory.* So I'll use three specific game metaphors to illustrate what interpersonal communication *is,* and what it *is not.*[2]

Communication as Bowling. Bowling is the number one participation sport in the United States. Although it doesn't have the glamour of tennis or the addictive quality of jogging, more people try to convert a ten-pin spare than work on their backhand or run in a 5K race. A bowling model of message delivery is probably the most widely held view of communication as well. I think that's unfortunate.

In the bowling model, the bowler is the sender. He or she addresses the pins—the target audience. The bowler then delivers the ball—the message. It rolls down the lane—the channel for the message and clutter in the lane/channel can deflect the ball/message. It strikes the passive pins/audience with a predictable effect.

In this one-way model of communication, the speaker/bowler must take care to select a precisely crafted message/ball and practice diligently to deliver it the same way every time. Of course that only makes sense if target listeners are interchangeable static pins waiting to be bowled over by our words—which they aren't. Communication theory that emphasizes message content to the neglect of relational factors simply isn't practical.

The bowling analogy also fails because the pins don't roll the ball back at the bowler. In the days before automatic pinsetters, I once angered the "pin boy" who was working the lane. My ball came back with spit in the finger holes. Real-life interpersonal communication is sometimes messy, often unpredictable, and it always involves more than just the speaker's action. This realization has led some observers to propose an interactive model for interpersonal communication.

Communication as Ping-Pong. Unlike bowling, Ping-Pong is not a solo game. This fact alone makes it a better analogy for interpersonal communication. One party puts the conversational ball in play and the other gets into position to receive. It takes more concentration and skill to receive than serve because while the speaker/server knows where the message is going, the listener/receiver doesn't. Like a verbal or nonverbal message, the ball may appear straightforward, yet have a deceptive spin.

50

"I'm suddenly filled with a strong but vague sense of foreboding."

Ping-Pong is a back-and-forth game; players switch roles continuously. One moment the person behind the paddle is an initiator, the next second that same player is a reactor, gauging the effectiveness of his or her shot by the way the ball comes back. The repeated adjustment essential for good play closely parallels the feedback process described in a number of interpersonal communication theories, yet there are still three inherent flaws in the table-tennis analogy.

In the first place, Ping-Pong is played in a controlled environment where the platform is stable, the bounce is true, and the ball is not deflected by the wind. In contrast, most face-to-face communication occurs in a storm of distraction.

The second defect is that the game is played with one ball, which at any given time is headed in a single direction. That's similar to the game of Password where one player says a word and then the other responds with another word. Back and forth they go in a turn-taking ritual until communication is successful. A true model of interpersonal encounters would have people sending and receiving balls at the same time.

The third problem is that Ping-Pong is a competitive game—someone wins and someone loses. In successful dialogue, both people win.

Communication as Charades. The game of charades better captures the simultaneous and cooperative nature of interpersonal communication. A charade is neither an action, like a strike in bowling, nor an interaction, like a rally in Ping-Pong. It's a transaction.

Charades is a mutual game. Although a team of two or more may compete against others, the actual play is cooperative. One member draws a title or slogan from a batch of possibilities and then tries to act it out visually for teammates in a silent minidrama. The goal is to get at least one partner to say the exact words on the slip of paper. Of course, the actor is prohibited from talking out loud.

Suppose you drew the saying, "God helps those who help themselves." That sentiment might not square with your idea of "amazing grace," but that's not the point. Your job is to create mental pictures for others that will cause them to utter those identical words. For *God* you might try folding your hands and gazing upwards. For *helps* you could act out washing dishes or changing a flat tire. By pointing at a number of real or imaginary people you may elicit a response of *them*, and by this point a partner may shout out, "God helps those who help themselves." Success.

Like charades, interpersonal communication is a mutual, ongoing process using verbal and nonverbal messages with another person to create and alter the images in both of our minds. Communication between us begins when there is some overlap between two images, and is effective to the extent that overlap increases. But even if our mental pictures were congruent, communication would be partial as long as we interpreted them differently. The idea that "God helps those who help themselves" could strike one person as a hollow promise, while the other might regard it as a divine stamp of approval for hard work.

All four theories in this section reject a simplistic one-way bowling analogy and an interactive Ping-Pong model of interpersonal communication. Instead, they view interpersonal communication in a way more akin to charades—a complex transaction in which overlapping messages simultaneously affect and are affected by the other person and multiple factors.

Chapter 4 presents George Herbert Mead's symbolic interactionism, a wide-ranging theory that links language with perception, thinking, self-concept, and culture. Mead regarded the ability to communicate with words as the essence of being human. He was interested in the way we attach labels to people and their actions—especially our own.

Similar to Mead, Barnett Pearce and Vernon Cronen believe that through communication, people create their own social reality. Chapter 5 presents their coordinated management of meaning (CMM) which suggests that all of us use communication to coordinate our actions with the behavior of others, to make sense of that interaction, and to remind ourselves that some things in life are not yet known.

Chapter 6 traces the development of Judee Burgoon's expectancy violations theory that forecasts how others will respond when a communicator acts in inappropriate ways. Her early model included the surprising prediction that there are times when talking at a distance "too close" or "too far" may actually help a person achieve a communication goal. She later expanded the theory to include a variety of nonverbal behaviors such as touch, eye contact, and facial expression, and she now uses it to explain the effects of verbal violations as well.

Together with David Buller, Burgoon has also crafted a theory that explores the interpersonal dynamics of deception in face-to-face interaction. Chapter 7 outlines Buller and Burgoon's interpersonal deception theory, which rejects the simplistic notion that it's easy to spot when others are lying. The intricacy of the theorists' explanation is typical of all four theories in this section. If you care about self-concept, conflict, nonconformity, and deception, you won't be bored.

Symbolic Interactionism
of George Herbert Mead

Jodie Foster received a best actress Oscar nomination for her 1994 portrayal of a backwoods Appalachian woman raised in almost total isolation. The film, *Nell*, covers a three-month period of the young woman's life immediately following the death of her mother.[1] Nell is discovered by Jerry Lovell, a small-town doctor who is quickly joined by Paula Olsen, a psychologist from a big city university medical center. Both are appalled and fascinated by this grown up "wild child" who cowers in terror and makes incomprehensible sounds.

Nell is based on the play *Idioglossia*, a Greek term meaning a personal or private language. As Jerry and Paula come to realize, Nell's speech is not gibberish. Her language is based on the King James version of the Bible, which her mother read to her out loud for over twenty years. Yet because the mother had suffered a stroke that left one side of her face paralyzed, the words Nell learned were unintelligible to anyone else.

Early in the film Paula labels Nell "autistic" and tries to have her committed to a psych ward for observation. Jerry, on the other hand, treats Nell as a frightened human being and tries to get to know her by learning her dialect. Although fiction, the movie is an intriguing story about the civilizing influence of language. As such, it could easily have been scripted by a symbolic interactionist. I'll use scenes from the film to illustrate the key ideas of George Herbert Mead, his student Herbert Blumer, and others who adopt an interactionist approach.

Mead was a philosophy professor at the University of Chicago for the first three decades of the twentieth century. As a close personal friend of the renowned pragmatist John Dewey, he shared Dewey's applied approach to knowledge. Mead thought that the true test of any theory is whether or not it is useful in solving complex social problems. He was a social activist who marched for women's suffrage, championed labor unions in an era of robber-baron capitalism, and helped launch the urban settlement house movement with pioneer social worker Jane Addams.

Although Mead taught in a philosophy department, he is best known by sociologists as the teacher who trained a generation of the best minds in their field. Strangely, he never set forth his wide-ranging ideas in a book or systematic treatise. After he died in 1934, his students pulled together class notes and conversations with their mentor and published *Mind, Self, and Society* in his name. It was only then that his chief disciple, Herbert Blumer at the University of California–Berkeley, coined the term *symbolic interactionism.* The words capture what Mead claimed was the most human and humanizing activity that people can engage in—talking to each other.

Blumer stated three core principles of symbolic interactionism that deal with *meaning, language,* and *thought.*[2] These premises lead to conclusions about the creation of a person's *self* and socialization into a larger *community.* The rest of this chapter discusses these topics one by one. As you will see, all of these themes are prominent in the story of Nell.

MEANING: THE CONSTRUCTION OF SOCIAL REALITY

Blumer starts with the premise that humans act toward people or things on the basis of the meanings they assign to those people or things. The viewer of *Nell* can see this principle played out in the radically different responses that Jodie Foster's character elicits from the people she meets. The county sheriff regards Nell as crazy and suggests she be put in a padded cell. His chronically depressed wife sees Nell as a free spirit and joins her in a lighthearted game of patty-cake. The chief psychiatrist at the medical center views this child-of-the-wild case as a chance to make research history and insists the patient be brought to the center for study. And because a group of sleazy guys in a pool hall are convinced that Nell will mindlessly mimic any action she sees, they approach her as easy sexual prey. As for the doctor who found her, Jerry assumes Nell is fully human and seeks to become her friend. She in turn calls Jerry her guardian angel.

Which of these interpretations is correct? Who is the *real* Nell? From Mead's pragmatic standpoint, the answer doesn't make much difference. Once people define a situation as real, it's very real in its consequences.[3] And with the possible exception of Jerry, all of the people in the story regard Nell as totally other than themselves—an oddity to be explored or exploited.

In June Wagner's one-woman play *The Search for Signs of Intelligent Life in the Universe,* Trudy the bag lady views society from her perspective on the street. Her words underscore the interactionist position that meaning-making is a community project:

> It's my belief we all, at one time or another,
> secretly ask ourselves the question,
> "Am *I* crazy?"
> In my case, the answer came back: A resounding
> YES!
>
> You're thinkin': How does a person know if they're crazy or not? Well, sometimes you don't know. Sometimes you can go through life suspecting you *are* but never

really knowing for sure. Sometimes you know for sure 'cause you got so many people tellin' you you're crazy that it's your word against everyone else's. . . .

After all, what is reality anyway? Nothin' but a collective hunch.[4]

LANGUAGE: THE SOURCE OF MEANING

Blumer's second premise is that meaning arises out of the social interaction that people have with each other. In other words, meaning is not inherent in objects; it's not preexistent in a state of nature. Meaning is negotiated through the use of language—hence the term *symbolic interactionism*.

As human beings, we have the ability to name things. We can designate a specific object (*person*), identify an action (*scream*), or refer to an abstract idea (*crazy*). Occasionally a word sounds like the thing it describes (*smack, thud, crash*), but usually the names we use have no logical connection with the object at hand. Symbols are arbitrary signs. There's nothing inherently small, soft, or lovable in the word *kitten*.[5] It's only by talking with others—symbolic interaction—that we come to ascribe that meaning and develop a universe of discourse.

Mead believed that symbolic naming is the basis for human society. The book of Genesis in the Bible states that Adam's first job was to name the animals—the dawn of civilization. Interactionists claim that the extent of knowing is dependent on the extent of naming. Although language can be a prison that confines us, we have the potential to push back the walls and bars as we master more words. You know from your experience of taking the SAT or ACT College Board exams that half the questions center on linguistic aptitude. The construction of the test obviously reflects agreement with the interactionist claim that intelligence is the ability to symbolically identify much of what we encounter. When Paula realizes the extent of Nell's personal vocabulary, she can no longer treat Nell as incompetent or ignorant.

But symbolic interaction is not just a means for intelligent expression; it's also the way we learn to interpret the world. A symbol is "a stimulus that has a learned meaning and value for people."[6] Consider the puzzle posed by the following story:

A father and his son were driving to a ball game when their car stalled on the railroad tracks. In the distance a train whistle blew a warning. Frantically, the father tried to start the engine, but in his panic, he couldn't turn the key, and the car was hit by the onrushing train. An ambulance sped to the scene and picked them up. On the way to the hospital, the father died. The son was still alive but his condition was very serious, and he needed immediate surgery. The moment they arrived at the hospital, he was wheeled into an emergency operating room, and the surgeon came in, expecting a routine case. However, on seeing the boy the surgeon blanched and muttered, "I can't operate on this boy—he's my son."[7]

How can this be? How do you explain the surgeon's dilemma? If the answer isn't immediately obvious, I encourage you to close the book and think it through. The problem as presented introduces an article that appears in a fascinating book of readings that is my recommended resource for symbolic interactionism. Douglas Hofstadter, the man who poses the problem, is adamant that readers think it through until they figure out the answer. There's no doubt, he assures us, that we'll know it when we get it.

I first heard this puzzle in a slightly different version about a decade ago. I'm ashamed to admit that it took me a few minutes to figure out the answer. My chagrin is heightened by the fact that my doctor is the wife of a departmental colleague and my daughter-in-law is a physician as well. How could I have been taken in?

Hofstadter's answer to my question is that the words we use have *default assumptions*. Since the story contains no reference to the doctor's gender, and the majority of physicians in America are men, we'll likely assume that the surgeon in the story is male. While such an assumption may have some basis in fact, the subtle tyranny of symbols is that we usually don't consciously think about the mental jump we're making. Unless we're brought up short by some obvious glitch in our taken-for-granted logic, we'll probably conjure up a male figure every time we read or hear the word *surgeon*. What's more, we'll probably assume that the way we think things are is the way they ought to be. That's how most of the "normal" people in *Nell* operated. They labeled Nell *strange, weird,* or *deviant*—assuming that those who are different are also demented.

A final note on language. In the first paragraph of this chapter I introduced the main characters in the movie *Nell*. Other than the typical masculine spelling of Jerry Lovell's first name, I made no reference as to whether the doctor is a man or a woman. If you had heard the name rather than read it, would you have consciously held open the possibility that Jerry (or Geri) might be female? If so, good for you.

THOUGHT: TAKING THE ROLE OF THE OTHER

Blumer's third premise is that an individual's interpretation of symbols is modified by his or her own thought processes. Symbolic interactionists describe thinking as an inner conversation. Mead called this inner dialogue *minding*.

Minding is the pause that's reflective. It's the two-second delay while we mentally rehearse our next move, test alternatives, anticipate others' reactions. Mead says we don't need any encouragement to look before we leap. We naturally talk to ourselves in order to sort out the meaning of a difficult situation. But first, we need language; the requirement for thinking is that we have learned to interact symbolically.

Lion King and Lassie movies aside, Mead believed that animals act "instinctively" and "without deliberation."[8] They are unable to think reflectively because, with few exceptions, they are unable to communicate symbolically. The human animal comes equipped with a brain that is hardwired for thought. But that alone is not sufficient for thinking. Interactionists maintain that "humans require social stimulation and exposure to abstract symbol systems to embark upon conceptual thought processes that characterize our species."[9] Language is the software that activates the mind.

Throughout the first half of *Nell*, Jerry and Paula are hard-pressed to explain Nell's ability to reflect rather than merely react. They understand that Nell interacted with her mother, but are puzzled as to how communication with a single reclusive and taciturn adult would offer the social stimulation that learning a language requires.[10] According to interactionist principles, there's no way that a person who has had almost zero human contact would be able to develop a language or think through her responses. Yet through cinematic flashbacks, viewers learn that Nell had a twin sister who was her constant companion during her early childhood development. Until her sister died, Nell's life was rich in social stimulation, twin speak, and shared meaning. As her past comes to light, Jerry and Paula gain an understanding of Nell's capacity to think. Symbolic interaction has activated cognitive processes that, once switched on, won't shut down.

Mead's greatest contribution to our understanding of the way we think is his notion that human beings have the unique capacity to *take the role of the other*. Early in life, kids role-play the activities of their parents, talk with imaginary friends, and take constant delight in pretending to be someone else. As adults, we continue to put ourselves in the place of others and act as they would act, although the process may be less conscious. Mead was convinced that thought is the mental conversation we hold with others.

In Harper Lee's novel *To Kill a Mockingbird*, Scout stands on Boo Radley's porch and recalls her father's words, "you never really know a man until you stand in his shoes and walk around in them."[11] That's a clear statement of what symbolic interactionism means by role-taking. The young, impulsive girl takes the perspective of a painfully shy, emotionally fragile man. Note that she doesn't *become* him—that would be *Invasion of the Body Snatchers*. She does, however, look out at the world through his eyes. More than anything else, what she sees is herself.

THE SELF: REFLECTIONS IN A LOOKING GLASS

Once we understand that *meaning, language,* and *thought* are tightly interconnected, we're able to grasp Mead's concept of the *self*. Mead dismissed the idea that we could get glimpses of who we are through introspection. He claimed, instead, that we paint our self-portrait with brush strokes that come from "taking the role of the other"—imagining how we look to another person. Interactionists call this mental image *the looking-glass self*.

Mead borrowed the phrase from sociologist Charles Cooley, who adapted it from a poem by Ralph Waldo Emerson. Emerson wrote that each close companion

Is to his friend a looking-glass
Reflects his figure that doth pass.[12]

Symbolic interactionists are convinced that the self is a function of language. Without talk there would be no self-concept, so one has to be a member of a community before consciousness of self sets in.[13] To the extent that we have novel conversations with new acquaintances, the self is always in flux. We can only imagine the wrenching change in self-concept that a real-life Nell would experience when thrust into interviews with psychologists, reporters, and lawyers.

According to Mead, the self is an ongoing process combining the "I" and the "me." The "I" is the spontaneous driving force that fosters all that is novel, unpredictable, and unorganized in the self. For those of you intrigued with brain hemisphere research, the "I" is akin to right-brain creativity. Nell's dance-like movements that simulated trees blowing in the wind sprang from the "I" part of self. So did Jerry's spur-of-the-moment musical accompaniment. (Surely if he'd thought about it ahead of time he'd have selected a song other than Willie Nelson's "Crazy.") When Paula goes ballistic over his lack of professionalism, he can only respond that sometimes people do things on impulse. Like Jerry, we know little about the "I" because it's forever elusive. Trying to examine the "I" part of the self is like viewing a snowflake through a lighted microscope. The very act causes it to vanish.

The "me" is viewed as an object—the image of self seen in the looking-glass of other people's reactions. Do you remember in grammar school how you learned to use the personal pronoun *me* in a sentence as the *object* of a verb? Because of the role-taking capacity of the human race, we can stand outside our bodies and view ourselves as objects. This reflexive experience is like having the Goodyear blimp hover overhead, sending back video images of ourselves while we act. Mead described the process this way: "If the 'I' speaks, the 'me' hears."[14] And again, "the 'I' of this moment is present in the 'me' of the next moment."[15]

An early turning point in the film comes when Jerry is with Nell in her cabin. She runs to a wardrobe mirror and reaches out to her reflected image and says, "may," a word Jerry understands to mean "me." She then pulls back and hugs herself while saying "tay," a word he interprets as "I." In the next scene, therapists viewing Paula's videotape of the sequence are impressed by this perfect case of Nell seeing her objective self as distinct from her subjective self. As a result of her actions, they have little doubt as to Nell's humanity and sanity. She has an intact self.[16]

COMMUNITY: THE SOCIALIZING EFFECT OF OTHERS' EXPECTATIONS

If Nell interacted solely with Jerry, the looking-glass self she'd construct from his response would form her self-concept—her "me." But as she meets and interacts with more people, she receives multiple reflections. According to Mead, she would then combine all of these looking-glass selves and end up with a composite picture he called the *generalized other.* The term is a synonym for our "me."

Our generalized other is the sum total of responses and expectations that

Reprinted from The Saturday Evening Post © 1973.

we pick up from the people around us. We naturally give more weight to the views of significant others, but even a chance comment or dirty look from a stranger can have a powerful impact on our self-image.

There is no "me" at birth. The "me" is formed only through continual symbolic interaction—first with family, next with playmates, then in institutions such as schools. As the generalized other develops, this imaginary composite person becomes the conversational partner in an ongoing mental dialogue. In this way, kids participate in their own socialization. The child gradually acquires the roles of those in the surrounding community. Mead would have us think of the "me" as the organized community within the individual.

Although *Nell* consistently portrays Mead's interactionist concepts, there's one discordant note at the end of the film. The final scene shows Nell five years later with the people she first met. Nell has obviously changed their lives. For example, Jerry and Paula are now married and have a daughter who reminds the viewer of Nell as a child. The sheriff's wife is no longer depressed and she attributes her transformation to Nell. Despite the fact that Nell has been thrust into a wider world of lawyers, reporters, and salesclerks who label her behavior deviant and insist she conform to societal roles, she seems strangely unaffected by their judgment or expectations. The character that Jodie Foster plays radiates an inner peace and contentment. The community in the form of her generalized other has not held sway. Of course, symbolic interactionists would remind us that the story of Nell is fiction.

A SYMBOLIC SAMPLER OF APPLIED INTERACTIONISM

Since Mead believed that a theory is valuable to the extent that it is useful, I've pulled together six separate applications of symbolic interactionism. Not only will this provide a taste of the practical insights the theory has generated, it will give you a chance to review some of the theoretical ideas covered in the chapter.

Creating reality. Shakespeare wrote "All the world's a stage, and all the men and women merely players."[17] In his book *The Presentation of Self in Everyday Life,* University of California–Berkeley sociologist Erving Goffman develops the metaphor of social interaction as a dramaturgical performance.[18] Goffman claims that we are all involved in a constant negotiation with others to publicly define our identity and the nature of the situation. He warns that "the impression of reality fostered by a performance is a delicate, fragile thing that can be shattered by minor mishaps."[19] His colleague, Joan Emerson, outlines the cooperative effort required to sustain the definition of a gynecological exam as a routine medical procedure.[20] The doctor and nurse enact their roles in a medical setting to assure patients that "everything is normal, no one is embarrassed, no one is thinking in sexual terms." The audience is satisfied only when the actors give a consistent performance.

Study of meaning. Mead advocated research through participant observation. Like Jerry in the movie *Nell,* the researcher systematically sets out to share in the lives of the people under study. The participant observer adopts the stance of an interested—yet ignorant—visitor who listens carefully to what people say in order to discover how they interpret their world. Mead had little sympathy for clinically controlled behavioral experiments or checklist surveys. The results might be quantifiable, but the lifeless numbers ignore the meaning the experience had for the person. Mead would have liked the wrangler who said that the only way to understand horses is to smell like a horse, eat from a trough, and sleep in a stall. That's participant observation! Undoubtedly, Mr. Ed's stable lad was a symbolic interactionist.

Generalized other.   The sobering short story "Cipher in the Snow" tells the true account of a boy who is treated as a nonentity by his parents and teachers and by other children. Their negative responses gradually reduce him into what they perceive him to be—nothing. He eventually collapses and dies in a snowbank for no apparent reason. The interactionist would describe his death as symbolic manslaughter.[21]

Naming.   Here's a partial list of epithets I've heard used in public places over the last year. They were all spoken in a demeaning voice. *Dummy, ugly, slob, fag, nigger, retard, fundamentalist, liberal, Neanderthal, slut, liar.* Sticks and stones can break my bones, but names can REALLY hurt me. Name-calling can be devastating because the epithets force us to view ourselves in a warped mirror. The grotesque images aren't easily dispelled.

Self-fulfilling prophecy.   One implication of the looking-glass self idea is that each of us has a significant impact on how others view themselves. That kind of interpersonal power is often referred to as a "self-fulfilling prophecy," the tendency for our expectations to evoke responses in others that confirm what we originally anticipated. The process is nicely summed up by Eliza Doolittle, a woman from the gutter in George Bernard Shaw's play *Pygmalion:* "The difference between a lady and a flower girl is not how she behaves, but how she's treated."[22]

Symbol manipulation.   Saul Alinsky was a product of the "Chicago School" of sociology at a time when Mead was having his greatest influence. But instead of pursuing a life of scholarship, Alinsky became a community organizer and applied what he learned to empower the urban poor. For example, in the early 1960s he helped found The Woodlawn Organization (TWO) to oppose his alma mater's complicity in substandard neighborhood housing. He searched for a symbol that would galvanize Woodlawn residents into united action and stir the sympathies of other Chicago residents. He earlier described his technique for selecting a symbolic issue:

> You start with the people, their traditions, their prejudices, their habits, their attitudes and all of those other circumstances that make up their lives. It should always be remembered that a real organization of the people . . . must be rooted in the experiences of the people themselves.[23]

Alinsky found his symbol in the rats that infested the squalid apartments. TWO's rallying cry became "Rats as big as cats." Not only did the city start to crack down on slum landlords, for the first time Woodlawn residents gained a sense of identity, pride, and political clout.

CRITIQUE: A THEORY TOO GRAND?

Most readers of *Mind, Self, and Society* are struck by the baffling array of concepts that Mead tries to cover. The theory's fluid boundaries, vague concepts, and undisciplined approach don't lend themselves to an easy summary. There are no *Cliffs Notes* for this one. Perhaps Mead was precise when he presented his ideas in class, but their exact meaning was blurred in the years before his students compiled the manuscript. Whatever the explanation is, the theory suffers from a lack of clarity.

Symbolic interactionism may also suffer from overstatement. Mead repeatedly declared that our capacity for language—the ability to use and interpret abstract symbols—was what distinguished humans from other animals. My graduate assistant is the mother of a three-year-old son who has a permanent peripheral nerve disorder. His eyes, ears, and other sense receptors work fine, but tragically the messages they send get scrambled on the way to his brain. Doctors say that he is, and always will be, unable to talk or interact with others on a symbolic level. After reading an early draft of this chapter, she asked, "So this means that Caleb is less human?" Her haunting question serves as a caution to any theorist who claims to have captured the essence of humanity.

Issues of clarity and human nature aside, symbolic interactionism is a remarkable endeavor. University of California–Riverside sociologist Randall Collins has labeled Mead "America's greatest sociological thinker."[24] Mead crafted an interconnecting network of ideas that has greater breadth than any other theory discussed in this book. I could have easily presented his ideas in the section on cognitive processing, relationship development, or intercultural communication.

Although Mead's ideas are best known by students of sociology, symbolic interactionism offers great insight into the creation of symbolic messages and their impact on the one who speaks and the one who hears. Most of the humanities-oriented communication theorists I feature in this book owe an intellectual debt to Mead's thinking. Look for ideas from symbolic interaction in Bormann's symbolic convergence theory, Pearce and Cronen's coordinated management of meaning, Geertz and Paconowsky's cultural approach to organizations, Burke's dramatism, Fisher's narrative paradigm, Philipsen's speech codes theory, and Kramarae's muted group theory. That impressive list of significant others could give a boost to any theorist's looking-glass self.

QUESTIONS TO SHARPEN YOUR FOCUS

1. Blumer's three core *premises of symbolic interactionism* deal with *meaning, language,* and *thought.* According to Blumer, which comes first? Can you make a case for an alternative sequence?

2. What do interactionists believe are the crucial differences between *human beings* and *animals?* What would you add or subtract from the list?

3. As Mead used the terms, is a *looking-glass self* the same thing as a person's *me?* Why or why not?

4. Think of a time in your life when your concept of *self* changed significantly. Do you believe that *self-fulfilling prophecy* played a major role in the shift?

A SECOND LOOK

Recommended resource: Peter Kollock and Jodi O'Brien (eds.), *The Production of Reality,* Pine Forge, Thousand Oaks, Calif., 1994.

Original statement: George Herbert Mead, *Mind, Self, and Society,* University of Chicago, Chicago, 1934.

Development of Mead's ideas: Herbert Blumer, *Symbolic Interactionism,* Prentice-Hall, Englewood Cliffs, N.J., 1969, pp. 1–89.

Summary statement: Herbert Blumer, "Symbolic Interaction: An Approach to Human Communication," in *Approaches to Human Communication,* Richard W. Budd and Brent Ruben (eds.), Spartan Books, New York, 1972, pp. 401–419.

Systematizing Mead's ideas: John D. Baldwin, *George Herbert Mead,* Sage, Newbury Park, Calif., 1986.

Dramaturgical metaphor: Erving Goffman, *The Presentation of Self in Everyday Life,* Doubleday Anchor, Garden City, N.Y., 1959.

Effects of social isolation: Kingsley Davis, "Final Note on a Case of Extreme Isolation," *American Journal of Sociology,* Vol. 3, 1947, pp. 432–437.

Applied interactionist activism: Donald Reitzes, Dietrich Reitzes, "Saul D. Alinsky: An Applied Urban Symbolic Interactionist," *Symbolic Interaction,* Vol. 15, 1992, pp. 1–24.

Communication issues: Bruce E. Gronbeck, "Symbolic Interactionism and Communication Studies: Prolegomena to Future Research," in *Communication and Social Structures,* D. R. Maines and C. J. Couch (eds.), Charles C. Thomas, Springfield, Ill., 1988, pp. 323–340.

Critique: Peter Hull, "Structuring Symbolic Interaction: Communication and Power," *Communication Yearbook 4,* Dan Nimmo (ed.), Transaction Books, New Brunswick, N.J., 1980, pp. 49–60.

CHAPTER 5

Coordinated Management of Meaning

of W. Barnett Pearce & Vernon Cronen

Barnett Pearce (The Fielding Institute) and Vernon Cronen (University of Massachusetts) are convinced that persons-in-conversation co-construct their own social realities and are simultaneously shaped by the worlds they create. In the late 1970s, when the two authors first suggested that our talk and action create the social environment in which we live, their idea was a radical departure from mainstream wisdom in the field of communication. Pearce and Cronen were frustrated by the cause-and-effect language of the behavioral sciences that was then in vogue, so they freely borrowed concepts and terms from philosophy, linguistics, and interpretive psychology. Today, many theorists hold that the joint use of language creates, shapes, and limits the diverse social worlds in which we live, but the coordinated management of meaning theory (CMM) is still the most comprehensive statement of *social construction* crafted by communication scholars.

THE SOCIAL CONSTRUCTIONIST IDEAL: COSMOPOLITAN COMMUNICATORS WHO ARE CURIOUS PARTICIPANTS IN A PLURALISTIC WORLD

Pearce and Cronen contrast their social constructionism with Shannon and Weaver's information-transmission model of communication that dominated our discipline for twenty-five years (see Chapter 3). They spot three stark differences that place the theories in two distinct camps:[1]

Social World as Singular versus Social World as Plural. Empirical researchers want to discover a reality *out there*. Truth may be elusive, but it is of one piece. Conversely, social constructionists are convinced that the events and objects of the social world are *made* rather than *found*. Since diverse people are involved in creating the social universe, it is clearly pluralistic. As a result, social constructionists assume one of two notions about ultimate truth. One, they believe that there are many truths, each deriving from a different tradition. Or two, they hold to the idea of a single truth that has multiple and contradictory faces, yet all are valid.

Quest for Certainty versus Exercise of Curiosity.   Information theorists strive to reduce uncertainty—entropy is an enemy. Constructionists, however, are curious about the way individuals act out their lives under ever-changing conditions. These interpretive researchers have an affinity for ambiguity, paradox, and irony that exposure to different groups can foster. Pearce notes that the Golden Rule serves people well when they interact with others from the same culture. But the multicultural perspective of social constructionists suggests that it's unfair to regard everyone else as a "native" in our own culture—holding *them* accountable to *our* standards.[2]

Spectator Knowledge versus Participant Knowledge.   The transmission model places the scientist outside the communication process looking in—a detached spectator of the human scene. In contrast, social constructionists seek positions of active involvement in what they study. They emphasize that knowing *about* something isn't as important as answering the question, *What shall I do?* For Pearce and Cronen, the ultimate goal of theorizing is to gain practical wisdom about how to *act*.

Figure 5.1 charts these issues in a three-dimensional model. The lower-left box represents the sector of traditional empirical research. The upper-right box represents the zone in which social constructionists feel at home. In his book, *Interpersonal Communication: Making Social Worlds*, Pearce sketches a vision of quality communication as viewed from this space:

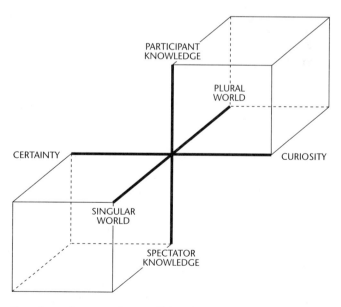

FIGURE 5.1   Two Opposite Agendas: Traditional Scientific Versus Social Constructionist

From a social constructionist perspective, good communication occurs when you and others are able to coordinate your actions sufficiently well that your conversations comprise social worlds in which you and they can live well—that is, with dignity, honor, joy and love.[3]

Pearce refers to this type of interaction as *cosmopolitan* communication, and he uses the same adjective to describe communicators who consistently converse in this socially eloquent way. When applied to individuals, the term "cosmopolitan" calls to mind a citizen-of-the-world who is able to interact comfortably with others who come from diverse cultural backgrounds, hold different values, and express discrepant beliefs. Pearce points out that true cosmopolitan communicators are rare because they need "the wisdom of a sage, the patience of a saint, and the skills of a therapist."[4] Yet CMM advocates are hopeful that their description of how persons-in-conversation co-construct their own social worlds will help thoughtful students of communication create a more benign universe.

PERSONS-IN-CONVERSATION—CREATING BONDS OF UNION

Pearce and Cronen adopt the term *persons-in-conversation* to designate communication as seen from inside the process.[5] According to CMM, that's the best place to figure out what's going on. The theory draws heavily on the experience of therapists, addiction counselors, mediators, and communication consultants who are part of the conversation when clients seek to alter the social realities in which they live. As a volunteer mediator for the past ten years at an urban center for conflict resolution, I'm particularly interested in the CMM analysis of alternative methods to settle disputes. Each time I go I wonder what kind of conflict I'll face—a lovers' quarrel, tension between tenant and landlord, a child-custody dispute, personal injury, graffiti vandalism, or neighborhood strife. I feel like Pearce's curious participant in a highly pluralistic world. In the rest of the chapter I'll draw on my mediation experience to illustrate the core principles of CMM—principles that are intellectual resources for cosmopolitan communicators.

Figure 5.2 presents artist M. C. Escher's 1955 lithograph *Bond of Union*, which is a striking illustration of CMM notions about persons-in-conversation. Consider the following points:

1. The experience of persons-in-conversation is the primary social process of human life. Pearce notes that this core idea runs counter to the prevailing intellectual view of "communication as an odorless, colorless vehicle of thought that is interesting or important only when it is done poorly or breaks down."[6] He suggests that the ribbon in Escher's drawing represents the process of communication. It isn't just one of the things the pair does or a tool they use to achieve some other end. On the contrary, their communication literally forms who they are and creates their relationship. *Bond of Union* depicts the process of communication as highly consequential.

Mediators see themselves as facilitating the process, helping parties "to arrive at an agreement in their own words which resolves *their* dispute as *they* define it."[7] Like most mediators, I start the process by explaining how mediation

FIGURE 5.2   M. C. Escher's *Bond of Union*

works, setting the ground rules, and then inviting each party to tell his or her story without interruption. I ask questions to clarify what each party wants, and then encourage the two sides to talk with each other about the problem(s) they face. At some point I meet privately with each person to explore thoughts he or she might be hesitant to voice in open session. When the parties are back together, I urge them to think of alternatives that could give *both* of them what they need. If they concur on a joint plan of action, I write up their agreement. Although I shape the process, they control its outcome. They are free to craft whatever works for them, and either party can end the mediation at any time. The staff of the center constantly remind mediators to "trust the process; it works."

  2. The way people communicate is often more important than the content of what they say.   The mood and manner that persons-in-conversations adopt play a large role in the social construction process. Pearce notes that the faces in *Bond of Union* have no substance; they consist in the twists and turns of the spiraling ribbon:

> Were the ribbon straightened or tied in another shape, there would be no loss of matter, but the faces would no longer exist. This image works for us as a model of the way the process of communication (the ribbon) creates the events and objects of our social worlds (the faces) not by its substance but by its form.[8]

The parties in mediation are often stuck in a destructive pattern of interaction. They call each other racists, liars, or jerks; they describe the other person's action as criminal, cruel, or crazy. Since Pearce regards language as "the single most powerful tool that humans have ever invented for the creation of social worlds,"[9] he thinks it's tragic when people in conflict are caught up in a language game that both are bound to lose. Even if they wanted to find a win-win solution, they usually don't know the rules of "getting to yes."[10] As a mediator, I try to help parties by taking the toxin out of the language they use. For example, I might reframe an event by using the term "incident" rather than crime, "harmful" in place of cruel, and "unexpected" instead of crazy. The facts or substance of a deed remain the same, yet by neutralizing the language that describes it, the shape or configuration of the conflict changes.

3. The actions of persons-in-conversation are reflexively reproduced as the dialogue continues.   Reflexivity means that our actions have effects that bounce back and affect us. The endless ribbon in *Bond of Union* loops back to *re*form each person. If Escher's figures were in conflict, each person would be wise to ask, "If I win this argument, what kind of person will I become?"

The spheres suspended in space can be seen as the external universe that is also co-constructed by the intertwined actors. "When we communicate," writes Pearce, "we are not just talking about the world, we are literally participating in the creation of the social universe."[11] For years, environmentalists have stressed that we have to live in the world that we produce. By fouling the air we breathe, we pollute the quality of our lives—as residents of Bangkok, Bucharest, and Mexico City know all too well. Pearce and Cronen are *social ecologists* who raise questions about the long-term effects of our communication practices. Like pragmatist John Dewey, they say that "making sense" of our social universe means "coming into agreement in action."[12] In mediation, I try to keep disputants focused on action by asking, "What can you decide today that will allow you to live together in peace tomorrow?"

Would the persons-in-conversation shown in Figure 5.2 realize that they are creating the social universe in which they talk and act? To the extent that they are cosmopolitan communicators, they would. According to CMM, cosmopolitan communicators are people with a multicultural attitude who are *mindful* about communication. In that sense, they are communication theorists. They are aware of their part in producing and sustaining their social universe and are consciously working at it. Pearce would want them (and us) to understand that *stories* are the most important technology of that co-construction project.

STORIES TOLD, STORIES LIVED, STORIES NOT YET TOLD

Unlike typical court proceedings, mediation gives clients the chance to tell their story in their own way. As a mediator, I offer myself as a neutral third party who is willing to listen—not as a judge to decide guilt or innocence, nor as a counselor prepared to offer advice. The stories told are often highly emotional, filled with vivid detail, and tightly structured to support the speaker's interpretation of the conflict. But the storyteller has trouble sustaining an idealized narrative in the presence of an adversary who's seen the story lived out in practice. As one woman said to her former husband, "Your story would make a good novel. But I don't need to read the book—I've seen the play."

Pearce and Cronen note that there's an inherent tension between the stories told and the stories lived. For example, I want to present myself as having Mother Teresa's compassion for the poor, Harvard University's Robert Coles' ability to captivate students, and Michael Jordan's natural grace on the basketball court ("I'd like to be like Mike"). But guests at the local homeless shelter, students in my comm theory course, and ball-playing friends keep me honest. (And I'm not alone. Even Mike has trouble being like Mike.)

Pearce thinks it's a mistake to try to reduce our lives to either stories we tell or stories we live. Stories told are how persons-in-conversation attempt to achieve meaning or *coherence* in life. Stories lived are how we try to *coordinate* our lives with others. These two human endeavors are the basis for the theory's title, Coordinated Management of Meaning. Pearce and Cronen also want to reserve a space in conversations for experiencing *mystery*—a concept I label "stories not yet told." Achieving coherence, coordinating actions, and experiencing mystery are the work of persons-in-conversation. Given that every human engages in multiple conversations, we all have a lifetime job.

Coherence—A Unified Context for Stories Told

The stories we tell are open to many interpretations. Consider how I might open a private meeting with one party in the midst of a mediation. Adopting a relaxed posture and a conversational tone, I say:

> Nick, this is our time together. Whatever you want to say is just between us. I won't share any of it with Kara unless you tell me it's O.K. (pause) So, how do you think it's going?

According to CMM, this *speech act* only makes sense within the multiple contexts of the specific episode, our relationship, my self-identity, and my culture—four frames that shape and are shaped by what I said.[13]

Episode.   An episode is a communication routine that has boundaries and rules—a recurrent language game. Pearce and Cronen describe the sequence as "nounable." This label placed on an episode answers the question, *What does he think he's doing?* For me, the speech act above frames the mediation episode known as "caucus," and what I think I'm doing is reducing Nick's anxiety enough that we can have an open conversation. Of course, Nick could read my speech act differently. He might label the one-on-one meeting a "counseling session" or, less charitably, "the third degree."

Relationship.   Just as punctuation provides a context for the printed word, the relationship between persons-in-conversation suggests how a speech act is to be taken. Some mediators attempt to ensure neutrality by remaining emotionally distant from the disputants. I take a different approach—I try to be "for" everyone at the table. I work to create trust through interpersonal warmth offered equally to all parties. In that relational context, I view my speech act as an assurance of unconditional positive regard, which is helpful for the other. (See the phenomenological tradition in Chapter 3.)

Self-Concept.   My invitation to speak frankly in caucus is genuine. I really want to hear what Nick is thinking, even if he's still mad at Kara or feels that mediation (or the mediator) is wasting his time. Perhaps if I struggled with my self-image as a competent mediator, my speech act would be more of a plea for help than an assurance of confidentiality. But my basic comfort in a "third-party neutral" role helps me create a safe environment where Nick can talk freely.

Culture.   Mediators comprise a 'culture' whose members recognize each other as sharing a common set of practices, values, and interpretations."[14] Specifically, mediators regard the court system as costly, time-consuming, and adversarial as opposed to the free, quick, cooperative service they offer. I'm part of that culture, so my speech act is clothed in moral obligation. Down deep I believe that Nick *ought* to take advantage of this opportunity to settle the dispute peaceably.

Pearce's *atomic model* illustrates the way that episode, relationship, self-concept, and culture interact with every speech act. His *serpentine model* shows that—from the outside—communication looks like "a game-like pattern of social interaction comprised of a sequence of acts, each of which evokes and responds to the acts of other persons."[15] I've combined the two images in Figure 5.3.

Look first at any of the nuclear clusters. They show that every speech act is wedded to four different contexts. Although the interlocking ellipses are drawn the same size, for any given social utterance the contexts of episode, relationship, self-concept, and culture aren't equally important in determining the coherence of a story told. CMM suggests that they form a hierarchy of increasing influence on the narrative. But their order of importance varies across people and situations. For example, many high school seniors talk about "The Prom" in a way that elevates the *episode* to mythic proportions but seems to have little to do with a romantic *relationship*. The interpretive trick, of course, is to figure out which context is dominant in any particular conversation. That's one reason why a CMM analysis of communication is more art than science.

Now note the serpentine flow of the conversation between the parties. Similar to Escher's *Bond of Union*, this model suggests that both parties affect—and are affected by—each other. It would be inappropriate to refer to the context (singular) of a conversation, because the contexts are co-evolving even as the people speak. Perhaps this is the most striking feature of the model. It leaves no room for isolated speech acts; everything in a conversation is connected to everything else. In fact, the second speech act is the only portion of the conversation shown in Figure 5.3 that we could reasonably discuss. We know with that segment what went before and what came after—factors that should affect how we interpret the act.

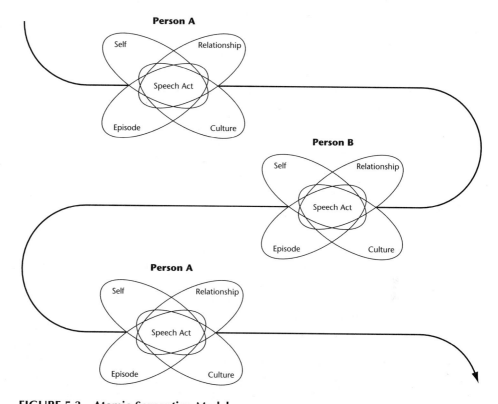

FIGURE 5.3   Atomic-Serpentine Model
(A synthesis of Barnett Pearce's atomic and serpentine models of communication, from *Interpersonal Communication: Making Social Worlds.*)

Do you get the impression from the atomic-serpentine model that even a "simple" conversation is an incredibly complex and open-ended process? If so, Pearce would be pleased. He thinks it's impossible to say what a statement means in a simple declarative sentence—even when the statement was made by you. Sometimes in a discussion Pearce is asked, "What does that mean?" He's tempted to reply, "I'm not completely sure yet; we haven't finished our conversation."[16]

Coordination—The Meshing of Stories Lived

According to Pearce, *coordination* refers to the "process by which persons collaborate in an attempt to bring into being their vision of what is necessary, noble, and good and to preclude the enactment of what they fear, hate, or despise."[17] This definition clearly describes what most humans want to accomplish throughout their lives, and what most mediators hope to facilitate when they meet with people in conflict. When parties craft a solution, a signed written agreement maps their plan to coordinate their future actions—even if only to the extent of staying out of each other's way. But coordination is

difficult when two people have a separate sense of what is necessary, noble, and good. Pearce and Cronen call these different *logics of meaning and action,* and maintain that any attempt to analyze a conversation must take into account the different *logical force* experienced by each participant.

Logical force is the moral obligation a person feels to act in a given way. To the spectator, it looks as if the actor is following a predetermined script or obeying a rigid rule. I often hear disputants preface their remarks with "I must," "I've got to," or some other variation of John Wayne's classic line, "A man's got to do what a man's got to do." But for persons operating *within* the logic of a given language game, no other conversational response comes to mind. What outsiders view as "knee-jerk reactions," participants regard as "common sense."

Although people in conflict often feel trapped by the language games in which they live, they can decide to coordinate their future actions without sharing a common interpretation of the events surrounding their dispute. Pearce and two other communication theorists who are mediators analyzed the deep structure of reality that surfaces in mediation.[18] They concluded that as long as a course of action seems appropriate to both parties, the different meaning each ascribes to the plan won't hinder an effective agreement.

Mystery—A Sense of Wonder for Stories Not Yet Told

Pearce notes that "with a single exception, all societies of which records remain have told themselves stories that included descriptions of the mysterious."[19] The exception is our "enlightened" society, which systematically debunks gods, ghosts, and giants. The authors of CMM believe that any attempt to reduce our lives to mere facts is a mistake and will ultimately fail. They applaud artists, poets, priests, children, science fiction writers, and anyone else who recognizes that there is always another story that could have been told—and who have the sense to realize that sometimes the best things cannot (or will not) be said.

For Pearce, mystery is "the essence of a 'cosmopolitan' attitude that views one's own life . . . as a manifestation or part of something greater; it is a reminder of what is 'beyond' the immediate, present moment."[20] He regards persons-in-conversation who save a space for the mysterious as "characterized by rapt attention, open-mindedness, a sense of wonder, perhaps even awe."[21] I was privileged to see this quality in the director of an inner-city medical clinic that had been "tagged" by a teenage graffiti artist. She puzzled over why he had defaced the building, but the tone of her question made it an invitation rather than an accusation. Haltingly, he said, "It's the only way I can say who I am." By the end of the session they had agreed that he and his friends would paint over the wall with a mural that expressed the dreams of the community. I think the three of us left the room in awe at this unexpected outcome.

In his book *Human Communication and the Human Condition,* Pearce pulls together the three concepts of coordination, coherence, and mystery by comparing communication to the process of drawing lines:

> For *coordination*, it is only necessary that those who interact with each other draw the lines at the same place—this allows them to "dance" with each other. For *coherence* it is only necessary that there be some lines drawn somewhere—this allows us to tame the terrors of history and impose meaning and order on the world. But *mystery* is the reminder that such lines are ultimately arbitrary distortions. . . . Without such reminders, hard-eyed men and women forget that [a word] is the basis for coordination and coherence, not a map of "reality."[22]

THE PRACTICE OF COSMOPOLITAN COMMUNICATION: COORDINATION WITHOUT COHERENCE

Pearce and Cronen describe CMM as a practical theory. Given their commitment to cosmopolitan communication, understanding the world seems less important to them than "providing a way of intelligently joining into the activity of the world so as to enrich it."[23] Of course, that's what mediators think they are doing. The center where I serve has a peer-review committee to check whether they are. While observing the mediator in an actual session, the reviewer tries to answer three questions: (1) Is the mediator competent? (2) Is he or she safe? (3) Is he or she an artist? In mediation, therapy, or any other social intervention, CMM proponents care deeply about these three issues.

Competence.   A mediator is competent to the extent that he or she helps people in conflict coordinate their future actions. It's doubtful that disputing parties will ever interpret each other's behavior in the same way, but the goal of mediation is an agreement on how parties will treat each other. A mediator's focus on coordination rather than coherence reflects the cosmopolitan ideal of CMM, which gives primacy to stories lived rather than stories told:

> Stories lived are the co-constructed patterns of joint-actions that others and we perform; stories told are the explanatory narratives that people use to make sense of stories lived.[24]

Pearce's distinction between stories lived and stories told provides a rationale for urging people with incompatible worldviews to act jointly for the common good. For example, conservative activists and radical feminists may join forces temporarily to protest a pornographic movie. Although they have discrepant views of social justice and different reasons for condemning the film, they might agree on a unified course of action. People can coordinate effectively without mutual understanding.

Safety.   Mediators, like referees, are safe only to the extent that they stay neutral. It is deceptively easy to become an advocate for a position that seems fair or to identify with someone from a similar background. Even when mediators remain impartial, they may yield to the temptation to push parties to reach an agreement. Yet most experienced mediators take the ethical stance that "efforts toward consensus, if pursued with very much zeal, are pernicious."[25]

Pearce and other CMM advocates are part of the Public Dialogue Consortium, a group of professional practitioners dedicated to bringing cosmopolitan communication into community forums where accusatory diatribe passes for serious discussion of issues. They work hard "to create circumstances in which people in the community who disagree with, distrust, and simply don't like each other can communicate 'safely'."[26] Members of the Consortium say that cosmopolitan communication, systematic eloquence, dialogue, love—or whatever else we might call it—allows people to find ways of coordinating with others with whom they do not and perhaps should not agree.

Artistry.   In order to serve as a mediator, a volunteer must be rated as both safe and competent.[27] Artistry is considered a welcome bonus. Pearce uses the term *mastery* to describe this same ability to artfully improvise when facing a novel situation. He contrasts game playing (playing by the rules) with game mastery (achieving coordination by transcending the rules). The artistic game master appreciates irony, wit, paradox, and creativity. He or she has the rhetorical sensitivity to know when the rules won't work, and changes the game.

My moment of mastery came in a mediation where a teenager faced an assault and battery charge from a classmate he had injured in a fight. Both guys were students at the high school that I had attended decades earlier. Receiving only monosyllable responses to my questions, I searched for a way to break out of this muted language game. Smiling at the scowling faces, I informed them that I too had been in a fight in the same gym. I then started singing what I dimly remembered as the school's team "fight song." Their joint laughter was the beginning of coordination. As for coherence, it was never really an issue.

CRITIQUE: WHAT DO THEY THINK THEY ARE DOING?

There's a professor at the college where I teach who gives one-question essay exams. Students are fond of characterizing their breadth: "Describe how the universe works. Use examples." Pearce and Cronen's coordinated management of meaning reads like an answer to that question. CMM is an impressive macrotheory of face-to-face communication, by far the most ambitious effort to spring from the ranks of speech communication scholars. Yet the very scope of the theory makes its central tenets difficult to pin down. Perhaps Pearce and Cronen make the job more difficult by not being consistent in how they define their terms or in the way they state their claims.[28] Pearce wryly admits that "social constructionism scarcely suffers from overly-precise definitions."[29] And Cronen acknowledges the charge of critics that CMM is "a black hole in space" that sucks in almost every issue of human existence; "CMM's creators keep dragging it into all sorts of issues that do not seem to be the proper place for communication scholars."[30]

In terms of clarity, cultural theorist Gerry Philipsen (see Chapter 31) questions the moral stance of CMM. He says that the value assumptions underlying CMM seem to have shifted over the past two decades, but the theorists haven't clearly articulated their ethical position.[31] The recent book *Moral Conflict: When Social Worlds Collide* by Pearce and University of New Mexico communication theorist Stephen Littlejohn may answer that concern. Seeking to pin down the characteristics of cosmopolitan communication, Pearce and Littlejohn describe a *transcendent eloquence* that enhances coordination between disparate moral communities. For example, how can "pro choice" secular humanists and "pro life" religious conservatives act civilly toward each other, much less collaborate? The authors say that because transcendent eloquence seeks human welfare as a worthy "end in itself," it is neither "blindly relativistic" nor a moral "neutral ground."[32] Coordination is the ultimate goal of CMM, but this won't happen without some degree of moral coherence. Participants in conflict can act together only if they value doing so. Thus, CMM is morally committed to helping disputants accept and act on the belief that combatants are worth more than the combat. If the theory helps you reach this goal, you won't mind a few fluid terms.

QUESTIONS TO SHARPEN YOUR FOCUS

1. *Social constructionists* want to be *curious participants* in a *pluralistic world.* How willing are you to give up certainty, a detached perspective, and the idea of truth as singular to join them?

2. Can you provide a rationale for placing this treatment of CMM immediately after the chapter on *symbolic interactionism?*

3. The film *Forrest Gump* was remarkable in that Forrest's *stories told* matched his *stories lived.* To what extent did this congruence help Forrest be a *competent, safe, artistic,* or *cosmopolitan* communicator?

4. CMM suggests that we can take part in joint action without shared understanding—*coordination* without *coherence.* Can you think of an example from your own life?

A SECOND LOOK

Recommended resource: W. Barnett Pearce, *Communication and the Human Condition,* Southern Illinois University, Carbondale, Ill., 1989.

Early statement of theory: W. Barnett Pearce and Vernon E. Cronen, *Communication, Action, and Meaning: The Creation of Social Realities,* Praeger, New York, 1980.

Social constructionism: W. Barnett Pearce, "A Sailing Guide for Social Constructionists," in *Social Approaches to Communication,* Wendy Leeds-Hurwitz (ed.), Guilford, New York, 1995, pp. 88–113.

Atomic and serpentine models of social creation: W. Barnett Pearce, *Interpersonal Communication: Making Social Worlds,* HarperCollins, New York, 1994, pp. 30–40.

Ethical implications: Vernon E. Cronen, "Coordinated Management of Meaning Theory and Postenlightenment Ethics," in *Conversation on Communication Ethics,* Karen Joy Greenberg (ed.), Ablex, Norwood, N.J., 1991, pp. 21–53.

Intellectual heritage: Vernon E. Cronen, "Coordinated Management of Meaning: The

Consequentiality of Communication and the Recapturing of Experience," in *The Consequentiality of Communication*, Stuart Sigman (ed.), Lawrence Erlbaum Associates, Hillsdale, N.J., 1995, pp. 17–65.

CMM applied to conflict mediation: Jonathan Shailor, *Empowerment in Dispute Mediation: A Critical Analysis of Communication*, Praeger, Westport, Conn., 1994.

Transcendent eloquence: W. Barnett Pearce and Stephen W. Littlejohn, *Moral Conflict: When Social Worlds Collide*, Sage, Thousand Oaks, Calif., 1997.

Critique: Gerry Philipsen, "The Coordinated Management of Meaning Theory of Pearce, Cronen and Associates," in *Watershed Research Traditions in Human Communication Theory*, Donald Cushman and Branislav Kovačić (eds.), State University of New York–Albany, 1995, pp. 13–43.

CHAPTER 6

Expectancy Violations Theory

of Judee Burgoon

One morning, years ago, I was walking back to my office puzzling over classroom conversations with four students. All four had made requests. Why, I wondered, had I readily agreed to two requests but just as quickly turned down two others? Each of the four students had spoken to me individually during the class break. Andre wanted my endorsement for a graduate scholarship, and Dawn invited me to eat lunch with her the next day. I said yes to both of them. Belinda asked me to help her on a term paper for a class with another professor, and Charlie encouraged me to play water polo with guys from his house that night. I said no to these requests.

Sitting down at my desk, I idly flipped through the pages of *Human Communication Research* (HCR). The year was 1978, and this relatively new behavioral science journal had arrived in the morning mail. I was still mulling over my uneven response to the students when my eyes zeroed in on an article entitled "A Communication Model of Personal Space Violations." "That's it," I blurted out to our surprised department secretary. I suddenly realized that, in each case, my response to the student may have been influenced by the conversational distance between us.

I mentally pictured the four students making their requests—each from a distance that struck me as inappropriate in one way or another. Andre was literally in my face, less than a foot away. Belinda's two-foot interval invaded my personal space, but not as much. Charlie stood about seven feet away—just outside the range I would have expected for a let's-get-together-and-have-some-fun-that-has-nothing-to-do-with-school type of conversation. Dawn offered her luncheon invitation from across the room. At the time, each of these moves seemed somewhat strange. Now I realized that all four students had violated my expectation of an appropriate interpersonal distance.

Consistent with my practice throughout this book, I've changed the names

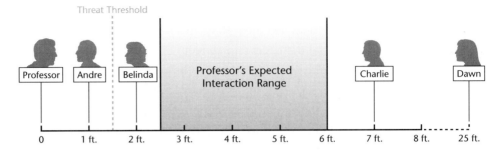

FIGURE 6.1 **Expectancy Violations in a Classroom Setting**

of these former students to protect their privacy. In this case, I've made up names that start with the letters A, B, C, and D to represent the increasing distance between us when we spoke. (Andre was the closest; Dawn, the farthest away.) Figure 6.1 plots the intervals relative to my expectations.

Judee Burgoon, a communication scholar then teaching at the University of Florida, wrote the journal article that stimulated my thinking. The article was a follow-up piece on the nonverbal expectancy violations model that she had introduced in HCR two years earlier. Since my own dissertation research focused on interpersonal distance, I knew firsthand how little social science theory existed to guide the study of nonverbal communication. I was therefore excited to see Burgoon offering a sophisticated theory of personal space. The fact that she was teaching in a communication department and had published her work in a communication journal was value added. I eagerly read Burgoon's description of her nonverbal expectancy violations model to see whether it could account for my mixed response to the various conversational distances chosen by the four students.

PERSONAL SPACE EXPECTATIONS: CONFORM OR DEVIATE?

Burgoon defined personal space as the "invisible, variable volume of space surrounding an individual that defines that individual's preferred distance from others."[1] She claimed that the size and shape of our personal space depends on our cultural norms and individual preferences, but it's always a compromise between the conflicting approach-avoidance needs that we as humans have for affiliation and privacy.

The idea of personal space wasn't original with Burgoon. In the 1960s, Illinois Institute of Technology anthropologist Edward Hall coined the term *proxemics* to refer to the study of people's use of space as a special elaboration of culture.[2] He entitled his book *The Hidden Dimension* because he was convinced that most spatial interpretation is outside our awareness. He claimed that Americans have four proxemic zones, which nicely correspond with the four interpersonal distances selected by my students:

1. Intimate distance: 0 to 18 inches (Andre)
2. Personal distance: 18 inches to 4 feet (Belinda)
3. Social distance: 4 to 10 feet (Charlie)
4. Public distance: 10 feet to infinity (Dawn)

Hall's book was filled with examples of "ugly Americans" who were insensitive to the spatial customs of other cultures. Hall strongly recommended that, in order to be effective, we learn to adjust our nonverbal behavior to conform to the communication rules of our partner. We shouldn't cross a distance boundary uninvited.

Cartoon by Peter Steiner. Reprinted with permission.

In his poem "Prologue: The Birth of Architecture," poet W. H. Auden echoes Hall's analysis and puts us on notice that we violate his personal space at our peril:

> Some thirty inches from my nose
> The frontier of my Person goes,
> And all the untilled air between
> Is private pagus or demesne.
> Stranger, unless with bedroom eyes
> I beckon you to fraternize,
> Beware of rudely crossing it:
> I have no gun, but I can spit.[3]

Burgoon's nonverbal expectancy violations model offered a counterpoint to Hall and Auden's advice. She didn't argue with the idea that people have definite expectations about how close others should come. In fact, she would explain Auden's thirty-inch rule as based on well-established American norms, plus the poet's own idiosyncrasies. But contrary to popular go-along-to-get-along wisdom, Burgoon suggested that there are times when it's best to break the rules. She believed that under some circumstances, violating social norms and personal expectations is "a superior strategy to conformity."[4]

An Applied Test of the Original Model

Whether knowingly or not, each of the four students making a request deviated from my proxemic expectation. How well did Burgoon's 1978 model predict my responses to these four different violations? Not very well. So that you can capture the flavor of Burgoon's early speculation and recognize how far her current theory has come, I'll outline what the model predicted my responses would be, and in each case compare that forecast to what I actually did.

Andre.   According to Burgoon's early model, Andre made a mistake when he crossed my invisible "threat threshold" and spoke with me at an intimate eyeball-to-eyeball distance. The physical and psychological discomfort I'd feel would hurt his cause. But the model missed on that prediction since I wrote the recommendation later that day.

Belinda.   In her 1978 article, Burgoon suggested that noticeable deviations from what we expect cause us to experience a heightened state of arousal. She wasn't necessarily referring to the heart-pounding, sweaty palms reaction that drives us to fight or flight. Instead, she pictured violations stimulating us to review the nature of our relationship with the person who acted in a curious way. That would be good news for Belinda if I thought of her as a highly rewarding person. But every comment she made in class seemed to me a direct challenge, dripping with sarcasm. Just as Burgoon predicted, the two-foot gap Belinda chose focused my attention on our rocky relationship, and I declined her request for help in another course. Score one for the nonverbal expectancy violations model.

Charlie.   Charlie was a nice guy who cared more about having a good time than he did about studies. He knew I loved water polo, but he may not have realized that his casual attitude toward the class was a constant reminder that I wasn't as good a teacher as I wanted to be. In her 1978 *Human Communication Research* article, Burgoon wrote that a person with "punishing power" (like Charlie) would do best to observe proxemic conventions, or better yet, stand slightly farther away than expected. Without ever hearing Burgoon's advice, Charlie did it right. He backed off to a distance of seven feet—just outside the range of interaction I anticipated. Even so, I declined his offer to swim with the guys.

Dawn.   According to this nonverbal expectancy violations model, Dawn blew it. Because she was an attractive communicator, a warm, close approach would have been a pleasant surprise. But her decision to issue an invitation from across the room would seem to guarantee a poor response. The farther she backed off, the worse the effect would be. There's only one problem with this analysis: Dawn and I had lunch together in the student union the following day.

Obviously, my attempt to apply Burgoon's original model to conversational distance between one teacher and four of his students didn't meet with much success. The theoretical scoreboard read:

Nonverbal expectancy violations model: **1**

Unpredicted random behavior: **3**

Burgoon's first controlled experiments didn't fare much better. But where I was ready to dismiss the whole model as flawed, she was unwilling to abandon *expectancy violation* as a key concept in human interaction. At the end of the 1978 journal article she hinted that some of her basic assumptions might need to be tested and reevaluated.

Of course that was then; this is now. Over the last two decades Judee Burgoon and her students have crafted a series of sophisticated laboratory and field studies to discover and explain the effects of expectancy violations. One of the reasons I chose to write about her theory is that the current version is an excellent example of ideas continually revised as a result of experimental disconfirmation. As she has demonstrated, in science, failure can lead to success.

A CONVOLUTED MODEL BECOMES AN ELEGANT THEORY

When applied to theories, the term *elegant* suggests "gracefully concise and simple; admirably succinct."[5] That's what expectancy violations theory has become. Burgoon has dropped concepts that were central in earlier versions, but that never panned out. Early on, for example, she abandoned the idea of a "threat threshold." Even though that hypothetical boundary made intuitive sense, repeated experimentation failed to confirm its existence.

Burgoon's retreat from "arousal" as an explanatory mechanism has been more gradual. She originally stated that people felt physiologically aroused when their proxemic expectations were violated. Later she softened the concept to "an orienting response" or a mental "alertness" that focuses attention on the violator. She now views arousal as a side effect of a partner's deviation, and no longer considers it a necessary link between expectancy violation and communication outcomes such as attraction, credibility, persuasion, and involvement.

By removing extraneous features, Burgoon has streamlined her model. By extending its scope, she has produced a complete theory. Her original nonverbal expectancy violations model was concerned only with spatial violations—a rather narrow focus. But by the mid-1980s, Burgoon realized that proxemic behavior is part of an interconnected system of nonlinguistic cues. It no longer made sense to study interpersonal distance in isolation. She began to apply the model to a host of other nonverbal variables—facial expression, eye contact, touch, and body lean, for example. Burgoon continues to expand the range of expectancy violations. While not losing interest in nonverbal communication, she now applies the theory to emotional, marital, and intercultural communication as well. Consistent with this broad sweep, she has dropped the *nonverbal* qualifier and refers to her theory as "expectancy violations theory," and abbreviates it EVT. From this point on, so will I.

What does EVT predict? Burgoon sums up her empirically driven conclusions in a single paragraph. It is my hope that my long narrative account of the theory's development helps you appreciate the two decades of work that lie behind these simple lines.

> Expectancies exert significant influence on people's interaction patterns, on their impressions of one another, and on the outcomes of their interactions. Violations of expectations in turn may arouse and distract their recipients, shifting greater attention to the violator and the meaning of the violation itself. People who can assume that they are well regarded by their audience are safer engaging in violations and more likely to profit from doing so than are those who are poorly regarded. When the violation act is one that is likely to be ambiguous in its meaning or to carry multiple interpretations that are not uniformly positive or negative, then the reward valence of the communicator can be especially significant in moderating interpretations, evaluations, and subsequent outcomes. . . . In other cases, violations have relatively consensual meanings and valences associated with them, so that engaging in them produces similar effects for positive- and negative-valenced communicators.[6]

CORE CONCEPTS OF EVT

A close reading of Burgoon's summary suggests that EVT offers a "soft determinism" rather than hard-core covering laws (see Chapter 1). The qualifying terms *may, can be, more likely,* and *relatively* reflect her belief that too many factors affect communication to allow us ever to discover simple cause-and-effect relationships. She does, however, hope to show a link between surprising interpersonal behavior and attraction, credibility, influence, and involvement. These are the potential outcomes of expectancy violation that Burgoon and her students explore. In order for us to appreciate the connection, we need to understand three core concepts of EVT: *expectancy, violation valence,* and *communicator reward valence.* I'll illustrate these three variables by referring back to my students' proxemic behavior and to another form of nonverbal communication—touch.

Expectancy

When I was a kid, my mother frequently gave notice that she *expected* me to be on my best behavior. I considered her words to be a warning or a wish rather than a confident forecast of my future actions. That's *not* how Burgoon uses the word. She and her colleagues "prefer to reserve the term 'expectancy' for what is predicted to occur rather than what is desired."[7] Figure 6.1 shows that I anticipated conversations with students to take place at a distance of 2½ to 6 feet. How did this expectation arise? Burgoon suggests that I mentally processed the context, type of relationship, and characteristics of the others in order to gauge what they would do.

Context begins with cultural norms. Three feet is too close in England or Germany, but too far removed in Saudi Arabia, where you can't trust people who won't let you smell their breath. Context also includes the setting of the conversation. A classroom environment dictates a greater speaking distance than would be appropriate for a private chat in my office.

Relationship factors include similarity, familiarity, liking, and relative status. In one study, Burgoon discovered that people of all ages and stations in life anticipate that lower-status people will keep their distance. Because of our age difference and teacher–student relationship, I was more surprised by Andre's and Belinda's invasions of my personal space than I was by Charlie's and Dawn's remote stances.

Communicator characteristics include all of the age/sex/place-of-birth demographic facts asked for on application forms, but they also include personal features that may affect expectation even more—physical appearance, personality, and communication style. Dawn's warm smile was a counterpoint to Belinda's caustic comments. Given this difference, I would have assumed that Dawn would be the one to draw close and Belinda the one to keep her distance. That's why I was especially curious when each woman's spatial "transgression" was the opposite of what I would have predicted.

We can do a similar analysis of my expectation for touch in that classroom situation. Edward Hall claimed that the United States is a "noncontact culture," so I wouldn't anticipate touch during the course of normal conversation.[8] Does this mean that Latin American or Southern European "contact cultures" wouldn't have expectations for nonverbal interaction? By no means. Burgoon is convinced that all cultures have a similar *structure* of expected communication behavior, but that the *content* of those expectations can differ markedly from culture to culture. Touch is fraught with meaning in every society, but the who, when, where, and how of touching is a matter of culture-specific standards and customs.

Burgoon's exploratory studies show that Americans in task relationships expect little or no touching—a handshake or perhaps brief handholding. Touches to the leg, arm, or face are thought unusual, and unless the other person is highly attractive, an arm around the shoulder or waist is highly unlikely. Women expect to be touched more than men.

As a male in a role relationship, it never occurred to me that students might make physical contact while making their requests. If it had, Dawn would have been the likely candidate. But at her chosen distance of 25 feet, she'd need to be a bionic woman to reach me. As it was, I would have been shocked if she'd violated my expectation and walked over to give me a hug. (As a lead-in to the next section, note that I didn't say disturbed, distressed, or disgusted.)

Violation Valence

We usually give others a bit of wiggle room to deviate from what we regard as standard operating procedure. But once we deal with someone who pushes the limits of expected behavior, we switch into an evaluation mode. According to Burgoon, we first try to interpret the meaning of the violation, and then figure out whether or not we like it.

The meaning of some violations is easy to spot. As a case in point, no one would agonize over how to interpret a purposeful poke in the eye with a sharp stick. It's a hostile act, and if it happened to us, we'd be livid. Many nonverbal behaviors are that straightforward. For example, moderate to prolonged eye contact in Western cultures usually communicates awareness, interest, affection, and trust. A level gaze is welcome; shifty eyes are not. As Emerson wrote, "The eyes of men converse as much as their tongues, with the advantage that the ocular dialect needs no dictionary. . . ."[9]

When a behavior has a socially recognized meaning, communicators can easily figure out whether to go beyond what others expect. If the valence is negative, do less than expected. If the valence is positive, go for the max. Burgoon validated this advice when she studied the effect of expectancy on marital satisfaction.[10] She questioned people about how much intimate communication they expected from their partner versus how much focused conversation they actually got. Of course, intimacy was ranked as positive. Partners who received about as much intimacy as they expected were moderately satisfied with their marriages. But people were most satisfied with their marriages when they had more good talks with their partners than they originally thought they would.

On the other hand, some expectancy violations are ambiguous and open to multiple interpretations. For example, the meaning of unexpected touch can be puzzling. Is it a mark of total involvement in the conversation, a sign of warmth and affection, a display of dominance, or a sexual move? Distance violations can also be confusing. Andre isn't from the Middle East, so why was he standing so close? I don't bark or bite, so why did Dawn issue her invitation from across the room? According to EVT, it's at times like these that we consider the reward valence of the communicator as well as the valence of the violation.

Before we look at the way communicator reward valence fits into the theory, you should know that Burgoon has found few nonverbal behaviors that are ambiguous when seen in a greater context. A touch on the arm might be enigmatic in isolation, but when experienced along with close proximity, forward body lean, a direct gaze, facial animation, and verbal fluency, almost everyone interprets the physical contact as a sign of high involvement in the conversation.[11] Or consider actor Eric Idle's words and nonverbal manner in a *Monty Python* sketch. He punctuates his question about Terry Gilliam's wife with a burlesque wink, a leering tone of voice, and gestures to accompany his words: "Nudge nudge. Know what I mean? Say no more . . . know what I mean?"[12] Taken alone, an exaggerated wink or a dig with the elbow might have many meanings, but as part of a coordinated routine, both gestures clearly transform a questionable remark into a lewd comment.

There are times, however, when nonverbal expectancy violations are truly equivocal. The personal space deviations of my students are cases in point. Perhaps I just wasn't sensitive enough to pick up the cues that would help me make sense out of their proxemic violations. But when the meaning of an action is unclear, EVT theory says that we interpret the violation in light of how the violator can affect our lives.

Communicator Reward Valence

EVT is not the only theory that describes our human tendency to size up other people in terms of the potential rewards they have to offer. Social penetration theory suggests that we live in an interpersonal economy in which we all "take stock" of the relational value of others we meet (see Chapter 9). The questions "What can you do *for* me?" and "What can you do *to* me?" often cross our minds. Burgoon is not a cynic, but she thinks the issue of reward potential moves from the background to the foreground of our minds when someone violates our expectation and there's no social consensus as to the meaning of the act. She uses the term *communicator reward valence* to label the results of our mental audit of likely gains and losses.

The reward valence of a communicator is the sum of the positive and negative attributes that the person brings to the encounter plus the potential he or she has to reward or punish in the future. The resulting perception is usually a mix of good and bad and falls somewhere on a scale between those two poles. I'll illustrate communicator characteristics that Burgoon frequently mentions by reviewing one feature of each student that I thought about right after their perplexing spatial violations.

Andre was a brilliant student. Although writing recommendations is low on my list of fun things to do, I would bask in reflected glory if he were accepted into a top graduate program.

Belinda had a razor-sharp mind and a tongue to match. I'd already felt the sting of her verbal barbs and thought that thinly veiled criticism in the future was a distinct possibility.

Charlie was the classic goof-off—seldom in class and never prepared. I try to be evenhanded with everyone who signs up for my classes, but in Charlie's case I had to struggle not to take his casual attitude toward the course as a personal snub.

Dawn was a beautiful young woman with a warm smile. I felt great pleasure when she openly announced that I was her favorite teacher.

My views of Andre, Belinda, Charlie, and Dawn probably say more about me than they do about the four students. I'm not particularly proud of my stereotyped assessments, but apparently I have plenty of company in the criteria I used. Burgoon notes that the features that impressed me also weigh heavily with others when they compute a reward valence for someone who is violating their expectations. Status, ability, and good looks are standard "goodies" that enhance the other person's reward potential. The thrust of the conversation is even more important, however. Most of us value words that communicate acceptance, liking, appreciation, and trust. We're turned off by talk that conveys disinterest, disapproval, distrust, and rejection.

Why does Burgoon think that the expectancy violator's power to reward or punish is so crucial? Because puzzling violations force victims to search the social context for clues to their meaning.[13] Thus, an ambiguous violation embedded in a host of favorable signals takes on a positive cast. Mixed signals from a punishing communicator stiffen our resistance.

Now that I've outlined EVT's core concepts of expectancy, violation valence, and communicator reward valence, you can better understand the bottom-line advice that Burgoon's theory offers. Should you communicate in a totally unexpected way? If you're certain that the novelty will be a pleasant surprise, the answer is yes. If you know that your outlandish behavior will offend, don't do it. Finally, when others don't know how to interpret your far-out behavior, their overall attitude toward you will loom large. So, if like Belinda and Charlie you have reason to suspect a strained relationship, and the meaning of a violation would be unclear, stifle your deviant tendencies and do your best to conform to expectations. But when you know you've already created a positive personal impression (like Andre or Dawn), a surprise move is not only safe, it will likely enhance the positive effect of your message.

CRITIQUE: WORK IN PROGRESS

I have a friend who fixes my all-terrain cycle whenever I bend it or break it. "What do you think?" I ask Bill. "Can it be repaired?" His response is always the same: "Man made it! Man can fix it!"

Judee Burgoon shows the same resolve as she seeks to adjust and redesign an expectancy violations model that has never worked quite as well in practice as its theoretical blueprint says it should. Almost every empirical test she runs seems to yield mixed results. For example, her early work on physical contact suggested that touch violations are often ambiguous. However, a sophisticated experiment she ran in 1992 showed that unexpected touch in a problem-solving situation was almost always welcomed as a positive violation, regardless of the status, gender, or attractiveness of the violator. (It seems expectancy violations research keeps producing its own unwanted surprises.) Burgoon concedes that we can't yet use EVT to generate specific predictions regarding touch outcomes. In fact, she calls for further descriptive work before applying the theory to *any* nonverbal behavior.[14] She's particularly troubled by two of EVT's shortcomings:

> First, EVT does not fully account for the overwhelming prevalence of reciprocity that has been found in interpersonal interactions. Second, it is silent on whether communicator valence supersedes behavior valence or vice versa when the two are incongruent (such as when a disliked partner engages in a positive violation).[15]

Some state legislatures have adopted a "lemon law"—a statute requiring auto dealers to replace a buyer's new car when it has a major defect that persists despite the shop's best attempts to fix it. Do repeated failures to predict outcomes when a person stands far away, moves in too close, or reaches out to touch someone imply that Burgoon ought to trade in her expectancy violations model for a new theory?[16] From my perspective, the answer is no.

Taken as a whole, Burgoon's expectancy violation model continues to meet four of the five criteria of a good scientific theory as presented in Chapter 2. Her theory advances a reasonable explanation for the effects of expectancy violations during communication. The explanation she offers is relatively simple and has actually become less complex over time. The theory has testable hypotheses that the theorist is willing to adjust when her tests don't support the prediction. Finally, the model offers practical advice on how to better achieve important communication goals of increased credibility, influence, and attraction. Could we ask for anything more? Of course.

We could wish for predicted effects of nonverbal violations that prove more reliable than the *Farmer's Almanac* forecast of long-range weather trends. Burgoon's revised version of EVT does do better than the original model. The ex post facto scoreboard for my responses to students' proxemic violations now stands at four hits, no misses. But until the theory gains a track record of accurate prediction ahead of time, it will be more speculation than science.

Burgoon and most other researchers in the field now acknowledge that any single nonverbal signal is part of an entire behavioral system; any attempt to say "This *means* that" or "This will *cause* that" is shaky at best. What expectancy violations theory does do is highlight some of the crucial components of the system.

QUESTIONS TO SHARPEN YOUR FOCUS

1. What *proxemic* advice would you give to communicators who believe they are seen as *unrewarding*?

2. Except for handshakes, *touch* is *unexpected* in most casual relationships. Is there a cultural *violation valence* for a light touch on the arm, a brief touch on the cheek, or a shoulder hug?

3. The sign on the door of a restaurant reads: "No shoes, no shirt, no service." What are other posted notices that communicate *nonverbal expectations?*

4. EVT and coordinated management of meaning (see Chapter 5) hold diverse assumptions about the nature of *knowledge, reality,* and *communication study.* Can you draw the distinctions?

A SECOND LOOK

Recommended resource: Judee K. Burgoon and Jerold Hale, "Nonverbal Expectancy Violations: Model Elaboration and Application to Immediacy Behaviors," *Communication Monographs,* Vol. 55, 1988, pp. 58–79.

Original model: Judee K. Burgoon, "A Communication Model of Personal Space Violations: Explication and an Initial Test," *Human Communication Research,* Vol. 4, 1978, pp. 129–142.

Expectancy: Judee K. Burgoon and Beth A. LePoire, "Effects of Communication Expectancies, Actual Communication, and Expectancy Disconfirmation on Evaluations of Communicators and Their Communication Behavior," *Human Communication Research,* Vol. 20, 1993, pp. 67–96.

Valence of touch, posture, and proximity: Judee K. Burgoon and Joseph Walther, "Nonverbal Expectancies and the Evaluative Consequences of Violations," *Human Communication Research,* Vol. 17, 1990, pp. 232–265.

Expectation and valence of touch: Judee K. Burgoon, Joseph Walther, and E. James Baesler, *Human Communication Research,* Vol. 19, 1992, pp. 237–263.

Communicator reward valence: Judee K. Burgoon, "Relational Message Interpretations of Touch, Conversational Distance, and Posture," *Journal of Nonverbal Behavior,* Vol. 15, 1991, pp. 233–259.

Cross-cultural application: Judee K. Burgoon, "Cross-Cultural and Intercultural Applications of Expectancy Violations Theory," in *Intercultural Communication Theory,* Richard Wiseman (ed.), Sage, Thousand Oaks, Calif., 1995, pp. 194–214.

Emotional communication application: Judee K. Burgoon, "Interpersonal Expectations, Expectancy Violations, and Emotional Communication," *Journal of Language and Social Psychology,* Vol. 12, 1993, pp. 30–48.

First date expectancy violations: Paul A. Mongeau and Colleen M. Carey, "Who's Wooing Whom II? An Experimental Investigation of Date-Initiation and Expectancy Violation," *Western Journal of Communication,* Vol. 60, 1996, pp. 195–213.

Empirical test: Beth A. LePoire and Judee K. Burgoon, "Two Contrasting Explanations of Involvement Violations: Expectancy Violations Theory Versus Discrepancy Arousal Theory," *Human Communication Research,* Vol. 20, 1994, pp. 560–591.

CHAPTER 7

Interpersonal Deception Theory

of David Buller and Judee Burgoon

University of Arizona communication theorists David Buller and Judee Burgoon have conducted over two dozen experiments in which they ask participants to deceive another person. The researchers explain that people often find themselves in situations where they make statements that are less than completely honest in order to "avoid hurting or offending another person, to emphasize their best qualities, to avoid getting into a conflict, or to speed up or slow down a relationship."[1] Put yourself in the situation described below and consider how you might respond:

> You've been dating Pat for nearly three years and feel quite close in your relationship. Since Pat goes to a different school upstate, the two of you have agreed to date other people. Nevertheless, Pat is quite jealous and possessive. During the school year you see Pat only occasionally, but you call each other every Sunday and talk for over an hour. On Friday one of your friends invites you to a party on Saturday night, but the party is "couples only," so you need a date. There's no way that Pat could come down for the weekend. You decide to ask someone from your Comm class who you've been attracted to so that you can go to the party. The two of you go and have a great time. On Sunday afternoon, there's a knock on your door and it's Pat. Pat walks in and says, "I decided to come down and surprise you. I tried calling you all last night, but you weren't around. What were you doing?"[2]

Buller and Burgoon focus on three types of response you might give if you decide not to tell the truth, the whole truth, and nothing but the truth. First, you could lie: "I was at the library getting ready for my Comm Theory exam." Second, you could tell part of the truth while leaving out important details: "I went to a party at a friend's apartment." Or third, you could be intentionally vague or evasive: "I went out for a while."

Following the lead of others who study verbal deceit, Buller and Burgoon

*"Sorry, sir. The Liars' Club Convention isn't at this hotel.
I'm afraid someone gave you the wrong information."*

Reprinted from the Saturday Evening Post © 1983.

label these three strategies *falsification, concealment,* and *equivocation.* The three differ in that falsification creates a fiction, concealment hides a secret, and equivocation dodges the issue. Yet all three messages fall under the umbrella concept of *deception,* which Buller and Burgoon define as "a message knowingly transmitted by a sender to foster a false belief or conclusion by the receiver."[3]

Would Pat be able to spot the deception? Interpersonal deception theory says probably not. Yet most people are confident they could and it's doubtful that this jealous romantic partner would be an exception.[4] Working on the popular assumption that nonverbal communication is hard to fake, Pat would probably check your facial expression and listen to the sound of your voice to confirm or disconfirm your answer.

Folk wisdom provides a rationale for monitoring nonverbal cues for signs of deceit. When people won't look us straight in the eye, we assume they have something to hide. We also tend to believe that nervous laughter and hurried speech reflect the fear of being caught in a lie.

Although this thinking represents "common sense," the bulk of deception research shows that these particular nonverbal cues are not reliable indicators of deception.[5] A chuckling, fast-talking person who avoids eye contact is just as likely to be telling the truth as someone who displays the socially accepted signs of sincerity. When tested under controlled laboratory conditions, people rarely are more than 60 percent accurate in their ability to spot deception, while a just-by-chance 50 percent detection rate is more common. It appears that Pat may never know for sure what you did or how you felt on Saturday night.

AN EMERGENT THEORY OF THOUGHTFUL INTERACTION

David Buller and Judee Burgoon discount the value of highly controlled studies designed to isolate unmistakable cues that people are lying. They agree that human beings are rather poor lie detectors, but they don't think that the typical one-way communication experiment is a helpful way to explore the reason why. They point out that past research has usually involved people listening to

---

1. What deceivers and respondents think and do varies according to the amount of interactive give-and-take that's possible in the situation.

2. What deceivers and respondents think and do varies according to how well they know and like each other.

3. Deceivers make more strategic moves and leak more nonverbal cues than truth tellers.

4. With increased interaction, deceivers make more strategic moves and display less leakage.

5. Deceivers and respondents' expectation for honesty (truth bias) is positively linked with interactivity and relational warmth.

6. Deceivers' fear of being caught and the strategic activity that goes with that fear are lower when truth bias is high, and vice versa.

7. Motivation affects strategic activity and leakage: (a) People who deceive for their own self-gain make more strategic moves and display more leakage. (b) The way respondents first react depends on the relative importance of the relationship and their initial suspicion.

8. As relational familiarity increases, deceivers become more afraid of detection, make more strategic moves, and display more leakage.

9. Skilled deceivers appear more believable because they make more strategic moves and display less leakage than unskilled deceivers.

FIGURE 7.1   Propositions of Interpersonal Deception Theory
(Buller and Burgoon, "Interpersonal Deception Theory," abridged and paraphrased)

scripted messages recorded by strangers with whom they've had no chance to interact. This static approach to deception ignores communication dynamics and focuses instead on internal thought processes—behind-the-eyes explanations for liars' manipulative behavior or the naïve acceptance of gullible listeners. Buller notes that "rarely is it acknowledged that receivers react to deceivers' messages and that these reactions alter the communication exchange and, perhaps, deception's success."[6] At the start of the 1990s he proclaimed the need for an *interpersonal* deception theory that would

> explain the interplay between active deceivers and detectors who communicate with multiple motives, who behave strategically, whose communication behaviors mutually influence one another to produce a sequence of moves and countermoves, and whose communication is influenced by the situation in which the deception transpires.[7]

Interpersonal deception theory is the result. Figure 7.1 is a paraphrased digest of the eighteen propositions that appeared in a 1996 issue of *Communication Theory* dedicated solely to exploring Buller and Burgoon's theory. Although the theorists consider their model as "work in progress," they are committed to

---

10. A deceiver's perceived credibility is positively linked to interactivity, the respondent's truth bias, and the deceiver's communication skill, but goes down to the extent that the deceiver's communication is unexpected.

11. A respondent's accuracy in spotting deception goes down when interactivity, the respondent's truth bias, and the deceiver's communication skill go up. Detection is positively linked to the respondent's listening skills, relational familiarity, and the degree to which the deceiver's communication is unexpected.

12. Respondents' suspicion is apparent in their strategic activity and leakage.

13. Deceivers spot suspicion when it's present. Perception of suspicion increases when a respondent's behavior is unexpected. Any respondent reactions that signal disbelief, doubt, or the need for more information increase the deceiver's perception of suspicion.

14. Real or imagined suspicion increases deceivers' strategic activity and leakage.

15. The way deception and suspicion are displayed within a given interaction changes over time.

16. In deceptive interactions, reciprocity is the most typical pattern of adaptive response.

17. When the conversation is over, the respondent's detection accuracy, judgment of deceiver credibility, and truth bias depend on the deceiver's final strategic moves and leakage as well as the respondent's listening skill and remaining suspicions.

18. When the conversation is over, the deceiver's judgment of success depends on the respondent's final reaction and the deceiver's perception of lasting suspicion.

FIGURE 7.1   (Continued)

a set of unchanging assumptions concerning interpersonal communication in general, and deception in particular. Most of these assumptions surface in their propositions, but two core ideas stand out.

Interpersonal communication is interactive.   If the encounter between you and Pat actually took place, both of you would be active participants, constantly adjusting your behavior in response to feedback from each other. Whatever story you tell, you shouldn't expect Pat to remain verbally and nonverbally mute. One way or another, you'll get a response. In order to capture the reality of two-way communication in flux, I've substituted the term *respondent* for the more passive term "listener" in my paraphrase of Buller and Burgoon's propositions. Interaction, rather than individuality, is at the core of their theory.

Strategic deception demands mental effort.   A successful deceiver must consciously manipulate information to create a plausible message, present it in a sincere manner, monitor reactions, prepare follow-up responses, and get ready for damage control of a tarnished image—all at the same time. People differ in their ability to deal with these complex mental tasks, but at some point the strategic requirements of deception can produce cognitive overload. If you choose to be less than honest in your surprise encounter with Pat, you might find yourself unable to attend to every aspect of deception, and some of your communication behavior will go on "automatic pilot." The resulting nonstrategic display is likely to be in the form of nonverbal behavior that you wouldn't even think about. Buller and Burgoon use the term *leakage* to refer to unconscious nonverbal cues that signal an internal state.[8] Over half of their eighteen propositions involve the important distinction between strategic and nonstrategic activity.

I urge you to make a strategic decision to mull over the eighteen propositions listed in Figure 7.1. They are the skeletal links of interpersonal deception theory. The theory will come alive for you if you call to mind a deceptive interaction in which you've played a part, either as deceiver or respondent, and then apply each proposition to that encounter. In the following sections I'll flesh out portions of this bare-bones propositional framework by examining what Buller and Burgoon say about the linguistic strategy of deceivers, their nonstrategic leakage, the suspicious reactions of respondents, and the behavioral adjustments that deceivers make.

STRATEGIC INFORMATION MANAGEMENT: THE LANGUAGE AND LOOK OF LIARS

At root, deception is accomplished by manipulating information. Whether through falsification, concealment, or equivocation, liars use words to accomplish their ends. As Sir Walter Scott wrote:

> O what, a tangled web we weave,
> When first we practise to deceive![9]

Buller and Burgoon agree, but not necessarily on moral grounds. They judge a deceptive act on the basis of the deceiver's motives, not on the act itself. That evaluation is complicated, however, because every deceptive act has at least three aims—to accomplish a specific task or instrumental goal, to establish or maintain a relationship with the respondent, and to "save face" or sustain the image of one or both parties. The web of words the deceiver weaves has to work on multiple levels.

The language used to achieve a specific task can be as varied as the people who feel a need to deceive. Yet Buller and Burgoon suggest that the interpersonal and identity motivations inherent in deception stimulate a recurring "text" which marks the communication as less than honest. Even though respondents probably won't spot these signs in the ebb and flow of interaction, the theorists list four message characteristics that reflect strategic intent.

1. Uncertainty and vagueness.   If you don't want Pat to know about Saturday night, you'll probably keep your answer short and noncommittal. If you say, "I worked late," the brevity precludes detail and there's nothing concrete for Pat to challenge. Another typical way to not be pinned down is to speak in the passive voice and use indefinite pronouns. ("It was impossible to get things done before then.")

2. Nonimmediacy, reticence, and withdrawal.   If Pat shows up unexpectedly and demands to know why you weren't in last night, you'll probably wish you weren't there now. That desire to be out of the situation is often encoded in nonverbal actions. You might turn away to make coffee, sit further apart than usual, or lean back rather than forward as you answer. We should expect a moment of silence before you answered, and frequent pauses during your response would be common. Words also show nonimmediacy when the speaker changes verbs from present to past tense—a linguistic move that says in effect, "I'm history."

3. Disassociation.   While nonimmediacy is a strategy of symbolically removing yourself from the situation, disassociation is a way of distancing yourself from what you've done. If you talk about your Saturday night date, you are liable to choose language that shifts much of the responsibility to others. *Levelers* are inclusive terms that do this by removing individual choice. ("But Pat, everyone <u>always</u> goes out on Saturday night.") *Group references* also suggest shared responsibility. ("<u>We</u> <u>all</u> went over to Holly's party <u>together.</u>") *Modifiers* downplay the intensity of unwelcome news. ("<u>Sometimes</u> I get <u>kinda</u> lonely staying home on Saturday night.") All of these linguistic constructions sever the personal connection between the actor and the act of deception.

4. Image- and relationship-protecting behavior. When people "practice to deceive," they usually recognize that nonverbal leakage could provide telltale signs that the words they speak aren't what they know to be true. Since discovery could hurt their reputations and threaten their relationships, they consciously strive to suppress the bodily cues that might signal deception. To mask the cues that leak out despite their best efforts, they try to appear extra sincere. Deceivers in dialogue tend to nod in agreement when the respondent speaks, avoid interrupting, and smile frequently. As Buller and Burgoon note, "it appears that smiling may be a simple, all-purpose strategy enacted to cover up deceit."[10] Jim Carrey's grinning presence in the film *Liar, Liar* epitomizes this typical diversionary tactic.

Those who desire a clear-cut way to separate truth telling from deception might hope that these four telltale signs of strategic messages would provide an either/or litmus test for discerning honesty. But the world of interpersonal communication is not that simple. Almost <u>all</u> communication is intentional, goal directed, and mindful. According to Proposition 3, deceptive communication is simply more so.

Five of Buller and Burgoon's propositions show that multiple factors strongly affect the extent of a deceiver's strategic behavior. They claim that this plan-based activity increases when the situation is highly interactive (Prop. 4), when the parties know each other well (Prop. 8), when the deceiver particularly fears discovery (Prop. 6), when the deceiver's motivation is selfish (Prop. 7), and when the deceiver has good communication skills (Prop. 9). It's not a stretch to think that all five of these intensifying factors would come into play if you decide to conceal, equivocate, or falsify. If so, your mind will be whirling.

Buller and Burgoon firmly believe that strategic moves aid successful deception. Yet even with all the high-intensity cognitive effort you might bring to the encounter, there's no guarantee that you'd pull it off. Interpersonal deception theory suggests that the outcome would depend not only on the quality of your message, but also on the nonstrategic cues you can't control.

LEAKAGE—THE TRUTH WILL COME OUT (MAYBE)

A century ago, psychiatric pioneer Sigmund Freud stated the case for using nonverbal cues to detect deception. Referring to a patient who wouldn't be truthful about his darkest thoughts and feelings, Freud observed, ". . . if his lips are silent, he chatters with his fingertips; betrayal oozes out of him at every pore."[11] Buller and Burgoon agree that behavior outside of the deceiver's conscious control can signal dishonesty, and they basically endorse the well-known four-factor model of deception developed by University of Rochester social psychologist Miron Zuckerman to explain why this leakage occurs.[12]

First, deceivers' intense *attempt to control* information can produce performances that come across as too slick or "canned." Nonstrategic information leaks usually go hand-in-hand with strategic activity. Second, lying causes physiological *arousal*. That's why a polygraph, which measures only autonomic responses, is called a "lie detector." Third, the predominant *felt emotions* that accompany deceit are guilt and anxiety. Although "duping delight" is always a possibility, most people feel bad about lying and are likely to show it. Finally, the complex *cognitive factors* involved in deception can tax the brain beyond its capacity. Cognitive overload means some behaviors go untended.

In a statistical procedure called *meta-analysis*, Zuckerman combined the results of thirty-five different leakage studies conducted by various researchers to see what unintentional nonverbal behaviors usually accompany deception.[13] Freud's drumming fingers made the list as part of a category called "self adapters"—fidgety hand movements unrelated to what is said. Other telltale signs were:

- increased blinking and enlarged pupils
- frequent speech errors (grammatical mistakes, repetitions, slips of the tongue)
- increased speech hesitations (awkward pauses, "ahs, ers, ums")
- higher voice pitch
- increased discrepancies between verbal and nonverbal channels

Note that smiling and other facial expressions didn't make the list. As University of Virginia social psychologist Bella DePaulo states, "Facial cues . . . are indeed faking cues."[14] Apparently most of us are aware of our face's capacity to convey complex messages, and therefore we strategically monitor and control that display far more than we do our tone of voice or body movement.

Buller and Burgoon contribute to the discussion of leakage by moving beyond a concern with micro-behaviors and focusing on the decline of the deceiver's overall performance. Reflective of Burgoon's work with expectancy violations (see Chapter 6), the theorists claim that an unexpected move signals something is wrong. As Propositions 4, 9, and 10 suggest, a skilled communicator operating in an interactive context has a better chance of crafting a deceptive performance that won't seem strange. But ultimately, whether or not the deceiver "pulls off" the deception depends on how suspicious the respondent actually is.

RESPONDENTS' DILEMMA: TRUTH BIAS OR SUSPICION?

Five of Buller and Burgoon's propositions refer to our persistent expectation that people will tell the truth (Prop. 5, 6, 10, 11, 16). First labeled a "truth bias" by communication researchers Steven McCornack (Michigan State University) and Malcolm Parks (University of Washington),[15] Burgoon and Buller have confirmed that respondents tend to regard interpersonal messages as honest, complete, direct, relevant, and clear—even when the speaker is lying.[16] So no matter what you might say about Saturday night, Pat would probably believe you.

Why are people so easily fooled? McCornack claims that there exists an implied *social contract* that all of us will be honest with each other—a mutual agreement that our messages will reflect reality as we know it. Since deception voids that contract, it's hard for us to believe that people will casually plunge us into social chaos.[17] Other deception researchers suggest that the expectation of honesty is a *cognitive heuristic,* a mental short cut used to bypass the huge clutter of verbal and nonverbal signals that bombard us throughout every conversation. Unless deception is obvious from the start, we "seize and freeze" on early signs of sincerity and effectively seal ourselves off from conflicting indicators. Whatever the reason for our assumption of veracity, Buller and Burgoon are convinced that people who know and like each other are particularly resistant to doubting each others' words. The theorists suggest that parties in close, warm relationships are motivated to find truth in whatever their friend, romantic partner, or family member says, and thus overlook or rationalize away statements that others might find questionable.[18]

Despite a powerful and prevailing truth-bias in face-to-face interaction, people can come to doubt the honesty of another's words. Pat may well be suspicious of what you say. Buller and Burgoon define *suspicion* as a "state of doubt or distrust that is held without sufficient evidence or proof."[19] As such, they picture suspicion as a mid-range mind-set, located somewhere between truth and falsity:

TRUTH _____ **SUSPICION** _____ **LIE**

We've already looked at the strategic and nonstrategic behavior of deceivers that might cause others to become suspicious. Verbal tactics of vagueness, nonimmediacy, and disassociation can make respondents wary; nonverbal signs of emotional stress and mental meltdown may put listeners on guard. In fact, any communication that strikes respondents as strange or out of character is liable to trigger misgivings about the message or the messenger. Of course, some suspicions may be planted before the interaction even begins. From past experience, Pat may know that you aren't always truthful. Certainly this jealousy will create a built-in skepticism toward any explanation you might offer. Or a prior warning from a third party could taint the whole interaction.

Given the many ways that respondents could become suspicious, we might imagine that deceivers would lose their truth-bias advantage and have their deception unmasked for what it is. Not so. Buller and Burgoon have found that it's actually difficult to induce a deep-seated skepticism.[20] On the rare occasions when respondents are highly suspicious, their doubts usually diminish after a few minutes of interaction.

When respondents doubt a deceiver's honesty, they tend to avoid direct confrontation in order to hide their suspicions. Instead, they adopt "a take charge interview style but one that is conducted under a pleasant guise."[21] Smiling often, they gently probe for more information rather than directly challenging the deceiver's statements. Buller and Burgoon have discovered scant evidence that these probes help respondents unmask deception. On the contrary, the theorists find that throughout the interaction, respondents are "oblivious to, or accepting of, sender deceit and may even assist, wittingly or unwittingly, in its creation."[22] Even though Buller and Burgoon's empirical commitment contrasts sharply with Pearce and Cronen's interpretive stance (see Chapter 5), interpersonal deception theory and CMM reach a common conclusion—namely that persons-in-conversation co-construct their own social realities. This construction project continues as the deceiver reacts to the respondent's suspicions.

PUTTING DOUBTS TO REST: DECEIVER ADJUSTMENT TO RESPONDENT SUSPICION

In the early stages of her work on interpersonal deception, Judee Burgoon stated that researchers should view deception as a "chain of offensive and defensive maneuvers on the part of both participants."[23] Propositions 12–18 describe the ongoing interaction in that adversarial "game." Just as unexpected words and nonverbal leakage reveal the strategic thinking and emotional stress that accompany deception, so respondents' suspicions can be seen through their own nontypical behaviors—even when they try to appear natural. The deception game isn't balanced, however, because unlike truth-bias players who don't even know they are playing, deceivers always know the name of the game and usually have more to lose if they fail. With this heightened motivation, deceivers are usually more successful at sensing suspicion than respondents are at spotting deception. Not surprisingly, as soon as deceivers see signs of doubt, they change their behavior in a way intended to alleviate their partner's distrust. According to Buller and Burgoon, they usually reciprocate the mood and manner of the person they are trying to mislead.

Reciprocation is a process of adjusting communication behavior to mesh with the style of the other. When the respondent shows high involvement through animated speech and forward body lean, the deceiver becomes similarly engaged. On the other hand, deceivers can match a nonchalant style with their own laid-back approach. A strong accusation can be countered with an angry retort, a pleasant query answered with a warm smile. Thus, deceivers whose initial words are met with skepticism show more variety in their communication behavior than do those who face apparent acceptance.

Truth tellers react the same way. When falsely accused or confronted by suspicion they try to tailor messages that will alleviate doubt. But in the context of suspected deception, their adaptation may strike the respondent as devious—a self-fulfilling prophecy labeled the "Othello error."[24] It's an apt reference to the Moorish king's unfounded fear of Desdemona's unfaithfulness, an escalating obsession that ended in tragedy. Although most suspicious reactions don't have Shakespearean consequences, the Bard's play depicts a "recursive spiral of sender and receiver cognitions influencing behaviors and subsequent cognitions during an interaction" that Buller and Burgoon think is typical of most interpersonal interactions where honesty is an issue.[25] Their theory explains why detection of deception (and detection of truth telling) is a hit-and-miss business. If you decide to lie about Saturday night, Pat may well be fooled. If you decide to tell the truth, Pat may not believe you. Interpersonal deception theory explains why.

CRITIQUE: WHY IS A SCIENTIFIC THEORY OF DECEPTIVE COMMUNICATION SO COMPLICATED?

David Buller and Judee Burgoon have created a theory that offers multiple explanations for what takes place during deceptive communication. Interactive contexts, strategic manipulation of language, nonverbal leakage, truth biases, suspicious probes, and behavioral adaptation are just a few of the explanatory concepts they use to capture the dynamics of deception. To some observers, interpersonal deception theory looks like the mousetrap pictured in Chapter 2.

Given that relative simplicity is the mark of a high quality scientific theory, is it reasonable that this one is so complex?

Other deception theories with a narrower focus are definitely more concise. For example, I was able to explain Zuckerman's four-factor model of nonverbal leakage in a few paragraphs. McCornack offers an equally simple model of deception that has direct causal links:[26]

Relational Closeness	→	Detection Confidence	→	Truth Bias	→	Less Detection Accuracy

The question is whether or not simple constructions can reflect the complexity of real-life deceptive give-and-take. Buller and Burgoon are convinced they can't. They insist that deception is essentially a *communication* activity. Every factor that affects interpersonal encounters remains in play:

> It is a frustrating and challenging reality that communication is a complex interplay between two or more people whose actions are responsive to their own cognitions, the partner's behavior, and the context and relationship in which interaction takes place. . . . We have reached a juncture in the study of deception where researchers must attack this complexity if we are to advance our understanding of this common communication phenomenon.[27]

I could argue that their theory needs to be <u>more</u> complicated. Although most of the propositions in Figure 7.1 are cast as straightforward predictions, we aren't told how to resolve conflicting forces affecting deception. For example, Proposition 6 claims that deceivers' fear of detection will decrease when respondents' truth bias goes up. Proposition 8 forecasts that deceivers' fear of detection will increase as relational familiarity goes up. So far so good. But what happens to deceiver anxiety when conversational parties share a strong truth bias <u>and</u> a common past? These opposing dynamics exist in many close relationships, yet the theory doesn't suggest which force is stronger. Given the absence of rules to sort out conflicting claims, it's not surprising that Buller and Burgoon pepper their discussion with qualifying terms such as *may, sometimes, tend to be, are likely to,* and *perhaps.*

For me, the simplicity of interpersonal deception theory is found in its practical advice. When talking with others, I should doubt my ability to detect deception. Most of us think we are great lie detectors; this theory suggests we aren't. Once we no longer assume that we have an uncanny knack to ferret out the truth, we diminish our chance of being fooled. We also decrease the danger of making snap judgments that do violence to others. I once heard a macho teenager boast that he could tell whether a girl was a virgin by looking into her eyes, regardless of what she said. That's the kind of arrogance that could easily tarnish a reputation.

Interpersonal deception theory underscores the complexity of deception when people can respond to each other face-to-face. It's hard to know for sure when someone isn't telling the truth. But before the difficulty of detection prompts you to lie to Pat—or anyone else for that matter, consider the thoughts in the brief ethical reflections that follow this chapter. Buller and Burgoon may be silent on the morality of deception; ethical theorists are not.

QUESTIONS TO SHARPEN YOUR FOCUS

1. In an *interactive context,* what *linguistic* features of the message and *nonverbal* signs of *leakage* in the messenger are probable indicators of deception?

2. Which of the eighteen propositions paraphrased in Figure 7.1 clearly show that interpersonal deception theory has a *cognitive* explanation for *communication behavior* during deception?

3. Buller and Burgoon claim that accurate detection of deception is difficult, yet most people knew Bill Clinton was lying about Monica Lewinsky long before he confessed. How would the authors explain this apparent contradiction?

4. What deceptive *strategy* would you use if you decided not to tell the truth to a close friend or relative—*falsification, concealment,* or *equivocation?* Which strategy is most likely to seem unexpected or strange? Why?

A SECOND LOOK

Recommended resource: David B. Buller and Judee K. Burgoon, "Interpersonal Deception Theory," *Communication Theory,* Vol. 6, 1996, pp. 203–242.

Deceptive communication—planned and otherwise: David B. Buller and Judee K. Burgoon, "Deception: Strategic and Nonstrategic Communication," in *Strategic Interpersonal Communication,* John Daly and John Woman (eds.), Lawrence Erlbaum Associates, Hillsdale, N.J., 1994, pp. 191–223.

Truth versus deception—differences in message content: Judee K. Burgoon, David B. Buller, Laura K. Guerrero, Walid Afifi, and Clyde Feldman, "Interpersonal Deception: XII. Information Management Dimensions Underlying Deceptive and Truthful Messages," *Communication Monographs,* Vol. 63, 1996, pp. 50–69.

Suspicion of deceit: Judee K. Burgoon, David B. Buller, Amy S. Ebesu, Cindy H. White, and Patricia A. Rockwell, "Testing Interpersonal Deception Theory: Effects of Suspicion on Communication Behaviors and Perceptions," *Communication Theory,* Vol. 6, 1996, pp. 243–267.

Probing strategies to discover dishonesty: Pamela J. Kalbfleisch, "The Language of Detecting Deceit," *Journal of Language and Social Psychology,* Vol. 13, 1994, pp. 469–496.

Leakage cues: Miron Zuckerman and Robert Driver, "Telling Lies: Verbal and Nonverbal Correlates of Deception," *Multichannel Integrations of Nonverbal Behavior,* Aron Siegman and Stanley Feldstein (eds.), Lawrence Erlbaum Associates, Hillsdale, N.J., 1985, pp. 129–148.

Affect of deceit: David B. Buller and Judee K. Burgoon, "Emotional Expression in the Deception Process," in *Handbook of Communication and Emotion: Research, Theory,*

Applications, and Contexts, Peter Andersen and Laura Guerrero (eds.), Academic Press, San Diego, 1998, pp. 381–402.

Practical implications of deception research: Pamela J. Kalbfleisch, "Deceit, Distrust and the Social Milieu: Application of Deception Research in a Troubled World," *Journal of Applied Communication Research,* Vol. 20, 1992, pp. 308–334.

Rival theory: Steven McCornack, "Information Manipulation Theory," *Communication Monographs,* Vol. 59, 1992, pp. 1–16.

Critique: Bella M. DePaulo, Matthew Ansfield, and Kathy L. Bell, "Theories About Deception and Paradigms for Studying It: A Critical Appraisal of Buller and Burgoon's Interpersonal Deception Theory and Research," *Communication Theory,* Vol. 6, 1996, pp. 297–310.

Most of us have found ourselves in communication situations where deception seemed an attractive option. Responding to Buller and Burgoon's suggestion that there are times when we want "to avoid hurting or offending another person," a student named Mark in my communication theory class posed the following real-life dilemma:

> I was waiting tables at the restaurant when I noticed my buddy Phil remove something from the cash drawer. The next day the manager announced that the register was fifty dollars short. She pulled me aside and asked me if I'd seen anyone dipping into the till. What should I say? If I tell the truth, Phil could lose his job and I might lose my friend. If I lie, I break trust with my boss and feel torn up inside. What do you think I ought to have said?

Students in the class looked for ways that Mark could duck the question or give a vague response. The manager, however, insisted on a straight answer. Mark never revealed what he said, but he wanted to discuss what was right, what would work out best, and to whom he should be *loyal* in this uncomfortable situation. These are the core issues of ethics. The ethical theories outlined below approach Mark's dilemma from these three different angles.

IMMANUEL KANT'S CATEGORICAL IMPERATIVE

German philosopher Immanuel Kant believed that any time we speak, we have a moral obligation to tell the truth. He wrote that "truthfulness in statements which cannot be avoided is the formal duty of an individual to everyone, however great may be the disadvantage accruing to himself or another."[1] Others might wink at white lies, question whether people deserve a straight answer, justify verbal deception for the hearer's own good, or warn of dire consequences that can result from uncensored truth. From Kant's perspective, there are no mitigating circumstances. We tell a lie every time we say something with intent to deceive. Lying is wrong—always.

Would Kant at least concede that Mark faces a tragic moral choice? Doesn't his duty to say what he saw clash with an obligation of loyalty to his friend Phil? According to Kant, no. He held that "a conflict of duties and obligations is inconceivable."[2] If Mark does what he ought to do—tell the truth—he'll find that ethical requirements are never contradictory.

Kant came to this absolutist position through the logic of his *categorical imperative,* a term that means "duty without exception." He stated the categorical imperative as a universal law: "Act only on that maxim which you can will to become a universal law."[3] In effect, Kant directed us to always ask the question, "What if everybody did that?" If we can't live with the answer, we have a solemn duty not to do the deed.

The categorical imperative is a method for determining right from wrong. Mark needs to ask himself the question, "What if everybody lied?" The answer of course is that if everyone lied all of the time, we could never be sure about any message. Stripped of reliable meaning, all language would be suspect. Promises would not be kept. Trust would disintegrate. Anarchy would reign. Since no rational being can live in a state like that, Kant's verdict is clear. Lying is always wrong! Case closed. Kant doesn't waffle on moral issues.

Even in the classic case of a humanitarian hiding Jews from the Nazi Holocaust, the categorical imperative requires that truth be served. If the Gestapo questions a householder about sheltering enemies of the state, he or she should respond truthfully. Both the protector and the protected may be sent to a death camp, but to throw away their dignity as human beings is a fate worse than death. In the words of a sports-minded colleague who teaches ethics, "Kant plays ethical hardball without a mitt."

AUGUSTINE'S DIVINE WILL

Augustine said, "Love God and do what you will." This maxim reflects the fifth-century Catholic bishop's belief that people who truly love God will desire to bring all their actions in line with his divine will. Augustine drew a sharp contrast between a person's symbolic citizenship in one of two ancient cities—Babylon and Jerusalem. Residents of Babylon are lovers of pleasure, the world, and themselves. Citizens of Jerusalem are lovers of God and they desire to submit to his law. "Let each one question himself as to what he loveth," Augustine wrote, "and he shall find of which [city] he is a citizen."[4]

Contemporary divine will advocates are less metaphorical, but they are equally convinced that making ethical choices is a matter of deciding where our basic loyalties lie. If we pledge allegiance to a higher being, we can pray the centuries-old prayer to

> See Thee more clearly,
> Love Thee more dearly,
> Follow Thee more nearly,
> Day by Day.[5]

Augustine believed that those who sincerely desire to follow God will discern truth telling as a central tenet of the divine will. Speech was given to humans by God so that they could make their thoughts known to each other.

> To use speech, then, for the purpose of deception, and not for its appointed end, is a sin. Nor, are we to suppose that there is any lie that is not a sin because it is sometimes possible, by telling a lie to do service to another.[6]

Augustine's essay "On Lying" makes it clear that he would join with Kant in urging Mark to tell the truth, no matter how painful the consequences. Yet unlike Kant, Augustine recognized gradations in the seriousness of lies. For example, lies aimed at helping others aren't as bad as those that aim to hurt.

"'Honesty is the best policy.' O.K.! Now, what's the <u>second</u>-best policy?"

From Augustine's perspective, Mark is less culpable if he lies to save Phil's job than if he falsely accuses another man to get him in trouble. The theologian was convinced, however, that any lie hurts our relationship with God. Just because some lies are less offensive to God than others, that's no reason to excuse ourselves from telling the truth. Thus Augustine concluded, "If any lies, like other sins, steal upon us, they should seek not to be justified but to be pardoned."[7]

SISSELA BOK'S PRINCIPLE OF VERACITY

Philosopher Sissela Bok is the author of *Lying: Moral Choice in Public and Private Life*.[8] The bulk of her book is an in-depth analysis of possible justifications for lying to a variety of people—enemies, peers, clients, students, children, other liars, patients who are dying, and so forth. By looking at lies from the perspective of all who are affected by them, Bok hopes to establish when, or if, lies can be justified.

Bok rejects Kant and Augustine's absolute prohibition of lying. She believes that "there are at least some circumstances which warrant a lie . . . foremost among them, when innocent lives are at stake, and where only a lie can deflect the danger."[9] But she also rejects a consequentialist ethic, which judges an act on the basis of whether we think it will result in harm or benefit. Consequentialism represents a kind of "bottom line" accounting which treats an act as morally neutral until we figure out if it will have positive or negative outcomes. Bok doesn't view lies as neutral! She is convinced that all lies drag around an initial negative weight that must be factored into any ethical equation. Her *principle of veracity* asserts that "truthful statements are preferable to lies in the absence of special considerations."[10]

Bok contends that we need the principle of veracity because liars engage in a tragic self-delusion. When they count the cost of deceit, they usually anticipate only their own short-term losses. Liars downplay the impact of their falsehood on the persons deceived, and almost always ignore the long-term effects on themselves and everyone else. They overlook the fact that all lies contribute to an erosion of confidence in people's word.

> Trust and integrity are precious resources, easily squandered, hard to regain. They can thrive only on a foundation of respect for veracity.[11]

Although Bok's principle of veracity allows people to lie in order to prevent a grievous wrong, it doesn't provide an ethical justification for Mark to deceive his boss. If he's tempted to lie, Bok says that he should apply the *test of publicity*.[12] Ordinarily that would involve openly checking with a variety of fair-minded people to see if they would endorse lying in this situation. But since Mark's boss demands an immediate answer, he just has time to mentally take the role of others (see Chapter 4). If he calls to mind a true cross-section of reasonable people (including the manager and customers at the restaurant), he'll realize that he has no warrant to lie and therefore he'll decide to tell the truth. Lying requires a compelling reason; truth telling does not.

In their search for communication that is ethical, these three theorists travel separate paths. Kant uses logic to discern human duty. Augustine urges commitment to align the heart toward God. Bok calls for a test of public justification. Despite their different approaches, all three end up at a place where truth is treasured and falsehood is shunned. Their conclusions offer scant encouragement for anyone looking for an ethically sound way to justify lies in daily life. Would you really want it otherwise?

COGNITIVE PROCESSING

The way we think has a profound effect on how we perceive other people, how we talk with them, and how they respond to our communication. The story of three umpires talking shop before a game illustrates three different approaches to cognitive processing.

The first umpire declared, "Some's balls, some's strikes—I calls them as they is." He denied that his thoughts had any impact on his perception of the game. The second umpire said, "Some's balls, some's strikes—I calls them as I sees them." He recognized that what he saw might not match the action on the field. The third umpire stated, "Some's balls, some's strikes—but they ain't nothin' till I calls them!" He understood that, for all practical purposes, the only game that really counted was the one being played out behind his eyes.

Cognitive theorists—scholars who think about thinking—align themselves with the third umpire. They are convinced that reality is not so much a matter of what's going on *out there* as it is of what's going on *in here*—in the mind. The trick, of course, is to figure out a way to get at it.

Suppose you come to class one day and your instructor places a black box on the table and invites you to take a closer look. You note that there's a hole in one end marked "input" and a matching hole on the other end labeled "output." Every student has a chance to feed objects into the first hole and watch what comes out on the other side. You observe that the output bears a vague resemblance to what went in. At the end of the hour, your instructor tells you to write an essay about what's going on inside the box.

The self-appointed task of cognitive theorists is similar to that class assignment. They compare and contrast what enters and exits the mind. Based on systematic similarities and differences between input and output, they construct a model of mental structures and mental processes. They often refer to their field of study as *information processing.*

The allusion to the world of computers is not accidental. What you know about word processing on an IBM PC or an Apple Mac may help you understand the different roles of structure and process in the mind. The computer hardware is the structure. What the software does when we strike a function key is the process. A four-year-old boy at a playground explained to me the difference between mental structure and mental process without ever using those terms. "My mind is like a jungle gym," he said. "Thinking is like climbing all over it."

Most cognitive theorists believe that information processing can be divided into five stages. Don't think of these stages in a rigid lock-step sequence; the progression of the five is similar to the five interconnected rings that symbolize the Olympic Games. There is partial overlap and duplication of function.

The functions are presented below, starting at the input end of the mental black box:

1. Sensory Input. The mind doesn't take in all raw data indiscriminately. Some is filtered out, some is swallowed whole, much is altered to fit preconceptions and prior expectations.

2. Central Processing. This takes place at the workbench of the mind, where meaning is attached to information. Most studies of interpersonal perception are less concerned with

INSIDE ONE'S MEMORY BANK

By the time you're forty, all available drawers are completely filled.

HOW TO SWIM	HOW TO BOWL	WATER-HEATER INFO	LOCAL ZIP CODES	BUS ROUTES
PEOPLE'S BIRTHDAYS	NAMES OF SON'S FRIENDS	NAMES OF DAUGHTER'S FRIENDS	HOW TO DRIVE	BOARD-GAME RULES
HOW TO RIDE A BIKE	ENGLISH GRAMMAR	STATE CAPITALS	PLOT OF "ANNA KARENINA"	MAKING LANYARDS
GRADE-SCHOOL TEACHERS	HIGH-SCHOOL FRENCH	N.Y.C. SUBWAY SYSTEM	CURRENT EVENTS	
OLD "TWILIGHT ZONE" PLOTS	ALL ABOUT PARAKEETS	COOKING SKILLS	DISCO	

You learn something new, something else gets thrown out.

> Gwyneth Paltrow and Ben Affleck are on the outs!

People think they can get around this by cramming stuff into already-in-use drawers, but they're sadly mistaken.

And in the end everything turns into material whose only function is to keep one's head from collapsing in on itself.

> Move over, American history, backgammon, and how to make good drip coffee, 'cause here comes **MY NEW FAX MACHINE!!!**

STYROFOAM PEANUTS	GOOSE DOWN	SAWDUST	WOOD CHIPS
DRIED BEANS	SHREDDED NEWSPAPER	GRAVEL	COTTON BATTING
CONCRETE	SILICONE	KAPOK	PLASTER OF PARIS

sensory stimuli than they are with the meanings people ascribe to them.

3. Information Storage. We don't create separate mental files for each bit of information that comes to mind. Long-term memory groups data in previously chosen categories. A phone conversation could be classified according to whom we are talking with, the topic of discussion, the length of the call, or how we felt about it afterward. The same information will be remembered differently depending on the material with which it's associated.

4. Information Retrieval. What comes out of long-term memory is not necessarily what went in. When we call up facts or images, we're quite capable of filling in the blanks or coloring in the pictures so that the material makes as much sense now as it did when we filed it away.

5. Utilization. How does the retrieved and transformed information affect our speech and nonverbal behavior? We haven't explained the cognitive process until we deal with the actions our thoughts produce.

Most communication scholars focus on the output end of cognitive processing, but they differ as to which prior stage has the greatest impact on message production. Researchers who study attention zero in on *sensory input.* Theorists concerned with memory concentrate on *information storage* and *retrieval.* Chapter 8 presents Jesse Delia's constructivism, a theory that cleaves the system at the point of *central processing.* Constructivists suggest that individual differences in cognitive complexity (central processing) affect a person's ability to adapt a message to a specific audience (utilization).

Although I feature only one theory in this section, a number of the chapters in the text have a strong cognitive component. For example, both theories discussed in the upcoming section on influence claim that human beings are hard-wired to process persuasive messages in a certain way (see Chapters 13 and 14). The scholars differ on schematics, but they agree that common mental structures and thought processes exist. Their quest to discover regularities inside the black box mark them as cognitive *scientists.* Interpretive thinkers, on the other hand, concentrate on creative thought and conscious choice.

CHAPTER 8

Constructivism

of Jesse Delia

While this course may be your first look at communication theory, constructivists believe that you already have an implicit theory of communication which helps you interpret and shape your social environment. The constructivist project is headed by Jesse Delia, former chair of the department of Speech Communication at the University of Illinois, now dean of Liberal Arts and Sciences there. Constructivists picture us as carpenters trying to construct or restore the relational world in which we live. Using this imagery, you might think of your implicit theory as a tool you use to align your culture, your cognitions, and your communication.

Since we aren't usually aware of the interpretive scheme we use to make sense of our social world, Delia and a network of constructivist researchers use Walter Crockett's open-ended Role Category Questionnaire (RCQ) to help us "get inside our head."[1] So that you fully understand the theory and what it says about your communication, take ten minutes to respond to the RCQ items before you are sensitized to what the survey is measuring.

ROLE CATEGORY QUESTIONNAIRE

Think of people about your same age whom you know well. Select one person that you like, and also pick someone you dislike. Once you have two specific people in mind, spend a moment to mentally compare and contrast them in terms of personality, habits, beliefs, and the way they treat others. Don't limit yourself to similarities and differences between the two; let your mind play over the full range of characteristics that make them who they are.

Now take a piece of paper and for about five minutes describe the person you enjoy so that a stranger would understand what he or she is like. Skip physical characteristics, but list all of the attributes, mannerisms, and reactions to others that identify who he or she is. Please do that now.

When you've finished the description, do the same thing for the person you don't like. Again, write down any and all personal characteristics or actions that you associate with that person. Spend about five minutes on this description.

PERSONAL CONSTRUCTS AS EVIDENCE OF COGNITIVE COMPLEXITY

The core assumption of constructivism is that "persons make sense of the world through systems of personal constructs."[2] Constructs are the cognitive templates or stencils we fit over "reality" to bring order out of chaos. The Role Category Questionnaire is designed to sample the interpersonal constructs in our mental toolbox that we bring to the construction site of meaning.

Much like sets of opposing terms (hot-cold, good-bad, fast-slow), constructs are contrasting features we use to classify perceptions. The police artist has an identification kit with which an eyewitness can construct the face of a suspect. By systematically altering the shape of the chin, size of the nose, distance between the eyes, line of the hair, and so forth, the witness can build a likeness of the person in question. However, the RCQ doesn't bother with physical features. It centers on the categories of personality and action that we use to define the character of another person.

The arena of politics offers a familiar example of the way we use constructs to describe another individual. All of us have our own bipolar dimensions of judgment that we apply to politicians. Some typical scales are liberal-conservative, honest-crooked, competent-inept. The politically astute observer may draw on dozens of these interpretive orientations to describe shades of difference. There are *conservatives,* and there are *social* conservatives. Then there are *articulate* social conservatives. Some of them are *belligerent,* and so forth. On the other hand, those who are politically unsophisticated may use only one value-laden construct as they watch the six o-clock news. They see only saints or scoundrels.

Researchers who use the RCQ are trying to determine the respondent's degree of cognitive complexity as they form interpersonal impressions. They are more concerned with the *structure* of the writer's constructs than with the actual judgments being made. Along that line, someone has said that there are two kinds of people in the world—those who think there are two kinds of people in the world, and those who don't. The constructivist believes that the first kind of person is cognitively immature, because he or she is able to see others only in terms of black or white. But the second kind of person has grown into a sophisticated observer of the human scene, capable of depicting people using a vast range of colors, shades, and hues. When it comes to thinking about people, the Role Category Questionnaire was designed to separate the kids from the adults.

THE THREE FACES OF COGNITIVE COMPLEXITY: DIFFERENTIATION, ABSTRACTION, AND INTEGRATION

Your descriptions on the RCQ can be scored for three different facets of cognitive complexity: differentiation, abstraction, and integration. *Differentiation* is defined as the number of separate personality constructs used to describe the target person. *Abstraction* is the degree to which the respondent sees visible behavior in terms of internal traits, motives, and dispositions. *Integration* has to do with recognizing and reconciling conflicting impressions. Scoring for differentiation is easy, but analyzing the test for abstraction and integration is both tricky and cumbersome. Because the three measures correlate moderately well, most researchers are content to count the number of constructs and assume they've tapped the entire dimension of cognitive complexity. I'll take you through a shorthand version of the scoring procedure.

Let's assume you decided to write about a friend named Chris and a co-worker named Alex. Add up the number of different descriptions you used to describe both people. As a rule of thumb, consider that each new term represents an additional mental construct. Seeing Chris as both *sharp* and *competent* would earn two points. So would a judgment that Alex is *hurried* and *never has time*. But there are exceptions to the one-term-equals-one-construct rule.

Adjectives and adverbs that merely modify the extent of a characteristic don't reflect additional constructs. Score just one point if you wrote that Chris is *totally sincere*. Since idioms such as *good ole boy* have a single referent, they get a single point as well. On their own, physical descriptions (*tall*) and demographic labels (*Irish*) say nothing about character, so skip over them. Apart from these rules, close calls should get the benefit of the doubt and score an extra point.

The combined score of both descriptions is an index of interpersonal construct differentiation. I've seen single scores as low as 3 and as high as 45, but typical adult populations average between 20 and 25. Are these scores a good measure of cognitive complexity? Delia makes a good case for the RCQ's validity. His claim that cognitive complexity develops with a child's chronological age is reflected in progressively higher scores as youngsters grow older. He also claims that individual differences between adults should be relatively stable over time. This standard has been met through good test-retest reliability.

Finally, he notes that a pure test of personality should not be confounded by other character traits or extraneous factors. Research has established that RCQ scores are independent of IQ, empathy, writing skill, and extroversion. Some critics have charged that it's merely a measure of loquacity or wordiness, but constructivists maintain that high scores on this free-response test take more than the gift of gab.

Now that you have an idea of what's involved in cognitive complexity, we'll consider the main hypothesis of constructivism. Delia and his colleagues claim that people who are cognitively complex in their perceptions of others have a communication advantage over those with less-developed mental structures. These fortunate individuals have the ability to produce sophisticated messages that have the best chance to achieve their communication goals.

SOPHISTICATED COMMUNICATION: PERSON-CENTERED MESSAGES . . . AND MORE

Early constructivist writing claimed that *person-centered messages* were the epitome of sophisticated communication. As Delia used the phrase, it referred to "messages which reflect an awareness of and adaptations to subjective, affective and relational aspects of the communication contexts."[3]

The study by Ruth Ann Clark and Delia of second- to ninth-grade school-children is a prototype of constructivist research that links person-centered messages to cognitive complexity.[4] It focused on the children's ability to adapt persuasive appeals to different target listeners. After taking the RCQ orally, the kids were given the role-play task of convincing a woman they didn't know to keep a lost puppy.

Naturally, the quality of messages differed. Some children showed no realization that the woman's perspective on the matter might be different from their own. Other kids recognized the difference but failed to adapt their message to this reality. A more sophisticated group took notice of the difference and were able to imagine what the woman was thinking. ("My husband will think I'm a sucker for every stray in town.") They then could make an attempt to refute the counterarguments they knew their appeal would raise. The most sophisticated messages also stressed the advantages that would come to her if she complied with the request. ("Having a dog for a companion will take away some of the loneliness you feel at night when your husband is out of town. He'll also feel better when he knows you've got a furry friend.")

Constructivists assume that strategic adaptation is a developmentally nurtured skill. Consistent with their belief, Clark and Delia found that the quality of messages improved as the age of the children increased. But differences in construct differentiation not due to chronological age also had a significant impact. Cognitively complex students were two years ahead of their same-age classmates in ability to encode person-centered messages. So the older kids who possessed cognitive complexity beyond their years were best able to take the perspective of the other and tailor the message to the individual listener.

Scholars who study communication use different terms to describe the capacity to create person-centered messages: *rhetorical sensitivity,*[5] *taking the role of the other* (see Chapter 4), *identification* (see Chapter 21), *self-monitoring, audience awareness, listener adaptation.* Whatever we call it, the creation of person-centered messages is a sophisticated communication skill. Constructivists say that cognitively complex people can do it better.

Note that they don't claim the person always *does* it, only that he or she has a capacity that others don't. Fatigue, pressure to conform, or other situational factors can mute the advantage. The way constructivists put it is that cognitive complexity is a "necessary but not sufficient condition" of person-centered messages.[6]

Truly sophisticated messages reflect more than the speaker or writer's efforts at audience adaptation. They also are crafted to accomplish *multiple goals.* Consider the workplace plight of a young single woman named Laura, whose married male boss suggests meeting together to talk about her career. Then at their business lunch he comes on to her—suggesting a sexual affair. Through no fault of her own, Laura's been placed in a complex situation that calls for a multifunctional message.[7] In order to stop the harassment, protect her job, keep a working relationship with her boss, and preserve her professional identity and reputation, Laura needs to craft a response that works on a number of levels at the same time. Sophisticated communicators have the tools to pull it off.

MESSAGE DESIGN LOGIC—THE MISSING LINK BETWEEN COMPLEXITY AND SOPHISTICATED COMMUNICATION

Until the work of Barbara O'Keefe in the late 1980s, constructivists were unable to nail down the reason why high construct differentiation usually leads to more effective communication. Like a terse bumper sticker, they proclaimed, COGNITIVELY COMPLEX PERSONS CAN DO IT BETTER, yet they weren't sure why. O'Keefe, a colleague of Delia at the University of Illinois, offered an "inside the head" explanation that continues to strike a responsive chord among cognitive scholars.[8] She suggested that people hold one of three distinct notions about how communication works. She called these *message design logics,* and each is an implicit theory of the ways in which messages can be shaped to serve as means to ends.

Expressive Design Logic

People who work from an expressive design logic accept the premise that "language is a medium for expressing thoughts and feelings."[9] They merely say what they think and feel so others will know what they think and feel. Their only goal is open and honest communication, and the idea of speaking to achieve a specific purpose is somewhat suspect. These folks distrust lawyers, politicians, salesmen, preachers, and anyone else who has a "way with words." Like Horton, Dr. Seuss' elephant who claimed that he meant what he said and said what he meant, people who employ an expressive design logic believe that words carry their own meaning.[10] There's no need for interpretation.

When asked, "Why did you say this *now*?" the expressive speaker refers to something said or done that triggered the comment. As with the concept of logical force in Pearce and Cronen's CMM theory (see Chapter 5), the person feels he or she had no choice but to respond this way. For example, if Laura holds an implicit theory of expressiveness, she might react to her boss's proposition with little thought of consequences:

> You are the most rude and disgusting man I have ever met. You're nothing but a dirty old man. Where do you get off thinking you could force me to have an affair with you? You make me sick.[11]

Conventional Design Logic

A second group of people assume that "communication is a game played co-operatively, according to socially conventional rules and procedures."[12] A conventional player equates effective communication with appropriateness. One learns the rules of the game, and plays accordingly when the cooperative nature of the enterprise calls for hedges, compliments, apologies, or detailed narrative. According to O'Keefe, a conventional design logic shapes messages that do what they have to do to accomplish the speaker's main goal.

When asked, "Why did you say this *now*?" the conventional speaker answers that the words were the appropriate thing to say under the present circumstances. Given Laura's overriding desire to end her boss's sexual harassment, her professional colleagues would applaud a just-say-no response to the cad:

> There's absolutely no chance I will have an affair with you, and if you try to fire me over this I won't keep quiet about it. That kind of behavior is not appropriate in the workplace. Besides that, you're married. Don't approach me again.[13]

Rhetorical Design Logic

Most people regard the communication context as a factor that limits a speaker's options. That's not the view of those who adopt a rhetorical design logic. They work from the premise that "communication is the creation and negotiation of social selves and situations."[14] This idea parallels the central theme of CMM—that persons-in-conversation co-construct their own social realities. Nothing is fixed; everything is in flux.

When it helps achieve their goals, rhetorically sensitive communicators are just as good at sharing their feelings as people who speak in an expressive mode. They can also match the conventional communicator's ability to discern and adapt to conversational custom. But they have the additional ability to craft novel messages that redefine the situation in a way that defuses conflict. In this way they are proactive in seeking harmony and consensus, while downplaying the raw use of power.

When asked, "Why did you say this *now*?" the rhetorical speaker answers in terms of pursuing specific goals—usually multiple. Note how a rhetorically sensitive Laura might use context as a resource as she tries to parry her boss's sexual advance, salvage her job, and save face, both for herself *and* for him:

> We've got a great working relationship now, and I'd like us to work well together in the future. So I think it's important for us to talk this out. You're a smart and

clear-thinking guy and I consider you to be my friend as well as my boss. That's why I have to think you must be under a lot of unusual stress lately to have said something like this. I know what it's like to be under pressure. Too much stress can really make you crazy. You probably just need a break.[15]

Do different message design logics really explain why cognitively complex people can fashion sophisticated communication? Based on O'Keefe's initial research, the answer seems to be yes. She asked college students to imagine they were in a class in which a group project was a major part of the final grade. As group leaders, they were responsible for dealing with a member who didn't have his work done, with the deadline just twenty-four hours away. (Sound familiar?) She asked each "leader" to write what he or she would say to regulate the behavior of the undependable student.

As expected, average construct differentiation scores on the RCQ were lowest (20) for those who used an expressive design logic, a bit higher (21) for those who employed a conventional design logic, and definitely highest (25 points) for those who utilized a rhetorical design logic. O'Keefe also discovered that most (80 percent) of the rhetorically sensitive messages were written by women. Although we can never get inside the "black box" of the mind, O'Keefe's findings suggest that different design logics are indeed operative.

BENEFICIAL EFFECTS OF SOPHISTICATED COMMUNICATION

Figure 8.1 portrays the linkages that constructivists have forged. Cognitive complexity facilitates a rhetorical message design logic, which in turn produces sophisticated communication. That part of the chain is well established. Constructivist researchers have now turned to exploring the positive effects of sophisticated messages on every conceivable form of communication outcome. We've already seen that these messages can be more persuasive. In this section I'll highlight the findings in three other areas of research that my students have found particularly interesting.

Comforting messages try to ease the emotional distress experienced by others. Purdue University communication professor Brant Burleson has developed a nine-stage hierarchical scale to code the degree of solace a message of support offers. At the bottom end are messages that virtually deny the thoughts and feelings of the person who is hurting: "You shouldn't be so upset about losing your boyfriend. After all, there are lots of fish in the sea." Midlevel messages take the other's distress seriously: "Gee, I'm sorry you guys broke up. I guess things like this happen though. Breaking up just seems to be a part of relationships." Top-of-the-line, sophisticated support messages explicitly validate the other's feelings and often add additional perspective on the situation: "I know it must hurt. I know you're feeling a lot of pain and anger right now. And that's OK, 'cause I know you were really involved; you guys were together a long time and you expected things to work out differently."[16]

As you might suspect, sophisticated messages are usually experienced as more comforting than clumsy attempts at social support. You hope that's

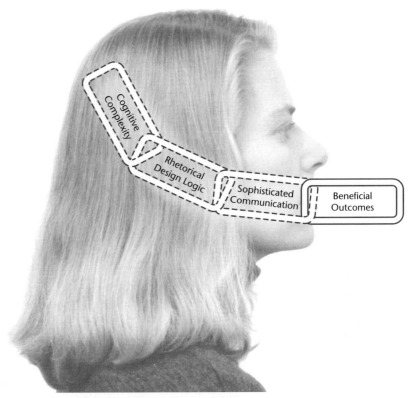

FIGURE 8.1   The Chain of Sophisticated Communication

reward enough for the friend who offers well-chosen words in a time of need. But Burleson notes that other positive outcomes accrue to the sensitive comforter:

> Compared to persons using less sophisticated comforting strategies, users of sophisticated strategies are better liked and more positively evaluated by both message recipients and observers. Further, users of sophisticated comforting strategies report feeling better both about themselves and those they try to help.[17]

Relationship maintenance is a process distinct from relationship development. As discussed in the next section of the book, voluntary relationships usually begin through mutual attraction, self-disclosure, and reduction of uncertainty. (See Chapters 9 and 10.) Once the relationship is established, however, its ongoing health requires periodic affirmation, conflict resolution, and the type of comforting communication described above. As with any interpersonal skill, some people are better at maintenance than others. Burleson and Wendy Samter of the University of Delaware figured that people with sophisticated communication skills would be especially good at sustaining close friendships. It turns out they were only partially right.[18]

To test their hypothesis, Burleson and Samter reviewed their own previous studies on friendship as well as the work of other researchers. They discovered a consistent pattern, which they labeled the "similar skills model." To their surprise, individuals' ability to give ego-support, resolve conflict, and provide comfort in times of stress did little to guarantee that their close personal relationships would survive and thrive. But the degree of similarity with their partner did. Friendships tended to last when partners possessed matching verbal skills—high or low. Apparently, highly refined communication skills are an advantage only when a friend has the sophistication to appreciate them. And a person with few of these abilities may be more comfortable spending time with someone who likes the same activities, can tell a good story, and isn't always "talking about feelings" or "pushing that touchy-feely crap."[19]

Organizational effectiveness isn't determined by a single sophisticated message. According to constructivist theory, high performance and promotion reflect a continual use of person-centered communication that seeks to achieve multiple goals with customers and co-workers. Employees who do it better should climb the corporate ladder faster.

Beverly Sypher (University of Kansas) and Theodore Zorn (University of North Carolina) conducted a longitudinal study of ninety white-collar workers at a large Eastern insurance company.[20] At the start of the study they measured cognitive complexity with the RCQ, tested for perspective-taking ability, and gauged communication skill by asking employees to write a charitable fund-raising appeal. As expected, workers with highly developed social constructs wrote letters that were more persuasive. Four years later, Sypher and Zorn checked each employee's progress within the company. Cognitively complex workers had better-paying jobs and were moving up through the ranks of the company faster than their less complex colleagues. Any time we deal with people, cognitive complexity seems to play a significant role.

SOCIALIZING A NEW GENERATION OF SOPHISTICATED SPEAKERS

In early editions of this text I chided constructivists for not addressing the question of how cognitively complex thinkers get that way. That's no longer a fair criticism. Burleson, Delia, and James Applegate of the University of Kentucky have recently marshaled evidence that complex thinking is a culturally transmitted trait. Specifically, they suggest that parents' capacity for complex social thinking is recreated in their children through complex messages of nurture and discipline.[21] Their claim is an extension of the truism that culture is produced and reproduced through the communication of its members.

Suppose, for example, that a five-year-old boy picks a flower from a neighbor's yard without permission and presents it to his mother. Almost any parent can scold the kid for stealing. ("Taking people's things without asking is wrong. Now go and apologize for taking the flower.") But it requires a mother with a complex set of interpersonal constructs to create a sophisticated message that encourages reflection and helps her son focus on the motivation, feelings, and intentions of others—mental exercises that increase the child's own cognitive complexity. After thanking her son for the gift, such a mom might say:

> When people work hard to have things (flowers) they usually want to keep them to appreciate them. Mrs. Jones might have given you a flower if you'd asked, but taking things from people without asking upsets them a lot.

Who is most likely to use this form of sophisticated socialization? According to Burleson, Delia, and Applegate, parents from more advantaged socio-economic backgrounds are likely candidates. They inhabit a world of intricate work environments, role systems, and social expectations. This more complicated social world stimulates the development of more complex ways of thinking and communicating. And once developed, complex ways of thinking and acting tend to perpetuate themselves. The **culture → complexity → communication** path seems to ensure that, cognitively speaking, the rich get richer. This cognitive fact of life was obvious to me in a paper submitted by Jane, a forty-year-old grad student in my interpersonal communication class. She recorded the precocious words of her seven-year-old daughter, Sunny, a child raised in the midst of sophisticated adult conversation.

> Mom, is nonverbal communication like when you don't point your face at me when we're talking about my day? Or when you say "Uh-huh" and "Really?" but your face doesn't move around like you really care what we're talking about. When you walk around cooking or Dad writes while we're talking, I feel like I'm boring. Sometimes when you guys talk to me it sounds like you're just teaching, not talking.

Constructivists would note that Sunny can reflect on her social world because communication from mother Jane has been anything but plain.

CRITIQUE: SECOND THOUGHTS ABOUT COGNITIVE COMPLEXITY

Delia launched his interpretive theory of cognitive differences in the 1970s when most communication scientists were trying to discover laws of behavior that applied equally to everyone. While these empirical researchers were assessing communication effectiveness by crunching the numbers from standardized attitude scales, Delia called for "free response data" that could reflect subtle differences in mental processes. He believed that open-ended responses would also force researchers to become theoretically rigorous.

The message design logics outlined by Barbara O'Keefe meet Delia's criteria. So do the other hierarchies of multiple-goal and person-centered messages described earlier in the chapter. But constructivists' total reliance on the RCQ to gauge cognitive complexity is another story. It's difficult to accept that a single number adequately reflects the intricate mental structures and processes that take place behind the eyes. It seems curious to ask respondents for their perception of two other people and then reduce their rich narratives to a mere frequency count of constructs. The total number may predict interesting communication differences, but explanatory depth is lacking.

A prophetic ethical voice also seems to be missing. If cognitive complexity is the key to interpersonal effectiveness, and if construct differentiation is enhanced by a privileged upbringing, advocates of the theory should devote some effort to creating reflective settings for kids that will help disadvantaged black-and-white thinkers develop the ability to see shades of gray. There are precedents for such a reform agenda.

Once medical researchers discovered the brain-deadening effects of lead poisoning, they were quick to mount a public campaign to stop the use of lead-based paint. Likewise, teachers lobbied for "Project Head Start" when they realized that food-for-the-stomach was a prerequisite of food-for-thought. Obviously poverty, peeling paint, and poor nutrition are linked together, and constructivist research suggests that a childhood devoid of reflection-inducing communication is part of the same vicious circle. Constructivist research is open to the charge of elitism unless the theorists issue a clear call for remedial efforts that will help narrow the gap between the "haves" and the "have-nots."

More than most theorists, Delia is capable of spearheading a reform movement to shape public policy. Early on, he made a strong call for a "reflective analysis of the implicit assumptions and ordering principles underlying research questions and methods."[22] He's launched a research program that models that commitment, and others have enlisted in the cause. As one of the few well-known theories about communication to spring from within the discipline, constructivism is especially worthy of your consideration.

QUESTIONS TO SHARPEN YOUR FOCUS

1. How many points for *differentiation* would the phrase "humorous and totally funny" score on the *Role Category Questionnaire?*

2. Look at the "Calvin and Hobbes" cartoon on page 113. How would *constructivists* explain Calvin's success in getting a horsey ride from his father?

3. Recall a situation that, in retrospect, called for a *person-centered message* that worked on *multiple goals*. What did you say? What *design logic* did your words reflect?

4. Sometimes during an argument, one kid will chide another with the words "Aw, grow up!" According to constructivists, the phrase offers good advice in a way that's ineffective. Why?

A SECOND LOOK

Recommended resource: Brant R. Burleson, "The Constructivist Approach to Person-Centered Communication: Analysis of a Research Exemplar," in *Rethinking Communica-*

tion, Vol. 2, Brenda Dervin, Lawrence Grossberg, Barbara J. O'Keefe, and Ellen Wartella (eds.), Sage, Newbury Park, Calif., 1989, pp. 29–36.

Comprehensive statement: Jesse Delia, Barbara O'Keefe, and Daniel O'Keefe, "The Constructivist Approach to Communication," in *Human Communication Theory,* F.E.X. Dance, (ed.), Harper and Row, New York, 1982, pp. 147–191.

State-of-the-art review: Brant Burleson and Scott Caplan, "Cognitive Complexity," in *Communication and Personality: Trait Perspectives,* James McCroskey, John Daly, and Matthew Martin (eds.), Hampton Press, Cresskill, N.J., 1998, pp. 233–286.

Role category questionnaire: Brant R. Burleson and Michael S. Waltman, "Cognitive Complexity: Using the Role Category Questionnaire Measure," in *A Handbook for the Study of Human Communication,* Charles Tardy (ed.), Ablex, Norwood, N.J., 1988, pp. 1–35.

Constructs: James Applegate, "Constructs and Communication: A Pragmatic Integration," in *Advances in Personal Construct Theory,* Vol. 1, R. Neimeyer and G. Neimeyer (eds.), JAI, Greenwich, Conn., 1990, pp. 197–224.

Message design: Barbara O'Keefe, "The Logic of Message Design: Individual Differences in Reasoning about Communication," *Communication Monographs,* Vol. 55, 1988, pp. 80–103.

Social support: Brant Burleson, "Comforting Messages: Significance, Approaches, and Effects," in *Communication of Social Support,* Brant Burleson, Terrance Albrecht, and Irwin Sarason (eds.), Sage, Thousand Oaks, Calif., 1994, pp. 3–28.

Relationship maintenance: Brant Burleson and Wendy Samter, "A Social Skills Approach to Relationship Maintenance," in *Communication and Relationship Maintenance,* Daniel Canary and Laura Stafford (eds.), Academic Press, San Diego, 1994, pp. 61–90.

Organizational communication: Beverly Davenport Sypher and Theodore Zorn, "Communication-Related Abilities and Upward Mobility: A Longitudinal Investigation," *Human Communication Research,* Vol. 12, 1986, pp. 420–431.

Developing cognitive complexity: Brant Burleson, Jesse Delia, and James Applegate, "The Socialization of Person-Centered Communication: Parental Contributions to the Social-Cognitive and Communication Skills of Their Children," in *Perspectives in Family Communication,* Mary Anne Fitzpatrick and Anita Vangelisti (eds.), Sage, Thousand Oaks, Calif., 1995, pp. 34–76.

Review and Critique: John Gastil, "An Appraisal and Revision of the Constructivist Research Program," in *Communication Yearbook 18,* Brant Burleson (ed.), Sage, Thousand Oaks, Calif., 1995, pp. 83–104.

RELATIONSHIP DEVELOPMENT

Think about your closest personal relationship. Is it one of "strong, frequent and diverse interdependence that lasts over a considerable period of time?"[1] That's how UCLA psychologist Harold Kelley and eight co-authors define the concept of *close relationship*. Although their definition could apply to parties that don't even like each other, most theorists reserve the term *close* for relationships that include a positive bond. That's how I'll use the term in this section.

The close relationship you thought of likely falls into one of three categories: romance, friendship, or family. Each type has characteristics that set it apart from the other two:

Friendship is the most voluntary and least programmed of all close relationships.[2] The contrast with kinship is particularly stark. We don't choose our relatives, but we can pick our friends. And once we do, the course of friendship is free from romantic rings, family responsibilities, and legal regulations that give society a stake in other types of relationship. Yet to say that friendship is free is not to suggest that it's random. Long-time friends usually share a rough equality of talents and social status; we typically select friends who are similar to ourselves in age, background, interests, and values. The very freedom and mutuality that make friendship attractive are also the qualities that render it fragile. Friends who become disaffected tend to drift apart because there's little community structure undergirding the relationship.

Romance is set apart from friendship and family by two qualities—sexual passion and exclusiveness. Although anyone who has recently "fallen in love" needs no convincing, Yale University psychologist Robert Sternberg concludes that mate love requires a combination of intimacy, passion, and commitment.[3] Intimacy by itself is the strong liking reflective of friendship. Passion alone is sexual infatuation or being "in lust." Commitment without intimacy or passion is typical of an arranged marriage at the start, or a marriage of convenience near its end. But when two people experience intimacy, passion, and commitment together, the relationship is usually closer than friendship or kinship.

Family members have a history. Years of shared experience provide close relatives with a knowledge that allows them to predict the responses of their parents, children, or siblings. Self-disclosure may be crucial in a developing romance or friendship, but except in times of crisis, close relatives feel they already know what's going on inside other family members. Intimate communication within families often begins with words like, "Remember when . . . ," rather than, "Let me tell you about . . . ." But not all memories are pleasant. Greater friction exists within the family than would be tolerated in most friendships. Hostility is normally expressed symbolically through sullen silence, dirty looks, sarcastic comments, or angry words. Yet even in the face of emotional or physical abuse, most people still return to family in times of trouble. As poet Robert Frost reminds us, "Home is the place where, when you have to go there, they have to take you in."[4] The idea of kin is so deeply rooted within us that it's the most common metaphor for describing close-

DILBERT reprinted by permission of United Features Syndicate, Inc.

ness.[5] "Blood is thicker than water," family members explain, implying that when push comes to shove, biology takes precedence over baptism—or any other ideological tie that binds.

Despite differences among friendship, romance, and family ties, the quality of closeness in each of these relationships is remarkably similar. All three types of intimacy can provide enjoyment, trust, sharing of confidences, respect, mutual assistance, and spontaneity.[6] The question is, how do we develop a close relationship?

Two distinct approaches have dominated the theory and practice of relational development. One tradition is the **phenomenological**

approach typified by humanistic psychologist Carl Rogers (see Chapter 3). Rogers believed that people draw close to others when: (1) their outward behavior is congruent with their inner feelings; (2) they unconditionally accept others for who they are, not for what they do; and (3) they listen to what others say with the aim of understanding what it's like to be them. Rogers' thoughts have permeated the textbooks and teaching of interpersonal communication.[7] The topics of self-disclosure, nonverbal warmth, empathic listening, and trust are mainstays in the introductory course.

The other approach assumes that relationship behavior is shaped by the **rewards and costs of interaction.** In 1992 University of Chicago economist Gary Becker won the Nobel Prize in economics on the basis of his application of supply and demand market models to predict the behavior of everyday living, including love and marriage. News commentators expressed skepticism that matters of the heart could be reduced to cold numbers, but the economic metaphor had dominated social science discussion of interpersonal attraction for the last three decades. The basic assumption of most relational theorists is that people interact with others in a way that maximizes their personal benefits and minimizes their personal costs.

Numerous parallels exist between the stock market and relationship market:

1. Law of supply and demand. A rare, desirable characteristic commands higher value on the exchange.

2. Courting a buyer. Most parties in the market prepare a prospectus that highlights their assets and downplays their liabilities.

3. Laissez-faire rules. "Let the buyer beware." "All's fair in love and war." "It's a jungle out there."

4. Expert advice. Daily newspapers around the country carry syndicated advice columns by Sylvia Porter and Ann Landers. Whether the topic is money or love, both columnists suggest cautious risk-taking.

5. Investors and traders. Investors commit for the long haul; traders try to make an overnight killing.

Some readers will reject the economic model of personal relationships as cynical and degrading. In his famous book *The Art of Loving,* humanist Erich Fromm insists, however, that the metaphor accurately captures the contemporary practice of love: "Two persons thus fall in love when they feel they have found the best object available on the market, considering the limitations of their own exchange value."[8]

Even from these brief summaries, you can tell that a humanistic model of relational development is quite different from an economic model of social exchange. Yet both traditions affect the two theories presented in Chapters 9 and 10.

Altman and Taylor's social penetration theory suggests that people draw close to each other through the type of honest self-disclosure that occurs in Rogerian counseling. They use a social exchange analysis to predict whether or not parties will take that risk.

Berger's uncertainty reduction theory claims that we have a deep desire to know what we can expect from the other person before we invest in a relationship—a reliable market forecast, as it were. But the relational variables he considers crucial read like a list of humanistic values—nonverbal warmth, intimate self-disclosure, reciprocal vulnerability, liking, and so on.

The two theories in this section regard communication as the means by which people can draw close. They both consider instant intimacy a myth; relationships take time to develop and they don't always proceed on a straight-line trajectory toward that goal. In fact most relationships never even get close. Yet some people do stay friends, romantic partners, and close kin for life. Both the client-centered counseling and marketplace exchange models suggest that we need to be concerned with the other person's needs as well as with our own. Perhaps relational longevity has less to do with what each party gets out of the relationships than with what each puts into it.

CHAPTER 9

Social Penetration Theory

of Irwin Altman & Dalmas Taylor

A friend in need is a friend indeed.
Neither a borrower nor a lender be.

A rolling stone gathers no moss.
Still waters run deep.

To know him is to love him.
Familiarity breeds contempt.

Proverbs are the wisdom of the ages boiled down into short, easy-to-remember phrases. There are probably more maxims in use about interpersonal relationships than about any other topic. But are these truisms dependable? As we can see in the pairings above, the advice they give often seems contradictory.

Consider the plight of Pete, a new freshman student at a residential college, as he enters the dorm to meet his roommate for the first time. Pete has just waved good-bye to his folks and already feels a sharp pang of loneliness as he thinks of his girlfriend back home. He worries about how she'll feel about him when he goes home at Thanksgiving. Will she illustrate the reliability of the old adage that "absence makes the heart grow fonder," or will "out of sight, out of mind" be a better way to describe the next few months?

Pete finds his room and immediately spots the familiar shape of a lacrosse stick. He's initially encouraged by what appears to be a common interest, but he's also fascinated by a campaign button that urges him to vote for a candidate for Congress who is on the opposite end of the political spectrum from Pete. Will "birds of a feather flock together" hold true in their relationship, or will "opposites attract" better describe their interaction?

Just then Jon, his roommate, comes in. For a few minutes they trade the stock phrases that give them a chance to size up each other. Something in Pete makes him want to tell Jon how much he misses his girlfriend, but a deeper sense of what is an appropriate topic of conversation on first meeting someone prevents him from sharing his feelings quite this soon. On a subconscious level, perhaps even a conscious one, Pete is torn between acting on the old adage "misery loves company," or on the more macho one, "big boys don't cry."

Pete obviously needs something more than commonsense sayings to help him understand relational dynamics. A few years before Pete was born, social psychologists Irwin Altman and Dalmas Taylor proposed a theory called "social penetration process" that explains how relational closeness develops. Altman is Distinguished Professor of Psychology at the University of Utah, and Taylor, recently deceased, was Provost and Professor of Psychology at Lincoln University in Pennsylvania. They would predict that Pete and Jon will end up as best friends only if they proceed in a "gradual and orderly fashion from superficial to intimate levels of exchange as a function of both immediate and forecast outcomes."[1] In order to capture the process, we first have to understand the complexity of people.

PERSONALITY STRUCTURE: A MULTILAYERED ONION

Altman and Taylor compare people to onions. This isn't their attempt at commentary on the human capacity to offend. It is their description of the multilayered nature of personality. Peel the outer skin from an onion, and you'll find another beneath it. Remove that layer and you'll expose a third, and so on. Pete's outer layer is his public self that's accessible to anyone who cares to look. The outer layer includes a myriad of details that certainly help describe who he is but are held in common with others at the school. On the surface, people see a tall, 18-year-old male, a business major from Michigan who lifts weights and gets lots of phone calls from home.

If Jon can look beneath the surface, he'll discover the semiprivate attitudes that Pete reveals only to some people. Pete is sympathetic to liberal causes, deeply religious, and prejudiced against fat people.

Pete's inner core is made up of his values, self-concept, unresolved conflicts, and deeply felt emotions. This is his unique private domain, which is invisible to the world but has a significant impact on the areas of his life that are closer to the surface. Perhaps not even his girlfriend or parents know his most closely guarded secrets about himself.

CLOSENESS THROUGH SELF-DISCLOSURE

Pete becomes accessible to others as he relaxes the tightened boundaries and makes himself vulnerable. This can be a scary process, but Altman and Taylor believe it's only by allowing Jon to penetrate well below the surface that Pete can draw truly close to his roommate.

There are many ways to show vulnerability. Pete could give up the territoriality that marks his desk and dresser drawers as his private preserve, share his clothes, or read a letter from his girlfriend out loud. Nonverbal paths to openness include mock roughhousing, eye contact, and smiling. But the main route to deep social penetration is through self-disclosure.

Figure 9.1 helps you imagine a wedge being pushed point first into an onion. The depth of penetration represents the degree of personal disclosure. To get to the center, the wedge must first slice through the outer layers. Altman and

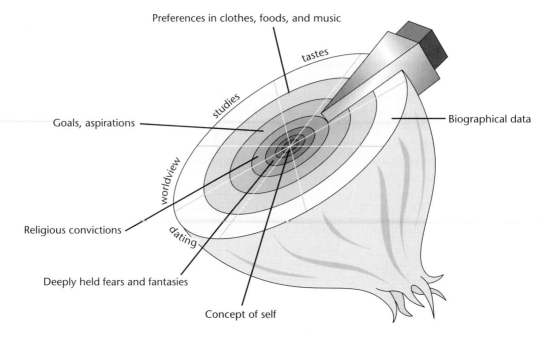

Preferences in clothes, foods, and music

tastes

studies

Goals, aspirations

Biographical data

worldview

Religious convictions

dating

Deeply held fears and fantasies

Concept of self

FIGURE 9.1   Penetration of Pete's Personality Structure

Taylor claim that on the surface level this kind of biographical information exchange takes place easily, perhaps at first meeting. But they picture the layers of onion skin as tougher and more tightly wrapped as the wedge nears the center.

Recall that Pete was hesitant to share his longing for his girlfriend with Jon. If he admits these feelings, he's opening himself up for some heavy-handed kidding or emotional blackmail. In addition, once the wedge has penetrated deeply, it will have cut a passage through which it can return again and again with little resistance. Future privacy will be difficult. Realizing both of these factors, Pete may be extra cautious about exposing his true feelings. Perhaps he'll fence off this part of his life for the whole school term. According to social penetration theory, a permanent guard will limit the closeness these two young men can achieve.

THE DEPTH AND BREADTH OF SELF-DISCLOSURE

The depth of penetration is the degree of intimacy. Although Altman and Taylor's penetration analogy strikes some readers as sexual, this was not their intent. The analogy applies equally to intimacy in friendship and romance. Figure 9.1 diagrams the closeness Jon has gained if he and Pete become friends during the year. In their framework of social penetration theory, Altman and Taylor have outlined the following observations about the process that will have brought Pete and Jon to this point:

1. Peripheral items are exchanged more frequently and sooner than private information. When the point of the wedge has barely reached the intimate area, the trailing edges have cut a wide swath through the outer rings. The relationship is still at a relatively impersonal level ("big boys don't cry"). University of Connecticut communication professor Arthur VanLear analyzed the content of conversation in developing relationships. His study showed that 14 percent of talk revealed nothing about the speaker, 65 percent dwelled on public items, 19 percent shared semiprivate details, and only 2 percent disclosed intimate confidences. Further penetration will bring Pete to the point where he can share deeper feelings ("misery loves company").

2. Self-disclosure is reciprocal, especially in the early stages of relationship development. The theory predicts that new acquaintances like Pete and Jon will reach roughly equal levels of openness, but it doesn't explain why. Pete's vulnerability could make him seem more trustworthy, or perhaps his initial openness makes transparency seem more attractive. It's also possible that the young men feel a need for emotional equity, so that a disclosure by Pete leaves Jon feeling uneasy until he's balanced the account with his own payment—a give-and-take exchange in which each party is sharing deeper levels of feeling with each other. Whatever the reason, social penetration theory asserts a law of reciprocity.

3. Penetration is rapid at the start but slows down quickly as the tightly wrapped inner layers are reached. Instant intimacy is a myth. Not only is there internal resistance to quick forays into the soul, there are societal norms against telling too much too fast. Most relationships stall before a stable intimate exchange is established. For this reason, these relationships fade or die easily following separation or a slight strain. A comfortable sharing of positive and negative reactions is rare. When it is achieved, relationships become more important to both parties, more meaningful, and more enduring.

4. Depenetration is a gradual process of layer-by-layer withdrawal. A warm friendship between Pete and Jon will deteriorate if they begin to close off areas of their lives that had earlier been opened. Relational retreat is a sort of taking back of what has earlier been exchanged in the building of a relationship. Altman and Taylor compare the process to a movie shown in reverse. Surface talk still goes on long after deep disclosure is silenced. Relationships are likely to terminate not in an explosive flash of anger but in a gradual cooling off of enjoyment and care.

While depth is crucial to the process of social penetration, breadth is equally important. Note that in Figure 9.1 I have segmented the onion much like an orange to accurately represent how Pete's life is cut into different areas—dating, studies, and so forth. It's quite possible for Pete to be candid about every intimate detail of his romance, yet remain secretive about his father's alcoholism or his own minor dyslexia. Because only one area is accessed, the relationship depicted in the onion drawing is typical of a summer romance—depth without breadth. Of course, breadth without depth describes the typical

"Since we're both being honest, I should tell you I have fleas."

"Hi, how are you?" casual relationship. A model of true intimacy would show wedges inserted deeply into every area.

REGULATING CLOSENESS ON THE BASIS OF REWARDS AND COSTS

Will Pete and Jon become good friends? According to social penetration theory, it all depends on the cost-benefit analysis that each man performs as he considers the possibility of a closer relationship. Right after their first encounter, Pete will sort out the pluses and minuses of friendship with Jon, computing a bottom-line index of relational satisfaction. Jon will do the same regarding Pete. If the perceived mutual benefits outweigh the costs of greater vulnerability, the process of social penetration will proceed.

I previewed this kind of economic analysis in the introduction to the present section on relationship development. Altman and Taylor's version draws heavily on the social exchange theory of psychologists John Thibaut and Harold Kelley.[2] Thibaut was at the University of North Carolina until his death in 1986; Kelley is at UCLA and continues to study the key concepts of social exchange—relational outcome, relational satisfaction, and relational stability.

Since Altman and Taylor believe that principles of social exchange accurately predict when people will risk self-disclosure, I'll describe these concepts in some detail.

Outcome: Rewards Minus Costs

Thibaut and Kelley attempt to quantify the value of different outcomes for an individual. They let a single number represent the rewards minus the costs of a given course of action. For example, Pete might arbitrarily sum up the benefits of reaching out to Jon in friendship as a **+14.** Pete is a stranger to campus, so he strongly desires someone to talk to, eat with, and just be around when he's not in class or studying. Jon's interest in lacrosse, easy laugh, and laid-back style make him an attractive candidate. But Pete is aware of a potential downside as well. If he reveals some of his inner life, his roommate may scoff at his faith in God or ridicule his liberal "do-gooder" values. Pete's not ashamed of his convictions, but he hates to argue, and he regards the risk of discord as a **–6.** Since a social exchange approach says that the outcome of an interaction is the combination of rewards (+14) and costs (–6), Pete would calculate the outcome of a close relationship with Jon as a promising **+8.** Of course, that assessment could change as he gets to know Jon better.

The idea of totaling potential benefits and losses to determine behavior isn't new. Since philosopher John Stuart Mill stated his principle of utility,[3] there's been a compelling logic to the minimax principle of human behavior. The minimax principle claims that people seek to maximize their benefits and minimize their costs. So the higher we index a relational outcome, the more attractive we find the behavior that might make it happen.

Social exchange theorists assume that we can accurately gauge the payoffs of a variety of interactions and that we have the good sense to choose the action that will provide the best result. Altman and Taylor aren't sure that the input we receive is always reliable, but that's not the issue. What matters to them is that we base our decision to open up with another person on the perceived benefit-minus-cost outcome.

Early in a relationship, we tend to see physical appearance, similar backgrounds, and mutual agreement as benefits ("birds of a feather flock together"). Disagreement and deviance from the norm are negatives. But as the relationship changes, so does the nature of interaction that friends find rewarding. Deeper friendships thrive on common values and spoken appreciation, and we can even enjoy surface diversity ("opposites attract").

Since Pete sees much more benefit than cost in a relationship with Jon, he'll start to reveal more of who he is. If the negatives outweighed the positives, he'd try to avoid contact with Jon as much as possible. Since they've just been assigned as roommates, Pete doesn't have the option to withdraw physically from Jon. But a negative assessment could cause him to hold back emotionally for the rest of the year.

Satisfaction—Comparison Level (CL)

Evaluating outcomes is a tricky business. Even if we convert intangible benefits and costs into quantifiable figures, their psychological impact may vary. A relational result of +8 has meaning only when contrasted with other outcome levels. Social exchange theory offers two standards of comparison that Pete and others use to evaluate their outcomes. The first benchmark deals with relative satisfaction—how happy or sad an interpersonal outcome makes a participant feel. Thibaut and Kelley call it the *comparison level*.

A person's comparison level (CL) is the threshold above which an outcome seems attractive. If your CL for clerical employment is an hourly wage of $8, you'd be happy to work for $10 an hour, but feel exploited if you received only $6 for your labor. Satisfaction depends on expectation.

Our CL for friendship, romance, or family ties is pegged by our relational history. We judge the value of a relationship by comparing it to the baseline of past experience. If Pete had little history of close friendship in high school (+2), a +8 relationship with Jon would look quite attractive. If, on the other hand, he's accustomed to being part of a close-knit group of intimate friends (+16), hanging out with Jon could pale by comparison.

Sequence plays a large part in evaluating a relationship. The result from each interaction is stored in the individual's memory. Experiences that take place early in a relationship can have a huge impact because they constitute a large proportion of the total relational history. One unpleasant experience out of ten is merely troublesome; one out of two can end a relationship before it really begins. Trends are also important. If Pete first senses a coolness from Jon but later feels warmth and approval, the shift will heighten Jon's attractiveness to a level higher than if Pete had perceived positive vibes from the very beginning.

Stability—Comparison Level of Alternatives (CL$_{alt}$)

Thibaut and Kelley suggest that there is a second standard by which we evaluate the outcomes we receive. They call it the *comparison level of alternatives* (CL$_{alt}$), and the level is pegged by the best payoffs available outside the current relationship. Stated another way, the CL$_{alt}$ is the worst outcome a person will accept and still stay in a relationship. As more attractive outside possibilities become available, or as existent outcomes slide below an established CL$_{alt}$, relational instability increases. Here again, a social exchange explanation reads like a stock market analysis. That's why some advocates label a social exchange approach a "theory of economic behavior."

The concept of CL$_{alt}$ doesn't speak to the issue of attraction or satisfaction, but it does explain why people sometimes stay in abusive relationships. For example, social workers describe the plight of the battered wife as "high cost, low reward." Despite her anguish, the woman feels trapped in the distressing situation because the option of being alone in the world appears even worse

(Outcome > CL_{alt}). She'll leave only when she perceives an outside alternative that promises a better life (CL_{alt} > Outcome).

The relative values of Outcome, CL, and CL_{alt} go a long way in determining whether a person is willing to become vulnerable in order to have a deeper relationship. The optimum situation is when both parties find:

$$Outcome > CL_{alt} > CL$$

Using Pete as an example, the notation shows that he forecasts a friendship with Jon that would be more than satisfying. The tie with Jon will be stable because there's no other relationship on campus that is more attractive. Yet Pete wouldn't feel trapped because he has other satisfying options available should this one turn sour. We see, therefore, that social exchange theory explains why Pete is primed for social penetration. If Jon's calculations are similar, the roommates will begin the process of mutual vulnerability that Altman and Taylor describe, and reciprocal self-disclosure will draw them close.

CRITIQUE: PULLING BACK FROM SOCIAL PENETRATION

Social penetration is an established and familiar explanation of how closeness develops, yet over 300 subsequent studies suggest that the path to intimacy described on the previous pages is not completely accurate. Just as Altman and Taylor describe friends as continually reappraising their relationship in light of new experiences, it makes sense for us to reevaluate the theory's predictions that fail to be supported by real-life data.

Contrary to the initial prediction that reciprocity of self-disclosure would be highest in the exploratory stage of relationships, VanLear found mutual sharing most frequently in the semiprivate middle range of penetration.[4] The discrepancy may be due to the unexpected speed of self-revelation. The evidence shows friendships form by a quick thrust of the disclosure blade rather than a measured insertion. University of Mississippi psychologist John Berg discovered that college roommates often decide within a few weeks whether or not they will stay together the following year.[5]

The original theory made no mention of the gender difference in vulnerability, but Altman and Taylor's latest summary of research concludes that males are less open than females. If Pete and Jon were Pam and Joan, the breadth, depth, and pace of disclosure would likely be greater.

The initial statement of Altman and Taylor's theory described the breakup of relationships as a reverse penetration process in which both parties methodically seal off inner layers of their lives and slowly drift apart. In order to test this hypothesis, Chicago psychologists Betsy Tolstedt, at Hines Hospital, and Joseph Stokes, at the University of Illinois, analyzed the conversation of long-term romantic partners at the time when their relationships were falling apart. They discovered that feelings of pain and anger caused the process of breaking up to be more chaotic than the theory would predict. Consistent with reports from marriage counselors, their findings indicate that the depth of self-disclosure often increases dramatically in the final stages of deterioration.[6]

Altman has had second thoughts about his basic assumption that openness is the predominant quality of relationship development. He speculates that the desire for privacy may counteract what he first thought was a unidirectional quest for intimacy. He now proposes a "dialectic model," which assumes that "human social relationships are characterized by openness or contact and closedness or separateness between participants."[7] He believes that the tension between openness and closedness results in cycles of disclosure and withdrawal. There is no guarantee that Pete's waves of accessibility will be in sync with the ebb and flow of Jon's openness. Two recent studies by VanLear confirm that there is periodic cycling between openness and closedness in both friendships and romantic relationships.[8] Chapter 12 shows how other communication scholars have continued to develop a dialectical perspective. Long-term closeness is a chancy prediction.

Although Altman and Taylor have found it necessary to modify their original theory, their image of wedges penetrating deeply into a multilayered onion has proved to be a helpful model of intimacy development. If Pete and Jon are typical roommates, they will likely permit only partial penetration. But as long as mutual vulnerability produces more pleasure than pain, they will continue to draw closer.

Altman and Taylor's wholesale use of a reward-cost analysis to explain the impetus for penetration raises at least two questions. First, can a complex blend of advantages and disadvantages be reliably reduced to a single number? Second, assuming we do quantify relational outcomes, are we so consistently selfish that we always opt to do what we calculate is in our own best interest?

University of North Dakota psychologist Paul Wright believes that Pete and Jon could reach a point of such closeness that their relationship would no longer be driven by a self-centered concern for personal gain. When friendships have what Wright calls "an intrinsic, end-in-themselves quality," people regard good things happening to their friends as rewards in themselves.[9] Jon would get just as excited about Pete's successful employment interview as he would if he got the job himself. This rare kind of selfless love involves a relational transformation, not just more self-disclosure.[10] Altman and Taylor's theory doesn't speak about the transition from "me" to "we," but it apparently takes place only after an extended process of social penetration.

QUESTIONS TO SHARPEN YOUR FOCUS

1. The onion model in Figure 9.1 is sectioned into eight parts, representing the *breadth* of a person's life. How would you label these eight regions of interest in your life?

2. Jesus said, "There is no greater love than this: to lay down one's life for one's friends."[11] Given the *minimax principle* of human behavior used in a *social exchange* analysis, how is such a sacrifice possible?

3. Social penetration theory is usually thought of as a theory of *self-disclosure.* What are some other ways of showing *vulnerability* in a relationship?

4. The romantic truism "to know her is to love her" seems to contradict the relational adage "familiarity breeds contempt." Given the principles of social penetration theory, can you think of a way both statements might be true?

A SECOND LOOK

Recommended resource: Irwin Altman and Dalmas Taylor, *Social Penetration: The Development of Interpersonal Relationships,* Holt, New York, 1973.

State of the art: Dalmas Taylor and Irwin Altman, "Communication in Interpersonal Relationships: Social Penetration Processes," in *Interpersonal Processes: New Directions in Communication Research,* Michael Roloff and Gerald Miller (eds.), Sage, Newbury Park, Calif., 1987, pp. 257–277.

Dialectic revision: Irwin Altman, Anne Vinsel, and Barbara Brown, "Dialectic Conceptions in Social Psychology: An Application to Social Penetration and Privacy Regulation," in *Advances in Experimental Social Psychology,* Vol. 14, Leonard Berkowitz (ed.), Academic Press, New York, 1981, pp. 107–160.

Reward-cost analysis: Dalmas Taylor and Irwin Altman, "Self-Disclosure as a Function of Reward-Cost Outcomes," *Sociometry,* Vol. 38, 1975, pp. 18–31.

Self-disclosure reciprocity: C. Arthur VanLear, "The Formation of Social Relationships: A Longitudinal Study of Social Penetration," *Human Communication Research,* Vol. 13, 1987, pp. 299–322.

Cycles of self-disclosure: C. Arthur VanLear, "Testing a Cyclical Model of Communicative Openness in Relationship Development: Two Longitudinal Studies," *Communication Monographs,* Vol. 58, 1991, pp. 337–361.

Social exchange theory: John W. Thibaut and Harold H. Kelley, *The Social Psychology of Groups,* John Wiley & Sons, New York, 1952.

Study of roommates: John Berg, "Development of Friendship between Roommates," *Journal of Personality and Social Psychology,* Vol. 46, 1984, pp. 346–356.

Intrinsic rewards of friendship: Paul H. Wright, "Self-Referent Motivation and the Intrinsic Quality of Friendship," *Journal of Social and Personal Relationships,* Vol. 1, 1984, pp. 115–130.

CHAPTER 10

Uncertainty Reduction Theory

of Charles Berger

No matter how close two people eventually become, they always begin as strangers. Let's say you've just taken a job as a driver for a delivery service over the Christmas holidays. After talking with the other drivers, you conclude that your income and peace of mind will depend on working out a good relationship with Heather, the radio dispatcher. All you know for sure about Heather is her attachment to Hannah, a 100-pound Labrador retriever who never lets Heather out of her sight. The veteran drivers joke that it's hard to tell the difference between the voices of Heather and Hannah over the radio. With some qualms you make arrangements to meet Heather (and Hannah) over coffee and donuts before your first day of work. You really have no idea what to expect.

Charles Berger believes that it's natural to have doubts about our ability to predict the outcome of initial encounters. Berger, a professor of communication who is now at the University of California, Davis, notes that "the beginnings of personal relationships are fraught with uncertainties."[1] Unlike social penetration theory, which tries to forecast the future of a relationship on the basis of projected rewards and costs (see Chapter 9), Berger's uncertainty reduction theory focuses on how human communication is used to gain knowledge and create understanding.

> Central to the present theory is the assumption that when strangers meet, their primary concern is one of uncertainty reduction or increasing predictability about the behavior of both themselves and others in the interaction.[2]

Interpersonal ignorance is not bliss; it's frustrating! Berger contends that our drive to reduce uncertainty about new acquaintances gets an extra boost from any of three prior conditions.[3]

a. *Anticipation of future interaction:* We know we will see them again.

b. *Incentive value:* They have something we want.

c. *Deviance:* They act in a weird way.

Heather hooks you on all three counts. You know you're going to be dealing with her for the next few weeks, she can make you or break you financially according to the routes she assigns, and she has this strange attachment to Hannah. According to Berger, when you add these three factors to your natural curiosity, you'll *really* want to solve the puzzle of who she is.

Berger believes that our main purpose in talking to people is to "make sense" out of our interpersonal world. That's why you're having breakfast with a stranger and her dog. If you brought your own hound to the meeting, chances are the two dogs would circle and sniff each other, trying to get some idea of what their counterpart was like. Humans are no different; we're just a bit more subtle as we use symbols instead of smells to reach our conclusions.

UNCERTAINTY REDUCTION: TO PREDICT AND EXPLAIN

Berger's focus on predictability is straight from Shannon and Weaver's information theory (see Chapter 3). "As the ability of persons to predict which alternative or alternatives are likely to occur next decreases, uncertainty increases."[4] He also owes a debt to Fritz Heider's view of people as intuitive psychologists. Heider, the father of attribution theory, believed that we constantly draw inferences about why people do what they do.[5] We need to predict *and* explain. If Heather's going to bark at you on the radio, you want to understand why.

Berger notes that there are at least two kinds of uncertainty that you face as you set out for your first meeting with Heather. Because you aren't sure how you should act, one kind of uncertainty deals with *behavioral* questions. Should you shake hands? Who pays for the donuts? Do you pet the dog? Often there are accepted procedural protocols to ease the stress that behavioral uncertainty can cause. Good manners go beyond common sense.

A second kind of uncertainty focuses on *cognitive* questions aimed at discovering who the other person is as a unique individual. What does Heather like about her job? What makes her glad? Sad? Mad? Does she have other friends, or does she lavish all her attention on Hannah? When you first meet a person, your mind may conjure up a wild mix of his or her potential traits and characteristics. Reducing cognitive uncertainty means acquiring information that allows you to discard many of these possibilities. *That's* the kind of uncertainty reduction Berger's theory addresses.

AN AXIOMATIC THEORY: CERTAINTY ABOUT UNCERTAINTY

Berger proposes a series of axioms to explain the connection between his central concept of uncertainty and eight key variables of relationship development: verbal output, nonverbal warmth, information seeking, self-disclosure, reciprocity, similarity, liking, and shared networks.[6] Axioms are traditionally regarded as self-evident truths that require no additional proof. (All people are created equal. The shortest distance between two points is a straight line.

What goes up must come down.) Here are Berger's eight truths about initial uncertainty.

> *Axiom 1:* Given the high level of uncertainty present at the onset of the entry phase, as the amount of verbal communication between strangers increases, the level of uncertainty for each interactant in the relationship will decrease. As uncertainty is further reduced, the amount of verbal communication will increase.

When you first sit down with Heather, the conversation will be halting and somewhat stilted. But as words begin to flow, you'll discover things about each other that make you feel more confident in each other's presence. When your comfort level rises, the pace of the conversation will pick up.

> *Axiom 2:* As nonverbal affiliative expressiveness increases, uncertainty levels will decrease in an initial interaction situation. In addition, decreases in uncertainty level will cause increases in nonverbal affiliative expressiveness.

When initial stiffness gives way to head nods and tentative smiles, you'll have a better idea of who Heather is. This assurance leads to further signs of warmth, such as prolonged eye contact, forward body lean, and pleasant tone of voice.

> *Axiom 3:* High levels of uncertainty cause increases in information-seeking behavior. As uncertainty levels decline, information-seeking behavior decreases.

What is it about Heather that prompted the other drivers to warn you not to start off on the wrong foot? You simply have no idea. Like a bug with its antennae twitching, you carefully monitor what she says and how she acts in order to gather clues about her personality. But you become less vigilant after she explains her pet peeve with drivers who complain about their assignments on the radio. Whether or not you think her irritation is justified, you begin to relax because you have a better idea of what to expect.

> *Axiom 4:* High levels of uncertainty in a relationship cause decreases in the intimacy level of communication content. Low levels of uncertainty produce high levels of intimacy.

Like Altman and Taylor (Chapter 9), Berger equates intimacy of communication with depth of self-disclosure. Demographic data revealing that Heather was raised in Toledo and that you are a communication major are relatively nonintimate. These typify the opening gambits of new acquaintances who are still feeling each other out. Heather's comment that she feels more loyalty from Hannah than from any person is a gutsy admission that raises the intimacy level of the conversation to a new plane. People express attitudes, values, and feelings when they have a good idea what the listener's response will be.

> *Axiom 5:* High levels of uncertainty produce high rates of reciprocity. Low levels of uncertainty produce low levels of reciprocity.

Self-disclosure research confirms the notion that people tend to mete out the personal details of their lives at a rate that closely matches their partner's willingness to share intimate information.[7] Reciprocal vulnerability is especially important in the early stages of a relationship. The issue seems to be one of power. When knowledge of each other is minimal, we're careful not to let the other person one-up us by being the exclusive holder of potentially embarrassing information. But when we already know the ups and downs of a person's story, an even flow of information seems less crucial. Berger would not anticipate long monologues at your first get-together with Heather; future meetings might be a different story.

> *Axiom 6:* Similarities between persons reduce uncertainty, while dissimilarities produce increases in uncertainty.

"I always know what Harry's going to say, and he always knows what I'm going to say, so, by and large, we just don't bother."

© The New Yorker Collection 1986 Gahan Wilson from cartoonbank.com. All Rights Reserved.

The more points of contact you establish with Heather, the more you'll feel you understand her inside and out. If you are a dog lover, the two of you will click. If, however, you are partial to purring kittens, Heather's devotion to this servile beast will cause you to wonder if you'll ever be able to figure out what makes her tick.

Axiom 7: Increases in uncertainty level produce decreases in liking; decreases in uncertainty produce increases in liking.

This axiom suggests that the more you find out about Heather, the more you'll appreciate who she is. It directly contradicts the cynical opinion that "familiarity breeds contempt," affirming instead that "to know her is to love her."

Axiom 8: Shared communication networks reduce uncertainty, while lack of shared networks increases uncertainty.

This axiom was not part of Berger's original theory, but his ideas triggered extensive research by other communication scholars who soon moved uncertainty reduction theory beyond the confines of two strangers meeting for the first time. Berger applauds this extension. "The broadening of the theory's scope suggests the potential usefulness of reconceptualizing and extending the original formulation."[8] For example, Malcolm Parks (University of Washington) and Mara Adelman (Seattle University) discovered that men and women who communicate more often with their romantic partners' family and friends have less uncertainty about the person they love than those whose relationships exist in relative isolation.[9] Networking couples also tend to stay together. On the basis of these findings, Berger incorporated this axiom into his formal design.

THEOREMS: THE LOGICAL FORCE OF UNCERTAINTY AXIOMS

Once we grant the validity of the eight axioms, it makes sense to pair two of them together to produce additional insight into relational dynamics. The combined axioms yield an inevitable conclusion when inserted in the well-known pattern of deductive logic:

$$\text{If } A = B$$
$$\text{and } B = C$$
$$\text{then } A = C$$

Berger does this for all possible combinations, thereby generating twenty-eight theorems. For example:

If similarity reduces uncertainty (axiom 6)
and reduced uncertainty increases liking (axiom 7)
then similarity and liking are positively related (theorem 21)

In this case, the result isn't exactly earthshaking. The connection between similarity and liking is a long-established finding in research on interpersonal attraction.[10] When viewed as a whole, however, these twenty-eight logical

	Ax 1 Verbal Communication	Ax 2 Nonverbal Warmth	Ax 4 Self-Disclosure	Ax 3 Information Seeking	Ax 5 Reciprocity	Ax 7 Liking	Ax 6 Similarity	Ax 8 Shared Networks
Ax 1 Verbal Communication		1 +	2 +	3 −	4 −	5 +	6 +	22 +
Ax 2 Nonverbal Warmth	1 +		7 +	8 −	9 −	10 +	11 +	23 +
Ax 4 Self-Disclosure	2 +	7 +		12 −	13 −	14 +	15 +	24 +
Ax 3 Information Seeking	3 −	8 −	12 −		16 +	17 −	18 −	25 −
Ax 5 Reciprocity	4 −	9 −	13 −	16 +		19 −	20 −	26 −
Ax 7 Liking	5 +	10 +	14 +	17 −	19 −		21 +	27 +
Ax 6 Similarity	6 +	11 +	15 +	18 −	20 −	21 +		28 +
Ax 8 Shared Networks	22 +	23 +	24 +	25 −	26 −	27 +	28 +	

FIGURE 10.1   Theorems of Uncertainty Reduction Theory
(Adapted from Berger and Calabrese, "Some Explorations in Initial Interaction and Beyond.")

extensions sketch out a rather comprehensive theory of interpersonal development—all based on the importance of reducing uncertainty in human interaction.

Instead of listing all twenty-eight theorems, I've plotted the relationships they predict in Figure 10.1. The chart reads like a mileage table you might find in a road atlas. Select one axiom along the top and another down the side. The intersection between the two shows the number of Berger's theorem and the type of correlation it asserts. A plus sign (+) shows that the two interpersonal variables rise or fall together. A minus sign (−) indicates that as one increases, the other decreases. Will the warmth of Heather's nonverbal communication increase as the intimacy of her self-disclosure deepens? Theorem 7 says it will. Suppose you grow fond of Heather as a friend. Will you seek to find out more about her? Theorem 17 says you won't. (More on this later.)

STRATEGIES TO COPE WITH CERTAIN UNCERTAINTY

Ten years after introducing uncertainty reduction theory, Berger switched his research focus to the thought processes that people go through in order to produce the messages they speak. He concluded that most social interaction is goal-driven; we have reasons for saying what we say. Berger labeled his work "A Plan-Based Theory of Strategic Communication" because he was convinced that we continually construct cognitive plans to guide our social action.[11] According to Berger, *"plans* are mental representations of action sequences that may be used to achieve goals."[12] Your breakfast with Heather offers a working example.

Your main reason for getting together with the dispatcher is to maximize your income over the Christmas holidays. Your overall strategy to reach that goal is to build a good working relationship with Heather, since she assigns the routes. The term "overall" is appropriate because Berger claims that plans are "hierarchically organized with abstract action representations at the top of the hierarchy and progressively more concrete representation toward the bottom."[13] In order to build that relationship, you intend to converse in a friendly and professional manner. In this case, "friendly" means smiling, admiring her dog, and holding eye contact when she speaks. You'll show professionalism by arriving on time, wearing a clean, pressed uniform, and revealing knowledge of the neighborhood. Figure 10.2 diagrams that plan. If you switch strategies at the top—seeking pity for a poor, struggling college student, for example—the alteration will cascade down the hierarchy, requiring changes in many of the behaviors and lots of mental effort.

Even if you are a cognitively complex person who has created a sophisticated rhetorical message plan (see Chapter 8), Berger claims you can't be sure that you'll reach your goal. You may have a great plan, but execute it poorly. Heather may interpret words that you mean one way to mean something else. Or she may have her own goals and plans that will inevitably thwart yours. Berger has come to the conclusion that uncertainty is central to <u>all</u> social interaction. "The probability of perfect communication is zero."[14]

Although Berger originally considered uncertainty reduction theory and the study of plan-based message production as separate projects, he now sees an intersection between the two bodies of research. Berger asks, "How do indi-

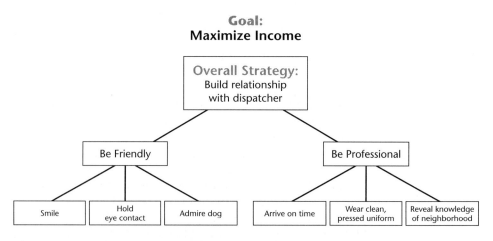

Figure 10.2   A Hierarchical Plan of Goal-Directed Communication

viduals cope with the inevitable uncertainties they must face when constructing messages?" And again, "How can a person hedge against embarrassment, anger, rejection and other downside risks associated with deploying a given message?"[15] The strategies described below are some of his answers.

Seeking information. Berger outlines three approaches we can use to find out how others might react to our messages. Using a *passive strategy*, we unobtrusively observe others from a distance. This fly-on-the-wall tactic works best when we spot others reacting to people in informal or "backstage" settings. (The strategy sounds like normal "scoping" behavior on any college campus.) In an *active strategy*, we ask a third party for information. We realize that our mutual acquaintance will probably give a somewhat slanted view, but most of us have confidence in our ability to filter out the bias and gain valuable information. With an *interactive strategy*, we talk face-to-face with the other person and ask specific questions. This is the quickest route to reduce uncertainty, but continual probing in social settings begins to take on the feel of a cross-examination or "the third degree." Our own self-disclosure offers an alternative way to elicit information from others without seeming to pry. By being transparent, we create a safe atmosphere for others to respond in kind—something that the "law of reciprocity" suggests they will do (see Chapter 9).

Choosing plan complexity. The complexity of a message plan is measured two ways—the level of detail the plan includes and the number of contingency plans prepared in case the original one doesn't work. If it's crucial that you make top dollar in your holiday delivery job, you're likely to draw from memory or newly create a plan far more complex than the sample shown in Fig. 10.2. You'll also have a fall-back plan in case the first one fails. On the other hand, you don't know much about Heather's goals or feelings, and high uncertainty argues for a less complex plan which you can adjust "on-line" when you get a feel for who she is and what she wants. This simpler approach is preferred for another reason. Enacting a complex plan takes so much cognitive effort that there's usually a deterioration in verbal and nonverbal fluency, with a resultant loss in credibility.

Hedging. The very real possibility of plan failure suggests the wisdom of providing ways for both parties to "save face" when at least one of them has miscalculated. Berger catalogues a series of planned hedges that allow a somewhat gracious retreat. For instance, you may be quite certain about what you want to accomplish in your meeting with Heather, yet choose words that are *ambiguous* so as not to tip your hand before you find out more about her. You might also choose to be equivocal in order to avoid the embarrassment that would come from a refusal of a specific request for preferred treatment in route assignment. *Humor* can provide the same way out. You could blatantly propose to use a portion of the saved time and good tips that come from prime assignments to stop at the butcher shop for a juicy bone for Hannah—but make the offer in a joking tone of voice. If Heather takes offense, you can respond, "Hey, I was just kidding."

The Hierarchy Hypothesis.   What happens to action choices when plans are frustrated? Berger's Hierarchy Hypothesis asserts that "when individuals are thwarted in their attempts to achieve goals, their first tendency is to alter lower level elements of their message."[16] For example, when it's obvious the person we're talking to has failed to grasp what we are saying, our inclination is to repeat the same message—but this time louder. The tactic seldom works, but it takes less mental effort than altering strategic features higher up in the action plan. Berger describes people as "cognitive misers" who would rather try a quick fix than expend the effort to repair faulty plans.[17] There's no doubt that on-line modifications are taxing, but when the issue is important, the chance to be effective makes it worth the effort. An even better hedge against failure is to find a "true friend" who will critique your action plan <u>before</u> you put it into effect.[18] As an Old Testament proverb warns, "Without counsel, plans go wrong."[19]

CRITIQUE: NAGGING DOUBTS ABOUT UNCERTAINTY

In a state-of-the-art update on uncertainty reduction theory, Charles Berger admits that his original statement contained "some propositions of dubious validity."[20] Critics quickly point to theorem 17, which predicts that the more you like people, the less you'll seek information about them.

> Frankly, it is not clear why information-seeking would decrease as liking increased other than being required by deductive inference from the axiomatic structure of uncertainty reduction theory. In fact, it seems more reasonable to suggest that persons will seek information about and from those they like rather than those they dislike.[21]

That's the blunt assessment of Kathy Kellermann at the University of California, Santa Barbara, who originally participated in Berger's research program. We might be willing to dismiss this apparent error as only one glitch out of twenty-eight theorems, but the tight logical structure that is the genius of the theory doesn't provide that option. Theorem 17 is dictated by axioms 3 and 7. If the theorem is wrong, the axioms are suspect. Kellermann targets the motivational assumption of axiom 3 as the problem.

Axiom 3 assumes that lack of information triggers a search for knowledge. But Kellermann and Rodney Reynolds now at Regent University studied motivation to reduce uncertainty in more than a thousand students at ten universities, finding that "wanting knowledge rather than lacking knowledge is what promotes information-seeking in initial encounters with others."[22] Their conclusion is illustrated by the story of a teacher who asked a boy, "What's the difference between *ignorance* and *apathy*?" The student replied, "I don't know, and I don't care." (He was right!) Kellermann and Reynolds also failed to find that anticipated future interaction, incentive value, or deviance gave any motivational kick to information seeking as Berger claimed they would. So it seems that Berger's suggestion of a universal drive to reduce uncertainty during initial interaction is questionable at best, yet it remains part of the theory.

Another attack on the theory comes from Michael Sunnafrank at the University of Minnesota in Duluth. He challenges Berger's claim that uncertainty reduction is the key to understanding early encounters. Consistent with Altman and Taylor's social penetration model presented in the previous chapter, Sunnafrank insists that the early course of a relationship is guided by its "predicted outcome value."[23] He's convinced that maximizing rewards is more important than figuring out personality. If this is true, you'll be more concerned with establishing a smooth working relationship with Heather at your first meeting than you will be in figuring out what makes her tick.

Who's right—Berger or Sunnafrank? Berger thinks there's no contest. He maintains that any predictions you make about the payoffs of working with Heather are only as good as the quality of your current knowledge. To the extent that you are uncertain of how an action will affect the relationship, predicted outcome value has no meaning.

Even though the validity of Berger's theory is in question, his analysis of initial interaction is a major contribution to communication scholarship. He recently observed that "the field of communication has been suffering and continues to suffer from an intellectual trade deficit with respect to related disciplines; the field imports much more than it exports."[24] Uncertainty reduction theory was an early attempt by a scholar trained within the discipline to reverse that trend. His success at stimulating critical thinking among his peers can be seen by the fact that every author cited in this chapter is a member of a communication faculty.

Although some of Berger's axioms may not perfectly reflect the acquaintance process, his focus on the issue of reducing uncertainty is at the heart of communication inquiry. Appealing for further dialogue and modification rather than wholesale rejection of the theory, Berger asks:

> What could be more basic to the study of communication than the propositions that (1) adaptation is essential for survival, (2) adaptation is only possible through the reduction of uncertainty, and (3) uncertainty can be both reduced and produced by communicative activity?[25]

It's a sound rhetorical question.

QUESTIONS TO SHARPEN YOUR FOCUS

1. An *axiom* is a self-evident truth. Which one of Berger's axioms seems least self-evident to you?

2. Check out *theorem 13* in Figure 10.1. Does the predicted relationship between *self-disclosure* and *reciprocity* match the forecast of social penetration theory?

3. What is your *goal* for the class period when *uncertainty reduction theory* will be discussed? What is your *hierarchical action plan* to achieve that goal?

4. The relationship between *information-seeking* and *liking* in *theorem 17* is only one out of twenty-eight predictions. Why do critics take doubts about its validity so seriously?

A SECOND LOOK

Recommended resource: Charles R. Berger, "Communicating Under Uncertainty," in *Interpersonal Processes: New Directions in Communication Research,* Michael Roloff and Gerald Miller (eds.), Sage, Newbury Park, Calif., 1987, pp. 39–62.

Original statement: Charles Berger and Richard Calabrese, "Some Explorations in Initial Interaction and Beyond: Toward a Developmental Theory of Interpersonal Communication," *Human Communication Research,* Vol. 1, 1975, pp. 99–112.

Strategies for uncertainty reduction: Charles R. Berger, "Beyond Initial Interaction: Uncertainty, Understanding, and the Development of Interpersonal Relationships," in *Language and Social Psychology,* H. Giles and R. St. Clair (eds.), Blackwell, Oxford, 1979, pp. 122–144.

Further development: Charles R. Berger and J. J. Bradac, *Language and Social Knowledge: Uncertainty in Interpersonal Relations,* Arnold, London, 1982.

Current state of the art: Charles R. Berger and William B. Gudykunst, "Uncertainty and Communication," in *Progress in Communication Sciences,* Vol. 10, Brenda Dervin and Melvin Voigt (eds.), Ablex, Norwood, N.J., 1991, pp. 21–66.

Comparison with other uncertainty theories: Charles R. Berger, "Uncertainty and Information Exchange in Developing Relationships," in *A Handbook of Personal Relationships,* Steve Duck (ed.), John Wiley and Sons, New York, 1988, pp. 239–255.

Coping with uncertain response: Charles R. Berger, "Message Production under Uncertainty," in *Developing Communication Theories,* Gerry Philipsen and Terrance Albrecht (eds.), State University of New York, Albany, 1997, pp. 29–55.

Plan-based strategic communication: Charles R. Berger, *Planning Strategic Interaction,* Lawrence Erlbaum Associates, Mahwah, N.J., 1997.

Critique: Michael Sunnafrank, "Predicted Outcome Value During Initial Interactions: A Reformulation of Uncertainty Reduction Theory," *Human Communication Research,* Vol. 13, 1986, pp. 3–33.

Critique: Kathy Kellermann and Rodney Reynolds, "When Ignorance Is Bliss: The Role of Motivation to Reduce Uncertainty in Uncertainty Reduction Theory," *Human Communication Research,* Vol. 17, 1990, pp. 5–75.

RELATIONSHIP MAINTENANCE

The term *maintenance* may call to mind an auto repair shop where workers with oil-stained coveralls and grease under their fingernails struggle to fix a worn-out engine. The work is hard, the conditions are messy, and the repair is best performed by mechanics who have some idea what they're doing.

This image of rugged work is appropriate when thinking about the ongoing effort required to maintain a close relationship. In many ways, forming a close bond is much easier than sustaining it. The beginning stages of intimacy are often filled with excitement at discovering another human being who sees the world as we do, with the added touch of wonder that the person we like likes us as well. As the relationship becomes more established, however, conflict, jealousy, distrust, and boredom can be the friction that threatens to pull the engine apart. The owner's manual of a new "Intimacy" should warn that periodic maintenance is necessary for friends, romantic partners, and even blood relatives to make it for the long haul.

"They're a perfect match—she's high-maintenance, and he can fix anything."

147

STRATEGY TYPES AND EXAMPLES OF RELATIONSHIP MAINTENANCE

A. Change external environment
1. **Barren and hostile** "I get us to focus on a mutual enemy or an adverse external condition."
2. **Fertile and benign** "I have a candlelight dinner with my spouse."

B. Communication strategies
3. **Talk** "I spend more time talking with my spouse."
4. **Symbolic contact** "I call my spouse during the day just to say 'Hi'."
5. **Openness and honesty** "I am open and honest with my spouse."
6. **Talk about the day** "I talk about my day with my spouse."
7. **Share feelings** "I share my feelings with my spouse."

C. Metacommunication
8. **Talk about the problems** "I talk about the problems in our relationship with my spouse."
9. **Interim progress reports** "I have regular, periodic talks about our relationship with my spouse."
10. **Cool off before talking** "I wait until I've cooled off before I discuss our problem with my spouse."
11. **Tell spouse his or her faults** "I tell my spouse his or her faults and the damage they do to our relationship."

D. Avoid metacommunication
12. "I keep quiet and let our problem pass."

E. Antisocial strategies
13. **Argument** "I argue or fight with my spouse."
14. **Ultimatums** "I give my spouse an ultimatum or I threaten to end the relationship."
15. **Insolence** "I am rude, insulting, impolite, and disrespectful to my spouse."
16. **Sullenness** "I sulk, pout, and give my spouse the silent treatment."
17. **Hyper-criticalness** "I nag and criticize my spouse."
18. **Be obstinate** "I am stubborn; I refuse to give in to or compromise with my spouse."
19. **Verbally imply relationship has no future** "I tell my spouse that the marriage has no future."
20. **Break contact** "I walk out of the house without telling my spouse when I will return."
21. **Act cold** "I give my spouse the cold shoulder."
22. **Refuse self-disclosure** "I don't provide my spouse with my customary degree of disclosure about myself."
23. **Refuse favors** "I refuse to supply my spouse with my usual favors or I refuse to accept favors I plainly need from my spouse."
24. **Threaten exclusiveness/common space/common future** "I have an affair, pretend to have an affair, or flirt with a third party."

FIGURE RM.1   Fifty Strategies for Relationship Maintenance in Marriage
(Adapted from Baxter and Dindia, "Marital Partners' Perceptions of Marital Maintenance Strategies.")

F. Prosocial strategies

25. **Be nice** "I am courteous and polite to my spouse; I show my spouse repect."
26. **Be cheerful** "I am cheerful, good-natured, and pleasant to my spouse."
27. **Refrain from criticism** "I refrain from criticizing my spouse."
28. **Give in** "I give in to or compromise with my spouse."
29. **Verbally imply relationship has future** "I bring up topics such as buying a home or having children that indicate the relationship will be there in the future."
30. **Be warm** "I am friendly, kind, sympathetic, understanding, and supportive of my spouse."
31. **Listen better** "I try to be a better listener to my spouse."
32. **Do favors** "I do a favor for my spouse."
33. **Ensure exclusiveness/common space/common future** "I assure my spouse of my fidelity."

G. Ceremonies

34. **Origin celebrations** "I remember my spouse's birthday, our wedding anniversary, Valentine's Day, and other special days."
35. **Reminiscence** "I reminisce with my spouse about past pleasurable experiences we shared together."
36. **Discuss the end of the relationship** "I discuss with my spouse what it would be like if the relationship ended through divorce or death."
37. **Ceremonies of atonement** "I kiss and make up with my spouse."
38. **Communion celebrations** "I have us eat out at a favorite or expensive restaurant."
39. **Verbal expressions of affection** "I tell my spouse I love him or her."
40. **Nonverbal expressions of affection** "I hug and kiss my spouse."
41. **Compliments** "I compliment my spouse."
42. **Gift-giving** "I give my spouse a gift."

H. Anti-rituals/spontaneity

43. "I surprise my spouse."

I. Togetherness

44. **Time together** "I spend more time with my spouse."
45. **Shared activity** "I do more things with my spouse."
46. **Spend time with network** "I spend time with my spouse together with our children, family, or friends."

J. Seek/allow autonomy

47. "I allow my spouse time to be alone or to do things with other people and I take time to be alone or to do things with other people."

K. Seek external assistance

48. **Seek outside help** "I seek help outside our marriage; for example, I have us attend an enrichment retreat or go to a marriage counselor."
49. **Joint use of prayer/religion** "I pray with my spouse or attend church with my spouse."
50. **Individual use of prayer/religion** "I pray by myself for guidance about our marriage."

Inasmuch as the image of auto upkeep and repair communicates the importance of "servicing" a relationship, the metaphor of mechanical labor is appropriate. But personal relationships aren't inanimate objects with interchangeable parts that can be adjusted with a wrench. Expanding the *maintenance* metaphor to living organisms underscores the importance of individualized attention in relational health. Most clients of HMOs (health maintenance organizations) are satisfied only when they receive personal attention from doctors and nurses that they have come to know.

Humanistic communication writer John Stewart refers to a pair's personal relationship as a "spiritual child," born as the result of their coming together.[1] His analogy stresses that a relationship requires continual care and nurture for sustained growth. When people ignore the spiritual children they've created, the results are sick and puny relationships. Although Stewart thinks it's impossible to totally kill a relationship as long as one of the "parents" is still alive, child abuse or abandonment will result in a stunted or maimed relationship.

Figure RM.1 lists fifty maintenance strategies grouped into eleven overarching categories. Although the list refers specifically to marriage partners, many of the same strategies are employed by friends and family members. In addition to providing a provocative checklist for analyzing your own efforts at relational maintenance, the classification offers a helpful way to illustrate three theories that focus on this topic.

I've already presented Thibaut and Kelley's exchange perspective as an integral part of social penetration theory (see Chapter 9). These theorists regard interpersonal behavior as the logical result of the external rewards and costs referred to in category A of the strategy list. From a social exchange perspective, antisocial and prosocial maintenance strategies (E and F) are attempts to exercise relational control through the use of selective rewards and punishments.

Chapter 11 presents Paul Watzlawick's interactional view of dysfunctional relationships. He describes the typical family as an interconnected system. Like it or not, what happens to one individual in the system has an impact on every other member. He believes that an excess or absence of overt talk about communication is a symptom of a family in trouble. This problem would show up in the metacommunication strategy types (C and D). Watzlawick's emphasis on using a therapist or counselor to help reframe family communication patterns suggests the benefits of seeking outside help (K).

Although communication researcher Leslie Baxter compiled the maintenance strategies listed in Figure RM.1, she and Barbara Montgomery are uneasy with the implication that the goal of maintenance and repair is to restore a relationship to its original condition. They are convinced that relational partners are caught in conflicting desires for connectedness and separateness (I and J), certainty and uncertainty (G and H), openness and closedness (B). For Baxter and Montgomery, relationship maintenance isn't as much about achieving stability as it is about coping with the stress inherent in every intimate bond. Since relationships are always in flux, they prefer to refer to the process of *sustaining* a relationship rather than using the term *maintenance*, which implies that change is bad. Chapter 12 presents their theory of relational dialectics.

CHAPTER 11

The Interactional View
of Paul Watzlawick

The Franklin family is in trouble. A perceptive observer could spot their difficulties despite their successful facade. Sonia Franklin is an accomplished pianist who teaches advanced theory and technique to students in her own home. Her husband Stan will soon become a partner in a Big Six accounting firm. Their daughter Laurie is an honor student, an officer in her high school class, and the number two player on the tennis team. But Laurie's younger brother, Mike, has dropped all pretense of interest in studies, sports, or social life. His only passion is drinking beer and smoking pot.

Each of the Franklins reacts to Mike's substance abuse in different but less than helpful ways. Stan denies that his son has a problem. Boys will be boys, and he's sure Mike will grow out of this phase. The only time he and Mike actually talked about the problem, Stan said, "I want you to cut back on your drinking—not for me and your mother—but for your own sake."

Laurie has always felt responsible for her kid brother and is scared because Mike is getting "wasted" every few days. She makes him promise that he'll quit using and continues to introduce him to her straight friends in the hope that he'll get in with a good crowd.

Sonia worries that alcohol and drugs will ruin her son's future. One morning when he woke up with a hangover, she wrote a note to the school saying Mike had the flu. She also called a lawyer to help Mike when he was stopped for drunk driving. Although she promised never to tell his father about these incidents, she chides Stan for his lack of concern. The more she nags, the more he withdraws.

Mike feels caught in a vicious circle. Smoking pot helps him relax, but then his family gets more upset, which makes him want to smoke more, which. . . . During a tense dinner-table discussion he lashed out: "You want to know why I use? Go look in a mirror." Although the rest of the family sees Mike as "the problem," psychotherapist Paul Watzlawick would describe the whole family system as disturbed. He formed his theory of social interaction by looking at dysfunctional patterns within families in order to gain insight about healthy communication.

THE FAMILY AS A SYSTEM

Picture a family as a mobile suspended from the ceiling. Each figure is connected to the rest of the structure by a strong thread tied at exactly the right place to keep the system in balance. Tug on any string, and the force sends shock throughout the whole network. Sever a thread, and the entire design tilts in disequilibrium.

The threads in the mobile analogy represent communication rules that hold the family together. Watzlawick believes that in order to understand the movement of any single figure in the family system, one has to examine the communication patterns among all its members. He regards the communication that the family members have among themselves about their relationships as especially important.

Watzlawick (pronounced VAHT-sla-vick) is a senior research fellow at the Mental Research Institute, Palo Alto, California, and clinical professor (emeritus) of psychiatry at Stanford University. He is one of about twenty scholars and therapists who were inspired by and worked with anthropologist Gregory Bateson. The common denominator that continues to draw the Palo Alto Group together is a commitment to study interpersonal interaction as part of an entire system. They reject the idea that individual motives and personality traits determine the nature of communication within a family. In fact, the Palo Alto researchers care little about *why* a person acts in a certain way, but they have a great interest in *how* that behavior affects everyone in the group.

A systems approach to family relationships defies simplistic explanations of why people act as they do. For example, some pop psychology books on body language claim that a listener standing in a hands-on-hips position is skeptical about what the speaker is saying. Watzlawick is certainly interested in the reaction others have to this posture, but he doesn't think that a particular way of standing should be viewed as part of a cause-and-effect chain of events:

$$a \rightarrow b \rightarrow c \rightarrow d$$

Relationships are not simple, nor are they "things" as suggested by the statement, "We have a good relationship." Relationships are complex functions in the same sense that mathematical functions link multiple variables:

$$x = b^2 + \frac{2c}{a} - 5d$$

Just as x will be affected by the value of a, b, c, or d, so the hands-on-hips stance could be due to a variety of attitudes, emotions, or physical conditions. Maybe the stance does show skepticism. But it also might reflect boredom, a feeling of awkwardness, aching shoulder muscles, or self-consciousness about middle-aged "hip-handles."

Watzlawick uses the math metaphor throughout the book *Pragmatics of Human Communication.* Along with co-authors Janet Beavin and Don Jackson,

Watzlawick presents key axioms that describe the "tentative calculus of human communication." These make up the "grammar of conversation," or, to use another analogy that runs through the book, "the rules of the game."

There is nothing particularly playful about the game the Franklins are playing. Psychologist Alan Watts says that "life is a game where rule No. 1 is: This is no game, this is serious."[1] Watzlawick defines game as "sequences of behavior governed by rules." Even though Sonia and Stan are involved in an unhealthy "game without end" of nag-withdrawal-nag-withdrawal, they continue to play because it serves a function for both of them. (Sonia feels superior; Stan avoids hassles with his son.) Neither party may recognize what's going on, but their rules are a something-for-something bargain. Mike's drinking and his family's distress may fit into the same category. (Getting drunk not only relieves tension temporarily, it's a great excuse for sidestepping the pressure to excel, which is the name of the game in the Franklin family.)

Lest we be tempted to see the Franklins' relationships as "typical" of all families dealing with addiction, Watzlawick warns that each family plays a one-of-a-kind game with homemade rules. Just as CMM claims that persons-in-conversation co-construct their own social worlds (see Chapter 5), the Palo Alto Group insists that each family system creates its own reality. That conviction shapes their approach to family therapy:

> In the systemic approach, we try to understand as quickly as possible the functioning of this system: What kind of reality has this particular system constructed for itself? Incidentally, this rules out categorizations because one of the basic principles of systems theory is that "every system is its own best explanation."[2]

AXIOMS OF INTERPERSONAL COMMUNICATIONS

The network of communication rules that governs the Franklins' interaction makes it extremely difficult for any of them to change their behavior. Watzlawick, Beavin, and Jackson use the label *family homeostasis* to describe what many family counselors agree is the tacit collusion of family members to maintain the status quo. Interactional theorists believe that we'll fail to recognize this destructive resistance to change unless we understand the following axioms, or rules, of communication.[3]

One Cannot Not Communicate

You've undoubtedly been caught in situations where you feel obliged to talk but would rather avoid the commitment to respond that's inherent in all communication. For example, you come home from a date, and your mother meets you inside the door and says, "Tell me all about it." Or perhaps you need to study, but your roommate wants to chat.

In an attempt to avoid communication, you could bluntly state that your test the following morning makes studying more important than socializing.

But voicing your desire for privacy can stretch the rules of good behavior and it often results in an awkward silence that speaks loudly about the relationship.

You could flood your mother with a torrent of meaningless words about the evening, merely say it was "fine" as you duck into your room, or plead tiredness, a headache, or a sore throat. Watzlawick calls this the "symptom strategy" and says it suggests, "*I* wouldn't mind talking to you, but something stronger than *I*, for which I cannot be blamed, prevents me." But whatever you do, it would be naive not to realize that your mother will analyze your behavior for clues about the evening's activities. His face an immobile mask, Mike Franklin may mutely encounter his parents. But he communicates in spite of himself by his facial expression and his silence. Those nonverbal messages will obviously have an impact on the rest of his family. A corollary to the first axiom is that "one cannot *not* influence."[4]

Communication = Content + Relationship

The heading is a shorthand version of the formal axiom: "Every communication has a content and relationship aspect such that the latter classifies the former and is therefore metacommunication."[5] Watzlawick chose to rename the two aspects of communication that Gregory Bateson had originally called "report" and "command." Report or content is *what* is said. Command or relationship is *how* it's said. Figure 11.1 outlines the distinction that is crucial to the interactional model.

Neither the equation above nor the contrasting terms in Figure 11.1 quite capture the way relationship surrounds content and provides a context or atmosphere for interpretation. It's the difference between data fed into a computer and the program that directs how the data should be processed. In written communication, punctuation gives direction as to how the words should be

Content	Relationship
Report	Command
What is said	How it is said
Verbal channel	Nonverbal channel
Communication	Metacommunication
Cognitive	Affective
Computer data	Computer program
Words	Punctuation

FIGURE 11.1   Interactional View of Two Aspects of Communication

understood. Shifting a question mark to an exclamation point alters the meaning of the message. Right? Right! In spoken communication, however, it is the tone of voice, emphasis on certain words, facial cues, and so forth, that direct how the message was meant to be interpreted.

Watzlawick refers to the relational aspect of interaction as "metacommunication." It is communication about communication. Metacommunication says, "This is how I see myself, this is how I see you, this is how I see you seeing me. . . ." According to Watzlawick, relationship messages are always the most important element in any communication—healthy or otherwise. But when a family is in trouble, metacommunication dominates the discussion. Mike Franklin's dinner-table outburst is an example of pathological metacommunication that shakes the entire family system. The Palo Alto Group is convinced it would be a mistake for the Franklins to ignore Mike's attack in the hope that the tension will go away. Sick family relationships only get better when family members are willing to talk with each other about their patterns of communication.

The Nature of a Relationship Depends on How Both Parties Punctuate the Communication Sequence

Consider the relational tangle described in one of the "Knots" composed by British psychotherapist R. D. Laing to describe sick family systems:

> He can't be happy
>> when there's so much suffering in the world
> She can't be happy
>> if he is unhappy
>> She wants to be happy
> He does not feel entitled to be happy
> She wants him to be happy
>> and he wants her to be happy
> He feels guilty if he is happy
>> and guilty if she is not happy
> She wants both to be happy
> He wants her to be happy
> So they are both unhappy[6]

The poem describes the discouraging cycle pictured at the top of the next page. Outside observers see a reciprocal pattern of guilt and depression that has no beginning or end. But the woman enmeshed in the "knot" punctuates the sequence by starting at point *p, r,* or *t.* She thus regards the man as selfish, the cause of her unhappiness. Equally ensnared in the system, the man punctuates the sequence by designating her depression at point *q* or *s* as the initial event. Therefore, he sees his guilt as the result of her being a happiness junkie. Asking either of them, "Who started it?" would merely feed into their fruitless struggle for control.

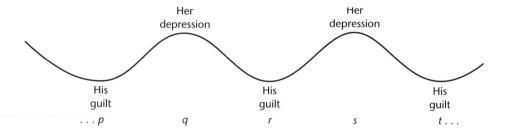

Watzlawick notes that "what is typical about the sequence and makes it a problem of punctuation is that the individual concerned conceives of himself only as reacting to, but not as provoking, these attitudes."[7] This is true for both adult Franklins. Stan sees himself as withdrawing from Sonia only because of her constant nagging. Sonia feels certain that she wouldn't harp on the issue if Stan would face the problem of Mike's drinking.

All Communication Is Either Symmetrical or Complementary

This axiom continues to focus on metacommunication. While definitions of *relationship* include the issues of belongingness, affection, trust, and intimacy, the interactional view pays particular attention to questions of control, status, and power. Remember that Bateson's original label for relationship communication was *command.* According to Watzlawick, symmetrical interchange is based on equal power; complementary communication is based on differences in power. He makes no attempt to label one type as good and the other as bad. Healthy relationships have both kinds of communication.

In terms of ability, the women in the Franklin family have a symmetrical relationship; neither one tries to control the other. Sonia has expertise on the piano; Laurie excels on the tennis court. Each of them performs without the other's claiming dominance. Fortunately, their skills are in separate arenas. Too much similarity can set the stage for an everything-you-can-do-I-can-do-better competition.

Sonia's relationship with Mike is complementary. Her type of mothering is strong on control. She hides the extent of Mike's drinking from his father, lies to school officials, and hires a lawyer on the sly to bail her son out of trouble with the police. By continuing to treat Mike as a child, she maintains their dominant–submissive relationship. Although complementary relationships aren't always destructive, the status difference between Mike and the rest of the Franklins is stressing the family system.

The interactional view holds that there is no way to label a relationship on the basis of a single verbal statement. Judgments that an interaction is either symmetrical or complementary require a sequence of at least two messages—a statement from one person, and a response from the other. While at Michigan State University, communication researchers Edna Rogers-Millar and Richard

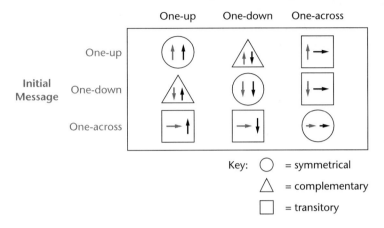

FIGURE 11.2   Matrix of Transactional Types
(Adapted from Rogers and Farace, "Analysis of Relational Communication in Dyads: New Measurement Procedures.")

Farace devised a coding scheme to categorize ongoing marital interaction on the crucial issue of who controls the relationship.

One-up communication (↑) is movement to gain control of the exchange. A bid for dominance includes messages that instruct, order, interrupt, contradict, change topics, or fail to support what the other person said. One-down communication (↓) is movement to yield control of the exchange. The bid for submission is evidenced by agreement with what the other person said. Despite Watzlawick's contention that all discourse is either symmetrical or complementary, Rogers-Millar and Farace code one-across communication (→) as well. They define it as transitory communication that moves toward neutralizing control.

Figure 11.2 presents the matrix of possible relational transactions. The pairs that are circled show a symmetrical interaction. The pairs in triangles indicate complementary relations. The pairs in squares reveal transitory communication. Rogers-Millar's later research showed that bids for dominance (↑) do not necessarily result in successful control of the interaction (↑↓).[8]

TRAPPED IN A SYSTEM WITH NO PLACE TO GO

Family systems are highly resistant to change. This inertia is especially apparent in the home of someone who has an addiction. Each family member occupies a role that serves the status quo. In the Franklin family, Mike, of course, is the one with "the problem." With the best of intentions, Sonia is the "enabler" who cushions Mike from feeling the pain caused by his chemical abuse. Stan is the "deny-er," while Laurie is the family "hero" who compensates for her brother's failure. Family therapists note that when one person in a distressed family gets better, another member often gets worse. If Mike stopped drinking and using pot, Laurie might quit the tennis team, ignore her studies, or start smoking marijuana herself. Dysfunctional families confirm the adage, "the more things change, the more they stay the same."

Watzlawick sees family members as often caught in the "double bind" of mutually exclusive expectations, which Bateson originally described. Parental messages such as "You ought to love me" or "Be spontaneous!" place children in an untenable position. The children are bound to violate some aspect of the injunction no matter how they respond. (Love can only be freely given; spontaneity on demand is impossible.) The paradox of the double bind is that the high-status party in a complementary relationship insists that the low-status person act as if the relationship were symmetrical—which it isn't. Stan's *demand* that his son stay sober for his *own sake* places Mike in a no-win situation. He can't obey his dad and be autonomous at the same time.

REFRAMING: CHANGING THE GAME BY CHANGING THE RULES

How can the Franklin family break out of their never-ending game and experience real change in the way they relate to each other? According to Watzlawick, effective change for the whole family will come about only when members are helped to step outside the system and see the self-defeating nature of the rules under which they're playing. He calls this process of changing the punctuation "reframing."

> To reframe . . . means to change the conceptual and/or emotional setting or viewpoint in relation to which a situation is experienced and to place it in another frame which fits the "facts" of the same concrete situation equally well or even better, and thereby changes its entire meaning.[9]

Watzlawick compares reframing to the process of waking up from a bad dream. He points out that during a nightmare you may run, hide, fight, scream, jump off a cliff, or try dozens of other things to make things better, but nothing really changes. Relief comes only when you step outside the system by waking up. Without the intervention of a timely alarm clock or a caring roommate, relief can be a long time coming.

Reframing is the sudden "ah-hah" of looking at things in a new light. Suppose you talked with Watzlawick about your struggles to keep up with the assignments for your comm theory class. You've chosen to be a communication major, so you believe you ought to *like* studying the material. Since you don't, you think there's something wrong with you. You also know that your family is making a financial sacrifice for you to be in college, so you feel guilty that you aren't getting good grades or experiencing deep gratitude for their help. In fact, you resent having to be grateful.

"I don't want you to go for a walk because I want you to go for a walk. I want you to go for a walk because you want to go for a walk."

If you described these dilemmas to Watzlawick, he would want you to reframe your attitudes as *unrealistic* and *immature*—nightmarish interpretations for most college students. Even under the best of circumstances, he'd explain, studying is an unpleasant necessity and to believe that it should be fun is ridiculous. As far as your folks are concerned, they have a right to your gratitude, but this doesn't mean you have to *enjoy* being thankful. So it's up to you. You can "continue in these immature outlooks or have the adult courage to reject them and to begin to look at life as a mixture of pleasant and unpleasant things."[10] The facts haven't changed, but he's given you a new way to interpret them. If you accept Watzlawick's frame, you'll probably cope better and feel less pain.

For the Franklins, reframing means they must radically change their perspective. One way to do this is by adopting the view of Alcoholics Anonymous (AA) that Mike's addiction is a disease over which he has no control. His drinking is not a sign of moral weakness or a voluntary rebuff of his family's values—he drinks because he's an alcoholic. The AA interpretation would imply that the Franklins need to abandon their fruitless search for someone to blame. Despite Mike's look-in-the-mirror accusation, the members of his family aren't responsible for his addiction. They didn't cause it, they can't cure it, and they can't control it. It's a disease. Does that mean Mike's not responsible for being chemically dependent? Right . . . but he *is* responsible for putting all of his energy into getting well.

Accepting a new frame implies rejecting the old one. The Franklins must admit that their so-called solutions are as much a problem as their son's drinking. Mike will never seek treatment for his illness as long as his family continues to shield him from the consequences of his behavior. Reframing will help Sonia see that writing excuses and hiring lawyers may be less caring than letting her son get kicked out of school or allowing his driver's license to be suspended.

Adapting a tough-love perspective or any new interpretive frame is usually accomplished only with outside help. For Watzlawick, that means therapy. As a social constructionist, he wouldn't try to discover the "real" reason Mike drinks or worry if it's "true" that some people are genetically predisposed to addiction. In his view, the purpose of therapy is the lessening of pain. He would regard the disease model of addiction as an alternative construction—another fiction, but perhaps for the Franklin family, a useful and less painful one.[11]

Conversely, self-help groups called Families Anonymous (FA) are intensely committed to the addiction model as *the* way to realign the family network. Just as AA gives support to the recovering alcoholic, FA offers support for those who face chemical dependency within their own families. At each meeting, participants read aloud a brief selection entitled "Helping," in which they pledge to avoid manipulation, control, overprotectiveness, and any attempts to make the addicted family member fit a standard or image. The reading closes with radical words for worried parents: "I can change myself. Others I can only love."[12] That's changing the game by changing the rules.

CRITIQUE: ADJUSTMENTS NEEDED WITHIN THE SYSTEM

Janet Beavin Bavelas coauthored *Pragmatics of Human Communication* with Watzlawick in 1967. Twenty-five years later, she reviewed the status of the axioms that are the central focus of the interactional view.[13] Based on the research program she conducted at the University of Victoria in Canada, Bavelas recommends modifying some axioms of the theory. Her proposal serves as an informed critique of the original theory.

The first axiom claims that we cannot not communicate. Perhaps because of the catchy way it's stated, this axiom has been both challenged and defended more than the others. Although Bavelas is fascinated by the way people avoid eye contact or physically position themselves so as to communicate to others that they don't want to communicate, she now concedes that not all nonverbal behavior is communication. Observers may draw inferences from what they see, but in the absence of a sender-receiver relationship and the intentional use of a shared code, Bavelas would describe nonverbal behavior as *informative* rather than *communicative*.

As Figure 11.1 shows, the Palo Alto Group treated the verbal and nonverbal channels as providing different kinds of information. Bavelas now thinks that the notion of functionally separate channels dedicated to different uses is wrong. She suggests a "whole message model" that treats verbal and nonverbal acts as completely integrated and often interchangeable. In effect, she has erased the light vertical line that divides Figure 11.1 down the middle—a major shift in thinking.

The content/relationship distinction of another axiom is still viable for Bavelas. Like Watzlawick, she continues to believe that the content of communication is always embedded in the relationship environment. Looking back, however, she thinks they confused readers by sometimes equating the term *metacommunication* with all communication about a relationship. She now wants to reserve the word for explicit communication about the process of communicating. Examples of metacommunication narrowly defined would be Laurie Franklin telling her brother, "Don't talk to me like a kid," and Mike's response, "What do you mean by that?" Laurie's raised eyebrow and Mike's angry tone of voice would be part of their tightly integrated packages of meaning.

Overall, systems theories involving people are difficult to evaluate because of their *equifinality*—a characteristic that means a given behavioral outcome could be caused by any or many factors that are interconnected. Because of this feature, it's hard to know when the system is out of whack. However, I find Bavelas' disenchantment with a theoretical system that she helped create a reason to question its validity.

Despite these doubts, I'm impressed with the impact that Watzlawick and his associates have had on the field of interpersonal communication. The publication of *Pragmatics of Human Communication* marked the beginning of widespread study of the way communication patterns sustain or destroy relationships. Their interactional view has also encouraged communication scholars to go beyond narrow cause-and-effect assumptions. The entanglements Watzlawick describes reflect the complexities of real-life relationships that most of us know. In that, the theory is a forerunner of the dialectical perspective featured in the next chapter.

QUESTIONS TO SHARPEN YOUR FOCUS

1. *Systems theorists* compare the family system to a mobile. What part of the mobile represents *metacommunication*? If you were constructing a mobile to model your family, how would you depict *symmetrical* and *complementary* relationships?

2. For decades, the United States and the former Soviet Union were engaged in a nuclear arms race. How does Watzlawick's axiom about the *punctuation of communication sequences* explain the belligerence of both nations?

3. Can you make up something your instructor might say that would place you in a *double bind?* Under what conditions would this be merely laughable rather than frustrating?

4. Read one of the letters printed in the "Ann Landers" or "Dear Abby" column of your daily newspaper. How could you *reframe* the situation the writer describes?

A SECOND LOOK

Recommended resource: Paul Watzlawick, Janet Beavin, and Don Jackson, *Pragmatics of Human Communication,* W. W. Norton, New York, 1967.

Seminal ideas of the Palo Alto Group: Gregory Bateson, "Information and Codification," in *Communication,* Jurgen Ruesch and Gregory Bateson (eds.), W. W. Norton, New York, 1951, pp. 168–211.

System theory: B. Aubrey Fisher, "The Pragmatic Perspective of Human Communication: A View from System Theory," in *Human Communication Theory,* Frank E. X. Dance (ed.), Harper & Row, New York, 1982, pp. 192–219.

Control, metacommunication, and context: Arthur Bochner and Dorothy Krueger, "Interpersonal Communication Theory and Research: An Overview of Inscrutable Epistemologies and Muddled Concepts," in *Communication Yearbook 3,* Dan Nimmo (ed.), Transaction Books, New Brunswick, N.J., 1979, pp. 197–211.

Relational control: L. Edna Rogers and Richard Farace, "Analysis of Relational Communication in Dyads: New Measurement Procedures," *Human Communication Research,* Vol. 1, 1975, pp. 222–239.

Reframing: Paul Watzlawick, John H. Weakland, and Richard Fisch, *Change,* W. W. Norton, New York, 1974, pp. 92–160.

Pathological punctuation: R. D. Laing, *Knots,* Pantheon Books, New York, 1970.

Therapeutic strategies for change: Paul Watzlawick, *The Language of Change,* W. W. Norton, New York, 1978, pp. 91–160.

Whether one cannot not communicate: Theodore Clevenger, Jr., "Can One Not Communicate? A Conflict of Models," *Communication Studies,* Vol. 42, 1991, pp. 340–353.

Theory adjustments: Janet Beavin Bavelas, "Research into the Pragmatics of Human Communication," *Journal of Strategic and Systemic Therapies,* Vol. 11. No. 2, 1992, pp. 15–29.

Critique: Carol Wilder, "The Palo Alto Group: Difficulties and Directions of the Interactional View for Human Communication Research," *Human Communication Research,* Vol. 5, 1979, pp. 171–186.

CHAPTER 12

Relational Dialectics

of Leslie Baxter & Barbara Montgomery

Leslie Baxter and Barbara Montgomery are central figures in a growing group of communication scholars who are interested in the intimate communication that takes place in close relationships. Baxter directs an extensive program of research at the University of Iowa. Montgomery is dean of communication for the School of Humanities and Social Sciences at Millersville University.

The first time Baxter conducted a series of in-depth interviews with people about their personal relationships, she quickly gave up any hope of discovering scientific laws that neatly ordered the experiences of friends and lovers.

> I was struck by the contradictions, contingencies, non-rationalities, and multiple realities to which people gave voice in their narrative sense-making of their relational lives.[1]

She saw no law of gravity to predict interpersonal attraction, no coefficient of friction that would explain human conflict. She found, instead, people struggling to respond to conflicting pulls or tugs they felt within their relationships. Working independently of Baxter, Montgomery's experience was much the same.

Baxter and Montgomery each analyzed tensions inherent in romantic relationships and began to catalogue the contradictions that couples faced. They soon recognized the commonality of their work, and co-authored a book on relating based on the premise that "relationships are organized around the dynamic interplay of opposing tendencies as they are enacted in interaction."[2]

Both scholars make it clear that the forces that strain romantic relationships are also at work among close friends and family members. They applaud the work of William Rawlins at Purdue University, who concentrates on the "communicative predicaments of friendship," and the narrative analysis of Art Bochner at the University of South Florida, who focuses on the complex contradictions within family systems. Whatever the form of intimacy, Baxter and Montgomery's basic claim is that "personal relationships are indeterminate processes of ongoing flux."[3]

Relational dialectics highlight the tension, struggle, and general messiness of close personal ties. The best way we can grasp Baxter and Montgomery's perspective is to examine a romantic narrative similar to the ones Baxter found so gripping in her early studies.

One of the most compelling pictures of intimate communication to appear in the last decade is the film *Children of a Lesser God*. The movie portrays the rocky relationship between a teacher of the hearing impaired and a young woman who has been deaf since birth. Their love affair provides an excellent example of the tension Baxter and Montgomery identify through their research on romantic relationships.

The phrase "children of a lesser god" is a poignant self-reference often made by those who are born into a silent world. The words reflect the muted experience of Sarah, a beautiful 25-year-old woman portrayed by actress Marlee Matlin, who herself cannot hear. Sarah's life is "on hold" as she mops floors at a private academy for deaf children where she had been a star pupil. Although Sarah is able to sign as fast as others can talk, she refuses to lip-read or to speak out loud. Anyone desiring to get close to Sarah must enter her world of silence.

Actor William Hurt plays James, an engaging and talented speech teacher who is new to the school. He draws near to Sarah, seeing her initially as a challenging "project" and later as an enchanting partner. They create an intimate bond, but the relationship is never without deep tension and visible stress. The first time the pair communicate by signing, James sits down in a chair opposite Sarah. She responds by standing up. When he stands up, she sits down. The byplay is a foretaste of the conflict to come.

THE PUSH-ME-PULL-YOU DIALECTICS OF CLOSE RELATIONSHIPS

Some viewers might be tempted to blame the couple's on-again, off-again relationship on Sarah's physical disability or her feisty disposition. But Baxter and Montgomery caution us not to look at personal traits when we want to understand the nature of close relationships. Neither biology nor biography can account for the struggle of contradictory tendencies that James and Sarah experience in the story. James and Sarah are an unusual couple, but the tensions they face are common to all personal relationships.

Contradiction is the central concept of relational dialectics. *Contradiction* refers to "the dynamic interplay between unified oppositions."[4] A contradiction is formed "whenever two tendencies or forces are interdependent (the dialectical principle of unity) yet mutually negate one another (the dialectical principle of negation)."[5] In the story, James and Sarah feel the contradiction of being stretched in two directions at the same time—toward both intimacy and independence. According to Baxter, every personal relationship faces that same tension. Rather than bemoaning this relational fact of life, Baxter and Montgomery suggest that couples take advantage of the opportunity it provides: "From a relational dialectics perspective, bonding occurs in both interdependence with the other and independence from the other."[6] One without the other diminishes the relationship.

Baxter and Montgomery draw heavily on the thinking of Mikhail Bakhtin, a Russian intellectual who survived the Stalinist regime. Bakhtin saw dialectical tension as the "deep structure" of all human experience. On the one hand, a centripetal or centralizing force pulls us together with others. On the other hand, a centrifugal or decentralizing force pushes us apart.

In order to picture Bakhtin's simultaneous and conflicting forces, imagine yourself playing "crack the whip" while skating with a group of friends. You volunteer to be the outermost person on a pinwheeling chain of skaters. As you accelerate, you feel the centripetal pull from the skater beside you who has a viselike grip on your wrist. You also feel the opposing centrifugal force that threatens to rip you from your friend's grasp and slingshot you away from the group. Skill at skating doesn't reduce the conflicting pressures. In fact, the more speed you can handle, the greater the opposing forces.

Unlike the thesis-antithesis-synthesis stages of Marxist dialectical theory, Bakhtin's fusion-fission opposites have no ultimate resolution. Relationships are always in flux; the only certainty is certain change. For Bakhtin, this isn't necessarily bad news. He saw dialectical tension as providing an opportunity for dialogue, an occasion when partners could work out ways to mutually embrace their conflicting desires for unity *with,* and differentiation *from,* each other.

Most westerners are bothered by the idea of paradox, so Baxter and Montgomery work hard to translate the concept into familiar terms. At the start of her research interviews, Baxter introduces a dialectical perspective without ever using the phrase itself. She talks about people experiencing within themselves certain "pulls" or "tugs" in different directions. Her words call up the image of Dr. Doolittle's "pushmi-pullyu."[7] The unicornlike beast epitomizes built-in dialectical tension—one body, but two heads facing in opposite directions. The pushmi-pullyu animals of Dr. Doolittle's world were rare. According to Leslie Baxter and Barbara Montgomery, the push-me-pull-you contradictions of our relational world are not.

THREE RELATIONAL DIALECTICS: CONNECTEDNESS-SEPARATENESS, CERTAINTY-UNCERTAINTY, OPENNESS-CLOSEDNESS

While listening to hundreds of men and women talk about their relationships, Baxter spotted at least three contradictions that challenge the traditional wisdom of the theories described earlier in the relationship development section. Recall that Altman and Taylor's social penetration theory assumes that partners want more *closeness;* Berger's uncertainty reduction theory posits a quest for interpersonal *certainty;* most conceptions of intimacy valorize the guileless *open self.* From the accounts she heard, Baxter concluded that these desires are only part of the story.

Although most of us embrace the traditional ideals of closeness, certainty, and openness in our relationships, our actual communication within family, friendship, and romance seldom follows a straight path toward these goals.

Internal Dialectic (within the relationship)	**External Dialectic** (between couple and community)
Connectedness - Separateness	Inclusion - Seclusion
Certainty - Uncertainty	Conventionality - Uniqueness
Openness - Closedness	Revelation - Concealment

FIGURE 12.1   Typical Dialectical Tensions Experienced by Relational Partners
(Based on Baxter and Montgomery, *Relating: Dialogues and Dialectics.*)

According to Baxter and Montgomery, that's because we also seek the exact opposite—autonomy, novelty, and privacy. As we face the resultant dilemmas, we can't just choose one side or the other. Conflicting forces in relationships aren't reducible to a series of "either/or" decisions. The "both/and" nature of dialectical pressures guarantees that our relationships will be complex, messy, and always somewhat on edge.

The left-hand column of Figure 12.1 charts three important arenas where Baxter sees dialectical tensions played out *within* a relationship. The right-hand column lists similar opposing forces that cause strains *between* a couple and their community. Unlike the typical they-all-lived-happily-ever-after love story, the portrayal of James and Sarah's relationship in *Children of a Lesser God* is credible because the pair continually struggles with these dialectics—and other ones as well. Accordingly, the figure suggests that these oppositional pairs are just the start of a longer list of internal and external contradictions that confront partners as they live out their relationship in real time and place. For example, Rawlins finds that friends continually have to deal with the paradox of judgment and acceptance. In this section, however, I'll limit my review to the three internal contradictions that Baxter and Montgomery discuss.

Connectedness and Separateness

Baxter and Montgomery regard the contradiction between connectedness and separateness as a primary strain within all relationships. If one side wins this me-we tug-of-war, the relationship loses:

> No relationship can exist by definition unless the parties sacrifice some individual autonomy. However, too much connection paradoxically destroys the relationship because the individual identities become lost.[8]

Throughout *Children of a Lesser God*, Sarah evidences a "stay away close" ambivalence that illustrates the connectedness-separateness dilemma. For example, from the time she first melts against James while dancing, she shows a strong desire for a close and lasting bond. Even after a bitter breakup, she confesses to her mother that she's lonely without him. And at the end of the film she declares to James, "I don't want to be without you."

But Sarah also experiences a need for separateness at least as strong as her drive for connection. When James tries to make small talk by asking why she likes cleaning floors, she emphatically signs that the job gives her the chance to work alone—in silence! (End of conversation.) Her fierce independence is fueled by a fear of being hurt. After James tells her that a girl once broke his heart, Sarah claims that no one could hurt her. If ever forced to admit that another person has caused her pain, she would "shrivel up and die."

Bakhtin wrote that dialectical moments were occasions for honest dialogue. Out of the agony of her conflicting desires for both intimacy and independence, Sarah communicates a relational truth that could have been scripted by Bakhtin or Baxter, who believe that bonding occurs only as parties experience an interdependence with *and* an independence from each other. Sarah slowly draws the

"At this point, my privacy needs are interfering with my intimacy goals."

open thumb and forefinger of each hand together with the explanation, "This sign—to connect—simple, but it means so much more when I do this." Sarah then closes together the thumb and forefinger of each hand to form interlocking links of a chain and continues:

> Now it means to be joined in a relationship—separate, but one. That's what I want. But you think for me—think for Sarah—as though there were no "I." "She will be with me, quit her job, learn how to play poker, leave Orin's party, learn how to speak." That's all you, not me. Until you let me be an "I" the way you are, you can never come inside my silence and know me. And I won't let myself know you. Until that time, we can't be like this—joined.

Certainty and Uncertainty

Berger's uncertainty reduction theory makes a strong case for the idea that people want predictability in their relationships (see Chapter 10). Baxter and Montgomery don't question our human search for interpersonal certainty, but they are convinced that Berger makes a mistake by ignoring our equal desire for novelty. We want the bit of mystery, the touch of spontaneity, the occasional surprise that are necessary for having fun. Without the spice of variety to season our time together, the relationship becomes bland, boring, and, ultimately, emotionally dead.

The certainty-uncertainty dialectic weaves through Sarah and James' relationship. As she admits at the end of the film, Sarah constantly uses her anger to push James away. When this doesn't work, she withdraws from the conversation. The emotional distance is safe and predictable. We see this recurring hit-and-run tactic when James, in street clothes, crouches down at the edge of a swimming pool and begins to declare his love to Sarah, who is in the water. She quickly kicks away from the side of the pool. But the patterned interaction takes a novel twist when James loses his balance as he imploringly says, "Sarah, I think I'm falling in lo—, into the pool with you." His unexpected entry into the water breaks through her defenses and she swims to him for their first kiss.

Not all surprises are welcome. As the love relationship between James and Sarah deepens, he promises he will never ask her to speak. Yet in a moment of passion, he begs her just once to say his name. Despite his protest that the plea "just came out," this sudden request breaks trust and shatters a comfortable routine. In this case Sarah desires certainty, whereas James wants novelty. Throughout much of the film their desires are the other way around, but the dialectic is always present.

Openness and Closedness

Halfway through *Children of a Lesser God* James asks Sarah, "What do you hear? I mean, is it just silence?" Sarah's response indicates the depth of her isolation, "No one has ever gotten in there to find out." James then asks if she will ever let him in, but his question is met only with stillness—Sarah's silence. From this scene we might conclude that Sarah is simply an extremely private person; yet earlier in the film she had openly revealed the humiliating details of adolescent sexual encounters. The two scenes seem contradictory.

You might recall that Irwin Altman, one of the founders of social penetration theory, ultimately came to the conclusion that self-disclosure and privacy operated in a cyclical or wavelike fashion over time.[9] Baxter and Montgomery pick up on Altman's recognition that relationships aren't on a straight-line path to intimacy. They see the pressures for openness and closedness waxing and waning like phases of the moon. The existence of an openness-closedness dialectic means that a person's need to "tell all" is countered by a natural desire for secrecy. If Sarah's communication seems somewhat schizophrenic, it's because the dialectical forces for transparency and discretion are hard to juggle.

PARALLEL DIALECTICS BETWEEN COUPLE AND COMMUNITY: INCLUSION-SECLUSION, CONVENTIONALITY-UNIQUENESS, REVELATION-CONCEALMENT

By now you can appreciate why Baxter and Montgomery claim that personal relationships are always in flux. The inherent contradictions within friendship, romance, and kinship make it impossible for pairs to relax into any sort of settled state. Even as partners struggle with the internal strains of a relationship vis-à-vis each other, as a couple they also face parallel yin-yang tensions with people in their social networks and the community at large. The right-hand column of Figure 12.1 displays three *external* dialectics that match the internal ones I've already reviewed. James and Sarah had to confront each of these contradictions as they became a couple in the context of a school community.

Inclusion and Seclusion

According to Baxter and Montgomery, a couple needs an abundance of privacy until the two parties have worked out a unique code of meanings and the relationship has jelled. In American culture, deliberate exclusion of outsiders is an act that crystallizes the pair as a social unit. The more they assert their autonomy from society, the more they establish a unique subculture. Yet even for the most devoted partners, tolerance for isolation wears thin after a while. Other people can be a source of stimulation to overcome the ho-hum predictability that settles in on a secluded pair. Third parties can also provide the social support that legitimizes the relationship of friends or lovers.

In *Children of a Lesser God,* Sarah and James spend almost all their free time alone with each other. Attempts to integrate their dyadic subculture with larger social networks turn out to be dismal flops. Sarah is patronized by the faculty at the headmaster's poker party. She also feels alienated from James' students who are learning to talk. James feels equally left out in the frantic silence of signing at a reception where all the guests are deaf. He peevishly blows across the top of a Coke bottle just to hear a sound. James and Sarah's fictional relationship is still fresh when the film ends, but the couple's inability to work out a balance between inclusion and seclusion with outsiders doesn't bode well for the future of their relationship.

Conventionality and Uniqueness

The school where James teaches discourages innovation. During the employment interview the headmaster warns James that no one there is trying to change the world. The message is clear—go along to get along.

Baxter and Montgomery note that society has a stake in seeing its relational patterns reproduced. Excessive uniqueness makes others feel uncomfortable. But pressure to conform is only one force a couple feels. Since a carbon-copy relationship doesn't provide the sense of uniqueness necessary for intimacy, a close pair also experiences a pressure to be different. Here again, the couple is caught in a dilemma.

James ignores the headmaster's advice to conform. His love affair with Sarah is anything but conventional. He is "normal"; she cannot hear and does not speak. He's a trained professional; she scrubs floors. The couple argue often and their confrontations are punctuated with obscene gestures. They don't "fit in." Yet even in the midst of their maverick relationship, James assumes that he and Sarah will enact traditional roles. They will marry and have children; she will quit her job; he will take care of her. The contradictory forces of conventionality and uniqueness are always at work.

Revelation and Concealment

Just as the contradiction between openness and closedness is a central tension a couple encounters within a relationship, the decision about what to tell others is a fundamental dilemma partners face within their social networks. Baxter and Montgomery note that each possible advantage of "going public" is offset by a corresponding potential danger. For example, approval from significant others could legitimate the relationship, but there's no guarantee support will be forthcoming. Or one partner might gain added pleasure by sharing the news with a friend or relative, but the confidant may be indiscreet and gossip with others.

Public disclosure is a relational rite of passage signaling a partner that the tie that binds them together is strong. But this kind of reassurance comes at the cost of privacy—a nonrecurring resource that gives a couple some breathing room to work out problems. Aware that strategic management of their "public relations" is a crucial matter, most couples mete out information bit by bit to carefully selected friends. But occasionally news of their bond "leaks out" through nonverbal behavior. This happened with James and Sarah. Mr. Franklin, the school's director, sees James running barefoot from Sarah's apartment. Franklin conveys his knowledge of the romance when he later returns James' shoe—retrieved from the bottom of the swimming pool. The only verbal acknowledgment that either man gives of this new state of affairs is

Franklin's indirect warning, "Be careful, Jimbo." A couple's link to the outside world will always be problematic.

DEALING WITH DIALECTICAL TENSION: COMPETENCE IN THE FACE OF CONTRADICTION

Confronted with the ongoing contradictions cited above, how is it that some close relationships manage to survive and, in a few instances, thrive? Baxter and Montgomery catalogue eight strategies that people use in order to cope with the opposing pressures that come with the relational territory. As you will see, some of the strategies are used more often than others, and not all prove equally satisfying. From a dialectical perspective, the ultimate effectiveness of a strategy depends on how well it realizes, reflects, and re-creates the contradictory nature of social reality.[10] A couple is interactionally competent to the extent that they can sustain an honest dialogue about the tension.

1. **Denial** is the not particularly helpful practice of continually responding to one pole of a dialectic while ignoring the other. For example, throughout much of the film, Sarah opts for separateness over connection, closedness instead of open expression, and surprise in lieu of predictability. Sarah isn't necessarily pleased with the choices she's made, and in this she's not alone. Baxter discovered that romantic partners who used denial strategies were often dissatisfied with how they handled the tension between autonomy and connection.[11]

2. **Disorientation** is a nonfunctional response that arises from an utter feeling of helplessness. Rather than denying the contradictions they confront, relational partners are overwhelmed by them. Whatever the result—fight, freeze, or flight—dialogue about the dilemma stops. When Sarah and James were stuck between the worlds of speech and silence, a disoriented James lashed out. A frightened Sarah ran away.

3. **Spiraling alteration** between contrasting poles is the process of separating the dialectical forces over time by responding to one pull now, the other pull later. According to Baxter and Montgomery, the ebb and flow practice of a first-one-then-the-other pole is the most common response of partners to the separateness-connection paradox. Such an irregular spiraling shift certainly describes James' efforts to connect with Sarah. His moves to draw close emotionally and physically are interspersed with fierce arguments or solitary retreats into music that only he can hear. These times of autonomy end with an apology, and then a new cycle of connectedness and separation begins—but never from quite the same place as before.

4. **Segmentation** is a tactic of compartmentalization by which partners isolate different aspects of their relationship. Some issues and activities resonate with one dialectical tug, while other concerns and actions resonate with the opposing pull. Sarah, for example, is transparent with James about her history with boys and her feelings of anger. On the other hand, her reason for avoiding speech is a taboo topic in their relationship.[12] Baxter and Montgomery claim

that along with denial and spiraling inversion, segmentation is a typical way that people deal with dialectics.

5. *Balance* is a compromise approach that promotes ongoing dialogue because partners see both dialectical poles as equally legitimate. However, attempts to strike a happy medium falter because they muffle or mute the full force of conflicting demands. Sarah tries to take pleasure in James' passion for a Bach sonata, but her request for him to "show me the music" merely increases his sadness. He turns off the stereo and signs, "I can't enjoy it . . . because you can't." The attempt to balance opposing forces is based on a view of intimacy as a "zero-sum game." Whenever one party wins, the other loses, and the supply of benefits is never sufficient to meet the demand.

6. *Integration* offers a way for parties to simultaneously respond to opposing forces without dilution or delusion. Montgomery illustrates the process by quoting the words of a couple who embraced their opposing relational needs for certainty and uncertainty: "We have one steadfast rule that every Friday night we do something new that we've never done before."[13] Baxter suggests that a "traditional" married couple could conceive of their relationship as unique because they've stayed together for thirty-five years.

7. *Recalibration* is the process of temporarily reframing a situation so that the tugs and pulls on partners no longer seem to be in opposite directions. At various points in the film, James labels Sarah's distancing as "stubbornness," an interpretation that allows him to assume that she will, in time, seek only intimacy. But recalibration is a mental gymnastic that offers no permanent resolution to a very real dilemma. Ultimately James has to contend with Sarah's dual desires for intimacy and autonomy—a tension that will always be in force.

8. *Reaffirmation* involves an active recognition by both partners that dialectical tensions will never go away. Instead of bemoaning this relational fact of life, these rare couples acknowledge and celebrate the rich complexity of their relationship. "If we weren't so close," they remind each other, "we wouldn't be having all these problems."

In the final scene of *Children of a Lesser God,* Sarah reaffirms her intense desire for connectedness *and* separateness by closing together the thumb and forefinger of each hand to form the interlocking links of a chain. She asks James, "Do you think we could find a place where we can meet—not in silence, and not in sound?" From Baxter and Montgomery's dialectical perspective, the answer is in doubt. Even if the couple were to find such a place, other contradictions would intrude. Close relationships are always in flux. Hollywood may offer the impression that James and Sarah "lived happily ever after," but a true-to-life tag line for their story would read, "and the struggle continues." That realistic assessment might seem discouraging. Yet when we appreciate the fact that healthy relationships need both connectedness and separateness, certainty and uncertainty, closeness and openness, the prospect of future dialectical work seems more like a promise than a threat.

CRITIQUE: WHAT DO WE DO WITH A RELATIONAL MESS?

Figure 12.2 is an attempt to picture the complexity of real-life relationships as described by Baxter and Montgomery. Note that each of the relational forces discussed in this chapter is drawn in tension with every other pole. For example, *openness* is not only in opposition with *closedness,* but with *certainty, separateness, conventionality,* and all the other relational forces.

This chaotic jumble of contradictions is far removed from such ideal notions of communication as *shared meaning, warm communion,* or *increasing certainty.* Yet I find that the authors' image of intimacy resonates with the experience of many students in my classes. Does this first-person testimony validate the relational dialectics perspective? For Baxter and Montgomery, it does. Traditional social scientists aren't so sure. They are bothered by the anecdotal nature of the support that dialectical researchers present.

Baxter and Montgomery claim that the only way we'll spot the messiness of relationships is by being willing to listen to varied voices that offer inconsistent accounts of relational communication, which is laced with multiple contradictions. While not discounting empirical data, they urge scholars to pay attention to everyday conversations, diary entries, historical narratives, and stories people tell themselves in novels and movies. This means that the film *Children of a Lesser God* validates, as well as illustrates, the dialectical perspective. I urge you to pay a visit to your local video store so that you can decide for yourself.

If we accept the basic premise that close relationships are "indeterminate processes of ongoing flux," do we automatically become cynics who sneer at friendship, romance, and family solidarity? Not necessarily. A jaundiced view of intimacy is often the result of failed relationships. A realistic appreciation of the effort required to sustain a close relationship can strengthen our resolve not to bail out when things are turbulent.

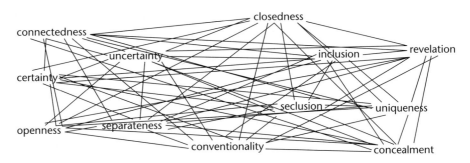

FIGURE 12.2 **The Messiness of Personal Relationships**

Barbara Montgomery goes one step further. At the conclusion of an article on relational dialectics she suggests that living in the midst of contradictions can actually be fun.

> I have been told that riding a unicycle becomes enjoyable when you accept that you are constantly in the process of falling. The task then becomes one of continually playing one force against another, countering one pull with an opposing motion and adapting the wheel under you so that you remain in movement by maintaining and controlling the fall. If successful, one is propelled along in a state of sustained imbalance that is sometimes awkward and sometimes elegant. From a dialectical perspective, sustaining a relationship seems to be a very similar process.[14]

QUESTIONS TO SHARPEN YOUR FOCUS

1. How many different synonyms and terms can you list that capture what Baxter and Montgomery mean by the word *dialectic?*

2. Which of the nine theories discussed in previous chapters would Baxter and Montgomery consider simplistic or antidialectical?

3. What *conflicting pulls* place the most strain on your closest personal relationship? What *strategy* do you and your partner use to deal with that *tension?*

4. Why wouldn't typical scale items like the one below reveal dialectical tension even if it exists?

What do you want from your partner?

Intimacy   :____:____:____:____:____:____:____: Independence

A SECOND LOOK

Recommended resource: Leslie A. Baxter and Barbara M. Montgomery, *Relating: Dialogues and Dialectics*, Guilford, New York, 1996.

Relational implications of Bakhtin's worldview: Leslie A. Baxter, "Thinking Dialogically about Communication in Personal Relationships," in *Uses of "STRUCTURE" in Communication Studies*, Richard L. Conville (ed.), Praeger, Westport, Conn., 1994, pp. 23–37.

Bakhtin—primary source: Mikhail Bakhtin, *The Dialogic Imagination*, Michael Holquist (ed.), Caryl Emerson and Holquist (trans.), University of Texas, Austin, 1981.

Bakhtin—secondary source: John Shotter and Michael Billig, "A Bakhtinian Psychology: From Out of the Heads of Individuals and into the Dialogues between Them," in *Bakhtin and the Human Sciences*, Michael Bell and Michael Gardiner (eds.), Sage, Thousand Oaks, Calif., 1998, pp. 13–29.

Relationship maintenance: Barbara Montgomery, "Relationship Maintenance Versus Relationship Change: A Dialectical Dilemma," *Journal of Social and Personal Relationships*, Vol. 10, 1993, pp. 205–224.

Relationship maintenance: Leslie Baxter and E. P. Simon, "Relationship Maintenance Strategies and Dialectical Contradiction in Personal Relationships," *Journal of Social and Personal Relationships,* Vol. 10, 1993, pp. 225–242.

Couples and/or culture: Barbara Montgomery, "Communication as the Interface Between Couples and Culture," *Human Communication Yearbook 15,* Stanley Deetz (ed.), Sage, Newbury Park, 1992, pp. 475–507.

Future research: Leslie A. Baxter and Barbara M. Montgomery, "Rethinking Communication in Personal Relationships from a Dialectical Perspective," in *A Handbook of Personal Relationships,* 2nd edition, Steve Duck (ed.), John Wiley & Sons, New York, 1997, pp. 325–349.

Friendship dialectics: William Rawlins, *Friendship Matters: Communication, Dialectics, and the Life Course,* Aldine de Gruyter, New York, 1992.

Family dialectics: Arthur Bochner and E. Eisenberg, "Family Process: System Perspectives," in *Handbook of Communication Science,* Charles Berger and Stephen Chaffee (eds.), Sage, Beverly Hills, Calif., 1987, pp. 540–563.

Relationships in flux: Richard Conville, *Relational Transitions,* Praeger, New York, 1991.

Comparing, contrasting, and critiquing different dialectical approaches: Barbara M. Montgomery and Leslie A. Baxter (eds.), *Dialectical Approaches to Studying Personal Relationships,* Lawrence Erlbaum Associates, Mahwah, N.J., 1998.

INFLUENCE

We live in a world of intentional interpersonal influence. It's hard to go through the day without having two or three people try to persuade you to spend time, energy, or money on something important to them. The *Godfather* genre of films equates persuasion with physical force; *Pulp Fiction* is a notable example. Yet even when said with a smile, the announcement that someone is going to make an offer that can't be refused is more interesting to the field of psychopathology than it is to communication scholars. Most rhetorical and communication theorists reserve the term *persuasion*

for intentional influence that is more voluntary than coerced. Few persuasion situations are strictly one or the other.

Some persuasion researchers focus solely on the verbal strategies people use to elicit behavioral compliance to their wishes. A study of compliance-gaining strategies usually asks people to imagine being in an uncomfortable interpersonal situation.[1] For example, the guy next door is hosting a wild midnight party while you're trying to sleep, your roommate's obnoxious guest has already stayed a week; or you need to borrow a car from someone you

"The old persuasive approach is out. From now on, they put out their campfires or you bite them."

barely know. The researcher then questions you about the tactics you'd use to get the other person to do what you want.

Typically, you would rank a predetermined list of compliance-gaining strategies—promises, threats, explanations, hints, compliments, warnings, accusations, direct requests, and so forth.

Advocates of compliance-gaining inquiry stress the importance of finding out what verbal strategies people actually use, rather than focusing on what they could say or might do to achieve their goal. Although the studies provide rich descriptive data, they aren't theory based and they have yet to generate insights with which to build new theory. There has been little explanation of why people select the tactics they do, prediction of what they would do next time, evaluation of how well the tactics work, or concern with application to other situations.

In contrast with the effort to catalogue compliance-gaining strategies, most persuasion theorists focus on voluntary shifts in attitude that come in response to verbal messages. Attitudes are internal responses made up of what people think, feel, and intend to do. Since attitudes can be known only through self-report, researchers usually ask lots of questions:

"What do you honestly believe?" (*Cognitive*)

"Is your heart really in it?" (*Affective*)

"What do you plan to do?" (*Behavioral*)

For many years, social scientists defined the combined answers as a "predisposition to respond" and were content to regard marks on unidimensional seven-point scales as synonymous with a person's inner attitude. See the example at the foot of this page.

But the marginal relationship between a person's stated opinion and subsequent behavior has proved a continual embarrassment for those who claim that attitudes predict actions. Although it makes the study of persuasion more complicated, researchers are increasingly treating attitudes as multidimensional constructs.[2]

In their textbook on persuasion, Richard Petty and John Cacioppo group theories of attitude change into seven major approaches:[3]

1. **Conditioning and Modeling.** Approaches that assume people seek to "maximize their benefits and minimize their costs." Persuasion is successful when people vicariously observe or directly experience rewards for "right" opinions and behavior. Social exchange theory (see pages 130–133) operates within this framework.

2. **Message-Learning.** Approaches that place a premium on the content of persuasion. Lasting influence depends on attention, comprehension, and retention of messages. Aristotle's *Rhetoric* (see Chapter 20) emphasizes the importance of logical appeals.

3. **Perceptual-Judgmental.** Approaches that are less concerned with what a message states than how it is interpreted by the person who hears it. The same message can strike two people as radically different. Chapter 13 presents Muzafer Sherif's social judgment theory. It examines the effect of different

Cigarette smoking causes cancer.

1	2	3	4	5	6	7
Strongly Disagree	Disagree	Slightly Disagree	No Opinion	Slightly Agree	Agree	Strongly Agree

amounts of discrepancy between the position advocated and the stand of the recipient.

4. **Motivational.** Approaches that focus on needs as forces for change. Persuasion scholars have concentrated on the need for consistency as a stimulus to attitude change. For example, Leon Festinger's cognitive dissonance theory makes the counterintuitive prediction that we are most likely to change our attitudes to match our actions when we are given but a minimal justification for changing that behavior.[4]

5. **Attributional.** Approaches that stress the power of self-fulfilling prophecy. Symbolic interactionism (see Chapter 4) emphasizes the self-fulfilling effect of the looking-glass selves that form our generalized other. Attributional theories consider attribution of attitude as a persuasive technique. Rather than raise resistance by pointing out a lack or failing in the other person, the advocate affirms the existence of the desired attitude as if it were already firmly in place.

6. **Combinatory.** Approaches that consider the way new ideas are weighted and averaged into previously held beliefs. These theories employ precise mathematical models to describe how the information is processed.

7. **Self-Persuasion.** Approaches that regard self-generated arguments as more potent agents of change than any external message. The process can be triggered by role-playing, by active involvement in a cause, or merely by wrestling with ideas that are linked to the attitude.

Despite the fact that some of these approaches offer conflicting explanations for changes in attitude, no one set of theories has emerged as the best way to view the persuasion process. Petty and Cacioppo's elaboration-likelihood model is a cognitive model that attempts to pull together the wisdom found in each approach. They see two distinct routes to attitude change in the mind of a person who hears or reads a persuasive message. The central route involves active consideration of message content; the peripheral route uses the credibility of the message source and other persuasion cues to determine a response. Chapter 14 presents Petty and Cacioppo's model, which explores the likelihood that people will use the central route and scrutinize the message.

CHAPTER 13

Social Judgment Theory

of Muzafer Sherif

My son Jim is an airline pilot. As he walks through the airport he hears all sorts of comments about air safety. I've listed eleven statements that reflect the range of attitudes he has heard expressed. Read through these opinions, and taste the diversity of viewpoint they represent.

- **a.** Air traffic controllers are overworked.
- **b.** All life is risk. Flying is like anything else.
- **c.** Complex jet planes are disasters waiting to happen.
- **d.** The crowded skies are a myth.
- **e.** Flying is safer than taking a train.
- **f.** Many pilots are flying while they are under the influence of alcohol.
- **g.** The most dangerous part of flying is the drive to the airport.
- **h.** Most mistakes are fatal at 30,000 feet.
- **i.** There are old pilots. There are bold pilots. There are no old, bold pilots.
- **j.** American pilots are the best-trained in the world.
- **k.** United States government regulations ensure well-maintained airplanes.

Take a few minutes to mark your reactions to these statements. If you follow each instruction given below before jumping ahead to the next one, you'll have a chance to experience what social judgment theory predicts.

1. To begin, read through the items again and underline the single statement that most closely represents your point of view.
2. Now look and see whether any other items seem reasonable. Circle the letters in front of these acceptable statements.
3. Reread the opinions and determine the one that strikes you as most objectionable. Run a line through the whole sentence.

4. Finally, cross out the letters in front of any other statements that are objectionable to you. By crossing out these unreasonable ideas, it's possible that all eleven statements will end up marked one way or another. It's also possible that you'll leave some items unmarked.

ATTITUDES AS LATITUDES: ACCEPTANCE, REJECTION, AND NONCOMMITMENT

I've just taken you through on paper what social judgment theory says happens in the head. We hear a message and immediately judge where it should be placed on the attitude scale in our mind. According to Carolyn Sherif, Muzafer Sherif, and Roger Nebergall, this subconscious sorting out of ideas occurs at the instant of perception. We weigh every new idea by comparing it with our present point of view. They call their analysis of attitudes "the social judgment-involvement approach," but most scholars refer to it simply as "social judgment theory." Although Carolyn Sherif is the first author of the book describing the process, it is commonly acknowledged that her husband took the lead in the theory's development and testing.

A psychologist who was associated with the University of Oklahoma, Muzafer Sherif had already published two landmark studies demonstrating how individuals are influenced by reference groups, groups that members use to define their identity. His "autokinetic effect" research stimulated scores of later studies analyzing conformity pressure;[1] his "robber's cave" study explored ways to reduce intergroup conflict.[2] Both studies found that people's perceptions are altered dramatically by group membership. Social judgment theory extended his concern with perception to the field of persuasion.

Sherif believed that each of the four steps listed above is necessary to determine your attitude toward airline safety, or any other attitude structure. He wrote that an "individual's stand is not represented adequately as a point along a continuum. Different persons espousing the same position may differ considerably in their tolerance around this point."[3]

He saw an attitude as an amalgam of three zones. The first zone is called the "latitude of acceptance." It's made up of the item you underlined and any others you circled as acceptable. A second zone is the "latitude of rejection." It consists of the opinions you crossed out as objectionable. The leftover statements, if any, define the "latitude of noncommitment." These were the items that you found neither objectionable nor acceptable. They're akin to marking "undecided" or "no opinion" on a traditional attitude survey. Sherif said we need to know the location and width of each of these interrelated latitudes in order to describe a person's attitude structure.

Suppose Jim encounters a man named Ned who is grumbling in the airport about the dangers of flight. Jim wants to persuade Ned that flying is safer than sleeping in his own bed. Social judgment theory recommends that he try to figure out the breadth and location of Ned's three latitudes before presenting his

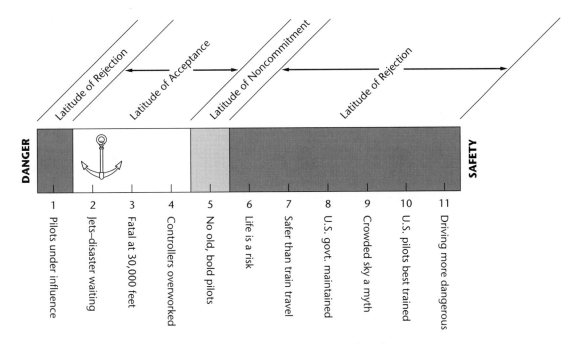

FIGURE 13.1   Ned's Cognitive Map Regarding Air Safety

case. Figure 13.1 shows where Ned places those eleven statements along the mental yardstick he uses to gauge safety. Armed with knowledge about the location and breadth of the three latitudes, my son would realize that Ned's high ego-involvement in the topic of air safety will cause him to twist any words of reassurance.

EGO-INVOLVEMENT—THE CERTAINTY OF THOSE WHO CARE

Ego-involvement refers to how crucial an issue is in our lives. Is it important? Is it central to our well-being? Does our attitude on the matter go a long way in defining who we are?

Some people walking down the concourse at the airport are mere visitors. They are meeting Aunt Juanita's plane, picking up a suitcase for a friend, or perhaps having a business lunch at the airport restaurant. These folks are all for smooth flights and no crashes, but air safety isn't their major concern. They don't stew over it, argue about it, or get sweaty palms when they hear a jet take off. According to Sherif, they have low ego-involvement.

For Ned and others, the issue is central. As frequent flyers, they swap horror stories of near misses with fellow travelers, read accounts of accidents in the newspaper, and shudder when they recall a rough landing on a foggy night.

People who fit this profile are highly ego-involved. Some even join an airline passenger association that lobbies Congress for stricter safety regulations. One way Sherif defined high ego-involvement was "membership in a group with a known stand." My son's pilot's license, ALPA union card, and employment with a major airline are indications that he's at least as ego-involved in the issue as Ned. Of course, his confidence in airline safety is at the other end of the spectrum.

Three features of Ned's attitude structure are typical of people with high ego-involvement in an issue. The first indication is that his latitude of noncommitment is almost nonexistent. People who don't care about an issue usually have a wide latitude of noncommitment, but Ned has only one statement in that category. He may not be sure about old, bold pilots, but he has definite opinions on everything else.

Second, Ned rejects all six statements that offer, in varying degrees, assurances of safety. According to social judgment theory, a wide latitude of rejection is a sign of high ego-involvement. Ned has intense feelings about the potential dangers of flying; he sees safety as a black-and-white issue. Persons with low ego-involvement would probably see more grays. Note that the effects of high ego-involvement on perception may be similar to those of low cognitive complexity (see Chapter 8). In both cases we may end up blurring together differences that could make a difference.

Finally, the "jets are disasters waiting to happen" statement, which best represents Ned's point of view, is relatively extreme. I've marked the place on the scale with a large anchor. Sherif said that's what our favored position does; it anchors all our other thoughts about the topic. If air safety were only a casual concern for Ned, it would be fitting to represent his stand with a small anchor that could easily be dragged to a new position. But since his fear of flying is deep-seated, a hefty anchor is more appropriate.

People who hold extreme opinions on either side of an issue almost always care deeply. While it's possible to feel passionately about middle-of-the-road positions, social judgment theory states that massive attitude anchors are usually found toward the ends of the scale. Extreme positions and high ego-involvement go together. That's why religion, sex, and politics are taboo topics in the wardroom of a U.S. Navy ship at sea. When passions run deep, radical opinions are common, and there's little tolerance for diversity.

Everything I've presented up to this point is Sherif's conception of the cognitive structure of attitudes. We need to understand the relationship between ego involvement and latitudes of acceptance, rejection, and noncommitment in order to appreciate the mental processes that social judgment theory says occur when a person takes notice of a message.

According to Sherif, persuasion is a two-step process. The first stage occurs when people hear (or read) a message and automatically evaluate where they think it falls vis-à-vis their own position. That's the perceptual judgment part of social judgment. In the second stage, people adjust their attitude toward or away from the message they heard. The next two sections outline these two processes.

JUDGING THE MESSAGE: CONTRAST AND ASSIMILATION ERRORS

Sherif claimed that we use our own anchored attitude as a comparison point when we hear a discrepant message. He believed there was a parallel between systematic biases in psychophysical judgments and the way we determine other people's attitudes. I've set up three pails of water in my class to illustrate this principle. Even though the contents looked the same, the water in the left bucket was just above freezing, the water in the right bucket was just below scalding, and the water in the middle bucket was lukewarm. A student volunteered to put his left hand in the left bucket and his right hand in the right bucket at the same time. Twenty seconds was about all he could take. I then asked him to plunge both hands in the middle bucket and to judge the temperature of the water. Of course this was a baffling request, because his left hand "told" him the water was hot, while his right hand sent a message that it was cold.

Sherif hypothesized a similar *contrast* effect when people who are "hot" for an idea hear a message on the topic that doesn't have the same fire. Judged by their standard, even warm messages strike them as cold. Sherif's *social judgment-involvement* label nicely captures the idea of a link between ego-involvement and perception. Highly committed people have large latitudes of rejection. Any message that falls within that range will be perceived by them as more discrepant from their anchor than it really is. The message is mentally pushed away to a position that is farther out, and the hearer doesn't have to deal with it as a viable option.

All of this is bad news for Jim. Suppose he walks up to Ned and calmly explains that the crowded skies are a myth. On his last five flights he's never seen another plane, much less had to dodge one. If Ned hears this as Jim intended, that message is a 9 on his mental scale. However, social judgment theory says he probably won't hear it that way. Despite Jim's well-intentioned effort, his words will strike nervous Ned as self-serving pilot propaganda. Unless a message is crystal clear, the contrast effect telescopes all unacceptable positions and pushes them farther away. Jim's supposedly reassuring words of ample separation between aircraft will register at a 10 or 11 rather than a 9.

Contrast is a perceptual distortion that leads to polarization of ideas. But it happens only when a message falls within the latitude of rejection. *Assimilation* is the opposite error of judgment. It's the rubber band effect that draws an idea toward the hearer's anchor so that it seems that she and the speaker share the same opinion. Assimilation takes place when a message falls within the latitude of acceptance. For example, suppose Jim tells Ned that air traffic controllers are overworked. Although that message is at 4 on Ned's cognitive map, he will hear it as more similar to his anchoring attitude than it really is, perhaps a 3.

"I'm happy to say that my final judgment of a case is almost always consistent with my prejudgment of the case."

Sherif was unclear as to how people judge a message that falls within their latitude of noncommitment. Most interpreters assume that neither bias would kick in and that the message would be heard roughly as intended.

DISCREPANCY AND ATTITUDE CHANGE

Judging how close or far a message is from our own anchored position is the first stage of attitude change. Shifting our anchor in response is the second. Sherif thought that both processes usually take place below the level of consciousness.

According to social judgment theory, once we've judged a new message to be within our latitude of acceptance, we will adjust our attitude somewhat to accommodate that new input. The persuasive effect will be positive but partial. We won't travel the whole distance, but there will be some measurable movement toward the speaker's perceived position. How much movement? Sherif wasn't specific, but he did claim that the greater the discrepancy, the more hearers will adjust their attitudes *as long as the message falls within their latitude of acceptance.*

If we've judged a new message to be within our latitude of rejection, we may also adjust our attitude, but in this case *away from* what we think the speaker is advocating. Since people who are highly ego-involved in a topic have broad ranges of rejection, most messages aimed to persuade them are in danger of actually driving them further away. This predicted "boomerang effect" suggests that people are often *driven* rather than *drawn* to the attitude positions they occupy.

Even though Sherif crafted a cognitive theory, the mental processes he describes are quite mechanical, or unthinking. He reduced interpersonal influence to the issue of the distance between the message and the hearer's position:

> Stripped to its bare essential, the problem of attitude change is the problem of the degree of discrepancy from communication and the felt necessity of coping with the discrepancy.[4]

The only space for volition in social judgment theory is the choice of alternative messages available to the speaker or writer.

PRACTICAL ADVICE FOR THE PERSUADER

Sherif would have advised Jim to avoid messages that claim flying is safer than driving or train travel. Ned simply won't believe them, and they may push him even deeper into his anti-aviation stance. For maximum influence, Jim should select a message that's right on the edge of Ned's latitude of acceptance. Admit that radar operators are overworked, but stress the care pilots take to compensate for possible controller mistakes. Or use the statement about the old, bold pilot, showing him how the airline systematically screens out daredevils. According to social judgment theory, this strategy will result in a small amount of positive persuasion.

Jim wants more. But Sherif would have cautioned that it's all Jim can get in a one-shot attempt. If he were talking to an open-minded person with a broad latitude of acceptance, a bigger shift would be possible. But when he's dealing with a highly ego-involved traveler, he has to work within a narrow range. True conversion from one end of the scale to the other is a rare phenomenon. The only way to get large-scale change is through a series of small, successive movements. Persuasion is a gradual process.

It's also a social process. The lack of interpersonal bond between Jim and Ned limits the amount of influence that's possible. If Ned heard strong reassurances of airline safety from his friends and family, it might occasion a major shift. Sherif noted that "most dramatic cases of attitude change, the most widespread and enduring, are those involving changes in reference groups with differing values."[5]

EVIDENCE THAT ARGUES FOR ACCEPTANCE

Research on the predictions of social judgment theory requires highly ego-involving issues. For example, one recent study that supports the theory's two-stage hypothesis presented a pro-choice message on abortion to members of a pro-life activist organization.[6] Another queried people on their attitude toward public disclosure of HIV test results.[7] An early experiment employed a topic vitally important to college students—sleep.[8] Before the study, most of the undergraduates accepted the conventional wisdom that the human body functions best with eight hours of sleep at night. They read an article written by an expert in the field that claimed young adults actually need much less. The message was the same for all with one crucial difference. Some students were told they needed eight hours, some seven, some six, and so on, right down the line. The final group actually read that humans need no sleep at all! Then all of them had a chance to give their opinions.

Sherif's theory suggests that the fewer hours recommended, the more students will be swayed until they begin to regard the message as patently ridiculous. The results shown in Figure 13.2 confirm this prediction. Persuasion increased as the hours advocated were reduced to three, a message that caused students to revise their estimate of optimum sleep down to 6.3 hours. Anything less than three hours fell outside their latitude of acceptance and ceased to be as effective.

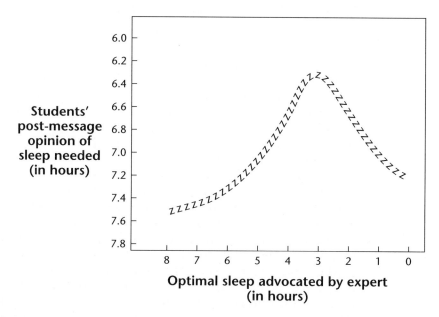

FIGURE 13.2   Sleep Study Results
(Adapted from Bochner and Insko, "Communicator Discrepancy, Source Credibility and Opinion Change.")

Three things have become clear as the theory has been tested:

1. A highly credible speaker can stretch the hearer's latitude of acceptance. When the "expert" in the sleep study was a Nobel Prize-winning physiologist rather than a YMCA director, persuasion increased.

2. Ambiguity can often serve better than clarity. When George Bush said on the campaign trail that he wanted a "kinder, gentler nation," nobody knew exactly what he meant, but it sounded good, so the statement fell within their latitude of acceptance. Tanya Donnelly, the lead singer for "Belly," takes the same approach. She says that she writes lyrics that are intentionally vague so as to appeal to a wider audience.[9]

3. There are some people who are dogmatic on every issue. "Don't confuse me with the facts," they say. "My mind is made up." These cantankerous souls have a chronically wide latitude of rejection.

A striking story of social judgment theory in action comes from a university development director I know who was making a call on a rich alumnus. He anticipated that the prospective donor would give as much as $10,000. He made his pitch and asked what the wealthy businessman could do. The man protested that it had been a lean year and that times were tough—he couldn't possibly contribute more than $20,000. The fundraiser figured that he had seriously underestimated the giver's latitude of acceptance and that $20,000 was on the low end of that range. Without missing a beat he replied, "Trevor, do you really think that's enough?" The alumnus wrote a check for $25,000.

CRITIQUE: HOW WIDE IS YOUR THEORETICAL LATITUDE OF ACCEPTANCE?

How do you feel about the ploy described above? The persuasive technique obviously worked, but the application of social judgment theory raises some thorny ethical questions. Is it legitimate for fund-raisers to alter their pitch based on a potential donor's latitude of acceptance? Is it all right for politicians to be intentionally vague so their message has broad appeal? Or consider my son's genuine desire to allay the fears of the flying public. The theory claims Jim will be more effective by presenting a soft-sell message at midscale rather than stating his genuine conviction that flying is safer than driving. Is this honest?

There are other problems with the theory that you might ponder as well. Like all cognitive explanations, social judgment theory assumes a mental structure and process that goes on "behind the eyes" where no one can see it. Do people really carry a set of scales around in their head that they use to gauge every idea they hear? How do we know? And if Sherif's three latitudes are really there, how can persuasion practitioners discover where they fall? That's what audience analysis and market research are all about, but it's hard to imagine Jim handing a questionnaire to a jittery traveler in the departure lounge.

As one who would like to have a positive influence, I appreciate Sherif's warning of the potential backlash I may create when I push a proposal that falls deep within the other's latitude of rejection. This could easily happen if I'm more concerned with *presenting my message* than I am with *understanding the other person's point of view.* You should know, however, that most research, including the sleep study, fails to find the forecast boomerang effect. The radical claim that students never need to sleep continued to have a positive, although diminished impact.

Despite the questions that surround social judgment theory, it is an elegant conception of the persuasion process. There's an intuitive appeal to the idea of crafting a message that's positioned right at the edge of the listener's latitude of acceptance in order to be as effectively discrepant as possible. That would be my recommendation to Jim as he confronts a variety of air travelers. I wonder in which of his three latitudes my advice will fall.

QUESTIONS TO SHARPEN YOUR FOCUS

1. How does the concept of *attitudes as latitudes* help you understand your attitude toward the various requirements of this course?

2. Suppose you find out that the fellow sitting next to you is *highly ego-involved* in the issue of gun control. Based on social judgment theory, what three predictions about his attitude structure would be reasonable to make?

3. What practical advice does social judgment theory offer you if you want to ask your boss for a raise?

4. Do you have any *ethical qualms* about applying the wisdom of social judgment theory? Why or why not?

A SECOND LOOK

Recommended resource: C. Kiesler, B. Collins, and N. Miller, *Attitude Change,* John Wiley & Sons, New York, 1969, Chapter 6, pp. 238–301.

Original conception: Carolyn Sherif, Muzafer Sherif, and Roger Nebergall, *Attitude and Attitude Change: The Social Judgment-Involvement Approach,* W. B. Saunders, Philadelphia, 1965.

Theory update: D. Granberg, "Social Judgment Theory," in *Communication Yearbook 6,* M. Burgoon (ed.), Sage, Beverly Hills, Calif., 1982, pp. 304–329.

Ego-involvement: W. W. Wilmot, "Ego-Involvement: A Confusing Variable in Speech Communication Research," *Quarterly Journal of Speech,* Vol. 57, 1971, pp. 429–436.

Attitudes as latitudes: Kenneth Sereno and Edward Bodaken, "Ego-Involvement and Attitude Change: Toward a Reconceptualization of Persuasive Effect," *Speech Monographs,* Vol. 39, 1972, pp. 151–158.

Assimilation and Contrast: J. Richard Eiser, *Social Judgment,* Brooks/Cole, Pacific Grove, Calif., 1990, pp. 53–76.

Test of two-stage hypothesis: Gian Sarup, Robert Suchner, and Gitanjali Gaylord, "Contrast Effects and Attitude Change: A Test of the Two-Stage Hypothesis of Social Judgment Theory," *Social Psychology Quarterly,* Vol. 54, 1991, pp. 364–372.

Message discrepancy: Stan Kaplowitz and Edward Fink, "Message Discrepancy and Persuasion," in *Progress in Communication Sciences: Advances in Persuasion,* Vol. 13, George Barnett and Frank Boster (eds.), Ablex, Greenwich, Conn., 1997, pp. 75–106.

Sleep study: S. Bochner and C. Insko, "Communicator Discrepancy, Source Credibility and Opinion Change," *Journal of Personality and Social Psychology,* Vol. 4, 1966, pp. 614–621.

Contemporary treatment: Daniel J. O'Keefe, "Social Judgment Theory," in *Persuasion: Theory and Research,* Sage, Newbury Park, Calif., 1990, pp. 29–44.

CHAPTER 14

Elaboration Likelihood Model

of Richard Petty & John Cacioppo

Like a number of women whose children are out of the home, Rita Francisco has gone back to college. Her program isn't an aimless sampling of classes to fill empty hours—she has enrolled in every course that will help her become a more persuasive advocate. Rita is a woman with a mission.

Rita's teenage daughter was killed when the car she was riding in smashed into a stone wall. After drinking three cans of beer at a party, the girl's eighteen-year-old boyfriend lost control on a curve while going eighty miles per hour. Rita's son walks with a permanent limp as a result of injuries received when a high school girl plowed through the parking lot of a 7-Eleven on a Friday night. When police obtained a DUI (driving under the influence) conviction, it only fueled Rita's resolve to get young drinking drivers off the road. She has become active with Mothers Against Drunk Driving (MADD) and works to convince anyone who will listen that "Zero Tolerance" laws, which make it illegal for drivers under the age of 21 to have any measurable amount of alcohol in their system, should be strictly enforced. Rita also wants to persuade others that young adults caught driving with more than 0.02 percent blood alcohol content should automatically lose their drivers licenses until they are 21.

This is a tough sell on most college campuses. While her classmates can appreciate the tragic reasons underlying her fervor, few subscribe to what they believe is a drastic solution. Rita realizes that students could easily dismiss her campaign as the ranting of a hysterical parent and is determined to develop the most effective persuasive strategy possible. She wonders if she would have more success by presenting well-reasoned arguments for enforcing zero tolerance or lining up highly credible people to endorse her proposal.

THE CENTRAL ROUTE VS. THE PERIPHERAL ROUTE: ALTERNATIVE PATHS TO PERSUASION

Ohio State psychologist Richard Petty thinks Rita is asking the right question. He conducted his Ph.D. dissertation study using the topic of teenage driving to test the relative effectiveness of high-source credibility and strong-message arguments. He found that the results varied depending on which of two mental routes to attitude change a listener happened to use. Petty labeled the two cognitive processes the "central route" and the "peripheral route." He sees the distinction as helpful in reconciling much of the conflicting data of persuasion research. Along with his Ohio State colleague John Cacioppo, he launched an intensive program of study to discover the best way for the persuader to activate each route.

The central route involves message elaboration. Elaboration is "the extent to which a person carefully thinks about issue-relevant arguments contained in a persuasive communication."[1] In an attempt to process new information rationally, people using the central route scrutinize the ideas, try to figure out if they have true merit, and mull over their implications. Similar to Buller and Burgoon's claim about deception and Berger's characterization of strategic message plans, elaboration requires high levels of cognitive effort. (See Chapters 7 and 10.)

The peripheral route offers a shorthand way to accept or reject a message "without any active thinking about the attributes of the issue or the object of consideration."[2] Instead of doing extensive cognitive work, recipients rely on a variety of cues that allow them to make quick decisions. Robert Cialdini of Arizona State University lists six cues that trigger a "click, whirr" programmed response.[3] These cues allow us to fly the peripheral route on automatic pilot:

1. Reciprocation—"You owe me."
2. Consistency—"We've always done it that way."
3. Social proof—"Everybody's doing it."
4. Liking—"Love me, love my ideas."
5. Authority—"Just because I say so."
6. Scarcity—"Quick, before they're all gone."

Figure 14.1 shows a simplified version of Petty and Cacioppo's elaboration likelihood model (ELM) as it applies to Rita's situation. Although their model with its twin-route metaphor seems to suggest two mutually exclusive paths to persuasion, the theorists stress that the central route and the peripheral route are poles on a cognitive processing continuum that shows the degree of mental effort a person exerts when evaluating a message.[4] The elaboration scale at the top represents effortful scrutiny of arguments on the left-hand side, and mindless reliance on non-content cues on the right. Most messages receive middle ground attention between these poles, but there's always a trade-off. The more Rita's listeners work to discern the merits of strict zero tolerance enforcement, the less they'll be influenced by peripheral factors such as their friends' scoffing laughter at her suggestion. Conversely, the more her hearers are affected by content-irrelevant factors such as Rita's age, accent, or appearance, the less they will be impacted by her ideas. We'll work down the model one level at a time in order to understand Petty and Cacioppo's predictions about the likelihood of Rita's message being scrutinized by students at her college.

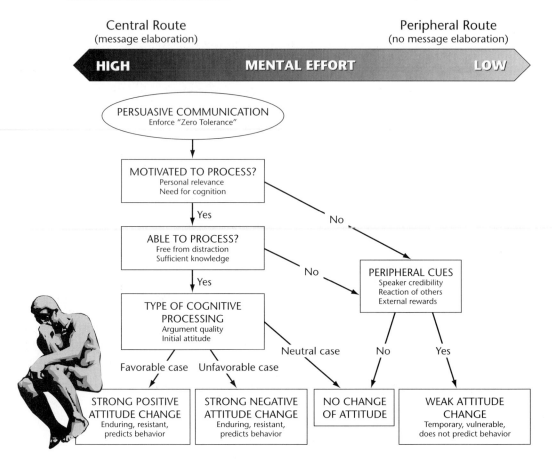

FIGURE 14.1   The Elaboration Likelihood Model
(Adapted from Petty and Cacioppo, "The Elaboration Likelihood Model: Current Status and Controversies.")

MOTIVATION FOR ELABORATION: IS IT WORTH THE EFFORT?

Petty and Cacioppo assume that people are motivated to hold correct attitudes. The authors admit that we aren't always logical, but they think we make a good effort not to kid ourselves in our search for truth. We want to maintain reasonable positions.

Yet a person can only scrutinize a limited number of ideas. We are exposed to so many persuasive messages that we would experience a tremendous information overload if we tried to interact with every variant idea we heard or read about. The only way to solve this problem is by being "lazy" toward most issues in life. Petty and Cacioppo claim we have a large-mesh mental filter that allows items we regard as less important to flow through without being processed. But statements about things that are personally relevant are trapped and tested. In the terminology of social judgment theory, we're motivated to elaborate only ideas with which we are highly ego-involved.

There are few things in life more important to young Americans than the right to drive. A license is the closest thing our society has to an adolescent rite of passage; for some it is a passport to freedom. It seems unlikely, therefore, that students would regard Rita's zero tolerance proposal as trivial. Yet threatening the loss of license may have less personal relevance to students who don't drink, or to those who already make sure they don't drive when they drink. And if students over 21 aren't worried about who's driving on the road, they too may feel that Rita's proposal has little to do with them. So ELM's authors would regard teenage students who drive after drinking a few beers as especially motivated to grapple with arguments about automatic drivers-license suspension.

Petty and Cacioppo maintain that as long as people have a personal stake in accepting or rejecting an idea, they will be much more influenced by what a message says than by the characteristics of the person who said it. But when a topic is no longer relevant, it gets sidetracked to the periphery of our mind where credibility cues take on a greater importance. Without the motivation of personal relevance, there probably will be no elaboration.

The theorists do recognize, however, that some people have a need for cognitive clarity, regardless of the issue. In fact, they've developed a "Need for Cognition Scale" to identify individuals who are most likely to elaborate message arguments.[5] Four of the items state:

> I usually end up deliberating about issues even when they don't affect me personally.
>
> I prefer my life to be filled with puzzles that I must solve.
>
> I prefer to think about small, daily projects to long-term ones.
>
> Thinking is not my idea of fun.

If you substantially agree with the first two statements and take issue with the last two, Petty and Cacioppo would anticipate that you'd be a person who works through many of the ideas and arguments you hear.

ABILITY FOR ELABORATION: CAN THEY DO IT?

Once people have shown an inclination to think about the content of a message (motivation), the next issue is whether or not they are *able* to do so. Since Rita's immediate audience consists of men and women who have duly impressed a college admissions officer, you would think the question of ability would be moot. But issue-relevant thinking (elaboration) takes more than intelligence. It also requires an opportunity to concentrate.

Distraction disrupts elaboration. Rita's classmates will be hard-pressed to think about her point of view if it's expressed amid the din of the student union snack bar where you can't hear yourself think. Or perhaps she presents her solution for highway safety when the students are trying to concentrate on something else—an upcoming exam, a letter from home, or an instant mental replay of the winning shot in an intramural basketball game.

Rita may face the same challenge as television advertisers who have only the fleeting attention of viewers. Like them, Rita can use repetition to ensure that her main point comes across, but too much commotion will short-circuit a reasoned consideration of the message, no matter how much repetition is used. In that case, students will use the peripheral route and judge the message by cues that indicate whether Rita is a competent and trustworthy person.

TYPE OF ELABORATION: OBJECTIVE VS. BIASED THINKING

As you can see from the downward flow in the central path of their model (Figure 14.1), Petty and Cacioppo believe that all motivation and ability strongly increase the likelihood that a message will be elaborated in the minds of listeners. Yet as social judgment theory suggests, they may not process the information in a fair and objective manner. Rita might have the undivided attention of students who care deeply about the right to drive but discover that they've already built up an organized structure of knowledge concerning the issue.

When Rita claims that the alcohol-related, fatal crash rate for young drivers is double that of drivers over 21, a student may counter with the fact that teenagers drive twice as many miles and are therefore just as safe as adults. Whether or not the statistics are true or the argument is valid isn't the issue. The point is that those who have already thought a lot about drinking and driving safety will probably be biased in the way they process Rita's message.

Petty and Cacioppo refer to biased elaboration as top-down thinking in which a predetermined conclusion colors the supporting data underneath. They contrast this with objective elaboration, or bottom-up thinking, which lets facts speak for themselves. Biased elaboration merely bolsters previous ideas. Perhaps you've seen a picture of Rodin's famous statue, *The Thinker*, a man sitting with his head propped in one hand. If the thinker already has a set of beliefs to contemplate, Petty and Cacioppo's research shows that additional thought will merely fix them in stone. Rita shouldn't assume that audience elaboration will always help her cause; it depends on whether it's biased elaboration or objective elaboration. It also depends on the quality of her arguments.

ELABORATED ARGUMENTS: STRONG, WEAK, AND NEUTRAL

If Rita manages to win an unbiased hearing from students at her school, Petty and Cacioppo say her cause will rise or fall on the perceived strength of her arguments. The two theorists have no absolute standard for what distinguishes a cogent argument from one that's specious. They simply define a strong message as one that generates favorable thoughts when it's heard and scrutinized.

Petty and Cacioppo predict that thoughtful consideration of strong arguments will produce major shifts in attitude change in the direction desired by the persuader. Suppose Rita states the following:

> National Safety Council statistics show that drivers in the 16–20 age group account for 15 percent of the miles driven in the United States, yet they are responsible for 25 percent of the highway deaths that involve alcohol.

This evidence could give cause for pause and careful consideration. Her fellow students may not be comfortable with the facts, but some of them might find the statistics quite compelling. According to the ELM, the enhanced thinking of those who respond favorably will cause their change in position to persist over time, resist counterpersuasion, and predict future behavior—the "triple crown" of interpersonal influence.

However, persuasive attempts that are processed through the central route can have dramatically negative effects as well. Despite her strong convictions, Rita may be able to make only a weak case for changing the current law.

> When underage drinkers are arrested for violating zero tolerance rules of the road, automatic suspension of their licenses would allow the Secretary of State's office to reduce its backlog of work. This would give government officials time to check driving records so they could keep dangerous motorists off the road.

This weak argument is guaranteed to offend the sensibilities of anyone who thinks about it. Rather than compelling listeners to enlist in Rita's cause, it will only give them a reason to oppose her point of view more vigorously. The elaborated idea will cause a boomerang effect that will last over time, defy other efforts to change it, and break out into behavior. These are the same significant effects that the elaborated strong argument produces, but in the opposite direction.

Rita's ideas could produce an ambivalent reaction. Listeners who carefully examine her ideas may end up feeling neither pro nor con toward her evidence. Their neutral or mixed response obviously means that they won't change their attitudes as a result of processing through the central route. Instead, thinking about the pros and cons of the issue serves to reinforce their original attitudes, whatever they may be.

PERIPHERAL CUES: AN ALTERNATIVE ROUTE OF INFLUENCE

Although the majority of this chapter has dealt with the central cognitive route to attitude change, most messages are processed on the less effortful peripheral path. Signposts along the way direct the hearer to favor or oppose the persuader's point of view without ever engaging in an inner dialogue over the merits of the proposal. Petty and Cacioppo call the resultant shifts attitude changes without "issue-relevant thinking."[6]

As explained earlier, the hearer who has chosen the peripheral route relies on a variety of cues as an aid in reaching a quick decision. The most obvious cues are tangible rewards linked to agreement with the advocate's position.

"In the interest of streamlining the judicial process, we'll skip the evidence and go directly to sentencing."

Food, sex, and money are traditional inducements to change. I once overheard the conclusion of a transaction between a young man and a college senior who was trying to persuade him to donate blood in order to fulfill her class assignment. "Okay, it's agreed," she said. "You give blood for me today, and I'll have you over to my place for dinner tomorrow night." Although this type of social exchange has been going on for centuries, Petty and Cacioppo would still describe it as peripheral. Public compliance to the request for blood? Yes. Private acceptance of its importance? Not likely.

For many students of influence, speaker or source credibility is the most interesting cue on the peripheral route. Four decades of research confirm that people who are likable and have expertise on the issue in question can have a persuasive impact regardless of what arguments they present. Rita's appearance, manner of talking, and background credentials will speak so loudly that some students won't hear what she says. Which students? According to Petty and Cacioppo, the unmotivated or unable students who switched to the peripheral path.

Listeners who believe that Rita's twin tragedies have given her wisdom beyond their own will shift to a position slightly more sympathetic to her point of view. The same holds true for those who see her as pleasant and warm. But there are students who will regard her grammatical mistakes as a sign of ignorance, or they'll be turned off by a maternal manner that reminds them of a lecture from Mom. These peripheral route critics will become a bit more skeptical of Rita's position. Note that attitude change on this outside track can be either positive or negative, but it lacks the robust persistence, invulnerability, or link to behavior that we see in change that comes from message elaboration.

Some of the most effective peripheral cues are endorsements from highly popular or respected public figures. Understanding the importance of identification for persuasion (see Chapter 21), Rita scans the pages of *Rolling Stone* to see if Billy Corgan of Smashing Pumpkins might have said something critical about teenage drivers. He's a local boy who's made it big, and the group's music is widely acclaimed by students at her college. By somehow associating her message with credible people, she can achieve a slight change in student attitudes. Yet it probably wouldn't last long, stand up to attack, or affect their behavior. Petty and Cacioppo say that a small and fragile change is all that can be expected through the peripheral route.

PUSHING THE LIMITS OF PERIPHERAL POWER

What if Smashing Pumpkins' tour bus were run off the road by a drunk teenage driver and guitarist James Iha met the same fate as Rita's daughter? Would his tragic death and Corgan's subsequent avowal that "friends don't let friends drive drunk" cue students to a permanent shift in attitude and behavior? Fortunately the group is still intact,[7] but a high-profile tragedy in the sports world suggests that the effect of even powerful peripheral cues is short-lived at best.

In 1991 basketball superstar Earvin "Magic" Johnson held a candid press conference to announce that he had tested positive for HIV. The story dominated network news coverage for days. University of South Florida psychologists Louis Penner and Barbara Fritzsche had just completed a study showing that many people had little sympathy for AIDS victims who had contracted the disease through sexual transmission. When asked to volunteer a few hours to help a patient stay in school, over half of the women but none of the men in the study volunteered. Penner and Fritzsche extended their study when they heard of Magic Johnson's illness.[8] They wondered if the tragedy that had befallen this popular star and his pledge to become an advocate for those with the disease would cause students to react more positively toward people with AIDS.

For a while it did. The week after Johnson's announcement, 80 percent of the men offered assistance. That number tapered off to 30 percent, however, within a few months. The proportion of women helping dipped below 40 percent in the same period. Penner and Fritzsche observed that people didn't grapple with the substance of Magic Johnson's message; rather, they paid attention to the man who was presenting it. Consistent with ELM's main thesis, the researchers concluded: "changes that occur because of 'peripheral cues' such as . . . being a well liked celebrity are less permanent than those that occur because of the substantive content of the persuasion attempt."[9] They might also have added that the effects of star performer endorsements are subject to the sharp ups and downs of celebrity status. After Penner and Fritzsche conducted their study, Magic Johnson's return to the NBA was the subject of cover stories in *Time* and *Newsweek*.

Although most ELM research has measured the effects of peripheral cues by studying credibility, a speaker's competence or character could also be a stimulus to effortful message elaboration. For example, the high regard that millions of sports fans had for Magic might for the first time have made it possible to scrutinize proposals for the prevention and treatment of AIDS without a moral stigma biasing each idea. Or the fact that Johnson's magic wasn't strong enough to repel the AIDS virus might cause someone to think deeply: "If it happened to a guy like Magic, it could happen to me." Even though Figure 14.1 identifies *speaker credibility*, *others' reaction*, and *external rewards* as variables that promote mindless acceptance via the peripheral route, Petty and Cacioppo note that it's impossible to compile a list of cues that are strictly peripheral.[10] Whatever the cue, if it motivates the listener to scrutinize the message, it is no longer a "no brainer."

CHOOSING A ROUTE: PRACTICAL ADVICE FOR THE PERSUADER

Petty and Cacioppo's advice for Rita (and the rest of us) is clear. She needs to determine the likelihood that her listeners will give their undivided attention to evaluating her proposal. If it appears that they have the motivation and ability to elaborate the message, she had best come armed with facts and figures to support her case. A pleasant smile, emotional appeals, or the loss of her daughter won't make any difference.

Since it's only by thoughtful consideration that her listeners could experience a lasting change in attitude, Rita probably hopes they can go the central route. Yet if they do, it's still difficult to build a compelling persuasive case. If she fails to do her homework and presents weak arguments, the people who are ready to think will shift their attitude to a more antagonistic position.

If Rita determines that her hearers are unable or unwilling to think through the details of her plan, she'll be more successful choosing a delivery strategy that emphasizes the package rather than the contents. This could include a heartrending account of her daughter's death, a smooth presentation, and an ongoing effort to build friendships with the students. Perhaps bringing home-made cookies to class or offering rides to the mall would aid in making her an attractive source. But as we've already seen, the effects will probably be minimal.

It's not likely that Rita will get many people to elaborate her message in a way that ends up favorably for her cause. Most persuaders avoid the central route because the audience won't go with them or they find it is too difficult to generate compelling arguments. But Rita really doesn't have a choice.

Drivers licenses (and perhaps beer) are so important to most of these students that they'll be ready to dissect every part of her plan. They won't be won over by a friendly smile. Rita will have to develop thoughtful and well-reasoned arguments if she is to change their minds. Given the depth of her conviction, she thinks it's worth a try.

CRITIQUE: ELABORATING THE MODEL

For the last twenty years, ELM has been a leading, if not *the* leading theory of persuasion and attitude change. Petty, Cacioppo, and their students have published almost one hundred articles on different parts of the model, and their initial dual process conception has stimulated additional research, application, and critique. In a recent status review, the theorists state that "the term 'elaboration' is used to suggest that people add something of their own to the specific information provided in the communication."[11] Consistent with their definition, Petty and Cacioppo have elaborated their original theory by making it increasingly more complex, less predictive, and less able to offer definitive advice to the influence practitioner. This is not the direction a scientific theory wants to go.

I have been unable to capture all of these elaborations in a short chapter, but Miami University communication researcher Paul Mongeau and communication consultant James Stiff believe that Petty and Cacioppo face an even greater problem. Specifically, they charge that "descriptions of the ELM are sufficiently imprecise and ambiguous as to prevent an adequate test of the entire model."[12] One place this stands out is ELM's silence as to what makes a strong or weak argument. Perhaps this omission is due to the difficulty of testing how good a case the speaker actually made.

Petty and Cacioppo define a good message as "one containing arguments such that when subjects are instructed to think about the message, the thoughts they generate are fundamentally favorable."[13] In other words, the arguments are regarded as strong if the people are persuaded, but weak if folks are turned off. Like my childhood friend described in Chapter 2, ELM seems to have its own "never-miss shot." Until such time as the ELM theorists can identify what makes a case weak or strong apart from its ultimate effect on the listener, it doesn't make much sense to include argument strength as a key variable within the model.

Yet even if Cacioppo and Petty's theory is too vague or their view of argument strength is too slippery, their elaboration likelihood model is impressive because it pulls together and makes sense out of diverse research results that have puzzled communication theorists for years. For example, why do most people pay less attention to the communication than they do to the communicator? And if speaker credibility is so important, why does its effect dissipate so quickly? ELM's explanation is that few listeners are motivated and able to do the mental work that is required for a major shift in attitude. The two-path hypothesis also helps clarify why good evidence and reasoning can sometimes have a life-changing impact but usually make no difference at all.

Attitude-change research often yields results that seem confusing or contradictory. Petty and Cacioppo's ELM takes many disjointed findings and pulls them together into a unified whole. This integrative function of the elaboration likelihood model makes it a valuable theory of influence.

QUESTIONS TO SHARPEN YOUR FOCUS

1. Can you think of five different words or phrases that capture the idea of *message elaboration?*

2. What *peripheral cues* do you usually monitor when someone is trying to influence you?

3. Petty and Cacioppo want to persuade you that their elaboration likelihood model is a mirror of reality. Do you process their arguments for its accuracy closer to your *central route* or your *peripheral route?* Why not the other way?

4. Students of persuasion often wonder whether *high credibility* or *strong arguments* sway people more. How would ELM theorists respond to that question?

A SECOND LOOK

Recommended resource: Richard E. Petty and John T. Cacioppo, *Communication and Persuasion: Central and Peripheral Routes to Attitude Change,* Springer-Verlag, New York, 1986.

Effect of involvement: Richard E. Petty and John T. Cacioppo, "Involvement and Persuasion: Tradition versus Integration," *Psychological Bulletin,* Vol. 107, 1990, pp. 367–374.

Secondary resource: Daniel J. O'Keefe, "Elaboration Likelihood Model," in *Persuasion: Theory and Research,* Sage, Newbury Park, Calif., 1990, pp. 95–129.

Postulates and research: Richard E. Petty and John T. Cacioppo, "The Elaboration Likelihood Model of Persuasion," in *Advances in Experimental Social Psychology,* Vol. 19, Leonard Berkowitz (ed.), Academic Press, Orlando, Fla., 1986, pp. 124–205.

Message arguments versus source credibility: Richard E. Petty, John T. Cacioppo, and R. Goldman, "Personal Involvement as a Determinant of Argument-Based Persuasion," *Journal of Personality and Social Psychology,* Vol. 41, 1981, pp. 847–855.

Need for cognition: John Cacioppo, Richard Petty, Jeffrey Feinstein, & Blair Jarvis, "Dispositional Differences in Cognitive Motivation: The Life and Times of Individuals Varying in Need for Cognition," *Psychological Bulletin,* Vol. 119, 1996, pp. 197–253.

Effects of evidence: John Reinard, "The Empirical Study of the Persuasive Effects of Evidence: The Status After Fifty Years of Research," *Human Communication Research,* Vol. 15, 1988, pp. 3–59.

Effects of credibility: H. W. Simons, N. M. Berkowitz, and R. J. Moyer, "Similarity, Credibility and Attitude Change: A Review and a Theory," *Psychological Bulletin,* Vol. 73, 1970, pp. 1–16.

Mindless cues: Robert B. Cialdini, *Influence: Science and Practice,* 2d ed., Scott Foresman, Glenview, Ill., 1988.

Critiques of ELM: "Forum: Specifying the ELM," *Communication Theory,* Vol. 3, 1993. (Paul Mongeau and James Stiff, "Specifying Causal Relationships in the Elaboration Likelihood Model," pp. 65–72. Mike Allen and Rodney Reynolds, "The Elaboration Likelihood Model and the Sleeper Effect: An Assessment of Attitude Change Over Time," pp. 73–82.)

Current status: Richard Petty and Duane Wegener, "The Elaboration Likelihood Model: Current Status and Controversies," in Shelly Chaiken and Yaacov Trope (eds.), *Dual Process Theories in Social Psychology,* Guilford, N.Y., 1999, pp. 41–72.

E t h i c a l   R e f l e c t i o n s

MARTIN BUBER'S DIALOGIC ETHICS

Martin Buber was a German Jewish philosopher and theologian who immigrated to Palestine prior to World War II and died in 1965. His ethical approach focuses on relationships between people rather than on moral codes of conduct. "In the beginning is the relation," Buber wrote. "The relation is the cradle of actual life."[1]

Buber contrasted two types of relationships—*I-It* versus *I-Thou*. In I-It relationships we treat the other person as a thing to be used, an object to be manipulated. Created by monologue, an I-It relationship lacks mutuality. Parties come together as individuals intent on creating only an impression. Deceit is a way to maintain appearances.

In an I-Thou relationship we regard our partner as the very one we are. We see the other as created in the image of God and resolve to treat him or her as a valued end rather than as a means to our own end. This implies that we will seek to experience the relationship as it appears to the other person. Buber says we can only do this through dialogue.

For Buber, *dialogue* is a synonym for ethical communication. Dialogue is mutuality in conversation that creates the "between," the "interhuman," the "transaction" through which we help each other to be more human. Dialogue is not only a morally appropriate act, it is also a way to discover what is ethical in our relationship. It thus requires self-disclosure to, confirmation of, and vulnerability with the other person.

Buber used the image of the "narrow ridge" to picture the tension of dialogic living. On one side of the moral path is the gulf of subjectivism, where there are no standards. On the other side is the plateau of absolutism, where rules are etched in stone:

> On the far side of the subjective, on this side of the objective, on the narrow ridge, where I and Thou meet, there is the realm of the Between.[2]

Duquesne University communication ethicist Ron Arnett notes that "living the narrow-ridge philosophy requires a life of personal and interpersonal concern, which is likely to generate a more complicated existence than that of the egoist or the selfless martyr."[3] Despite that tension, many interpersonal theorists have carved out ethical positions similar to Buber's philosophy. Consistent with CMM's foundational belief that persons-in-conversation co-construct their own social realities (see Chapter 5), Barnett Pearce is attracted to Buber's position that dialogue is the place where values are determined. Bakhtin, of course, shares Buber's dialogical view of personhood whereby all people feel dual tugs toward opposites—dialogue *and* manipulation, for example. (See Chapter 12.)

During his lifetime, Buber's dialogic ethics were often compared to the value Carl Rogers placed on congruence, empathic listening, and unconditional positive regard. (See Chapter 3.) The two men met only once for a public dialogue at the University of Michigan. They discussed the similarity of Rogers' psychological concept of "acceptance" with Buber's ethical ideal of "confirmation."[4] I was a sophomore on campus at the time and lived one block from the hall where they spoke. I wish that back then I had had the ethical sensibility to have gone. My loss.

THOMAS NILSEN'S SIGNIFICANT CHOICE

Consistent with the democratic values of a free society, University of Washington emeritus professor Thomas Nilsen proposes that persuasive speech is ethical to the extent that it maximizes people's ability to exercise free choice. Since many political, religious, and commercial messages are routinely designed to bypass rather than appeal to a listener's rational faculties, Nilsen upholds the value of significant choice in unequivocal terms:

> When we communicate to influence the attitudes, beliefs, and actions of others, the ethical touchstone is the degree of free, informed, rational and critical choice—significant choice—that is fostered by our speaking.[5]

For Nilsen, significant choice is the test of ethical influence because "only a self-determining being can be a moral being; without significant choice, there is no morality."[6] As support, he cites two classic essays on the freedom of speech. John Milton's *Aeropagitica*[7] argues against prior restraint of any ideas, no matter how heretical. John Stuart Mill's *On Liberty*[8] advocates a free marketplace of ideas because the only way to test an argument is to hear it presented by a true believer who defends it in earnest.

Throughout history, philosophers, rhetoricians, and influence practitioners have compared persuasion to a lover making fervent appeals to his beloved—wooing an audience, for example. Nilsen's ethic of significant choice is nicely captured in the courtship analogy because true love cannot be coerced; it must be freely given. Inspired by Danish philosopher Søren Kierkegaard's description of the ethical religious persuader as lover,[9] I have elsewhere presented a typology of false (unethical) lovers:[10]

> *Smother lovers* won't take no for an answer; their persistence is obnoxious.
>
> *Legalistic lovers* have a set image of what the other should be.
>
> *Flirts* are in love with love; they value response, not the other person.
>
> *Seducers* try deception and flattery to entice the other to submit.
>
> *Rapists* use force to have their way; conformity pressure and guilt inducement are tools of mind rape.

"Tell me more about this Christianity of yours. I'm terribly interested."

Reproduced by permission of Punch.

In differing degrees, all five types of persuader violate the human dignity of the persons they pursue by taking away the chance for choice that is informed and free.

Nilsen obviously would approve persuasive appeals that encourage message elaboration through ELM's central route, just as he would condemn the fundraiser's deceptive ploy described on page 187. Do emotional appeals automatically short-circuit our ability to make rational choices or do they free us up to consider new options? Significant choice, like beauty and credibility, may be in the eye of the beholder.

PART THREE

Group and Public Communication

GROUP DECISION MAKING

A cynic once said that a camel is a horse put together by a committee. Though many share this pessimistic view, the results of research in business, education, and government show that problem-solving groups often come up with solutions that are superior to anything thought of by individual members. Referred to as "synergy," the recurrent finding that the group product is greater than the sum of its parts has stimulated efforts to explain the typical process of group decision making.

Fifty years ago, Robert Bales of Harvard University developed a method of discussion analysis that distinguishes twelve types of verbal behavior.[1] A typical committee meeting requires the classification of ten to fifteen comments a minute. Figure DM.1 shows Bales' list of categories and some of the interrelationships he built into his system of observation.

The middle area of Bales' system (sections B and C) is for statements that focus on accomplishing the group task. The outer areas (sections A and D) are for comments that reflect relationships within the group. By coding everything a person says, an observer using Bales' categories is able to develop a profile of preferred interaction style for each group member. The results confirm that some people

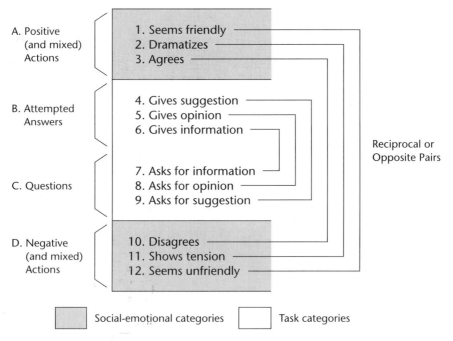

FIGURE DM.1   Bales' Categories for Interaction Process Analysis
(From Bales, *Personality and Interpersonal Behavior.*)

concentrate on getting the job done, while others are much more concerned with social-emotional issues. Task-oriented individuals are the pistons that drive the group machine. Relationship-oriented members are the lubricant that prevents excessive friction from destroying the group. Good groups require both kinds of people.

You can see in Figure DM.1 that Bales' twelve categories are divided into a half-dozen reciprocally matched pairs. *Asks for information* is balanced by *gives information. Seems friendly* is juxtaposed with *seems unfriendly.* The only pair that doesn't present an obvious mirror image is *dramatizes—shows tension.* As you may recall from the discussion of Bormann's symbolic interaction theory in Chapter 2, Bales originally called category 2 *relieves tension.* He found, however, that most tension-reducing comments had a storytelling or dramatic quality that served to get the group moving when it was stuck, so he decided that the term *dramatizes* was a more accurate label.

Bales discovered that good groups maintain a rough balance among each of the six pairs. For example, a group's initial discussion is more productive when people hear answers (category 6) to their questions about the nature of their task (category 7). But the group process stalls if members seek facts that no one has, or if everyone volunteers information that nobody wants.

Contrary to those who would like to eliminate all group conflict, Bales found that a 2:1 ratio of positive to negative comments is optimum for the social-emotional category pairs shown in Figure DM.1 (1 and 12, 2 and 11, 3 and 10). Although a high proportion of cutting remarks could tear a group apart, a healthy dose of voiced skepticism is necessary to reach a quality decision. Twenty years later, Harvard psychologist Irving Janis popularized the term "groupthink" as a label for inferior decision making that occurs when group members have an inordinate desire for group harmony.

Members value unity so much that they refuse to voice doubts even when they see the group headed in a dangerous direction.[2]

Bales' emphasis on group balance or equilibrium reflects his systems approach to group decision making. You've already had some exposure to systems thinking through Shannon and Weaver's information theory and Watzlawick's interactional view that regards the family as a system (see Chapters 3 and 11). Bales' version suggests that decision-making groups face problems posed by task requirements, social-emotional needs, and environmental factors, and he regarded the process of communication as the chief method by which groups satisfy these requirements.

Systems theorists offer the following general model of group decision making:

$$INPUT \rightarrow PROCESS \rightarrow OUTPUT$$

For example, we could think of *information* as input, *talk* as process, and *decisions* as output.[3] This model can help us locate the work of many communication theorists who are concerned with group decision making. Bales' interaction analysis addresses the input-process connection. So does Bormann's symbolic interaction theory. Yet neither Bales nor Bormann tracks the specific effects of member discussion on the quality of a group's final decision. The first theory in this section deals with the link between process and output.

Chapter 15 presents Randy Hirokawa and Dennis Gouran's functional perspective. Building on the task concerns of Bales, these theorists focus on the specific function communication plays in reaching a quality group judgment. Their ultimate goal is to offer practical advice on how participants can act to ensure better group decisions.

Scott Poole's adaptive structuration theory is concerned with the entire input-process-output group decision-making system. Adapting sociologist Anthony Giddens' concept of structuration, Poole says that group members use rules and resources (input) in interaction (process) to produce and reproduce group decisions (output). The intriguing feature of structuration is that the decision is not only *affected* by the input of the group, but also bounces back and *affects* those same rules and resources. Chapter 16 explains this concept in detail.

Psychologists who study group process often focus on member composition. These analysts tend to assume that the personality and opinion of participants will automatically determine the ultimate outcome. The theorists featured in this section disagree. They believe that communication is neither a waste of time nor a corrosive agent that disfigures what would have been an elegant solution to the problem. Both theories carve a space for the quiet, powerless, or marginalized members of groups to speak out in order that the group might produce better decisions. If we suspect that a camel is a horse put together by a committee, we should remember that the ungainly looking beast turns out to be an ideal solution for a group of desert nomads.

"We may as well go home. It's obvious that this meeting isn't going to settle anything."

Functional Perspective on Group Decision Making

of Randy Hirokawa & Dennis Gouran

Have you ever wondered how your communication professors got their jobs? Over a fifteen-month period, I served on four departmental search committees appointed to select final candidates for positions in rhetoric, theater, journalism, and broadcast production. Of course the whole department expected each group to come up with top-notch candidates, and consistent with a discipline that values rational discourse, they likely assumed that we'd make our high-quality decisions after systematic and reasoned discussion.

As the committee meetings piled up, however, I wondered if the time and energy we put into discussing the applicants might not be wasted effort. Given the mix of communication interests, academic knowledge, and personal prejudices that committee members brought to the table, weren't our final choices likely to be made on political rather than rational grounds? Even if we could be objective, I feared that our free-for-all debate over candidates would so cloud our judgment that we'd end up making second-rate choices.

Nagging doubts about the role of group discussion are reflected and magnified in oft-heard criticisms that cynical committee members voice when they talk in the corridor after a meeting:[1]

"If you want something done, do it yourself."

"Too many cooks spoil the broth."

"A committee is a group that keeps minutes and wastes hours."

"Committees lure fresh ideas down a cul-de-sac and quietly strangle them."

Communication professors Randy Hirokawa (University of Iowa) and Dennis Gouran (Pennsylvania State University) believe that these pessimistic views are unwarranted. Assuming that group members care about the issue, are reasonably intelligent, and face a challenging task that calls for more facts, new ideas, or clear thinking, Hirokawa and Gouran are convinced that group interaction has a positive effect on the final decision. Hirokawa speaks of *quality* solutions.[2] Gouran refers to decisions that are *appropriate*.[3] Both scholars regard talk as the social tool that helps groups reach better conclusions than they otherwise might. As the Hebrew proverb suggests, "Without counsel plans go wrong, but with many advisers they succeed."[4]

The functional perspective described in this chapter illustrates the wisdom of joint interaction. Gouran laid the groundwork for the theory with his early writing on group decision making. Hirokawa developed the core principles of the theory during his graduate studies, and today his research tests and refines this theory. On the assumption that you might be interested in a behind-the-scenes look at the faculty hiring process, I'll draw on my search committee experience to illustrate Hirokawa and Gouran's functional perspective.

FOUR FUNCTIONS FOR EFFECTIVE DECISION MAKING

Consistent with Bales and other pioneer researchers, Hirokawa and Gouran draw an analogy between small groups and biological systems. Complex living organisms must satisfy a number of functions such as respiration, circulation, digestion, and elimination of bodily waste if they are to survive and thrive in an ever-changing environment. In like manner, Hirokawa and Gouran see the group decision-making process as needing to fulfill four task requirements if members are to reach a high-quality solution. Hirokawa and Gouran refer to these conditions as *requisite functions* of effective decision making—thus the "functional perspective" label.[5] The four functions are: (1) problem analysis, (2) goal setting, (3) identification of alternatives, and (4) evaluation of positive and negative consequences.

1. Analysis of the Problem

Is something going on that requires improvement or change? To answer that question, group members must take a realistic look at current conditions. Defenders of the status quo are fond of saying, "If it ain't broke, don't fix it." But as Hirokawa warns, any misunderstanding of the situation tends to be compounded when members make their final decision. He also notes that the clearest example of faulty analysis is a failure to recognize a potential threat when one really exists.[6] After people acknowledge a need to be addressed, they still must figure out the nature, extent, and probable cause(s) of the problem that confronts the group.

Most communication departments have little difficulty analyzing the situation when a faculty member resigns or retires—departments move quickly to initiate a search for a new hire. To the extent that an opening provides the opportunity to shore up a weak area or enhance the reputation of an already recognized concentration, a vacancy is a nice problem to have. My department's searches for a rhetorician, a theater director, and a broadcast production person presented no apparent difficulties. In each case, we formed a search committee, drafted and published a position description throughout the profession, and checked with friends on other campuses to see who might be interested.

The journalism search, however, was another matter. This newly created position had been on the books for two years, but none of us seemed in a hurry to fill it. We were holding out for one of two nationally recognized reporters who had expressed interest in coming to Wheaton. But the timing wasn't right. We did, however, have confidence that the students were well-served by a part-time instructor who had few academic credentials, yet was a marvelous mentor. No problem, right? Then, for the first time, someone on our rather dormant committee asked whether we'd be able to keep the full-time faculty line if we didn't fill it for another year. She was addressing the function of problem analysis, and her question forced us to take a realistic look at the situation. When we consulted the dean, he said, in effect, "Use it or lose it." We quickly switched into an active search mode.

2. Goal Setting

Because group members need to be clear on what they are trying to accomplish, Hirokawa and Gouran regard discussion of goals and objectives as the second requisite function of decision making. A group needs to establish criteria by which to judge proposed solutions. If the group fails to satisfy this task requirement, it's likely that personal prejudice or organizational politics will drive the choice rather than reason.[7]

Faculty involved in our search for a rhetorician agreed unanimously that a successful candidate should possess an earned doctorate, have taught at the college level for at least five years, and be a scholar publishing actively in communication journals. Because our school is first and foremost a teaching institution, we also insisted that finalists demonstrate their ability to engage our students in a live classroom situation. Finally, consistent with Wheaton's worldview that all truth is God's truth, we informed applicants that we were looking for a scholar with a faith commitment who was unafraid to pursue knowledge from a liberal arts perspective. This rather exacting set of standards reduced our pool of applicants, but the criteria gave us increased confidence in our final decision.

3. Identification of Alternatives

In their original statement of the functional perspective, Hirokawa and Gouran stressed the importance of marshaling a number of alternative solutions from which group members could choose:

"Gentlemen, the fact that all my horses and all my men couldn't put Humpty together again simply proves to me that I must have <u>more</u> horses and <u>more</u> men."

If no one calls attention to the need for generating as many alternatives as is realistically possible, then relatively few may be introduced, and the corresponding possibility of finding the acceptable answer will be low.[8]

Limited choice was never an issue in our search for a drama coach. More than 150 candidates applied for the opening. In the initial stage, all we had to do was open the envelopes. The broadcast production search was a different story, however. We wanted a person with industry experience, a doctorate or a master of fine arts degree, and equal abilities to teach radio *and* television production. Numerous audio technicians with radio experience applied for the post, but only a few had the advanced degree we required. And none of these applicants had a background in video production. After three months we had no viable alternatives.

At that point, one of our members reminded us that we were a *search* committee and suggested that we get off our butts and start beating the bushes for candidates who met our criteria. So we held a brainstorming session where everyone kicked in ideas on ways to extend the search. As a result, phone, fax, and e-mail messages tapped into a network of production houses, station managers, deans, and college presidents. By fulfilling the functional requirement of generating relevant alternatives, the group discovered two candidates who not only met our basic criteria but also brought desired ethnic diversity to an all-Anglo department.

4. Evaluation of Positive and Negative Characteristics

After a group has identified alternative solutions, participants must take care to test the relative merits of each option against the criteria they believe are important. This point-by-point comparison doesn't take place automatically. Hirokawa and Gouran warn that groups get sloppy and often need one member to remind the others to consider both the positive and negative features of each alternative.

As a case in point, the search committee was tremendously impressed with the credentials, talent, and personality of Mark, the leading candidate for the position of theater director. He brought extensive experience on the stage, had directed a well-received production of *The Diviners* as guest director the year before, and showed an interpersonal warmth that connected with students and faculty alike. All of our drama majors signed a petition urging that we select him for the position. It took our committee "realist" to point out that Mark had never worked in an academic setting. If he came, we shouldn't underestimate the difficulty this creative artist would have adapting to the routine chores of grading, academic advising, committee meetings, and filling out reports.

We almost made the opposite error in another search. An otherwise strong applicant had not received tenure at his current school, and the circumstances surrounding that denial seemed to dominate our discussion to the exclusion of his many strengths. The same pragmatic committee member urged us to spend time examining the applicant's positive characteristics, which far outweighed the negative.

Hirokawa notes that some group tasks have a *positive bias* in that spotting the favorable characteristics of alternative choices is more important than identifying negative qualities.[9] For example, the recommendation forms for "Teacher of the Year" at my school accentuate the positive. "Good enough" is not good enough to get the award. Hirokawa says that other group tasks have a *negative bias*—the unattractive characteristics of choice options carry more weight than positive attributes. Tenure committee deliberations at colleges where there's a premium on teaching rather than research tend to be more influenced by instructors' shortcomings. That's because committee members are loath to condemn future generations of students to mediocre teachers who've been granted job security for life.

PRIORITIZING THE FUNCTIONS

The word *prioritizing* can mean developing a logical progression, or it can refer to deciding what is most important. In much of their writing, Hirokawa and Gouran maintain that both are nonissues. The theorists repeatedly state that all four functions need to be accomplished to maximize the probability of a high-quality decision, but that no single function is inherently more central than the others.[10] Likewise, no one group agenda or plan of attack seems to get the job done better. As long as the group ends up dealing with all four functions, the route its members take doesn't appear to make much difference. Hirokawa does add, however, that groups that successfully resolve particularly tough problems often take a common decision-making path.[11]

Figure 15.1 portrays the path that seems to offer a natural problem-solving progression. Groups start with problem analysis, then deal with goal setting and identifying alternatives, and end by evaluating the positive and negative characteristics of each alternative before making the final choice. This decision-making flow parallels the advice I heard on National Public Radio's *Car Talk*. Asked how car owners should handle close-call decisions on auto repair, mechanics Tom and Ray Magliozzi ("Click and Clack, the Tappet Brothers") gave a street-smart answer that ran something like this:

> First, figure out if it's broke. Then, make up your mind how good you want to fix it. Or before that ask your mechanic to list the choices you've got. Either way, you gotta do both. Finally, weigh the bang-for-the-buck that each job gives. Then decide.

Hirokawa also recognizes that the requirements of a given task may make a specific function less important than it normally is. For example, to the extent that the task is obvious to everyone, problem definition and goal setting will have less impact on the quality of the solution than time spent generating and evaluating solutions. That was the case in our departmental search for a broadcast production specialist. We already knew what we wanted.

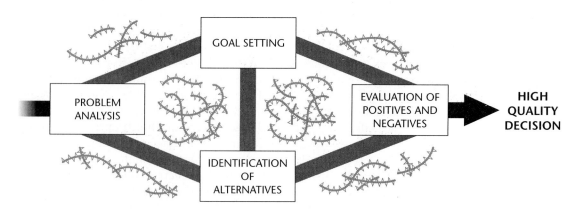

FIGURE 15.1   An Effective Decision-Making Path from a Functional Perspective

A different task, however, might make a problem definition a functional priority. Suppose the dean told our department that we had to decide once-and-for-all whether or not we wanted a journalism program. Up or down—which would it be? The closed-ended nature of the task would obviously reduce the importance of generating alternatives. On the other hand, developing a set of criteria by which to make a decision would (or should) be the committee's highest priority.

THE ROLE OF COMMUNICATION IN FULFILLING THE FUNCTIONS

Most communication scholars believe that discussion among members has a significant effect on the quality of group decisions. Traditional wisdom suggests that talk is the medium or conduit through which information travels between participants.[12] Verbal interaction makes it possible for members to (1) distribute and pool information, (2) catch and remedy errors, and (3) influence each other. Similar to Shannon and Weaver's concept of channel noise causing a loss of information (see Chapter 3), group researcher Ivan Steiner claimed that[13]

$$\begin{matrix} \text{actual group} \\ \text{productivity} \end{matrix} = \begin{matrix} \text{potential} \\ \text{productivity} \end{matrix} - \begin{matrix} \text{losses due} \\ \text{to processes} \end{matrix}$$

It follows that communication is best when it doesn't obstruct or distort the free flow of ideas.

While not rejecting this traditional view, Hirokawa believes that communication plays a more active role in crafting quality decisions. Like social constructionists (see Chapter 5), he regards group discussion as a tool or instrument that group members use to create the social reality in which decisions are made.[14] Discussion exerts its own impact on the end product of the group.

How does this work in practice? Think of the lines in Figure 15.1 as safe trails through a dense thicket—paths that connect the four key task functions and lead ultimately to the goal of a high-quality group decision. Members can easily wander off that goal path and get caught up in a tangle of pricker-bushes that thwart the group's progress. The bushes in this analogy represent distractions or barriers that retard movement toward the goal. Gouran and Hirokawa list a number of thorny obstacles—ignorance of the issue, faulty facts, misguided assumptions, sloppy evaluation of options, illogical inferences, disregard of procedural norms, and undue influence by powerful members. They believe that people go astray through talk, but they also believe that communication has the power to pull them back onto the goal-directed path.

Consistent with these convictions, Hirokawa and Gouran outline three types of communication in decision-making groups:

1. Promotive—interaction that moves the group along the goal path by calling attention to one of the four requisite decision-making functions.

2. Disruptive—interaction that diverts, retards, or frustrates group members' ability to achieve the four task functions.

3. Counteractive—interaction that members use to get the group back on track.

Hirokawa and Gouran suggest that most comments from group members disrupt rather than promote progress toward the goal. They conclude, therefore, that "effective group decision-making is perhaps best understood as a consequence of the exercise of counteractive influence."[15] In other words, someone has to say something to get the group back on track.

Hirokawa has made repeated efforts to develop a conversational coding system that classifies the function of specific statements. Much like Bales' interaction categories outlined in the introduction to decision making, Hirokawa's Function-Oriented Interaction Coding System (FOICS) requires researchers to categorize each functional utterance, which is "an uninterrupted statement of a single member that appears to perform a specified function within the group interaction process."[16]

Using FOICS, raters are asked to make two judgments: (1) Which of the four requisite functions, if any, does an utterance address? and (2) Does the utterance facilitate (promote) or inhibit (disrupt) the group's focus on that function? Ideally, this 4×2 classification scheme provides eight discrete categories of communication. Researchers can then use the data to examine the effect of verbal interaction on the decision outcome. In practice, however, raters find it difficult to agree on how a statement should be coded. Hirokawa is keenly aware that a single comment may serve multiple functions, and that words that appear helpful on the surface may have a hidden power to disrupt, or vice versa. He continues to work on refining the methodology.

TEST TUBE GROUPS IN THE LABORATORY

Hirokawa is a social scientist who firmly believes that the purpose of research is to test theory. His 1988 investigation of forty-two newly formed three-person groups is typical of more than a dozen controlled laboratory studies designed to test the functional perspective over the last two decades. Hirokawa asked these ad hoc student groups to develop specific recommendations for fair and reasonable discipline of a student caught cheating on a term-paper assignment. As a way to determine the quality of their advice, he submitted each decision to two teacher-administrators who had lots of previous experience dealing with plagiarism.

Hirokawa videotaped the forty-two discussions and tried to assess the role of communication by asking trained raters to analyze the discussion using a modified version of the FOICS categories. He also asked a separate group of trained observers to judge how well each group met the requisite functions of assessing the problem, setting criteria, and evaluating the positive and negative qualities of each alternative course of action. Note that he left out the task function of *identifying alternatives*. Even though that function was an integral part of the original theory, Hirokawa dropped it from his research design for almost a decade. Recently, however, he has reiterated the importance of generating options and he now measures whether groups fulfill that function in their deliberations.

Three separate analyses of the data confirmed that the groups reached questionable conclusions when members failed to perform the function of problem analysis or when they didn't evaluate the negative consequences of each option. Evidence for the necessity of setting criteria for acceptable choices and evaluating their positive consequences was less compelling. Overall, Hirokawa regards the results as "additional support for the functional perspective," because they confirm "that the quality of a group's decision is directly related to its ability to satisfy important decisional functions."[17]

The FOICS analysis of communication failed to identify the impact of any particular utterance. Although Hirokawa was able to establish a strong link between fulfilling two requisite functions and the quality of a group's decision, he was unable to isolate specific comments that moved the group along its goal path. His raters could spot the *quantity* of statements that "spoke" to each task function, but they had a tough time gauging the *quality* of those contributions—and Hirokawa is convinced that "group decision-making performance is dependent more on the *quality*, rather than the *quantity*, of functional utterances."[18] Coding comments is an ongoing problem for empirical researchers who want to study the nature and effects of communication. Hirokawa ruefully cites the tongue-in-cheek comment of Thomas Scheidel, the department chair at the University of Washington:

> All group communication researchers should employ the method of interaction analysis once in his/her career . . . to learn never to use it again.[19]

PRACTICAL ADVICE FOR AMATEURS AND PROFESSIONALS

How can you and I use the functional perspective to facilitate better group decisions? We can start with a healthy dose of humility concerning the wisdom of our own opinions. Hirokawa and Gouran report that groups often abandon the rational path due to the persuasive efforts of members who are convinced they alone have the right answer. Their discussion style proclaims, "Don't confuse me with the facts, my mind's made up," and they wear down the opposition. We can make sure that we don't come to the table with the sort of closed-minded attitude that contributes to the problem rather than the solution. We should also be wary of pushing any "intuitive hunch" or "gut feeling" that we can't back up with reasonable evidence. These are errors to avoid.

We can also take proactive measures to promote clear thinking within the group. In almost every article they write, Gouran and Hirokawa acknowledge their intellectual debt to the early twentieth-century American pragmatist philosopher John Dewey.[20] Dewey's pragmatism was based on the hopeful assumption that practical decisions can be brought under more intelligent control through the process of rational inquiry.[21] He advocated a six-step process of *reflective thinking* that parallels a doctor's approach to treating a patient:[22]

1. Recognize symptoms of illness.
2. Diagnose the cause of the ailment.

3. Establish criteria for wellness.

4. Consider possible remedies.

5. Test to determine which solutions will work.

6. Implement or prescribe the best solution.

Note that Hirokawa and Gouran's four requisite functions are almost exact replicas of steps 2, 3, 4, and 5 in Dewey's reflective-thinking process. Both lists recommend that group members discuss issues in a way that promotes problem analysis, goal setting, finding alternatives, and evaluation of these options. When we're tempted to make remarks that will detract from the process, Hirokawa and Gouran suggest that we bite our tongues. And when others say things that sidetrack the group from fulfilling the four functional requisites, the theorists urge us to counter with a comment aimed at getting the group back on a rational path.

You may be hesitant to counteract the dubious logic of a powerful leader or a high-status member of the group, but Gouran and Hirokawa don't advocate direct criticism. Instead, they recommend a strategy of insisting on a careful process. By raising questions, calling for more alternatives, and urging a thorough evaluation of evidence, a low-status member can have a high-power impact on the quality of the final decision.

CRITIQUE: IS RATIONALITY OVERRATED?

In their review of the small group communication literature, John Cragan and David Wright conclude that there are three leading theories.[23] One is Bormann's symbolic convergence theory, discussed in Chapter 2. The second is Scott Poole's adaptive structuration theory, which I introduce in Chapter 16. The third is Hirokawa and Gouran's functional perspective. In their 1993 *Communication Yearbook* critique of the functional perspective, Purdue University communication researchers Cynthia Stohl and Michael Holmes explain why it is so highly regarded:

> The basic premise of the perspective, that communication serves task functions and the accomplishment of those functions should be associated with effective group decisions, is intuitively appealing and sensible.[24]

As a result, many communication scholars endorse the theory as a model for group discussion and decision making. One of my students is so convinced that he wrote, "A list of the four functions should be woven into the carpet of every committee room." But the exclusive focus on rational talk in this model may be the reason why researchers get mixed results when they test the theory's predictions.[25]

Until recently, Hirokawa's response to the problem of partial support has been to tighten his research procedures. By working in a controlled setting with zero-history groups, he hoped to ensure that extraneous factors wouldn't contaminate the results. In like manner, his FOICS method of coding conversation all but ignores comments about relationships inside or outside the group. Yet by treating relational statements as a distraction, Hirokawa commits the same mistake that the late Aubrey Fisher admitted he made in his own task-focused research:[26]

> The original purpose of the investigation . . . was to observe verbal task behavior free from the confounding variables of the socioemotional dimension. That purpose, of course, was doomed to failure. The two dimensions are interdependent.[27]

Not only do political and social factors help shape the group's decision, they also go a long way in determining whether it will be effective in the long run.

Stohl and Holmes' critique frames the same issue in a slightly different way. They contend that most real-life groups have a prior decision-making history and are embedded within a larger organization. They advocate adding a *historical function* that requires the group to talk about how past decisions were made. They also recommend an *institutional function* that is satisfied when members discuss the reality of power brokers and stakeholders who aren't at the table, but whose views clearly affect and are affected by the group decision. During the search committee discussion of journalism candidates, for example, a senior faculty member observed, "Two years ago we recommended hiring a journalist without an advanced degree, and we got slapped down by the dean and the faculty personnel committee. Let's not fight that losing battle again." She served us well by dealing with historical and institutional functions that Hirokawa and Gouran ignore.

In 1995 Hirokawa moved the functional perspective out of the laboratory and into the field—literally. He joined a four-person medical team that served rural Iowa communities that had no physician. Members of the team were *student* health professionals—a future doctor, dentist, pharmacist, and nurse. The group jointly discussed the symptoms, diagnosis, potential quality of life, and treatment options for each patient. Hirokawa observed them satisfying the requirements that he and Gouran outlined in their functional perspective. He discovered that the quality of medical service they offered was more satisfying to the patients and less expensive to the state than when an established physician visited the community on an individual basis. Hirokawa has no doubts about the vitality of the functional perspective in the real world where life-and-death decisions are made.

QUESTIONS TO SHARPEN YOUR FOCUS

1. Hirokawa and Gouran claim that small groups are like living *systems*. Do you see parallels between the four *functional requisites* of task groups and the body's need for respiration, circulation, digestion, and elimination?

2. A recent analysis of over a dozen empirical studies showed that *evaluation of the negative consequences of alternative choices* is more important in reaching good group decisions than *problem analysis, goal setting,* or *identification of alternatives.*[28] Why might this be so?

3. Think of a time when you've been part of a task group that strayed from the *goal path.* What *counteractive statement* could you have made that might have brought it back on track?

4. Why might you find it frustrating to use Hirokawa's *Function-Oriented Interaction Coding System* to analyze a group discussion?

A SECOND LOOK

Recommended resource: Dennis Gouran, Randy Hirokawa, Kelly Julian, and Geoff Leatham, "The Evolution and Current Status of the Functional Perspective on Communication in Decision-Making and Problem-Solving Groups," in *Communication Yearbook 16,* Stanley Deetz (ed.), Sage, Newbury Park, Calif., 1993, pp. 573–600.

Original statement: Dennis Gouran and Randy Hirokawa, "The Role of Communication in Decision-Making Groups: A Functional Perspective," in *Communications in Transition,* Mary Mander (ed.), Praeger, New York, 1983, pp. 168–185.

Role of communication: Randy Hirokawa and Dirk Scheerhorn, "Communication in Faulty Group Decision-Making," in *Communication and Group Decision-Making,* Randy Hirokawa and M. Scott Poole (eds.), Sage, Beverly Hills, Calif., 1986, p. 69.

Integration with other theory: Randy Hirokawa and Abran Salazar, "An Integrated Approach to Communication and Group Decision-Making," in *Managing Group Life: Communicating in Decision-Making Groups,* Lawrence Frey and J. Kevin Barge (eds.), Houghton Mifflin, Boston, 1997, pp. 156–181.

Empirical test: Randy Hirokawa, "Group Communication and Decision-Making Performance: A Continued Test of the Functional Perspective," *Human Communication Research,* Vol. 14, 1988, pp. 487–515.

Coding group interaction: Randy Hirokawa, "Functional Approaches to the Study of Group Discussion," *Small Group Research,* Vol. 25, 1994, pp. 542–550.

Field study: Elizabeth Graham, Michael Papa, and Mary McPherson, "An Applied Test of the Functional Communication Perspective of Small Group Decision-Making," *Southern Communication Journal,* Vol. 62, 1997, pp. 269–279.

Critique: Cynthia Stohl and Michael Holmes, "A Functional Perspective for Bona Fide Groups," *Communication Yearbook 16,* 1993, pp. 601–614.

CHAPTER 16

Adaptive Structuration Theory

of Marshall Scott Poole

For much of the twentieth century, small group researchers thought they had spotted a universal pattern of communication that all groups use when they make a decision. Although the names and number of the different stages depended on who did the labeling and counting, scholars generally agreed there was a good fit between this single-sequence model and the actual phases that groups go through as members reach agreement:[1]

> *Orientation*—efforts are unfocused because group goals are unclear; relationships are uncertain; members need more information.

> *Conflict*—factions disagree on approach to the problem and argue against other viewpoints; members justify their own positions.

> *Coalescence*—tensions are reduced through peaceful negotiation; members allow others to "save face" by adopting solutions acceptable to all.

> *Development*—group concentrates on ways to implement a single solution; members are involved and excited.

> *Integration*—group focuses on tension-free solidarity rather than task; members reward each other for cohesive efforts.

PHASING OUT THE PHASE MODEL

Despite widespread acceptance of this one-size-fits-all phase model of group decision making, Scott Poole, now a professor of communication at Texas A&M University, wasn't convinced. Beginning with his dissertation research in 1980 and extending throughout the entire decade, he sought to find out *if* and *when* ongoing groups actually conform to the single-sequence model when making tough decisions on important issues. Poole tracked forty-seven specific decisions made by twenty-nine different groups in natural settings—real people making real decisions.[2]

Early in his research, Poole discovered that only a third of the groups actually followed the discussion pattern laid out in the single-sequence model. Yet just as Hirokawa and Gouran offer their functional perspective as a preferred procedure for task groups to adopt (see Chapter 15), Poole was still hopeful that the five phases offered a blueprint for reaching high-quality decisions. He wrote that "the unitary sequence provides a logically-ideal format for decision-making—as John Dewey and others have noted—and it may well be the simplest effective path a decision-making group could follow."[3]

Yet the longer Poole examined the complexity of group decision making, the less optimistic he became that any theory or model would be able to predict a specific sequence of action. By the end of the decade, he was disenchanted with the scientific quest to discover a fixed pattern of group behavior. He became convinced that group dynamics were far too complicated to be reduced to a few propositions or a predictable chain of events. He also grew uncomfortable with the model's objectivist assumption that group and task structures dictate the way a decision is made. In effect, it claims that communication has no significant impact on the process or the outcome; group members are just along for a five-stage ride.

Poole still thought that group members were affected by social structures such as group composition, communication networks, status hierarchies, task requirements, group norms, and peer pressure. But he no longer saw these structures as determining how the group reached a decision or what that decision might be. He was convinced that what people say and do makes a difference.

Given this commitment, Poole and two other communication scholars, Robert McPhee (Arizona State University) and David Seibold (University of California, Santa Barbara), became intrigued by the work of British sociologist Anthony Giddens. Giddens suggested that people in society are *active agents* in the sense that they are "able to act otherwise" and have the capacity "to make a difference."[4] In Giddens' macrotheory of societal structuration, Poole saw core ideas that could be adapted and applied to the microlevel of small group activity. (McPhee went on to apply structuration in an organizational context; Seibold used it to analyze the structure of arguments.) A familiarity with Giddens' concept of structuration will help you better understand the theory of adaptive structuration that Poole subsequently developed.

STRUCTURATION: PRODUCTION AND REPRODUCTION THROUGH USE OF RULES AND RESOURCES

Anthony Giddens is the director of the London School of Economics and the chief intellectual advisor to British Prime Minister Tony Blair. Colleagues call him "the most important English social philosopher of our time."[5] Giddens openly admits that *structuration* "is an unlovely term at best,"[6] yet he believes that no other word adequately captures the process of societal structures shaping people's actions, while at the same time being shaped by those actions.

Specifically, structuration refers to **"the production and reproduction of the social systems through members' use of rules and resources in interaction."**[7]

By using the word _interaction_, as opposed to the more passive _behavior_, Giddens reflects his conviction that people are relatively free to act as they will. They aren't merely pawns in the game of life or unsuspecting dupes controlled by unseen forces that they can't resist. He says that every social actor knows a lot about the way society works, and when asked, these competent social agents can explain most of what they do.[8]

Giddens uses the phrase _rules and resources_ interchangeably with the term _structures_. _Rules_ are implicit formulas for action, recipes for how to "get on" in life.[9] Giddens' conception of rules parallels that of Pearce and Cronen in CMM (see Chapter 5). As they use the term, rules are neither scientific nor societal laws. Rather, rules are participants' sense of how to play the game. _Resources_ refer to all of the relevant personal traits, abilities, knowledge, and possessions people bring to an interaction. Resources are almost always in short supply and tend to be unequally distributed within a society. Structuration is a fluid process because rules and resources (structures) are constantly changing.

Production of social systems is a process akin to the "creation of realities" in CMM, although Giddens is referring to sweeping changes across an entire society. It happens when people use rules and resources in interaction. So does reproduction. _Reproduction_ occurs whenever actions reinforce features of systems already in place, and thus maintain the status quo.

Poole applies and extends these key concepts of structuration within small groups, but a brief example of societal structuration may help you picture the kind of large-scale process that Giddens imagines. The sexual revolution that began in the 1960s illustrates how the widespread adoption of new rules and resources dramatically transformed patterns of physical intimacy. Through faithful use [rule] of "the Pill" [resource] prior to sexual intercourse [interaction], women increased their control over their own bodies [production]. The change in contraception meant men worried less about unwanted pregnancy, thus reinforcing [reproduction] the sexual double standard that it is men's role to push for greater physical intimacy, and women's responsibility to say when to stop [rule].

Giddens' concept of structuration is the core idea that spawned adaptive structuration theory. Poole calls his theory _adaptive structuration_ because he sees members of task groups intentionally adapting rules and resources to accomplish their decision-making goals. His "adaptive" label also seems appropriate because he's tailored Giddens' macrosociological principles to the microworld of small groups. When applied to group interaction, structuration obviously describes a process more intricate than the five-phase model outlined at the start of this chapter. That's fine with Poole. He believes that the "value of a theory of group decision making hinges on how well it addresses the complexities of interaction,"[10] and recommends ethnography as a way to explore structuration.[11]

OPPORTUNITY FOR PARTICIPANT OBSERVATION

Knowing that I'd be writing this chapter, I recently adopted a participant-observer role within a newly formed decision-making group so that I could identify and illustrate key principles of Poole's adaptive structuration theory. The group I selected governs the Opportunity International Network. I'll briefly describe the work of Opportunity so that you can picture the task the group faces.

Opportunity International is a nonprofit microenterprise development organization that works in twenty-eight countries of the Two-Thirds World, countries where many of the people live on the equivalent of a dollar a day. Its mission is to provide opportunities for people in chronic poverty to transform their lives. Opportunity's strategy is to create jobs, stimulate small businesses, and strengthen communities among the poor. Its method is to work through indigenous partner agencies that provide small business loans, training, and counsel. Most of the staff and volunteers are motivated by Jesus' call to serve the poor.[12]

In 1997 fifty-seven Opportunity <u>implementing</u> partner agencies in poverty areas around the world created 150,000 jobs by making 100,000 small loans. The typical loan was about $200 and the payback rate was 94 percent. Money to make these loans came from five Western <u>support</u> partner agencies that raised thirteen million dollars in contributions from individual, corporate, and government donors. Opportunity–U.S. raised two-thirds of those funds, and historically, Americans have had the biggest say in where the money goes. Until recently, some might have suggested that Opportunity's governance illustrates a cynical rendition of the Golden Rule: "He who has the gold, rules."

Increasingly, both support and implementing partners within Opportunity have come to recognize the inefficiency and inequity of a few funders making operational decisions for local organizations around the world. In the fall of 1997, representative staff and board members from each partner agency came together and formed the Opportunity International Network—a framework of autonomous yet interdependent organizations held together by a common motivation, mission statement, and set of core values. The Network is guided by a twelve-member board of individuals from around the world—six from implementing partners and six from support partners. In the rest of the chapter I'll present key elements of adaptive structuration theory that I find helpful in understanding what took place at our first Network board meeting. I'll follow the same *interaction, rules and resources, production and reproduction* succession that I used to parse Giddens' concept of structuration.

CRITICAL INTERACTIONS: DECISIONS WITH AN EYE TOWARD MORALITY, COMMUNICATION, AND POWER

The Network board's first action was to select a businessman from Ghana to serve as its Chair. His considerable stature in his own country made him a prime candidate, but before the board voted, members discussed matters of morality, communication, and power—issues that Poole and Giddens agree are fundamental in any social interaction. People talked about how their choice of leader might reflect and affect Opportunity's core values of respect and commitment to the poor. [*Morality*] Members agreed that choosing a non-western leader would send an encouraging message to the Network, namely that implementing partners now have a strong say in running the organization. [*Communication*] And everyone affirmed their obligation to act on behalf of the entire Network, not just in their own agency's interest. [*Power*] Poole notes that these three elements are mixed together in every group action. He says that it's "hard to use moral norms without considering their interpretation—a matter of meaning—and how they are 'made to count'—a matter of power."[13]

The way we selected our leader illustrates Poole's optimistic assumption that group members are "skilled and knowledgeable actors who reflexively monitor their activities as they navigate a continuous flow of intentionality."[14] Subsequent events confirm his added belief that even well-thought-out decisions always have unanticipated consequences—both good and bad. To our delight, in his first months in office this soft-spoken man from Ghana raised a million dollars for program expansion in the Philippines, introduced Opportunity's work to President and Mrs. Clinton when they visited Africa, and accepted an invitation for a skybox seat at the United Center to watch Michael Jordan win a playoff basketball game. (For this diehard Bulls fan, it's hard to rate which of these achievements was most impressive.)

On the downside, our leader's nondirective style allowed two or three individuals to monopolize most of the board's discussions. During a break the first day, an Asian woman said softly, "He should make sure that those of us from implementing partners have a chance to speak." On the second day of our meeting I sensed the growing frustration of members who had difficulty jumping into the fast-paced discussion, so I pointed out our lack of balance and urged that everyone be given equal time to contribute. My intentions were good, but Poole's structuration research suggests my advocacy may have actually made the situation worse.[15] Even though some of the muted members later thanked me for speaking up for them, my action may have encouraged implementing partner dependency by reinforcing a tendency to wait for an invitation before voicing an opinion.

The Network board experience that I've described so far highlights two key points of adaptive structuration theory. First, communication in small task groups makes a difference. We might know the structure of a group, the nature of its task, and even the history and personality of each member. Yet it's impossible to predict what decisions the group will make without hearing what's been said. Communication matters.

Second, adaptive structuration theory has a "critical edge."[16] Recall that critical theories strive to reveal unfair social practices and free people from oppressive systems (see Chapter 3). By highlighting the way that undemocratic group processes can be altered, Poole hopes to empower people who are now treated as second-class citizens.

THE USE AND ABUSE OF RULES AND RESOURCES

Poole refers to small group *rules* as "propositions that indicate how something ought to be done or what is good or bad."[17] Although rarely put into words, these rules contain members' collective practical wisdom on how best to reach the group goal. The *resources* that individuals bring to the task are "materials, possessions, or attributes that can be used to influence or control the actions of the group or its members."[18] As a research strategy, Poole selects a few structures that appear to be pivotal and then examines them in greater depth.

Personal relationships quickly emerged as a resource for the Network board. An individual's status and influence rose as that member showed personal interest in others. Two corporate CEOs provided a fascinating contrast in relational styles. Although neither man knew others, one went out of his way to establish ties before the first meeting. He traveled to three other countries to spend time with some of his new colleagues. I felt his warmth when he asked for copies of books I had written and later showed that he had spent time reading them. The other corporate leader made no attempt to reach out to others. Even though he "hosted" the first meeting in his country, he failed to invite the group to his home, join with others at dinner, or go sightseeing with the rest of us. Not only did he lack the resource of personal relationships with others, he violated the tacit rule that members should seek to be friends—or at least be friendly.

I imagine the second CEO may be impatient with the group's relational expectation. "After all," he might reason, "I was put on the Board to make astute business decisions, not to join a social clique." His likely frustration highlights Poole's claim that rules and resources can constrain group members from acting freely. Conversely, one who makes the effort to understand and use these structures can become an effective player—as did his counterpart.

A group's rules and resources are often borrowed from parent organizations or from the larger culture. Poole calls the process *appropriation.* Given that the Network board draws people from nine different cultures to the same table, Poole wouldn't be surprised if their appropriated rules and resources for making decisions didn't square with *Robert's Rules of Order.* He anticipates the Network board's experience when he writes, "Different groups may appropriate the political norm of majority rule in a variety of ways. One group may regard the rule as a last resort, to be used only if consensus cannot be attained. . . ."[19]

Consensus was the only decision path acceptable to most implementing partners, but the support partners were unwilling to abandon clearly stated motions and official votes. So we ended up appropriating both structures! If even one member was hesitant, no vote was taken. When we finally crafted a plan that all twelve could embrace, our Chair called for a unanimous vote—a ritual to seal our mutual commitment.

The bulk of Poole's structuration research has explored how groups use computerized group decision support systems (GDSS)—high tech media that have the potential to improve meetings and help make better decisions. I won't attempt to explain the hardware and software of computer-assisted meetings, but structures built into the system (such as anonymous input of ideas, or one vote per group member) are designed to promote democratic decision making. Just as we refer to "the spirit of the law," Poole and Gerardine DeSanctis (University of Minnesota), his colleague in studying how groups adapt computer technologies, call the designer's intent the "spirit of the technology." They explain that *"spirit* is the principle of coherence that holds a set of rules and resources together."[20]

The same spirit of democratic decision making was the impetus for the Network board's use of Power Point technology on the day we were to set a strategic direction for the entire organization. As we went around the table five times, each person in turn stated a single goal that he or she believed the Opportunity Network should achieve over the next few years. Each statement was simultaneously keyed into the computer and projected on the wall for the author to edit or others to question. Researching a similar procedure, Poole quotes a GDSS user's response: "By typing our thoughts on the screen, we were forced to listen to each other—something we hadn't always done before."[21] Our experience was equally positive. Members who might have been marginalized because English is their second language finally had equal space on the wall for their ideas. They also could read words they otherwise would have missed. In Poole's terms, this was a *faithful* appropriation of the technology—consistent with the spirit of the resource.

Sometimes groups appropriate rules or resources in ways that thwart their intended use. Poole describes this as an *ironic* appropriation, and I spotted it in the way the Network board processed the sixty suggestions that surfaced in the five "go-rounds." With our computer technology, we could have moved items around and combined goals that appeared similar. But after making a few false starts, the board gave up and appointed a three-person subcommittee to sort through the raw data and return the next morning with their recommendations. Since the founding spirit of the Network was to give all stakeholders a say in governance, it does seem ironic that members gave up their voice at that crucial juncture.

PRODUCTION AND REPRODUCTION—THE REASON FOR GROUP CHANGE AND/OR STABILITY

So far my description of adaptive structuration theory has focused on group <u>process</u>—members' use of rules and resources in interaction. Poole is also interested in group <u>product</u>—that which is produced and reproduced through the interaction. Clearly, decision-making groups produce decisions. The minutes of the Network board reflect nineteen decisions, all unanimous. But the action that sent shock waves throughout the Network was the one that set exceedingly high standards for our global outreach: "In the five-year period 1998–2002, we will provide 2 million loans to poor families with an overall default rate of no more than 2 percent."

At first, people around the Network were stunned by the scope of this vision; they didn't know whether to laugh or cry. As one U.S. colleague asked, "Were you folks smoking opium over there?" Yet three months later, both support and implementing partner agencies were working harder than ever to discover innovative ways to make the vision a reality. There's no doubt that by using available rules and resources, the Network board had produced a change in the larger system. But Poole would be even more curious to know the effect of the structuration process on the rules and resources of the group.

Poole believes that Giddens' *duality of structure* concept is the key to discovering that effect. Duality of structure refers to the idea that rules and resources are both the *medium* and the *outcome* of interaction.[22] In terms of group decision making, this means that the decision is *affected by* the rules and resources of the group, but at the same time it has an *effect upon* those same structures. This is crucial to Poole because it helps explain why groups are sometimes stable and predictable—as the single-sequence model suggests—yet why they are often changing and unpredictable. According to Poole, it depends on how group members appropriate rules and resources:

> Both stability and change are products of the same process. Structures are stable if actors appropriate them in a consistent way, reproducing them in similar form over time. Structures may also change, either incrementally or radically through structuration.[23]

Stability.   We can't know from a single meeting of the board whether or not the rules and resources I've described will be used the same way in the future. I suspect that consensus seeking and relationship building will continue to be enacted in their present form and become group norms. Even while apart, board members are reproducing these rules and resources as they talk to partner agen-

DILBERT reprinted by permission of United Features Syndicate, Inc.

cies about the five-year goals we set. We remind them that this vision was unanimously approved, and later send e-mail messages to Network board colleagues sharing our excitement at the staff's response. Because structures exist by virtue of being put into practice—a use-it-or-lose-it structurational principle—these cohesiveness-building rules and resources may be reproduced essentially intact and be formed into solidified structures much like sedimented rock.

Change.   Reproduction does not necessarily mean replication. Even when a group appears stable, the rules and resources that members use can change gradually over time through the process Poole calls *interpenetration of structures.* Since any group action draws upon multiple rules and resources, Poole's phrase helps us picture how one structure might affect (or infect) the other. Think again of the way the Network board has folded voting into a consensus structure. If no one ever casts a negative vote because agreement has already been reached, the consensus structure has mediated the meaning of the voting structure.

Although the board was able to create a way for majority rule and rule by consensus to co-exist, Poole notes that there are times when group structures are in direct contradiction, each undermining the other. As an example, the board charter states that "Network board members shall serve the entire Network, not just a specific constituency." Yet all twelve seats are tied to a specific country or region of the world, and each sending body naturally expects their representative to look after its interests. The interpenetration of these contradictory structures may well occur when the board begins to grapple with a global budget. The allocation of funds could trigger change that's revolutionary rather than evolutionary.

HOW SHOULD WE THEN LIVE . . . IN A GROUP?

Browsing through a bookstore recently, I spotted the intriguing title *How Should We Then Live?* The question goes way beyond the scope of this chapter, but a scaled-down version seems appropriate. The core claim of adaptive structuration theory is that groups create themselves, yet members don't always realize they are crafting and reinforcing the tools that do the work.[24] If Poole is right, how should we then live our lives with others in a task group that makes decisions? The answer is implicit in the hierarchy shown below: *Step up from a passive role to having an active voice within your group!*

Some people make things happen.

Some people watch things happen.

Some people have things happen to them.

Some people don't even know things are happening.

Poole is hopeful that a knowledge of how rules and resources work will equip low-power members to become agents of change within their groups: "If actors are unaware of a factor or do not understand how it operates, then it is likely to be a strong influence. To the extent that members are aware of a factor, they can use it or even change it."[25] Are you a group member with little or no say in the decisions made by others? Poole would encourage you to alter what you do and say in little ways. Small moves won't threaten high-power members who often tend to resist change. Yet if you are consistent and persistent, these small changes can shift the direction of the group and your role in it.[26] How shall we live our lives in groups? Aware, free, as active change agents who make things happen. That's the critical edge of adaptive structuration theory.

CRITIQUE: TIED TO GIDDENS—FOR BETTER OR WORSE

Along with symbolic convergence theory and the functional perspective (see Chapters 2 and 15), adaptive structuration theory is one of the three leading theories of group communication.[27] That's because Poole makes a serious attempt to deal with the dilemma of free will and determinism in the context of group decision making. In essence, he asks: What happens when an irresistible force (freely chosen human action) meets an immovable object (group structures that are no respecters of persons)? *Structuration* is his answer—a resolution that privileges human choice. Poole's assessment of his theory's strength is similar:

> The advantage of this theory is that it mediates the seeming dichotomy between action and structure that is inherent in much group research. It gives an account of how group members produce and maintain social structures, which acknowledges creativity and self-reflexivity.[28]

The high standing of Poole's theory within the communication discipline is also enhanced by its grounding in Giddens' concept of structuration. For the academic community, this close tie provides the kind of scholarly clout that other theorists get by claiming Aristotle, Darwin, Freud, or Marx as intellectual ancestors. But Poole's faithful adaptation of Giddens' ideas and terminology comes at a cost. The range and complexity of Giddens' thinking overwhelms most readers, and his ideas are couched in a prose style that even his admirers describe as *dense, thick, unforgiving,* and *impenetrable.* Poole's writing is more accessible, yet Giddens' heaviness still comes through. Ironically, Poole reports that Giddens doesn't recognize his ideas when they're applied in a micro-analysis of small group structuration. Apparently, the British sociologist pictures sedimented structures building across an entire society over decades rather than layers of rules and resources forming within a group after a few meetings.

Poole acknowledges that structuration is a tough concept to grasp and apply. (As a teacher, he reserves adaptive structuration theory for his graduate classes.) He critiques all group communication theories—his own included—for failing to capture the imagination of students and practitioners:

> We have not intrigued, puzzled, or spoken to most people's condition. I fear we have overemphasized technique and propositional soundness at the expense of creativity. Creativity and a certain element of playfulness are just as important as sound theory construction.[29]

Surprisingly, Poole's indebtedness to Giddens has not resulted in a group theory that's blatantly critical of oppressive structures. Poole does try to raise consciousness of unseen power dynamics that affect group discussion and he encourages members to act assertively. But this soft critical edge seems tame for a theory so deeply rooted in the ideas of Giddens, a leading figure in the critical tradition.

Ken Chase, a colleague at Wheaton, puts much of the responsibility on Giddens. Chase claims that the mark of a good critical theorist is that he or she "avoids separating ethical responsibility from theory construction and, accordingly, provides theory with an internal standard for moral argument."[30] Although structuration theory takes communication seriously and claims that morality is an issue in all interaction, Giddens doesn't suggest what that moral stance should be. Neither Giddens nor Poole provides a steady moral compass for ethical communication. Critical theorists featured later in the book aren't nearly so hesitant (see Chapters 19, 24, 33, 34). They leave no doubt as to what kind of communication they're for, and what they oppose.

QUESTIONS TO SHARPEN YOUR FOCUS

1. Poole refers to group communication as *action* rather than *behavior.* How does his choice of words reflect a rejection of the *phase* or *single-sequence model* of group decision making?

2. Poole and Giddens regard the *duality of structure* as the key to understanding *structuration.* In what way could consensus as *rule and resource* be both the *medium* and *outcome* of an *interaction?*

3. Suppose you've been elected by communication majors to represent student opinion to department faculty. In what way is your role both a *rule* and a *resource?* How could you *produce* and/or *reproduce* student influence?

4. Why do you or don't you consider *adaptive structuration theory* to be a separate theory from Giddens' *structuration theory?* Should both names appear in the chapter heading? (Poole and Giddens?) (Giddens and Poole?)

A SECOND LOOK

Recommended resource: Marshall Scott Poole, "Group Communication and the Structuring Process," in *Small Group Communication: Theory & Practice,* 7th edition, Robert Cathcart, Larry Samovar, and Linda D. Henman (eds.), Brown & Benchmark, Madison, Wis., 1996, pp. 85–95.

Expanded treatment: Marshall Scott Poole, David Seibold, and Robert McPhee, "The Structuration of Group Decisions," in *Communication and Group Decision Making,* 2nd edition, Sage, Thousand Oaks, Calif., 1995, pp. 114–146.

Initial statement: Marshall Scott Poole, David Seibold, and Robert McPhee, "Group Decision-Making as a Structurational Process," *Quarterly Journal of Speech,* Vol. 71, 1985, pp. 74–102.

Giddens' theory of structuration: Anthony Giddens, *The Constitution of Society: Outline of the Theory of Structuration,* University of California, Berkeley, 1984, pp. 281–284, 373–377.

Profile of Giddens: Robert Boynton, "The Two Tonys," *The New Yorker,* October 6, 1997, pp. 66–74.

GDSS research: Marshall Scott Poole and Gerardine DeSanctis, "Microlevel Structuration in Computer-Supported Group Decision Making," *Human Communication Research,* Vol. 19, 1992, pp. 5–49.

Structuration in organizations: Robert McPhee, "Formal Structure and Organizational Communication," in *Organizational Communication: Traditional Themes and New Directions,* Robert McPhee and Phillip Tompkins (eds.), Sage, Beverly Hills, Calif., 1985, pp. 149–178.

Rules for decision making: Sunwolf and David Seibold, "Jurors' Intuitive Rules for Deliberation: A Structurational Approach to Communication in Jury Decision Making," *Communication Monographs,* Vol. 65, 1998, pp. 282–307.

Self critique: Marshall Scott Poole, "Do We Have Any Theories of Group Communication?" *Communication Studies,* Vol. 41, 1990, pp. 237–247.

Critique of structuration theory: John Thompson, "The Theory of Structuration," in *Social Theory of Modern Societies: Anthony Giddens and His Critics,* David Held and John Thompson (eds.), Cambridge University, Cambridge, England, 1989, pp. 56–76.

ORGANIZATIONAL COMMUNICATION

Organizational theorists offer a variety of helpful ways to view what's going on when people come together for complex activity. Most organizational analysis considers communication to be the central task of management, if not of all employees. The five approaches below use different metaphors to picture the place of communication in corporate life.

1. The Mechanistic Approach. This functional approach visualizes organizations as machines designed to accomplish specific goals. According to this metaphor, workers are interchangeable parts that function smoothly as long as their range of motion is clearly defined and their actions are lubricated with an adequate hourly wage. Whether working under a supervisor on the General Motors assembly line, a manager at the golden arches of McDonald's, or a militaristic coach in the NFL, employees receive a downward flow of communication about how to do their jobs. Human engineering places a premium on control, efficiency, and rationality. However, the cool impersonality of management may grind down any sense of personal responsibility or human creativity among the work force.

2. The Human Relations Approach. In direct contrast to the mechanistic model, the human relations approach sees individuals as the essential ingredients of any organization. Workers are people, and people are not necessarily the unmotivated, passionless robots the mechanistic approach assumes them to be. Strongly influenced by Carl Rogers' optimistic view of human nature, the human relations ap-proach suggests that given the opportunity to get involved in a challenging task, people will respond with enthusiasm and creativity. Humanistic managers assume that nonauthoritarian relationships in the workplace will facilitate two-way communication and free workers to maximize their full human potential.

3. The General Systems Approach. The word *system* is used to describe many of the important realities of our life—a weather system, telephone system, accounting system, digestive system, or defense system. System refers to the overall process that transforms raw material or input from the environment (warm air, messages, numbers, food, or soldiers) into finished products or output (thunderstorms, communication, balance sheets, energy, or armies). In each case the whole is greater than the sum of its parts. Chapter 17 presents Karl Weick's model of organizations as information systems—coordinated activities in need of constant realignment in order to survive in a changing environment.

4. The Cultural Approach. Symbolic interactionists assume that human beings act toward things on the basis of meanings that the things have for them (see Chapter 4). Given impetus by the theoretical and ethnographic insights of anthropologist Clifford Geertz, cultural researchers look for shared meanings that are unique to a given group of people. Chapter 18 describes the interpretive frame that Michael Pacanowsky uses to decipher corporate culture. For Pacanowsky and other interpretive theorists, culture is not something

"And so you just threw everything together? . . . Mathews,
a posse is something you have to <u>organize</u>."

an organization *has;* culture is something an organization *is.*

5. The Political Approach. An increasing number of organizational scholars focus on the overt and covert struggles for power that take place in every organization. For ex-ample, Stanley Deetz analyzes managerial practices that perpetuate an unequal distribution of power and extend corporate control to all areas of life. Chapter 19 presents Deetz' critical theory of communication, which suggests that corporations could—and should—be more democratic.

CHAPTER 17

Information Systems Approach to Organizations

of Karl Weick

My father worked at a large metropolitan newspaper. I was 6 years old when he first took me to experience the final hour before the morning edition was "put to bed." The place was alive with activity—shouted orders, quick telephone calls, and copy boys running last-minute changes to the composing room. The whole scene was like watching a huge animal struggling for survival.

Many systems theorists regard the image of a living organism as an appropriate metaphor to apply to all organizations—one model fits all. Even though mosquitoes, sparrows, trout, and polar bears represent vastly different species in the animal kingdom, they all have systems to provide for nourishment, respiration, reproduction, and elimination of bodily waste.

Karl Weick is uncomfortable comparing organizations to live *bodies*, but he definitely regards organizing as a lively *process*. Weick is the Rensis Likert Professor of Organizational Behavior and Psychology at the University of Michigan. Whether he's examining a publishing company, IBM, the city council, or a local jazz band, Weick focuses on the common process of organizing (verb) rather than the static structure of the organization (noun). He sees his approach as capturing a slice of life; traditional analysis is like performing an autopsy.

Weick equates organizing with information processing; information is the common raw material that all organizations process. But the communication an organization receives is often equivocal. That means a given message has more than one possible interpretation. Weick's model of organizing describes how people make sense out of these confusing verbal inputs.

THE GOAL OF ORGANIZING: MAKING SENSE OUT OF EQUIVOCAL INFORMATION

Weick's idea of organizing as a way to make sense out of equivocal information is conceptually close to Shannon and Weaver's information theory and Berger's uncertainty reduction theory. (See Chapters 3 and 10.) You'll recall that Shannon and Weaver define information as the reduction of uncertainty, and Berger assumes that increasing predictability is our primary concern when we meet someone new. Early on, Weick seemed to use the terms *uncertainty* and *equivocality* interchangeably:

> The activities of organizing are directed toward the establishment of a workable level of certainty. An organization attempts to transform equivocal information into a degree of unequivocality with which it can work and to which it is accustomed.[1]

However, in his more recent book, *Sensemaking in Organizations,* Weick draws a clear distinction between the two ideas.[2]

As Weick uses the term, uncertainty denotes a lack of information. People who are uncertain look for more facts and a way to interpret them. Equivocality, on the other hand, refers to ambiguity. The problem is one of confusion rather than ignorance—too many possible meanings rather than not enough. When words or events are equivocal, people don't need more information. They need a context or framework to help them sort through the data they already have—a filter to help them screen out interpretations that would turn out to be counterproductive. Let's take a look at a typical example of equivocality in an information-processing system you know well—your college.

Suppose your instructor assigns a term paper in which you are to compare and contrast any two communication theories. By this point in your academic career, you know the ins and outs of writing a term paper, but this assignment is quite ambiguous. Would you be wise to pick a pair of theories that reflect your core commitment to the social sciences or the humanities, or would it be better to select one from each camp? Does your instructor want you to quote extensively from primary sources, or is there a premium on original thinking? Which would be a bigger mistake—a once-over-lightly, three-page analysis or an inflated twenty-page tome that's obvious overkill? You are on your own because the teacher is away at a conference until the night before the paper is due. Besides, in response to earlier questions, he or she merely said, "Do whatever you think best."

Faced with this highly equivocal situation, you'd probably start by spending as much time checking with other students in the class as you would in the library checking out the readings I've listed in the "Second Look" section. Class members who are in touch with each other would probably coalesce on a way to approach the assignment. Weick cites the words of communication specialists George Huber and Richard Daft to show how important this kind of face-to-face interaction is in any organization:

"I wish you would make up your mind, Mr. Dickens. Was it the best of times or was it the worst of times? It could scarcely have been both."

> When confronted with an equivocal [ambiguous, confusing] event, managers use language to share perceptions among themselves and gradually define or create meaning through discussion, groping, trial and error, and sounding out.[3]

I'll continue to use life at a college or university to illustrate Weick's model of organizing as a system of processing equivocal information.

THE UNIVERSITY AS A LOOSELY COUPLED SYSTEM

Over fifty years ago, University of Chicago Chancellor Robert Hutchins bemoaned the chaos that confronts the young adult who steps onto the university campus. There are courses running from art to zoology, but Hutchins claimed that neither the students nor the professors can integrate truths presented within a department, much less between separate disciplines. Weick agrees that "university organizations have *goals* that are inconsistent, ill defined, and loosely coupled; *technology* that no one understands; and *participants* who vary in how much time and effort they invest in the organization."[4] But he doesn't share Hutchins' pessimism.

Weick believes that the degree of complexity and diversity within the organization needs to match the level of ambiguity of the data it processes. He calls this "requisite variety." Since university students and faculty are dealing with vast amounts of confusing information, Weick is convinced they will fail to accomplish their varied tasks of "sensemaking" unless they organize in a complicated array of interpersonal networks. He advises deans and department heads not to panic in the face of disorder. Instead, he encourages members who are working in an equivocal information environment to "complicate themselves." Most organizations function quite well even though no one person knows for sure what's going on.

Business consultants often describe organizations according to the mechanistic approach—employees are cogs in a corporate machine which is geared to produce widgets. Weick adopts the general systems approach, but he thinks the principles of mechanical engineering have little to offer the student of organizational life. Rather than using a mechanical model, he prefers a biological one, the same type used in the Bible to describe relationships in the early Christian church:

> For the body does not consist of one member but of many. . . . If the ear should say, "Because I am not an eye, I do not belong to the body," that would not make it any less a part of the body. If the whole body were an eye, where would be the hearing? . . . God arranged the organs in the body, each one of them, as he chose. . . . There are many parts, yet one body. The eye cannot say to the hand, "I have no need of you."[5]

The passage illustrates the interconnectedness that Weick regards as the primary feature of organizing life. Sometimes the bonds are tight. For example, McDonald's quality-control directives ensure that the french fries you get near campus will taste like the ones served under the golden arches in your home neighborhood. In other cases the linkage is quite loose. A drought in Idaho may adversely affect the taste of potatoes served in McDonald's *and* the student union cafeteria. But almost all events are coupled to each other in some way.

In order that you might experience loose coupling firsthand, Weick urges you to tour buildings on your campus and note whether there are more statues and busts of college donors than there are of famous people. He claims that this seemingly isolated feature of university life could well be linked with a closed-stack policy in the library, the percentage of the campus budget that goes for beautification, the average distance from faculty offices to washrooms, and whether or not faculty names are printed alphabetically in the college catalog or are listed in order of academic rank.

Weick describes the basic unit of interconnectedness as the *double interact*. A double interact consists of three elements—act, response, and adjustment.

You write a research proposal, the professor says it's too wordy, you cut it down to a single page.

Student 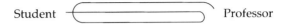 Professor

Double interact loops are the building blocks of every organization. These communication cycles are the reason Weick focuses more on relationships within an organization than he does on an individual's talent or performance. He believes that many outside consultants gloss over the importance of the double interact because they depart the scene before the effects of their recommended action bounce back to have an impact on the actor.

The university is a prime example of double interacts in a loosely coupled system. Loose coupling refers to the fact that feedback loops in the history department have little in common with the double interacts occurring in the school of business, and neither set is tightly linked with the cycles of information within the service department that's responsible for the care and maintenance of the college buildings and grounds. Although Hutchins deplored the absence of common goals and commitment, Weick sees it as a strength. Loose coupling allows the university to absorb shocks, scandals, and stupidity without destroying the system. An incompetent professor, surly registrar, or dull student won't be cause to shut the doors.

THE UNIVERSITY AS A SYSTEM OPEN TO THE ENVIRONMENT

In 1844, Charles Darwin's *The Origin of the Species* presented his theory of evolution.[6] His survival-of-the-fittest position states that organisms live in a harsh environment. Some are not well suited to survive and thus quickly die. Others have whatever it takes to live, so they reproduce. Natural selection results in a form of life better suited to its surroundings:

$$\text{Variation} \rightarrow \text{Selection} \rightarrow \text{Retention}$$

Weick applies Darwin's theory to organizations. He thinks we should consider the social-cultural environment as a jungle where survival is the name of the game, an ultimate goal even more important than accomplishing the stated aims of the organization. The March of Dimes is a case in point. That charitable organization was founded for the specific purpose of funding research to discover a way to prevent polio. In 1954 Dr. Jonas Salk discovered a vaccine for the virus, and in 1960 Dr. Albert Sabin developed an effective oral strain that virtually ended the crippling childhood disease. One might think that the charity would celebrate victory and gratefully disband. But the March of Dimes fundraising system proved to have greater resistance to death than polio. The organization adapted to a changing environment by switching its focus to birth defects, and three decades later is still soliciting money.

Weick contends that some people organize in a way better adapted to survive than do others. The fierce competition among schools for new students and the steady disappearance of small private colleges support his view. Weick notes one major difference between biological evolution and group survival, however. A given animal is what it is; variation comes through mutation. But the nature of an organization can change when its members alter their behavior. University of Colorado economist Kenneth Boulding labeled adaptation through change "survival of the fitting."

My childhood visit to my father's office left a lasting impression of organizational fluidity. He pointed out the official organizational chart that hung on the wall. The bold vertical lines of authority flowing down the pyramid gave the impression of a controlled and orderly flow of communication. But then he pulled his unofficial pencil version from the top drawer of his desk. It was smudged with erasures and cluttered by dotted lines criss-crossing the page. "That's who is really talking to each other this week," he said. Weick would have liked my father's approach. He tells managers to continually "rechart the organizational chart."

THE THREE-STAGE PROCESS OF SOCIAL-CULTURAL EVOLUTION

According to Weick, social-cultural evolution is a three-stage process that begins with enactment:

$$\text{Enactment} \rightarrow \text{Selection} \rightarrow \text{Retention}$$

Enactment: Don't Just Sit There; Do Something

The term *ivory tower* is often used to suggest that universities are separate and aloof from the world that surrounds them. Weick regards any notion of fixed barriers between an organization and its environment as erroneous. Consider the relationship between a university basketball team and its various publics. In addition to double interacts with the players, the coach has to respond to professors calling for strict academic standards, alumni clamoring for victory, reporters wanting interviews, television's dictates for odd starting times, the administration's demands for ethical recruitment, and the whims of parents and high school coaches who are convinced that their boy is the next Michael Jordan.

The example not only shows the absence of firm boundaries that mark where an organization stops and the environment begins, it is also consistent with Weick's belief that organizations create their own environment. Achieving a slot in the NCAA playoffs will create alumni pride, a climate certain to result in increased giving. In the terms of open-systems theory, the environment is as much an output as it is an input. Through the process of enactment, people organizing together invent their environment rather than merely discover it.

Action is the root idea of enactment. Weick is convinced that the failure to act is the cause of most organizational ineffectiveness. He advises the manager to wade into the swarm of equivocal events and "unrandomize" them. The only way a leader can fail the test of organizing is by doing nothing.

Weick is well known for his counterintuitive maxims for managers:

Act, then think!
Leap, then look!
Ready, fire, aim!

He believes that action is a precondition for sensemaking. He suggests that shy people may be more confused because they are hesitant to act, an inertia that robs them of the opportunity to crystalize meaning. Once people act, they generate tangible outcomes in a social context, and this helps them to look back and discover what is really happening and what needs to be done next.[7]

I recently had the opportunity to watch Weick's advice played out in discussions between the young president of a small church-affiliated college and male students who petitioned the administration for condom dispensers in the dorm. Although the proposal for coin-operated machines in the men's washrooms was specific, the meaning behind the request was equivocal. Did the ad hoc group have a sincere concern about the dangers of AIDS and unwanted pregnancy on campus, or were they using the issue as a way to attack the moral fiber of the school? Was the request an admirable case of student activism or merely a challenge to all authority?

As soon as he heard about the issue, the president, William Hill, set up a series of meetings and informal discussions to clarify the situation. Although talking about the issue may not strike you as bold action, remember that Weick regards processing information as the essence of organizing. Language is action. Whenever managers say something, they are actually creating a new environment rather than merely describing a situation. That's why Weick thinks most organizations need to have more meetings rather than fewer. President Hill's act of initiating honest dialogue created a positive climate among students and gave him a basis for selecting a specific interpretation of their behavior.

Selection: Retrospective Sensemaking

Weick defines *selection* as "retrospective sensemaking," and he thinks the concept is beautifully captured by the response of a little girl who was told to be sure of her meaning before she spoke. "How can I know what I think till I see what I say?" she replied.[8]

Retrospective sensemaking is an organizer's answer to the recurring question of meaning: "Knowing what I know now, should I change the way I label and connect the flow of experience?" But we can only interpret actions that we've already taken. That's why Weick thinks chaotic action is better than orderly inaction. Common ends and shared means are the result of effective organizing, not a prerequisite. Planning comes after enactment.

President Hill received information that he could interpret in different ways (equivocality). He immediately invited the six students making the request to come to his office to talk (enactment). After the meeting was over, he looked back on the dialogue and tried to imagine a reasonable history that led up to the conference (selection). Weick says that Hill had two organizational tools to help make his selection—rules and cycles.

Assembly *rules* are stock responses that have served well in the past and have become standard operating procedure. Whether codified in oral tradition or stated in the company manual, these rules represent the corporate wisdom about how to process information. Undoubtedly, Hill's school has a pool of guidelines relevant to the student request for condom dispensers:

> All requests should be put in writing.
> Never appear to give in to student pressure.
> In sexual matters, just say no.
> Controversial issues should be sent to the trustees.

Yet each of these rules seems less than satisfying in this many-faceted situation. Weick would claim their inadequacy is due to the ambiguity inherent in the request. Rules are fine when equivocality is low, but they fail to remove uncertainty from a situation when many conflicting interpretations are possible.

The second tool for selection is the act-response-adjustment *cycle* of the double interact. These verbal loops can take the form of interviews, meetings, open briefings, conferences, phone calls, discussions, exchange of memos, working lunches, or chats over the watercooler. Like a full turn of the crank on an old-fashioned clothes wringer, each communication cycle squeezes equivocality out of the situation. Weick claims the more equivocal the information an organization has to process, the more communication cycles it requires to reduce ambiguity to an acceptable level. He postulates an inverse relationship between rules and cycles. As cycles increase to handle complex data, reliance on rules goes down.

A series of communication cycles between Hill and Bob Lott (spokesperson for the petitioning group) went a long way to reduce uncertainty that each had about the other's intent:

> HILL: It's great to see that students care about social issues on campus.
> LOTT: Thanks for being willing to talk with us right away. The former president would have ignored the issue, and we'd never get a straight answer.
> HILL: This one is a tough issue. When it comes to AIDS, there's no such thing as safe sex with more than one partner. Condoms aren't 100 percent effective.
> LOTT: We don't want to encourage loose behavior, but sometimes in a moment of passion during dorm visitation a guy and a girl may have sex without taking proper precautions. Chaplain Thurgood at Pinehurst College said, "I'd do anything in my power to prevent one abortion or one case of AIDS." That's how we feel.
> HILL: I feel the same way. But I fear that your suggestion would encourage dangerous sex rather than make it safe. Would you guys be willing to cut out closed-door visitation to reduce the risk?
> LOTT: (Long pause) We'll have to think that one over.

You may or may not agree with either man's stance, but through this sequence of double interacts both parties eliminated potential misinterpretations of the other's actions. Hill rejected the notion that students were trying to embarrass the school, but he also concluded that they weren't willing to sacrifice their visitation rights to achieve public health goals. Hill ultimately decided against installing condom dispensers. Although Hill's decision was not popular with the students, because of his openness to discuss the issue in a reasoned manner, they did not perceive him as a weak leader or an authoritarian prude. The positive cast that each put on the other's behavior is consistent with Weick's preference for affirmation over criticism. In Hill's and Lott's case, the foundation for positive interpretations had been laid through the president's participation in pickup games of basketball in the gym.

Although much of Weick's overall model remains to be tested, two innovative studies confirm that organizational members employ rules to process unambiguous data, but use communication cycles to process highly equivocal information. Organizational communication professors Linda Putnam of Texas A & M University and Ritch Sorenson of Iowa State University designed a sixteen-hour simulation for two imaginary fireworks companies, periodically feeding in messages of varying ambiguity.[9] Participants applied more rules when the meaning was clear, and fewer rules when the meaning was obscure.

Hofstra University dean and communication professor Gary Kreps ran a field test on the year-long proceedings of a university faculty senate.[10] He gauged the equivocality of twenty-four separate motions and then tracked the debate within the body. As Weick predicted, equivocal proposals generated more double interacts among members than motions that appeared straightforward. Taken together, these studies show that there is an inverse relationship between rules and cycles that varies according to input ambiguity.

Retention: Treat Memory as a Pest

Retention in organizations is like biological reproduction in nature. It's the way systems remember. President Hill's college isn't as loosely coupled as a state university, so his manner of responding to the condom proposal may become a dominant action in corporate policy. But even small schools aren't so tightly knit that a leader's actions and interpretations automatically become the norm for all college staff. Most employees will never hear how the president responded, much less recall it at a later date.

Weick thinks that's fortunate. Too much retention creates a network of rules that reduces a person's flexibility to respond to complex information.

However, Weick recognizes that some degree of collective memory provides stability for people who are working together. What is a corporate image if not a record of interpersonal relationships, causal maps of how things work within the organization, and stories of successful penetrations of the outside environment? That's why universities publicize faculty and student achievements, preserve accounts of experiences on campus, and catalogue the honors received by famous alumni. But the weight of tradition can stifle the flexibility needed to ensure survival in an uncertain future. Weick seeks an ongoing tension between stability and innovation. He fears that managers give too much credence to past experience and suggests they should "treat memory as a pest."

Weick urges leaders to continually discredit much of what they think they know—to doubt, argue, contradict, disbelieve, counter, challenge, question, vacillate, and even act hypocritically. Company manuals are collections of recipes that suggest that each course will turn out right if you follow the rules. Weick prefers the crazed-chef approach, which encourages the cook to make up the recipe as he or she goes along. Organizations fail because they lose flexibility by relying too much on the past.

CRITIQUE: THE PLUSES AND MINUSES OF METAPHOR

Karl Weick manages to do what few systems theorists have done in the past—make a general theory interesting. He accomplishes this through a variety of provocative metaphors, vivid examples, and startling statements. He writes that "all interesting theories share the quality that they constitute an attack on the assumptions taken for granted by an audience."[11] He guarantees attention by continually challenging the conventional wisdom of managers who seek to simplify procedures and minimize conflict.

His sociocultural application of Darwin's evolution theory shares the advantages and drawbacks of all metaphors. On the positive side, the biological model explains the hard-to-understand concept of systems in terms of something we know intimately—our living body. It also highlights features of organizations that we might otherwise miss—the ultimate goal of survival, the body's ability to innovate, and especially, its constant exchange with the environment.

Yet the living-information-systems model has its danger. It would be easy to become so caught up in the figure of speech that the metaphor becomes an ideology. Some who regard organizations as actual living organisms have taken the way the body *is* as evidence of how an organization *ought* to be. For example, many apologists for the free enterprise system offer social Darwinism as justification for cutthroat capitalism. Or we might argue that since the healthy body has a functional unity, any conflict within an organization is a sign of illness. Weick, however, doesn't treat the metaphor as proof, and he shouldn't be held responsible for the mistakes of people who do.

Some managers do hold Weick responsible for his shoot-from-the-hip advice. They say that it's easy for Weick to urge a quick-draw managerial response when he's not the one who will be hurt by stray shots from his "ready, fire, aim" maxim.

Weick answers their criticism with the true story of a small Hungarian army patrol that was lost for three days in the Swiss Alps.[12] The soldiers had given up hope and resigned themselves to dying until one of them found a map in his pocket. With new hope, they used the map to discover their bearings and made it back to their home base. It was only then that they discovered that the map was of the Pyrenees, not the Alps! When you're lost, says Weick, any old map will do. When you are confused, any strategic plan is better than inaction because it animates and orients people. Act first, think later.

Weick has offered a provocative theory that has stimulated a great deal of discussion. If his theory strikes you as somewhat equivocal, consider the ambiguity an occasion for double interacts with your instructor to reduce the uncertainty.

QUESTIONS TO SHARPEN YOUR FOCUS

1. Weick's *"Act now, plan later"* advice seems to contradict Hirokawa and Gouran's functional perspective, which encourages rational deliberations (see Chapter 15). Can you think of a way that both theorists might be right?

2. Weick says that *"meetings make sense."* Using Weick's concept of *requisite variety,* can you explain why Weick thinks most organizations need to have more meetings rather than fewer?

3. What organization do you know that is *tightly coupled?* How does it deal with *equivocal messages* from its *environment?* Does this method of *information processing* help or hinder its survival?

4. Does Weick's advocacy of *retrospective sensemaking* apply to your learning in this course? When would *rules* serve well? What opportunities do you have for *double interacts?*

A SECOND LOOK

Recommended resource: Karl E. Weick, *The Social Psychology of Organizing,* 2d ed., Addison-Wesley, Reading, Mass., 1979.

Theory update: Karl E. Weick, "Organizing Improvisation: 20 Years of Organizing," *Communication Studies,* Vol. 40, 1989, pp. 241–248.

Sensemaking: Karl E. Weick, *Sensemaking in Organizations,* Sage, Thousand Oaks, Calif., 1995.

Living system metaphor: Gareth Morgan, "Nature Intervenes: Organizations as Organisms," in *Images of Organization,* Sage, Beverly Hills, Calif., 1986, pp. 39–76.

Loosely coupled systems: J. Douglas Orton and Karl E. Weick, "Loosely Coupled Systems: A Reconceptualization." *Academy of Management Review,* Vol. 15, 1990, pp. 202–223.

Academic organization: Karl Weick, "Educational Organizations as Loosely Coupled Systems," *Administrative Science Quarterly,* Vol. 21, 1976, pp. 1–21.

Retrospective sensemaking: Anne Donnellon, Barbara Gray, and Michael Burgoon, "Communication, Meaning, and Organized Action," *Administrative Science Quarterly,* Vol. 31, 1986, pp. 43–55.

Rules and equivocal messages: Linda Putnam and Ritch Sorenson, "Equivocal Messages in Organizations," *Human Communication Research,* Vol. 8, 1982, pp. 114–132.

Cycles and ambiguous proposals: Gary Kreps, "A Field Experimental Test and Reevaluation of Weick's Model of Organizing," in *Communication Yearbook 4,* Dan Nimmo (ed.), Transaction Books, New Brunswick, N.J., 1980, pp. 389–398.

Critique of Weick's model: B. Aubrey Fisher, "The Enactment of Communication," Annual meeting of the Speech Communication Association, 1980.

18

Cultural Approach to Organizations

of Clifford Geertz & Michael Pacanowsky

Princeton anthropologist Clifford Geertz writes that "man is an animal suspended in webs of significance that he himself has spun."[1] He pictures culture as those webs. In order to travel across the strands toward the center of the web, an outsider must discover the common interpretations that hold the web together. Culture is shared meaning, shared understanding, shared sensemaking.

Geertz has conducted field research in the islands of Indonesia and on the Moroccan highlands, rural settings remote from industrial activity. His best known monograph is an in-depth symbolic analysis of the Balinese cockfight. Geertz has never written a treatise on the bottom line, never tried to decipher the significance of the office Christmas party, and never met a payroll, a disqualifying sin in the eyes of many business professionals. Despite his silence on the topic of big business, Geertz' interpretive approach has proved useful in making sense of organizational activity.

In the field of speech communication, former University of Colorado professor Michael Pacanowsky has applied Geertz' cultural insights to organizational life. He says that if culture consists of webs of meaning that people have spun, and if spun webs imply the act of spinning, "then we need to concern ourselves not only with the structures of cultural webs, but with the process of their spinning as well."[2] That process is communication. It is communication that "creates and constitutes the taken-for-granted reality of the world."[3]

CULTURE AS A METAPHOR OF ORGANIZATIONAL LIFE

The use of culture as a root metaphor was undoubtedly stimulated by western fascination with the economic success of Japanese corporations. When American business leaders traveled to the Far East a decade ago to study methods of production, they discovered that the superior quantity and quality of Japan's industrial output had less to do with technology than it did with workers' shared cultural value of loyalty to each other and to their corporation. Organizing looks radically different depending on how people in the host culture structure meaning. Communal face-saving in Japan is foreign to the class antagonism of Great Britain, or the we're-number-one competitive mind-set of the United States.

Today the term *corporate culture* means different things to different people. Some observers use the phrase to describe the surrounding environment that constrains a company's freedom of action. (U.S. workers would scoff at singing a corporate anthem at the start of their working day.) Others use the term to refer to a quality or property of the organization. (Acme Gizmo is a friendly place to work.) They speak of *culture* as synonymous with *image, character,* or *climate.* But Pacanowsky is committed to Geertz' symbolic approach, and thus considers culture as more than a single variable in organizational research:

> Organizational culture is not just another piece of the puzzle; it is the puzzle. From our point of view, culture is not something an organization *has;* a culture is something an organization *is.*[4]

WHAT CULTURE IS; WHAT CULTURE IS NOT

Geertz admits that the concept of culture as "systems of shared meaning" is somewhat vague and difficult to grasp. Unlike popular usage, which equates culture with concerts and art museums, he refuses to use the word to signify "less primitive." No modern anthropologist would fall into the trap of classifying people as high- or low-culture.

Culture is not whole or undivided. Geertz points out that even close-knit societies have subcultures and countercultures within their boundaries. For example, employees in the sales and accounting departments of the same company may eye each other warily—the first group calling the accountants "number crunchers" and "bean counters," the accountants in turn labeling members of the sales force "fast talkers" and "glad-handers." Despite their differences, both groups may regard the blue-collar bowling of production workers as a strange ritual compared with their own weekend rite of a round of golf.

For Pacanowsky, the web of organizational culture is the residue of employees' performances—"those very actions by which members constitute and reveal their culture to themselves and to others."[5] He notes that job performance may play only a minor role in the enactment of corporate culture.

> People do get the job done, true (though probably not with the singleminded task-orientation communication texts would have us believe); but people in organizations also gossip, joke, knife one another, initiate romantic involvements, cue new employees to ways of doing the least amount of work that still avoids hassles from a supervisor, talk sports, arrange picnics.[6]

Geertz calls these cultural performances "an ensemble of texts . . . which the anthropologist strains to read over the shoulder of those to whom they properly belong."[7] The elusive nature of culture prompts Geertz to label its study a "soft science." It is "not an experimental science in search of law, but an interpretive one in search of meaning."[8] The corporate observer is one part scientist, one part drama critic.

The fact that symbolic expression requires interpretation is nicely captured in a story about Pablo Picasso recorded by York University (Toronto) writer Gareth Morgan.[9] A man commissioned Picasso to paint a portrait of his wife. Startled by the nonrepresentational image on the canvas, the woman's husband complained, "It isn't how she really looks." When asked by the painter how she really looked, the man produced a photograph from his wallet. Picasso's comment: "Small, isn't she?"

THICK DESCRIPTION—WHAT ETHNOGRAPHERS DO

Geertz refers to himself as an ethnographer. You'll recall that I first introduced his name when I presented ethnography as one of the four main communication research methodologies (see Chapter 1). Just as geographers chart the physical territory, ethnographers map out social discourse. They observe, they record, they analyze. There's no shortcut for the months of participant observation required to collect an exhaustive account of interaction. Without that raw material, there would be nothing to interpret.

Geertz spent years in Indonesia and Morocco developing his deep description of two separate cultures. Pacanowsky initially invested nine months with W. L. Gore & Associates, best known for their Gore-Tex line of sports clothing and equipment. Like Geertz, he was completely open about his research goals, and during the last five months of his research he participated fully in problem-solving conferences at the company. Later, Pacanowsky spent additional time at the W. L. Gore plants in Delaware as a consultant. In order to become intimately familiar with an organization *as members experience it*, ethnographers must commit to the long haul. Pacanowsky has recently committed to the long haul of working full-time at Gore. Earlier, however, he cautioned against "going native." The researcher must

> . . . maintain a posture of radical naïveté and allow himself or herself to experience organizational life as "strange," so that he or she will be sure to prompt organizational members for the resources (or knowledge) they are drawing upon which allow them to take for granted those very same organizational experiences.[10]

The daily written accounts of intensive observation invariably fill the pages of many ethnographic notebooks. The visual image of these journals stacked on top of each other would be sufficient justification for Geertz to refer to ethnography as "thick description." The term, however, describes the intertwined layers of common meaning that underlie what a particular people say and do. Analysis of corporate culture requires interpretation as well as observation. It's not enough to preserve copies of office memos or to make transcripts of meetings. Thick description is tracing the many strands of a cultural web and tracking evolving meaning.

Thick description starts with a state of bewilderment. "What the devil's going on?" Geertz asks himself as he wades into a new culture. The only way to reduce the puzzlement is to observe as if one were a stranger in a foreign land. This could be difficult for a manager who is already enmeshed in a specific corporate culture. He or she might overlook many of the signs that point to common interpretation. Worse yet, the manager might assume that office humor or the company grapevine has the same significance for people in this culture as for those in a previous place of employment. Geertz says it will always be different.

Behaviorists would probably consider employee trips to the office watercooler of little interest. If they did regard water breaks worth studying, they would tend to note the number of trips and length of stay for each worker. Ethnographers would be more interested in the significance the seemingly mundane activity had for these particular employees. Instead of a neat statistical summary, they'd record pages of dialogue at the watercooler. Pacanowsky fears that a frequency count would only bleach human behavior of the very properties that interest him. Classifying performances across organizations would yield superficial generalizations at the cost of localized insight. He'd rather find out what makes a particular tribal culture unique.

Although Pacanowsky would pay attention to all cultural performances, he would be particularly sensitive to the imaginative language members used, the stories they told, and the nonverbal rites and rituals they practiced. Taken together, these three forms of communication provide helpful access to the unique shared meanings within an organization.

METAPHORS: TAKING LANGUAGE SERIOUSLY

When used by members throughout an organization (and not just management), metaphors can offer the ethnographer a starting place for accessing the shared meaning of a corporate culture. Pacanowsky records a number of prominent metaphors used at W. L. Gore & Associates, none more significant than the oft-heard reference within the company to Gore as a "lattice organization."[11] If one tried to graph the lines of communication at Gore, the map would look like a *lattice* rather than the traditional pyramid shaped organizational chart. The cross-hatched lines would show the importance of one-on-one communication and reflect that no person within the company needs permission to talk to anyone else. Easy access to others is facilitated by an average plant size of 150 employees and voice mail and paging systems that encourage quick responses.

This lack of hierarchical authority within the lattice organization is captured in the egalitarian title of "associate" given to every worker. People do have differential status at Gore, but it comes from technical expertise, a track record of good judgment, and evidence of follow-through that leads to accomplishment.

The company's stated objective (singular) is "to make money and have fun."[12] The founder, Bill Gore, is famous for popping into associates' offices and asking, "Did you make any money today? Did you have any fun today?" But work at Gore is not frivolous. The *waterline* operating principle makes it clear that associates should check with others before making significant decisions:

> Each of us will consult with appropriate Associates who will share the responsibility of taking any action that has the potential of serious harm to the reputation, success, or survival of the Enterprise. The analogy is that our Enterprise is like a ship that we are all in together. Boring holes above the waterline is not serious, but below the waterline, holes could sink us.[13]

After nine months of studying communication performances at W. L. Gore & Associates, Pacanowsky floated three different metaphors of his own to describe crucial features of that unique culture.[14] In its passion for decentralization and its extraordinary orality, he saw Gore as a *cluster of peasant villages.* In its attraction for people who love to create something new but want to fit in with other like-minded players, Gore is like a *large improvisational jazz group.* And inasmuch as a sizable group of Gore associates thinks that the company's innovative charter is the best thing since the invention of the wheel while a smaller but significant group is cynical about its idealistic goals, Pacanowsky compared the people at Gore to *factions in colonial America.* For both the discovery and communication of corporate culture, ethnographers find metaphor a valuable tool.

THE SYMBOLIC INTERPRETATION OF STORY

Stories that are repeated over and over provide a convenient window through which to view corporate webs of significance. Pacanowsky asks, "Has a good story been told that takes you to the heart of the matter?"[15] He focuses on the script-like qualities of narratives that line out an employee's part in the company play. Although workers have room to improvise, the anecdotes provide clues as to what it means to perform a task in this particular theater. Stories capture memorable performances and pass on the passion the actor felt at the time.

Pacanowsky suggests three types of narrative that dramatize organizational life. *Corporate stories* carry the ideology of management and reinforce company policy. Every McDonald's franchisee hears about the late Ray Kroc, who, when he was chairman of the board, picked up trash from the parking lot when he'd visit a store. *Personal stories* are those company personnel tell about themselves, often defining how they would like to be seen within the organization. *Collegial stories* are positive or negative anecdotes told about others in the organization. Since these aren't usually sanctioned by management, collegial accounts pass on how the organization "really works."

Stories at Dixie

Throughout most of my life, I've had access to some of the cultural lore of Dixie Communications, a medium-sized corporation that operates a television station and a newspaper in a southern city. Like so many other regional companies, Dixie has been taken over by an out-of-state corporation that has no local ties. The brief narratives below are shorthand versions of stories heard again and again throughout the company.

Although the original publisher has been dead for twenty-five years, old-timers fondly recall how he would spend Christmas Eve with the workers in the press room. Their account is invariably linked with reminders that he initiated health benefits and profit sharing long before it became a union demand. (Corporate)

The publisher ran another newspaper in the north and so was away much of the time. No announcement was ever made about when he would return. When the janitor polished the brass banister in the main lobby and hummed "Happy Days Are Here Again," everyone knew "the big brass" would arrive shortly. (Corporate)

The current comptroller is the highest-ranking "local boy" in the corporation. He often tells the story about the first annual audit he performed long before computers were installed. Puzzled when he ran across a bill for fifty pounds of pigeon feed, he discovered that the company used homing pigeons to send in news copy and circulation orders from a town across the bay. The story usually concludes with an editorial comment about pigeons being more reliable than the new machines. His self-presentation reminds listeners that he has always been cost-conscious, yet it also aligns him with the human side of the "warm people versus cold machines" issue. (Personal)

The theme of absentee ownership runs throughout many of the stories told around the plant. On-site inspections by the CEO of the parent company are limited to overnight stays. The man comes straight from the airport carrying his suitcase. Rumor has it that he brings it to carry the cash profits back up north. The term *carpetbagger* is often part of the story. (Collegial)

Shortly after the takeover, a department head encouraged the new publisher to meet with his people for a few minutes at the end of the day. The new boss declined the invitation on the grounds of efficiency: "To be quite candid, I don't want to know about a woman's sick child or a man's vacation plans. That kind of information makes it harder to fire a person." Spoken in a cold, superior tone, the words *quite candid* are always part of the story. (Collegial)

Both Geertz and Pacanowsky caution against any analysis that says "This story means. . . ." Narratives contain a mosaic of significance and defy a simplistic one-on-one translation of symbols. Yet taken as a whole, the five stories above reveal an uneasiness with the new management. This interpretation is consistent with repeated metaphorical references to the old Dixie as "family" and the new Dixie as "a faceless computer."

FICTION AS A FORM OF SCHOLARLY DISCOURSE

Not only has Pacanowsky shown that narratives are a prime source of cultural wisdom for the ethnographer, he has also demonstrated that scholars can use a fictional format to convey the results of their research. Pacanowsky has published an imaginative account in the *Quarterly Journal of Speech* that captures the angst felt within a subculture of academics. In the introduction he claims that "fictional descriptions, by the very nature of their implicitness and impressionism can fully capture (can I be so strong?) both the bold outlines and the crucial nuances of cultural ethos."[16] On the next page, Figure 18.1 contains an excerpt of a conversation between two speech communication professors during an annual convention. Although fictional, it is autobiographical to the extent that Pacanowsky and the character of Jack in the story are members of the same subculture.

RITUAL: THIS IS THE WAY IT'S ALWAYS BEEN, AND ALWAYS WILL BE

Geertz wrote about the Balinese rite of cockfighting because the contest represented more than a game. "It is only apparently cocks that are fighting there. Actually it is men." The cockfight is a dramatization of status. "Its function is interpretive: It is a Balinese reading of Balinese experience, a story they tell themselves about themselves."[17]

Pacanowsky agrees with Geertz that some rituals (like the Balinese cockfight) are "texts" which articulate *multiple* aspects of cultural life.[18] These rituals are nearly sacred, and any attempt to change them meets with strong resistance. Although the emphasis on improvisation and novelty reduces the importance of ritual at Gore, organizational rites at more traditional companies weave together many threads of corporate culture.

Over a generation ago, workers in the classified advertising department at Dixie created an integrative rite that survives to the present. The department is staffed by over fifty telephone sales representatives who work out of a large common room. At Dixie, these representatives not only take the "two lines/two days/two dollars" personal ads over the phone, they also initiate callbacks to find out if customers were successful and might want to sell other items. Compared with similar operations at other papers, classified advertising at Dixie is a major profit center with low employee turnover. The department continues to have the "family atmosphere" of pre-merger Dixie. Most of the phone representatives are women under the age of 40. They regard Max, the male manager who has held his position for over thirty years, as a "father confessor"—a warm, nonjudgmental person with a genuine concern for their lives. Whenever a female employee has a baby, Max visits her in the hospital and offers help to those at home preparing for her return. Women announce their pregnancy by taping a dime within a large picture frame on the outer wall of Max's office, inscribing their name and anticipated day of delivery.

This rite of integration serves multiple functions for the women:

> At a time of potential anxiety, it is an occasion for public affirmation from the larger community.

> The rite is a point of contact between work and those outside of Dixie. Employees often take pride in describing the ritual to customers and friends.

Slouching Towards Chicago

He and Radner were such different people, and they were not really close friends. But at every convention, they would get together over dinner and appraise their professional careers and personal lives in a surprisingly intimate manner. One year, Radner had side-splitting tales to tell of his affair with the wife of his department chairman. The next year, he cried as he worked his way through the details of his divorce. For his part, Jack was inclined to reflect on the transitions of his life—how strangely happy he was to have gotten married in a church, how being a father brought him to heights of joy and depths of anger he'd never before felt capable of experiencing, how he would become seized by intense physical cold on those occasions when he really thought about his father's death. "Our lives in review" was the way Jack thought about those dinners with Radner.

"You know," said Radner, "in seven years, I have authored or co-authored 48 convention papers, and published 14 articles in refereed journals, and had 10 chapters invited for various textbooks and readers."

"Numbers have always been important to you," said Jack with a laugh. "That's why you're such a fine quantitative type."

"Hey, don't patronize me. Your career is cranking along, too."

"I hardly have—let's see what is it? 48 plus 14 plus 10?—seventy odd articles at this point."

"Maybe not, but you're a known item in the field. People read your work. They talk about it. They get worked up about it. I mean, I hate to admit it, but it's true. Nobody really gets up about my stuff. It's solid, but nobody gets worked up about it. But your stuff—"

"Hype. I get calls in the night from 24-year-old groundbreakers-to-be who can't add. 'I have to put together my prospectus and I don't want to do a traditional, quantitative study, and I read your article in *QJ*, and I wondered if you could send me anything else you've written that I can use to, you know, develop my position, I mean, everybody here is so traditional, I don't know if they'll let me do an interpretive study . . .' on and on."

"But that's what I mean. People get excited."

"I don't. You know what I want? What I want more than 70 articles or people getting excited or calling me up? What I want is to write one good solid book-length piece of interpretive research. No more diddly articles. No more 'this is what we should be doing.' Just one solid book. And then I'd get excited."

"Why don't you then?"

"I can't!" Jack pounded the table with his fist. "I gotta worry about tenure. I gotta worry about building my vita. So I piss away my time on these damned convention papers, on these 'take-a-potshot-at-the-other-guy' articles instead of—"

"Oh, come on. You're going to get tenure. Why don't you stop doing this other shit and work on a book?"

It was not a question that Jack had never heard before, not with the frequency with which he would launch into his 'pissing my life away' refrain. But maybe it was because it was during "life in review" that the question suddenly hit him with a force and an eerieness that he hadn't felt before. He was silent for a moment. "Because," he said finally, shaken with the realization, "I don't know if I really have it in me to write a book. And it scares me to think I might find that out."

FIGURE 18.1 Excerpt from "Slouching Towards Chicago" by Michael Pacanowsky

Although the dime-on-the-wall practice originated with the workers, the authorized chronicle of decades of expected births proclaims a sense of permanence. It says in effect: "The company doesn't consider motherhood a liability; your job will be here when you get back."

From the management's standpoint, the rite ensures that there will be no surprises. Max has plenty of time to schedule the employee's maternity leave, arrange for another salesperson to cover her accounts, and anticipate stresses that she might be encountering.

It is tempting to read economic significance into the fact that employees use dimes to symbolize this major change in their lives. But the women involved refer to the small size of the token rather than its monetary value. Geertz and Pacanowsky would caution that this is *their* story, and we should listen to *their* interpretation.

THE MANAGER AS CHANGE AGENT

The current popularity of the cultural metaphor is undoubtedly due to business leaders' desire to shape interpretation within the organization. Symbols are the tools of management. Executives don't operate forklifts or produce widgets; they create a vision, state goals, process information, send memos, and engage in other symbolic behavior. If they believe that culture is the key to commitment, productivity, and sales, the possibility of changing culture becomes a seductive idea. Creating favorable metaphors, planting organizational stories, and establishing rites would seem an ideal way to create a corporate myth that would serve managerial interests.

But can culture be created? Geertz regards shared interpretations as naturally emerging from all members of a group rather than consciously engineered by leaders. Managers may articulate a new vision in a fresh vocabulary, but it is the workers who smile, sigh, snicker, or scoff. For example, Martin Luther King's "I Have a Dream" speech, which will be discussed in Chapter 20, was powerful because he touched a chord that was already vibrating within millions of listeners.

DILBERT reprinted by permission of United Features Syndicate, Inc.

Shared meanings are hard to dispel. Symbol watchers within a company quickly discount the words of management if they don't square with performance. Yet even if culture *could* be changed, there still remains the question of whether it *should* be. Symbolic anthropologists have traditionally adopted a non-intrusive style appropriate to examining fine crystal—look, admire, but don't touch. Managers who regard themselves as agents of cultural change create bull-in-a-china-shop fears for consultants who have ethical concerns about how their corporate analyses might be used. University of Massachusetts management professor Linda Smircich notes that ethnographers would draw back in horror at the idea of using their data to extend a tribal priest's control over the population, yet most communication consultants are hired by top management to do just that.[19]

CRITIQUE: IS THE CULTURAL APPROACH USEFUL?

By now you understand that Geertz would regard the quest to alter culture as both inappropriate and virtually impossible. This purist position exposes him to criticism from pragmatists who want not only to understand organizational communication but also to influence it. While granting that culture is a helpful metaphor, pragmatists point out that most employees join a company long after they've been socialized into the values of the larger society. They also claim that corporate cultures like Gore & Associates are rare. Most organizations have a series of bureaucratic rules and procedures that seem to replace the shared interpretations that are Geertz and Pacanowsky's "superglue" of culture. Pragmatists also despair of having the time or funding to carry out the thick description Geertz' view of culture dictates.

None of these objections attack the basic validity of an interpretive approach that takes corporate communication seriously. Contrary to the traditional approach of consultants who are funded by the organizations they study, the purpose of thick description is not to help managers increase production or to get things running smoothly. The aim of most symbolic analysis is to create a better understanding of what it takes to function effectively within a given culture. In most organizations, members are free to decide whether or not they want to belong. A sensitive cultural analysis could help them make an intelligent choice. Perhaps managers fail to appreciate the value of thick description because they have yet to make an effort to sort out the webs of significance within their organization. The answer, like culture, is a matter of interpretation.

QUESTIONS TO SHARPEN YOUR FOCUS

1. Based on the concept of organizational culture as systems of *shared meaning*, how would you describe the culture at your school to a prospective student?

2. Consider Pacanowsky's "Slouching Towards Chicago" as an *ethnographer's thick description*. What can you deduce about Jack and Radner's subculture from the fragment of narrative in Figure 18.1?

3. Think of your extended family as an *organizational culture.* What single family *ritual* might you analyze to *interpret* the webs of significance you share to someone visiting your home?

4. What favorite *story* do you tell to others about your current or most recent place of employment? Would you classify it as a *corporate, personal,* or *collegial* narrative? Why?

A SECOND LOOK

Recommended resource: Clifford Geertz, The *Interpretation of Cultures,* Basic Books, New York, 1973. (See especially "Thick Description: Toward an Interpretive Theory of Culture," pp. 3–30; and "Deep Play: Notes on the Balinese Cockfight," pp. 412–453.)

Culture as performance: Michael Pacanowsky and Nick O'Donnell-Trujillo, "Organizational Communication as Cultural Performance," *Communication Monographs 50,* 1983, pp. 127–147.

Non-managerial orientation: Michael Pacanowsky and Nick O'Donnell-Trujillo, "Communication and Organizational Cultures," *Western Journal of Speech Communication,* Vol. 46, 1982, pp. 115–130.

Cultural metaphor: Gareth Morgan, "Creating Social Reality: Organizations as Cultures," in *Images of Organization,* Sage, Newbury Park, Calif., 1986, pp. 111–140.

Corporate ethnography: Michael Pacanowsky, "Communication in the Empowering Organization," in *Communication Yearbook 11,* James Anderson (ed.), Sage, Newbury Park, Calif., 1988, pp. 356–379.

Corporate stories: Joanne Martin, Martha Feldman, Mary Jo Hatch, and Sim Sitkin, "The Uniqueness Paradox in Organizational Stories," *Administrative Science Quarterly,* Vol. 28, 1983, pp. 438–453.

Rites: Harrison Trice and Janice Beyer, "Studying Organizational Cultures Through Rites and Ceremonials," *Academy of Management Review,* Vol. 9, 1984, pp. 653–669.

Current scholarship: Peter J. Frost, Larry F. Moore, Meryl Reis Louis, Craig C. Lundberg, and Joanne Martin (eds.), *Reframing Organizational Culture,* Sage, Newbury Park, Calif., 1991.

Managing organizational culture: Sonja A. Sackmann, "Managing Organizational Culture: Dreams and Possibilities," *Communication Yearbook 13,* James A. Anderson (ed.), Sage, Newbury Park, Calif., 1990, pp. 114–148.

Interpretive vs. functional approach: Linda L. Putnam, "The Interpretive Perspective: An Alternative to Functionalism," in *Communication and Organizations: An Interpretive Approach,* Linda L. Putnam and Michael Pacanowsky (eds.), Sage, Newbury Park, Calif., 1982, pp. 31–54.

CHAPTER 19

Critical Theory of Communication Approach to Organizations

of Stanley Deetz

The 1989 film *Roger & Me* dramatizes the three-year quest of filmmaker Michael Moore to personally interview Roger Smith, the inaccessible board chairman of General Motors.[1] An early scene in the film shows Smith announcing the company's plan to close eleven factories, a "cost-cutting" measure that laid off 30,000 workers in Flint, Michigan, birthplace of GM, the world's largest industrial corporation. Moore tells the audience he wanted to invite Roger Smith to spend a day in Flint talking with jobless workers and their families. He later refers to his film as "dark comedy, social satire, 'mockumentary' "[2] because it contrasts the smug affluence of isolated corporate managers with the desperate poverty of people who can't find jobs. Critics described the film as wickedly funny and many listed it in their "Top Ten Flicks of the Year."

Roger & Me personalizes the consequences of corporate "downsizing." Moore repeatedly shows a sheriff's deputy evicting people from their homes while piling their belongings on the sidewalk. ("Nothing personal; I'm just doing my job.") He also chronicles the increased rates of violent crimes, mental illness, and family breakup that follow the massive layoffs. During this period, *Money* magazine ranked Flint as the worst city in the United States to live in. Viewers are convinced when Moore interviews an out-of-work woman who has a sign in front of her house: "Rabbits for Sale—Pets or Meat." The "Bunny Lady" talks about hard times while holding a large white rabbit, absently stroking its fur. She then clubs, skins, and guts the animal in under a minute, explaining matter-of-factly that this is what she has to do to survive.

Moore's film taps a growing concern of Americans that something is wrong with the way decisions are reached at the highest levels of business and government. While auto industry advocates complain that slick editing created the unfair impression that Flint was gutted by corporate decree, no one disputes the devastating impact of AT&T's 1995 decision to lay off 40,000 employees in the midst of high corporate profits. The choices GM and AT&T made illustrate that many major corporate decisions are reached with little regard to their effects on employees, communities, or the environment. As Michael Moore demonstrated, the modern corporation is protected from direct public control, yet it is the place where the crucial decisions that affect the everyday lives of citizens are made.

University of Colorado communication professor Stanley Deetz has developed a critical communication theory to explore ways to ensure the financial health of corporations while increasing the representation of diverse—and often noneconomic—human interests. He does this by first showing that corporations have become political as well as economic institutions. He then employs advances in communication theory to point out how communication practices within corporations can distort decision making. Finally, he outlines how workplaces can become more productive and democratic through communication reforms.

CORPORATE COLONIZATION OF EVERYDAY LIFE

Deetz views multinational corporations such as GM, AT&T, IBM, Time-Warner, and Amoco as the dominant force in society—more powerful than the church, state, or family in their ability to influence the lives of individuals. For example, over 90 percent of the mass media outlets—newspapers, broadcast, cable, telephone lines, and satellites—are owned by just a handful of corporations.[3] Deetz notes that continual reporting of the Dow-Jones Industrial Average underscores the absence of an equivalent index of the arts, health care, or environmental quality. Media preoccupation with corporate well-being makes presidential candidate Steve Forbes' curious claim that "economics and values are the same thing" sound almost reasonable.[4]

The corporate executive suite is the place where most decisions are made regarding the use of natural resources, development of new technologies, product availability, and working relations among people. Deetz says that corporations "control and colonize" modern life in ways that no government or public body since the feudal era ever thought possible.[5] Yet the fallout of corporate control is a sharp decrease in the quality of life for the vast majority of citizens.

Within the lifetime of most of today's college students, the average American workweek has increased from forty to fifty hours, and leisure time has declined by a corresponding ten hours. Despite the fact that 85 percent of families with children now have mothers working outside the home, their real standard of living has *decreased* over the last two decades. The number of full-time workers whose income has fallen below the poverty line has increased by half, yet compensation for chief executive officers (CEOs) has risen from 24 times to over 175 times that of the average worker.[6] Deetz suggests that "we need to consider in depth what type of 'business' this is, who the moral claimants are, how privilege is organized, and what the possible democratic responses are."[7]

Deetz' theory of communication is "critical" in that he wants to critique the easy assumption that "what's good for General Motors is good for the country." More specifically, he wants to examine communication practices in organizations that undermine fully representative decision making, thus reducing the quality, innovation, and fairness of company policy.

INFORMATION VERSUS COMMUNICATION: A DIFFERENCE THAT MAKES A DIFFERENCE

Deetz begins his analysis by challenging the view that communication is the transmission of information. Even though a majority of human communication scholars now dismiss Shannon and Weaver's information theory (see Chapter 3), the conduit model is still taken for granted in organizations and in everyday life. There's an intuitive appeal in the idea that words refer to real things—that by using the right words we can express state-of-the-art knowledge. As Deetz notes, "Clearly, the public really wants to believe in an independent reality."[8] He warns, however, that as long as we accept the notion that communication is merely the transmission of information, we will continue to perpetuate corporate dominance over every aspect of our lives.

Consider GM's annual report. The sanitized numbers present themselves as facts compiled and categorized according to "standard accounting procedures." Yet Deetz contends that each line item is constitutive—created by corporate decision makers who had the power to make their decisions stick. What seems to be value-free information is really meaning in formation. The end-of-the-year audit is not fact—it's artifact.

In place of the *information model* of messages, Deetz presents a *communication model* that regards language as the principal medium through which social reality is produced and reproduced. He states that "language does not represent things that already exist. In fact, language is a part of the production of the thing that we treat as being self-evident and natural within the society."[9] Humanists like I. A. Richards have long pointed out that meanings are in people, not in words (see Chapter 3). But Deetz moves even further away from a representational view of language when he raises the question, "*Whose* meanings are in people?" Once we accept that organizational forms are continually created and recreated through language, we'll understand that GM divisions not only produce cars, they also produce meaning.

People who adopt the lingo of big business may not be aware that they are putting corporate values into play. For example, the bottom line on a profit-and-loss statement is only that—the last line on the financial report. Yet a CEO's continual use of the term *the bottom line* to justify all managerial decisions produces a perceived reality that shuts out non-financial considerations. When

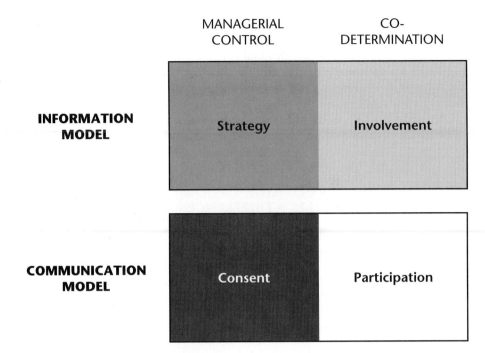

FIGURE 19.1   Organizational Practices
(Based on Deetz, *Transforming Communication, Transforming Business,* Chapter 7)

ordinary citizens begin to use this economic idiom to characterize the deciding or crucial factor in their own family decisions, they reinforce and expand the influence of corporate thinking in life without even realizing they are doing so.

Figure 19.1 contrasts Deetz' communication approach to organizational practices with an information approach that regards language as neutral and neutered. Like Pearce and Cronen (see Chapter 5), Deetz considers communication to be the ongoing social construction of meaning. But his critical theory differs from CMM in that he thinks that the issue of power runs through all language and communication. Deetz would not be surprised that GM workers or the people of Flint, Michigan, had no say in plant closures, or that filmmaker Michael Moore was refused an interview with board chairman Roger Smith. He believes that managerial control often takes precedence over representation and long-term company health.

> The fundamental issue in my analysis is control and how different groups are represented in decision making. . . . Since industrialization, managers in American corporations have primarily operated from a philosophy of control.[10]

The left side of Figure 19.1 represents corporate decision processes that systematically exclude the voices of people who are affected by the decisions. Deetz calls the practice discursive closure or, more simply, *managerial control.* The right side of the figure pictures decision processes that invite open dialogue among all stakeholders. Deetz calls the practice *codetermination*. Coupled with the constitutive view of communication, codetermination represents the "collaborative collective constructions of self, other, and the world"[11] that Deetz believes are the product of participatory democracy.

The 2 × 2 nature of Figure 19.1 yields four different ways that public decisions—including corporate ones—can be made: *strategy, consent, involvement,* and *participation*. Deetz' analysis of these four corporate practices provides the core of his critique of managerialism.

STRATEGY—OVERT MANAGERIAL MOVES TO EXTEND CONTROL

In *Roger & Me*, Michael Moore uses Roger Smith to personify all that's wrong with General Motors. Although Deetz is sympathetic with Moore's goal of exposing corporate callousness, he makes it clear that individual managers are not the problem. The real culprit is *managerialism*. Deetz describes managerialism as discourse based on "a kind of systematic logic, a set of routine practices, and ideology" that values control above all else.[12] Stockholders want profits and workers desire freedom, but management craves control.

Moore gives the viewer a glimpse of managerial control when he films the autocratic way that Smith runs the GM annual stockholders meeting. Many workers experience that dictatorial style daily in the expressed and implied messages that come down from the top:

"Because I'm the boss."

"Because I say so."

"If you don't like it, quit."

"It's my way or the highway."

Some employees do object by saying, in effect, "Take this job and shove it," but this doesn't increase representation. Choice is often limited to loyalty or exit— "love it or leave it." Without an option of "voice," workers have no say in the decisions that affect them during the majority of their waking hours. Deetz argues that while control of this sort is disappearing in most enlightened corporations, new forms of control based in communication systems impede any real worker voice in structuring their work.

Stockholders face the same either/or dilemma. They can choose to hold their shares or sell them, but neither option offers a way to influence corporate policy. Although management presents itself as making decisions on behalf of stockholders (the owners), Deetz says that the interests of the two groups are often not the same. Because of stock options and "golden parachutes," top management has benefited more than any other group from the merger mania of the last two decades. Whereas long-term growth would help the average investor, quick profits and tight control of costs is the manager's ticket up the corporate ladder. Regardless of a company's product line or service, "control is the management product and is most clearly the one on which individual advancement rests."[13]

Initially, managers may regard efficiency as a means to the end of higher profits. Deetz is convinced, however, that the desire for control soon becomes a valued end in itself. The desire for control can exceed the desire for corporate performance. Talking in terms of money is often more for control than respect for efficiency or profits.

> The control drive of managerialism seeks the medium of its extension, and money is it. . . . Everything that cannot be adequately translated into money is implicitly suppressed, and all competing rights of decisions regarding one's life are made marginal.[14]

Nowhere is this quest for control more apparent than in the corporate aversion to public conflict. The managerial rule of thumb seems to be that conflict is to be "dealt with" rather than openly discussed. Managers are rewarded for "putting out fires," "running a tight ship," or "making things run smoothly." The impersonal nature of these metaphors suggests that executives should place responsibility to the company ahead of personal feelings or ethical concerns. In the corporate context, claims of "company policy" and "just doing my job" provide sufficient moral justification for suppressing almost any act of employee resistance or dissent.

Other than accelerating advancement on the managerial career path, there is little evidence that strategic control has beneficial effects. Deetz claims that most corporate successes (or failures) are the result of factors beyond managerial control.[15] Control does have distinct disadvantages, however. The cost is high and workers resent the constant surveillance. Frequent references to "clearing out the deadwood" or "trimming the fat" create an understandable jumpiness among employees, and sometimes their fear is acted out in covert rebellion. For example, smart buyers were wary of cars that came off the GM assembly line in Flint after Smith announced plans to close the plants. Because dominance has these drawbacks, most modern managers prefer to maintain control through the voluntary consent of the worker rather than by relying on the strategic use of raw power.

CONSENT—COVERT CONTROL WITHOUT OBJECTION

Deetz is not against capitalism, but he's convinced that corporations are greedy. "They expect more than a fair day's work for a fair day's pay; they want love, respect, and above all loyalty."[16] Even though the company gets the workers' most rested, alert, and chemical-free portion of the day, apparently that's not enough. Management insists that allegiance to the company should come before family, friends, church, and community. Through the process Deetz calls "consent," most employees willingly give that loyalty without getting much in return. "*Consent* is the term I use to designate the variety of situations and processes in which someone actively, though unknowingly, accomplishes the interests of others in the faulty attempt to fulfill his or her own interests. The person is complicit in her or his own victimization."[17]

DILBERT reprinted by permission of United Features Syndicate, Inc.

Lynn, a former student of mine, wrote an "application log" entry for Deetz' critical theory that poignantly captures the human cost of consent:[18]

> My father was very loyal to his company in the interest of moving up the ladder for pay increases. When my brother and I were babies and toddlers, my family lived in four different places in three years because the company required that we move. Later on, my father spent much of his time traveling and lived in New York for over six months while the rest of us lived in Baltimore. During my high school years, he worked until about eight or nine o'clock in the evening even though it wasn't demanded of him. His entire department was often there because it was common practice to spend that much time getting the job done.
>
> I would love to see the ideal world where employees have a lot more power in their communication within a large company. I think that it would possibly save families like mine from growing up without a full-time father.
>
> I can see further implications. If employees, especially men, feel like they have more power in the workplace, they will be less likely to come home and feel the need to prove their power at home by demeaning their wives in many different ways. I think that if Deetz' proposals ever worked on a wide scale, our country would see a decrease in domestic violence.

How do companies manage to strike such an unfair bargain with their employees? It's tempting to point to the workaholism of Lynn's father as the core of the problem, but Deetz lays more of the blame on managerial control of workplace language, information, forms, symbols, rituals, and stories. Although these are the practices that Pacanowsky and other interpretive scholars treat as indicators of a given organizational culture (see Chapter 18), Deetz views them as attempts to produce and reproduce a culture that is sympathetic to managerial interests. All corporations have their own sets of constitutive practices. The question he asks is not "What do these mean?" Rather, it is "Whose meanings are these?"

Deetz suggests that the force of an organizational practice is strongest when no one even thinks about it. If someone were to question such a routine, employees would be hard pressed to explain why it is standard operating procedure. The best response they could muster would be a nonanswer: "That's the way it's done around here." Practices that have this "taken-for-granted" quality are often equated with common sense. Without a clear understanding that communication produces rather than reflects reality (the bottom half of Figure 19.1), employees will unknowingly consent to the managerial mentality that wants to expand corporate control.

INVOLVEMENT—FREE EXPRESSION OF IDEAS

For anyone who has a stake in corporate decisions (all of us?), shifting from the left to the right side of Figure 19.1 is a crucial move. In political terms, it represents a switch from autocracy to liberal democracy—from managerial decisions made behind closed doors to open discussions where all have the opportunity to express their opinions.

Employee involvement in corporate choices began with a suggestion box mounted on a wall. In some companies, this invitation for expression evolved over decades into open forums that look like early-American town meetings. At their best, these attempts at corporate democracy are based on a commitment to free speech and the value of an open marketplace of ideas. (See Nilsen's ethic of significant choice, p. 203–205). Deetz notes, however, that this liberal democracy model only works in companies where everyone shares a common set of values.[19] In today's heterogeneous, postmodern society, that's seldom the case.

As Deetz surveys corporate communication practices, he concludes that "the right of expression appears more central than the right to be informed or to have an effect."[20] Through involvement in discussions of company policy, employees have a chance to air their grievances, state their desires, and recommend alternative ways of working. Many managers use these sessions as a way to give employees a chance to let off steam. But free expression falls far short of having a "voice" in corporate decisions. Advocacy is not negotiation. When workers find out that their ideas aren't represented in the final decision, they quickly become cynical about the process. Deetz thinks this is tragic:

> The combination of belief in a "reality" *and* cynicism is disastrous for a
> democracy. The belief that all claims are merely opinions is used to stop
> discussions rather than start them.[21]

PARTICIPATION—STAKEHOLDER DEMOCRACY IN ACTION

Deetz' theory of communication is critical, but not just negative. While he strongly criticizes the managerial strategy of ever-increasing control over workers, engineering their consent, and granting them free expression without giving them a voice in decisions, he also believes that joint, open decisions in the workplace are possible. Deetz is convinced that "meaningful democratic participation creates better citizens and better social choices, and provides important economic benefits."[22] One of the goals of his theory is to reclaim the possibility of open negotiations of power.

The first move Deetz makes is to expand the list of people who should have a say in how a corporation is run. He sees at least six groups of stakeholders with multiple needs and desires.[23]

Investors want security of principal and a decent return on their investment.

Workers want a reasonable wage, safe working conditions, a chance to take pride in their labor, security of employment, and time for their families.

Consumers want quality goods and services at a fair price.

Suppliers want a stable demand for their resource with timely payment upon delivery.

Host communities want payment for services provided, stable employment, environmental care, and the quality of family and public life enhanced rather than diminished.

Greater society and the world community want environmental care, economic stability, overall civility, and fair treatment of all constituent groups (racial, ethnic, sexual . . .).

Deetz notes that some stakeholders have taken greater risks and made longer term investments in a company than typical owners of stock or top-level managers.[24] He believes it's imperative that those who are affected by corporate decisions have a say in how such decisions are made. Of course, this stance runs counter to traditional notions of exclusive stockholder rights or managerial prerogatives, but Deetz says there's no legitimate basis for privileging one group of stakeholders over another. He reminds us that nature did not make corporations—we did.

The rights and responsibilities of people are not given in advance by nature or by a privileged, universal value structure, but are negotiated through interaction.[25]

Participants in the negotiation that Deetz envisions might include people shown in *Roger & Me*—board chairman Roger Smith; an assembly line worker; a Chevy owner; deputy Dan, who evicts people from their homes; and the Bunny Lady. Perhaps filmmaker Moore would enter in as a representative of society at large. Certainly the discussion would be heated. From Deetz' perspective, that would be fine.

Managerialism impedes democratic stakeholder participation through a process Deetz calls *systematically distorted communication.* Unlike strategic control, which is open and deliberate, systematically distorted communication operates without employees' overt awareness. When this happens, expectations and norms within a group setting restrict what can be openly expressed, or even thought. Deetz emphasizes that the workers deceive themselves because they believe they are interacting freely, while in reality only certain options are available. As an example, Deetz notes that arbitrary authority relations within an organization "may be disguised as legitimate divisions of labor." That way any talk about power relations must assume the validity of the status quo, thus reproducing the organizational hierarchy rather than challenging it. Real interactive decisions can't be made in such a context.

Systematically distorted communication requires suppression of potential conflict. This process, which Deetz calls *discursive closure,* occurs in a variety of ways. For example, certain groups of people within the organization may be classified as "disqualified" to speak on important issues. Arbitrary definitions can be labeled as "natural" to avoid further discussion. The values that guided a manager's judgment call may be kept hidden, so it appears to be an objective decision. A group may discourage members from talking about certain subjects. Or the organization may allow the discussion of a topic such as gender-linked job classification or pay differences, but discount its importance or quickly divert attention to other issues.

Deetz would have managers take the role of mediators rather than persuaders, coordinating the conflicting interests of all parties affected by corporate decisions. He understands that even those who are committed to open dialogue would feel insecure as they relinquished control. He suggests a good way to start is to "complicate" their perceptions of subordinates by being around them, talking with them, learning their hopes, dreams, fears, values, and needs. Michael Moore was right. Roger Smith needed to go to Flint.

SATURN CORPORATION—A MODEL OF STAKEHOLDER PARTICIPATION

About the time that Michael Moore was trying to interview Roger Smith, General Motors created a wholly owned subsidiary to build a car that could compete with Japanese imports in quality and price—the Saturn. Deetz cites the Saturn Corporation as an example of the benefits to be had when discussion and negotiation take the place of managerial control. The Saturn case is particularly impressive because all 7000 employees at the Spring Hill, Tennessee, plant participate in workplace decisions, and the innovations they create take place in the context of a highly competitive industry with entrenched labor and management bureaucracies. As it turns out, Saturn does much of what Deetz recommends:[26]

1.   *Create a workplace in which every member thinks and acts like an owner.* Early on, when managers suggested a short-term relaxation of quality to catch up on dealer demand, workers protested and ultimately convinced them that it was in the company's long-term interest to build a car that consumers would trust.

2.   *The management of work must be reintegrated with the doing of work.* Saturn management and labor work side-by-side in six- to fifteen-member teams. Team members have a say in selecting their leaders, so accountability flows both ways.

3.   *Quality information must be widely distributed.* At Saturn, all information, including financial, is shared openly among all employees. Workers can find out what they need to know to make informed decisions; they are also involved in the production of knowledge.

4.   *Social structure should grow from the bottom rather than be enforced from the top.* Saturn work teams have the authority, responsibility, and resources to budget, schedule work, assign jobs, inspect quality, control inventory, hire and train new workers, schedule vacations, coordinate with other teams, and perform all of the functions that will make them productive.

Although not everything runs smoothly at the Saturn factory, the car they produce there does. Every year, *Consumer Reports* selects it as one of the best in its class. As you might expect, worker satisfaction, commitment, and loyalty are high. So far, Saturn's profits are steady, but not as spectacular as GM hoped they'd be. Of course, the annual report doesn't show the value of a socially responsible company or the value of technology transfer to other GM factories.

Deetz is encouraged that democracy in the workplace is financially viable. He notes that if Saturn were to fail, critics would blame stakeholder participation. It's curious, he says, "that thousands of control-oriented and irresponsible companies fail each year. Rarely is their control orientation or social irresponsibility even mentioned as a reason."[27]

CRITIQUE: IS WORKPLACE DEMOCRACY JUST A DREAM?

Deetz' approach to corporate decision making is inherently attractive because it is built on values that many of us in the field of communication share. By reserving a seat at the decision-making table for every class of stakeholder, Deetz affirms the importance of democratic participation, fairness, equality, diversity, and cooperation.

Without question, Deetz' insistence on the constitutive nature of all communication can help us understand consent practices in the workplace. Yet his advocacy of stakeholder rights and participatory democracy isn't necessarily furthered by his constructionist view of communication. In fact, his reform agenda could be hindered. If, contrary to the U.S. Declaration of Independence, there are no self-evident truths on which to stand, then everything is in play and it doesn't make much sense to assume that we have a *right* to participate in decisions that affect us.

Political realism may be another problem. As applied to corporate life, Deetz' theory is a critique of managerialism. University of Wisconsin–Milwaukee communication professor Robert McPhee offers a somewhat tongue-in-cheek summary: "If we just didn't find it natural and right and unavoidable to hand power over to managers, everything would be very different and our problems would be solved."[28] Although a caricature, this capsule statement underscores the problematic nature of the stakeholder negotiations that Deetz pictures and the incredible difficulty of getting all parties to sit at the table as equals. In assessing the current scholarship, corporate climate, and best practices of workplace democracy, University of Montana communication professor George Cheney and seven co-authors conclude that "the possibilities for the survival of 'postbureaucratic,' relatively egalitarian organizations remain debatable."[29] They add that "evidence weighs heavily against the long-term maintenance of the 'integrity' of highly democratic organizations," but they, like Deetz, are hopeful that small, highly adaptable, process-oriented companies can lead the way in sustaining participatory democracy among stakeholders.

Deetz admits that a positive alternative to managerialism is difficult to work out in conception and in practice.[30] He'd like to do better, but democracy has never been neat and tidy. Perhaps it's asking too much of one theory that it both reform commonsense conceptions of communication *and* private business at the same time. Moving from the dark quadrant of *consent* to the clear quadrant of *participation* in Figure 19.1 is a quantum leap. Deetz is encouraged, however, by the number of companies that have begun to implement at least modified stakeholder models of decision making. He hopes that his theory will further the dialogue and hasten that trend. To that end I close this chapter with his words.

> Corporations are political sites, because they make critical decisions for the public. Considering them as simply private economic entities overlooks both the significance of these public choices and the legitimacy of the interests of a variety of stakeholders beyond owners. Management . . . has focused on control, rather than operating as a coordinator of these diverse stakeholder interests. . . . Morally and practically we must expand the capacity to represent wider segments of society and their values.[31]

QUESTIONS TO SHARPEN YOUR FOCUS

1. Deetz contrasts *information* models, which assume language *reflects* reality, with *communication* models, which assume reality emerges out of a relationship among self, others, language, and the world. What other theories already covered fit the communication model?

2. Managers use *strategy* and *consent* to maintain *control* over subordinates. According to Deetz, which practice is more effective? Why?

3. The *stakeholder model* requires *participation,* not just *involvement.* What is the difference between the two practices?

4. To what extent do you agree with the following statement: "Autocracy at work is the price we pay for *democracy* after hours." Does it apply equally to work in the classroom?

A SECOND LOOK

Recommended resource: Stanley Deetz, *Transforming Communication, Transforming Business: Building Responsive and Responsible Workplaces,* Hampton, Cresskill, N.J., 1995.

Critical foundation: Stanley Deetz, *Democracy in an Age of Corporate Colonization: Developments in Communication and the Politics of Everyday Life,* State University of New York, Albany, 1992.

Overview of organizational communication: Stanley Deetz, "Conceptual Foundations for Organizational Communication Studies," in *The New Handbook of Organizational Com-*

munication, Fred Jablin and Linda Putnam (eds.), Sage, Thousand Oaks, Calif., 1997, in press.

Communication vs. advocacy: Stanley Deetz, "The Future of the Discipline: The Challenges, the Research, and the Social Contribution," in *Communication Yearbook 17*, Stanley Deetz (ed.), Sage, Newbury Park, Calif., 1994, pp. 565–600.

International Communication Association 1997 Presidential Address: Stanley Deetz, "Communication in the Age of Negotiation," *Journal of Communication*, Vol. 47, No. 4, 1997, pp. 118–135.

State-of-the-art review: George Cheney, et al., "Democracy, Participation, and Communication at Work: A Multidisciplinary Review," in *Communication Yearbook 21*, Michael Roloff (ed.), Sage, Thousand Oaks, Calif., 1998, pp. 35–91.

Organizational politics: "Interests, Conflict, and Power: Organizations as Political Systems," Gareth Morgan, *Images of Organizations*, Sage, Newbury Park, Calif., 1986, pp. 141–198.

Stories as power: Dennis Mumby, "The Political Function of Narrative in Organizations," *Communication Monographs*, Vol. 54, 1987, pp. 113–127.

Review and critique: Branislav Kovačić, "The Democracy and Organizational Communication Theories of Deetz, Mumby, and Associates," in *Watershed Research Traditions in Communication Theory*, Donald Cushman and Branislav Kovačić (eds.), State University of New York, Albany, N.Y., 1995, pp. 211–238.

PUBLIC RHETORIC

Despite what you read in the newspapers, *rhetoric* is not necessarily a dirty word. For citizens in ancient Greece, knowing how to speak in public was part of their democratic responsibility. Rhetorical ability was a survival skill in the rough-and-tumble politics of the Roman Forum. "For the very great majority of students, higher education meant taking lessons from the rhetor, learning the art of rhetoric from him."[1] Following the decay of Rome, the church explored the use of rhetoric to preserve and spread the faith. As the Renaissance took hold, the study of rhetoric moved to the university, as one of the core subjects of the trivium—logic, grammar, and rhetoric. In each setting, teachers and practitioners championed the art of rhetoric as a means of ensuring that speakers of truth would not be at a disadvantage when trying to win the hearts and minds of an audience.

Aristotle defined rhetoric as "an ability, in each particular case, to see the available means of persuasion."[2] It centers attention on the intentional act of using words to have an effect. I use the term *public rhetoric* in this section to refer to a speaking context in which the speaker has an opportunity to monitor and adjust to the response of his or her immediate audience. Rhetoricians have always had a special interest in judicial argument, legislative debate, political rallies, religious sermons, and messages given at special celebrations.

The Greeks and Romans distinguished five parts, or divisions, of the study of rhetoric:

1. *Invention*—discovery of convincing arguments
2. *Arrangement*—organizing material for best impact
3. *Style*—selection of appropriate language
4. *Delivery*—coordinating voice and gestures
5. *Memory*—mastery and rehearsal of content

With the possible exception of memory, these "five canons of rhetoric" require that a speaker first analyze and then adapt to a specific group of listeners. We can, of course, react to the idea of audience adaptation in two different ways. If we view speakers who adjust their message to fit a specific audience in a positive light, we'll praise their rhetorical sensitivity and flexibility. If we view them negatively, we'll condemn them for their cynical pandering and lack of commitment to the truth. Rhetorical thought across history swings back and forth between these two conflicting poles. The words of most rhetoricians reflect the tension they feel between "telling it like it is" and telling it in a way that the audience will listen.

The Greek philosopher Plato regarded rhetoric as mostly flattery. Far from seeing it as an art, he described rhetoric as a "knack"—similar to cooking or the clever use of cosmetics. Both are attempts to make things seem better than they really are.[3] In spite of his scorn, Plato imagined an ideal rhetoric based on a speaker's understanding of listeners with different natures and dispositions.

> He must then discover the kind of speech that matches each type of nature. When that is accomplished, he must arrange and adorn each speech in such a way as to present complicated and unstable souls with complex speeches, speeches exactly attuned to every

changing mood of the complicated soul—while the simple soul must be presented with a simple speech.[4]

Plato's ideal discourse was an elite form of dialogue meant for private, rather than public, consumption. This philosophic, one-on-one mode of communication is known as *dialectic* (not to be confused with Marx's economic theory). Unlike typical oratory in Athens, where speakers addressed large audiences on civic issues, Plato's dialectic focused on exploring eternal Truths in an intimate setting.

Plato hoped that philosophic dialectic would supplant public rhetoric. It took Plato's best student, Aristotle, to rejuvenate rhetoric as a serious academic subject. More than 2,000 years ago, Aristotle's *Rhetoric* systematically explored the topics of speaker, message, and audience. Chapter 20 presents his theory of rhetoric, the majority of which has stood the test of time. His ideas form a large proportion of the advice presented in contemporary public speaking texts. Aristotle defined rhetoric as the art of discovering all available means of persuasion, but this conception doesn't solve the problem of how to get audiences to listen to hard truths.

Religious rhetors live within the same paradox. In many ways the apostle Paul seemed to personify the lover of diverse souls that Plato had earlier described. In his first letter to the Corinthians, Paul reminds the people of Corinth that he made a conscious decision to let his message speak for itself ("My speech and my proclamation were not with plausible words of wisdom"[5]). Yet further on in the letter he outlines a conscious rhetorical strategy ("I have become all things to all people, that I might by all means save some"[6]). Four centuries later, Augustine continued to justify the conscious use of rhetoric by the church. Why, he asked, should defenders of truth be long-winded, confusing, and boring, when the speech of liars was brief, clear, and persuasive?

The tension between the logic of a message and the appeal it has for an audience wasn't easily resolved when the university

"I see our next speaker needs no introduction. . . ."

Reproduced by permission of WM Hoest Enterprises, Inc.

became the seat of rhetoric. British philosopher Francis Bacon sought to integrate the two concerns when he wrote that "the duty of rhetoric is to apply Reason to Imagination for the better moving of the will."[7] French scholar Peter Ramus offered a more radical solution to the problem. He split the five canons of rhetoric into two parts. Invention, arrangement, and memory became the province of logic. That left only style and delivery for rhetoricians to explore, and for centuries rhetoric was more concerned with form than substance.

American teachers of rhetoric rediscovered Aristotle in the early 1900s; neo-Aristotelianism became *the* standard for rhetorical research and practice. But not all scholars are content to analyze speeches using Aristotle's categories of logical, emotional, and ethical proof. At least two twentieth-century rhetoricians have offered conscious alternatives to Aristotle's way of thinking.

Kenneth Burke's dramatism proposes a "new rhetoric." He claims that speaker identification with an audience is a better way to understand the human drama than Aristotle's "old rhetoric" of persuasion. Walter Fisher argues that the "rational world paradigm" of Aristotle is too limited. He regards all communication as story and offers his "narrative paradigm" as a new way to understand both private and public rhetoric. I present Burke's dramatism in Chapter 21 and Fisher's narrative paradigm in Chapter 22.

Despite the claims of newness by Burke and Fisher, each theorist has to deal with the old question that Aristotle faced: "How do you move an audience without changing your message or losing your integrity?" As you read, see which theorist comes up with an answer that's most satisfying to you.

CHAPTER 20

The Rhetoric

of Aristotle

Aristotle was a student of Plato in the golden age of Greek civilization, four centuries before the birth of Christ. He became a respected instructor at Plato's Academy but disagreed with his mentor over the place of public speaking in Athenian life.

Ancient Greece was known for its traveling speech teachers called Sophists. Particularly in Athens, these teachers trained aspiring lawyers and politicians to participate effectively in the courts and deliberative councils. In hindsight, they appear to have been innovative educators who offered a needed and wanted service.[1] Yet since they had no theoretical basis for the advice they gave, philosophers and skeptics criticized their methods. Plato scoffed at the Sophists' oratorical devices, dismissing their crowd-pleasing techniques as similar to the knack of cookery or the flattering use of cosmetics—both of which he perceived as being aimed at making something appear better than it really is. His suspicion is mirrored today in the negative way people use the term *mere rhetoric* to label the speech of "tricky" lawyers, "mealy-mouthed" politicians, "spellbinding" preachers, and "fast-talking" salespeople.

Aristotle, like Plato, deplored the demagoguery of speakers' using their skill to move an audience while showing a casual indifference to the truth. Yet unlike Plato, he saw the tools of rhetoric as a neutral means by which the orator could either accomplish noble ends or further fraud: " . . . by using these justly one would do the greatest good, and unjustly, the greatest harm."[2] Aristotle believed that truth has a moral superiority that makes it more acceptable than falsehood. But unscrupulous opponents of the truth may fool a dull audience unless an ethical speaker uses all possible means of persuasion to counter the error. Speakers who neglect the art of rhetoric have only themselves to blame when their hearers choose falsehood. Success requires wisdom *and* eloquence.

Both the *Politics* and *Ethics* of Aristotle are polished and well-organized books compared with the rough prose and arrangement of his text on rhetoric. The *Rhetoric* apparently consists of Aristotle's reworked lecture notes for his course at the Academy. Despite the uneven nature of the writing, the *Rhetoric* is a searching study of audience psychology. Sophistic training for public address was practically useful, but it wasn't carefully grounded or rigorously organized. But Aristotle raised rhetoric to a science by systematically exploring the effects of the speaker, the speech, and the audience. He regarded the speaker's use of this knowledge as an art. Quite likely, the text your communication department uses for its public speaking classes is basically a contemporary recasting of the audience analysis provided by Aristotle 2,300 years ago.

RHETORIC: MAKING PERSUASION PROBABLE

Aristotle saw the function of rhetoric as the discovery in each case of "the available means of persuasion." He never spelled out what he meant by persuasion, but his concern with noncoercive methods makes it clear that he ruled out force of law, torture, and war. His threefold classification of speech situations according to the nature of the audience shows that he had affairs of state in mind.

The first in Aristotle's classification is courtroom (forensic) speaking, which addresses judges who are trying to decide the facts of a person's guilt or innocence. Prosecutor Marcia Clark and attorney Johnnie Cochran's closing arguments at the O. J. Simpson trial are examples of judicial rhetoric centering on accusation and defense. The second, political (deliberative) speaking, attempts to influence legislators or voters who decide future policy. The 1996 presidential debates gave Bill Clinton and Bob Dole a chance to sway undecided voters. The third, ceremonial (epideictic) speaking, heaps praise or blame on another for the benefit of spectators. Lincoln gave his Gettysburg Address in order to honor "the brave men, living and dead, who struggled here."

Because his students were familiar with the question-and-answer style of Socratic dialogue, Aristotle classified rhetoric as a counterpart or offshoot of dialectic. Dialectic is one-on-one discussion; rhetoric is one person addressing many. Dialectic is a search for truth; rhetoric tries to demonstrate truth that's already been found. Dialectic answers general philosophical questions; rhetoric addresses specific, practical ones. Dialectic deals with certainty; rhetoric deals with probability. Aristotle saw this last distinction as particularly important: Rhetoric is the art of discovering ways to make truth seem more probable to an audience that isn't completely convinced.

RHETORICAL PROOF: LOGOS, ETHOS, PATHOS

According to Aristotle, the available means of persuasion are based on three kinds of proof: logical (*logos*), ethical (*ethos*), and emotional (*pathos*). Logical proof comes from the line of argument in the speech, ethical proof is the way the speaker's character is revealed through the message, and emotional proof is the feeling the speech draws out of the hearers. Some form of *logos*, *ethos*, and *pathos* is present in every public presentation, but perhaps no other modern-day speech has brought all three proofs together as effectively as Martin Luther King, Jr.'s "I Have a Dream" delivered in 1963 to civil rights marchers in

Washington, D.C. We'll look at this speech throughout the rest of the chapter to illustrate Aristotle's rhetorical theory.

Case Study: "I Have a Dream"

At the end of August 1963, a quarter of a million people assembled at the Lincoln Memorial in a united march on Washington. The rally capped a long, hot summer of sit-ins protesting racial discrimination in the south. (The film *Mississippi Burning* portrayed one of the tragic racial conflicts of that year.) Two months before the march, President John F. Kennedy submitted a civil rights bill to Congress that would begin to rectify the racial injustices, but its passage was seriously in doubt. The organizers of the march hoped that it would put pressure on Congress to outlaw segregation in the south, but they also wanted the demonstration to raise the national consciousness about economic exploitation of blacks around the country.

Martin Luther King shared the platform with a dozen other civil rights leaders, each limited to a five-minute presentation. King's successful Montgomery, Alabama, bus boycott, freedom rides, and solitary confinement in a Birmingham jail set him apart in the eyes of demonstrators and TV viewers. The last of the group to speak, King had a dual purpose. In the face of a Black Muslim call for violence, he urged blacks to continue their nonviolent struggle without hatred. He also implored white people to get involved in the quest for freedom and equality, to be part of a dream fulfilled rather than contribute to an unjust nightmare.

A few years after King's assassination, I experienced the impact his speech had had upon the African-American community. Teaching public address in a volunteer street academy, I read the speech out loud to illustrate matters of style. The students needed no written text. As I came to the last third of the speech, they recited the eloquent "I have a dream" portion word for word with great passion. When we finished, all of us had moist eyes.

David Garrow, author of the Pulitzer Prize-winning biography of King, called the speech the "rhetorical achievement of a lifetime, the clarion call that conveyed the moral power of the movement's cause to the millions who watched the live national network coverage."[3] King shifted the burden of proof onto those who opposed racial equality. Aristotle's three rhetorical proofs can help us understand how he made the status quo of segregation an ugly option for the moral listener.

Logical Proof: Lines of Argument That Make Sense

Aristotle focused on two forms of logical proof—the *enthymeme* and the *example*. He regarded the enthymeme as "the strongest of the proofs."[4] An enthymeme is merely an incomplete version of a formal deductive syllogism. Logicians might create the following syllogism out of one of King's lines of reasoning:

Major or general premise: All people are created equal.

Minor or specific premise: I am a person.

Conclusion: I am equal to other people.

Typical enthymemes, however, leave out a premise that is already accepted by the audience: "All men are created equal. . . . I am equal to other men." In terms of style, the enthymeme is more artistic than a stilted syllogistic argument. But as retired University of Wisconsin rhetorician Lloyd Bitzer notes, Aristotle had a greater reason for advising the speaker to suppress the statement of a premise that the listeners already believe.

> Because they are jointly produced by the audience, enthymemes intuitively unite speaker and audience and provide the strongest possible proof. . . . The audience itself helps construct the proof by which it is persuaded.[5]

Most rhetorical analysis looks for enthymemes embedded in one or two lines of text. In the case of "I Have a Dream," the whole speech is one giant enthymeme. If the logic of the speech were to be expressed as a syllogism, the reasoning would be as follows:

Major premise: God will reward nonviolence.

Minor premise: We are pursuing our dream nonviolently.

Conclusion: God will grant us our dream.

King used the first two-thirds of the speech to establish the validity of the minor premise. White listeners are reminded that blacks have been "battered by the storms of persecution and staggered by winds of police brutality." They have "come fresh from narrow jail cells," and are "veterans of creative suffering." Blacks are urged to meet "physical force with soul force," not to allow "creative protest to degenerate into physical violence," and never to "satisfy our thirst for freedom by drinking from the cup of bitterness and hatred." The movement is to continue nonviolent.

King used the last third of the speech to establish his conclusion; he painted the dream in vivid color. It included King's hope that his four children would not be "judged by the color of their skin, but by the content of their character." He pictured an Alabama where "little black boys and black girls will be able to join hands with little white boys and white girls as sisters and brothers." And in a swirling climax, he shared a vision of all God's children singing, "Free at last, free at last. Thank God Almighty we are free at last." But he never articulated the major premise.

This line of argument makes no sense unless King and his audience were already committed to the truth of the major premise—that God would reward their commitment to nonviolence. Aristotle stresses that audience analysis is crucial to the effective use of the enthymeme. The centrality of the church in American black history, the religious roots of civil rights protest, and the crowd's frequent response of "My Lord" suggest that King knew his audience well. He never stated what to them was obvious, and this strengthened rather than weakened his logical appeal.

The enthymeme uses deductive logic—moving from global principle to specific truth. Arguing by example uses inductive reasoning—drawing a final conclusion from specific cases. Since King mentioned few examples of discrimination, it might appear that he failed to use all possible means of logical persuasion. But pictures of snarling police dogs, electric cattle prods used on peaceful demonstrators, and signs over drinking fountains stating "Whites only" appeared nightly on TV news. As with the missing major premise of the enthymeme, King's audience supplied their own vivid images.

Ethical Proof: Perceived Source Credibility

According to Aristotle, it's not enough for a speech to contain plausible argument. The speaker must *seem* credible as well. Many audience impressions are formed before the speaker ever begins. As poet Ralph Waldo Emerson cautioned over a century ago, "Use what language you will, you can never say anything but what you are."[6] Some who watched Martin Luther King on television undoubtedly tuned him out because he was black. But Aristotle was more interested in audience perceptions that are shaped by what the speaker does or doesn't say. In the *Rhetoric* he identified three qualities that build high source credibility—intelligence, character, and goodwill.

1. Perceived Intelligence. The quality of intelligence has more to do with practical wisdom and shared values than it does with training at Plato's Academy. Audiences judge intelligence by the overlap between their beliefs and the speaker's ideas. ("My idea of an agreeable speaker is one who agrees with me.") King quoted the Bible, the United States Constitution, the patriotic hymn "My Country 'tis of Thee," Shakespeare's *King Lear,* and the Negro spiritual "We Shall Overcome." With the exception of bomb-throwing terrorists and racial bigots, it's hard to imagine anyone with whom he didn't establish a strong value identification.

2. Virtuous Character. Character has to do with the speaker's image as a good and honest person. Even though he and other blacks were victims of "unspeakable horrors of police brutality," King warned against a "distrust of all white people" and against "drinking from the cup of bitterness and hatred." It would be difficult to maintain an image of the speaker as an evil racist while he was being charitable toward his enemies and optimistic about the future.

3. Goodwill. Goodwill is a positive judgment of the speaker's intention toward the audience. Aristotle thought it possible for an orator to possess extraordinary intelligence and sterling character, yet still not have the listeners' best interest at heart. King was obviously not trying to reach "the vicious racists" of Alabama, but no one was given a reason to think that King bore them ill will. His dream included "black men and white men, Jews and Gentiles, Protestants and Catholics."

"We find the defendent guilty on all charges, Your Honor. On the positive side, we really liked his openness and energy."

Although Aristotle's comments on *ethos* were stated in a few brief sentences, no other portion of his *Rhetoric* has received such close scientific scrutiny. The results of sophisticated testing of audience attitudes show that his three-factor theory of source credibility stands up remarkably well. Listeners definitely think in terms of authoritativeness (intelligence) and trustworthiness (character). Sometimes goodwill seems to fold into questions of character, and at other times a new dimension of speaker dynamism or energy surfaces. But whether the third category of credibility is goodwill or dynamism, Martin Luther King exuded all three.

Emotional Proof: Striking a Responsive Chord

Aristotle believed that the effective speaker must know how to stir up various emotions in the audience. He catalogued a series of opposite feelings, then explained the conditions under which each mood is experienced, and finally described how the speaker can get an audience to feel that way. Aristotle scholar and translator George Kennedy claims that this analysis is "the earliest systematic discussion of human psychology."[7] If Aristotle's advice sounds familiar, it may be a sign that human nature hasn't changed much in 2,300 years.

Anger (vs. Mildness).   Aristotle's discussion of anger was an early version of Freud's frustration-aggression hypothesis. People feel angry when they are thwarted in their attempt to fulfill a need. Remind them of interpersonal slights, and they'll become irate. Show them that the offender is sorry, deserves praise, or has great power, and the audience will calm down.

Love or Friendship (vs. Hatred).   Consistent with present-day research on attraction, Aristotle considered similarity as the key to mutual warmth. The speaker should point out common goals, experience, attitudes, and desires. In the absence of these positive forces, a common enemy can be used to create solidarity.

Fear (vs. Confidence).   Fear comes from a mental image of potential disaster. The speaker should paint a vivid word picture of the tragedy, showing that its occurrence is probable. Confidence can be built up by describing the danger as remote.

Shame (vs. Shamelessness).   We feel embarrassed or guilty when loss is due to our own weakness or vice. The emotion is especially acute when a speaker recites our failings in the presence of family, friends, or those we admire.

Indignation (vs. Pity).   We all have a built-in sense of fairness. As the producers of *60 Minutes* have discovered, it's easy to arouse a sense of injustice by describing an arbitrary use of power upon those who are helpless.

Admiration (vs. Envy).   People admire moral virtue, power, wealth, and beauty. By demonstrating that an individual has acquired life's goods through hard work rather than mere luck, admiration will increase.

THE FIVE CANONS OF RHETORIC

Although the organization of Aristotle's *Rhetoric* is somewhat puzzling, scholars and practitioners synthesize his words into four distinct standards for measuring the quality of a speaker: the construction of an argument (invention), ordering of material (arrangement), selection of language (style), and techniques of delivery. Later writers add memory to the list of skills the accomplished speaker must master. As mentioned in the introduction to this section on public rhetoric, the five canons of rhetoric have set the agenda of public address instruction for over 2,000 years. Aristotle's advice strikes most students of public speaking as refreshingly up to date.

Invention.   To generate effective enthymemes and examples, the speaker draws on both specialized knowledge about the subject and general lines of reasoning common to all kinds of speeches. Imagining the mind as a storehouse of wisdom or an informational landscape, Aristotle called these stock arguments *topoi*, a Greek term that can be translated as "topics" or "places." As

Cornell University literature professor Lane Cooper explains, "In these special regions the orator hunts for arguments as a hunter hunts for game."[8] When King argues "We refuse to believe that there are insufficient funds in the great vaults of opportunity of this nation," he marshalls the specific American topic or premise that the United States is the land of opportunity. When he contends that "many of our white brothers, as evidenced by their presence here today, have come to realize that their destiny is tied up with our destiny," he establishes a causal connection that draws from Aristotle's general topics of cause/effect and motive.

Arrangement.   According to Aristotle, you should avoid complicated schemes of organization. "There are two parts to a speech; for it is necessary first to state the subject and then to demonstrate it."[9] The introduction should capture attention, establish your credibility, and make clear the purpose of the speech. The conclusion should remind your listeners what you've said and leave them feeling good about you and your ideas. Like speech teachers today, Aristotle decried the practice of starting with jokes that have nothing to do with the topic, insistence on three-point outlines, and waiting until the end of the speech to reveal the main point.

Style.   Aristotle believed that "to learn easily is naturally pleasant to all people," and that "metaphor most brings about learning."[10] Furthermore, he taught that "metaphor especially has clarity and sweetness and strangeness."[11] King was a master of metaphor:

> The Negro lives on a *lonely island* of poverty in the midst of a *vast ocean* of material prosperity.

> To rise from the *dark and desolate valleys* of segregation to the *sunlit path* of racial justice.

King's use of metaphor was not restricted to images drawn from nature. Perhaps his most convincing metaphor was an extended analogy picturing the march on Washington as people of color coming to the federal bank to cash a check written by the Founding Fathers. America had defaulted on the promissory note and had sent back the check marked "insufficient funds." But the marchers refused to believe that the bank of justice was bankrupt, that the vaults of opportunity were empty. These persuasive images gathered listeners' knowledge of racial discrimination into a powerful flood of reason:

> Let justice roll down like waters
> and righteousness like a mighty stream.[12]

Memory.   Aristotle's students needed no reminder that good speakers are able to draw upon a collection of ideas and phrases stored in the mind. But Roman teachers of rhetoric found it necessary to stress the importance of memory. In our present age of word processing and TelePrompTers, memory seems to be a lost art. Yet the stirring conclusion of King's speech departed from his prepared text and effectively pulled together lines he had used before. Unlike

King and many Athenian orators, most of us aren't speaking in public every day. For us, the modern equivalent of memory is rehearsal.

Delivery. Audiences reject delivery that seems planned or staged. Naturalness is persuasive; artifice, just the reverse. Any form of presentation that calls attention to itself takes away from the speaker's proofs.

CRITIQUE: STANDING THE TEST OF TIME

For many teachers of public speaking, criticizing Aristotle's *Rhetoric* is like doubting Einstein's theory of relativity or belittling Shakespeare's *King Lear.* Yet the Greek philosopher often seems less clear than he urged his students to be. Scholars are puzzled by a failure to define the exact meaning of *enthymeme,* a confusing system of classifying metaphor according to type, and the blurred distinctions between deliberative (political) and epideictic (ceremonial) speaking. At the beginning of the *Rhetoric,* Aristotle promised a systematic study of *logos, ethos,* and *pathos,* but he failed to follow that three-part plan. Instead, it appears that he grouped the material in a speech-audience-speaker order. We must remember, however, that Aristotle's *Rhetoric* consists of lecture notes rather than a treatise prepared for the public.

Some present-day critics are bothered by the *Rhetoric*'s view of the audience as passive. Speakers in Aristotle's world seem to be able to accomplish any goal as long as they prepare their speeches with careful thought and an accurate audience analysis. Other critics wish Aristotle had considered a fourth component of rhetoric, the situation. Any analysis of King's address apart from the context of the march on Washington would certainly be incomplete.

In the eyes of some readers, Aristotle waffled on a basic ethical issue that all speakers confront. Book One of the *Rhetoric* says that it's wrong to play on the emotions of an audience. ("That is the same as if someone made a straight-edge rule crooked before using it."[13]) Yet Book Three says that impression management is the central task of the speaker. Of course, ethicists today continue to struggle with the legitimacy of using emotional appeals to influence an audience, so perhaps Aristotle's ambivalence is just another example of the *Rhetoric*'s timeless wisdom.

Referring to Aristotle's manuscript in a rare moment of sincere appreciation, the French skeptic Voltaire declared what many speech communication teachers would echo today: "I do not believe there is a single refinement of the art that escapes him."[14] Despite the shortcomings and perplexities of this work, it remains a foundational text of our discipline—a starting point for scientists and humanists alike.

QUESTIONS TO SHARPEN YOUR FOCUS

1. For most people today, the term *rhetoric* has bad associations. What synonym or phrase captures what Aristotle meant, yet doesn't carry a negative connotation?

2. What *enthymemes* have advocates on each side of the abortion issue employed in their public *deliberative rhetoric*?

3. Aristotle divided *ethos* into issues of *intelligence, character,* and *goodwill.* Which quality is most important to you when you hear a campaign address, sermon, or other public speech?

4. Most scholars who define themselves as rhetoricians identify with the humanities rather than the sciences. Can you support the claim that Aristotle took a *scientific approach to rhetoric*?

A SECOND LOOK

Recommended resource: Aristotle, *On Rhetoric: A Theory of Civil Discourse,* George A. Kennedy (ed. and trans.), Oxford University, New York, 1991.

Rhetoric as art: George A. Kennedy, "Philosophical Rhetoric," in *Classical Rhetoric,* University of North Carolina, Chapel Hill, 1980, pp. 41–85.

Rhetoric as science: James L. Golden, Goodwin F. Berquist, and William E. Coleman, *The Rhetoric of Western Thought,* Kendall/Hunt, Dubuque, Iowa, 1976, pp. 25–39.

Key scholarship: Richard Leo Enos and Lois Peters Agnew (eds.), *Landmark Essays on Aristotelian Rhetoric,* Lawrence Erlbaum Associates, Mahwah, N.J., 1998.

Enthymeme: Lloyd F. Bitzer, "Aristotle's Enthymeme Revisited," *Quarterly Journal of Speech,* Vol. 45, 1959, pp. 399–409, also in Enos and Agnew, pp. 179–191.

Metaphor: Samuel Levin, "Aristotle's Theory of Metaphor," *Philosophy and Rhetoric,* Vol. 15, 1982, pp. 24–46.

Dimensions of source credibility: J. C. McCroskey, "Scales for the Measurement of Ethos," *Speech Monographs,* Vol. 33, 1968, pp. 67–72.

Rhetoric and ethics: Eugene Garver, *Aristotle's Rhetoric: An Art of Character,* University of Chicago, Chicago, 1994.

History of rhetoric: Thomas Conley, *Rhetoric in the European Tradition,* Longman, New York, 1990.

Analysis of King's speech: Alexandra Alvarez, "Martin Luther King's 'I Have a Dream,' " *Journal of Black Studies,* Vol. 18, 1988, pp. 337–357.

King's oral rhetoric: Carolyn Calloway-Thomas and John Louis Lucaites (eds.), *Martin Luther King, Jr., and the Sermonic Power of Public Discourse,* University of Alabama, Tuscaloosa, 1993.

King's written rhetoric: Martin Luther King, Jr., "Letter from a Birmingham Jail," in *Why We Can't Wait,* Harper & Row, New York, 1963, pp. 77–100.

March on Washington: David J. Garrow, *Bearing the Cross,* William Morrow, New York, 1986, pp. 231–286.

CHAPTER 21

Dramatism

of Kenneth Burke

American audiences want straightforward advice from their film critics. Roger Ebert and the late Gene Siskel created the successful television show *Sneak Previews* by describing a movie's plot, showing a brief clip, commenting on the quality of acting, and recommending whether people should see the film or skip it. The thumbs-up–thumbs-down nature of their judgment left little room for trying to discern the writer's purpose or the director's motivation. In this sense, Siskel and Ebert were *reviewers* of cinema rather than *critics*.

Kenneth Burke, on the other hand, was a critic. Along with the symbolic theorists we've already discussed (Bormann, Geertz and Pacanowsky, Pearce and Cronen, Mead), Burke believes that language is a strategic human response to a specific situation. "Verbal symbols are meaningful acts from which motives can be derived." He considers clusters of words as dances of attitudes. According to Burke, the critic's job is to figure out why a writer or speaker selected the words that were choreographed into the message. The task is ultimately one of assessing motives.

Until his death in 1993 at the age of 96, Burke picked his way through the human "motivational jungle" using the tools of philosophy, literature, psychology, economics, linguistics, sociology, and communication. He spent his young adult years in Greenwich Village, a New York bohemian community that included e.e. cummings and Edna St. Vincent Millay. Like many intellectuals during the depression of the 1930s, Burke flirted with communism but was disillusioned by Stalin's intolerance and brutality. Although he never earned a college degree, he taught for fifteen years at Bennington College in Vermont and filled visiting lectureships at Harvard, Princeton, Northwestern, and the University of Chicago.

Burke's writing shows an intellectual breadth and depth that leads admirers to refer to him as a Renaissance man. He called himself a "gypsy scholar" and responded to questions about his field of interest by asking, "What am I but a word man?" *Dramatism* was Burke's favorite word to describe what he saw going on when people open their mouths to communicate.

As Burke viewed it, life is not *like* a drama; life *is* drama. The late Harry

Chapin (who happened to be Burke's grandson) captured some of the tragedy and comedy of everyday life by putting words to music in "story songs." My personal favorite is "Cat's in the Cradle," the timeless tale of a father too busy to spend time with his son. Any male who hears the song realizes that he has a part in the drama rather than the role of a passive listener.

The latest somebody-done-somebody-wrong song on country radio makes it clear that a critic's skills could be helpful in understanding human motivation. But it wasn't until 1952 that University of Illinois rhetorician Marie Hochmuth Nichols alerted the field of speech to the promises of Burke's dramatistic methodology.[1] Since that time, thousands of communication scholars have used his perspectives of identification, dramatistic pentad, and guilt-redemption cycle as ways to analyze public address.

IDENTIFICATION: WITHOUT IT, THERE IS NO PERSUASION

Although a great admirer of Aristotle's *Rhetoric*, Burke was less concerned with enthymeme and example than he was with a speaker's overall ability to identify with an audience.

> The key term for the "old rhetoric" was *persuasion* and its stress upon deliberative design. The key term for the "new rhetoric" is *identification* and this may include partially unconscious factors in its appeal.[2]

Identification is the common ground that exists between speaker and audience. Burke used the word *substance* as an umbrella term to describe a person's physical characteristics, talents, occupation, background, personality, beliefs, and values. The more overlap there is between the substance of the speaker and the substance of the listener, the greater the identification. Behavioral scientists have used the term *homophily* to describe perceived similarity between speaker and listener,[3] but Burke preferred religious language to scientific jargon. Borrowing from Martin Luther's description of what takes place at the communion table, Burke said identification is "consubstantiation." The theological reference calls to mind the oft-quoted Old Testament passage where Ruth pledges solidarity with her mother-in-law, Naomi: "For where you go I will go, and where you lodge I will lodge; your people shall be my people, and your God my God."[4] That's identification.

Audiences sense a joining of interests through style as much as through content. Burke said that the effective communicator can show consubstantiality by giving signs in language and delivery that his or her properties are the same as theirs. The style of a typical tent evangelist probably turns off a cosmopolitan New Yorker more than the content of the message. The mood and manner of revival-style preaching signal a deep division between the evangelist and the urbane listeners. To the extent that the speaker could alter the linguistic strategy to match the hearers' sophisticated style, they'd think the speaker was "talking sense."

Burke said that identification works both ways. Audience adaptation not only gives the evangelist a chance to sway the audience, it also serves to help the preacher fit into the cultural mainstream. But identification in either direction will never be complete. If nothing else, our tennis elbow or clogged sinuses constantly remind us that we are separate from the rest of the human race. But without some kind of division in the first place, there would be no need for identification. And without identification, there is no persuasion.

THE DRAMATISTIC PENTAD

Burke regarded persuasion as the communicator's attempt to get the audience to accept his or her view of reality as true. The "dramatistic pentad" is a tool to analyze how the speaker tries to do it. The five-pronged method is a shorthand way to "talk about their talk about." Burke's pentad directs the critic's attention to five crucial elements of the human drama—act, scene, agent, agency, and purpose.

> In a well-rounded statement about motives, you must have some word that names the act (names what took place in thought or deed), and another that names the scene (the background of the act, the situation in which it occurred); also you must indicate what person or kind of person (agent) performed the act, what means or instruments he used (agency), and the purpose.[5]

Although Burke was an advocate of creativity, he believed the critic's choice of labels should be constrained by the language that the speaker actually selects. Burke recommended a content analysis that identifies key terms on the basis of frequency and intensity of use. The speaker's "god term" is the word to which all other positive words are subservient. When critics discover the god term, they should avoid dictionary definitions as a way of determining its exact meaning. A speaker's god term is best understood by the other words that cluster around it, known by the company it keeps. In like fashion, a "devil term" sums up all that a speaker regards as bad, wrong, or evil. Consistent with the Sapir-Whorf hypothesis described in the socio-cultural section of Chapter 3, Burke's analysis sees words as "terministic screens" which dictate interpretations of life's drama.[6]

Burke illustrated the importance of taking language seriously by having the reader imagine a parallel pentad with substitute terms:

act	scene	agent	agency	purpose
response	situaton	subject	stimulus	target

He said that the dramatistic pentad on the top assumes a world of intentional action, whereas the scientific terms on the bottom describe motion without purpose.

The dramatistic pentad is deceptively similar to the standard journalistic practice of answering who, what, where, when, why, and how in the opening paragraph of a story. Because Burke regarded himself as an interpreter rather than a reporter, he was not content merely to label the five categories. By evaluating the ratio of importance between individual pairs (scene-agency, agent-act), the critic can determine which element provides the best clue to the speaker's motivation.

The pentad offers a way to determine why the speaker selected a given rhetorical strategy to identify with the audience. When a message stresses one element over the other four, it reveals a speaker's philosophy or worldview.

Act.   A critic's label for the act pictures what was done. A speech that features dramatic verbs demonstrates a commitment to realism.

Scene.   The description of the scene gives a context for where and when the act was performed. Public speaking that emphasizes setting and circumstance downplays free will and reflects an attitude of situational determinism ("I had no choice").

Agent.   The agent is the person or people who performed the act. Some messages are filled with references to self, mind, spirit, and personal responsibility. This focus on character and the agent as instigator is consistent with philosophical idealism.

Agency.   Agency is the means the agent used to do the deed. A long description of methods or technique reflects a "get-the-job-done" approach that springs from the speaker's mind-set of pragmatism.

Purpose.   The speaker's purpose is the stated or implied goal of the address. An extended discussion of purpose within the message shows a strong desire on the part of the speaker for unity or ultimate meaning in life, common concerns of mysticism.

Burke was somewhat confusing in his use of the terms *purpose* and *motivation*. Is the concern for purpose (as one of the five terms of the pentad) separate from the quest for underlying motivation, which the entire dramatistic metaphor is designed to uncover? Perhaps it's the distinction between an immediate localized goal, and the ultimate direction of all human activity. According to this view, the pentad can be seen as offering a static photograph of a single scene in the human drama. The guilt-redemption cycle, the third perspective, would be the plot of the whole play.

GUILT-REDEMPTION CYCLE: THE ROOT OF ALL RHETORIC

The immediate purpose of a speech may vary according to the scene or agent, but Burke was convinced that the ultimate motivation of all public speaking is to purge ourselves of an ever-present, all-inclusive sense of guilt. Guilt is his catch-all term to cover every form of tension, anxiety, embarrassment, shame, disgust, and other noxious feelings that he believed intrinsic to the human condition. His "Definition of Man" is a discouraging counterpoint to the optimism of Carl Rogers. (Like most writers of an earlier generation, Burke used the word *man* to designate human beings of both genders. Given his record of using words to startle and stretch his readers, if he were writing today, one wonders if he might suddenly recast his definition in exclusively feminine symbols. But in order to remain faithful to what he wrote, I won't alter his gender-loaded references.)

> Man is
> the symbol-using inventor of the negative
> separated from his natural condition by instruments
> of his own making
> goaded by the spirit of hierarchy
> and rotten with perfection.[7]

Burke started out by acknowledging our animal nature, but like Mead (see Chapter 4) he emphasized this uniquely human ability to create, use, and abuse language. The rest of his definition makes it clear that the capacity to manipulate symbols is not an unmixed blessing. The remaining lines suggest three linguistic causes for the sense of inner "pollution."

By writing "inventor of the negative," Burke claimed that it's only through manmade language that the possibility of choice comes into being. There is no "Don't" or "Thou shalt not" in nature. Symbolic interaction is a precondition of "no-ing."

The phrase "separated from his natural condition by instruments of his own making" bounces off the traditional description of a human as a "tool-using animal." Here again, Burke suggested that our technological inventions get us into trouble. Murphy's Law states that anything that can go wrong will.[8] When it comes to interpersonal relations, Burke thought Murphy was an optimist.

Burke wrote extensively about hierarchies, bureaucracies, and other ordered systems which rank how well people observe society's negative rules. He was convinced that no matter how high you climb on the performance ladder, you'll always feel a strong sense of embarrassment for not having done better. The guilt-inducing high priests of the hierarchy are the professional symbol users of society—teachers, lawyers, journalists, artists, and advertising copy writers.

The final phrase, "rotten with perfection," is an example of what Burke called "perspective by incongruity."[9] The device calls attention to a truth by linking two incongruous words. Burke used the technique to point out that the harder we strive to be perfect, the more rotten we feel. The realization of a "perfect 10" (Ten Commandments, an Olympic dive) only intensifies our sense of imperfection. Perfection makes us more aware of our "original sin" and heightens our desire to find someone on whom we can dump our load of guilt. Burke believed that getting rid of guilt is the basic plot of the human drama. At its root, rhetoric is the public search for a perfect scapegoat.

Redemption Through Victimage

Those who have rejected or never had a religious commitment may be impatient with Burke's continual use of theological terms. Surprisingly, he made no claim to be a man of faith, nor did he ask his readers to believe in God.

The world was going down the tubes. They needed a
scapegoat. They found Wayne.

Regardless of whether or not you accept the Christian doctrine of human sin and divine redemption, Burke claimed that the "purely social terminology of human relations can not do better than to hover about that accurate and succinct theological formula."[10] He regarded theology as a field that has fine-tuned its use of language and urged the social critic to look for secular equivalents of the major religious themes of guilt and purification. This quest brought him to view rhetoric as a continual pattern of redemption through victimage.

Burke said that the speaker has two choices. The first option is to purge guilt through self-blame. Described theologically as "mortification," this route requires confession of sin and a request for forgiveness. Yet even obvious candidates (Richard Nixon, O.J. Simpson, Bill Clinton) find it excruciatingly difficult to admit publicly that they are the cause of their own grief. Since it's much easier for people to blame their problems on someone else—the second option—Burke suggested that we look for signs of victimage in every rhetorical act. He was sure that we would find it.

Victimage is the process of designating an external enemy as the source of all our ills. The list of candidates is limited only by our imagination—eastern liberals, Muslim fundamentalists, the Colombian drug cartel, the military-industrial complex, blacks, Communists, Jews, chauvinistic males, homosexuals, the police, rich capitalists, and so forth. Since Operation Desert Storm, Americans would probably nominate Iraq's president Saddam Hussein, whose massively callous acts make him seem the personification of evil. Perfect guilt requires a perfect victim. God terms are only as powerful as the devil terms they oppose.

Burke was not an advocate of redemption through victimization, but he said he couldn't ignore the historical pattern of people uniting against a common enemy ("congregation through segregation"). We've already discussed his claim that identification is the central strategy of the new rhetoric. The easiest way for an orator to identify with an audience is to lash out at whatever or whomever the people fear ("My friend is one who hates what I hate").

A RHETORICAL CRITIQUE USING DRAMATISTIC INSIGHT

Many rhetorical critics in speech communication have adopted Burke's techniques of literary criticism to inform their understanding of specific public address events. I asked Ken Chase, a colleague at Wheaton, and Glen McClish at San Diego State University to perform a Burkean analysis of Malcolm X's famous speech "The Ballot or the Bullet." The critique that follows is the result of their combined insight.

Malcolm X, "The Ballot or the Bullet"

Often paired with Martin Luther King, Jr., Malcolm X was one of the most influential civil rights speakers of the 1960s. Malcolm's rhetoric, though, was more militant, angry, and for many African Americans, more realistic than the idealism of King's "I Have A Dream." Malcolm delivered his famous speech, "The Ballot or the Bullet," in April 1964, only eleven months before his assassination.

By viewing public rhetoric as an attempt to build a particular social order, Kenneth Burke helps reveal the power of "The Ballot or the Bullet." Malcolm's address portrays America as a nation that promises full equality, dignity, and freedom for all its citizens, yet African Americans have never received their birthright. Epitomizing his commitment to Black Nationalism, Malcolm urges his brothers and sisters to start their own businesses and elect their own leaders. At the same time he attacks white politicians who impede civil rights. The audience at the Corey Methodist Church in Cleveland, Ohio, interrupted Malcolm X with applause and laughter over 150 times during the lengthy oration.

Malcolm asserts that the struggle for civil rights is not only the work of his fellow Black Muslims, but is shared by all concerned African Americans. By strategically aligning himself with Christian ministers like King and Adam Clayton Powell, he minimizes the alienation his Islamic faith could potentially create. He emphasizes the shared heritage of all African Americans: "Our mothers and fathers invested sweat and blood. Three hundred and ten years we worked in this country without a dime in return. . . ." In this way, Malcolm creates a strong sense of *identification* as he coaxes his audience to share his so-cial purpose and his means for achieving it.

The title of the speech, "The Ballot or the Bullet," refers to the means, or *agency*, by which the *agents*—African Americans—can *act* as citizens to accom-plish the *purpose* of equality, dignity, and freedom. Malcolm strategically places his audience within the larger context of American history and the international struggle for human rights. It is this *scene* which motivates the militant message that African Americans will proclaim—"We've got to fight until we overcome."

Malcolm's emphasis on the means to achieve his purpose ("by whatever means necessary") results in a high agency-purpose ratio—an indicator of his pragmatic motivation. The ballot enforces civil rights legislation; the bullet de-fends blacks from white violence. The bullet also warns white society that equality must not be delayed: "Give it to us now. Don't wait for next year. Give it to us yesterday, and that's not fast enough."

Malcolm criticizes his brothers and sisters for failing to show the courage, knowledge, and maturity that are necessary to reap the full benefits of citizen-ship. It is the white man, however, who has enslaved, lynched, and oppressed the Africans living on American soil, and it is he who must bear the brunt of collective *guilt*. Through *victimage*, the white man and his society become the *scapegoat* that must be sacrificed for the *redemption* of blacks. Within the drama of African-American life, "Black Nationalism" serves as the *god term* which em-bodies the spirit of the movement. Conversely, "White man" is the *devil term* that epitomizes all who oppose equality, dignity, and freedom for all.

CRITIQUE: EVALUATING THE CRITIC'S ANALYSIS

Kenneth Burke was perhaps the foremost rhetorician of the twentieth century. Burke wrote about rhetoric; other rhetoricians write about Burke. Universities offer entire courses on Burkean analysis. On two separate occasions the Na-tional Communication Association featured the man and his ideas at its na-tional convention. The Kenneth Burke Society holds conferences and competi-tions which give his followers the opportunity to discuss and delight over his wide-ranging ideas. He obviously had something to say.

The problem for the beginning student is that he said it in such a round-about way. Burke was closely tied to symbolic interactionism (see Chapter 4) and complexity seems to be characteristic of much of the writing within that tradition. Even advocates like Nichols feel compelled to explain why Burke was frequently confusing and sometimes obscure: "In part the difficulty arises from the numerous vocabularies he employs. His words in isolation are usually simple enough, but he often uses them in new contexts."[11] Clarity is compro-mised further by Burke's tendency to flood his text with literary allusions. Un-less a student is prepared to grapple with Coleridge's "The Rime of the Ancient Mariner," Augustine's *Confessions,* and Freud's *The Psychopathology of Everyday Life*—all on the same page—Burke's mental leaps and breadth of scholarship will prove more frustrating than informative.

Yet Burke enthusiasts insist that the process of discovery is half the fun. Like a choice enthymeme, Burke's writing invites active reader participation as he surrounds an idea. And no matter what aspect of rhetoric that idea addresses, the reader will never again be able to dismiss words as "mere rhetoric." Burke has done us all a favor by celebrating the life-giving quality of language.

Without question, the dramatistic pentad is the feature of Burke's writing that has gained the most approval. The integrated procedure offers five artistic "cookie cutters" for the critic to use in slicing human interaction into digestible, bite-sized morsels. Many have found it helpful in pinpointing a speaker's motivation and the way the speech functions to serve that need or desire.

Burke's concept of rhetoric as identification is a major advance in a field of knowledge which many scholars had thought complete. Rather than opposing Aristotle's definition, he gave it a contemporary luster by showing that common ground is the foundation of emotional appeal. Communication scientists can't test Burke's claim that unconscious identification produces behavior and attitude change, but they can confirm that perceived similarity facilitates persuasion.

Of all Burke's motivational principles, his strategies of redemption are the most controversial. Perhaps that's because his "secular religion" takes God too seriously for those who don't believe, yet not seriously enough for those who do. Both camps have trouble with Burke's unsubstantiated assumption that guilt is the primary human emotion which underlies all public address. There's no doubt that Malcolm X's "The Ballot or the Bullet" exploited a guilt-scapegoat linkage, but whether the same religious drama is played out in every important public event is another matter.

I appreciate Burke's commitment to an ethical stance that refuses to let desirable ends justify unfair means. He urged speakers not to make a victim out of someone else in order to become unified with the audience. True believers in the dramatistic gospel maintain that it's unwise to talk about communication without some understanding of Burke. The inclusion of this chapter is my response to their claim.

QUESTIONS TO SHARPEN YOUR FOCUS

1. Burke says that without *identification*, there is no persuasion. A number of the theories already covered deal with ideas or principles akin to identification. Can you name five?

2. Burke encourages the *rhetorical critic* to discover communicators' *motives* by analyzing the *God terms* and *Devil terms* they use. What are his God terms and Devil terms?

3. Apply the *dramatistic pentad* to the nonverbal rhetoric of a Friday night party on campus. Which of the five elements of the pentad would you stress to capture the meaning of that human drama?

4. Burke claims that all rhetoric ultimately serves to *expiate guilt through victimage*. If he's right, is it the speaker, the listener, or the victim's guilt that is being purged?

A SECOND LOOK

Recommended resource: Sonja Foss, Karen Foss, and Robert Trapp, *Contemporary Perspectives on Rhetoric*, Waveland, Prospect Heights, Ill., 1985, pp. 153–188.

Dramatism: Kenneth Burke, "Dramatism," in *The International Encyclopedia of the Social Sciences*, Vol. 7, David L. Sills (ed.), Macmillan, New York, 1968, pp. 445–451.

Key scholarship: Barry Brummet (ed.), *Landmark Essays on Kenneth Burke*, Hermagoras, Davis, Calif., 1993.

Identification: Kenneth Burke, *A Rhetoric of Motives*, Prentice-Hall, Englewood Cliffs, N.J., 1950, pp. 20–46.

Pentad: Kenneth Burke, *A Grammar of Motives*, Prentice-Hall, Englewood Cliffs, N.J., 1945, pp. xvii–xxv.

Guilt-redemption: Kenneth Burke, "On Human Behavior Considered 'Dramatistically,' " in *Permanence and Change*, Bobbs-Merrill, Indianapolis, 1965, pp. 274–294.

Human nature: Kenneth Burke, "Definition of Man," in *Language as Symbolic Action*, University of California, Berkeley, 1966, pp. 3–24.

Devil terms: Elizabeth Walker Mechling and Jay Mechling, "Sweet Talk: The Moral Rhetoric Against Sugar," *Central States Speech Journal*, Vol. 34, 1983, pp. 19–32.

Malcolm X speaks: Malcolm X, "The Ballot or the Bullet," in *Great Speakers and Speeches*, 2d ed., John L. Lucaites and Lawrence M. Bernabo (eds.), Kendall/Hunt, Dubuque, Iowa, 1992, pp. 277–286.

Application to speech communication: Marie Hochmuth Nichols, "Kenneth Burke and the New Rhetoric," *Quarterly Journal of Speech*, Vol. 38, 1952, pp. 133–144; also in Brummet, pp. 271–279.

Limits of dramatism: James W. Chesebro, "Extensions of the Burkean System," *Quarterly Journal of Speech*, Vol. 78, 1992, pp. 356–368.

Feminist critique: Celeste Michelle Condit, "Post-Burke: Transcending the Substance of Dramatism," *Quarterly Journal of Speech*, Vol. 78, 1992, pp. 349–355; also in Brummet, pp. 3–18.

22

Narrative Paradigm

of Walter Fisher

People are storytelling animals. This simple assertion is Walter Fisher's answer to the philosophical question, What is the essence of human nature?

Many of the theorists discussed in earlier chapters offer different answers to this key question of human existence. For example, Thibaut and Kelley's social exchange theory operates on the premise that humans are rational creatures. Berger's uncertainty reduction theory assumes that people are basically curious. Most pertinent for students of communication, Mead's symbolic interactionism insists that our ability to use symbols is what makes us uniquely human. (See Chapters 9, 10, and 4.)

Fisher doesn't argue against any of these ideas, but he thinks that human communication reveals something more basic than rationality, curiosity, or even symbol-using capacity. He is convinced that we are narrative beings who "experience and comprehend life as a series of ongoing narratives, as conflicts, characters, beginnings, middles, and ends."[1] If this is true, then "all forms of human communication need to be seen fundamentally as stories."[2]

Walter Fisher is Director of the Annenberg School of Communication at the University of Southern California. Throughout his professional life he has been uncomfortable with the prevailing view that rhetoric is only a matter of evidence, facts, arguments, reason, and logic that has its highest expression in courts of law, legislatures, and other deliberative bodies. In 1984 he proposed that offering good reasons has more to do with telling a compelling story than it does with piling up evidence or constructing a tight argument.[3]

Fisher soon became convinced that all forms of communication that appeal to our reason are best viewed as stories shaped by history, culture, and character. When we hear the word *story*, most of us tend to think of novels, plays, movies, TV sitcoms, and yarns told at night sitting around a campfire. Some of us also call to mind accounts of our past—tales we tell to others in which we are the central character. But Fisher regards *all* types of communication as story. Obviously, he sees differences in form between a Robert Frost poem, an Anne Tyler novel, or a performance of *King Lear* on the one hand, and a philosophical essay, historical report, political debate, theological discussion, or scientific treatise on the other. Yet if we want to know whether or not we should believe the "truth" each of these genres proclaims, Fisher maintains that all of them could and should be viewed as narrative. In 1984 Fisher introduced the term *narrative paradigm* to highlight his belief that there is no type of communication that is purely descriptive or didactic.

TELLING A COMPELLING STORY

Most religious traditions are passed on from generation to generation through the retelling of stories. The faithful are urged to "tell the old, old story" to encourage believers and convince those in doubt. American writer Frederick Buechner takes a fresh approach to passing on religious story. For example, he retells the eighth-century B.C. biblical story of the rocky marriage between Hosea and Gomer in twentieth-century form. Buechner's account of forgiveness provides a vehicle for examining Fisher's narrative paradigm in the rest of the chapter.

The story begins when the startling "word of the Lord" comes to the Israeli prophet Hosea that he is to marry a prostitute. He chooses Gomer.[4]

> She was always good company—a little heavy with the lipstick maybe, a little less than choosy about men and booze, a little loud, but great at a party and always good for a laugh. The prophet Hosea came along wearing a sandwich board that read "the End is at Hand" on one side and "Watch Out" on the other.
>
> The first time he asked her to marry him, she thought he was kidding. The second time she knew he was serious but thought he was crazy. The third time she said yes. He wasn't exactly a swinger, but he had a kind face, and he was generous, and he wasn't all that crazier than everybody else. Besides, any fool could see he loved her.
>
> Give or take a little, she even loved him back for a while, and they had three children whom Hosea named with queer names like Not-pitied-for-God-will-no-longer-pity-Israel-now-that-it's-gone-to-the-dogs so that every time the roll was called at school, Hosea would be scoring a prophetic bullseye in absentia. But everybody could see the marriage wasn't going to last, and it didn't.
>
> While Hosea was off hitting the sawdust trail, Gomer took to hitting as many night spots as she could squeeze into a night, and any resemblance between her next batch of children and Hosea was purely coincidental. It almost killed him, of course. Every time he raised a hand to her, he burst into tears. Every time she raised one to him, he was the one who ended up apologizing.
>
> He tried locking her out of the house a few times when she wasn't in by five in the morning, but he always opened the door when she finally showed up and helped get her to bed if she couldn't see straight enough to get there herself. Then one day she didn't show up at all.
>
> He swore that this time he was through with her for keeps, but of course he wasn't. When he finally found her, she was lying passed out in a highly specialized establishment located above an adult bookstore, and he had to pay the

management plenty to let her out of her contract. She'd lost her front tooth and picked up some scars you had to see to believe, but Hosea had her back again and that seemed to be all that mattered.

He changed his sandwich board to read "God is love" on one side and "There's no end to it" on the other, and when he stood on the street corner . . . nobody can say how many converts he made, but one thing that's for sure is that, including Gomer's, there was seldom a dry eye in the house.[5]

NARRATION AND PARADIGM: DEFINING THE TERMS

Fisher defines *narration* as "symbolic actions—words and/or deeds—that have sequence and meaning for those who live, create, or interpret them."[6] Hosea's life and Buechner's account of it clearly qualify as narrative. But Fisher's definition is broad and is especially notable for what it doesn't exclude. On the basis of his further elaboration,[7] I offer this expanded paraphrase of the definition above:

> Narration is communication rooted in time and space. It covers every aspect of our lives and the lives of others in regard to character, motive, and action. The term also refers to every verbal or nonverbal bid for a person to believe or act in a certain way. Even when a message seems abstract—is devoid of imagery—it is narration because it is embedded in the speaker's ongoing story that has a beginning, middle, and end, and it invites listeners to interpret its meaning and assess its value for their own lives.

Under Fisher's expanded definition, the didactic God-is-love phrase on Hosea's sandwich board is the premise for the *Greatest Story Ever Told*. Those who dwell in the story cannot help loving as Hosea did. When the term *narrative* is applied this way, we may have trouble imagining any serious communication which doesn't qualify as narration. That's precisely Fisher's point. He believes that all messages are best viewed as story, not necessarily in their form, but because they cause us to spin out their implications for the way we live *our* story.

Fisher uses the term *paradigm* to refer to a "conceptual framework." You'll remember from Delia's constructivism that the perception of people is not so much a matter of the physics of sight and sound as it is one of interpretation (see Chapter 8). Meaning isn't inherent in events; it's attached at the workbench of the mind. A paradigm is a universal model which calls for people to view events through a common interpretive lens.

In *The Structure of Scientific Revolutions*, Thomas Kuhn argues that an accepted paradigm is the mark of a mature science. Responding to this challenge, communication scientists in the 1970s sought to discover a universal model that would explain communication behavior.[8] Fisher's narrative paradigm is an interpretive counterpart to their efforts. Fisher offers a way to understand all communication and to direct rhetorical inquiry. He doesn't regard the narrative paradigm as a specific rhetoric. Rather, he sees it as "the foundation on which a complete rhetoric needs to be built. This structure would provide a comprehensive explanation of the creation, composition, adaptation, presentation, and reception of symbolic messages."[9]

PARADIGM SHIFT: FROM RATIONAL-WORLD PARADIGM TO NARRATIVE PARADIGM

Fisher begins his book *Human Communication as Narration* with a reference to the opening line of the Gospel of John: "In the beginning was the word (*logos*)." He notes that the Greek word *logos* originally included story, reason, rationale, conception, discourse, thought—all forms of human communication. Imagination and thought were not yet distinct. The story of Hosea and Gomer was *logos*.

According to Fisher, the writings of Plato and Aristotle reflect the early evolution from a generic to a specific use of *logos*—from story to statement. *Logos* had already begun to refer only to philosophical discourse, a lofty enterprise that relegated imagination, poetry, and other aesthetic concerns to a second-class status. Rhetoric fell somewhere between *logos* and poetic. It was the bastardized offspring of the somewhat seamy union between "pure logic" on the one hand and emotional stories that would stir up passions on the other. The Greek citizen concerned with truth alone should steer clear of rhetoric and consult an expert on wisdom—the philosopher.

Fisher notes that 2,000 years later the scientific revolution dethroned the philosopher-king. For the last few centuries the only knowledge that seems to be worth knowing in academia is that which can be spotted in the physical world. The person who wants to understand the way things are needs to check with a doctor, a scientist, an engineer, or other technical expert. Despite the elevation of technology and the demotion of philosophy, both modes of decision making are similar in their elitist tendencies to "place that which is not *formally* logical or which is not characterized by *expertise* within a somehow subhuman framework of behavior."[10] Fisher sees philosophical and technical discussion as the scholars' standard approach to knowledge. He calls this mind-set the *rational-world paradigm*. Hirokawa and Gouran's functional perspective on group decision making is a perfect example (see Chapter 15).

Fisher lists five assumptions of the prevailing rational-world paradigm. See if they match what you've been taught all along in school.

1. People are essentially rational.
2. We make decisions on the basis of arguments.
3. The type of speaking situation (legal, scientific, legislative) determines the course of our argument.
4. Rationality is determined by how much we know and how well we argue.
5. The world is a set of logical puzzles that we can solve through rational analysis.

Viewed through the rational-world paradigm, the story of Hosea is ridiculous. Hosea's marriage to Gomer is irrational. The only logical conclusion is that the man had an unhealthy sexual obsession with a destructive woman. Buechner's words present no plausible argument why Hosea's willingness to let Gomer walk all over him is a superior strategy to separation or divorce. Other than the Old Testament passage, the author offers no evidence that Hosea and Gomer are historical characters, that any kind of god exists, or that this supreme being actually commanded Hosea to marry a whore. The claim that Hosea and Gomer's dysfunctional marriage illustrates the divine-human relationship has no basis in fact. The story is absurd.

Fisher is convinced that the assumptions of the rational-world paradigm are too limited. He calls for a new conceptual framework (a paradigm shift) in order to better understand human communication. His narrative paradigm is built on five assumptions similar in form to the rational-world paradigm, but quite different in content.

1. People are essentially storytellers.
2. We make decisions on the basis of good reasons.
3. History, biography, culture, and character determine what we consider good reasons.
4. Narrative rationality is determined by the coherence and fidelity of our stories.
5. The world is a set of stories from which we choose, and thus constantly re-create, our lives.

Viewing human beings as storytellers who sometimes argue is a major conceptual shift. For example, in a logical system, values are emotional nonsense. From the narrative perspective, however, values are the "stuff" of stories. Working from a strictly logical standpoint, aesthetic proof is irrelevant, yet within a narrative framework, style and beauty play a pivotal role in determining whether or not we get into a story. Perhaps the biggest shift in thinking has to do with who is qualified to assess the quality of communication. Whereas the rational-world model holds that only experts are capable of presenting or discerning sound arguments, the narrative paradigm maintains that, armed with a bit of common sense, almost any of us can see the point of a good story and judge its merits as the basis for belief and action. Fisher would say that each of us will make his or her judgment about Buechner's account of Hosea (or any story) based upon *narrative rationality.*

NARRATIVE RATIONALITY: COHERENCE AND FIDELITY

According to Fisher, not all stories are equally good. Even though there's no guarantee that people won't adopt a bad story, he thinks that everybody applies the same standards of narrative rationality to whatever stories he or she hears. Will we accept an account of a marriage between a prophet and a prostitute—a story with the moral that true love is unremitting and forever, that it knows no bounds? Fisher believes that our answer depends on whether or not Buechner's account meets the twin tests of *narrative coherence* and *narrative fidelity*.

Narrative Coherence: Does the Story Hang Together?

Narrative coherence has to do with how probable the story appears to the hearer. Does the narrative "hang together"? Do the people and events it portrays seem to be of one piece? Are they part of an organic whole? Do the characters act consistently?

Buechner's version of Hosea and Gomer's relationship translates this ancient tale of unrequited love into a contemporary setting. To the extent that his modern-day references to roll calls in school, adult bookstores, and heavy lipstick consistently portray the present, the story has structural integrity. Fisher regards the internal consistency of a narrative as similar to lines of argument in a rational-world paradigm. In that sense, his narrative paradigm doesn't discount or replace logic. Instead, Fisher lists the test of reason as one, but only one, of the factors that affect narrative coherence.

Stories hang together when we're convinced that the narrator hasn't left out important details, fudged the facts, or ignored other plausible interpretations. We often judge the coherence of a narrative by comparing it with other stories we've heard that deal with the same theme. How does Buechner's account of a man's love for a prostitute stack up against films such as *Pretty Woman, Never on Sunday,* or *Leaving Las Vegas*? To the extent that Gomer's selfish behavior seems more realistic to us than the heart-of-gold motivation of pretty woman Julia Roberts, we'll credit Buechner's biblical update with coherence.

For Fisher, the ultimate test of narrative coherence is whether or not we can count on the characters to act in a reliable manner. We are suspicious of accounts where characters behave "uncharacteristically"; we tend to trust stories of people who show continuity of thought, motive, and action. Whether you regard Buechner's Hosea as a wonderfully forgiving husband or a nauseatingly spineless wimp, the constancy of his love for Gomer in spite of her unfaithfulness is a thread that gives the fabric of the story a tight weave.

Narrative Fidelity: Does the Story Ring True?

Narrative fidelity is the quality of a story that causes the words to strike a responsive chord in the life of the listener. A story has fidelity when it rings true with the hearers' experiences; it squares with the stories they might tell about themselves.

Have we, like Gomer, ever been caught up in the party scene, cheated on a faithful lover, been forgiven when we didn't deserve it, or shed tears over the hurt we've caused ourselves and others? To the extent that the details of the story portray the world we live in, the narrative has fidelity.

Fisher's book *Human Communication as Narration* has the subtitle *Toward a Philosophy of Reason, Value, and Action.* He believes a story has fidelity when it provides a logic of good reasons to guide our future actions. When we buy into a story, we buy into the type of character we should be. Thus, values are what set the narrative paradigm's logic of good reasons apart from the rational-world paradigm's mere logic of reasons.

The logic of good reasons centers on five value-related issues. Fisher says we are concerned with the values embedded in the message, the relevance of those values to decisions made, the consequence of adhering to those values, the overlap with the worldview of the audience, and conformity with what the audience members believe is "an ideal basis for conduct."[11] The last two concerns—congruity with the listeners' values and the actions they think best—form the basis for Fisher's contention that people tend to prefer accounts that fit with what they view as truthful and humane. But what specific values guide audiences as they gauge a story's truth or fidelity? Fisher suggests that there is an *ideal audience* or permanent public that identifies the values that a good story embodies:

> It appears that there is a permanent public, an actual community existing over time, that believes in the values of truth, the good, beauty, health, wisdom, courage, temperance, justice, harmony, order, communion, friendship, and oneness with the Cosmos—as variously as those values may be defined or practiced in "real" life.[12]

Fisher admits that other communities are possible—ones based on greed or power, for example. Yet he believes that when people are confronted by "the better part of themselves," these less idealistic value systems wouldn't be "entirely coherent or true to their whole lives, or to the life that they would most like to live."[13] Fisher believes, then, that the humane virtues of the ideal audience shape our logic of good reasons. If we are convinced that this audience of good people would squirm in discomfort at the stupid codependence of the prophet, Buechner's version of the biblical narrative will lack fidelity. But inasmuch as we think that these ideal auditors would applaud Hosea's love and forgiveness of Gomer, Buechner's words will have the ring of truth.

CRITIQUE: DOES FISHER'S STORY HAVE COHERENCE AND FIDELITY?

Fisher's narrative paradigm offers a fresh alternative to the neo-Aristotelian analysis which has dominated rhetorical thinking in the field of communication. His approach is radically democratic. When communication is viewed as narrative, people don't need specialized training to figure out whether a story holds together or has the ring of truth. Anyone with a little common sense is a competent rhetorical critic.

In *Human Communication as Narration,* Fisher applies the principles of narrative coherence and narrative fidelity to analyze various types of communication. He explains why a sometimes illogical President Ronald Reagan was aptly known as "The Great Communicator." He examines the false values of Willy Loman that lead to his downfall in *Death of a Salesman.* And he explores the consequences of adopting the rival philosophies embedded in the stories of two Greek thinkers—Socrates and Callicles. According to Fisher, the very fact that the narrative paradigm can be applied to this wide range of communication genres is strong evidence of its validity.

Of course, Fisher's theory is itself a story, and as you might expect, not everyone accepts his narrative tale. Critics dispute whether all communication really is story and whether Fisher's logic of good reasons is true to life. Ironically, the first concern is a matter of coherence and the second raises the issue of fidelity.

Fisher's claim that all communication is story begs two questions:

1. Are there any forms of communication where coherence is not an appropriate standard? University of Kansas rhetorical critic Robert Rowland suggests that some types of science fiction don't even try to make narrative sense. A variety of postmodern literature seems equally chaotic. The discovery of a communication genre unconcerned with consistency could be a serious blow to Fisher's universal claim. Of course, a literary critic could still use narrative coherence and fidelity as appropriate criteria in the cases where the text meets a more rigorous definition of story.

2. Even if we sign on to Fisher's sweeping statement that all human communication is narration, does this truth offer any meaningful insight? Fisher's definition of narration seems so broad that saying discourse is story may not be saying much. The problem is similar to popular psychology's wholesale diagnosis of families as dysfunctional. If the "dysfunctional" label is attached to every family system, the term loses descriptive power. There's no realistic way to support or refute the claim; perhaps by labeling all communication as narration, Fisher has purchased coherence at the cost of clarity.

Other critics charge that Fisher's logic of good reasons is the soft spot of his narrative paradigm. According to Fisher, a story's good reasons are good because they appeal to the values of the people who are likely to hear the tale. But one shortcoming of the narrative paradigm is its failure to specify how to recognize the values of a story and the values of an audience to see if they coincide.

William Kirkwood at East Tennessee State University claims there is a bigger problem with the logic of good reasons. Kirkwood says that a standard of narrative fidelity implies that good stories cannot and perhaps should not go beyond what people already believe and value. He charges that the logic of good reasons encourages writers and speakers to adjust their ideas to people rather than people to their ideas, and thus denies the "rhetoric of possibility."[14]

Fisher thinks this is ridiculous. He explicitly states that people have the capacity "to formulate and adopt new stories that better account for their lives or the mystery of life itself."[15] Certainly, the forgiveness that Hosea extends to Gomer goes beyond anything most of us have ever experienced on a human level, yet the story still strikes a responsive chord in many who hear it. Perhaps a good story can extend our aspirations to a level that we couldn't have imagined before we first heard the tale.

Finally, we might question the broad applicability Fisher claims for his approach. In the closing paragraph of *Human Communication as Narrative*, he declares, "The logic I have outlined and critically applied in interpreting and assessing political, aesthetic, and philosophical discourse is, I believe, a universal logic."[16] Yet the work of Geertz and Pacanowsky (see Chapter 18) strongly suggests that stories are culturally specific.

Is all communication story, and do we judge every message we hear on the basis of whether it holds together and rings true with our values? If you take Fisher's ideas seriously, you won't need me or a trained rhetorician to give you the final word. Like everyone else, you can spot the difference between a good and a bad story.

QUESTIONS TO SHARPEN YOUR FOCUS

1. Using Fisher's definition of *narration*, can you think of any types of communication that don't fit within the *narrative paradigm*?

2. Fisher claims that the *rational-world paradigm* dominates western education. Can you list courses you've had at college that adopt the assumptions of this conceptual framework?

3. What is the difference between *narrative coherence* and *narrative fidelity*?

4. You apply a *logic of good reasons* to the stories you hear. What are the *values* you hold that cause you to accept or reject Buechner's story of Hosea?

A SECOND LOOK

Recommended resource: Walter R. Fisher, *Human Communication as Narration: Toward a Philosophy of Reason, Value, and Action,* University of South Carolina, Columbia, 1987.

Departure from neo-Aristotelian rhetoric: Walter R. Fisher, "Toward a Logic of Good Reasons," *Quarterly Journal of Speech,* Vol. 64, 1978, pp. 376–384.

Original statement: Walter R. Fisher, "Narration as a Human Communication Paradigm: The Case of Public Moral Argument," *Communication Monographs,* Vol. 51, 1984, pp. 1–22.

Storytelling and narrativity in communication research: Journal of Communication, Vol. 35, No. 4, 1985, entire issue.

Paradigms: Thomas Kuhn, *The Structure of Scientific Revolutions,* University of Chicago, Chicago, 1962.

Political communication as story: Richard Johannesen, "A Rational World Ethic Versus a Narrative Ethic for Political Communication," in *Ethics in Human Communication,* 3d ed., Waveland, Prospect Heights, Ill., 1990, 253–263.

Scientific communication as story: Walter R. Fisher, "Narrative Rationality and the Logic of Scientific Discourse," *Argumentation,* Vol. 8, 1994, pp. 21–34.

Narrative ethics: Alan Bush and Victoria Davies Bush, "The Narrative Paradigm as a Perspective for Improving Ethical Evaluations of Advertisements," *Journal of Advertising,* Vol. 23, No. 3, 1994, pp. 31–41.

Telling the old story in a new way: Frederick Buechner, *Peculiar Treasures,* Harper & Row, New York, 1979.

Critique: Robert C. Rowland, "On Limiting the Narrative Paradigm: Three Case Studies," *Communication Monographs,* Vol. 56, 1989, pp. 39–54.

Critique: Barbara Warnick, "The Narrative Paradigm: Another Story," *Quarterly Journal of Speech,* Vol. 73, 1987, pp. 172–182.

E t h i c a l   R e f l e c t i o n s

ARISTOTLE'S GOLDEN MEAN

In his fourth-century B.C. rhetorical text, Aristotle defined rhetoric as the ability in every speaking situation "to see all available means of persuasion."[1] His book is the first systematic treatise on audience analysis and adaptation—an attempt to teach public speakers the science and art of impression management. Aristotle's approach to rhetoric begs the same question that is raised by Burke's emphasis on *identification* and Fisher's concern for perceived *narrative fidelity:* Is it ethical to alter a message to make it more acceptable for a particular audience?

The way I've phrased the question reflects a western bias to link morality with behavior. Does an *act* produce good or bad? Is it right or wrong to *do* a certain deed? Aristotle, however, spoke of ethics in terms of character rather than conduct, inner disposition instead of outer behavior. He took the Greek admiration for moderation and elevated it to a theory of virtue.

When Barry Goldwater was selected as the Republican party's nominee for president in 1964, he boldly stated: "Extremism in the defense of liberty is no vice . . . moderation in the pursuit of justice is not virtue."[2] Aristotle would have strongly disagreed. He assumed virtue stands between the two vices.[3] Aristotle saw wisdom in the person who avoids excess on either side. Moderation is best; virtue develops habits that seek to walk an intermediate path. This middle way is known as the "golden mean." That's because out of the four cardinal virtues—courage, justice, temperance, and practical wisdom—temperance is the one that explains the three others.

As for audience adaptation, Aristotle would council against the practice of telling people only what they want to hear, pandering to the crowd, or "wimping out" by not stating what we really think. He would be equally against a disregard of audience sensitivities, riding roughshod over listeners' beliefs, or adopting a take-no-prisoners, lay-waste-the-town rhetorical belligerence. The golden mean would lie in winsome straight talk, gentle assertiveness, and appropriate adaptation.

Whether the issue is truthtelling, self-disclosure, or risk-taking when making decisions, Aristotle's golden mean suggests other middle-way communication practices:

Extreme	*Golden Mean*	*Extreme*
Lies	Truthful statements	Brutal honesty
Secrecy	Self-disclosure	Soul-baring
Cowardice	Courage	Recklessness

The final line speaks to issues raised by Hirokawa and Gouran's functional perspective. Their emphasis on group member vigilance seeks to combat an irresponsible recklessness—a rash disregard of possible dire results if things go wrong. But Aristotle would remind us that cowardice is an equally tragic character flaw. As Weick's "Act then think" advice for managers suggests, the paralyzing fear that goes with paying too much attention to danger can prevent us from seizing the opportunity to accomplish much good. The virtue of courage is found in the middle way.

CORNEL WEST'S PROPHETIC PRAGMATISM

Cornel West is a pragmatist philosopher who is professor of African-American studies at Harvard University. Along with best-known American pragmatist John Dewey (see Chapter 15), West regards pragmatism as "a mode of cultural critical action that focuses on the ways and means by which human beings have, do, and can overcome obstacles, dispose predicaments, and settle problematic situations."[4] The moral obstacle West wants to overcome is the institutional oppression of "the disadvantaged, degraded, and dejected" people who struggle on the margins of society.[5] They face racism, sexual discrimination, and economic injustice. West agrees with the analysis of Christian realist Reinhold Niebuhr.[6] These evils exist not just because of ignorance or apathy—they are the result of pervasive human sin.

West is also sympathetic to a Marxist critique of capitalism,[7] but his own brand of pragmatism is deeply rooted in the narratives of the biblical scriptures:

> I have dubbed it "prophetic" in that it harks back to the Jewish and Christian tradition of prophets who brought urgent and compassionate critique to bear on the evils of their day. The mark of the prophet is to speak the truth in love with courage—come what may.[8]

In the public rhetoric section, we've already seen two examples of Hebrew prophets calling for social justice and response to God's forgiveness. Martin Luther King's "I Have A Dream" in Chapter 20 included the words of Amos in which the prophet implores, "Let justice roll down like waters and righteousness like a mighty stream." Chapter 22 examined the prophetic allegory of divine love pictured in Hosea's marriage to a prostitute. These passages have their counterparts in the best-known parables of Jesus. The parable of the Good Samaritan reminds believers that they are responsible to help those who are hurting; the parable of the Prodigal Son proclaims God's delight when his rebellious children return and are reunited.[9]

As a prophetic pragmatist, Cornel West would applaud the action-oriented approach of Poole's adaptive structuration theory so long as the ultimate goal or commitment of members using rules and resources is to empower rather than exploit the disadvantaged, degraded, and dejected who are excluded from the decision-making process. He would be even more enthusiastic over Deetz' call for stakeholders to have an effective say in decisions that affect their lives.

The ethical implications of West's prophetic pragmatism are not always clear-cut. In 1995 he took flak from most whites and many blacks for

supporting Nation of Islam Minister Louis Farrakhan's Million Man March on Washington. West acknowledges that he faced a tragic moral choice: "After all, I am a radical democrat devoted to a downward redistribution of wealth and a Christian freedom-fighter in the King legacy—which condemns any xenophobia, including patriarchy, homophobia, and anti-semitism."[10] These commitments put him at odds with Farrakhan's rhetoric. But West says that he and Farrakhan agreed on the importance of highlighting black suffering, and he was convinced by Dr. Martin Luther King's example of forming alliances and coalitions across racial, gender, class, and religious lines. And so he marched.

PART FOUR

Mass Communication

MEDIA AND CULTURE

Early mass communication theorists assumed that print and electronic media have an enormous power to mold opinion, arouse feelings, and sway behavior. They viewed the mass audience as defenseless and relatively passive—a herd of sheep that is easy prey for manipulative advertising or clever propaganda. The "powerful effects" model likened media messages to bullets fired from a machine gun into a crowd. A similar metaphor pictured print, film, and radio as hypodermic needles that inject something directly into the patient. The ability of Goebbel's Nazi propaganda to mobilize anti-Semitic feeling in the 1930s gave credence to the cause-and-effect notion of media influence.

Even while the United States movie industry cranked out patriotic films in the 1940s to bolster the national war effort, American social scientists began to question the tradition of powerful effects. Voting-behavior studies showed that audiences were much more active, resistant, and obstinate than had been first imagined. Media sociologists Elihu Katz of Hebrew University and Paul Lazarsfeld of Columbia University characterized society as "a honeycomb of small groups bound by a rich web of personal ties and dependencies,"[1] which help shield the individual from media influence. This "limited effects" model recommends looking at differences between people in order to explain the relatively small and scattered impact of mass media.

One line of research consistent with a limited-effects view examines reader, listener, and viewer motivation for attending to a particular type of message. For example, the "uses and gratifications" approach suggests that viewers are selective in the kinds of TV programs they watch.[2] People wanting *information* may tune in *The NewsHour with Jim Lehrer* on public television; individuals seeking to clarify their *personal identity* may watch *Oprah*; viewers searching for clues about *social interaction* may turn on *All My Children*; and people looking for *entertainment* may select *Mad About You*. Of course, some shows might satisfy all four desires, but most programs will affect only those who are predisposed to respond. Advocates of the limited-effects position believe that media constitute only one set of factors that influence people.

The European study of mass communication has focused on broad cultural issues rather than on specific media effects. Because the mass media standardize the symbolic environment, continental scholars have developed a list of questions that they believe every researcher should address.[3]

1. What is the mediating role of culture? Does culture constrain the media, or do the media alter culture?

2. Do the media reflect the diversity of a culture, or do they only portray the ideology of the dominant group within society?

3. What should be the crucial focus of mass communication study—the content of the message or the technology of the media?

4. What research methods are appropriate for analyzing the impact of the media—the quantitative statistical measures of social scientists or the qualitative textual analyses of literature, ethnography, and philosophy?

5. What is the role of the media specialist—neutral administrator of research funded by government and business or critic of societal injustice?

The three theories in this section speak to these cultural issues. Marshall McLuhan's theory of technological determinism (see Chapter 23) regards our present cultural upheaval as a direct result of the sensory bombardment we receive from the electronic media. His belief that "the medium is the message" contrasts with Roland Barthes' insistence that the *content* of the media makes a profound difference. Chapter 24 presents Barthes' semiotics, the study of media images and the way they can be co-opted to serve alternative ends. Stuart Hall's cultural studies theory described in Chapter 25 builds on Barthes' semiotic analysis. The objective of cultural studies is to unmask the role of the media in maintaining the status quo of power relationships in society. Pursuing cultural studies from an initial Marxist commitment, Hall is an advocate for people who are systematically relegated to the margins of society.

Although McLuhan, Barthes, and Hall reject the simplistic "hypodermic needle" model of mass media influence, their theories do represent a return to the concept of powerful effects. Despite their differences on a number of the crucial issues, each theorist believes that the media have a powerful effect because they articulate, interpret, and help create a society's culture. The media mediate culture.

CHAPTER 23

Technological Determinism

of Marshall McLuhan

In a memorable scene from Woody Allen's classic 1977 movie *Annie Hall*, the characters played by Allen and Diane Keaton are standing in a movie line in front of a man pontificating about film in general, and Marshall McLuhan's ideas in particular. When a frustrated Allen interrupts the monologue and challenges the speaker's interpretation of McLuhan, the man haughtily announces that he teaches a course at Columbia entitled, "TV, Media, and Culture." At that point Marshall McLuhan himself walks on screen and tells the man he understands nothing of McLuhan's work. He adds that it's amazing the man is allowed to teach a course in anything.

The fanciful scene works because many viewers were already acquainted with McLuhan and his ideas. The mild-mannered Canadian had earlier been featured in an extended *Playboy* interview and his picture had been on the cover of *Time* magazine. As director of the Center for Culture and Technology at the University of Toronto, McLuhan was that rare media commodity—an academic who could present revolutionary ideas in a way that captured the imagination of a wide audience.

Coming to his study of media and culture from a background in English literature, McLuhan pictured himself as a blind man tapping his cane in all directions to discover the nature of his media environment. He referred to his ideas as "probes," the tentative gropings of one who takes "the numb stance of the technological idiot." But there was nothing tentative about McLuhan's prophetic message. When asked what he was doing, the "Oracle of the Electronic Age" said he was telling all who would listen that we live at a unique time in history. The new electronic media have radically altered the way people think, feel, and act. We're in the midst of a revolution, yet most of us have yet to understand that the world will never be the same.

COMMUNICATION INVENTIONS: THE BALANCE POINTS OF HISTORY

McLuhan divided all human history into four periods, or epochs—a tribal age, a literate age, a print age, and an electronic age. He claimed the transitions between periods were neither gradual nor evolutionary; in each case the world was wrenched from one era into the next because of new developments in communication technology. The schematic in Figure 23.1 represents the Canadian professor's view of history. As you can see, he thought that those of us born in the twentieth century are living on the cusp of history.

According to McLuhan, the crucial inventions that changed life on this

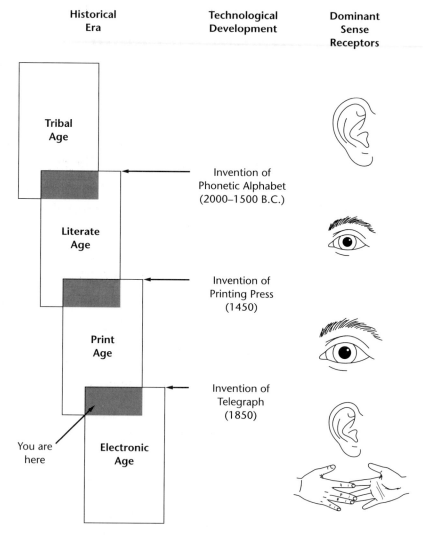

FIGURE 23.1 **Marshall McLuhan's Media Map of History**

planet were the phonetic alphabet, the printing press, and the telegraph. He was certain that their developers had little idea at the time that their technological innovations would revolutionize society, but if we'd only bother to open our eyes, we'd see that the phonetic alphabet catapulted the human race into an age of literacy and Gutenberg's press launched the industrial revolution.

> For the past 3500 years of the Western world, the effects of media—whether it's speech, writing, printing, photography, radio or television—have been systematically overlooked by social observers. Even in today's revolutionary electronic age, scholars evidence few signs of modifying this traditional stance of ostrichlike disregard.[1]

What almost everyone fails to see, said McLuhan, is that people alive today are caught up in a third radical breakthrough. Whatever answer Samuel Morse received when he first tapped out "What hath God wrought?" on his telegraph, the reply clearly didn't anticipate the social upheaval the electronic media would create.

WE SHAPE OUR TOOLS AND THEY IN TURN SHAPE US

At its core, McLuhan's theory is technological determinism. He held that inventions in technology invariably cause cultural change. Whereas Karl Marx's economic determinism argued that changes in modes of *production* determine the course of history, McLuhan concluded that it is specifically changes in modes of *communication* that shape human existence.

Belief in the pivotal role of communication innovation didn't originate with McLuhan. Noting the effect of the railroad in the wilderness, fellow Canadian Harold Innis had already suggested that sudden extensions of communication are reflected in cultural disturbances. But McLuhan was unique in claiming that channels of communication are the primary cause of cultural change. Family life, the workplace, schools, health care, friendship, religious worship, recreation, politics—nothing remains untouched by communication technology. Whereas Emerson regarded an institution as "the lengthened shadow of a man," McLuhan was sure that cultural institutions are lengthened shadows of human inventions—specifically the alphabet, the printing press, and the electronic media. As with all his ideas, he had a catchy way of putting it: "We shape our tools and they in turn shape us."

McLuhan regarded communication inventions as pivotal because he considered every new form of media innovation to be an extension of some human faculty. The book is an extension of the eye. The wheel is an extension of the foot. Clothing is an extension of the skin. Electronic circuitry (especially the computer) is an extension of the central nervous system. You can see by these examples that McLuhan avoids a narrow definition of media. Media are anything that amplify or intensify a bodily organ, sense, or function. Media not only extend our reach and increase our efficiency, they also act as a filter to organize and interpret our social existence.

THE MEDIUM IS THE MESSAGE

McLuhan was convinced that the way we live is largely a function of the way we process information. The phonetic alphabet, the printing press, and the telegraph were turning points in human history because they changed the way people thought about themselves and their world. Tom Wolfe, an analyst of popular culture, summarizes McLuhan's thesis:

> The new technologies . . . radically alter the entire way people use their five senses, the way they react to things, and therefore, their entire lives and the entire society. It doesn't matter what the content of a medium like TV is . . . twenty hours a day of sadistic cowboys caving in people's teeth or . . . Pablo Casals droning away on his cello.[2]

McLuhan said it more succinctly: "The medium is the message."

Students of McLuhan continue to debate what the theorist meant by this apparently simple equation. Sometimes he seemed to indicate that the words we choose are irrelevant ("The content or message of any particular medium has about as much importance as the stenciling on the casing of an atomic bomb"). On other occasions he made the significance of the symbols a matter of degree ("I'm not suggesting that content plays *no* role—merely that it plays a distinctly subordinate role"). Either way, he obviously believed that a medium changes people more than the sum of all the messages of that medium. He warns that the content of a medium "is like the juicy piece of meat carried by the burglar to distract the watchdog of the mind." The same words spoken face-to-face, printed on paper, or presented on television provide three different messages.

The word *message* lends itself to a pun which further illustrates McLuhan's conviction that the media work us over. "The medium is the *massage*," he claimed. The image he offers is of a burly masseur pummeling his client's body rather than giving him a soothing back rub. Television roughs up its viewers. He also described the turbulent 1960s with another variation on the theme:

"The medium is the *mass-age.*" Although McLuhan obviously had fun with his play on words, he was serious about the core idea. Be it oral, written, or electronic, the primary channel of communication changes the way we perceive the world. The dominant medium of any age dominates people.

PARSING THE PAST: A MEDIA ANALYSIS OF HISTORY

McLuhan supported his thesis of technological determinism by interpreting the sweep of human history from a media perspective.

1. The Tribal Age: An Acoustic Place in History

According to McLuhan, the tribal village was an acoustic place where the senses of hearing, touch, taste, and smell were developed far beyond the ability to visualize. The right hemisphere of the brain dominated the left hemisphere. The ear was king; hearing was believing. Members of this oral culture were unable to adopt the role of the detached observer—they acted and emotionally reacted at the same time. Conformity to the group was the rule rather than the exception.

McLuhan claimed that "primitive" people led richer and more complex lives than their literate descendants because the ear, unlike the eye, is unable to select the stimuli it takes in.

> By their dependence on the spoken word for information, people were drawn together into a tribal mesh . . . and since the spoken word is more emotionally laden than the written—conveying by intonation such rich emotions as anger, joy, sorrow, fear—tribal man was more spontaneous and passionately volatile.[3]

Then someone invented the alphabet.

2. The Age of Literacy: A Visual Point of View

McLuhan wrote that the phonetic alphabet fell into the acoustic world like a bombshell, installing sight at the head of the hierarchy of senses. People who could read exchanged an ear for an eye. Of course, the reader is free to disagree, illustrating McLuhan's belief that a private, left-brain "point of view" becomes possible in a visual society. Both writer and reader are separate from the text. Literacy jarred people out of collective tribal involvement into "civilized" private detachment. Writing made it possible to leave the tribe without being cut off from a flow of information.

McLuhan also claimed that the phonetic alphabet established the line as the organizing principle in life. In writing, letter follows letter in a connected, orderly line. Logic is modeled on that step-by-step linear progression. According to McLuhan, when literate people say, "I don't follow you," they mean, "I don't think you are logical." He alleged that the invention of the alphabet fostered the sudden emergence of mathematics, science, and philosophy in ancient Greece.

He cited the political upheaval in colonial Africa as evidence that literacy triggers an ear-to-eye switch that isolates the reader. When oppressed people learned to read, they became independent thinkers.

3. The Print Age: Prototype of the Industrial Revolution

If the phonetic alphabet made visual dependence possible, the printing press made it widespread. In *The Gutenberg Galaxy*, McLuhan wrote that repeatability is the most important characteristic of movable type, and a run of 100,000 copies of his book suggests that he's right. Because the print revolution demonstrated mass production of identical products, McLuhan called it the forerunner of the industrial revolution.

He saw other unintended side effects of Gutenberg's invention. The rise of nationalism followed the homogenization of fluid regional tongues into a fixed national language. Printing deified not only the Gutenberg Bible, but all written words. The press turns words into The Word, and McLuhan labeled literate people "natural suckers" for propaganda. But he regarded the fragmentation of society as the most significant outcome of the new innovation:

> Printing, a ditto device, confirmed and extended the new visual stress. It created the portable book, which men could read in privacy and in isolation from others.[4]

Many libraries have the words "The truth will set you free" carved in stone above the main entrance.[5] McLuhan said that the books inside free readers to be alienated from others in their literate culture. Like easel painting, the printed book glorifies individualism.

4. The Electronic Age: The Rise of the Global Village

According to McLuhan, the power of the printed word is over: "The age of print . . . had its obituary tapped out by the telegraph." Of course, Samuel Morse's invention was only the first of the electronic communication devices that would make the corner Radio Shack like a magic shop to previous generations.

Telegraph   Telephone   Radio

Film projector   Phonograph

Television   Photocopier   Answering machine

Computer   VCR   Compact disc

Holograph   Cellular phone   FAX

DVD   Modem   Internet

Before his death in 1980, McLuhan predicted that even the staggering cultural impact of this communication hardware would be insignificant compared with the upheaval caused by the computer software to come.

McLuhan insisted that the electronic media are retribalizing the human race. Instant communication has returned us to a prealphabetic oral tradition where sound and touch are more important than sight. We've gone "back to the future."

The day of the individualist, of privacy, of fragmented or "applied" knowledge, of "points of view" and specialist goals is being replaced by the over-all-awareness of a mosaic world in which space and time are overcome by television, jets and computers—a simultaneous, "all-at-once" world in which everything resonates with everything else as in a total electrical field.[6]

McLuhan pictured all of us as members of a single global village. The electronic media bring us in touch with everyone, everywhere, instantaneously. Closed human systems no longer exist. The rumble of empty stomachs in Kathmandu or tank treads in Kosovo vibrates in the living rooms of Kansas City. As the first postliterate generation, privacy for us is a luxury or a curse of the past. The planet is like a general store where nosy people keep track of everyone else's business—a twelve-way party line or an Ann Landers column "writ large." Citizens of the world are back in acoustic space.

Linear logic is useless in the electronic society that McLuhan described. Acoustic people no longer inquire, "Do you see my point?" Instead we ask, "How does that grab you?" What we feel is more important than what we think.

TELEVISION IS A COOL MEDIUM

The purpose of McLuhan's media-cultural analysis was to explain the social unrest of the 1960s and focus attention on the unprecedented changes that were still ahead as society moved fully into the electronic era. Because television had just become the dominant communication medium, most of McLuhan's efforts centered on describing the fundamental nature and revolutionary power of TV.

McLuhan classified media as either *hot* or *cool*. Hot media are high-definition channels of communication and are usually beamed at a single sense receptor. Print is a hot, visual medium. So are photographs and motion pictures. They package lots of data in a way that requires little work on the part of the viewer. McLuhan would have labeled the text of this book "hot" but judged the cartoons as "cool." Cool media's low-definition display draws a person in, requiring high participation to fill in the blanks.

McLuhan said a lecture is hot; discussions are cool. The hard sell is hot; the soft sell is cool. Plato's syllogisms were hot; Aristotle's enthymemes were cool. Despite radio's claim to be "the theater of the mind," he called it hot because the broadcast wave carries detailed information over a single channel. Yet he considered the telephone cool because its personal nature demands a response.

Note the parallel between McLuhan's categories of hot and cool and the distinctions between left-brain and right-brain functions. Hot media tend to be highly visual, logical, and private. They are organized to communicate packets of discrete information. Cool media tend to be aural, intuitive, and emotionally involving. Unlike the hot camera, which focuses on the figure in the foreground, cool (right-brain) media clarify the surrounding context and let perceivers insert themselves into the story. People naturally think of television as a visual medium, but McLuhan disputed that notion. He classified TV as an aural and tactile medium—very, very cool.

Television is cool because it requires involvement and participation to fill in its vague and blurry image. The low-definition video display presents a series of widely spaced dots which viewers must connect on their internal mental screens. Unlike radio or print, television doesn't bypass either sight or sound. You can probably study while listening to the radio, but for most people television doesn't work well as background.

LIVING ON THE EDGE OF AN ERA: SOME EXAMPLES

McLuhan supported his interpretation of history by offering numerous examples of media-induced change. I'll cite some of the evidence he offered in the areas of politics, education, and sex and drugs. I'll also include events that took place after he died that lend added credence to his ideas. I'm confident that McLuhan would have drawn on these subsequent events to support his theory of technological determinism.

Politics

Political leaders in the electronic age can survive without vision, but they can't make it without charisma. Larry King, Ted Koppel, and David Letterman are late-night heroes because they know how to talk to the nation on TV in the personal style the town crier used in a preprint era. McLuhan said that "the political candidate who understands TV—whatever his party, goals or beliefs—can gain power unknown in history."[7] Political journalists scoffed in 1992 when Bill Clinton played his saxophone on MTV and hosted an economic summit in the style of a television talk-show host. But the soon-to-be president showed that the generation gap was really a communication gap. He understood that baby boomers are children of the boom box rather than the soap box.

In 1969, McLuhan observed that "the Western world is being revolutionized by the electronic media as rapidly as the East is being Westernized."[8] The iron curtain could keep western people, products, and paper out of eastern Europe, but it couldn't stop the electronic media from carrying the message of freedom from other parts of the global village. Few recognized the extent of the electronic revolution, however. The sudden collapse of the Communist-bloc governments of eastern Europe in 1989 shocked political pundits. Based on his belief that social reality is determined by communication technology, McLuhan probably would have been surprised that it took so long.

Education

McLuhan charged that people living in the midst of innovation often cling to what *was*, as opposed to what *is*. He considered the educational establishment a prime example. By the time Johnny starts school, he has already watched over

10,000 hours of television. According to McLuhan, the child craves in-depth involvement, not linear detachment. "But suddenly, he is snatched from the cool, inclusive womb of television and exposed—within a vast bureaucratic structure of courses and credits—to the hot medium of print."[9] Johnny's friend Jenny discovers that unlike *Sesame Street,* her Tuesday class isn't sponsored by the number 4. Words plod along a blackboard one by one rather than prance in patterns on a user-friendly screen. McLuhan claimed that today's child knows that going to school is an interruption to his or her education. Because the teacher still considers video an audiovisual *aid* rather than the primary tool of learning, the information level for Jenny and Johnny takes a dip when they walk into the classroom.

The acoustic media are a threat to an educational establishment that has a vested interest in books. The establishment runs the schools as "intellectual penal institutions" with visual, print-oriented teachers as mindguards. The result is a triumphant and bitter cry of "School's out forever" in Alice Cooper's countercultural song.[10] The irony, from McLuhan's perspective, is that it is school—not hard rock—which stands against culture. If teachers would "plunge into the vortex of electronic technology," they could turn an outdated "ivory tower" into a modern-day "control tower."

Sex and Drugs

One of McLuhan's more controversial claims was that TV is a tactile medium as well as an acoustic one. He contended that "TV tattoos its message directly on our skins," and linked that "fact" to increased interpersonal touch, nudity, and public sexuality of recent decades. Because television is a medium of touch, when we "turn on" the set, we do the same thing to ourselves. McLuhan's first book, *The Mechanical Bride,* anticipated current fascination with the sensual possibilities of virtual reality.[11] He thought that the sexual revolution that began in the 1960s was the inevitable consequence of youth's trying to cope with the tension created by living in the historical seam between two conflicting media cultures.

He felt the same way about drugs. McLuhan regarded the use of marijuana, cocaine, and LSD as an attempt to achieve empathy with an electronic environment that offers the potential of an all-at-once, total involvement of the senses. As a devout Catholic, McLuhan was less than enthusiastic about the use of hallucinogenic drugs, but he tried to avoid moral judgments. When asked about the legalization of mind-expanding drugs, McLuhan responded:

> My personal point of view is irrelevant, since all such legal restrictions are futile and will inevitably wither away. You could as easily ban drugs in a retribalized society as outlaw clocks in a mechanical culture.[12]

THE DAWN OF A NEW ERA?

The recent revolution in communication technology raises a question of whether or not computers have wrenched us into an "interactive age" or "digital era" that is qualitatively distinct from the four historical epochs that McLuhan named. Although the answer is uncertain, "converged" multimedia systems are already on the horizon.

One early prototype melds cable television and digital telephone capability with the interactivity of the Internet. The device brings together features of all the previous epochs and introduces a potential new phase—interactivity. Never before have members of a media audience been able to co-construct and alter the story that they are experiencing. This is the promise of real-time inter-active media. Imagine watching *Saving Private Ryan,* but shifting the setting from Normandy to the South Bronx, or watching the Super Bowl, but having the ability to change the color of the uniforms to chartreuse and the announc-ers to Homer and Bart Simpson. Initial forays into the realm of virtual reality are already making such innovations possible.

The theoretical implications of this new technology are enormous, but diffi-cult to predict with precision. We may be entering an age in which McLuhan's categories become even more fuzzy or obsolete. How can we decide if a medium is "hot" or "cold" when it combines some of both? We may shape our tools and in turn be shaped by them, but in a virtual reality context, won't we immediately turn around and reshape them (and vice versa) in infinite feedback loops?

Futurists such as Donna Haraway are convinced that the line between hu-mans and their tools will inevitably vanish, and the age of the "cyborg" is now.[13] Even though our computers are not yet grafted onto our bodies, few of us in higher education could function without them. Artificial intelligence is just as essential to modern life as any other extension of the body that McLuhan analyzed. With cameras and televisions enhancing our eyes, satellite dishes in-creasing the sensitivity of our ears, and computers and the Internet augment-ing the power of our brains, the human body has finally become fully extended through communication technology. Whether we call this a new digital era or simply the logical development of the electronic age doesn't seem to make much difference. Either way, we're part of it.

CRITIQUE: HOW COULD HE BE RIGHT? BUT WHAT IF HE IS?

Pop artist Andy Warhol said that sometime in life every person enjoys fifteen minutes of fame. Marshall McLuhan had fifteen years. Academics tend to be suspicious of their colleagues who make money and become famous, so perhaps the man's enormous popularity gave added impetus to critics' scorn for his methods and message. The pages of *McLuhan: Hot & Cold* and *McLuhan: Pro & Con,* collections of essays that critique his ideas, are filled with denunciation.

"[McLuhan] prefers to rape our attention rather than seduce our understanding."[14]

"He has looted all culture from cave painting to *Mad* magazine for fragments to shore up his system against ruin."[15]

"The style . . . is a viscous fog through which loom stumbling metaphors."[16]

By labeling his ideas "probes" rather than "theory," McLuhan may have hoped to deflect criticism. But if this was his stratagem, it obviously didn't work. Fairleigh Dickinson communication professor Paul Levinson referred to McLuhan's "charming contempt for logic," but not everyone was charmed. George Gordon, chairman of the department of communication at Fordham University, labels his work "McLuhanacy" and dismisses it as totally worthless. Gordon stated, "Not one bit of *sustained* and *replicated* scientific evidence, inductive or deductive, has to date justified any one of McLuhan's most famous slogans, metaphors, or dicta."[17] Indeed, it's hard to know how one could go about proving that the phonetic alphabet created Greek philosophy, the printing press fostered nationalism, or that television is a tactile medium.

It is also hard to say that he was wrong because it's difficult to be certain what he said. As a writer, McLuhan often abandoned the linearity and order that he claimed were the legacy of print technology. As a speaker he was superb at crafting memorable phrases and ten-second sound bites, but his truths were enigmatic and seldom woven into a comprehensive system. For example, what does it mean to say that television is a "cool medium"? Would the recent development of high-resolution screens alter McLuhan's analysis? Because of the scattershot way he presented his insights, we'll never know.

Since deterministic theories maintain that everything in life is connected to a single factor—economics (Marx), sex (Freud), media (McLuhan)—there's no way to stand objectively outside the theory to support or discredit its claims. For those who regard testability as a mark of good theory, McLuhan's leaps of faith are a major hindrance to taking his ideas seriously. McLuhan, however, dismissed his detractors by describing them as left-brain critics who are incapable of understanding right-brain concepts. From within his system, who's to say that he is wrong?

Tom Wolfe reverses the question: "What if he's *right*? Suppose he is what he sounds like—the most important thinker since Newton, Darwin, Freud, Einstein and Pavlov?"[18] This kind of praise for McLuhan's ideas is more typical of media practitioners than academic theorists. Tony Schwartz, the acknowledged leader in the field of political advertising, credits McLuhan for his insight that attitudes are not ideas you put into a person with words. They are emotional responses that can be drawn out of people through association with familiar sounds. Electronic media don't instruct—they strike a responsive chord.

Malcolm Muggeridge echoes McLuhan's media-as-message dictum in his analysis of religious broadcasting. Drawing on his former experience as BBC television host and editor of the British humor magazine *Punch*, Muggeridge proclaims the folly of believing that the message of God's love can be presented on TV without being polluted. He notes, "Nothing TV deals with becomes more grand, beautiful, mysterious, or complicated."[19] He likens the efforts of TV evangelists to the misguided labor of a piano player in a brothel, pounding out the hymn "Abide with Me" in order to edify customers and inmates alike. The medium *is* the message.

Although it would be difficult to find anyone today who accepted all, or even most, of McLuhan's ideas, his historical analysis has heightened awareness of the possible cultural effects of new media technologies. Other scholars have been more tempered in their statements and rigorous in their documentation. But none has raised media consciousness to the level achieved by McLuhan with his catchy statements or dramatic metaphors. The late economist Kenneth Boulding, who headed the Institute of Behavioral Sciences at the University of Colorado, captured both the pro and con reactions to McLuhan by using a metaphor of his own: "It is perhaps typical of very creative minds that they hit very large nails not quite on the head."[20]

QUESTIONS TO SHARPEN YOUR FOCUS

1. What would McLuhan say about the impact of the *Internet* on the *global village*? Consider the fact that civic, political, and religious participation are declining in America.[21] Has electronic *technology* increased social connectedness?

2. McLuhan considers a motion picture film viewed in a theater a *hot medium.* Using his own rationale for television as a *cool medium,* can you defend the thesis that film should be classified "cool" as well?

3. What news have you seen recently on TV that illustrates McLuhan's belief that we now live in a *global village*?

4. Can you conceive of any way that McLuhan's theory of *technological determinism* could be proven false?

A SECOND LOOK

Recommended resource: Playboy interview: Marshall McLuhan, *Playboy,* March 1969, pp. 53–54, 56, 59–62, 64–66, 68, 70, 72, 74, 158.

Impact of print media: Marshall McLuhan, *The Gutenberg Galaxy,* University of Toronto, Toronto, 1962.

Impact of electronic media: Marshall McLuhan, *Understanding Media,* McGraw-Hill, New York, 1964.

McLuhan once-over-lightly: Marshall McLuhan and Quentin Fiore, *The Medium Is the Massage,* Random House, New York, 1967.

Early vs. late McLuhan: Bruce E. Gronbeck, "McLuhan as Rhetorical Theorist," *Journal of Communication,* Vol. 31, 1981, pp. 117–128.

Intellectual roots: Harold Innis, *The Bias of Communication,* University of Toronto, Toronto, 1964.

Methodology: Paul Levinson, "McLuhan and Rationality," *Journal of Communication,* Vol. 31, 1981, pp. 179–188.

Further developments in technological determinism: Walter Ong, *Orality and Literacy: The Technologizing of the Word,* Methuen, London, 1982.

Resonance in practice: Tony Schwartz, *The Responsive Chord,* Anchor, Garden City, N.Y., 1973.

Religious broadcasting: Malcolm Muggeridge, *Christ and the Media,* Eerdmans, Grand Rapids, Mich., 1977.

Rethinking McLuhan through critical theory: Paul Grosswiler, *Method Is the Message,* Black Rose, Montreal, 1998.

Critique: Gerald Stearn (ed.), *McLuhan: Hot & Cool,* Dial Press, New York, 1967.

Critique: Raymond Rosenthal (ed.), *McLuhan: Pro & Con,* Funk & Wagnalls, New York, 1968.

Critique: G. N. Gordon, "An End to McLuhanacy," *Educational Technology,* January, 1982, pp. 39–45.

CHAPTER 24

Semiotics

of Roland Barthes

During the 1991 Persian Gulf War, when the United States launched Operation Desert Storm against Saddam Hussein's Iraq, students at a Texas liberal arts college competed in a strange outdoor decorating contest. It began when members of a service organization tied large yellow ribbons on virtually every tree on campus. Shortly before the cease-fire, another student group responded by placing black ribbons on many of the same trees. The combined symbolic activity of the students stirred up feelings of bewilderment, frustration, and amusement within the campus community.

How should a communication scholar view these carefully placed, dueling strips of cloth? According to French literary critic and semiologist Roland Barthes (rhymes with "smart"), these public objects are sophisticated, multifaceted signs waiting to be read. Interpreting signs is the goal of semiology; Barthes held the Chair of Literary Semiology at the College of France when he was struck and killed by a laundry truck in 1980. In his highly regarded book *Mythologies,* Barthes sought to decipher the cultural meaning of a wide variety of visual signs—from sweat on the faces of actors in the film *Julius Caesar,* to a magazine photograph of a young African soldier saluting the French flag.

Although semiology (or semiotics, as it is better known in America) is concerned with *anything that can stand for something else,* Barthes was interested in seemingly straightforward signs that communicate ideological or connotative meaning and perpetuate the dominant values of society. Unlike most intellectuals, he frequently wrote for the popular press and occasionally appeared on television to comment on the foibles of the French middle class. His academic colleagues found his statements witty, disturbing, flashy, overstated, or profound in turn—but never dull. He obviously made them think. With the exception of Aristotle, the four-volume *International Encyclopedia of Communication* refers to Barthes more than any other theorist in this book.[1]

Barthes was a mercurial thinker who changed his mind about the way signs worked many times over the course of his career. Yet most current practitioners of semiotics follow the basic analytical concepts of his original theory.

Reproduced by permission of Creators Syndicate.

His approach provides great insight into the use of signs, particularly those channeled through the mass media.

WRESTLING WITH SIGNS

Barthes initially described his semiotic theory as an explanation of "myth." He later substituted the term *connotation* to label the ideological baggage that signs carry wherever they go, and most students of Barthes' work regard connotation as a better word choice to convey his true concern.

Barthes' theory of connotative meaning won't make sense to us, however, unless we first understand the way he views the structure of signs. His thinking was strongly influenced by the work of Swiss linguist Ferdinand de Saussure, who coined the term *semiology* and advocated its study.[2] To illustrate Barthes' core principles I'll feature portions of his essay on pro wrestling à la Hulk Hogan. We'll then have the semiotic resources to interpret the provocative power of ribbons on trees during Desert Storm.

1. A Sign Is the Combination of Its Signifier and Signified

The distinction between signifier and signified can be seen in Barthes' graphic description of the body of a wrestler who was selected by the promoter because he typified the repulsive slob:

> As soon as the adversaries are in the ring, the public is overwhelmed with the obviousness of the roles. As in the theatre, each physical type expresses to excess the part which has been assigned to the contestant. Thauvin, a fifty-year-old with an obese and sagging body . . . displays in his flesh the characters of baseness. . . . I know from the start that all of Thauvin's actions, his treacheries, cruelties and acts of cowardice, will not fail to measure up to the first image of ignobility he gave me. . . . The physique of the wrestlers therefore constitutes a basic sign, which like a seed contains the whole fight.[3]

According to Barthes, the image of the wrestler's physique is the *signifier.* The concept of ignobility or injustice is the *signified.* The combination of the two—the villainous body—is the *sign.*

This way of defining a sign differs from our customary usage of the word. We would probably say that the wrestler's body *is a sign of* his baseness—or whatever else comes to mind. But Barthes considers the wrestler's body to be just *part* of the overall sign; it's the signifier. The other part is the concept of hideous baseness. The signifier isn't a sign of the signified. Rather, they work together in an inseparable bond to form a unified sign.

Barthes' description of a sign as the correlation between the signifier and the signified came directly from Saussure. The Swiss linguist visualized a sign as a piece of paper with writing on both sides—the signifier on one side, the signified on the other. If you cut off part of one side, an equal amount of the other side automatically goes with it.

Is there any logical connection between the image of the signifier and the content of the signified? Saussure insisted that the relationship is arbitrary—one of correlation rather than of cause and effect. Barthes wasn't so sure. He was willing to grant the claim of Saussure (and I. A. Richards) that words have no inherent meaning. For example, there is nothing about *referee* as a verbal sign that makes it stand for the third party in the ring who is inept at making Thauvin follow the rules. But nonverbal signifiers seem to have a natural affinity with their signifieds. Barthes noted that Thauvin's body was so repugnant that it provoked nausea. He classified the relationship between signifiers and signifieds as "quasi-arbitrary." After all, Thauvin really did strike the crowd as vileness personified.

2. A Sign Does Not Stand on Its Own: It Is Part of a System

Barthes entitled his essay "The World of Wrestling," for like all other semiotic systems, wrestling creates its own separate world of interrelated signs:

> Each moment in wrestling is therefore like an algebra which instantaneously unveils the relationship between a cause and its represented effect. Wrestling fans certainly experience a kind of intellectual pleasure in *seeing* the moral mechanism function so perfectly. . . . Wrestlers, who are very experienced, know perfectly how to direct the spontaneous episodes of the fight so as to make them conform to the image which the public has of the great legendary themes of its mythology. A wrestler can irritate or disgust, he never disappoints, for he always accomplishes completely, by a progressive solidification of signs, what the public expects of him.[4]

Barthes notes that the grapplers' roles are tightly drawn. There is little room for innovation; the men in the ring work within a closed system of signs. By responding to the unwavering expectation of the crowd, the wrestlers are as much spectators as the fans who cheer or jeer on cue.

Wrestling is just one of many semiotic systems. Barthes also explored the cultural meaning of designer clothes, French cooking, automobiles, Japanese gift giving, household furniture, urban layout, and public displays of sexuality.

He attempted to define and classify the features common to all semiotic systems. This kind of structural analysis is called *taxonomy,* and Barthes' book *Elements of Semiology* is a "veritable frenzy of classifications."[5] Barthes later admitted that his taxonomy "risked being tedious," but the project strengthened his conviction that semiotic systems function the same way despite their apparent diversity.

Barthes believed that the significant semiotic systems of a culture lock in the status quo. The mythology that surrounds a society's crucial signs displays the world as it is today—however chaotic and unjust—as *natural, inevitable,* and *eternal.* The function of myth is to bless the mess. We now turn to Barthes' theory of connotation, or myth, which suggests how a seemingly neutral or inanimate sign can accomplish so much.

THE YELLOW RIBBON TRANSFORMATION: FROM FORGIVENESS OF STIGMA TO PRIDE IN VICTORY

According to Barthes, not all semiological systems are mythic. Not every sign carries ideological baggage. How is it that one sign can remain emotionally neutral while other signs acquire powerful inflections or connotations that suck people into a specific worldview? Barthes contends that a mythic or connotative system is a *second-order semiological system*—built off a preexisting sign system. The sign of the first system becomes the signifier of the second. A concrete example will help us understand Barthes' explanation.

In an *American Journal of Semiotics* article, Donald and Virginia Fry of Emerson College examined the widespread American practice of displaying yellow ribbons during the 1980 Iranian hostage crisis.[6] They traced the transformation of this straightforward yellow symbol into an ideological sign. Americans' lavish display of yellow ribbons during Operation Desert Storm a decade later adds a new twist to the Frys' analysis. I'll update their yellow ribbon example to illustrate Barthes' semiotic theory.

"Tie a Yellow Ribbon Round the Ole Oak Tree" was the best-selling pop song of 1972 in the United States.[7] Sung by Tony Orlando and Dawn, the lyrics express the thoughts of a convict in prison who is writing to the woman he loves. After three years in jail, the man is about to be released and will travel home by bus. Fearing her possible rejection, he devises a plan that will give her a way to signal her intentions without the potential embarrassment of a face-to-face confrontation.

Since he'll be able to see the huge oak planted in front of her house when the bus passes through town, he asks her to use the tree as a message board. If she still loves him, wants him back, and can overlook the past, she should tie a yellow ribbon around the trunk of the tree. He will know that all is forgiven and join her in rebuilding a life together. But if this bright sign of reconciliation isn't there, he'll stay on the bus, accept the blame for a failed relationship, and try to get on with his life without her.

The yellow ribbon is obviously a sign of acceptance, but one not casually offered. There's a taint on the relationship, hurts to be healed. Donald and Virginia Fry label the original meaning of the yellow ribbon in the song as "forgiveness of a stigma."

Yellow ribbons in 1991 continued to carry a "we want you back" message when U.S. armed forces fought in Operation Desert Storm. Whether tied to trees, worn in hair, or pinned to lapels, yellow ribbons still proclaimed, "Welcome home." But there was no longer any sense of shameful acts to be forgiven or disgrace to be overcome. Vietnam was ancient history and America was the leader of the "new world order." Hail the conquering heroes.

The mood surrounding the yellow ribbon had become one of triumph, pride, and even arrogance. After all, hadn't we intercepted Scud missiles in the air, guided "smart bombs" into air-conditioning shafts, and "kicked Saddam Hussein's butt across the desert"? People were swept up in a tide of "yellow fever." More than 90 percent of U.S. citizens approved of America's actions in the Persian Gulf. The simple yellow ribbon of personal reconciliation now served as a blatant sign of nationalism. What had originally signified forgiveness of a stigma now symbolized pride in victory.

THE MAKING OF MYTH: STRIPPING THE SIGN OF HISTORY

According to Barthes' theory, the shift from "forgiveness of stigma" to "pride in victory" followed a typical semiotic pattern. Figure 24.1 shows how it's done.

Barthes claimed that every ideological sign is the result of two interconnected sign systems. The first system is strictly descriptive—the signifier image and the signified concept combining to produce a denotative sign. The three elements of the sign system based on the "Tie a Yellow Ribbon . . ." lyrics are marked with Arabic numerals at the top left portion of the diagram. The three segments of the connotative system are marked with Roman numerals. Note that the sign of the first system does double duty as the signifier of the Gulf war connotative system. According to Barthes, this lateral shift, or connotative sidestep, is the key to transforming a neutral sign into an ideological tool. Follow his thinking step-by-step through the diagram.

The signifier (1) of the denotative sign system is the image of a yellow ribbon that forms in the mind of the person who hears the 1972 song. The content of the signified (2) includes the stigma that comes from the conviction of a crime and a term in jail, the prisoner's willingness to take responsibility for the three-year separation, and the explosive release of tension when the Greyhound passengers cheer at the sight of the oak tree awash in yellow ribbons. The corresponding denotative sign (3) is "forgiveness of a stigma." For those who heard the song on the radio, the yellow ribbon sign spoke for itself. It was a sign rich in regret and relief.

Current usage takes over the sign of the denotative system and makes it the signifier (I) of a secondary (connotative) system. The "welcome home" yellow ribbon is paired with the mythic content of a signified (II) that shouts to the

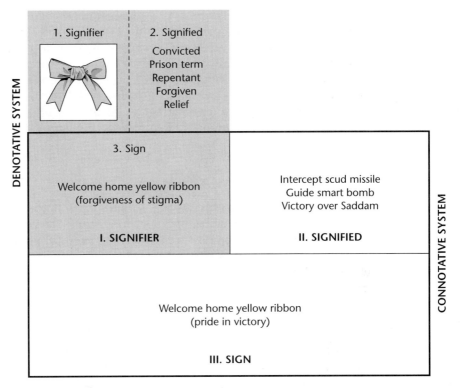

FIGURE 24.1 Connotation as a Second-Order Semiotic System
(Adapted from Barthes, "Myth Today")

world, "Our technology can beat up your technology." But as the symbol of the yellow ribbon is expropriated to support the myth of American nationalism, the sign loses its historical grounding.

As a mere signifier of the connotative system, the yellow ribbon is no longer rooted in the details of the song. It ceases to stand for three years of hard time in prison, repentance, wrongdoing, or forgiveness that gains meaning because there is so much to be forgiven. Now in the service of the mythic semiotic system, the yellow ribbon becomes empty, timeless, a form without substance. According to Barthes, that doesn't mean that the meaning of the original denotative sign is lost:

> The essential point in all this is that the form does not suppress the meaning, it only impoverishes it, it puts it at a distance, it holds it at one's disposal. One believes that the meaning is going to die, but it is a death with reprieve; the meaning loses its value, but keeps its life, from which . . . the myth will draw its nourishment.[8]

In the connotative system, the generalized image of a yellow ribbon is now paired with the signified content of victory in the Persian Gulf War as seen on

CNN. But since the signifier can't recall a historical or cultural past, the mythic sign (III) of which it is a part carries the "crust of falsity."[9] For example, there's no sense of American culpability in supplying arms to Saddam Hussein until the time he invaded Kuwait. And since mythic communication is unable to imagine anything alien, novel, or other, the sign sweeps away second thoughts about civilian deaths in Baghdad. The transformed yellow ribbon is now a lofty sign that allows no room for nagging doubts that love of oil may have been our country's prime motivation for championing the United Nation's "humanitarian" intervention.

UNMASKING THE MYTH OF A HOMOGENEOUS SOCIETY

Barthes was convinced that only those with semiotic savvy can spot the hollowness of connotative signs. For most Americans, the yellow ribbon will continue to elicit an unreflective "we're number one" feeling of national pride. Of course, it goes without saying that people will love their country. But that's precisely the problem with mythic signs. They *go without saying.* They don't explain, they don't defend, and they certainly don't raise questions. So it's up to the semiologist to expose or deconstruct the mythic system.

This same deconstructive urge inspired the left-leaning students of the antiwar student group to tie black ribbons on campus trees. In their view, the yellow ribbon signs placed by the student patriots merely perpetuated the destructive nationalism that gripped the country. Acting as fledgling semiologists, these social activists presented a competing sign to expose what they believed to be the jingoistic connotative system supported by the trees adorned with yellow ribbons.

Throughout his life, Roland Barthes deciphered and labeled the ideologies foisted upon naïve consumers of images. Although the starting-point signifiers varied, Barthes concluded that society's connotative spin always ends up the same. *Mythic signs reinforce the dominant values of their culture.* For example, the wrestling match we examined earlier seems at first glance to be no more than a harmless Saturday night diversion. Under Barthes' watchful eye, however, it's the site of dangerous mythmaking. He explains that the honorable wrestler's eventual triumph over the rule-breaking villain signifies a make-believe ideology of pure "justice." The "good guys win" simplicity of the spectacle provides false comfort for an audience that lives in a world of dubious morality and inherent inequality:

> What is portrayed in wrestling therefore is an ideal understanding of things; it is the euphoria of men raised for a while above the constitutive ambiguity of everyday situations and placed before the panoramic view of a univocal Nature, in which signs at last correspond to causes, without obstacle, without evasion, without contradiction.[10]

According to Barthes, ideological signs enlist support for the status quo by transforming history into nature—pretending that current conditions are the natural order of things. As with the ribbons and the wrestling match, every-thing that is personal, conditional, cultural, and temporal disappears. We are left with a sign that makes the world seem inevitable and eternal. Barthes' analysis calls to mind the final words of the "Gloria Patria," a choral response that many Christians sing in worship:

> As it was in the beginning,
> Is now and ever shall be,
> World without end. Amen. Amen.

For believers, singing these words about anything or anyone but God would be heresy. Without granting the exception, Barthes would concur. All his semiotic efforts were directed at unmasking what he considered the heresy of those who controlled the images of society—the naturalizing of history.

THE SEMIOTICS OF MASS COMMUNICATION: "I'D LIKE TO BE LIKE MIKE"

Like wrestlers and ribbons, most semiotic signs gain cultural prominence when broadcast through the electronic and print media. Because signs —as well as is-sues of power and dominance—are integral to mass communication, Barthes' semiotic analysis has become a seminal media theory. As Kyong Kim, author of a recent book on semiotics, concludes:

> Information delivered by mass media is no longer information. It is a commodity saturated by fantasized themes. Mass audiences are nothing more than consumers of such commodities. One should not forget that, unlike nature, the media's reality is always political. The mass signification arising in response to signs pouring from the mass media is not a natural process. Rather it is an artificial effect calculated and induced by the mass media to achieve something else.[11]

The advertisements that make commercial television so profitable also create layers of connotation that reaffirm the status quo. During the 1998 NBA playoffs, one of the most frequently aired spots featured Chicago Bulls' superstar Michael Jordan slam-dunking the basketball over a variety of helpless defenders. He then gulps down Gatorade while a host of celebrity and everyday admirers croon his praises. The most memorable of these adoring fans is a pre-school African Amer-ican boy who stares up in awe at the towering Jordan. "Sometimes I dream," we hear him sing, "that he is me." He *really* wants to be like Mike!

Obviously, the commercial is designed to sell Gatorade by linking it to the virtually unlimited achievement of basketball's greatest player. To partake of this liquid is to reach for the stars. In that sense, the little boy, rather than MJ himself, becomes the spot's crucial sign. Within this denotative system, the youngster's rapt gaze is the signifier, and his dream of becoming a famous ath-lete is the signified. The resultant denotative sign—a look of yearning—has the potential to move cartons of Gatorade off the shelf. But as the signifier of a sec-ondary connotative system, it has greater cultural impact.

At the connotative level, the original "look of yearning" suggests a new second-order signified—a more general kind of dreaming about one's future in which the ad's audience is invited to participate. Viewers are encouraged to wish for careers and goals that are virtually unobtainable, even in the best of circumstances. The CEO of Microsoft, the conductor of the New York Philharmonic, Hollywood's most glamorous talent, the President of the United States, and the world's leading AIDS researcher constitute the lofty heights surveyed by the gaze that the connotative shift implies. With its attractive visuals, uplifting soundtrack, and good-natured humor, the commercial functions as a glorification of *unfulfilled desire*, the very essence of its second-order sign. This is America after all, so think big, aim high, and don't be satisfied with anything but the top. Do what it takes—and purchase what is required—to be the very best. Ideologically speaking, it is this kind of naturalized longing that enslaves the average citizen and fuels the capitalist system. Although the commercial evokes a warm, fuzzy reaction from the viewer, it surreptitiously enforces our fundamental cultural myths about unlimited possibilities for success, myths that—according to Barthes—maintain the dominance of those who hold the reins of commerce and power.

Furthermore, Barthes would no doubt seek to expose the semiotic sleight of hand that subtly drains the second-order connotative system of the historical reality implicit in the original sign. At this denotative level, the African American boy's fixation with MJ is necessarily embedded in a long history of racial injustice and economic hardship. Michael Jordan's accomplishments, as well as the dream of his pint-sized fan, exist in a world in which African Americans must strive particularly hard to succeed. As the documentary *Hoop Dreams* brilliantly portrays, the desire-filled faces of the youngsters who populate the rough basketball courts of urban America also reflect the poverty, substance abuse, shattered families, and harsh, big-city surroundings that constantly threaten to engulf them. Nonetheless, the yearning connoted by the second-order system generated by the commercial is utterly stripped of this rather grim social reality. The boy, his life, and his dream are deftly co-opted by the system. Or so Barthes would argue.

CRITIQUE: DO MYTHIC SIGNS ALWAYS REAFFIRM THE STATUS QUO?

Barthes' interpretations of cultural signs are usually fascinating and frequently compelling. But are connotative systems always ideological, and do they inevitably uphold the values of the dominant class? Perhaps there are significant semiotic systems that suggest divergent perspectives or support alternative voices. To some students of signification, Barthes' monolithic Marxist approach to myth-making borders on a conspiracy theory. These interpreters are unwilling to accept the idea that all representation is a capitalistic plot, or that visual signs can't be used to promote resistance to dominant cultural values.

University of Pennsylvania political scientist Anne Norton expands Barthes' semiotic approach to account for other possibilities. For example, she argues that Madonna's MTV persona signifies an autonomous, independent sexuality that inspires young girls to control—rather than to be controlled by—their environments. In effect, Madonna's "construction of herself as a 'material girl' subverts the hierarchies and practices evolved by its dense tissue of references."[12]

In much the same vein, University of Texas media scholar Douglas Kellner writes that through Madonna's deliberate manipulation of stereotypes and imagery, female "wanna-be's" are "empowered in their struggles for *individual* identity." Although her provocative outfits and unabashed eroticism may seem at first glance to reinforce traditionally patriarchal views of women, her onstage character refigures her body as "the means to her wealth" and recasts her sexuality as "a form of feminine power."[13] In the same way, those black ribbons exemplified a counterculture connotative system that challenged the status quo. By hanging black crepe on trees, the protesters reminded a campus heavily supportive of Operation Desert Storm that war always means ghastly death for human beings on both sides. Stephen Spielberg's *Saving Private Ryan* offers the same gritty, connotative feel.

Perhaps the truth is somewhere in-between. In his book-length analysis of British working-class youth, sociologist Dick Hebdige studied the personal appearance and style of mods, punks, hipsters, teddy boys, and other counterculture groups. He argues that although their semiotic activity is eventually co-opted by mainline society, their deviant style often enjoys a brief time of subversive signification. For a while, the clothing, haircuts, and guitar riffs of the Sex Pistols signified that punk-rock group's stylistic challenge to the symbolic order of mainline society, but these signs of refusal soon became status quo clichés.[14]

Whether or not we accept Barthes' claim that all connotative signs reinforce dominant values, his semiotic approach to imagery remains a core theoretical perspective for a wide variety of communication scholars, particularly those who emphasize media and culture. For example, cultural studies guru Stuart Hall builds directly on Barthes' analysis of myth to establish his critique of the "hegemonic" effects of mass communication.[15] Hall's innovative analysis, though, deserves a chapter all its own.

QUESTIONS TO SHARPEN YOUR FOCUS

1. What are the *signifier* and *signified* of a favorite item of clothing or jewelry? Can you think of a way that this sign has already *been stripped of history*?

2. Why did Barthes think it was crucial to *unmask* or *deconstruct* the original *denotation* of a sign?

3. Identify at least one similar nonverbal *signifier* popularized through the *television* dramas *ER* and *Friends*. How do their *signifieds* differ?

4. "It's not over 'til the fat lady sings." What are the denotative *signifier, signified,* and *sign* to which this statement refers? What *connotative* shift has altered the meaning of the original sign?

A SECOND LOOK

Recommended resource: Roland Barthes, *Mythologies,* Annette Lavers (trans.), Hill and Wang, New York, 1972, especially "The World of Wrestling" and "Myth Today," pp. 15–25, 109–159.

Barthes' structuralism: Annette Lavers, *Roland Barthes: Structuralism and After,* Harvard University, Cambridge, Mass., 1982.

Essays on semiotics: Roland Barthes, *The Semiotic Challenge,* Richard Howard (trans.), Hill and Wang, New York, 1988.

Saussure on signs: Ferdinand de Saussure, *A Course in General Linguistics,* McGraw-Hill, New York, 1966.

Introduction to semiotics: Arthur Asa Berger, *Signs in Contemporary Culture,* Sheffield, Salem, Wisc., 1989.

Intermediate semiotics: Kyong Kim, *Caged in Our Own Signs: A Book About Semiotics,* Ablex, Norwood, N.J., 1996.

Applied semiotics: Wendy Leeds-Hurwitz, *Semiotics and Communication: Signs, Codes, Cultures,* Lawrence Erlbaum Associates, Hillsdale, N.J., 1993.

Interpreting media signs: John Fiske and John Hartley, *Reading Television,* Methuen, London, 1978.

Barthes' critique of Barthes: Roland Barthes, "Inaugural Lecture, College de France," in *A Barthes Reader,* Susan Sontag (ed.), Hill and Wang, New York, 1982, pp. 457–478.

CHAPTER 25

Cultural Studies

of Stuart Hall

Cultural studies picks up where semiotics leaves off. For that reason, I'll continue to use the Gulf War example to illustrate Stuart Hall's media theory. At the time when amateur semiologists were battling it out around tree trunks with yellow and black ribbons, a similar yet much larger conflict was being waged on television, through print, and in the minds of American media consumers. This media war was ideological, fought on both sides with formidable weapons of propaganda, live coverage, nationalism, and censorship. Yet Hall would argue that the semiotic skirmish on the college campus was merely a microcosm of what was taking place in the mass media. The yellow ribbons vastly outnumbered the black ones. The mass media supported the status quo in that they subtly drew people toward the ideological position of the majority who favored the invasion of Iraq.

Stuart Hall is a Jamaican-born professor of sociology at Open University, Milton Keynes, England. In previous pages you have read about the ideas of the Frankfurt School sociologists, Stanley Deetz and Roland Barthes (See Chapters 3, 19, and 24). Hall joins this group of critical scholars who critique "mainstream" communication research that is empirical, quantitative, and narrowly focused on discovering cause-and-effect relationships. Hall in particular doubts the scientific community's potential to find any useful answers to important questions about media influence. He rejects the "body counts" of survey research, which is "consistently translating matters that have to do with signification, meaning, language, and symbolization into crude behavioral indicators." For Hall, the issue is not what percentage of Americans supported U.S. participation and leadership in the fight against Saddam Hussein. Rather, the crucial question is how the media created unified support for the invasion of Iraq among a public that had previously been split on the issue.

Although critical theorists select different communication topics to study, they are similar in that all are heavily influenced by a Marxist interpretation of society, which is suspicious of any analysis that ignores power relationships. Critical theorists like Hall take Marx' epitaph as a mission statement for their work: "The philosophers have only *interpreted* the world in various ways; the point however, is to *change* it." The change that Hall and most critical theorists want to accomplish is to empower people who are on the margins of society, people who have little say in the direction of their lives and who are scrambling just to survive.

THE MEDIA ARE IDEOLOGICAL

Hall believes the mass media function to maintain the dominance of those already in positions of power. Broadcast and print outlets serve the Bill Gates, Steve Forbes, and Ted Turners of the world. Conversely, the media exploit the poor and powerless. Hall charges that the field of communication continues to be "stubbornly sociologically innocent." He is "deeply suspicious of and hostile to empirical work that has no ideas because that simply means that it does not know the ideas it has."[1] Noncritical researchers represent their work as pure science with no presuppositions, but every media theory by its very nature has ideological content. For example, the whole field of market research is based on the value assumption that capitalism is good.

As for mainstream mass communication research in the United States, Hall believes that it serves the myth of democratic pluralism—the pretense that society is held together by common norms including equal opportunity, respect for diversity, one person-one vote, individual rights, and rule of law. The usual finding that media messages have little effect celebrates the political claim that democracy works. Such research claims that the American dream has been empirically verified, and science beckons developing countries to become "fully paid up members of the consensus club."

Hall claims that typical research on individual voting behavior, brand loyalty, or response to dramatic violence fails to uncover the struggle for power that the media mask. He thinks it's a mistake to treat communication as a separate academic discipline (a view that may or may not endear him to your instructor). Academic isolation tends to separate messages from the culture they inhabit:

> All the repetition and incantation of the sanitized term *information,* with its cleansing cybernetic properties, cannot wash away or obliterate the fundamentally dirty, semiotic, semantic, discursive character of the media in their cultural dimensions.[2]

Therefore, Hall refers to his work as "cultural studies" rather than "media studies," and in the decade of the seventies he directed the Center for Contemporary Cultural Studies (CCCS) at the University of Birmingham. Under Hall, the staff of CCCS sought to articulate their perception of the cultural struggle between the haves and the have-nots. Hall uses the term *articulate* in the dual sense of *speaking out* on oppression and *linking* that subjugation with the communication media because they provide the terrain where meaning is shaped. He says he doesn't seek to be a "ventriloquist" for the masses, but does desire to "win some space" where their voices can be heard. The effort to jar people loose from their entrenched power positions often requires harsh words, but a "cozy chat among consenting scholars" won't dissolve the ideology that is the glue binding together most communication study.

The language Hall uses reflects his commitment to a broad Marxist interpretation of history. Since one of Hall's stated aims is to unmask the power imbalances within society, he says the cultural studies approach is valid if it "deconstructs" the current structure of a media research establishment that fails to deal with ideology. Just as Deetz wants to give a meaningful voice to stakeholders affected by corporate decisions (see Chapter 19), Hall wants to liberate people from an unknowing acquiescence to the dominant ideology of the culture. Obviously, critical theory and cultural studies are close relatives. However, Hall places less emphasis on rationality and more emphasis on resistance. As far as he's concerned, the truth of cultural studies is established by its ability to raise our consciousness of the media's role in preserving the status quo.

EARLY CULTURAL CRITICS

Cultural studies is a complex movement. In order to grasp Hall's theory, we must first understand its roots. Hall has tapped into the economic determinism of Marxist scholars from the Frankfurt School (see Chapter 3), the deep textual analysis of semiotics (see Chapter 24), and the philosophical/linguistic critique of a theorist I haven't mentioned before, Michel Foucault. Each of these European scholars knew and were influenced by each other's work.

By the end of World War II, it was clear that the revolt of the proletariat that Marx had predicted wasn't producing egalitarian societies free of oppression, nor were the dominant capitalist economies of the world deteriorating. The question was simply, why not?

Frankfurt School theorists were the first to take up the question. What Marx failed to predict, they concluded, was the modern era takeover of public discourse by private industry. They argued that working classes had not yet revolted because corporate-owned media were effective in tailoring messages that supported the capitalist system.[3] Both news and entertainment media present a picture of the world in which capitalism is natural, eternal, and unalterable.

As rather orthodox Marxists, the Frankfurt School theorists adhered to a hard-line economic determinism. Where Marx speaks of "the means of production" whose owners dominate society, the Frankfurt School theorists write of "the means of production of culture" whose owners have an undue influence over ideology and political power. The idea of "culture industries" is more heavy-handed than Hall's analysis thirty years later, but he agrees that the private control of public communication tends to maintain the status quo by constraining free expression. He also thinks that the average citizen is blissfully unaware of that fact.

Hall adopts the term *hegemony* when he refers to the cultural role of the media.[4] The word is little used by Americans, perhaps because it describes how many countries see the United States. Hegemony usually refers to the preponderant influence or domination of one nation over another. Hall employs the term to describe the subtle sway of society's haves over its have-nots. He emphasizes that media hegemony is not a conscious plot, it's not overtly coercive, and its effects are not total. The broadcast and print media present a variety of ideas, but then they tend to prop up the status quo by privileging the already accepted interpretation of reality. The result is that the role of mass media turns out to be "production of consent" rather than a "reflection of consensus" that already exists.

Notice that I haven't given any specific examples of culture industries or hegemony. That was the Frankfurt School's problem. They were strong on abstract analysis, but offered few case studies that would validate their claims. That's where Barthes' semiotics proved valuable.

Roland Barthes provided a way to start with concrete media images and systematically deconstruct their shift in meaning. Recall that one of Barthes' recurrent themes was that mythic signs reinforce the dominant values of culture. Through semiotic analysis in the previous chapter, we saw how the "all-is-forgiven" yellow ribbon was co-opted to become a mythic sign that validated American power and all-out victory. So we can appreciate that semiotics became the source of tangible illustrations of how societal power is preserved and communicated through everyday objects and symbols.

One of the problems semiotics has, however, is its inability to separate ideological or mythic signs from nonideological or oppositional signs. For example, at what point does wearing a Sex Pistols T-shirt change from being an anti-establishment sign of rebellion to being a sign of middle-age nostalgia and corporate sellout? Semiotics lacked an adequate explanation of why certain meanings get attached to certain symbols at certain historical times. Since Barthes had no answer, Hall turned to the ideas of the radical and eccentric French philosopher, Foucault.

Michel Foucault contends that both Marxists and semiologists are missing the point about the relationship between societal power and communication. He believes it's wrong to think of signs and symbols as somehow separate from mass media messages. The microlevel semiotics of yellow ribbons and the macrolevel CNN reports broadcast live from Baghdad are unified through their common discursive nature. What Foucault means is that they both require "frameworks of interpretation" in order to make sense. He believes that the framework people use is provided through the dominant discourse of the day.[5]

Foucault's concept of *discourse* established a bridge between semiotics and economic determinism. His construction can account for the changing nature of meaning over time, while keeping a steady eye on power relations. Hall describes the contribution of Foucault's work to the study of communication with revolutionary fervor: "The 'discursive turn' in the social and cultural sciences is one of the most significant shifts of direction in our knowledge of society which has occurred in recent years."[6] As I now turn to central tenets of Hall's cultural studies, remember that you are constantly hearing Foucault's voice in the background.

MAKING MEANING

In his book *Representation,* Hall states that the primary function of discourse is to *make meaning.* Many students of communication would agree that words and other signs contain no intrinsic meaning. That's why in I. A. Richards' semantic triangle, the line along the base that connects the word and its referent is dotted rather than solid (see Figure 3.2, Chapter 3). A catchy way of stating this reality is, "Words don't mean; people mean." But Hall asks us to push further and ask where *people get their meanings.* After all, humans don't come equipped with ready-made meanings either. Hall's answer is that they learn what signs mean though discourse—through communication and culture:

> Primarily, culture is concerned with the production and exchange of meanings—
> "the giving and taking of meaning"—between the members of a society or group.
> To say that two people belong to the same culture is to say that they interpret the
> world in roughly the same ways and can express themselves, their thoughts and
> feelings about the world in ways that will be understood by each other.[7]

To illustrate that meaning comes through discourse, Hall asks his readers how they know that a red light means *stop* and a green light means *go*? The answer is that someone, many years ago, told them so. The process is the same when we consider signs such as a picture of Saddam Hussein, the golden arches, or the word "welfare." But it is not enough that we simply recognize that meaning is created in discourse. We must also examine the *sources* of that discourse, especially the originators or "speakers" of it.

Hall was struck by Foucault's extensive study of mental illness, sexuality, and criminality in different historical eras. Foucault concentrated on what people were saying, what people were *not* saying, and *who* got to say it. As you might suspect, he discovered that throughout history, not everyone in society had equal voice and power. That's certainly true in America today. Undoubtedly, CNN founder Ted Turner has more discursive power than I have. Yet due to the fact that I've authored a college textbook, I'm aware that I have more power to frame meaning than many of the students who read it.

In terms of mental illness, Foucault found that the definition of what constitutes insanity and what to do about it have changed dramatically over time.[8] People with power drew arbitrary lines between the normal and abnormal, and these distinctions became "discursive formations" that had real, physical effects on those deemed to belong to each group.[9] Over time, these unquestioned and seemingly natural ways of interpreting the world became ideologies, which then perpetuated themselves through further discourse. The right to make meaning can literally be a crazy-making power.

CORPORATE CONTROL OF MASS COMMUNICATION

Hall has worked to move the study of communication away from the compartmentalized areas reflected in the organization of this text: relationship development, influence, media effects, gender and communication, and so on. He believes we should be studying the unifying "atmosphere" in which they all occur and from which they emanate—human culture. Yet consistent with Marxist theory, he also insists that communication scholarship should examine power relations and social structures. For Hall, stripping the study of communication away from the cultural context in which it is found and ignoring the realities of unequal power distribution in society have weakened our field and made it less theoretically relevant.

Hall and other cultural studies advocates wish to place the academic spotlight directly on the ways media representations of culture reproduce social inequalities and keep the average person more or less powerless to do anything but operate within a corporatized, commodified world. At least within the United States, the vast majority of information we receive is produced and distributed by corporations. If your family room television is tuned to CNN, and the table beneath it holds a copy of *Sports Illustrated*, your home is a virtual advertisement for a media conglomerate. Time-Warner owns *SI*, CNN, and most likely the cable company that brings the signal to your house.

As long as subscription rates don't go up, what difference does monopoly ownership make? Hall would answer that corporate control of such influential information sources prevents many stories from being told. Consider the plight of people in East Timor. That's hard to do if you've never heard about the "ethnic cleansing" of that Pacific island colony; somehow accounts of Indonesian-sanctioned brutality never made the evening news. But even if the story had been widely reported, Hall is sure it would have been delivered with a spin quite sympathetic to western multinational corporations. The ultimate issue for cultural studies is not *what* information is presented, but *whose* information it is.

THE MEDIA ROLE IN THE GULF WAR

The yellow ribbons that garnished trees all over the country during 1991 were an important symbolic activity for semiologists and those involved in cultural studies. Yet they were only one piece of an elaborate mosaic of cultural activity that worked toward a unified ideological end, whether intentional or not. Douglas Kellner, an early cultural studies pioneer, describes some of the significant but frequently overlooked ways in which an array of cultural products can be deployed to generate popular support for the dominant ideology.[10] If we were scripting the effort, the plan would be to regulate and mold the discourse so that some messages are first encoded by mass media, then decoded, internalized, and acted upon by the audience—all while other ideas remain unvoiced. Hall calls this "hegemonic encoding." Kellner says that the term describes actual media practice during the Gulf War.

According to Kellner, the major television networks were effective in disguising the war as theater. The media portrayal of the war erased the horrors of conflict, such as the loss of Iraqi civilian lives, by treating it as a major TV event filled with drama, heroism, and special effects:

> The media framed the war as an exciting narrative, as a nightly miniseries with dramatic conflict, action and adventure, danger to allied troops and civilians, evil perpetuated by villainous Iraqis, and heroics performed by American military planners, technology, and troops. Both CBS and ABC used the logo "Showdown in the Gulf" during the opening hours of the war . . . coding the event as a battle between good and evil. Indeed, the Gulf War was presented as a war movie with beginning, middle, and end.[11]

Perhaps no single image is more associated with the Gulf War than the on-board camera shots of "smart bombs" being delivered through ventilation shafts of Iraqi buildings. As this footage was replayed throughout the 100-day battle, the visual sequence emphasized the superiority of U.S. military technology and the surgical precision of modern warfare. Kellner points out that such images have multiple benefits for dominant ideological coding. Primarily, watching such gee-whiz weaponry at work impresses the viewer with its pinpoint precision and stealth, while suppressing the real purpose of the weapon—to destroy things and people.

The image of the bomb reducing the building to rubble is encoded to communicate the inherent superiority of the American military and the laughable folly of an Iraqi army trying to oppose it. Frequent replays of sophisticated weapons in action distract attention from the *morality* of the war, focusing instead on the tactical aesthetics. Kellner says that it is much easier to cheer for an effective weapons system than it is to engage the complex question of whether these weapons should be used at all. When they explode, they look really cool. And they are ours.

By avoiding the intrinsic ethical issues of using a military option, the media frame for the story could be designed for the *making* of war. Kellner says that instead of offering objective description from the battlefront, U.S. media took sides and became "active propagandists" for the Coalition forces. The appropriate narrative form was a simplistic "good guys vs. bad guys" showdown. Of course, this frame required the creation of heroes and villains, and the culture industries were more than willing to do their part.

Hall talks about the media's tendency to "commodify" whatever it presents, and the Gulf War was no exception. Kellner notes that war itself was a lucrative commodity. High ratings produced increased advertising revenue and T-shirts, buttons, bumper stickers, toys, videos, and even yellow ribbons went on sale within a couple of weeks. Much of the merchandise contained a not so subtle racial slur. One T-shirt depicted an Arab man on a camel with military planes flying overhead. The caption stated: "I'd fly 10,000 miles to smoke a Camel."[12]

Taken together, these texts, images and behaviors created a discourse that framed opposition to the war as a non-option. To be a "good American" was to

support the troops. Hall refers to this media process as "ideological discourses of constraint." The practical effect is to limit the range of alternatives and then make those restricted choices seem like that's all there ever could be.[13]

THE OBSTINATE AUDIENCE

The fact that the media present a preferred interpretation of human events is no reason to assume that the audience will correctly "take in" the offered ideology. I once heard Robert Frost recite his famous poem "Stopping by Woods on a Snowy Evening." After completing the last stanza—

> These woods are lovely, dark and deep,
> But I have promises to keep,
> And miles to go before I sleep,
> And miles to go before I sleep.[14]

—the New England poet said in a crusty voice, "Some people think I'm talking about death here, but I'm not." Yet poems, like media depictions, have a life of their own. Despite his words, I have continued to interpret the verse as referring to obligations to be met before we die.

Hall holds out the possibility that the powerless may be equally obstinate by resisting the dominant ideology and translating the message in a way more congenial to their own interests. He outlines three decoding options:

1. *Operating inside the dominant code.* The media produce the message; the masses consume it. The audience "reading" coincides with the "preferred reading."

2. *Applying a negotiable code.* The audience assimilates the leading ideology in general but opposes its application in specific cases.

3. *Substituting an oppositional code.* The audience sees through the establishment bias in the media presentation and mounts an organized effort to demythologize the news.

With all the channels of mass communication in the unwitting service of the dominant ideology, Hall has trouble believing that the powerless can change the system ("pessimism of the intellect"). Yet he is determined to do everything he can to expose and alter the media's structuring of reality ("optimism of the will"). Hall has a genuine respect for the ability of people to resist the dominant code. He doesn't regard the masses as cultural dupes who are easily manipulated by those who control the media, but he is unable to predict when and where the resistance will spring up.

Hall cites one small victory by activists in the organized struggle to establish that black is beautiful. By insisting on the term *black* rather than *Negro* or *colored*, people of African heritage began to give dignity in the 1970s to what was once a racial slur. Jesse Jackson's call for an African American identity is a continuing effort to control the use of symbols. This is not a matter of mere semantics as some would charge. Although there is nothing inherently positive or negative in any of these racial designations, the connotative difference is important because the effects are real. A similar campaign has transformed the term *Jamaican*. When Hall went to England, the word had an immigrant feel; today it conjures up romance, rum and Coke, and reggae music. The ideological fight is a struggle to capture language. Hall sees those on the margins of society doing semantic battle on a media playing field that will never be quite level.

CRITIQUE: HOW DO WE KNOW HE'S RIGHT?

In his early work, Marshall McLuhan was highly critical of television. Hall accuses McLuhan of being co-opted by the media establishment in his later years. He characterizes McLuhan's final position as one of "lying back and letting the media roll over him; he celebrated the very things he had most bitterly attacked." No one has ever accused Stuart Hall of selling out to the dominant ideology of western society. Many, however, question the wisdom of performing scholarship under an ideological banner.

Do such explicit value commitments inevitably compromise the integrity of research? Former Surgeon General C. Everett Koop lamented that pro-choice researchers always conclude that abortion does no psychological harm to the mother, whereas pro-life psychologists invariably discover that abortion leaves long-term emotional scars. Not surprisingly, the findings of the economically conservative American Enterprise Institute in Washington, D.C., differ greatly from the conclusions reached at the Center for Contemporary Cultural Studies under the direction of Hall. Ever since Copernicus thought the unthinkable, that the earth is not the center of the universe, truth has prospered by investigating what *is*, separately from what we think it *ought* to be. Hall seems to blur that distinction.

Is Hall's analysis of culture superior to the work of other cultural studies or critical theories? Without a standard of truth, there seems to be no reliable way to evaluate the quality of media criticism. One person's research conclusions are as good as another's. Hall has served the field of mass communication well by identifying hidden ideologies, but as yet offers no basis for preferring one over another. Liberation theology in Latin America reaches many of the same Marxist conclusions arrived at by Hall, but that movement cites Jesus' concern for the poor as its ultimate validation. Hall offers no court of appeal—embracing his cultural analysis is an act of faith or personal preference.

Hall's most positive contribution to mass communication study is his constant reminder that it's futile to talk about meaning without considering power at the same time. Cliff Christians, director of the Institute for Communication Research at the University of Illinois and a leading writer in the field of media ethics, agrees with Hall that the existence of an idealistic communication situation where no power circulates is a myth. Christians is lavish in his praise of Hall's article, which I've listed as the recommended resource: "His essay, like the Taj Mahal, is an artistic masterpiece inviting a pilgrimage."[15]

Stuart Hall has attracted tremendous interest and a large following. Samuel Becker, chairman of the communication studies department at the University of Iowa, describes himself as a besieged empiricist and notes the irony of Hall's attack. Hall knocks the dominant ideology of communication studies, yet he "may himself be the most dominant or influential figure in communication studies today."[16]

QUESTIONS TO SHARPEN YOUR FOCUS

1. *Hegemony* is not a household word in the United States. How would you explain what the term means to your roommate? Can you think of a metaphor or analogy that would clarify this critical concept?

2. What is the nature of Hall's complaint about *American media scholarship*?

3. Hall articulates the position that the *media encode the dominant ideology of our culture.* If you do not now agree with his thesis, what *evidence* could he muster that would convince you that he's right? What evidence would you provide to counter his argument?

4. In what way is Roland Barthes' *semiotic* perspective similar to Hall's cultural studies? (see Chapter 27). How do they differ?

A SECOND LOOK

Recommended resource: Stuart Hall, "Introduction" and "The Work of Representation," in *Representation: Cultural Representations and Signifying Practices,* Stuart Hall (ed.), Sage, London, 1997, pp. 1-64.

Critique of the dominant communication theory paradigm: Stuart Hall, "Ideology and Communication Theory," in *Rethinking Communication Theory,* Vol. 1, Brenda Dervin, Lawrence Grossberg, Barbara O'Keefe, and Ellen Wartella (eds.), Sage, Newbury Park, Calif., 1989, pp. 40–52. (See also multiple reactions following.)

Marxist interpretations: Samuel Becker, "Marxist Approaches to Media Studies: The British Experience," *Critical Studies in Mass Communication,* Vol. 1, 1984, pp. 66–80.

Open Marxism: Stuart Hall, "The Problem of Ideology—Marxism Without Guarantees," *Journal of Communication Inquiry,* Vol. 10, No. 2, 1986, pp. 28–44. (The whole issue is devoted to Stuart Hall.)

Ideology of the media: Stuart Hall, "The Rediscovery of 'Ideology': Return of the Repressed in Media Studies," in *Culture, Society and the Media,* Michael Gurevitch, Tony Bennett, James Curran, and Janet Woollacott (eds.), Methuen, London, 1982, pp. 56–90.

Media bias: Stuart Hall, I. Connell, and L. Curti, "The 'Unity' of Current Affairs Television," in *Working Papers in Cultural Studies No. 9,* Center for Contemporary Cultural Studies, University of Birmingham, Birmingham, England, 1976, pp. 51–93.

Manufacturing consent: Edward Herman and Noam Chomsky, *Manufacturing Consent: The Political Economy of the Mass Media,* Pantheon, New York, 1988.

Journalistic bias toward the status quo: Stuart Hall, "A World at One with Itself" and "The Determination of News Photographs," in *The Manufacture of News,* Stanley Cohen and Jock Young (eds.), Sage, Beverly Hills, Calif., 1981, pp. 147–156 and 226–243.

Media hegemony: Robert Goldman and Arvind Rajagopal, *Mapping Hegemony: Television News Coverage of Industrial Conflict,* Ablex, Norwood, N.J., 1991.

Articulation of black: Stuart Hall, "Signification, Representation, Ideology: Althusser and the Post-Structuralist Debates," *Critical Studies in Mass Communication,* Vol. 2, 1985, pp. 91–114.

Critical theory in American communication study: Hanno Hardt, "The Return of the 'Critical' and the Challenge of Radical Dissent: Critical Theory, Cultural Studies, and American Mass Communication Research," in *Communication Yearbook 12,* James A. Anderson (ed.), Sage, Newbury Park, Calif., 1989, pp. 558–600.

American cultural studies: Lawrence Grossberg, *Bringing It All Back Home: Essays on Cultural Studies,* Duke University Press, Durham, N. C., 1997.

Historical perspective: Stuart Hall, "Cultural Studies and Its Theoretical Legacies," in *Cultural Studies,* Lawrence Grossberg, Cary Nelson, and Paula Treichler (eds.), Routledge, New York, 1992, pp. 277–294.

MEDIA EFFECTS

In 1940, before the era of television, a team of researchers from Columbia University headed by Paul Lazarsfeld descended on Erie County, Ohio, an area that had reflected national voting patterns in every twentieth-century presidential election. By surveying people once a month from June to November, the interviewers sought to determine how the press and radio affected the people's choice for the upcoming presidential election.[1]

Contrary to the then accepted "hypodermic needle" model of direct media influence, the researchers found little evidence that voters were swayed by what they read or heard. Political conversions were rare. The media seemed merely to reinforce the decisions of those who had already made up their minds.

Lazarsfeld attributed the lack of media effect to "selective exposure." Republicans avoided articles and programs that were favorable to President Franklin Roosevelt; Democrats bypassed news stories and features sympathetic to Republican Wendell Willkie. The principle of selective exposure didn't always test out in the laboratory, where people's attention was virtually guaranteed, but in a free marketplace of ideas it accounted for the limited short-term effects of mass communication.

The Erie County results forced media analysts to recognize that friends and family affect the impact of media messages. They concluded that print and electronic media influence masses of people only through an indirect "two-step flow of communication." The first stage is the direct transmission of information to a small group of people who stay well informed. In the second stage, these opinion leaders pass on and interpret the messages to others in face-to-face discussion.

The two-step flow theory surfaced at a time of rapid scientific advancement in the fields of medicine and agriculture. The model accurately described the diffusion of innovation among American doctors and farmers in the 1950s, but the present era of saturation television has made alterations necessary. The first step of the revised two-stage theory of media influence is the transmission of information to a mass audience. The second step is validation of the message by people who the viewer respects.[2]

In 1953, Fredric Wertham's *Seduction of the Innocent* documented the glorification of violence in comic books.[3] Since then, mass communication researchers have sought to establish a relationship between media usage and aggression. Ad hoc studies have produced conflicting results, but two theory-based programs of research have established causal links between television and violent behavior.

University of Alabama media researcher Dolf Zillmann's excitation transfer theory recognizes that TV has the power to stir up strong feelings.[4] Although we use labels like "fear," "anger," "sex," "humor," and "love" to describe these emotional states, the physiological response is the same no matter what kind of TV program elicited the response. It's easy to get our emotional wires crossed when the show is over. Zillmann says that the heightened state of arousal takes a while to dissipate, and the leftover excitation can amplify any mood we happen to be feeling. If a man is mad at his wife, the emotional stimulation he gets from televised aggression can escalate into domestic violence. But Zillmann says that the arousal which comes from an erotic bedroom scene or a hilarious comedy often has the same effect.

Excitation transfer can account for violent acts performed immediately after TV viewing. But Stanford psychologist Albert Bandura's social learning theory takes it a step further and predicts that the use of force modeled on television today may erupt in antisocial behavior years later.[5] Although Bandura's theory can explain imitation in many contexts, most students of his work apply it specifically to the vicarious learning of aggression through television.

Communication scholars have shown surprisingly little interest in studying the dynamics of television advertising. However, practitioner Tony Schwartz theorizes that commercials are effective when they strike a responsive chord within the viewer.[6] He says that media persuasion is not so much a matter of trying to put an idea into consumers' heads as it is seeking to draw an emotional response out of them. The best commercials use sight and sound to resonate with an audience's past experience.

The first two theories in this section were instrumental in reestablishing a powerful-effects view of mass communication. Chapter 26 presents George Gerbner's cultivation theory, which postulates a relationship between heavy television viewing and people's worldview. Specifically, Gerbner suggests that exposure to vast amounts of symbolic violence on the screen conditions viewers to view the world as a mean and scary place. Chapter 27 outlines McCombs and Shaw's conception of the agenda-setting function of the media. Their theory originally claimed that the news media don't try to tell people what to think, but the selection of news in the broadcast and print media has a powerful effect on what the public will think about. Chapter 28 on the media equation presents a more radical hypothesis. Byron Reeves and Clifford Nass claim that people respond to computers, television, and other communication media as if they were human, so rules of interpersonal behavior will predict their responses.

Although the theories in this section offer different explanations for the media's impact, all of them hold that these effects can be objectively measured. In each case, the theorists present empirical evidence that support their claims.

CALVIN AND HOBBES © 1995 Watterson. Reprinted with permission of Universal Press Syndicate. All rights reserved.

CHAPTER 26

Cultivation Theory

of George Gerbner

What are the odds that you'll be involved in some kind of violent act within the next seven days? 1 out of 10? 1 out of 100? 1 out of 1,000? 1 out of 10,000?

According to George Gerbner, the answer you give may have more to do with how much TV you watch than with the actual risk you face in the week to come. Gerbner, dean emeritus of The Annenberg School for Communication at the University of Pennsylvania and founder of the Cultural Environment Movement claims that heavy television users develop an exaggerated belief in "a mean and scary world." The violence they see on the screen can cultivate a social paranoia that counters notions of trustworthy people or safe surroundings.

Like Marshall McLuhan, Gerbner regards television as the dominant force in shaping modern society. But unlike McLuhan, who viewed the medium as the message, Gerbner is convinced that TV's power comes from the symbolic content of the real-life drama shown hour after hour, week after week. At its root, television is society's institutional storyteller and a society's stories give "a coherent picture of what exists, what is important, what is related to what, and what is right."[1]

Until recently, the only acceptable storytellers outside the home were those passing down religious tradition. Today, the TV set is a key member of the household, with virtually unlimited access to every person in the family. Television dominates the environment of symbols, telling most of the stories, most of the time. Gerbner claims that people now watch television as they might attend church, "except that most people watch television more religiously."[2]

What do they see in their daily devotions? According to Gerbner—violence. During the turmoil of the late 1960s, the National Commission on the Causes and Prevention of Violence suggested that violence is as American as cherry pie.[3] Instead of being a deviant route to power, physical force and its threat are traditionally ways people gain a larger slice of the American dream. Gerbner says that violence "is the simplest and cheapest dramatic means to demonstrate who wins in the game of life and the rules by which the game is played."[4] Those who are immersed in the world of TV drama learn these "facts of life" better than occasional viewers.

Most people who decry violence on television are worried that all too receptive young viewers will imitate aggression on the screen. As noted in the introduction to this section, Stanford psychologist Albert Bandura's research suggests that this fear has some basis in fact, at least for a small minority of the audience.[5] Gerbner, however, is concerned with a much broader and potentially more harmful emotional effect—that television violence convinces viewers it is indeed "a jungle out there."

Gerbner's voice is only one of many that proclaim a link between communication media and violence. Critics have publicly warned against the chaotic effects of comic books, rock music, and video games as well as television. But the man who for many years was the editor of the *Journal of Communication* thinks that TV is a special case. For almost two decades he spearheaded an extensive research program that monitored the level of violence on television, classified people according to how much TV they watch, and compiled viewer perceptions of potential risk and other sociocultural attitudes. His cultivation explanation of the findings is one of the most talked-about and argued-over theories of mass communication.

AN INDEX OF VIOLENCE

Alarmed parents, teachers, and critics of television assume that the portrayal of violence has been escalating. But is the level of dramatic aggression really on the rise? As Director of the Cultural Indicators research project, Gerbner sought to develop an objective measure which would allow TV's friends and foes to discuss the trend on the basis of fact rather than feeling. He defined dramatic violence as "the overt expression of physical force (with or without a weapon, against self or others) compelling action against one's will on pain of being hurt and/or killed or threatened to be so victimized as part of the plot."[6]

The definition rules out verbal abuse, idle threats, and pie-in-the-face slapstick. But it includes the physical abuse presented in a cartoon format. When the coyote pursuing the roadrunner is flattened by a steamroller, or the Mighty Morphing Power Rangers crush their enemies, Gerbner labels the scene violent. He also counts auto crashes and natural disasters. From an artistic point of view, these events are no accident. The screenwriter inserted the trauma for dramatic effect. Characters die or are maimed just as effectively as if they'd taken a bullet in the chest.

For over two decades, Cultural Indicators researchers randomly selected a week during the fall season and videotaped every prime-time (8 to 11 P.M.) network show. They also recorded programming for children on Saturday and Sunday (8 A.M. to 2 P.M.). After counting up the incidents that fit their description, they gauged the overall level of violence with a formula that included the ratio of programs that scripted violence, the rate of violence in the programs that did, and the percentage of characters involved in physical harm and killing. They found that the annual index is remarkably stable.

EQUAL VIOLENCE, UNEQUAL RISK

Gerbner reports that regardless of whether the dramas are *NYPD Blue, Cops, Nash Bridges, Millennium,* or dozens of forgettable shows canceled after a thirteen-week run, the cumulative portrayal of violence varies little from year to year. Over half of prime-time programs contain actual bodily harm or threatened violence. *Home Improvement, Murphy Brown,* and *Friends* are not typical. Dramas that include violence average five traumatic incidents per viewing hour. Almost all the weekend children's shows major in mayhem. They average twenty cases an hour. By the time the typical TV viewer graduates from high school, he or she has observed 13,000 violent deaths.

On any given week, two-thirds of the major characters are caught up in some kind of violence. Heroes are just as involved as villains, yet there is great inequality as to the age, race, and gender of those on the receiving end of physical force. Old people and children are harmed at a much greater rate than young or middle-aged adults. In the pecking order of "victimage," African Americans and Hispanics are killed or beaten more than their Caucasian counterparts. Gerbner notes that it's risky to be "other than clearly white." It's also dangerous to be female. The opening lady-in-distress scene is a favorite dramatic device to galvanize the hero into action. And finally, blue-collar workers "get it in the neck" more often than white-collar executives.

"You do lovely needlepoint, grandma, but . . ."

Reproduced by permission of Punch.

If insurance companies kept actuarial tables on the life expectancy of television characters, they'd discover that the chance of a poor, elderly black woman's avoiding harm for the entire hour is almost nil. The symbolic vulnerability of minority-group members is even more striking given their gross underrepresentation in TV drama. Gerbner's analysis of the world of television records that 50 percent of the people are white, middle-class males, and women are outnumbered by men 3 to 1. Although one-third of our society is made up of children and teenagers, they appear as only 10 percent of the characters on prime-time shows. Two-thirds of the United States labor force have blue-collar or service jobs, yet that group constitutes a mere 10 percent of the players on television. African Americans and Hispanics are only occasional figures, but the elderly are by far the most excluded minority. Less than 3 percent of the dramatic roles are filled by actors over the age of 65.

In sum, Gerbner's Cultural Indicators project reveals that people on the margins of American society are put into a symbolic double jeopardy. Their existence is understated, but at the same time their vulnerability to violence is overplayed. When written into the script, they are often made visible in order to be a victim. Not surprisingly, these are the very people who exhibit the most fear of violence when the TV set goes off.

ESTABLISHING A VIEWER PROFILE

Equipped with the sure knowledge of TV drama's violent content, Gerbner and his associates gathered surveys of viewer behavior and attitudes. Although some later researchers have tried to create saturation exposure in an experimental setting, Gerbner says the nature of his cultivation hypothesis makes testing in the laboratory impossible. He believes that the effects of heavy TV viewing can be seen only after years of slow buildup. The pervasive presence of television also rules out a control group. Gerbner regards everyone as a consumer. His questions merely aim at distinguishing between "light" and "heavy" users.

Most of Gerbner's work establishes a self-report of two hours a day as the upper limit of light viewing. He labels heavy viewers as those who admit an intake of four hours or more. He also refers to the heavy viewer as "the television type," a more benign term than "couch potato" with its allusion either to a steady diet of television and potato chips, or a vegetable with many eyes. There are more heavy viewers than light viewers, but each group makes up about one-fourth of the general population. People whose viewing habits are in the two- to four-hour midrange make up the other half, but Gerbner wants to compare people with distinctly different patterns of television exposure.

Gerbner claims that television types don't turn on the set in order to watch *ER* or *Friends*. They simply want to watch television per se. Light viewers are more selective, turning the set off when a favorite program is over. Gerbner's reason for distinguishing the audience is to test whether those with heavy viewing habits regard the world as more dangerous than those with occasional or light viewing habits. Cultivation theory predicts they do.

PLOWING THE MIND: DEEP FURROWS VS. ONCE OVER LIGHTLY

Believing that violence is the backbone of TV drama and knowing that people differ in how much TV they see, Gerbner sought to discover the *cultivation differential*. That's his term for "the difference in the percent giving the 'television answer' within comparable groups of light and heavy viewers."[7] His survey targeted four attitudes.

1. *Chances of involvement with violence.* The question at the start of the chapter addresses this issue. Those with light viewing habits predict that their weekly odds of being a victim are 1 out of 100; those with heavy viewing habits fear the risk to be 1 out of 10. Actual crime statistics indicate that 1 out of 10,000 is more realistic. Of course, the prediction of those with heavy viewing habits may be due to their greater willingness to justify physical aggression. Children who are habitual TV watchers agree that it's "almost always all right [to hit someone] if you are mad at them for a good reason."

2. *Fear of walking alone at night.* Not surprisingly, more women than men are afraid of dark streets. But for both sexes, the fear of victimization correlates with time spent in front of the tube. People with heavy viewing habits tend to overestimate criminal activity, believing it to be ten times worse than it really is. In actuality, muggers on the street pose less bodily threat than injury from cars.

3. *Perceived activity of police.* People with heavy viewing habits believe that 5 percent of society is involved in law enforcement. Their video world is peopled with police, judges, and government agents. People with light viewing habits estimate a more realistic 1 percent. Gerbner's television type assumes that police officers draw their guns almost every day, which is not true.

4. *General mistrust of people.* Those with heavy viewing habits are suspicious of other people's motives. They subscribe to statements that warn people to expect the worst:

"Most people are just looking out for themselves."
"In dealing with others, you can't be too careful."
"Do unto others before they do unto you."
Gerbner calls this cynical mind-set the "mean world syndrome."

The Cultural Indicators evidence suggests that the minds of heavy TV viewers become fertile grounds for sowing thoughts of danger. If cultivation of the nonstop viewer does indeed occur, what's the mechanism that plows a furrow in their brow? Gerbner presents two explanations of how cultivation takes place—mainstreaming and resonance.

MAINSTREAMING

Mainstreaming is Gerbner's word to describe the process of "blurring, blending and bending" that those with heavy viewing habits undergo. He thinks that through constant exposure to the same images and labels, television types develop a commonality of outlook. Radio stations segment the audience to the point where programming for left-handed truck drivers who bowl on Friday nights is a distinct possibility. Instead of "narrowcasting" their programs, TV producers *broad*cast, in that they seek to "attract the largest possible audience by celebrating the moderation of the mainstream."[8] Television homogenizes its audience so that those with heavy viewing habits share the same orientations, perspectives, and meanings with each other. We shouldn't ask how close this collective interpretation is to the mainstream of culture. According to Gerbner, the television answer *is* the mainstream.

He illustrates the mainstream effect by showing how television types blur economic and political distinctions. TV glorifies the middle class, and those with heavy viewing habits assume that label no matter what their income. But those with light viewing habits who have blue-collar jobs accurately describe themselves as working-class people.

In like fashion, those with heavy viewing habits position themselves as political moderates. Most characters in TV dramas frown on political extremism—right or left. This middle-of-the-road ethic is apparently picked up by the constant viewer. It's only from the ranks of sporadic TV users that Gerbner finds people who label themselves "liberal" or "conservative."

Social scientists have come to expect political differences between rich and poor, blacks and whites, Catholics and Protestants, city dwellers and farmers. Those distinctions still emerge when sporadic television viewers respond to the survey. But Gerbner reports that traditional differences diminish among those with heavy viewing habits. It's as if the light from the TV set washes out any sharp features that would set them apart.

Even though those with heavy viewing habits call themselves moderates, the Cultural Indicators team notes that their positions on social issues are decidedly conservative. Heavy viewers consistently voice opinions in favor of low taxes, more police protection, and stronger national defense. They are against big government, free speech, homosexuals in the military, the Equal Rights Amendment, abortion, interracial marriage, open-housing legislation, and affirmative action.

Saturation viewing seems to bend television types toward the political right, although such viewers do support greater funding of social security, health services, and education. Gerbner labels the mix of attitudes and desires the "new populism" and sees its rise as evidence that those with heavy viewing habits have been sucked into the mainstream. The almost complete overlap between the "new populism" and the policies of Ronald Reagan could explain the former president's reputation as being the "great communicator" when he went directly to the people on television. His message was like an old friend they'd grown up with on prime-time TV.

RESONANCE

Gerbner also explains the constant viewer's greater apprehension by the process of *resonance*. Many viewers have had at least one firsthand experience with physical violence—armed robbery, rape, bar fight, mugging, auto crash, military combat, or a lover's quarrel that became vicious. The actual trauma was bad enough. But he thinks that a repeated symbolic portrayal on the TV screen can cause the viewer to replay the real-life experience over and over in his or her mind: "The congruence of the television world and real-life circumstances may 'resonate' and lead to markedly amplified cultivation patterns."[9] Heavy viewers who have experienced physical violence get a double dose.

For three years I was a volunteer advocate in a low-income housing project. Although I felt relatively safe walking through the project, police and social workers told stories of shootings and stabbings. Even peace-loving residents were no strangers to violence. I can't recall ever entering an apartment where the TV was silent. Gerbner would expect that the daily diet of symbolic savagery would reinforce people's experience of doorstep violence, making life even more frightening. The hesitation of most tenants to venture outside their apartments would seem to confirm his resonance assumption.

The mainstreaming and resonance hypotheses are after-the-fact explanations for Gerbner's finding that for the many people who watch lots of television, the world is a scary place. In contrast, he notes that most media effects research focuses on only the few people who imitate the violence they see on TV.

> But it is just as important to look at the large majority of people who become more fearful, insecure, and dependent on authority; and who may grow up demanding protection and even welcoming repression in the name of security.[10]

CRITIQUE: THE LINK BETWEEN TV EXPOSURE AND WORLDVIEW—SIGNIFICANT, SMALL, CRUCIAL

For most observers, Gerbner's claim that the dramatic content of television creates a fearful climate makes sense. How could the habitual viewer watch so much violence without it having a lasting effect? Yet over the last twenty years communication journals have been filled with the sometimes bitter charges and countercharges of critics and supporters. Opponents have challenged Gerbner's definition of violence, the programs he selects for content analysis, his decision to lump together all types of programs (action, soap operas, sitcoms, news, and so on), his assumption that there is always a consistent television answer, his nonrandom methods for selecting respondents, his simple hours-per-day standard for categorizing viewers as "light" or "heavy," his forced-choice technique to measure their perceived risk of being mugged, his statistical method of analyzing the data, his interpretation of correlational data, and much more.

Communication researchers Michael Morgan (University of Massachusetts) and James Shanahan (Cornell University) catalog the various criticisms of Gerbner's theory and systematically respond to their charges.[11] In a few cases these cultivation theory advocates grant the substance of a specific critique, yet they insist that by focusing on "methodological minutiae," critics divert attention from the powerful social role of television as society's storyteller. They contrast Gerbner's "big picture" perspective with what they believe is the "methodological exercise" approach of his critics:

> Efforts to provide greater specificity and precision have helped sharpen the analysis but often seem to result in losing track of the real social significance of it all. We suggest that, after 20 years, researchers put aside the quibbles to focus critically on the social role of television.[12]

Morgan and Shanahan suggest that at least a portion of the strident attack on cultivation theory is politically motivated. If so, we shouldn't be surprised. After all, cultivation theory refutes the television industry's easy assurance that symbolic violence does no harm. In addition, Gerbner's words contain a thinly veiled criticism of a Pat Buchanan type of conservative populism that the theorist believes is nightly supported by the narrative images of prime-time programming. Be that as it may, the main issue for us to decide is how to interpret the consistent yet small relationship that Gerbner and others have established between heavy TV viewing and belief in a mean and scary world.

In order to provide a map that will allow students of cultivation theory to maneuver through the minefield of confusing and sometimes conflicting findings, Morgan and Shanahan performed a *meta-analysis* on 82 separate cultivation studies. *Meta-analysis* is a technique of statistically blending independent studies that explore the same connection—in this case the link between hours in front of a TV set and the subsequent tendency to give "television answers" to questions about the likelihood of violence, sex role attitudes, political viewpoints, and so forth. They discovered an average correlation of +.091.[13]

What does this numerical index mean? There are three different ways to answer that question. In the first place, given the large sample sizes used in cultivation research, a correlation of +.091 is usually "statistically significant." That means it would seldom occur by chance if there weren't an actual relationship between viewing and viewpoint. In short, Gerbner predicted that exposure to television and social attitudes are linked; Morgan and Shanahan's analysis confirms that they are.

A second way to answer the question ("What does this mean?") is with the response, "Not much." Although the meta-analysis validates a statistically significant relationship between exposure to television and fearful attitudes, the connection is very weak. An index of +.091 is so close to zero that it doesn't suggest a difference that makes a difference.

To illustrate how small the correlation really is, think of putting everyone's fear of victimization into a pie—sour apple or bitter lemon might be appropriate. Suppose the pie was sliced into eight equal pieces, and that you ate a fifteenth portion of one piece. That single small bite would represent the amount of fear that can be explained by heavy television viewing. What's left over—almost the entire pie—is the fear people feel for reasons other than their exposure to televised violence.[14]

In response to this criticism, Shanahan and Morgan ask us to imagine a cherry pie of which only 1 percent is bourbon, or for that matter, anthrax. The taste and potential effect would surely be quite different. This leads to a third possible interpretation.

A final answer to the question of what the data might mean has to do with the crucial importance of the issue at hand. Fear of violence is a paralyzing emotion. As Gerbner repeatedly points out, worry can make people prisoners in their own homes, change the way they vote, affect how they feel about themselves, and dramatically lower their quality of life. With consistent evidence that heavy television viewing produces *some* effect on a person's worldview, Morgan and Shanahan call on media scholars to move beyond methodological arguments and to begin to develop theoretical perspectives that speak to the issue of who controls the production and distribution of cultural stories. Of course, Stuart Hall's cultural studies attempts to do precisely that (see Chapter 25).

As for Gerbner, in 1996 he founded the Cultural Environment Movement, a coalition of organizations and social activists who believe that it's vitally important who gets to tell the stories in a culture, and whose stories don't get told. They are committed to changing the stories that American television tells and are convinced that this will happen only when the public wrests back control of the airwaves from media conglomerates. Gerbner underscores the movement's agenda with repeated references to a line from Scottish patriot Andrew Fletcher:

> If a man were permitted to make all the ballads, he need not care who should make the laws of a nation.[15]

QUESTIONS TO SHARPEN YOUR FOCUS

1. How would you change Gerbner's *definition of dramatic violence* so that his index of TV violence would measure what you think is important?

2. What type of people are underrepresented in television drama? What type of people are overrepresented? Who are the victims of symbolic violence on the screen?

3. How do your *political* and *social values* differ from the *mainstream* attitudes of Gerbner's *television type*?

4. The *meta-analysis* finding of a +.091 relationship between TV exposure and worldview can be seen as *significant*, *small*, and/or *crucial*. How do these interpretations differ? Which is most salient for you?

A SECOND LOOK

Recommended resource: George Gerbner, Larry Gross, Michael Morgan, and Nancy Signorielli, "Growing Up with Television: The Cultivation Perspective," in *Media Effects: Advances in Theory and Research,* Jennings Bryant and Dolf Zillmann (eds.), Lawrence Erlbaum Associates, Hillsdale, N.J., 1994, pp. 17–41.

Violence index: George Gerbner, Larry Gross, Marilyn Jackson-Beeck, Suzanne Jeffries-Fox, and Nancy Signorielli, "Cultural Indicators: Violence Profile No. 9," *Journal of Communication,* Vol. 28, No. 3, 1978, pp. 176–207.

Mainstreaming and resonance: George Gerbner, Larry Gross, Michael Morgan, and Nancy Signorielli, "The 'Mainstreaming' of America: Violence Profile No. 11," *Journal of Communication,* Vol. 30, No. 3, 1980, pp. 10–29.

Research review and meta-analysis: Michael Morgan and James Shanahan, "Two Decades of Cultivation Research: An Appraisal and a Meta-Analysis," in *Communication Yearbook 20,* Brant Burleson (ed.), Sage, Thousand Oaks, Calif., pp. 1–45.

New directions: Nancy Signorielli and Michael Morgan (eds.), *Cultivation Analysis: New Directions in Media Effects Research,* Sage, Newbury Park, Calif., 1989.

Type of programming: Robert Hawkins and Suzanne Pingree, "Uniform Messages and Habitual Viewing: Unnecessary Assumptions in Social Reality Effects," *Human Communication Research,* Vol. 7, 1981, pp. 291–301.

Fear vs. likelihood of violence: Glenn G. Sparks and Robert M. Ogles, "The Difference Between Fear of Victimization and the Probability of Being Victimized: Implications for Cultivation," *Journal of Broadcasting & Electronic Media,* Vol. 34, No. 3, 1990, pp. 351–358.

Cognitive processing that supports cultivation: L. J. Shrum, "Psychological Processes Underlying Cultivation Effects," *Human Communication Research,* Vol. 22, 1996, pp. 482–509.

Four critiques: Anthony Doob and Glenn Macdonald, "Television Viewing and Fear of Victimization: Is the Relationship Causal?" *Journal of Personality and Social Psychology,* Vol. 37, 1979, pp. 170–179; Paul Hirsch, "The 'Scary World' of the Nonviewer and Other Anomalies," *Communication Research,* Vol. 7, 1980, pp. 403–456; Horace Newcomb, "Assessing the Violence Profile Studies of Gerbner and Gross," *Communication Research,* Vol. 5, 1978, pp. 264–282; Dolf Zillmann and Jacob Wakshlag, "Fear of Victimization and the Appeal of Crime Drama," in *Selective Exposure to Communication,* Dolf Zillmann and Jennings Bryant (eds.), Lawrence Erlbaum Associates, Hillsdale, N.J., 1985, pp. 141–156.

CHAPTER 27

Agenda-Setting Theory
of Maxwell McCombs & Donald Shaw

For some unexplained reason, in June 1972, five unknown men broke into the Democratic National Committee headquarters looking for undetermined information. It was the sort of local crime story that rated two paragraphs on page 17 of the *Washington Post*. Yet editor Ben Bradlee and reporters Bob Woodward and Carl Bernstein gave the story continual high visibility even though the public initially seemed to regard the incident as trivial.

President Nixon dismissed the break-in as a "third-rate burglary," but over the following year Americans showed an increasing public awareness of Watergate's significance. Half the country became familiar with the word *Watergate* over the summer. By April of 1973 that figure had risen to 90 percent. When television began gavel-to-gavel coverage of the Senate hearings on the matter a year after the break-in, virtually every adult in the United States knew what Watergate was about. Six months later President Nixon protested, "I am not a crook," and a half-year after that he was forced from office because the majority of citizens and their representatives had decided that he was.

THE ORIGINAL AGENDA: NOT WHAT TO THINK, BUT WHAT TO THINK ABOUT

Journalism professors Maxwell McCombs and Donald Shaw regard Watergate as a perfect example of the agenda-setting function of the mass media. They were not surprised that the Watergate issue caught fire after months on the front page of the *Washington Post*. McCombs and Shaw believe that the "mass media have the ability to transfer the salience of items on their news agendas to the public agenda."[1] They aren't suggesting that broadcast and print personnel make a deliberate attempt to influence listener, viewer, or reader opinion on the issues. Reporters in the free world have a deserved reputation for independence and fairness. But McCombs and Shaw say that we look to news professionals for cues on where to focus our attention. "*We* judge as important what the *media* judge as important."[2]

Although McCombs and Shaw first referred in 1972 to the agenda-setting function of the media—the idea that people desire media assistance in determining political reality—it had already been voiced by a number of current events analysts. In an attempt to explain how the United States had been drawn into World War I, Pulitzer Prize-winning author Walter Lippmann claimed that the media act as a mediator between "the world outside and the pictures in our heads."[3] In the past, McCombs and Shaw have often quoted University of Wisconsin political scientist Bernard Cohen's observation concerning the specific function the media serve: "The press may not be successful much of the time in telling people what to think, but it is stunningly successful in telling its readers what to think about."[4]

Starting with the Kennedy-Nixon contest in 1960, political analyst Theodore White wrote the definitive account of four presidential elections. Independently of McCombs and Shaw, and in opposition to the then current wisdom that mass communication had limited effects upon its audience, White came to the conclusion that the media shaped the election campaigns:

> The power of the press in America is a primordial one. It sets the agenda of public discussion; and this sweeping political power is unrestrained by any law. It determines what people will talk and think about—an authority that in other nations is reserved for tyrants, priests, parties and mandarins.[5]

A THEORY WHOSE TIME HAD COME

McCombs and Shaw's agenda-setting theory found an appreciative audience among mass communication researchers. The prevailing selective exposure hypothesis claimed that people would attend only to news and views that didn't threaten their established beliefs. The media were seen as merely stroking preexistent attitudes. After two decades of downplaying the influence of newspapers, magazines, radio, and television, the field was disenchanted with this limited-effects approach. Agenda-setting theory boasted two attractive features: It reaffirmed the power of the press while still maintaining that individuals were free to choose.

McCombs and Shaw's agenda-setting hypothesis represented a back-to-the-basics approach to mass communication research. Like the initial Erie County voting studies,[6] the focus is on election campaigns. The hypothesis predicts a cause-and-effect relationship between media content and voter perception. Although later work explores the conditions under which the media priorities are most influential, the theory rises or falls on its ability to show a match between the media's agenda and the public's agenda later on. McCombs and Shaw supported their main hypothesis with results from surveys they took while working together at the University of North Carolina in Chapel Hill. (McCombs is now at the University of Texas.) Their analysis of the 1968 race for president between Richard Nixon and Hubert Humphrey set the pattern for later agenda-setting research. The study provides an opportunity to examine in

©1993 WASHINGTON POST WRITERS GROUP WILEY

...AND HERE'S WHAT YOU CARE ABOUT TODAY...

THE BEGINNING OF THE NEWS MEDIA

detail the type of quantitative survey research that Stuart Hall and other critical theorists so strongly oppose.

MEDIA AGENDA AND PUBLIC AGENDA: A CLOSE MATCH

McCombs and Shaw's first task was to measure the media agenda. They determined that Chapel Hill residents relied on a mix of nine print and broadcast sources for political news—two Raleigh papers, two Durham papers, *Time*, *Newsweek*, the out-of-state edition of the *New York Times*, and the CBS and NBC evening news.

They established *position* and *length* of story as the two main criteria of prominence. For newspapers, the front-page headline story, a three-column story on an inside page, and the lead editorial were all counted as evidence of significant focus on an issue. For newsmagazines, the requirement was an opening story in the news section or any political issue to which the editors devoted a full column. Prominence in the television news format was defined by placement as one of the first three news items or any discussion which lasted over forty-five seconds.

Because the agenda-setting hypothesis refers to substantive issues, the researchers discarded news items about campaign strategy, position in the polls, and the personalities of the candidates. The remaining stories were then sorted into fifteen subject categories, which were later collapsed into five major issues. A composite index of media prominence revealed the following order of importance: foreign policy, law and order, fiscal policy, public welfare, and civil rights.

In order to measure the public's agenda, McCombs and Shaw asked Chapel Hill voters to outline what each considered the key issue of the campaign, regardless of what the candidates might be saying. People who were already committed to a candidate were dropped from the pool of respondents. The researchers assigned the specific answers to the same broad categories used for media analysis. They then compared the aggregate data from undecided voters with the composite description of media content. The rank of the five issues on both lists was nearly identical.

WHAT CAUSES WHAT?

McCombs and Shaw believe that the hypothesized agenda-setting function of the media is responsible for the almost perfect correlation they found between the media and public ordering of priorities.

Media agenda → Voters' agenda

But as critics of cultivation theory remind us, correlation is not causation. It's possible that newspaper and television coverage simply reflect public concerns that already exist.

Voters' agenda → Media agenda

The results of the Chapel Hill study could be interpreted as support for the notion that the media are just as market-driven in their news coverage as they are in programming entertainment. The findings are impressive but equivocal. A true test of the agenda-setting hypothesis must be able to show that a matching public agenda lags behind the media schedule of priorities, as shown in Figure 27.1. It also needs to show that neither the media agenda nor the public agenda is simply a mirror of reality—a reflection of what's going on in the world.

Pennsylvania State University communication researcher Ray Funkhouser performed an exhaustive retrospective search for newsmagazine stories during

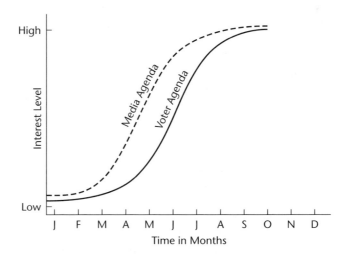

FIGURE 27.1   Time Lag Between Media and Voter Agendas
(Adapted from Westley, "What Makes It Change?")

the decade 1960 to 1970. He charted the rise and fall of media attention on issues and compared these trends with annual Gallup poll responses to a question about "the most important problem facing America." Funkhouser's results make it clear that the twin agendas aren't mere reflections of reality. The number of American troops in Vietnam increased until 1968, but news coverage peaked two years before. The same was true of urban violence and campus unrest. Press interest cooled down while cities and colleges were still heating up. It appears that Walter Lippmann was right—the actual environment and the pictures in our mind are two different worlds.

As with less ambitious agenda-setting studies, Funkhouser's study found a strong relationship between media and public agendas, but he wasn't sure that the Gallup poll responses really measured people's personal, emotional concerns:

> The correspondence between news articles and public opinion may be nothing more than the public's regurgitating back to the pollster what is currently in the news, with little or no relation to what the respondent himself feels is important.[7]

Even though Funkhouser failed to establish a definite chain of influence from media to the general public, two Yale researchers did.

Political scientists Shanto Iyengar and Donald Kinder conducted an experimental study at Yale University in which they spliced previously aired news features into tapes of current network newscasts.[8] For four days straight, three groups of New Haven residents came together to watch the evening news and fill out a questionnaire about their own concerns. Each group saw a different version—one version contained a daily story on environmental pollution, another had a daily feature on national defense, and a third offered a daily dose of news about economic inflation. Viewers who saw the media agendas that focused on pollution and defense elevated these issues on their own lists of concerns—definite confirmation of a cause-and-effect relationship between the media agenda and the public agenda. (As it turned out, inflation was already an important topic for most participants, so there wasn't any room for that issue to move up on the third group's agenda.)

The Funkhouser and Iyengar and Kinder articles are just two research reports of over 250 studies that have tested, refined, and expanded McCombs and Shaw's original hypothesis. Most of the subsequent work can be clustered under four general themes, which I summarize in the next four sections.

WHO ARE THE PEOPLE MOST AFFECTED BY THE MEDIA AGENDA?

Even in their original Chapel Hill study, McCombs and Shaw understood that "people are not automatons waiting to be programmed by the news media."[9] They suspected that some viewers might be more resistant to the media's political priorities than others—that's why they filtered out the responses of voters who were already committed to a candidate. In follow-up studies, McCombs and Shaw turned to the uses and gratifications tradition referred to in the section introduction and sought to discover exactly what kind of person was most susceptible to the media agenda. They've now concluded that people who have a willingness to let the media shape their thinking have a high *need for orientation.* Others refer to it as an "index of curiosity."

Need for orientation arises from high *relevance* and *uncertainty.* Because I'm a dog and cat owner, any story about cruelty to animals always catches my attention (high relevance). My feelings are mixed about scientific progress that comes from experimentation on live animals (high uncertainty). According to McCombs and Shaw, this combination would make me a likely candidate to be influenced by media stories about vivisection. If the news editors of *Time* and ABC think it's important, I probably will too.

WHICH ISSUES ARE BOOSTED BY MEDIA ATTENTION?

The media are more effective in establishing the importance of some topics than they are in raising the priority of others. Both broadcast and print sources seem to have the least effect on local "pocketbook" issues that confront the consumer on a day-to-day basis. Although a summit meeting among oil-producing nations may seem rather remote for the average American, the resultant cost of gasoline at the pump is not. People can and will get riled up about the issue without any help from the media.

Chronic social issues are much more dependent on media coverage to raise public consciousness and conscience. For example, journalist C. J. Bosso found that news organizations were slow to react to famine in Ethiopia in the 1980s.[10] But when the press and television finally picked up the story, the coverage occasioned great public concern and a massive relief effort. When the media later abandoned the issue, people concluded that the crisis was over and shifted their attention elsewhere. This study illustrates the consistent finding that most people can only concentrate on three to five news topics at a time. If the media bring a new issue to the fore, another topic will recede in the public's consciousness.[11]

The media seem particularly effective in creating public interest in political candidates and campaign strategy. By January 1992, news commentators had decided that Bill Clinton was the leader for the Democratic presidential nomination. "Before a vote was cast, and even though polls showed that more than half of all rank-and-file Democrats didn't even know who he was, Clinton was hailed on the covers of *Time, The New Republic,* and *New York* magazine."[12]

Although McCombs and Shaw at first dismissed this form of coverage as irrelevant to their agenda-setting hypothesis, they came to realize that the real issue in the campaign was the campaign. Most agenda-setting research since their prototype study finds that the media assign the highest news value to questions of campaign strategy. The ultimate issues are, *Who is going to win?* and *How is the candidate going to do it?*

While a doctoral candidate at the University of Pennsylvania, John Carey studied the political agenda during an off-year congressional election. He compared the media analysis of the campaign to the color commentary on a televised pro football game:

> The general game plan was laid out; strengths and weaknesses of supporting elements like the party organization were analyzed; field conditions like inflation and unemployment were considered; the present score (i.e. the polls) was matched against scores earlier in the game to see where the momentum was going; psychological elements like poor crowd reaction were suspected of taking a toll on one side; and key plays . . . were brought back again and again in a form of instant replay.[13]

Viewers seem to relish the rich smorgasbord of analysis that dominates political coverage. Perhaps their appetite for "inside dope" is another example of consumer tastes being shaped by a menu drawn up in the press and network kitchens—the public agenda following the media agenda.

FRAMING: TRANSFERRING THE SALIENCE OF ATTRIBUTES

Well into this decade, almost every article about the theory included a reiteration of the agenda-setting mantra—*the media aren't very successful in telling us what to think, but they are stunningly successful in telling us what to think about.* Throughout the last decade, however, McCombs has emphasized that the media do, in fact, influence the way we think. The specific process he cites is one that many media scholars discuss—*framing.*

James Tankard, one of the leading writers on mass communication theory, defines a media frame as "the central organizing idea for news content that supplies a context and suggests what the issue is through the use of *selection, emphasis, exclusion,* and *elaboration.*"[14] The final four nouns in that sentence suggest that the media not only set the agenda for what issues, events, or candidates are most important, but they also transfer the salience of specific attributes belonging to those potential objects of interest. My own "final four" experience may help explain the distinction.

I'm writing this section while visiting relatives in St. Petersburg, Florida. The *St. Petersburg Times* is filled with stories about the finals of the NCAA men's basketball tournament that starts here tomorrow. The field of 64 teams has now been narrowed to four, and it's hard to imagine anything the newspaper or television stations could do to make this Final Four event more salient for local residents. No one seems to talk about anything else.

What is it about the Final Four extravaganza that captures people's attention? For some it's the high quality of basketball play they expect to see. For others it's a rooting interest in a particular college. But beyond these inherent characteristics of a basketball tournament, there are many other potential features of the event that might come to mind:

Gambling—more money bet on this than the Super Bowl.

Party scene—a guy yells out, "This is where it's at."

Local economy—it's the weekend to keep Florida green.

Exploitation of players—how many will graduate?

Beach forecast—sunny and warm, all three days.

The morning paper carried separate stories on all of these features, but coverage on benefits to the local economy and the gambling angle were front page features that ran five times as long as the brief article on player exploitation buried inside.

We see, therefore, that there are two levels of agenda setting. The first level, according to McCombs, is the transfer of salience of an *attitude object* in the mass media's pictures of the world to a prominent place among the pictures in our head. (The Final Four becomes important to us.) This is the agenda-setting function that survey researchers have traditionally studied.

The second level of agenda setting is the transfer of salience of a bundle of *attributes* that the media associate with an attitude object to the specific features of the image projected on the walls of our minds.[15] (When I think of the Final Four, I imagine money changing hands for a variety of reasons. I don't think about GPAs or diplomas.) According to McCombs, the agenda setting of attributes mirrors the process of framing that Robert Entman describes in his article clarifying the concept:

> To frame is to select some aspects of a perceived reality and make them more salient in a communication text, in such a way as to promote a particular problem definition, causal interpretation, moral evaluation and/or treatment recommendation for the item described.[16]

A REVISED HEADLINE: NOT JUST WHAT TO THINK ABOUT, BUT HOW TO THINK ABOUT IT

Is there evidence that the process of framing as defined by agenda-setting theorists actually alters the pictures in the minds of people when they read the newspaper or tune in to broadcast news? Does the media's construction of an agenda with a cluster of related attributes create a coherent image in the minds of subscribers, listeners, and viewers? McCombs cites two national election studies in other countries that show this is how framing works. One was conducted in Japan,[17] the other in Spain.[18] I find compelling evidence in a third study conducted by Salma Ghanem for her doctoral dissertation under McCombs' supervision at the University of Texas.[19]

Ghanem analyzed the changing percentage of Texans who ranked crime as the most important problem facing the country between 1992 and 1995. The figure rose steadily from 2 percent in 1992 to more than one-third of the respondents in 1994, and then dipped back to a still high 20 percent. Ironically, even as public concern about crime was on the rise the first two years, the actual frequency and severity of unlawful acts was actually going down. On the basis of many first level agenda-setting studies like the Chapel Hill research, Ghanem assumed that the increased salience of crime was driven by a media that featured crime stories prominently and often. She found a high correlation (+.70) between the amount of media coverage and the depth of public concern.

Ghanem was more interested in tracking the transfer of salience of specific crime attributes—the second level of agenda setting. Of the dozen or so media frames for stories about crime, two bundles of attributes were strongly linked to the public's increasing alarm. The most powerful frame was one that cast crime as something that could happen to anyone. The stories noted that the robbery took place in broad daylight, or the shooting was random and without provocation. The second frame was where the crime took place. Out-of-state problems were of casual interest, but when a reported felony occurred locally or in the state of Texas, concern rose quickly. Note that both frames were features of news stories that shrank the psychological distance between the crimes they described and the average citizens who read or heard about them. Many concluded, "I could be next." The high correlations (+.78, +.73) between these media frames and the subsequent public concern suggests that attribute frames make compelling arguments for the choices people make after exposure to the news.

Framing is not an option. Reporters inevitably frame a story by the personal attributes of public figures they select to describe. For example, the media continually reported on the "youthful vigor" of Jack Kennedy while he was alive, but made no mention of his extramarital affairs, which were well known to the White House press corps. The 1988 presidential race was all but over after *Time* framed the contest between George Bush and Michael Dukakis as "The Nice Man vs. The Ice Man." And Republican spin doctors fought an uphill battle positioning their candidate once media stories focused on Bob Dole's lack of passion—"Dead Man Walking" was the quip of commentator Mark Shields. Media outlets are constantly searching for material that they regard as *newsworthy*. When they find it, they do more than tell their audiences *what to think about*.

McCombs and Shaw no longer subscribe to Cohen's classic remark about the media's limited agenda-setting role. They now headline their work with a revised and expanded version that describes agenda setting as a much more powerful media function:

> The media may not only tell us what to think about,
> they also may tell us how and what to think about it,
> and perhaps even what to do about it.[20]

WHO SETS THE AGENDA FOR THE AGENDA SETTERS?

Recall that Funkhouser found that topic selection in newsmagazines was out of sync with actual national and world events. In fact, 75 percent of the stories that come across a news desk are never printed for broadcast. Obviously, news doesn't select itself. Who sets the agenda for the agenda setters?

One view regards a handful of news editors as the guardians, or "gatekeepers," of political dialogue. Nothing gets put on the political agenda without the concurrence of eight men—the operation chiefs of Associated Press, the *New York Times,* the *Washington Post, Time, Newsweek,* ABC, NBC, and CBS. Although there is no evidence to support right-wing conservative charges that the editors are part of a liberal, eastern-establishment conspiracy, these key decision makers are undeniably part of a media elite that doesn't represent a cross-section of U.S. citizens. The media elite consists of middle-aged Caucasian males who attend the same conferences, banquets, and parties. As Watergate demonstrated, when one of them "puffs" a story, the rest of the nation's media climb aboard.

An alternative view regards the candidates themselves as the ultimate source of issue salience. In 1988, George Bush successfully focused media attention on Willie Horton, a convict who raped and murdered a woman while he was on a furlough from a prison in Massachusetts. Bush's media handlers (sometimes referred to as "spin doctors") turned the tragedy into a commentary on the Democratic governor's liberalism, and not a day went by without some effort to smear Dukakis with Horton's crime. By winning the election, Bush inherited the power that a president has to raise any issue to national prominence with a few remarks. He was able to put the tax issue on the table with his famous statement, "Read my lips—no new taxes!" But he was unable to get the issue off the table when he broke that pledge. He also tried to dismiss the economic recession as a "mild technical adjustment." The press and the populace decided it was major.

Current thinking on news selection focuses on the crucial role of public relations professionals working for government agencies, corporations, and interest groups. Even prestigious newspapers with large investigative staffs such as the *Washington Post* and the *New York Times* get over half of what they print straight from press releases and press conferences.[21]

"Interest aggregations" are becoming increasingly adept at creating news that must be reported. Columbia University sociologist Robert Merton coined this term to refer to clusters of people who demand center stage for their one overriding concern, whatever it might be—antiabortion, antiwar, anticommunism, antipollution, anti-free trade, anti-immigration. As the examples indicate, these groups usually rally around a specific action which they oppose. They stage demonstrations, marches, and other media events so that television and press will be forced to cover their issue. The net effect is that various power centers are vying for the right to be heard. The media seem to pay attention to those who grab it.

CRITIQUE: ARE THE EFFECTS TOO LIMITED, THE SCOPE TOO WIDE?

When McCombs and Shaw first proposed the agenda-setting hypothesis, they saw it as a sharp break from the limited effects model that had held sway in media research since the work of the "Founding Fathers" in the 1940s. Although not reverting to the old hypodermic needle model or magic bullet conception of media influence, McCombs and Shaw ascribed to broadcast and print journalism the significant power to set the public's political priorities. As years of careful research have shown, however, it doesn't always work. Perhaps the best that can be said is that the media agenda affects the salience of some issues for some people. As recently as 1994, McCombs suggested that "agenda setting is a theory of limited media effects."[22] That would be quite a comedown from its original promise.

The new dimension of framing reopens the possibility of a powerful media effects model. As Ohio State University journalism professor Gerald Kosicki states,

> media "gatekeepers" do not merely keep watch over information, shuffling it here and there. Instead, they engage in active construction of the messages, emphasizing certain aspects of an issue and not others.[23]

But Kosicki questions whether framing is even a legitimate topic of study under an agenda-setting banner. He sees nothing in McCombs and Shaw's original model that anticipates the importance of interpretive frames.

As McCombs is fond of pointing out, the evidence is there. In the lead article of a 1977 book that he and Shaw edited, they clearly previewed the current "New Frontiers" of agendas of attributes and framing:

> Agenda setting as a concept is not limited to the correspondence between salience of topics for the media and the audience. We can also consider the saliency of various attributes of these objects (topics, issues, persons or whatever) reported in the media. To what extent is our view of an object shaped or influenced by the picture sketched in the media, especially by those attributes which the media deem newsworthy?[24]

McCombs is even able to refer to a few early studies that explored the salience of attributes. For almost two decades, however, agenda-setting researchers took a different path, and framing was a subject for interpretive media scholars like Roland Barthes and Stuart Hall to explain.

McCombs' definition of framing is highly restrictive: "Framing is the selection of a restricted number of thematically related attributions for inclusion on the media agenda when a particular object is discussed."[25] It doesn't address the mood of a newspaper story that is set by the emotional connotation of the words that are used in the text.

In the case of broadcast news, the tone of voice and facial expression of the presenter also make a tremendous difference. Consider the affectively loaded phrases used in the ongoing abortion debate. The effect on the audience is significantly different if a story is framed as "freedom-of-choice versus antiabortion forces" rather than "right-to-life versus pro-abortion advocates." Even if a newswriter carefully refers to each group of defenders by each group's preferred designation ("freedom of choice" and "right to life"), that evenhandedness will be lost if a broadcaster slightly raises an eyebrow while saying one phrase or the other.

As for McCombs and Shaw, they believe their restrictive view of framing is an advantage. The popularity of framing as a construct in media studies has resulted in diverse and perhaps contradictory uses of the term. At least within agenda-setting theory, framing has a specific and straightforward meaning.

Whether or not we accept a restricted definition of *framing*, the agenda-setting function of the mass media has earned a firm place in media-effects literature. McCombs and Shaw have established a plausible case that some people look to print and broadcast news for guidance on which issues are really important. Agenda-setting theory also provides a needed reminder that news stories are just that—stories. The message always requires interpretation. For these reasons, McCombs and Shaw have accomplished the function they ascribe to the media. Agenda-setting theory has a priority place on the mass communication agenda.

QUESTIONS TO SHARPEN YOUR FOCUS

1. If the media aren't telling you what to think, why is their ability to tell you *what to think about* so important?

2. What *type of person* under *what type of circumstances* is most susceptible to the media's *agenda-setting function*?

3. Hillary Clinton is one of the most controversial public figures in America. How could you *frame* her visit to a children's hospital to make her look good? How could you do it to make her look bad?

4. Is there a recent issue that *news reporters and commentators* are now talking about all the time that you and the people you know don't care about? Do you think you'll still be unconcerned four months from now?

A SECOND LOOK

Recommended resource: Maxwell McCombs and Tamara Bell, "The Agenda-Setting Role of Mass Communication," in *An Integrated Approach to Communication Theory and Research,* Michael Salwen and Donald Stacks (eds.), Lawrence Erlbaum Associates, Hillsdale, N.J., 1996, pp. 89–105.

Prototype election study: Maxwell McCombs and Donald Shaw, "The Agenda-Setting Function of the Mass Media," *Public Opinion Quarterly,* Vol. 37, 1973, pp. 62–75.

Agendas of attributes: Maxwell McCombs, "New Frontiers in Agenda Setting: Agendas of Attributes and Frames," *Mass Comm Review 24,* 1997, in press.

Framing: Maxwell McCombs and Salma Ghanem, "The Convergence of Agenda Setting and Framing," in *Framing in the New Media Landscape,* Stephen Reese, Oscar Gandy, and August Grant (eds.), in press.

Descriptive research: Ray Funkhouser, "The Issues of the 60's: An Exploratory Study in the Dynamics of Public Opinion," *Public Opinion Quarterly,* Vol. 36, 1972, pp. 176–187.

Experimental research: Shanto Iyengar and Donald Kinder, *News That Matters,* University of Chicago, Chicago, 1987.

Rise and fall of a single issue: J. P. Winter and C. H. Eyal, "Agenda-Setting for the Civil Rights Issue," *Public Opinion Quarterly,* Vol. 45, 1981, pp. 376–383.

Anthology of agenda-setting research: David Protess and Maxwell McCombs, *Agenda Setting: Readings on Media, Public Opinion, and Policymaking,* Lawrence Erlbaum Associates, Hillsdale, N.J., 1991.

Recent scholarship: Maxwell McCombs, Donald L. Shaw, and David Weaver, *Communication and Democracy: Exploring the Intellectual Frontiers in Agenda-Setting Theory,* Lawrence Erlbaum Associates, Mahwah, N.J., 1997.

Critique: Gerald Kosicki, "Problems and Opportunities in Agenda-Setting Research," *Journal of Communication,* Vol. 43, 1993, No. 2, pp. 100–127.

CHAPTER 28

The Media Equation

of Byron Reeves & Clifford Nass

Byron Reeves and Clifford Nass are members of the communication department at Stanford University and the directors of the school's Social Responses to Communication Technology project. As the title suggests, both men are intrigued by the way people interact with television, computers, and other high-tech media. Based on a research program that explores this interface, Reeves and Nass are convinced that people treat communication media as if they were human. As opposed to many of the theoretical constructions described in earlier chapters, their media theory can be represented by a simple equation.[1]

THE MEDIA EQUATION: MEDIA = REAL LIFE

Reeves and Nass' book, *The Media Equation,* is not a science-fiction fantasy in which computers come alive and take over the world. The authors regard computer chips, software, transistors, and digital television as inanimate objects and expect them to remain that way. What their equation does suggest, however, is that we *respond* to communication media *as if* they were alive. The book's subtitle underscores this point: "How People Treat Computers, Television, and New Media Like Real People and Places."

The practical implication of the media equation is that once we turn on a television or boot up our computer, we follow all the rules of interpersonal interaction that we've practiced throughout life. Thus the word *interface* is particularly apt when describing human-media relations. This natural social response goes way beyond occasional words yelled at the television set or our frantic plea for the computer to retrieve lost data. Reeves and Nass maintain that the media equation is so basic that it "applies to everyone, it applies often, and it is highly consequential."[2] To make their point they recommend the following test:

"I love it when you talk dirty to me!"

1. Pick any well-established finding from the research literature of interpersonal communication. (For example—"People like to be praised by other people, even if the praise is undeserved.")

2. Cross out the second reference to *people* and substitute the word *media*. ("People like to be praised by media, even if the praise is undeserved.")

3. Then test this revised proposition using the same experimental methods that established the interpersonal principle. (Design computer messages to arbitrarily praise some people for their problem-solving ability while criticizing others for their faulty strategy. Then see if users who received compliments like the machine more and think it did a better job than do those who receive the critical messages.)

When Nass ran the experiment outlined above, he confirmed that computers that flattered their users were rated more helpful and better liked than critical machines.[3] This is not an isolated finding. Together, Reeves and Nass have published over forty reports of experiments supporting their claim that people respond to media in the same way they respond in face-to-face interactions with other people. Assuming the media equation is valid, students of media effects would do well to spend some time in the interpersonal communication and social psychology sections of the library rather than relying solely on mass communication literature or the latest reports of technological advances.

BEYOND INTUITION THAT PROTESTS: "NOT ME, I KNOW A PICTURE IS NOT A PERSON"

The media equation is clearly counterintuitive. As we watch TV or surf the net, none of us is convinced that we respond to images on the screen as if they were real. Children might mistake animated pictures of people for the real thing, but we know that they are merely *representations* of life. At best, they create only a second-hand reality. Even if others are fooled, we are not.

Reeves and Nass counter that "people respond socially and naturally to media even though they believe it is not reasonable to do so, and even though they don't think these responses characterize themselves."[4] Their rejoinder parallels social psychologist Philip Zimbardo's warning against the "not me" syndrome. Zimbardo writes that we often set ourselves apart from others by clinging to the illusion of personal invulnerability—the naïve belief that our attitudes and actions are not conditioned by situation or circumstance.[5] While a "not me" orientation preserves our belief that we are fully autonomous, that pride is dangerous, Zimbardo argues, because it reduces our vigilance to the power of outside forces to mold our lives. We thus become more vulnerable to them.

Students of communication also find the media equation strange because they are accustomed to thinking of media effects in terms of program *content*. We've already examined cultivation research that focuses on the effects of television violence and an agenda-setting analysis that monitors the types of stories covered by the news media. Other studies probe the effects of political ads, pornography, or depictions of paranormal phenomena.[6] In contrast, the media equation applies to electronic media, regardless of content. In this respect, the media equation is more similar to the technological determinism of McLuhan than to the content focus of Gerbner or McCombs and Shaw (see Chapters 23, 26, 27). Yet while McLuhan differentiates between hot and cool media, Reeves and Nass claim that their theory holds for all modern media.

Finally, the media equation defies accepted wisdom because we are accustomed to thinking of media as tools. McLuhan reinforced this idea when he said that we shape our tools, and they in turn shape us. But he probably had it only half right. Reeves and Nass strongly agree that the media affect our responses, but they think the tool metaphor leads us astray. Tools are *things* purchased at a hardware store. Tools can be picked up or turned on, and just as easily put down or switched off. We can be detached from a tool. Not so, they say, with television, computers, and other forms of virtual reality. The sights and sounds we encounter draw us in and elicit social responses that we've built up over a lifetime of human interaction. Media are more than just tools. Although Reeves and Nass realize their claim violates common sense, they insist that "media are full participants in our social and natural world."[7]

OLD BRAINS, NEW TECHNOLOGIES

Reeves and Nass credit the slow pace of evolution as the reason that the human race responds socially and naturally to media: "The human brain evolved in a world in which *only* humans exhibited rich social behaviors, and a world in which *all* perceived objects were real physical objects. Anything that *seemed* to be a real person or place *was* real."[8] So we haven't yet adapted to twentieth century media that not only depict lifelike images, but which themselves personify the characteristics of human actors. The Social Responses to Communication Technology group at Stanford maintains that the media equation holds true because of what now turns out to be a human biological limitation: "There is no neural function or anatomical region designed to help humans differentiate mediated and unmediated experience and to change mental processing accordingly."[9] Thus the media equation is an unconscious, automatic response—literally a "no brainer."

People can of course think themselves out of primitive, automatic responses to mediated experience. Reeves and Nass cite the familiar case of the visceral fear we might feel while watching a horror film. It's possible to lower our level of fright by continually reminding ourselves that "it's only a movie, it's only a movie." But this strategy takes a great deal of mental effort and makes it hard to follow the plot, so we usually don't do it. The theorists note that "the fact that the movie scared us in the first place is good evidence that media are real first, and false only after we think about it. There are vestiges of old brains in modern thinking."[10]

Thwarting the media equation is even more difficult within an interactive environment. We might think it would be easy to remember that any response from a computer was originally encoded by a programmer, but according to Nass, it's not. He ran a study showing that people consider computers rather than their programmers as the source of information on the screen.[11] In fact, he discovered that computer users don't normally think about programmers at all. They don't need to. The machine is more humanly present than the absent programmer.

Nass acknowledges that computers are different from people in a thousand different ways, but he points out that they are very much like people in a few significant ways: "Computers use language, respond based on multiple prior inputs, fill roles traditionally filled by humans, and produce human-sounding voices."[12] Perhaps that's all our slow-to-evolve human brains need:

> These extremely social cues have only been associated, up until recently, with other humans. Hence, when confronted with a machine that possesses even a few of these humanlike characteristics, it is possible that our most natural response is to behave socially toward it.[13]

PROVING THE EQUATION

In algebra, "proving" an equation means demonstrating that the terms on both sides of the equal sign are equivalent. A mathematician does this by performing the same computations to both sides of the equation in an attempt to reduce the complexity to a simple $x = x$ identity. It's a solo activity that involves no interaction with media hardware or interpersonal communication.

Proving the media equation is a more daunting task. The predicted relationship between responses to media and responses to people can best be symbolized as an $x = y$ equation. There's no mathematical logic that connects the two types of behavior. And due to the counterintuitive nature of the theorists' prediction, it's dangerous to rely on people's introspective accounts of why they do what they do. So evidence that we do in fact interact with media (x) the same way we do with people (y) must come from empirical research. Reeves and Nass insist that "empirical methods show what otherwise would not be known."[14]

The two theorists review a variety of media experiments that they've designed to parallel well-known studies of interpersonal communication. If their media equation is valid, their results on media-human interface should match established findings of relationships between people. I've selected three areas of research connected with communication theories discussed in this text to provide a sample of what they've found. The topics are *interpersonal distance, similarity and attraction,* and *source credibility.*

Interpersonal Distance

Although Burgoon expanded her expectancy violations theory to cover almost any breach of normal interpersonal behavior, she created and refined her original model based on the effects of violating personal space (see Chapter 6). She said that unanticipated physical proximity would trigger increased arousal, resulting in heightened attention to the nature of the relationship. When this happens, "violator valence" determines whether our response will be more or less favorable than it would have been had the other conformed to our proxemic norm.

The media equation suggests that any finding validated in interpersonal communication research should hold equally true in modern media usage. So when a television picture gets "up close and personal," viewers should be stimulated and respond the same way they would as if someone had walked into the room and approached to within a few inches. Reeves and Nass acknowledge that this claim seems rather far-fetched: "We can all safely say that real people don't reside inside of media or on a screen, so it shouldn't matter whether images of people make them appear close or far away. . . . After all, it's only a picture."[15] Yet the very improbability of their prediction makes it a good test of the media equation.

Participants in Reeves' experiment watched forty ten-second clips of different people talking about their favorite restaurant or their last vacation.[16] When one person looks at another person talking, the most important cue to the distance between them is the extent to which the other person's face fills the observer's field of vision. To simulate that effect in testing the media equation, Reeves and Nass controlled perceived distance in three different ways. First, they varied the distance between the viewer and the television set—four feet versus ten feet. Second, they varied the size of the screen—forty-one inches versus fifteen inches. And third, they varied the camera shot—a face filling the screen versus a full body shot, head-to-toe. When systematically rotated, these three variables offered eight different impressions of interpersonal distance. For example, mediated figures appeared furthest away when framed head-to-toe on a fifteen-inch screen at a distance of ten feet. Conversely, subjects who watched only four feet away from a face that filled the forty-one-inch screen literally had a mediated person "in their face."

Subjects' evaluations of each person in the video were rated on scales anchored with pairs of words such as *calm/anxious, pleasant/unpleasant,* and *violent/gentle.* That was the easy part. Finding a nonintrospective measure of attentiveness was tougher to do. Instead of using heartbeat, skin resistance, pupil dilation, or another nonspecific index of physiological arousal, Reeves rigged up a secondary reaction-time task that provided a measure of attention directed specifically toward the person on the screen. While watching the video, subjects were expected to press a button whenever they heard a random tone—much like the procedure in a hearing test. Because the human capacity for cognitive processing is limited (see Chapters 7, 8, and 10), the more viewers were absorbed in watching the person on the screen, the longer it took for them to react to the tone. On the other hand, a quick reaction to the sound was a reliable indicator that viewers weren't very involved with a specific speaker.

What did Reeves discover? When the figures on the screen "came too close," vigilance increased, and as Burgoon predicted, response toward their mediated presence became more intense. Mild approval became strong attraction; vague uneasiness turned into distinct irritation. In one sense, the study is unspectacular in that it merely replicates the findings of nonverbal communication research. Yet as Reeves and Nass suggest, the support it provides for the media equation is both surprising and impressive:

> People assume that a picture of a face, regardless of its size, is merely a symbol that stands for someone not actually present. But it is more. The size of a face can broadly influence psychological responses—from the mental energy required to attend . . . to thoughtful judgment of character.[17]

Similarity and Attraction

Perhaps the most well-validated principle of relational research is that perceived similarity increases attraction.[18] This "law of attraction" is now a standard feature of many communication theories. For example, you read earlier about Charles Berger combining two axioms of uncertainty reduction theory to create Theorem 21, a clear statement of the positive relationship between similarity and attraction (see Chapter 10). So if the media equation is really true, individuals should like a "similar" computer more than one they see as "different." To test this seemingly strange prediction, Nass and Reeves first set out to do what is almost a mantra in the field of computer design—"give computers some personality."[19]

When people judge personality, relational control turns out to be a crucial dimension. Where does the person fall on a *dominant–submissive* scale? With relatively little effort, Nass and Reeves were able to take identical computers and make one seem "dominant" and the other "submissive." They programmed the computers to offer users the same amount of help on a desert survival problem, yet to interact in different styles. Advice from the dominant computer was stated with certainty: "You should definitely rate the flashlight higher. It is your only reliable night signaling device." The submissive computer was more tentative: "Perhaps the flashlight should be rated higher? It may be your only reliable night signaling device." The dominant computer always went first and expressed a high level of confidence in its own opinions. The submissive computer always went last and expressed doubt about the wisdom of its judgments. The dominant computer was named "Max"; the submissive computer was named "Linus."

How successful was this manipulation? As it turned out, Stanford students easily identified the personality of the machines. Participants who worked with Max rated the computer as *domineering, authoritative, controlling,* and *forceful,* while those who used Linus considered the computer to be *submissive, timid,* and *shy.* Nass and Reeves note that this is a typical case of impression formation extending beyond the realm of human-human contact: "Our old brains automatically extrapolate when given a little hint."[20] But they also add, "It is not enough to demonstrate that computers can be endowed with personality, and that people are capable of recognizing that personality; rather, it must also be demonstrated that people *respond* to computer personalities in the same way that they respond to human personalities."[21]

In order to assess user response, Nass and Reeves employed a psychological test to identify students who had personalities that were decidedly dominant or submissive. Half of these students were paired with computers that were similar in personality—dominant-dominant or submissive-submissive. The other half worked with computers that had an opposite control orientation—dominant-submissive or submissive-dominant. When the desert survival exercise was over, the results were clear. Students matched with computers that displayed similar personalities were more socially and intellectually attracted to their machines than were students working with dissimilar computers. Or to use Watzlawick's terminology (see Chapter 11), students in *symmetrical* relationships (↑↑, ↓↓) liked their electronic partners better than did students in *complementary* relationships (↑↓, ↓↑).

The similarity-attraction relationship has practical implications for computer software and hardware design. True user-friendly media are those that match the personality of the operator. This is not a one-size-fits-all proposition. Hesitant users might like a doe-eyed, paper-clip helper who appears only when summoned, but aggressive users don't. They want an assertive machine that proactively inserts numbers, automatically corrects spelling, and makes jarring noises when users are about to do something stupid. Based on people's desire for this type of compatibility, Microsoft and Macintosh would do well to offer buyers a choice between a Linus and a Max.

As consultants to Microsoft and Silicone Valley high-tech companies, Reeves and Nass were pleased to demonstrate that creating a personality for a computer doesn't require sophisticated graphics, natural language processing, or artificial intelligence. As communication theorists, they were also gratified to report additional support for their media equation:

> When machines are endowed with personality-like characteristics, people will respond to them *as if* they have personalities, despite the fact that these individuals will claim that they do *not* believe the machines actually have personalities.[22]

Source Credibility

Beginning with Aristotle's emphasis on ethical proof (see Chapter 20), rhetorical scholars have shown a continuing interest in *who* says something as well as *what* is said. That interest has been more than matched by researchers schooled in the socio-psychological tradition of communication theory. The early Yale Attitude Studies established that the credibility of a message source has a strong effect on how listeners respond to the message (see Chapter 3). In like manner, our interpersonal communication is affected by the roles and reputations we bring to a relationship. As media theorists grounded in that socio-psychological tradition, Reeves and Nass think it also makes sense to talk about the credibility of mediated messages. The problem is figuring out who the source of the message really is. The media equation suggests that for all practical purposes, it's the electronic messenger.

If we think about it, we'll realize that the source of most news reported on television is an unseen news editor. But according to the media equation, we usually don't think about it. Even when the BBC labels the messenger a "newsreader," trying to concentrate on a faceless writer is a complicated and tiring task. Reeves and Nass conclude that "people automatically assign responsibility for messages to those who deliver them, even when the receiver knows the link is dubious. What is most *proximate* is the messenger, not someone in some other place."[23] That's why Peter Jennings, Dan Rather, and Wolf Blitzer *make* news, not just report it.

Credibility is in the eye of the beholder. The news anchors mentioned above are often viewed as filling a specific social role—they are specialists in public affairs. Is it possible that viewers could regard a television set as a specialist as well? The idea seems ludicrous, yet if the media equation is right, it could be quite natural to assign a specific role to a TV. After all, viewers have already attributed expertise to ESPN for sports, CNN for news, and the Weather Channel for the latest forecast. Perhaps it's not so far-fetched to think that a television set could serve the same function. As Reeves and Nass write, "Despite some hilarity as we planned the experiment, we were anxious to see if a social role could define a box of wires and glass."[24] Their prediction was that content on a television set that is labeled a *specialist* will be perceived as superior to identical content on a television set that carries a *generalist* label.

All participants in the study watched two videotapes. A *news* tape contained stories on business fraud, a wounded police officer, a book about suicide, and the closing of a military medical center. An *entertainment* tape contained segments from *Cheers, The Cosby Show, Roseanne,* and *Who's the Boss?* Half of the participants watched both tapes on a TV set labeled "News and Entertainment Television." The other half watched the news tape on a set labeled "News Television" and the entertainment tape on a different set labeled "Entertainment Television."

Despite all logic, viewers who watched the news tapes on the specialist television rated the reporters' stories as more *interesting, important, informative,* and *disturbing* than viewers who saw the same tape on a generalist set. In like fashion, viewers who saw the entertainment video on the specialist TV found it more *relaxing* and somewhat *funnier* than viewers who saw it on the generalist set. Viewers who watched the programs on specialist television sets even rated the clarity and color of the picture better! It takes a Machiavellian mind to figure out how advertisers might use this information to sell more TVs, but Reeves and Nass focus on the implications for their media equation:

> These studies provide perhaps the most compelling evidence yet that social responses to media are not dictated by "common sense." No viewer thinks that television sets have an ability to influence the content that they display. Nonetheless, people are influenced by labels, and the influence goes beyond their ability to analyze their own responses. . . . These social orientations to media indicate that it is natural for people to treat media socially, perhaps easier than treating media in any other way, including as a tool.[25]

Who is the source of a computer message when there is no proximate person presented on the screen? According to the media equation, the computer itself. This is obviously a controversial thesis, but if we actually do treat computers as if they were real people, that solid-state box is a more immediate source than any invisible programmer. Nass set up a simple experiment to explore whether computers, not their programmers, are actually considered the real source of information.[26] It is, of course, hard to demonstrate that people are *not* thinking about a programmer, but it's possible to see if there's a difference when one group is prompted to think of the programmer and the other group is not.

Two groups were tutored by a computer and later rated the responses they received in terms of how helpful and positive they were. One group was asked to think about the persons who programmed the computer, the other group received no special instructions:

> Half of the participants were told that they were working with programmers, and that the programmers had different ways of tutoring. They were also told that

they would be evaluated by the programmers after the session. The other half were told the exact same things, but the word "computer" was substituted for "programmer." When participants worked without a programmer, the computer referred to itself as "this computer." When a programmer was mentioned, the computer referred to itself as "I."

As Nass anticipated, there was a big difference between the two groups. People who were told to think about the person who programmed their computer rated the machine as less competent and less friendly than did those who were free to imagine any information source. From this Reeves and Nass conclude that it's possible for people to think about a distant source, but only if they are instructed to do so and only at great cost. Our natural or default response is to the most immediate source—the computer.

Adding Up the Evidence

The studies described above are only a small portion of the empirical evidence that Reeves and Nass offer in support of their media equation. For example, they've demonstrated that people will identify a computer as male or female based only on its "voice," and then respond to the metal box with a CPU in a typically gendered way.[27] The theorists have also shown that people tend to be polite to computers and will readily consider them teammates, yet are willing to "scapegoat" them when they are "different" and the situation turns sour.[28]

None of these studies "prove" that media equal real life. There's no way to use deductive logic to establish an $x = y$ identity—the ironclad certainty that responses to people and responses to media are the same and always will be. But in terms of increased probability, inductive support in the form of empirical evidence is mounting up. So far, Reeves and Nass have yet to discover a principle of interpersonal communication that doesn't apply to our treatment of television, computers, and other sophisticated electronic media.

CRITIQUE: AN INTRIGUING ONE-WAY RELATIONSHIP

Four decades before *The Media Equation* was written, another Stanford professor published a counterintuitive theory that captured the imagination of social psychologists and communication researchers. In his theory of cognitive dissonance, Leon Festinger suggested that the best way to induce attitude change in others is to offer them only a *minimal justification* to act in a way consistent with the desired position.[29] Like Festinger, Reeves and Nass not only challenge common wisdom, they also back up their media equation with an impressive array of empirical support. The theory's intriguing predictions and evolutionary explanation should generate widespread discussion in academia.

Insights generated by the media equation have already proven valuable for computer hardware and software companies. Reeves and Nass were instrumental in developing the "personality" of Microsoft's Office 97 graphics, and a Bill Gates' testimonial to the worth of their ideas is printed on the back cover of *The Media Equation.* Currently, the theorists serve as consultants to General Magic and Portico Products working on voice recognition software. But the basic message of their work for the industry is that computers don't need artificial intelligence, natural language processing, or sophisticated pictorial representation to elicit a typical interpersonal response from the user. The media equation phenomenon plus a few simple lines of text are enough to do the trick.

Consumer advocates and scholars working from a critical tradition are much less enthusiastic about the implications of the media equation. That's because even while Reeves and Nass advise technicians on ways to enhance the human qualities of media, they hold out little hope that people can easily resist these interpersonal advances. The theorists say that *knowledge* of the media equation is only a limited defense, but they offer no other, and have yet to turn their considerable research skills to figuring out how protesters might inject a resistance variable into the media equation. A *HotWired* review focused on this "administrative" bias: "Describing research and analysis in a jolly-professor/prankish-hacker way gives *The Media Equation* a friendly personality, but make no mistake: This is clearly a book of magic, full of dark and dangerous spells to bring others under control . . . ."[30]

My concern with the media equation stems from a seemingly offhand comment mentioned only in a footnote of a Nass and Reeves journal article. In that note, the theorists acknowledge that they use a conception of *interpersonal communication* taken from social psychology rather than from the field of communication.[31] The difference is not trivial. Most social-psych research treats interpersonal communication as *one-way* communication, which is best studied within a stimulus-response paradigm. Conversely, most communication scholars define interpersonal communication as the *construction of shared meaning,* and they study the two-way flow of messages, which create common interpretations.

University of Iowa communication researcher Steve Duck uses his own equation metaphor to show how the two definitions of interpersonal communication affect similarity research. He says that people's perception of similarity is not based on the similarity of experience itself (*experience = events*), rather it is founded on the similar construction of experience (*experience = subjective interpretation.*)[32] Duck writes that "talk about similarity is the place where similarity slides over from being an individual, perceptual object and becomes a social, relational action grounded in mutuality and jointly constructed interaction."[33]

Duck's analysis shows us that interpersonal similarity is much more complex than the mere matching of dominant or submissive personalities. In like manner, proxemic violations can't be measured with just a ruler, and credibility is still in the eye of the beholder. Reeves and Nass have obtained surprising and impressive results to support their contention that media effects parallel interpersonal effects. But until they show that the media equation works when applied to some of the shared meaning findings of constructivism, relational dialectics, or other complex interpersonal research programs, the media equation will seem more like a powerful metaphor than a mathematical certainty.

QUESTIONS TO SHARPEN YOUR FOCUS

1. The *media equation* states that our *responses to media* match how we *react in real life*. Since an equation is an *identity,* is it also true that our real life responses match the way we react to media?

2. Given sufficient time and money, how might you prove or disprove the contention that the slow pace of *evolution* is the reason our *old brain* responds *socially and naturally* to media?

3. What experience have you had with *television, computers,* or other *new electronic media* that supports or contradicts the media equation? Why might Reeves and Nass discount your *testimony*?

4. How could media equation researchers design an *experiment* to discover whether or not people *create shared meaning* with a computer?

A SECOND LOOK

Recommended resource: Byron Reeves and Clifford Nass, *The Media Equation: How People Treat Computers, Television, and New Media Like Real People and Places,* Cambridge University Press, New York, 1996.

Computers as social actors: Clifford Nass and J. S. Steuer, "Voices, Boxes, and Sources of Messages: Computers and Social Actors," *Human Communication Research,* Vol. 19, 1993, pp. 504–527.

Evolutionary explanations for social phenomena: Benjamin Detenber and Byron Reeves, "A Bio-Informational Theory of Emotion: Motion and Image Size Effects on Viewers," *Journal of Communication,* Vol. 46, 1966, No. 3, pp. 66–84.

Interpersonal/media distance: Byron Reeves, Matthew Lombard, Geetu Melwani, "Faces on the Screen: Pictures or Natural Experience?" Paper presented to the International Communication Association, Miami, 1992.

User/media similarity and attraction: Youngme Moon and Clifford Nass, "How 'Real' Are Computer Personalities? Psychological Responses to Personality Types in Human-Computer Interaction," *Communication Research,* Vol. 23, 1996, pp. 651–674.

User/media similarity and attraction: Clifford Nass, Youngme Moon, B. J. Fogg, Byron Reeves, and D. Christopher Dryer, "Can Computer Personalities Be Human Personalities?" *International Journal of Human-Computer Studies,* Vol. 43, 1995, pp. 223–239.

Media credibility: Clifford Nass, Byron Reeves, Glenn Leshner, "Technology and Roles: A Tale of Two TVs," *Journal of Communication,* Vol. 46, 1996, No. 2, pp. 121–128.

Gendered media: Clifford Nass, Youngme Moon, and Nancy Green, "Are Machines Gender-Neutral? Gender Stereotypic Responses to Computers," *Journal of Applied Social Psychology*, Vol. 27, 1997, pp. 864–876.

Critique: Steve Duck, *Meaningful Relationships,* Sage, Thousand Oaks, Calif., 1994, pp. 97–126.

JÜRGEN HABERMAS' DISCOURSE ETHICS

German philosopher and social theorist Jürgen Habermas doesn't offer a touchstone principle or set of guidelines by which to gauge degrees of ethical goodness. Instead, like Immanuel Kant, his countryman from an earlier century, this "Frankfurt School" critical theorist suggests a rational process through which people can determine right from wrong. But whereas Kant's categorical imperative (see page 103) can be applied by a single individual in private contemplation, Habermas' procedure for ethical decision making requires a diverse group of people engaged in public discourse. He asks in effect, "What ethical norms would members of an ideal communication community agree represent their mutual interests?"

Habermas imagines an *ideal speech situation* in which participants are free to listen to reason and speak their minds without fear of constraint or control.[1] He is convinced that noncoercive ethical consensus is possible only to the extent that three conditions or requirements are met.[2]

"Protocol or no, if he doesn't stop talking soon, I'm going to eat him."

Reprinted from The Saturday Evening Post © 1980.

1. *Requirement for access.* Anyone who meets minimum standards of communication competence has an equal opportunity to participate in the dialogue. So long as people can use a common language to share meaning, are capable of understanding each other's intentions, and can interact in an appropriate way, they have rights of equal access.

2. *Requirement for argument.* All individuals must be allowed to introduce ideas, call into question other ideas, and sincerely express their attitudes, needs, and desires.

3. *Requirement for justification.* Everyone is committed to a standard of universalizability. What makes ethical claims legitimate is their "acceptance not only among those who agree to live with and by them but by anyone *affected* by them."[3]

Habermas understands that thoroughly noncoercive dialogue is a utopian dream, yet he finds his conception of the ideal speech situation helpful in gauging the degree to which an ethical discussion is rational. Just as many jurists are more concerned with whether a trial is conducted fairly than they are with a jury's verdict, Habermas' discourse ethic "judges only the quality of the conditions for choice and not the quality of the choices themselves."[4] Applying this standard to American media, Theodore Glasser, director of the graduate program in journalism at Stanford University, asserts that today's news practitioners hurt rather than help rational ethical discussion.

Glasser has three major charges. First, "the moral relativism that pervades American journalism not only reduces questions of ethics to questions of conscience but effectively excludes larger moral issues that are not immediately a matter of individual choice."[5] Second, the press is quick to appeal to First Amendment rights to defend individual self-expression. But in line with discourse ethics, Glasser suggests that "freedom of expression exists as a *collective* right intended to protect the processes of deliberation and the opportunities for democratic participation."[6] Third, investigative journalism virtually ignores key issues of media ownership, control, and bias.[7] This self-serving silence demonstrates the importance of Habermas' insistence that *everyone* have a say in forming the professional ethics of media practitioners.

CLIFFORD CHRISTIANS' COMMUNITARIAN ETHICS

Clifford Christians is director of the doctoral program in communications at the University of Illinois and lead author of *Good News: Social Ethics and the Press*.[8] Although he values free speech, he doesn't share the near-absolute devotion to the First Amendment that seems to be the sole ethical commitment of many journalists. Christians rejects reporters' and editors' insistence on an absolute right of free expression that is based on the individualistic rationalism of John Locke and other Enlightenment thinkers. In our age of ethical relativism where "continue the conversation" is the best philosophy has to offer,[9] Christians believes that "discovering the truth" is still possible if we are willing to examine the nature of our humanity. The human nature he perceives is, at root, "personhood in community."[10]

Christians agrees with Martin Buber that the relation is the cradle of life. ("In the beginning is the relation.")[11] He is convinced, therefore, that *mutuality* is the essence of humanness. People are most fully human as "persons-in-relation" who live simultaneously for others and for themselves.

> A moral community demonstrates more than mere interdependence; it is characterized by mutuality, a will-to-community, a genuine concern for the other apart from immediate self-interest. . . . An act is morally right when compelled by the intention to maintain the community of persons; it is wrong if driven by self-centeredness."[12]

Christians understands that a commitment to mutuality would significantly alter media culture and mission. Communitarian ethics establishes *civic transformation* rather than objective information as the primary goal of the press. A reporter's aim thus becomes a revitalized citizenship shaped by community norms—morally literate and active participants, not just readers and audiences provided with data.[13] The theorists presented in the media effects and media and culture sections could be held to the same standard.

Christians applauds Gerbner's Cultural Indicators project in its attempt to change violent media content, yet he's skeptical that simply uncovering the negative effects of cultivated fear will bring about needed reform. Christians says that media criticism must be willing to reestablish the idea of moral right and wrong. Selfish practices aimed at splintering community are not merely misguided, they are evil.[14]

McLuhan's exposure of technology's morally deadening power could be a stimulus for local resistance to depersonalizing inventions. However, McLuhan's passive acceptance of all technological innovation has added to the problem rather than offering a solution.

Christians' communitarian ethics are based on the Christian tradition of *agape* love rather than Stuart Hall's Marxist interpretation of history. With an emphasis on establishing communal bonds, alienated people on the margins of society receive special attention from communitarians. Yet both scholars ultimately judge journalists on the basis of how well they use the media's power to champion the goal of social justice:

> Is the press a voice for the unemployed, food-stamp recipients, Appalachian miners, the urban poor, Hispanics in rural shacks, the elderly, women discriminated against in hiring and promotion, ethnic minorities with no future in North America's downsizing economy?[15]

PART FIVE

Cultural Context

INTERCULTURAL COMMUNICATION

When we think of *culture*, most of us picture a place—the South American culture of Brazil, the Mideast culture of Saudi Arabia, or the Far East culture of Japan. But Gerry Philipsen, a professor of communication at the University of Washington who specializes in intercultural communication, says that culture is not basically geographical. Nor is it essentially political or a matter of race. Philipsen describes *culture* as "a socially constructed and historically transmitted pattern of symbols, meanings, premises, and rules."[1] At root, culture is a code.

Ethnographers study the speech and nonverbal communication of people in order to crack that code. We've already looked at Mead's reliance on participant observation (see Chapter 4) and Geertz' use of thick description (see Chapter 18) to unravel the complex web of meanings that people share within a society or culture. In like manner, Philipsen spent three years in a multiethnic, blue-collar Chicago neighborhood studying what it means to speak like a man in "Teamsterville," the home of the late mayor Richard J. Daley and a place where the "Grabowski fans" of Mike Ditka's football world feel at home. Communication is used there to show solidarity with friends who are part of the neighborhood.[2]

After completing his ethnographic research in Teamsterville, Philipsen spent more than a year studying the communication patterns of a dispersed group he called the "Nacirema" (*American* backwards). He found a ritualized form of Nacirema talk about talk on display five times a week in the daytime television talk show *Donahue*—the forerunner of *Oprah*. Together with University of Massachusetts

communication professor Donal Carbaugh, Philipsen discovered that any appeal to a universal standard of ethical conduct was considered by persons in the audience to be an infringement of their right to be unique individuals. The ultimate issue of every conversation on *Donahue* was the presentation of "self."[3]

For many years the *Donahue* show originated in a Chicago television studio located within five miles of Teamsterville, yet the two cultures these communities reflect seem to be worlds apart. Philipsen was not content to merely describe the contrasting cultures he studied; he wanted to develop a general theory that would explore the relationship between communication and culture. Chapter 31 presents his speech codes theory, which seeks to explain—and even predict—the discourse within a language community.

Is there a way to measure the relative discrepancy between any two patterns of communication or systems of meanings? From a study of multinational corporations in more than fifty countries, Dutch researcher Geert Hofstede concluded that there are four crucial dimensions on which to compare cultures.[4]

1. *Power distance*—the extent to which the less powerful members of society accept that power is distributed unequally (Americans—small; Japanese—medium).

2. *Masculinity*—clearly defined sex roles with male values of success, money, and things dominant in society (Americans—high; Japanese—extremely high).

3. *Uncertainty avoidance*—the extent to which people feel threatened by ambiguity and create beliefs and institutions

to try to avoid it (Americans—low; Japanese—extremely high).

4. *Individualism*—people look out for themselves and their immediate family as opposed to identifying with a larger group that is responsible for taking care of them in exchange for group loyalty (Americans—extremely high; Japanese—low).

Many researchers agree that Hofstede's distinction between individualism and collectivism is the crucial dimension of cultural variability. The we-centered focus of Teamsterville sets it apart from individualistic American society in general, and from the extreme I-centered preoccupation of its Nacirema subculture in particular. Cultural anthropologist Edward Hall was the first to label the communication style of collectivistic cultures *high-context* and the style of individu-

alistic cultures *low-context*. The designation divides groups of people on the basis of how they interpret messages.

> A high-context communication or message is one in which most of the information is either in the physical context or internalized in the person, while very little is in the coded, explicit part of the message. A low-context communication is just the opposite, i.e., the mass of information is vested in the explicit code.[5]

Hall says that people in every culture communicate both ways. The difference is one of focus. Collectivistic Japanese have a message-context orientation; individualistic Americans rely more on message content.

The term *cross-cultural communication* is usually reserved for theory and research that compare specific interpersonal variables such as conversational distance, self-disclosure, or

Cats and fish enduring cultural exchange.

From *Bad Dogs*, John S. P. Walker [Alfred A. Knopf, 1982]
© 1982 John S. P. Walker, reprinted by permission of author.

styles of conflict resolution across two or more different cultures. Chapter 30 presents Stella Ting-Toomey's face-negotiation theory, which distinguishes people's approach to conflict based on the individualistic or collectivistic orientation of their culture. Although her original theory reflects a cross-cultural approach to communication, subsequent versions also suggest ways of bridging cultural differences.

William Gudykunst used a similar comparative approach when he first explored how the predictions of Berger's uncertainty reduction theory might need to be modified to accommodate cultural differences (see Chapter 10). He was intrigued with the possibility that high-context speakers might be more in doubt about a stranger's decorum or ability to act appropriately than they are with attitude similarity, self-disclosure, or other typical low-context concerns. But along with Barnett Pearce and Vernon Cronen (see Chapter 5), Gudykunst has grown increasingly interested in issues of intercultural encounters. What happens when a stranger tries to communicate effectively within a different culture? Chapter 29 presents Gudykunst's model of anxiety/uncertainty management, which offers an extensive and detailed answer to that question.

CHAPTER 29

Anxiety/Uncertainty Management Theory

of William Gudykunst

During my first sabbatical leave from Wheaton College I spent a month in the Philippine Islands. When a Filipino couple I knew heard that I was coming to their country, they asked me to spend a week with them on an "academic adventure." Ping and Lena were former graduate students of mine who occasionally taught at Mickelson College, a small church-related school in the remote province of the Davao del Sur. Lena had used a text of mine for a course at the school, and she invited me to be the commencement speaker at their graduation.

The students and staff at Mickelson are Belaan Indians. In addition to their native tongue, they speak a dialect of Cebuano; English is their third language and is taught in the school. To get to their campus from Manila, I had to fly first on a jet, then on a propeller plane. The trip continued by jeep and concluded with a six-hour pump boat ride over open water. Ping and Lena explained that the one hundred students and ten faculty faced multiple threats of disease, violent weather, Communist/Muslim insurgency, and piracy—in that order. Located on the top of a small mountain, the school had no electricity or running water. A banner in their chapel proclaimed, "Lo, I am with you always even unto the end of the world."[1] I felt I was there.

ENTER THE STRANGER

Bill Gudykunst's anxiety/uncertainty management (AUM) theory focuses on encounters between cultural in-groups and strangers. Gudykunst is professor of communication at California State University, Fullerton, and he developed his interest in intergroup communication when he served as an intercultural relations specialist for the U.S. Navy in Japan. His job was to help naval personnel and their families adjust to living in a culture that seemed very strange to Americans.

Although I've included AUM in the section on intercultural communica-tion, Gudykunst intends his theory to apply in any situation where differences between people spawn doubts and fears. For example, once a month I'm one of four men who cook breakfast, serve it, and clean up afterward at a local home-less center. I make it a point to talk with guests who show a desire for early morning conversation, but I'm never sure what topics are appropriate and I'm somewhat nervous about saying something that will embarrass them (or me). Throughout the chapter I will use the terms *intergroup* and *intercultural* inter-changeably to reflect the scope of the theory and the fact that we don't have to travel to a foreign land to either be or encounter a stranger.

Gudykunst assumes that at least one person in an intercultural encounter is a *stranger*.[2] Through a series of initial crises, strangers experience both anxi-ety and uncertainty—they don't feel secure and they aren't sure how to behave. Although strangers and in-group members experience some degree of anxiety and uncertainty in any new interpersonal situation, when the encounter takes place between people of different cultures, strangers are hyper-aware of cul-tural differences. They tend to overestimate the effect of cultural identity on the behavior of people in an alien society, while blurring individual distinctions ("When I was in the Philippines I noticed that all Filipinos are . . .").

As a stranger in a strange land, I experienced all the thoughts and feelings that Gudykunst describes. But lest we get hung up on our own doubts and in-securities, Gudykunst reminds us that my hosts at Mickelson were subject to the same pangs of anxiety and uncertainty that affected me. It was a novel sit-uation for them as well—I was only the second Caucasian visitor they'd had at their school in a decade.

Gudykunst makes it clear that AUM is a theory under construction. Early accounts cast his ideas into axioms written from the standpoint of the stranger. Recent efforts flip the perspective and describe intercultural encounters with strangers as experienced by members of the in-group. In an effort to avoid the ethnocentric trap of thinking that my view of the world is the way it *really* is, I'll illustrate Gudykunst's theory by applying it to the situation of my Philip-pine Belaan hosts. They wanted to bridge the culture gap through effective communication just as much as I did.

EFFECTIVE COMMUNICATION: THE RESULT OF MINDFULNESS

Gudykunst uses the term *effective communication* to refer to the process of min-imizing misunderstandings. Other authors use a variety of terms to convey the same idea—*accuracy, fidelity, understanding*.[3] According to Gudykunst, effective communication between Mickelson's president, Pol Quia, and me would not necessarily require that we draw close, share similar attitudes, or even speak with clarity—as welcome as these outcomes might be. Gudykunst would con-sider our communication effective if Pol and I could accurately predict and ex-plain each other's behavior to the extent that these actions tied into our discus-sion. In other words, no big surprises.

Figure 29.1 diagrams Gudykunst's basic theory of anxiety/uncertainty management.[4] The theory is designed to explain effective face-to-face communication, and the box at the far right of the figure represents that goal. Gudykunst asserts that cutting down on misunderstanding is hard work, especially when the stranger comes from a wildly different culture. I'll work back through the flowchart to show how he thinks a meeting of minds might occur. As Gudykunst's term *mindfulness* suggests, he doesn't think it happens by accident.

Like brushing our teeth or turning out the lights before we go to sleep, much of our everyday conversation seems to be part of a set routine. The way we answer the phone, place an order at McDonald's, or kid around with our friends becomes so habitual that we can do it without thinking. Someone watching us play out our lives could easily spot a number of *scripts* we seem to follow when we communicate with others.

Scripted behavior may serve us well when the roles are familiar and all the players know their lines, but Gudykunst cautions that mindless conversation in

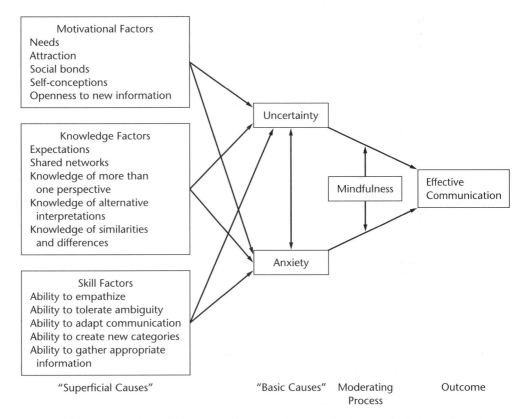

FIGURE 29.1   A Schematic Representation of the Basic Theory (Omitting Cultural Variability)
(From Gudykunst, "Toward a Theory of Effective Interpersonal and Intergroup Communication: An Anxiety/Uncertainty Management [AUM] Perspective")

a cross-cultural situation can escalate the tension and confusion that's already there. In order to reduce anxiety and uncertainty rather than create more, Pol Quia needs to pay attention to what he says and how I respond. I need to monitor my words and Pol's reaction as well.

William Howell, one of Gudykunst's mentors at the University of Minnesota, suggests four levels of communication competence:[5]

1. *Unconscious incompetence.* We misinterpret others' behavior and aren't even aware we're doing so. Ignorance is bliss.

2. *Conscious incompetence.* We know that we're misinterpreting others' behavior but don't do anything about it.

3. *Conscious competence.* We think about our communication and continually work at changing what we do in order to become more effective.

4. *Unconscious competence.* We've developed our communication skills to the point that we no longer have to think about how we speak or listen.

Gudykunst defines *mindfulness* as stage 3 in Howell's model. In fact, following Ellen Langer's notion of *mindful learning,* he thinks stage 4 is less competent than stage 3 and can be downright dangerous.[6] Someone operating at that level may look and feel like a "natural," but situations with strangers are often so fluid that unconscious competence can quickly turn into oblivious incompetence. The intercultural communicator who tries to fly on automatic pilot may quickly crash and burn. Cognitive choice, on the other hand, moderates the destructive force of doubt or fear.

ANXIETY AND UNCERTAINTY: TWIN OFFSPRING OF CULTURAL VARIABILITY

As the title of his theory suggests, Gudykunst believes that anxiety and uncertainty are the basic causes of communication failure in intergroup situations. These two causes of misinterpretation are closely related, yet Gudykunst sees them as different in that uncertainty is cognitive and anxiety is affective.

Gudykunst takes his ideas of uncertainty straight from Charles Berger's uncertainty reduction theory (see Chapter 10). Uncertainty includes the doubts we have about our ability to predict the outcome of our encounters with strangers. For example, would my gift of an *Encyclopedia Britannica* to the Mickelson library be regarded as an educational treasure or an insensitive judgment on their lack of academic resources? In that sense, uncertainty looks to the future. Yet it refers to the past as well.

As we mentally review an intergroup encounter, uncertainty describes our inability to explain why any of us acted as we did. For example, why did students carry cases of Coke up the mountain when I arrived at Mickelson? Was this effort in recognition of my status as honored visitor, an accommodation to my queasy North American stomach, or a tacit statement that there would be nothing stronger to drink during my stay? I wasn't sure.

Uncertainty is a thought; anxiety is a feeling. Gudykunst defines anxiety as

Shrew People: quick, carnivorous, usually nocturnal beings; small but more vicious than the better-known Mole People; eat five times their own body weight every day; cannibals.

"the feeling of being uneasy, tense, worried, or apprehensive about what might happen."[7] Just as people fall silent when they fear that their contrary opinions will cause them to be isolated, so both strangers and in-group members eye the future warily when their differences make mutual satisfaction seem unlikely. The district superintendent expressed this form of fear the night before the Mickelson graduation.

I had just delivered a forty-minute address to students and their families at the senior-class baccalaureate ceremony. Because most of the Belaan parents spoke no English, I stopped every few sentences for the superintendent to translate my words into their tongue. Therefore, the forty minutes consisted of twenty minutes of message plus twenty minutes of interpretation. After I was through, the obviously worried man took me aside and explained the local rhetorical facts of life. What I had said was fine, he told me, but it was way too brief. Unless I spoke at the graduation ceremony the next day for at least an hour—without an "interrupter"—the local citizens would regard the ceremony as of little consequence and the students would "lose face." Now I was worried.

The experience demonstrates the extent to which anxiety and uncertainty are linked to the degree of difference between the culture of the in-group and the culture from which the stranger comes. Gudykunst's model in Figure 29.1 doesn't portray the place of cultural variability, yet propositions within the theory make it clear that the wider the cultural gap, the higher the levels of anxiety and uncertainty that everyone will experience.

Anxiety and uncertainty aren't always bad. Gudykunst insists that a minimal level of both are necessary to keep us from getting lazy, bored, or overly confident in our predictions. Anxiety and uncertainty will motivate us to communicate better. But once they climb above a threshold of useful stimulation, anxiety and uncertainty are the causes of failed communication. As Gudykunst writes of the uncertainty that accompanies intercultural contact, he pictures the push-pull dialectic of certainty-uncertainty that Leslie Baxter and Barbara Montgomery describe for all relationships (see Chapter 12). In like manner, stranger-group anxiety is akin to tension created by the connectedness-separateness contradiction. Both are natural and even helpful in intercultural contacts, but when cultural differences are great, they can quickly escalate to a catastrophic level that destroys any chance of effective communication.

Gudykunst draws on Hofstede's dimensions of culture as a helpful way to gauge cultural variation.[8] According to Hofstede's research, the Philippines and the United States are almost identical in their strong emphases on masculinity and high tolerance for ambiguity. But the two cultures diverge sharply on the dimension of power position and collectivism versus individualism. I was a low-context egalitarian individualist invading the world of high-context hierarchical collectivists. No wonder they had some doubts and fears to overcome when I arrived.

MANAGING ANXIETY AND UNCERTAINTY WHEN CULTURES CLASH

The far left column of Figure 29.1 pulls together many factors that cause uncertainty and anxiety to rise or fall in a specific intercultural encounter. Don't let Gudykunst's label of "Superficial Causes" fool you into thinking that they are unimportant or trivial. They are superficial only in the sense that they are the surface factors that contribute to the basic or underlying issues of anxiety and uncertainty in intergroup encounters. Some of these motivational, knowledge, and skill variables explain why Mickelson faculty and students were able to communicate effectively with me during that first encounter and why I've gone back to Davao del Sur four times over the last fifteen years.

In the 1993 version of his theory, Gudykunst organized these multiple factors along traditional lines of *communication competence*. By way of illustration, consider the speakers who are highly competent in public speaking classes at your school. Students who get A's usually evidence three qualities—motivation, knowledge, and skill. It takes all three to be truly effective.

Some speakers have something to say (knowledge) and want to say it (motivation), but they leave the audience squirming because they don't have the skill to eliminate the *and ahs* and *you knows* from their delivery. The motivation and skill of a second group of speakers demonstrate that they have the gift of gab, but listeners will quickly tune out their smooth-sounding talk if it's clear they don't know their subject and their audience. And speakers in a third group have the requisite knowledge and skill to be effective, but their motivation to stand up and speak in front of others is definitely lacking. Either they just don't care or they're scared out of their wits.

Gudykunst lays out thirty-seven separate axioms that specify factors affecting the level of anxiety and uncertainty. He's tried to word them in a way that suggests what a stranger could do to reduce the fear and ignorance that threaten effectiveness.[9] I'll present ten of the axioms that I've found especially helpful in understanding my initial encounter with the native Filipino students and faculty at Mickelson College. As you will see, these axioms draw heavily on ideas advanced by other communication theorists. In that sense, AUM is a great review of much that you've already read in earlier chapters.

Motivation Factors

Axiom 7: An increase in our need for a sense of group inclusion when we interact with strangers will produce an increase in our anxiety.

Although I was raised in the individualistic culture of the United States, I personally feel the pull of connectedness much more than its dialectical counterpart, separateness (see Chapter 12). My Filipino hosts are part of a collectivist society that emphasizes social identity. As Axiom 7 suggests, our mutual strong needs for affiliation increased our initial edginess when we first met.

Axiom 31: An increase in our attraction to strangers will produce a decrease in our anxiety and an increase in our confidence in predicting their behavior.

At the end of my visit, Pol told me that our relationship was solidified with laughter. It started when I was afraid of crossing a ravine on a felled coconut tree, so I crawled across on all fours like an animal. The Belaans began to giggle at the ridiculous sight, and I couldn't help laughing with them. After that, whenever the conversation got dull, someone would grunt like a pig and we'd all break out laughing. As social penetration theory predicts, attraction led to vulnerability and self-disclosure (see Chapter 9).

Knowledge Factors

Axiom 12: An increase in our ability to complexly process information about strangers will produce an increase in our ability to accurately predict their behavior.

Delia's constructivism assumes that cognitively complex people are best equipped to take the perspective of others (see Chapter 8). As I talked with Bing Quia, the wife of Mickelson's president, she showed that she didn't think of people in either/or categories. Perhaps her interpersonal flexibility was due to her wider knowledge of Filipino society—she was the only adult at the school who wasn't Belaan by birth. Whatever the reason for her ability to differentiate personality constructs, Bing seemed to be able to sense my thoughts and feelings and express them to others in the group.

> *Axiom 25:* An increase in our awareness of strangers' violations of our positive expectations and/or their confirming our negative expectations will produce an increase in our anxiety and a decrease in our confidence in predicting their behavior.

Burgoon has extended her expectancy violations model to include verbal violations in intercultural contexts (see Chapter 6). Early in our conversations I asked the Mickelson faculty to tell me about problems they encountered as teachers. My bluntness was an invitation for public embarrassment. The question violated their expectation that I would take care not to say anything that would cause them to lose face, and the talk became tense. This was the low point of my five-day visit.

> *Axiom 41:* An increase in our knowledge of strangers' language (dialect, jargon, slang) will produce an increase in our ability to manage our anxiety and an increase in our ability to accurately predict their behavior.

In Chapter 3, "Mapping the Territory," I presented the semantic triangle that I. A. Richards introduced to help people understand the linguistic causes of misunderstanding. One of the remedies that Richards offered was an 850-word lexicon of basic English.[10] He believed that once mastered, these words are sufficient to communicate almost any idea. Although I didn't speak Cebuano or the local Belaan dialect, the faculty and students of Mickelson had a command of my native language that exceeded Richards' minimum vocabulary. As a result, they were able to dispel a number of their doubts and fears about my response to being on their campus. Of course, I benefited just as much.

> *Axiom 20:* An increase in the personal similarity we perceive between ourselves and strangers will produce an increase in our ability to manage our anxiety and our ability to accurately predict their behavior. Boundary Condition: Understanding group differences is critical only when strangers strongly identify with the group.

Burke used the term *identification* to refer to the similarities that make interpersonal communion possible (see Chapter 21). Despite our cultural differences, the folks at Mickelson and I shared a common religious faith and a joint concern with education. These commonalities made our cultural group loyalties pale by comparison, so the boundary condition in the axiom wasn't a factor. As if these similarities didn't provide enough common ground, I was shipwrecked with the district superintendent in a violent thunderstorm. That common life-threatening experience made thoughts of stranger-danger recede and drew us together in a common bond.

Axiom 37: An increase in networks we share with strangers will produce a decrease in our anxiety and an increase in our confidence in predicting their behavior.

This axiom is a direct extension of the one Berger added to his original uncertainty reduction theory (see Chapter 10). Ping and Lena, my former graduate students, were the only people the Mickelson staff and I knew in common, but they acted as enthusiastic go-betweens as they both sponsored me and endorsed my hosts.

Skill Factors

Axiom 21: An increase in our ability to categorize strangers in the same categories in which they categorize themselves will produce an increase in our ability to accurately predict their behavior.

For my Filipino hosts, who constantly struggled to survive in a harsh environment, my presence posed an additional complication. With some hesitation, one of the Belaan men asked me what they should do with my body if I were to die while I was there. After some thought, I suggested cremation—a novel suggestion in this remote province. He replied that they were open to the idea as long as they could send the ashes back to my family in America. Weick notes that double interacts are preferable to rules when dealing with equivocal information in a hostile environment (see Chapter 17). By initiating a communication cycle of speech act, response, and adjustment, my hosts increased their options and felt better as well.

Axiom 15: An increase in our ability to tolerate ambiguity when we interact with strangers will produce an increase in our ability to manage our anxiety and an increase in our ability to accurately predict strangers' behavior.

Given the slow pace of life in a remote setting without telephone, television, or daily mail, students at Mickelson found it difficult to understand my concern about returning to Manila on a specific day. After a few questions, however, they seemed to accept this stranger's preoccupation with schedule as a puzzle not worth worrying about. Even though I was the visitor to their culture, I sensed that they were compiling a "thick description" of my cultural values without having to make immediate sense of what they observed (see Chapter 18).

Axiom 16: An increase in our ability to empathize with strangers will produce an increase in our ability to accurately predict their behavior.

Carl Rogers claimed that empathic understanding is a necessary condition for relational health (see Chapter 3). It's even less of a stretch to imagine how the skill of empathic listening could reduce uncertainty about a stranger's motives and actions. On several occasions I discussed aspects of my personal life with Porferio, the district superintendent. His steady gaze and comfortable silences gave me the feeling that he was imagining what it was like to be me. If so, he was also reducing his uncertainty about his American visitor.

These ten examples provide a sample of the multiple factors that Gudykunst claims affect the anxiety and uncertainty that people experience when a stranger comes into their midst. The continual tie-in with other communication theory and research demonstrates Gudykunst's belief that intercultural communication is an extension of, rather than an exception to, principles of interpersonal communication. It's all a matter of degree. The stranger a stranger, the more everyone involved has to work mindfully at overcoming anxiety and uncertainty.

CRITIQUE: OVERWHELMED BY INTERGROUP VARIABLES

You may remember that Michael Sunnafrank is a severe critic of uncertainty reduction theory—the theory that was the original catalyst for AUM (see Chapter 10). Yet Sunnafrank acknowledges the impact and scope of Gudykunst's work: "Unarguably the most prolific communication research program in the 1980s is being conducted by Gudykunst and his associates."[11] This flow of scholarship continues unabated at the turn of the century as Gudykunst continually revises and extends the application of his theory.

There is a danger, however, that the student of communication could easily be overwhelmed by the sheer quantity and detail of Gudykunst's theoretical predictions. Berger's original uncertainty reduction theory contained seven axioms that generated twenty-one theorems when they were paired in all possible combinations. In contrast, Gudykunst's latest version of AUM sets forth ninety-four axioms, and he holds out the possibility of generating more. The most recent additions employ Hofstede's four dimensions of cultural variability (individualism–collectivism, uncertainty avoidance, power distance, and masculinity) and show how these affect the motivational, knowledge, and skill factors that I discussed earlier.

Many of these principles are fascinating. Consider Gudykunst's axiom that links collectivism with the ability to see people as they see themselves:

Axiom 68: An increase in collectivism will be associated with an increase in the ability to categorize strangers in the same categories they categorize themselves.

If this is true, my collectivistic Filipino hosts may have been better equipped to accurately predict the behavior of their individualistic guest than I was to predict theirs. This knowledge could make me a more mindful communicator the next time I go. Yet even though this axiom and others are helpful, I still find it hard to get my arms around ninety-four "self-evident truths."

In the final section of the book I discuss the compromises or "trade-offs" each theorist must make when constructing a theory. No theory can do it all. Gudykunst has made a conscious choice to create a theory in the "grand" tradition—a theory that addresses a vast array of communication variables in a variety of communication contexts. He then decided to cast his conclusions in specific axioms that are easily applied. One has to admire the ambitious scope of the project. What he has sacrificed, of necessity, is simplicity. As you can tell by the way I've set up this chapter, it's not a choice I would have made. Instead of listing the 94 axioms, I decided to illustrate a few. But as a serious student of communication theory and practice, I'm glad Gudykunst and some others are thinking big.

Consider for a moment if Gudykunst had made a different choice and tried to capture the essence of AUM in a single elegant statement. Since the bulk of the axioms focus on the causes or effects of anxiety and/or uncertainty, that's what summary Axiom 47 seems to do:

> *Axiom 47:* An increase in our ability to manage our anxiety about interacting with strangers *and* an increase in the accuracy of our predictions and explanations regarding their behavior will produce an increase in the effectiveness of our communication.

Yet even this core axiom is conditional. Gudykunst goes on to say that it holds only when we are "mindful" in the stranger's presence. He then adds that "anxiety and uncertainty below our minimum thresholds will not produce increases in our effectiveness; anxiety and uncertainty above our maximum threshold will produce decreases in effectiveness."[12] Since all of these qualifications seem to be necessary to capture the complexity of cross-cultural differences, maybe you're glad Gudykunst broke them down into bite-sized portions. Then again, maybe by virtue of their nonrecurring nature, intergroup encounters with strangers aren't susceptible to scientific scrutiny, prediction, or control.

Stella Ting-Toomey, Gudykunst's colleague at California State University, Fullerton, questions whether the whole uncertainty reduction approach doesn't reflect a western bias. She notes that the implicit goal of uncertainty reduction is to control one's environment—a theme that is "highly valued by Western, individualistic cultures but not necessarily by Eastern collectivistic cultures."[13] Gudykunst strongly objects, noting that according to Geert Hofstede's list, most Asian countries are high on uncertainty avoidance. (See the introduction to this section.)

Since Gudykunst and Ting-Toomey teach in the same department and co-author scholarly books and articles, the constructive dialogue will continue. But the issue Ting-Toomey raises is more far-reaching than the relative importance of reducing uncertainty. What's at stake is the question of whether or not a pan-human theory of intercultural communication is possible.[14] You'll have a chance to consider the issue of comparative theory and east-west differences when you read about Ting-Toomey's face-negotiation theory in the next chapter.

QUESTIONS TO SHARPEN YOUR FOCUS

1. When might the reduction of *anxiety* and *uncertainty* hinder rather than help facilitate *effective communication*?

2. Which of the ten *superficial causes* of anxiety and uncertainty I presented would apply to communication between teenagers and the elderly? Would they be different for encounters between heterosexuals and homosexuals?

3. In what situations might *mindfulness* hinder rather than help effective communication?

4. Think of the most culturally diverse *intercultural encounter* you've ever had. Which of Hofstede's four *dimensions of cultural variability* were highly discrepant?

A SECOND LOOK

Recommended resource: William B. Gudykunst, "Anxiety/Uncertainty Management (AUM) Theory: Current Status," in *Intercultural Communication Theory*, R. L. Wiseman (ed.), Sage, Thousand Oaks, Calif., 1995, pp. 8–58.

Preliminary statement: William B. Gudykunst, "A Model of Uncertainty Reduction in Intercultural Encounters," *Journal of Language and Social Psychology*, Vol. 4, 1985, pp. 79–97.

Initial formal statement: William B. Gudykunst, "Uncertainty and Anxiety," in *Theories in Intercultural Communication*, Young Yun Kim and William S. Gudykunst (eds.), Sage, Newbury Park, Calif., 1988, pp. 123–156.

Significant development: William B. Gudykunst, "Toward a Theory of Effective Interpersonal and Intergroup Communication: An Anxiety/Uncertainty Management (AUM) Perspective," in *Intercultural Communication Competence*, R. L. Wiseman and J. Koester (eds.), Sage, Newbury Park, Calif., 1993, pp. 33–71.

Relationship to uncertainty reduction theory: William Gudykunst, "The Uncertainty Reduction and Anxiety/Uncertainty Reduction Theories of Berger, Gudykunst, and Associates," in *Watershed Research Traditions in Communication Theory*, Donald Cushman and Branislav Kovačić (eds.), State University of New York, Albany, N.Y., 1995, pp. 67–100.

Integration of identity and uncertainty perspectives: William B. Gudykunst and Mitchell R. Hammer, "The Influence of Social Identity and Intimacy of Interethnic Relationships on Uncertainty Reduction Processes," *Human Communication Research*, Vol. 14, 1988, pp. 569–601.

Interpersonal vs. Intergroup relations: William Gudykunst and Robin Shapiro, "Communication in Everyday Interpersonal and Intergroup Encounters," *International Journal of Intercultural Relations*, Vol. 20, 1996, pp. 19–45.

Practical application: William Gudykunst, *Bridging Differences: Effective Intergroup Communication*, Sage, Thousand Oaks, Calif., 1998.

Intercultural training: William Gudykunst, "Applying Anxiety/Uncertainty Management (AUM) Theory to Intercultural Adjustment Training," *International Journal of Intercultural Relations,* in press.

Practical advice for communicating with strangers: William B. Gudykunst and Young Yun Kim, *Communicating with Strangers: An Approach to Intercultural Communication,* 2d ed., McGraw-Hill, New York, 1992.

Mindfulness: Ellen J. Langer, *The Power of Mindful Learning,* Addison-Wesley, Reading, Mass., 1997.

Critique: Stella Ting-Toomey, "Culture and Interpersonal Relationship Development: Some Conceptual Issues," in *Communication Yearbook 15,* James A. Anderson (ed.), Sage, Newbury Park, Calif., 1989, pp. 371–382.

CHAPTER 30

Face-Negotiation Theory

of Stella Ting-Toomey

When I presented Pearce and Cronen's coordinated management of meaning (see Chapter 5), I used some of my experiences as a mediator at a metropolitan center for conflict resolution to illustrate principles of the theory. As I indicated then, my role as mediator is to help people in conflict reach a voluntary agreement that satisfies both sides. I'm not a judge or a jury, and I work hard not to make moral judgments about who's right and who's wrong. A mediator acts as a neutral third party whose sole job is to facilitate the process of negotiation. That doesn't mean it's easy.

Most disputants come to the center in a last-ditch effort to avoid the cost and intimidation of a day in court. The service is free, and we do everything possible to take the threat out of the proceedings. But after failing or refusing to work out their differences on their own, people walk in the door feeling various degrees of anger, hurt, fear, confusion, and shame. On the one hand, they hope that the negotiation will help resolve their dispute. On the other hand, they doubt that talk around a table will soften hard feelings and change stubborn responses that seem to be set in stone.

The professional staff at the center instructs volunteers in a model of negotiation that maximizes the chance of people's reaching a mutually acceptable agreement. From the first day of training, the staff insists that "the mediator controls the process, not the outcome." Figure 30.1 lists a number of techniques that mediators use to ensure progress without suggesting the shape of the solution. Used artfully, the techniques work well. Despite the initial hostility of conflicting parties, 70 percent of the negotiations end in freely signed and mutually kept agreements.

The model of negotiation doesn't work equally well for everyone, however. Although the center serves a multiethnic urban area, my colleagues and I have noticed that the number of people of Asian origin seeking conflict mediation is disproportionately small. On rare occasions when Japanese, Vietnamese, Chinese, or Koreans do come to the office, the discussion seems to go round and round without getting anywhere. Even when participants reach agreement, they seem more relieved that it's over than pleased with the solution.

Assurance of impartiality: "Neither of you have met me before, right? I haven't got a stake in what you decide."

Guarantee of confidentiality: "What you say today is strictly between us. I'll rip up my notes before you leave the room."

Nonjudgmental listening: "I don't know anything about what brought you here. Beth, we'll start with you. Please tell me what happened."

Disputant equality: "Nate, thanks for not interrupting while Beth was telling her story. Now it's your turn. What do you want to tell me?"

Avoid "why" questions: Harmful—"Why did you do that?" Helpful—"What would you like to see happen?"

Validate feelings while defusing their force: "I can understand that you felt mad when you found the bike was broken."

Frequent summarization: "I'd like to tell you what I've heard you say. If I don't get it right, fill me in. Beth, I hear three concerns. . . ."

Blame self, not them: "Nate, I'm sorry. That slipped by me. Say it again so that I can get it right."

Private conferences: "I wanted to meet privately with you to see if there's anything you want to tell me in confidence that you didn't feel you could say with Beth in the room." (Always meet individually with both parties.)

Reframe issues of "right" and "wrong" into interests: "Beth, I'm not sure I understand. Tell me, how will Nate's going to jail give you what you need?"

Avoid advice: Harmful—"Here's a suggestion that might solve your problem." Helpful—"How do you think this issue might be settled?"

Brainstorming: "Let's see how many different solutions you can think of that might solve the problem. Just throw out any ideas you have and we'll sort through them later to see which ones might help."

Role play: "Nate, do you have any thoughts about what would make Beth comfortable?"

Mutual stroking: "I appreciate your hard work on this problem. I feel optimistic that both of you can come to an agreement."

Don't get stuck: "Let's move on to the issue of insurance. We can come back to this later on."

Reality testing: "How realistic is it to think that the bike can be put back in mint condition?"

Consider the alternative: "What are you going to do if you don't reach an agreement today?"

Reminder of voluntary participation: "This is your deal. No option is unreasonable as long as it serves what both of you need. But don't sign anything you aren't happy with. Either of you can walk out at any time."

Move toward agreement: "You've already agreed on a number of important issues. I'm going to begin to write them down."

No assignment of guilt: Harmful—"Nate admits he broke the bicycle and apologizes for his carelessness." Helpful—"Nate agrees to pay $140. Beth agrees to drop all charges."

Highly specific written agreements: "Nathanial Stamos agrees to pay Elizabeth Greenfield an amount of one hundred forty dollars with a money order delivered to her apartment at 792 East Highland at 7:00 P.M. Friday, September 24, 1999."

FIGURE 30.1   Techniques of Third-Party Mediation

Stella Ting-Toomey's face-negotiation theory helps to explain these cultural differences of responding to conflict. A communication department colleague of Gudykunst at California State University, Fullerton, Ting-Toomey assumes that people of every culture are always negotiating "face." The term is a metaphor for our public self-image, the way we want others to see us and treat us. *Facework* "refers to specific verbal and nonverbal messages that help to maintain and restore face loss, and to uphold and honor face gain."[1] Our identity can always be called into question, and the anxiety and uncertainty churned up by conflict render us especially vulnerable. Face-negotiation theory postulates that the facework of people from individualistic cultures like the United States will be strikingly different from the facework of people from collectivistic cultures like Japan or Korea. According to Ting-Toomey, when the facework is different, the style of handling conflict will vary as well.

COLLECTIVISM VS. INDIVIDUALISM

Ting-Toomey bases her face-negotiation theory on the distinction between collectivism and individualism. The most extensive differentiation between the two has been made by University of Illinois psychologist Harry Triandis. He says that there are three important distinctions between collectivism and individualism. They are the different ways of defining *self, goals,* and *duty.*[2]

Consider a man named Em. Collectivist Em might think of himself as a father, Christian, and teacher, while an individualistic textbook author would probably define himself simply as Em, independent of any group affiliation. Collectivistic Em wouldn't go against group goals, but his individualistic counterpart would naturally pursue personal interests. Collectivist Em would have been socialized to enjoy duty that requires sacrifice; individualistic Em would employ the minimax principle to determine a course of action that he would see as fun and personally beneficial (see Chapter 9).

More than two-thirds of the world's people are born into collectivistic cultures, while less than one-third of the population live in individualistic cultures.[3] To help you draw a clearer mental picture of the distinctions, I'll follow the lead of cross-cultural researchers who cite Japan and the United States as classic examples of collectivistic and individualistic cultures. Note that it would be equally appropriate to use China, Korea, or Vietnam to represent a collectivistic perspective. I could also insert Germany, Switzerland, or one of the Scandinavian societies as the model of an individualistic approach. It is Ting-Toomey's grouping of national cultures within the collectivistic and individualistic categories that separates her theory of conflict management from a mere listing of national characteristics, so feel free to make mental substitutions.

Triandis says that the Japanese value collective needs and goals over individual needs and goals. They assume that in the long run, each individual decision affects everyone in the group. Therefore, a person's behavior is controlled by the norms of the group. This *we*-identity of the Japanese is quite foreign to the *I*-identity of the American who values individualistic needs and goals over group needs and goals. The American's behavior is governed by the personal rules of a freewheeling self that is concerned with individual rights rather than group responsibilities. Marching to a different drummer is the rule in the United States, not the exception.

Triandis claims that the strong in-group identity of the Japanese people leads them to perceive others in us-them categories. It is more important for the Japanese to identify an outsider's background and group affiliation than the person's attitudes or feelings—not because they don't care about their guest, but because unique individual differences seem less important than group-based information. People raised in the United States show a different curiosity. They are filled with questions about the interior life of visitors from other cultures. What do they think? What do they feel? What do they plan to do? Americans assume that every person is unique, and they reduce uncertainty by asking questions to the point of cross-examination.

The cultural differences Triandis outlines above are similar to what Edward Hall notes when he distinguishes between high- and low-context cultures (see the introduction to this section). You'll recall that he uses these labels to refer to the relative importance of context when interpreting a message within a given culture. In a low-context society, what is said has great significance; meaning is found in words. Words are less important in a high-context society; meaning is couched in the nature of the situation and the relationship. When referring to culture, Ting-Toomey uses Triandis and Hall's terms interchangeably. The Japanese have a collectivistic/high-context culture; Americans have an individualistic/low-context culture.

With this understanding of the difference between collectivistic and individualistic cultures in mind, read through the description of mediation techniques in Figure 30.1. Taken as a whole, the list provides a reliable window to the values that guide this type of conflict resolution. Participants who come to the conflict center are treated as responsible individuals who can make up their own minds about what they want. The mediator encourages antagonists to deal directly with their differences and keeps the conversation focused on the possibility of a final agreement. While the mediator is careful never to pressure clients to reach an accord, the climate of immediacy suggests this is their best chance to put the whole mess behind them in an acceptable way and get on with their lives. The mediator works hard to make sure that the individual rights of both parties are respected.

Whether or not disputants reach an agreement, the mediation approach outlined in Figure 30.1 offers a safe place where no one need feel embarrassed. At least no one from an individualistic American culture! As it turns out, the very techniques designed to allow people to save face during negotiation pose an additional threat to face for collectivists. No wonder these people stay away or leave dissatisfied. Ting-Toomey's face-negotiation theory explains why this is so by sketching the different dimensions of face.

THE MULTIPLE FACES OF FACE

Although popular western wisdom regards *face* as an Asian preoccupation, Ting-Toomey and other relational researchers find it to be a universal concern. That's because face is an extension of self-concept, a vulnerable, identity-based resource. As Ting-Toomey notes, most of us sometimes blush. It's a telltale sign that we feel awkward, embarrassed, ashamed, or proud—all face-related issues.[4] In their well-developed theory of politeness, University of Cambridge linguists Penelope Brown and Stephen Levinson define face as "the public self-image that every member of society wants to claim for himself/herself."[5] Many Western writers regard face as an almost tangible good that can rise or fall like soybean futures on the commodity exchange at the Board of Trade. Taiwanese scholar L. Yutang calls face "a psychological image that can be granted and lost and fought for and presented as a gift."[6] The term includes the patrician concern for dignity, honor, and status. Yet it also covers arrogant "trash talk" after a slam-dunk on the basketball court—"in your face!" Ting-Toomey simply refers to face as "the projected image of one's self in a relational situation."[7]

Although an overall view of face as public self-image is straightforward and consistent with Mead's concept of the "generalized other" (see Chapter 4), Ting-Toomey highlights several issues that turn face into a multifaceted object of study. Face means different things to different people depending on their cultural and individual identities.

The question, "Whose face are you trying to save?" may seem ridiculous to most Americans or members of other individualistic cultures. The answer is obvious: "Mine!" Yet Ting-Toomey reminds us that there are many places in the world where face concerns focus on the other person. Even in the midst of conflict, people in these collectivistic cultures pay as much or more attention to maintaining the face of the other party as they do to preserving their own. Their answer to the face-concern question would honestly be a mutual "ours," or even an altruistic "yours."

Self-concerned *face-restoration* is the facework strategy used to stake out a unique place in life, preserve autonomy, and defend against loss of personal freedom. Not surprisingly, face-restoration is the typical face strategy across individualistic cultures. *Face-giving* out of concern for others is the facework strategy used to defend and support another person's need for inclusion. It means taking care not to embarrass or humiliate the other in public. Face-giving is the characteristic face strategy across collectivist cultures.

When your face is being threatened, are you more inclined to ward off the verbal blow before it hits, or do you repair the damage and reassert your strength after the punch? Ting-Toomey claims that people from collectivist societies use self-effacing strategies to proactively deflect potential face threats for both themselves and others. ("I'm so sorry. This was my fault.") That's mutual face-saving and giving. People in individualistic societies are more likely to retroactively restore their own lost face by justifying their actions or blaming the situation.[8] That's self-face-repair and restoration.

Of course, collectivism and individualism aren't all or nothing categories. The difference between other-face and self-face concerns is not absolute. Just as relational dialectics insists that everyone wants connectedness *and* separateness in a close relationship (see Chapter 12), so too all people desire affiliation and autonomy within their particular society. People raised in Japan or other Pacific Rim countries do have personal wants and needs; Americans and northern Europeans still desire to be part of a larger group. The cultural difference is always a matter of degree.

Yet when push comes to shove, most people from a collectivistic culture tend to privilege other-face over self-face. Given their high-context social environment, they are more likely to interpret communication on the basis of *who* said something under *what* circumstances than to parse words spoken for their lexical meaning. In like manner, people raised in an individualistic culture are normally more concerned with self-face than they are with other-face. The low-context nature of their social milieu makes it more likely that they will closely scrutinize specific words to figure out exactly what the speaker or writer meant.

FACE: LINKING CULTURE AND CONFLICT MANAGEMENT

By now it is obvious that there is a strong link between culture and face-management. Since the predominant concern of most people in collectivistic cultures is the face of others, their facework is giving face. Self-face is the predominant concern of most people in individualistic cultures, so their facework is protecting and restoring their own public self-image. For the last decade, Ting-Toomey's research has centered on establishing a link between the face-concerns of different cultures and people's predominant style of dealing with conflict. Reduced to bare bones, Ting-Toomey's face-negotiation theory suggests a two-step causal chain with face maintenance as the explanatory link between culture and style of conflict resolution:

$$\text{Type of culture} \rightarrow \text{Type of face maintenance} \rightarrow \text{Type of conflict management}$$

Based on the work of M. Afzalur Rahim, professor of management and marketing at Western Kentucky University, Ting-Toomey identified five distinct responses to situations where there is an incompatibility of needs, interests, or goals—avoiding, obliging, compromising, dominating, and integrating.[9] Suppose, for example, that you are the leader of a group of students working together on a class research project. Your instructor will assign the same grade to all of you based on the quality of the group's work, and that project evaluation will count for two-thirds of your final grade in the course. As often happens in such cases, one member of the group has just brought in a shoddy piece of work and you have only three days to go until the project is due. You don't know this group member well, but you do know that it will take 72 hours of round-the-clock effort to fix this part of the project. What mode of conflict management will you adopt?

Avoiding: "I would avoid open discussion of my differences with the group member."

Obliging: "I would give in to the wishes of the group member."

Compromising: "I would use give-and-take so that a compromise could be made."

Dominating: "I would be firm in pursuing my side of the issue."

Integrating: "I would exchange accurate information with the group member to solve the problem together."

Face-negotiation theory suggests that avoiding, obliging, compromising, dominating, and integrating vary according to their mix of concern for self-face and other-face. Figure 30.2 charts these five types of conflict management according to their culture-related face concern. Obliging, for example, is the behavior of choice for people who are concerned for the face of others, but not their own. Conversely, dominating is the act of someone concerned with their own face-repair, but not with face-giving to others. The clear area on the left side of the figure represents Ting-Toomey's original prediction that avoiding, obliging, and compromising would be the typical responses of people from collectivistic cultures. The shaded side on the right represents her initial expectation that members of individualistic cultures would tend to choose the dominating and integrating strategies. Given my experience as a mediator in interethnic conflict situations, I wouldn't have argued with these predictions.

Ting-Toomey tested her theory on almost a thousand university students in

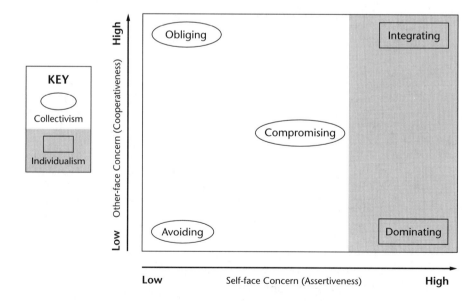

FIGURE 30.2 A Cultural Map of Five Conflict Management Styles
(Based on Ting-Toomey et al., "Culture, Face Maintenance, and Styles of Handling Interpersonal Conflict: A Study in Five Cultures")

Japan, China, South Korea, Taiwan, and the United States.[10] They were asked how they as leaders would deal with the slightly known student who needed to redo the shoddy work in three days in order for the group to complete the project. As anticipated, there was a strong relationship between type of culture and face concern. Individualistic American students showed a distinct preference for dominating strategies to rectify the problem, while collectivistic Asian students indicated they would either avoid bringing up the problem altogether or they would try to oblige any request the group member made. So far, so good.

The surprising findings involved the integrating and compromising styles of conflict. Ting-Toomey's face-negotiation theory claimed that students from the United States would select a direct problem-solving strategy more than the Asian students, who would be prone to compromise. The results in these areas were mixed. In retrospect, it seems that different cultural and ethnic groups ascribe their own meanings to the terms *integrate* and *compromise*. Traditionally, these solution-oriented styles have reflected a western approach to conflict management in workplace situations. For most Americans, integration is reaching a good solution, while for Asians, it is more of a relational term that means achieving peace with one another. If you reread the techniques of third-party mediation in Figure 30.1 with this distinction in mind, you'll see why people who come from Pacific Rim countries might be frustrated by the standard U.S. mediation practices of holding private conferences, reality testing, pushing for agreement, and especially insisting on highly specific, low-context written agreements.

BACK TO THE DRAWING BOARD: ADDING STYLES AND POWER

On the basis of the five-culture study, Ting-Toomey recognized the need to rethink some of the concepts of face-negotiation theory. She's concluded that the map of conflict styles shown in Figure 30.2 doesn't adequately identify the variety of strategies that people actually use, nor does it reflect the face reasons why they use them. She is also convinced that the collectivistic–individualistic distinction is not the only cultural variable to affect people's style of conflict management, so she's added the consideration of *power* to her theory.

New Conflict Styles

Almost all texts on dispute resolution refer to five main styles of conflict resolution: *avoiding, obliging, compromising, dominating,* and *integrating*. Although they sometimes go by different names—*withdrawing, giving-in, negotiating, competing,* and *problem-solving*—the five categories have been discussed and researched so often that they almost seem to be chiseled in stone. Yet Ting-Toomey and John Oetzel, her research colleague in the communication department at the University of New Mexico, remind us that these styles have surfaced in work situations in Western countries. Using an ethnically diverse sample, they have identified three additional styles of conflict management

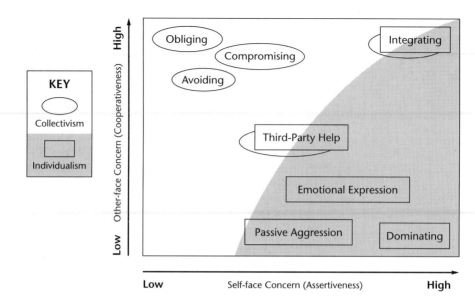

FIGURE 30.3   A Revised Cultural Map of Eight Conflict Management Styles
(Adapted from Stella Ting-Toomey and John Oetzel, *Managing Intercultural Conflict Effectively*, Sage, Thousand Oaks, Calif., in press)

that American individualistic-based scholarship has missed. The styles are *emotional expression, passive aggression,* and *third-party help*.[11] In the student project example described earlier, these styles might be expressed the following way:

Emotional expression: "Whatever my 'gut' and my 'heart' tell me, I would let these feelings show."

Passive aggression: "Without actually accusing anyone of being lazy, I'd try to make him or her feel guilty."

Third-party help: "I would enlist the professor to aid us in solving the conflict."

Figure 30.3 charts Ting-Toomey and Oetzel's new map of conflict styles, arranged according to their face concern. Two features are worth noting. First, *avoiding* and *compromising* are now located near *obliging* in high "other face" territory. Apparently these are simply different strategies that people in collectivist cultures use to accomplish the same end—giving face to the other party. Second, the ovals and rectangles that outline *integrating* and *third-party help* are superimposed to show that both collectivists and individualists use the strategies, yet interpret them differently. Ting-Toomey suggests that collectivists who adopt these styles focus on relational-level collaboration and concession, whereas individualists concentrate on solving the task problem in a way that brings closure.[12] Furthermore, collectivists prefer seeking help from a familiar third party, while individualists want advice from an impartial person they may not know.

Power Distance

In the introduction to this intercultural section, I presented power distance as an important dimension on which to compare cultures. You'll recall that Geert Hofstede defines *power distance* as the extent to which the less powerful members of society accept that power is distributed unequally. Although the United States and Japan provide ideal cultural illustrations for individualism and collectivism, respectively, neither one falls at an extreme on the scale of power distance. According to Hofstede, Israel is an exemplar of a culture with *small* power distance, while Mexico is a classic case of a *large* power distance society.

Israelis value equal rights and rewards based on personal performance. At work, employees expect to have a say in the decision-making process, so well-regarded employers use a democratic style of management. Conversely, Mexicans accept unequal power distributions, hierarchical roles, and rewards based on age. In the workplace, subordinates expect to be told what to do, so an esteemed boss is one who acts as a benevolent autocrat. When low-status members of society encounter face-threat in Israel, they typically defend themselves using self-face strategies. But their counterparts in Mexico tend to use self-effacing strategies to minimize the loss of face.[13]

Linking a newly identified style of conflict resolution with the issue of power, Ting-Toomey notes that third-party mediators in large power distance cultures are usually people who are highly regarded by both parties in the dispute (a wise,

"Mr. Kenny here will attempt to resolve our differences."

elder statesman, for example). The disputants may be willing to make concessions in order to "give face" to this honored mediator. In the process, they back away from confrontation without loss of face to either party. The interaction she describes is much too intricate to be predicted or explained by a simple causal proposition. The complexity illustrates the difficulty that Ting-Toomey faces as she works to combine the issue of power distance with face-negotiation theory's basic distinction between collectivistic and individualistic cultures.

APPLICATION: COMPETENT INTERCULTURAL FACEWORK

Ting-Toomey's ultimate goal for her theory goes beyond merely identifying the ways people in different cultures negotiate face or handle conflict. She believes that cultural *knowledge, mindfulness,* and facework *interaction skills* are the three requirements for effectively communicating across cultures. Imagine that you are a Japanese student in a U.S. college. As the appointed leader of the class research project, you feel it is your uncomfortable duty to talk with the nonproductive American member of the group. How might you achieve competent intercultural facework?

Knowledge is the most important dimension of facework competence. It's hard to be culturally sensitive unless you have some idea of the ways you might differ from your classmate. Ting-Toomey's theory offers basic insights about collectivistic and individualistic cultures, face-concerns, conflict styles, and power distance, all of which could help you understand the American student's perspective, and vice versa. If you've read this chapter carefully, this knowledge will put you in good stead.

Mindfulness shows a recognition that things are not always what they seem. It's a conscious choice to seek multiple perspectives on the same event. Perhaps the other's inferior work is not due to laziness but is the best he or she could do in this situation. The student might have a learning disability, an emotional problem, a lack of clarity about the assignment, or a desire to merely pass the course. Of course, your initiation of a conversation to discuss the project is also open to multiple interpretations. Ting-Toomey writes:

> Mindfulness means being particularly aware of our own assumptions, viewpoints, and ethnocentric tendencies in entering any unfamiliar situation. *Simultaneously,* mindfulness means paying attention to the perspectives and interpretive lenses of dissimilar others in viewing an intercultural episode.[14]

When you are mindful, you mentally switch off automatic pilot and process the situation and conversation through the central route of the mind as ELM suggests (see Chapter 14). But you also are freed up to empathize with the other student and approach the discussion with a fresh or creative mindset. The result could be a novel solution that takes advantage of your different ways of thinking.

Interaction skill is your ability to communicate appropriately, effectively, and adaptively in a given situation. Perhaps you are studying communication to gain that type of competence. Hopefully your department offers a course in interpersonal or intercultural communication that includes structured exercises, role plays, or simulations. Without "hands-on" learning and feedback from others on how you're doing, it's hard to improve. Volunteers at the center for conflict resolution practice their mediation skills through this kind of experiential learning. A number of the techniques listed in Figure 30.1 parallel skills that Ting-Toomey regards as crucial in cross-cultural communication. For example, *disputant equality, nonjudgmental listening, no assignment of guilt,* and *validating feelings* are all designed to preserve or give face to parties rather than threaten their public self-image. That would be a helpful skill to have when talking to the student in your research group. So would American-type straight talk that individualistic/low-context people understand. By using the two skills together, you might increase joint face and get the research project back on track.

CRITIQUE: CONFOUNDED BY INDIVIDUAL DIFFERENCES

Critiquing a theory is somewhat like playing king-of-the-hill. A scholar plants a theoretical flag—preferably on top of a mound of empirical or interpretive research, and then other theorists and researchers try to pull it down. Most of the theories included in this book have survived that kind of rough-and-tumble challenge. Seldom do theorists pull their own flag down; other scholars are more than willing to do it for them. Face-negotiation theory is different because the current challenge comes from its leading advocates—John Oetzel and Stella Ting-Toomey herself. So that you can understand how this is so, I will briefly review their discussion of individual differences within cultures.

Just as cultures vary along a scale anchored by *self-face* and *other-face*, Ting-Toomey also recognizes that people *within* a culture differ on the relative emphasis they place on these two face concerns. She uses the terms *independent* and *interdependent self* to refer to "the degree to which people conceive of themselves as relatively autonomous from, or connected to, others."[15] Psychologists Hazel Markus and Shinobu Kitayama call this dimension "self-construal" or the more familiar term, "self-image."[16]

The independent self values *I*-identity and is more self-face oriented, so this concept of self is prevalent within individualistic cultures like the United States. Yet due to the ethnic diversity of American society, there are people raised in the U.S. who are highly interdependent. The interdependent self emphasizes relational connectedness, is more concerned with other-face, and is therefore closely aligned with collectivism. Yet again, it would be dangerous to stereotype all members of a collectivist society as having the same self-construal. Culture is an overall framework for face-concern, but individuals within a culture have different images of self as well as varied views as to the degree to which they give others face or restore their own face in conflict situations.

The relational reality of self-image differences within two cultures is represented in the diagram on the next page. Each plus sign (+) stands for the self-construal of a person raised in a collectivistic society that socializes its members to be interdependent and includes everyone in face concerns. Each star (*) stands for the self-construal of a person raised in an individualistic culture that stresses independence and self-reliance. The cultures are obviously different. But the overlap shows that an American might focus so much on other-face that he or she would have a self-image more interdependent than a person raised in Japan with a relatively high independent self-construal.

```
                    Collectivistic Culture (Japan)
Other-   + + + + + + + + + + + + + + + +                            Self-
Face              * * * * * * * * * * * * * * * * * * * * * * * * * * * * * *   Face
                    Individualistic Culture (U.S.A.)
```

Ting-Toomey built her theory on the foundational idea that people from collectivistic/high-context cultures are noticeably different in the way they manage face and conflict situations than do people from individualistic/low-context cultures. In a dozen scholarly articles she has defended that basic conviction. Yet in two recent studies, Oetzel and Ting-Toomey discovered that "self-construal is a better predictor of conflict styles than ethnic/cultural background."[17] You can now see why face-negotiation theory is "in progress" and Ting-Toomey writes that "more theorizing effort is needed to 'decategorize' the colossal concepts of 'individualism' and 'collectivism' . . . into finer *culture-level*, explanatory-categories."[18]

Ting-Toomey and Oetzel are currently directing a cross-cultural study that ranges over five countries on three continents to further explore the relationship between cultural variability and individual self-image. Perhaps their network of researchers will find that self-construal is a necessary step on the path from culture to styles of conflict management:

$$\text{Type of culture} \rightarrow \text{Type of self-construal} \rightarrow \text{Type of face maintenance} \rightarrow \text{Type of conflict management}$$

If so, the distinction between collectivistic and individualistic cultures would still be important because culture would have a strong effect on an individual's self-construal. But the sense of individual identity would be one step closer to the person's preferred style of dealing with conflict, so naturally it would predict dispute behavior better than generalized culture.

Stella Ting-Toomey has spent a lifetime exploring the concept of face—both its cultural roots and its role in dealing with conflict. Given the mix of her Hong Kong Chinese upbringing, marriage to an Irish American, and a professional life spent at five universities across the United States focusing on multicultural issues, Ting-Toomey is not about to abandon the study of cultural collectivism–individualism and its impact on communication. But she wants to get it right and realizes her theory needs to become more complex to better predict how people will respond in a conflict situation. I appreciate her commitment.

QUESTIONS TO SHARPEN YOUR FOCUS

1. Are citizens of Saudi Arabia raised in an *individualistic* or *collectivistic* culture? Does that society have a large or small *power distance*? How did you decide?

2. Do you see yourself as having more of an *independent* or an *interdependent self*? Does this go with the flow of your culture or are you swimming upstream?

3. Both Ting-Toomey and Gudykunst say that *knowledge, mindfulness,* and *skill* are necessary for effective intercultural communication. How does their use of these terms differ? Is it a difference that makes a difference?

4. What *style of conflict management* would you use with the group member who did poor work? Do you think that your response is based on your culture, self-construal, sex, or status? What other factors affect your decision?

A SECOND LOOK

Recommended resource: Stella Ting-Toomey, "Intercultural Conflict Styles: A Face-Negotiation Theory," in *Theories in Intercultural Communication,* Young Yun Kim and William Gudykunst (eds.), Sage, Newbury Park, Calif., 1988, pp. 213–235.

Original conception: Stella Ting-Toomey, "Toward a Theory of Conflict and Culture," in *Communication, Culture, and Organizational Processes,* William Gudykunst, Lea Stewart, and Stella Ting-Toomey (eds.), Sage, Beverly Hills, Calif., 1985, pp. 71–86.

Updated theory: Stella Ting-Toomey and Atsuko Kurogi, "Facework Competence in Intercultural Conflict: An Updated Face-Negotiation Theory," in *International Journal of Intercultural Relations,* Vol. 22, 1998, pp. 187–225.

Introduction to concept of face: William Cupach and Sandra Metts, *Facework,* Sage, Thousand Oaks, Calif., 1994.

Comprehensive treatment of face: Stella Ting-Toomey (ed.), *The Challenge of Facework,* SUNY, Albany, N.Y., 1994.

Cross-cultural research on conflict management: Stella Ting-Toomey, Ge Gao, Paula Trubisky, Zhizhong Yang, Hak Soo Kim, Sung-Ling Lin, and Tsukasa Nishida, "Culture, Face Maintenance, and Styles of Handling Interpersonal Conflict: A Study in Five Cultures," in *International Journal of Conflict Management,* Vol. 2, 1991, pp. 275–296.

Collectivistic/individualistic culture: Harry C. Triandis, *Individualism & Collectivism,* Westview, Boulder, Colo., 1995.

Face-negotiation in culturally diverse groups: John Oetzel, "Explaining Individual Communication Processes in Homogeneous and Heterogeneous Groups through Individualism-Collectivism and Self-Construal," *Human Communication Research,* Vol. 25, 1998, pp. 202–224.

A personal account of face: Stella Ting-Toomey, "An Intercultural Journey: The Four Seasons," in *Working at the Interface of Cultures: Eighteen Lives in Social Science,* Michael Bond (ed.), Routledge, New York, 1997, pp. 202–215.

Intercultural communication: Stella Ting-Toomey, *Communicating Across Cultures,* Guilford, New York, 1999.

Insider's critique: John Oetzel, "The Effects of Self-Construals and Ethnicity on Self-Reported Conflict Styles," *Communication Reports,* Vol. 11, 1998, pp. 133–144.

CHAPTER 31

Speech Codes Theory

(The Ethnography of Communication) of Gerry Philipsen

After three years on the staff of a youth organization, I resigned to pursue full-time graduate work in communication at Northwestern University. Gerry Philipsen was one of my classmates. When I finished my Ph.D. course work, the labor market was tight; I felt fortunate to receive an offer to teach at Wheaton College. A while later I heard Gerry was doing youth work on the south side of Chicago. I remember thinking that while my career was progressing, Gerry's was going backward. How wrong I was. As articles in the *Quarterly Journal of Speech* soon made evident, Gerry Philipsen was doing ethnography.[1]

In Chapter One I introduced ethnography as a research method that places a premium on discovering the meanings that people share within a given culture. It is, for example, the approach of the symbolic interactionist who is a participant observer in the life of the community (see Chapter 4). We've already seen results of ethnographic research conducted in an organizational setting (see Chapter 18). Pacanowsky's analysis of the unique corporate culture of W. L. Gore & Associates illustrates anthropologist Clifford Geertz' claim that ethnography is "not an experimental science in search of law, but an interpretive science in search of meaning."[2]

While at Northwestern, Philipsen read an article by University of Virginia anthropologist and linguist Dell Hymes, "The Ethnography of Speaking." Hymes called for a "close to the ground" study of the great variety of communication practices around the world.[3] Philipsen decided to start in the Chicago community where he worked, a place he dubbed "Teamsterville," since driving a truck was the typical job for men in the community. For three years Philipsen talked to kids on street corners, to women on front porches, to men in corner bars, and to everyone at the settlement house where he worked so that he would be able to describe the speech code of Teamsterville residents. By *speech code*, Philipsen means "a system of socially constructed symbols and meanings, premises, and rules, pertaining to communicative conduct."[4]

Even though the people of Teamsterville spoke English, Philipsen noted that their whole pattern of speaking was radically different from the speech code he knew and heard practiced within his own family of origin, his friends at school, and across many talk shows on radio and TV. The stark contrast motivated him to conduct a second multiyear ethnographic study, which began while he was teaching speech communication at the University of California, Santa Barbara, and continued when he went to the University of Washington. Although most of his "cultural informants" were from Santa Barbara or Seattle, the speech-code community from which they were drawn is not confined to the west coast of the United States. He labeled them the "Nacirema" (*American* spelled backwards), because their way of using language was intelligible to, and practiced by, a majority of Americans. For many people reading this chapter, "Naciremas Are Us."

Philipsen defines the Nacirema culture by speech practices rather than geographical boundaries or ethnic background. For over two decades, Nacirema talk was epitomized by the speech of Phil Donahue, his guests, and his audience on the daytime *Donahue* show.[5] It's a style of speaking about self, relationships, and communication itself that emerged for Philipsen as he spent hundreds of hours listening to tapes of dinner-table conversations, life stories, and ethnographic interviews.

Philipsen shows how the Nacirema speech code is manifest in communications patterns of two Seattle women, but the patterns of communication that he and graduate student Tamar Katriel charted are built on a much larger research base. Just as cultural markers emerge gradually for the ethnographer, so the defining features of the Nacirema code will become more clear as you read the rest of the chapter. But for starters, one characteristic feature of that speech code is a preoccupation with metacommunication—their talk about talk.[6]

As Philipsen intended, the Teamsterville and Nacirema ethnographic studies provided rich comparative data on two distinct cultures. But he also wanted to go beyond mere description of interesting local practices. His ultimate goal was to develop a general theory that would capture the relationship between communication and culture. Such a theory would guide cultural researchers and practitioners in knowing what to look for, and offer clues on how to interpret the way people speak.

Based on Dell Hymes' suggestion, Philipsen first referred to his emerging theory as the "ethnography of communication." He has found, however, that many people can't get past the idea of ethnography as simply a research method, so now that his theory has moved from description to explanation and prediction, Philipsen labels his work "speech codes theory." Specifically, the theory seeks to answer questions about the existence of speech codes, their substance, the way they can be discovered, and their force on people within a culture.

Philipsen outlines the core of speech codes theory in five general propositions paraphrased below. He is hopeful, however, that their presentation could be intertwined with the story of his fieldwork and the contributions of other scholars that stimulated the conceptual development of the theory. I've tried to capture that narrative mix within the limited space of this chapter.

THE DISTINCTIVENESS OF SPEECH CODES

> *Proposition 1:* Wherever there is a distinctive culture, there is to be found a distinctive speech code.

Philipsen describes an ethnographer of speaking as "a naturalist who watches, listens, and records communicative conduct in its natural setting."[7] When he entered the working-class ethnic world of Teamsterville, Philipsen found patterns of speech that were strange to his ears. After many months in the community, he was less struck by the pronunciation and grammar that was characteristic of then Chicago Mayor Richard J. Daley than he was by the practice of "infusing a concern with place into every conversation."[8] He realized that Teamsterville residents say little until they've confirmed the nationality, ethnicity, social status, and place of residence of the person with whom they're speaking. Most conversations start (and often end) with the question, "Where are you from and what's your nationality?"

Philipsen gradually discovered that discussion of "place" is related to the issue of whether or not a person is from "the neighborhood." This concern wasn't merely a matter of physical location. Whether or not a person turned out to be from "around here" was a matter of cultural solidarity. Unlike Mr. Rogers' Neighborhood, Teamsterville did not welcome diversity. As Philipsen heard when he first entered a corner tavern, "We don't want no yahoos around here."

Whereas Philipsen discovered that Teamsterville conversation is laced with assurances of common place among those in the neighborhood, he found that speech among the Nacirema is a way to express and celebrate psychological uniqueness. Dinnertime is a speech event where all family members are encouraged to have their say. Everyone has "something to contribute," and each person's ideas are treated as "uniquely valuable."

In Teamsterville, children "were to be seen, not heard." Among the Nacirema, however, it would be wrong to try to keep a child quiet at the dinner table. Communication is the route by which kids develop "a positive self-image," a way to "feel good about themselves." Through speech, family members "can manifest their equality and demonstrate that they pay little heed to differences in status—practices and beliefs that would puzzle and offend a proper Teamsterviller."[9]

Philipsen was raised in a largely Nacirema speech community, but until his research in Teamsterville, he hadn't thought of his family's communication as a particular cultural practice. Its taken-for-granted quality illustrates the saying that's common among ethnographers: "We don't know who discovered water, but we're pretty sure it wasn't the fish."

THE SUBSTANCE OF SPEECH CODES

> *Proposition 2:* A speech code involves a culturally distinctive psychology, sociology, and rhetoric.

With this proposition, Philipsen takes a step back from the cultural relativism that characterizes most ethnographers. He continues to maintain that every culture has its own unique speech code; there's no danger we'll mistake a Nacirema discussion of personal worth with Teamsterville talk of neighborhood solidarity. But his second proposition asserts that whatever the culture, the speech code reveals structures of self, society, and strategic action. The Teamsterville code of when to speak and when to remain silent illustrates these three functions of social life.

Psychology.   According to Philipsen, every speech code "thematizes" the nature of individuals in a particular way. The Teamsterville code defines people as a bundle of social roles. In the Nacirema code, however, the individual is conceptualized as unique—someone whose essence is defined from the inside out.

Sociology.   Philipsen writes that "a speech code provides a system of answers about what linkages between self and others can properly be sought, and what symbolic resources can properly and efficaciously be employed in seeking those linkages."[10] Teamsterville men gauge their relative self-worth by the style of speaking that goes with the neighborhood. They respect and resent middle-class Northside residents who speak Standard English. On the other hand, they are reassured by their perceived ability to speak better than those they referred to as lower-class "Hillbillies, Mexicans, and Africans." Within the community, men speak the same way. Any attempt a man made to "improve" his speech would be regarded as an act of disloyalty and would alienate him from his friends.

According to the unwritten code of Teamsterville, speech is not a valued resource for dealing with people of lower status—wives, children, or persons from outside the neighborhood who are lower on the social hierarchy. Nor is it a resource for encounters with bosses, city officials, or other higher-status outsiders. In cases where that's necessary, a man draws on his personal connections with a highly placed intermediary who will state his case. Speech is reserved for symmetrical relationships with people matched on age, sex, ethnicity, occupational status, and neighborhood location. Words flow freely with friends.

Rhetoric.   Philipsen uses the term *rhetoric* in the double sense of "discovery of truth" and "persuasive appeal." Both concepts come together in the way Teamsterville young and adult men talk about women. To raise doubts about the personal hygiene or sexual purity of a man's wife, mother, or sister is to attack his honor. *Honor* is a code that grants worth to an individual on the basis of adherence to community values. The language of the streets in Teamsterville makes it clear that a man's social identity is strongly affected by the women he's related to by blood or marriage. "If she is sexually permissive, talks too much, or lacks in personal appearance, any of these directly reflects on the man and thus, in turn, directly affects his honor."[11]

In contrast, Philipsen discovered that a verbalized code of dignity holds sway among the Nacirema. *Dignity* refers to the worth that an individual has by virtue of being a human being. "Discourse spoken in a code of dignity

prejudices the talk—and the hearing of the talk—in favor of treating individuals in terms of their 'intrinsic humanity divested of all socially imposed roles or norms.'"[12] Within a code of dignity, personal experience is given a moral weight greater than logical argument or appeal to authority. Communication is a resource to establish an individual's uniqueness.

MEANINGS OF SPEAKING

Proposition 3: The significance of speaking depends on the speech codes used by speakers and listeners to create and interpret their communication.

Proposition 3 can be seen as Philipsen's speech code extension of I. A. Richards' maxim that words don't mean, people mean (see Chapter 3). If we want to understand the significance of prominent speech practices within a culture, we must listen to the way people talk about it and respond to it. It's their practice; they decide what it means.

No speech practice is more important among the Nacirema than the way they use the term *communication*. Philipsen and Tamar Katriel have shown that the Nacirema use this key word as a shorthand way of referring to "close, open, supportive speech."[13] These three dimensions set communication apart from speech that their informants dismissed as "mere communication," "small talk," or "normal chit-chat."

Close relationships contrast with *distant* affiliations, where others are "kept at arm's length."

Open relationships in which parties listen and demonstrate a willingness to change are distinct from *routinized* associations, where people are stagnant.

Supportive relationships in which people are totally "for" the other person stand in opposition to *neutral* interactions, where positive response is conditional.

You may have noticed my not-so-subtle switch from a description of *communication* to a discussion of *relationships*. Philipsen and Katriel say that Nacirema speakers use the two words almost interchangeably. In Burkean terms (see Chapter 21), when not qualified by the adjective *casual, communication* and *relationship* are "god terms" of the Nacirema. References to *self* have the same sacred status.

Although the people of Teamsterville know and occasionally use the word *communication*, it holds none of the potency that it has for the Nacirema. To the contrary, for a Teamsterville male involved in a relationship with someone of higher or lower status, communicating is considered an unmanly thing to do. Philipsen first discovered this part of the Teamsterville speech code through his work with youth at the community center. He ruefully recalls, "When I spoke to unruly Teamsterville boys in order to discipline them I was judged by them to be unmanly because, in such circumstances, I spoke."[14] The guys "naturally" expected this older male to use power or physical force to bring them in line.

They were confused when Philipsen, consistent with his Nacirema speech code, sat down with them to "talk things out." The only explanation that made sense to them was that their youth leader was a homosexual. Not until much later did their conclusion get back to him.

THE SITE OF SPEECH CODES

> *Proposition 4:* The terms, rules, and premises of a speech code are inextricably woven into speaking itself.

How can we spot the speech code of a given culture—our own or anyone else's? The answer is to analyze the speech of native speakers. Philipsen is convinced that speech codes are on public display as people speak; they are open to scrutiny by anyone who cares enough to take a long look. Proposition 4 suggests that it couldn't be otherwise.

Dell Hymes recommends that we start by looking for patterns as to who talks to whom, in what settings, toward what ends, and about what topics. It was this framework of inquiry that first helped Philipsen notice the importance of a man's "place" when men talked together in Teamsterville bars. Hymes also suggests that a good way to get at the meaning of speech events is by examining the words that people use to label them. For example, Tamar Katriel used this ethnographic technique when she returned to her native Israel and analyzed a distinctive style of speaking that Israeli Jews call *dugri*.[15] It's a blunt form of straight talk based on the assumption that the other person wants what's best for the community and is able to handle criticism. ("I tell you *dugri*, I don't like what you're doing.")

Philipsen focuses on highly structured cultural forms that often display the cultural significance of symbols and meanings, premises, and rules that might not be accessible through normal conversation. For example, *social dramas* are public confrontations in which one party invokes a moral rule to challenge the conduct of another. The response from the person criticized offers a way of testing and validating the legitimacy of the "rules of life" that are embedded in a particular speech code. Philipsen analyzes the late Mayor Daley's reply in the city council to charges of nepotism—in this case the appointment of his best friend's son to a political position.[16] By all accounts, Daley went ballistic. Most reporters regarded the speech as an irrational diatribe, yet his appeal to place, honor, and traditional gender roles resonated with the values of Teamsterville. When Philipsen asked people in the neighborhood if it was right for Daley to favor his friends, they responded, "Who should he appoint, his enemies?"

Totemizing rituals offer another window to a culture's speech code. They involve a careful performance of a structured sequence of actions that pays homage to a sacred object. Philipsen and Katriel spotted a "communication ritual" among the Nacirema that honors the sacred trinity of self, communication, and relationships.[17] Known as "a good talk," the topic is often a variation on the theme of how to be a unique, independent "self," yet still receive validation from close others. The purpose of the ritual is not problem-solving per se. Rather, people come together to express their individuality, affirm each other's identity, and experience intimacy.

The communication ritual follows a typical sequence: (1) Initiation—a friend voices a need to work through an interpersonal problem; (2) Acknowledgment—the confidant validates the importance of the issue by a willingness to "sit down and talk"; (3) Negotiation—the friend self-discloses, the confidant listens in an empathic and nonjudgmental way, the friend in turn shows openness to feedback and change; (4) Reaffirmation—both the friend and confidant try to minimize different views, and reiterate appreciation and commitment to each other. By performing the communication ritual correctly, both parties celebrate the central tenet of the Nacirema code: "Whatever the problem, communication is the answer."

THE DISCURSIVE FORCE OF SPEECH CODES

> *Proposition 5:* The artful use of a shared speech code is a sufficient condition for predicting, explaining, and controlling the form of discourse about the intelligibility, prudence, and morality of communication conduct.

Does the knowledge of people's speech codes in a given situation help an observer or participant *predict* or *control* what others will say and how they'll interpret what is said? Philipsen thinks it does. It's important, however, to clearly understand what Philipsen is *not* saying.

Let's assume that Philipsen is again working with youth and now knows the code of when a man should speak in Teamsterville. Proposition 5 does not claim he should or could keep an unruly kid in line with a smack on the head. Speech codes theory deals with only one type of human behavior—speech acts. Nor does it claim that fathers in Nacirema homes will always encourage their kids to talk at the dinner table. As we saw under Proposition 2, even when people give voice to a speech code, they still have the power, and sometimes the desire, to resist it. Perhaps the father had a bad day and wants some peace and quiet. Proposition 5 does suggest, however, that by a thoughtful use of shared speech codes, participants can guide metacommunication—the talk about talk. This is no small matter.

The dad-at-the-dinner-table example can help us see how prediction and control might work. Suppose a Nacirema father growls at his kids to finish their dinner without saying another word. Inasmuch as we understand the speech code of the family, we can confidently predict that his children will say that his demand is unfair, and his wife will object to his verbal behavior. As for artful control, she could choose to pursue the matter in private so that her husband wouldn't lose face in front of the children. She might also tie her objection to shared values. ("If you don't communicate with our kids they're going to grow up bitter and end up not liking you.") In this way she would tap into issues that her husband would recognize as legitimate, and set the moral agenda for the rest of the discussion about the way he talks with the kids.

The dinner-table example I've sketched is based on an actual incident discussed by Philipsen.[18] He uses it to demonstrate the rhetorical force of appealing to shared speech codes. While the scope of Proposition 5 is limited to metacommunication, talk about the clarity, appropriateness, and ethics of a person's communication is an important feature of everyday life. In the vernacular of the Nacirema, "It's a big deal." For people who study communication, it's even bigger.

PERFORMANCE ETHNOGRAPHY

In an extension and critique of the style of ethnography that Philipsen does, some researchers have stopped talking about *doing* ethnography in favor of *performing* ethnography. Much like Philipsen, Northwestern University performance ethnographer Dwight Conquergood spent several years with teenagers in the "Little Beirut" district of Chicago. Conquergood was living in a multiethnic tenement and performing participant observation among local street gangs. Performance ethnography is more than a research tool; it is grounded in several theoretical principles.

The first principle is that performance is both the *subject* and the *method* of performance ethnography. All social interactions are performance because, as Philipsen notes, speech not only reflects but also alters the world. Thus, Conquergood views the daily conversations of gang members while hangin' on the street corner as performances. Of particular interest to Conquergood are rituals, festivals, spectacles, dramas, games, and other metaperformances. The ritualistic "handshakes" and elaborate graffiti enacted by the gangs are examples of metaperformance because the gang members themselves recognize the actions to be symbolic. Neither fiction nor farce, metaperformances are reminders that life consists in "performances about performances about performances."[19]

Researchers also consider their work performative. Fieldwork is performance because it involves suspension of disbelief on the part of both the participant observer and the host culture. In the act of embodied learning, researchers recognize that they are doing ethnography *with* rather than *of* a people group—they are co-performers. Conquergood didn't merely observe the greetings of gang members on the street, he greeted people.

In reporting their fieldwork, performance ethnographers are no less concerned about performance. They consider the thick descriptions traditionally produced to be a bit thin. By taking speech acts out of dialogues and dialogues out of context, published ethnographies smooth all the voices of the field "into the expository prose of more or less interchangeable 'informants.'"[20] Thus, the goal of performance ethnographies is to produce actable ethnographies. As Conquergood states, "What makes good theatre makes more sensitive and politically committed anthropological writing."[21]

Conquergood performs his ethnographies through public reading and even acting the part of a gang member. This kind of performance enables the ethnographer to recognize the limitations of, and uncover the cultural bias in, his or her written work. For those participating as audience members, performance presents complex characters and situations eliciting understanding that's actively responsive rather than passive.

Performance ethnography almost always takes place among marginalized groups. The theoretical rationale underlying this fact is that oppressed people are not passive but create and sustain their culture and dignity. In the face of daily humiliations, they create "subtle, complex, and amazingly nuanced performances that subversively key the events and critique the hierarchy of power."[22] Consistent with the belief of critical theorists that communication theory shouldn't be neutral toward power structures and politics, Conquergood is committed to chronicling the performances of the oppressed in order to give them a voice in the larger society. He says of his own research among Chicago gangs, "What I have to do is create a space for an alternate hearing."[23]

CRITIQUE: DIFFERENT SPEECH CODES IN COMMUNICATION THEORY

A favorite grad school professor of mine was fond of saying, "You know you're in the wrong place on an issue if you aren't getting well roasted from all sides." By this "golden mean" standard, Gerry Philipsen is on the right academic path.

Most ethnographers applaud Philipsen's commitment to long-term participant observation, but they are critical of his efforts to generalize across cultures. Granted, he doesn't reduce cultural variation to a single issue such as an individualistic/low context—collectivistic/high context dichotomy. Philipsen's critics recoil, however, when he talks about explanation, prediction, and control—the traditional goals of science. Any theory that adopts these aims, no matter how limited its scope, strikes them as reductionist.

Theorists who operate from a feminist, critical, or cultural studies perspective (see Chapters 34, 19, and 25, respectively) charge that Philipsen is silent and perhaps naive about power relationships. His description of the Nacirema speech code fails to unmask patterns of domination, and he doesn't speak out against male hegemony in Teamsterville. Many of these theorists are also suspicious of what they consider Philipsen's reification of culture. Even though Philipsen says that people aren't automatons, these critics are concerned that by continually talking about culture as if it were a concrete thing, he contributes to a belief in cultural determinism.

As one trained in the empirical tradition, I could wish for a bit more scientific rigor before generalizations are made. Philipsen's grounded research in Teamsterville is impressive; his study of the Nacirema raises a number of questions. What are the boundaries of this speech community? Isn't it circular to first identify a dispersed speech community on the basis of common discursive practices and then do ethnographic research to determine their speech code? Were his two female informants representative of the culture or are they caricatures that are three standard deviations away from the norm? Has the language of this speech community so infused academic departments of communication that we as scholars are unable to objectively analyze the code?

Most of all, I could wish for a few more data sets than the two Philipsen presents. The Teamsterville and Nacirema codes are so diametrically opposed, it's tempting to divide the world into two cultural clusters:

Collectivistic	Individualistic
Hierarchical	Egalitarian
Code of Honor	Code of Dignity
A Man's World	A Woman's World
(Teamsterville)	(Nacirema)

This certainly isn't Philipsen's intention, but without an example of a culture that draws from both columns, there's no evidence to the contrary.

My concerns are minor compared to what I believe Philipsen has accomplished. He accepted Dell Hymes' challenge and became the first ethnographer of communication in our discipline. He has trained an increasing number of cultural scholars including Tamar Katriel, Donal Carbaugh, Kristine Fitch, and Brad "J" Hall, who have all performed their own ethnographic studies. Of most significance for this text, he has elevated ethnography from its former status as a seldom-used research method to its present position as an intriguing theoretical perspective. In light of the progress that Gerry Philipsen has already made, I am confident that further propositions and research evidence are on the way.

QUESTIONS TO SHARPEN YOUR FOCUS

1. Most of *speech code* theory is concerned with *cross-cultural* rather than *intercultural* communication. What is the difference? Which incidents described in the chapter are examples of intercultural encounters?

2. Which three *propositions* of the theory suggest a *scientific* approach to the study of speech codes?

3. Most scholars still think of Philipsen's work as the *ethnography of communication*. Why do you (or don't you) think *speech codes theory* is a better name? Why might *social identity theory* be a valid option?

4. Philipsen says that the *Nacirema* way of talking is the prevailing *speech code* in the United States. What *research* cited in this chapter supports his claim?

A SECOND LOOK

Recommended Resource: Gerry Philipsen, "A Theory of Speech Codes," in *Developing Communication Theory,* Gerry Philipsen and Terrance Albrecht (eds.), SUNY, Albany, N.Y., 1997, pp. 119–156.

Extended treatment: Gerry Philipsen, *Speaking Culturally: Explorations in Social Communication,* SUNY, Albany, N.Y., 1992.

Fieldwork in Teamsterville: Gerry Philipsen, "Speaking 'Like a Man' in Teamsterville: Culture Patterns of Role Enactment in an Urban Neighborhood," *Quarterly Journal of*

Speech, Vol. 61, 1975, pp. 13–22; Gerry Philipsen, "Places for Speaking in Teamsterville," *Quarterly Journal of Speech,* Vol. 62, 1976, pp. 15–25.

Fieldwork with Nacirema: Tamar Katriel and Gerry Philipsen, " 'What We Need Is Communication': Communication as a Cultural Category in Some American Speech," *Communication Monographs,* Vol. 48, 1981, pp. 302–317.

Original call for ethnography of communication: Dell Hymes, "The Ethnography of Speaking," in *Anthropology and Human Behavior,* T. Gladwin and W. C. Sturtevant (eds.), Anthropological Society of Washington, Washington, D.C., 1962, pp. 13–53.

Initial exploration of a third speech code: Gerry Philipsen, Eric Aoki, Theresa Castor, Lisa Coutu, Patricia Covarrubias, Lorelle Jabs, Melissa Kane, and Michaela Winchatz, "Reading *Waterlily* for Cultured Speech," *Iowa Journal of Communication,* Vol. 29, 1997, pp. 31–50.

Historical context for ethnography of communication: Wendy Leeds-Hurwitz, "Culture and Communication: A Review Essay," *Quarterly Journal of Speech,* Vol. 76, 1990, pp. 85–116.

Cultural terms for talk: Donal Carbaugh, "Fifty Terms for Talk: A Cross-Cultural Study," *International and Intercultural Communication Annual,* Vol. 13, 1989, pp. 93–120.

Review essay: Donal Carbaugh, "The Ethnographic Communication Theory of Philipsen and Associates, in *Watershed Research Traditions in Communication Theory,* Donald Cushman and Branislav Kovačić (eds.), SUNY, Albany, N.Y., 1995, pp. 241–265.

Dialogue on ethnography: "The Forum: Writing Ethnographies" (articles by Gerry Philipsen, John Fiske, and Donal Carbaugh), *Quarterly Journal of Speech,* Vol. 73, 1991, pp. 327–342.

Performance ethnography: Dwight Conquergood, "Homeboys and Hoods: Gang Communication and Cultural Space," in *Group Communication in Context,* Lawrence Frey (ed.), Lawrence Erlbaum Associates, Hillsdale, N.J., 1994, pp. 23–55.

Coding cultural history: Tamar Katriel, *Performing the Past: A Study of Israeli Settlement Museums,* Lawrence Erlbaum Associates, Mahwah, N.J., 1997.

Critique: James West, "Ethnography and Ideology: The Politics of Cultural Representation," *Western Journal of Communication,* Vol. 57, 1993, pp. 209–220.

GENDER AND
COMMUNICATION

Most of us believe that women and men interact differently. When we think about the differences (and most of us think about them a lot), we usually draw on the rich data of our lives to construct our own minitheories of masculine-feminine communication.

For example, I recently sat from 9 A.M. to 4 P.M. in a large room at the federal courthouse with a hundred other prospective jurors. We entered as strangers, but by mid-morning the women were sitting in clusters of three to seven engrossed in lively discussions. All the men sat by themselves. I thought about that stark difference as I went to my interpersonal communication class. Reviewing the class list, I realized that 70 percent of the students who took the course as an elective were female. Conversely, two-thirds of those who opted for my persuasion course were male. On the basis of this limited personal experience, I jumped to the conclusion that women talk more than men, and their communication goal is connection rather than influence.

Yet stereotyping is a risky business. The distinction between women's focus on intimacy and men's concern for power has held up well under scrutiny by communication researchers. But most studies of gender differences show that women actually talk *less* than men in mixed groups.

Linguist Robin Lakoff of the University of California, Berkeley, was one of the first scholars who attempted to classify regularities of women's speech that differentiate "women-talk" from "men-talk."[1] She claimed that women's conversation is characterized by:

1. Apologies ("I'm sorry I don't know how to explain this better").

2. Indirect requests ("It's cold in here with the window open").

3. Tag questions ("That was a good movie, don't you think?").

4. Qualifiers ("I sometimes think that it's rather boring going there").

5. Polite commands ("Thanks for not smoking while we drive").

6. Precise color terms ("That's a beautiful mauve jacket").

7. Absence of coarse language ("Oh my, I left the tickets at home").

8. Speaking less, listening more.

Lakoff concluded that women's speech is marked by tentativeness and submission. She also thought that the content of women's speech was trivial.

Unfortunately, Lakoff's conclusions were based mainly on personal reflection and anecdotal evidence—much like my courthouse and classroom theorizing. After two decades of research comparing the conversational styles of men and women, we now know that patterns of gender differences are more complicated than Lakoff first suggested. Current scholarship tempers her conclusions with at least three cautions.

1. There are more similarities among men and women than there are differences. After conducting a meta-analysis of hundreds of research studies that reported gender differences on topics such as talk time, self-disclosure, and styles of conflict management, University of Wisconsin—Milwaukee communication professor Kathryn Dindia found that the differences were actually quite small. She parodies the popular belief that men and women come from two different worlds in the way she summarizes her findings: "Men are from North Dakota, Women are from South Dakota."[2] Can you really spot a difference? If I tell you that Pat talks fast, uses big words, and holds eye contact—your chances of guessing whether Pat is male or female are just slightly better than fifty-fifty.[3]

2. Great variability of communication style exists among both women and men. Scores on the Sex-Role Inventory, developed by Stanford University psychologist Sandra Lipsitz Bem, illustrate this within-group diversity.[4] Bem asks people to rate themselves on a series of gender-related descriptions—many related to speech. A person who marks "soft-spoken," "eager to soothe hurt feelings," and "does not use harsh language" ranks high in femininity. A person who marks "assertive," "defends own beliefs," and "willing to take a stand" ranks high in masculinity. As you might expect, males tend to fit masculine sex roles and females tend to fit feminine sex roles, but the scores from a group of people of

"How is it gendered?"

©The New Yorker Collection 1999 Edward Koren from cartoonbank.com. All Rights Reserved.

the same sex are typically all over the map. Sometimes individuals—male or female—score high on both scales. Bem regards this combination as the best of both worlds and refers to these people with blended identities as *androgynous*. Obviously, gender-related speech isn't an either-or proposition.

3. Sex is a fact; gender is an idea.[5] Within the literature of the field, the sex-related terms *male* and *female* are typically used to categorize people biologically like they do at the Olympics—by chromosomes and genitalia. On the other hand, the terms *men* and *women* or *masculine* and *feminine* are usually employed to describe an idea that's been learned and reinforced from others. When we forget that our concept of gender is a human construction, we fall into the trap of thinking that there is a real-in-nature category called "man"—an early Clint Eastwood archetype who smokes Marlboros, doesn't eat quiche, won't cry, and does "what he's got to do." We would compound the error if we thought of the communication habits that Lakoff listed as "female" attributes. Sex is a given, but we negotiate or work out our concept of gender with others throughout our lives.

The three theories discussed in this section attempt to identify crucial differences between masculine and feminine styles of communication and explain why the differences persist. Chapter 32 presents Deborah Tannen's theory of genderlect styles, which attributes misunderstanding between men and women to the fact that women's talk focuses on connection, while men communicate to achieve status and maintain independence. The "genderlect" label reflects Tannen's belief that male-female conversation is cross-cultural communication. When inevitable mistakes occur, no one is particularly to blame. Although Dindia says Tannen ignores the striking similarities between men and women's communication, she regards Tannen's best seller, *You Just Don't Understand,* as the most responsible statement of the two-culture hypothesis.

Sandra Harding and Julia Wood agree that men and women have separate perspectives, but they don't regard them as equally valid. Because different locations within the social hierarchy affect what is seen, they think that women and other oppressed minorities perceive a different world than do those who view it from a position of privilege and power. Chapter 33 describes Harding and Wood's standpoint theory. It suggests that research starting from the lives of women, gays and lesbians, racial minorities, and the poor provides a less false view of the world than does typical academic research that comes from an advantaged perspective.

Rooted in feminist analysis, Cheris Kramarae's version of muted group theory regards talk between men and women as an unequal interchange between those who have power in the society and those who do not. As discussed in Chapter 34, Kramarae's belief is that women are less articulate than men in public because the words of our language and the norms for their use have been devised by men. As long as women's conversation is regarded as tentative and trivial, men's dominant position is secure. But just as men have a vested interest in accentuating the differences between men's and women's speech, muted group theory has a reformist agenda of contesting the masculine bias in language. Kramarae is convinced that as women become less muted, their control over their own lives will increase.

CHAPTER 32

Genderlect Styles

of Deborah Tannen

"Male-female conversation is cross-cultural communication."[1] This simple statement is the basic premise of Deborah Tannen's *You Just Don't Understand*, a book that seeks to explain why men and women often talk past each other.

Tannen is a linguistics professor at Georgetown University, and her research specialty is conversational style—not what people say but the way they say it. In her first book on conversational style she offers a microanalysis of six friends talking together during a two-and-a-half hour Thanksgiving dinner.[2]

Tannen introduces this sociolinguistic study with a quote from E. M. Forster's novel *A Passage to India*: "A pause in the wrong place, an intonation misunderstood, and a whole conversation went awry."[3] Forster's novel illustrates how people of goodwill from different cultures can grossly misunderstand each other's intentions. Tannen concludes that similar miscommunication occurs all the time between women and men. The effect may be more insidious, however, because the parties usually don't realize that they are in a cross-cultural encounter. At least when we cross a geographical border we anticipate the need to overcome a communication gap. In conversing with members of the opposite sex, Tannen notes, our failure to acknowledge different conversational styles can get us into big trouble. Most men and women don't grasp that "talking through their problems" with each other will only make things worse if their divergent ways of talking are causing the trouble in the first place.

Tannen's writing is filled with imagery that underscores the mutually alien nature of male and female conversation styles. When she compared the style of boys and girls in second grade, she felt she was looking at the discourse of "two different species." For example, two girls could sit comfortably face-to-face and carry on a serious conversation about people they knew. But when boys were asked to talk about "something serious," they were restless, never looked at each other, jumped from topic to topic, and talked about games and competition. These stylistic differences showed up in older kids as well. Tannen notes that "moving from the sixth-grade boys to the girls of the same age is like moving to another planet."[4] There is no evidence that we grow out of these differences as we grow up. She describes adult men and women as speaking "different words from different worlds," and even when they use the same terms, they are "tuned to different frequencies."

Tannen's cross-cultural approach to gender differences departs from much of feminist scholarship that claims that conversations between men and women reflect men's efforts to dominate women. She assumes that male and female conversational styles are equally valid: "We try to talk to each other honestly, but it seems at times that we are speaking different languages—or at least different genderlects."[5] Although the word *genderlect* is not original with Tannen, the term nicely captures her belief that masculine and feminine styles of discourse are best viewed as two distinct cultural dialects rather than as inferior or superior ways of speaking.

Tannen realizes that categorizing people and their communication according to gender is offensive to many women and men. None of us like to be told, "Oh, you're talking just like a (wo)man." Each of us regards her- or himself as a unique individual. But at the risk of reinforcing a simplistic reductionism that claims biology is destiny, Tannen insists that there *are* gender differences in the ways we speak.

> Despite these dangers, I am joining the growing dialogue on gender and language because the risk of ignoring differences is greater than the danger of naming them.[6]

WHEN HARRY MET SALLY: THE CLASH OF TWO CULTURES

Do men and women really live in different worlds? Tannen cites dialogue from Anne Tyler's *The Accidental Tourist,* Ingmar Bergman's *Scenes from a Marriage,* Alice Walker's *The Temple of My Familiar,* Erica Jong's *Fear of Flying,* and Jules Feiffer's *Grown Ups* to support her claim that the different ways women and men talk reflect their separate cultures.

Whenever I discuss Tannen's theory in class, students are quick to bring up conversations between Billy Crystal and Meg Ryan in the 1989 Rob Reiner film *When Harry Met Sally.* I'll use the words of Harry and Sally in the film written by Nora Ephron to illustrate the gender differences that Tannen proposes.

The movie begins as two University of Chicago students who have never met before share an eighteen-hour ride to New York City. Harry is dating Sally's good friend Amanda. Their different perspectives become obvious when Harry makes a verbal pass at his traveling companion just a few hours into the drive:

> SALLY: Amanda is my friend!
> HARRY: So?
> SALLY: So, you're going with her.
> HARRY: So?
> SALLY: So you're coming on to me.
> HARRY: No I wasn't. . . .
> SALLY: We are just going to be friends, O.K.?

HARRY: Great, friends, best thing. [Pause] You realize of course we could never be friends.

SALLY: Why not?

HARRY: What I'm saying is . . . , and this is not a come-on in any way, shape or form . . . , is that men and women can't be friends because the sex part always gets in the way.

SALLY: That's not true, I have a number of men friends and there is no sex involved.

HARRY: No you don't. . . .

SALLY: Yes I do.

HARRY: No you don't.

SALLY: Yes I do.

HARRY: You only think you do.

SALLY: You're saying I've had sex with these men without my knowledge?

HARRY: No, what I'm saying is that they all want to have sex with you.

SALLY: They do not.

HARRY: Do too.

SALLY: They do not.

HARRY: Do too.

SALLY: How do you know?

HARRY: Because no man can be friends with a woman that he finds attractive. He always wants to have sex with her.

SALLY: So you're saying that a man can be friends with a woman he finds unattractive?

HARRY: No, you pretty much want to nail them too.

Harry next meets Sally five years later on an airplane. He surprises her when he announces that he's getting married. Sally obviously approves, but the ensuing conversation shows that they are still worlds apart in their thinking:

SALLY: Well it's wonderful. It's nice to see you embracing life in this manner.

HARRY: Yeah, plus, you know, you just get to a certain point where you get tired of the whole thing.

SALLY: What whole thing?

HARRY: The whole life of a single guy thing. You meet someone, you have the safe lunch, you decide you like each other enough to move on to dinner. You go dancing, . . . go back to her place, you have sex, and the minute you're finished you know what goes through your mind? How long do I have to lie here and hold her before I can get up and go home? Is thirty seconds enough?

SALLY: [Incredulous tone] That's what you're thinking? Is that true?

HARRY: Sure. All men think that. How long do you like to be held afterward? All night, right? See that's the problem. Somewhere between thirty seconds and all night is your problem.

SALLY: I don't have a problem.

HARRY: Yeah you do.

The casual viewer of these scenes will hear little more than two individuals quarreling about sex. Yet neither conversation is about the desirability of sex per se, but about what sex means to the parties involved. Tannen's theory of genderlect suggests that Harry's and Sally's words and the way they are said reflect the separate worlds of men and women. Harry would probably regard Sally as a resident of *Mr. Rogers' Neighborhood,* while Sally might see Harry as coming from the *Planet of the Apes* or *Animal House.* But each person obviously finds the other's view alien and threatening. Sally, as a woman, wants intimacy. Harry, as a man, wants independence.

FEMININE FOCUS ON CONNECTION vs. MASCULINE FOCUS ON STATUS

Tannen says that more than anything else, women seek human connection. Harry's initial come-on irritated Sally because he was urging her to ignore her friendship with Amanda. She was further saddened at Harry's conviction that women and men can't be friends. But she was especially shocked at Harry's later revelation that, for him, the act of sex marked the end of intimacy rather than its beginning. Both times Harry insisted that he was speaking for all men. If what Harry said was true, Sally did indeed have a problem. Harry's words implied that true solidarity with a man would be difficult to achieve, if not impossible.

According to Tannen, men are concerned mainly with status. They are working hard to preserve their independence as they jockey for position on a hierarchy of competitive accomplishment. In both conversations, Harry was the one who introduced the topic, started to argue, talked the most, and enjoyed the last word. In other words, he won. For Harry, sexual intercourse represented achievement rather than communion. "Nailing" a woman was a way to score in a never-ending game of who's on top. A woman's desire for intimacy threatened his freedom and sidetracked him from his quest to be "one up" in all his relationships.

Harry's opinion that *all* men think like he does may strike you as extreme. Tannen agrees. She believes that some men are open to intimacy, just as some women have a concern for power. You'll recall that Baxter and Montgomery's relational dialectics assumes that everyone feels a tension between connectedness and separation in their relationships (see Chapter 12). Tannen agrees that many men and women would like to have intimacy *and* independence in every situation if they could, but she doesn't think it's possible. As a result, these differences in priority tend to give men and women differing views of the same situation.

> Girls and women feel it is crucial that they be liked by their peers, a form of involvement that focuses on symmetrical connection. Boys and men feel it is crucial that they be respected by their peers, a form of involvement that focuses on asymmetrical status.[7]

RAPPORT TALK vs. REPORT TALK

Why is Tannen so certain that women focus on connection while men focus on status? Her answer is that she listens to men and women talk. Just as an ethnographer pores over the words of native informants to discover what has meaning within their society, so Deborah Tannen scrutinizes the conversation of representative speakers from the feminine culture and the masculine culture in order to determine their core values. She offers numerous examples of the divergent styles she observes in everyday communication. These linguistic differences give her confidence that the connection-status distinction structures every verbal contact between women and men.

Consider the following types of talk, most of which are evident in the film *When Harry Met Sally.* At root, each of these speech forms shows that women value *rapport* talk, while men value *report* talk.

1. Public Speaking vs. Private Speaking

Folk wisdom suggests that women talk more than men. Tannen cites a version of an old joke that has a wife complaining to her husband: "For the past ten years you've never told me what you're thinking." Her husband caustically replies, "I didn't want to interrupt you." Tannen grants the validity of the wordy-woman–mute-male stereotype as it applies to a couple alone. She finds that women talk more than men in private conversations, and she endorses Alice Walker's notion that a woman falls in love with a man because she sees in him "a giant ear."[8] Sally continually tries to connect with Harry through words. She also shares the details of her life over coffee with her close friends Alice and Marie. But according to Tannen, Sally's rapport style of relating doesn't transfer well to the public arena where men vie for ascendancy and speak much more than women.

Harry's lecture style is typical of the way men seek to establish a "one-up" position. Tannen finds that men use talk as a weapon. The function of the long explanations they use is to command attention, convey information, and insist on agreement. Even Harry's rare self-disclosure to his buddy, Jess, is delivered within the competitive contexts of jogging, hitting a baseball in a batting cage, or watching a football game. When men retreat from the battle to the safety of their own home, they no longer feel compelled to talk to protect their status. They lay their weapons down and retreat into a peaceful silence.

Harry is unusual in that he's willing to talk about the nuances of his life with Sally. Most men avoid this kind of small talk. Yet in private conversation with Sally, Harry still speaks as though he were defending a case in court. He codifies rules for relationships, and when Sally raises a question, he announces an "amendment to the earlier rule." Men's monologue style of communication is appropriate for report, but not for rapport.

2. Telling a Story

Along with theorists Clifford Geertz, Michael Pacanowsky, and Walter Fisher (see Chapters 18 and 22), Tannen recognizes that the stories people tell reveal a great deal about their hopes, needs, and values. Consistent with men's focus on status and Billy Crystal's portrayal of Harry, Tannen notes that men tell more stories than women—especially jokes. Telling jokes is a masculine way to negotiate status. Men's humorous stories have a *can-you-top-this?* flavor that serves to hold attention and elevate the storyteller above his audience.

When men aren't trying to be funny, they tell stories in which they are heroes, often acting alone to overcome great obstacles. On the other hand, women tend to express their desire for community by telling stories about others. On rarer occasions when a woman is a character in her own narrative, she usually describes herself as doing something foolish rather than acting in a clever manner. This downplaying of self serves to put her on the same level with her hearers, thus strengthening her network of support.

3. Listening

A woman listening to a story or explanation tends to hold eye contact, to offer head nods, and to react with "yeah, uh-huh, mmmn, right" or other responses that indicate "I'm listening" or "I'm with you." For a man concerned with status, that overt style of active listening means "I agree with you," so he avoids putting himself in a submissive or "one-down" stance. Women, of course, conclude that men aren't listening, which is not necessarily true.

When a woman who is listening starts to speak before the other person is finished, she usually does so to add a word of agreement, to show support, or to finish a sentence with what she thinks the speaker will say. Tannen labels this "cooperative overlap." She says that from a woman's perspective, cooperative overlap is a sign of rapport rather than a competitive ploy to control the conversation. She also recognizes that men don't see it that way. Men regard any interruption as a power move to take control of the conversation, because in their world that's how it's done. Those who win the conversational game can take a don't-talk-while-I'm-interrupting-you stance and make it stick. Tannen concludes that these different styles of conversation management are the source of continuing irritation in cross-gender talk. "Whereas women's cooperative overlaps frequently annoy men by seeming to co-opt their topic, men frequently annoy women by usurping or switching the topic."[9]

4. Asking Questions

When Sally and Harry started out on their trip to New York, Sally produced a map and a detailed set of directions. It is safe to assume that Harry never used them. According to Tannen, men don't ask for that kind of help. Every admission of ignorance whittles away at the image of self-sufficiency that is so important for a man. "If self-respect is bought at the cost of a few extra minutes of travel time, it is well worth the price," she explains.[10]

Women ask questions to establish a connection with others. Even a five-minute stop at a gas station to check the best route to New York can create a sense of community, however brief. Tannen notes that when women state their opinions, they often tag them with a question at the end of the sentence ("That was a good movie, *don't you think*?"). Tag questions serve to soften the sting of potential disagreement that might drive people apart. They are also invitations to participate in open, friendly dialogue. But to men, they make the speaker seem wishy-washy.

Tannen's work on genderlect gives her the chance to speak on the lecture circuit and to do interviews on radio call-in shows. When she takes questions, she finds that women ask for information in a way that validates her expertise. Conversely, men questioners engage in a verbal sparring match, seeming satisfied only when they ask something that stumps or embarrasses her. Tannen admits that it's hard for her to understand why public face is so important to men. She quotes with approval the words of a wife in a short story: "I'd have been upset about making the mistake—but not about people *knowing*. That part's not a big deal to me." Her husband replied, "Oh, is it ever a big deal to me."[11]

5. Conflict

In the second half of *When Harry Met Sally*, Harry blows up at their friends Jess and Marie and then storms out of the room. After making an excuse for his behavior, Sally goes to him to try to calm him down.

> HARRY: I know, I know, I shouldn't have done it.
> SALLY: Harry, you're going to have to try and find a way of not expressing every feeling that you have every moment that you have them.
> HARRY: Oh, really?
> SALLY: Yes, there are times and places for things.
> HARRY: Well the next time you're giving a lecture series on social graces, would you let me know, 'cause I'll sign up.
> SALLY: Hey. You don't have to take your anger out on me.
> HARRY: Oh, I think I'm entitled to throw a little anger your way. Especially when I'm being told how to live my life by Miss Hospital Corners.
> SALLY: What's that supposed to mean?
> HARRY: I mean, nothing bothers you. You never get upset about anything.

This scene illustrates Tannen's description of most male-female strife. Men usually initiate the conflict. Since life is a contest, men are more comfortable with conflict and are less likely to hold themselves in check. By making an attempt to placate Harry and excuse his anger at their friends, Sally responds in what Tannen believes is an equally typical fashion. "To most women, conflict is a threat to connection—to be avoided at all costs."[12]

The dialogue illustrates another feature of conflict between men and women. As often happens, Sally's attempt to avert a similar outburst in the future sparks new conflict with Harry. Tannen says that men have an early warning system that's geared to detect signs that they are being told what to do. Harry bristles at the thought that Sally is trying to limit his autonomy, so her efforts backfire.

"NOW YOU'RE BEGINNING TO UNDERSTAND"

What if Tannen is right and all conversation between men and women is best understood as cross-cultural communication? Does this mean that genderlect can be taught like French, Swahili, or any other foreign language? Tannen offers a qualified "yes." She regards sensitivity training as an effort to teach men how to speak in a feminine voice, while assertiveness training is an effort to

"And do you, Deborah Tannen, think they know what they're talking about?"

teach women how to speak in a masculine voice. But she's aware of our ethno-centric tendency to think that it's the other person who needs fixing, so she expresses only guarded hope that men and women will alter their linguistic styles.

Tannen has much more confidence in the benefits of multicultural understanding. She believes that understanding each other's styles, and the motives behind them, is a first move in overcoming destructive responses.

> The answer is for both men and women to try to take each other on their own terms rather than applying the standards of one group to the behavior of the other. . . . Understanding style differences for what they are takes the sting out of them.[13]

Tannen suggests that one way to measure whether or not we are gaining cross-gender insight is a drop in the frequency of the oft-heard lament, "You just don't understand."

Sally says that in so many words when Harry declares his love for her at a New Year's Eve party after months of estrangement. "It just doesn't work that way," she cries. Yet Harry shows that he *does* understand what's important to Sally and that he can cross the cultural border of gender to connect through rapport talk.

> Then how 'bout this way. I love that you get cold when it's seventy-one degrees out. I love that it takes you an hour and a half to order a sandwich. I love that you get a little crinkle above your nose when you're looking at me like I'm nuts. I love that after I spend a day with you I can still smell your perfume on my clothes. And I love that you are the last person I want to talk to before I go to sleep at night.

Dumbfounded, Sally realizes that Harry understands a lot more than she thought he did, and he used her linguistic style to prove it. The viewer hopes that Sally has an equal understanding of report talk that is the native tongue of Harry and males who live in the land of the status hierarchy.

CRITIQUE: IS TANNEN SOFT ON RESEARCH AND MEN?

Is male-female conversation really cross-cultural communication? Tannen suggests we use the "aha factor" to test the validity of her interpretation:

> If my interpretation is correct, then readers, on hearing my explanation, will exclaim within their heads, "Aha!" Something they have intuitively sensed will be made explicit. . . . When the subject of analysis is human interaction—a process that we engage in, all our lives—each reader can measure interpretation against her/his own experience.[14]

If we agree to this subjective standard of validity, Tannen easily makes her case. For example, in the book *You Just Don't Understand,* she describes how women who verbally share problems with men are often frustrated by the masculine response tendency to offer solutions. According to Tannen, women don't want advice; they're looking for the gift of understanding. When I first read this section I had the kind of "aha" reaction that Tannen says validates her theory. I suddenly realized that her words described me. Any time my wife, Jean, tells me about a problem she's facing, I either turn coldly analytic, or dive in and try to fix things for the woman I love. I now know that Jean would rather hear me voice some version of "I feel your pain."

Apparently Tannen's analysis of common misunderstandings between men and women has struck a responsive chord in a million other readers. *You Just Don't Understand* has been a best-seller for over five years. But does a chorus of aha's mean that she is right? Psychic Jean Dixon might make ten predictions, and if only one comes true, that's the prophecy people remember and laud her for. They forget that the other nine turned out to be wrong. According to many social scientists, Tannen's "proof" may be like that.

Perhaps using selective data is the only way to support a reductionist claim that women are one way and men another. Tannen's theme of intimacy versus independence echoes one of the dialectics Leslie Baxter and Barbara Montgomery observe, but she suggests none of the flux, internal contradiction, or ongoing complexity of human existence that relational dialectics describes (see Chapter 12). Tannen's women and men are differentially programmed within their gendered culture to respond to the tension by virtually denying one pole or the other of the contradiction. Saying it's so may eventually make it so—self-fulfilling prophecy is a powerful force. But as I stated in the introduction to this section, most gender researchers spot more diversity *within* each gender than *between* them.

Communication scholars Ken Burke (not the Burke of Chapter 21), Nancy Burroughs-Denhart, and Glen McClish offer a rhetorical critique of Tannen's work.[15] They say that although Tannen claims both female and male styles are equally valid, many of her comments and examples tend to put down masculine values. Certainly Tannen is not alone in this practice. In a widely discussed article that appeared in the *Journal of Applied Communication Research,* Julia Wood and Christopher Inman (University of North Carolina) observe that the prevailing ideology of intimacy discounts the ways that men draw close to each other.[16] Rapport talk is only one route to connection.

A very different critique comes from feminist scholars. For example, German linguist Senta Troemel-Ploetz accuses Tannen of having written a dishonest book that ignores issues of male dominance, control, power, sexism, discrimination, sexual harassment, and verbal insults. "If you leave out power," she says, "you do not understand talk."[17] The two genderlects are anything but equal. "Men are used to dominating women; they do it especially in conversations. . . . Women are trained to please; they have to please also in conversations."[18]

Contrary to Tannen's thesis that mutual understanding will bridge the culture gap between the sexes, Troemel-Ploetz believes that "men understand quite well what women want but they give only when it suits them. In many situations they refuse to give and *women cannot make them give.*"[19] She thinks it's ridiculous to assume that men will give up power voluntarily. To prove her point, she suggests doing a follow-up study on men who read Tannen's best-seller. Noting that many women readers of *You Just Don't Understand* give the book to their husbands to read, Troemel-Ploetz states that if Tannen's theory is true, a follow-up study should show that these men are now putting down their papers at the breakfast table and talking empathetically with their wives. She thinks it will never happen.

The discussion of gender and power will continue in the next two chapters.

QUESTIONS TO SHARPEN YOUR FOCUS

1. Based on Tannen's *genderlect analysis,* do you agree with Harry that men and women can't be friends? Why or why not?

2. Apart from the topics of conflict, questions, listening, storytelling, and public versus private speaking, can you come up with your own examples of how *rapport talk* is different from *report talk*?

3. What are the practical implications for you if talk with members of the opposite sex is, indeed, *cross-cultural communication*?

4. Tannen's *"aha" factor* is similar to Carl Rogers' standard of basing our knowledge on personal experience (see Chapter 3). What are the dangers of relying solely on the "aha" factor?

A SECOND LOOK

Recommended resource: Deborah Tannen, *You Just Don't Understand*, Balantine, New York, 1990.

Conversational style: Deborah Tannen, *That's Not What I Meant!,* William Morrow, New York, 1986.

Linguistic microanalysis of conversation: Deborah Tannen, *Conversational Style: Analyzing Talk Among Friends,* Ablex, Norwood, N.J., 1984.

Strategies of conversational rapport: Deborah Tannen, *Talking Voices: Repetition, Dialogue, and Imagery in Conversational Discourse,* Cambridge University, Cambridge, 1989.

Gender differences in children's talk: Deborah Tannen, "Gender Differences in Topical Coherence: Creating Involvement in Best Friends' Talk," *Discourse Processes,* Vol. 13, 1990, pp. 73–90.

Defense of multiple methodologies: Deborah Tannen, "Discourse Analysis: The Excitement of Diversity," *Text,* Vol. 10, 1990, pp. 109–111.

Discourse analysis: Deborah Tannen, *Gender and Discourse,* Oxford University, Oxford, 1994/96.

Gendered language in the workplace: Deborah Tannen, *Talking From 9 to 5: Women and Men at Work—Language, Sex, and Power,* Avon, New York, 1994.

Linguistic analysis of class and gender: Jennifer Coates, *Women, Men, and Language, A Sociolinguistic Account of Gender Differences in Language,* 2d ed., Longman, London, 1993.

Parallel view of gender differences: Carol Gilligan, *In a Different Voice: Psychological Theory and Women's Development,* Harvard University, Cambridge, 1982.

Critique: Senta Troemel-Ploetz, "Review Essay: Selling the Apolitical," *Discourse and Society,* Vol. 2, 1991, pp. 489–502.

CHAPTER 33

Standpoint Theory
of Sandra Harding and Julia T. Wood

As you've seen throughout the book, many communication theories raise questions about knowledge. For example:

Can we know when people are lying to us?

What's the best way to reduce uncertainty about someone you've just met?

Does the "bottom line" in an annual report reflect corporate reality?

How can we find out whether or not television has a powerful effect?

Are men and women from different cultures?

If you're interested in communication, you'll want to find the answers. ("Inquiring minds want to know.") Standpoint theorists Sandra Harding and Julia Wood claim that one of the best ways to discover how the world works is to start the inquiry from the standpoint of women and other groups on the margins of society.

A standpoint is a place from which to view the world around us. Whatever our vantage point, its location tends to focus our attention on some features of the natural and social landscape while obscuring others. Synonyms for *standpoint* include *viewpoint, perspective, outlook,* and *position.* Note that each of these words suggests a specific location in time and space where observation takes place, while at the same time referring to values or attitudes. Sandra Harding and Julia Wood think the connection is no accident. As standpoint theorists, they claim that "the social groups within which we are located powerfully shape what we experience and know as well as how we understand and communicate with ourselves, others, and the world."[1] Our standpoint affects our worldview.

Harding is a philosopher of science who holds joint appointments in women's studies, education, and philosophy at the University of California, Los Angeles. To illustrate the effect of standpoint, she asks us to imagine looking into a pond and seeing a stick that appears to be bent.[2] But is it really? If we walk around to a different location, the stick seems to be straight—which it actually is. Of course, physicists have developed a theory of light refraction that explains why this visual distortion occurs. In like manner, standpoint theorists suggest that we can use the inequalities of gender, race, class, and sexual orientation to observe how different locations within the social hierarchy tend to generate distinctive accounts of nature and social relationships. Specifically, Harding claims that "when people speak from the opposite sides of power relations, the perspective from the lives of the less powerful can provide a more objective view than the perspective from the lives of the more powerful."[3] Her main focus is the standpoint of marginalized women.

Just as Harding is recognized as the philosopher who has most advanced the standpoint theory of knowledge among feminist scholars,[4] Julia Wood has championed and consistently applied standpoint logic within the field of communication. Wood is a professor of communication at the University of North Carolina at Chapel Hill, and was selected as the 1998 North Carolina Professor of the Year for her teaching and research. Wood regards all perspectives as partial, but she insists that some standpoints are "more partial than others since different locations within social hierarchies affect what is likely to be seen."[5] For communication researchers, taking women's standpoint seriously means heeding Wood's call to choose research topics that are responsive to women's concerns:

> Abiding concern with oppression leads many feminist scholars to criticize some of the topics that dominate research on relationships. When four women are battered to death by intimate partners every day in North America, study of how abusive relationships are created and sustained seems more compelling than research on heterosexual college students' romances. Is it more significant to study friendships among economically comfortable adolescents or social practices that normalize sexual harassment and rape?[6]

As a male researcher who has already studied romance and friendship on a private college campus, intellectual honesty compels me to explore the logic of Harding and Wood's standpoint agenda. But their standpoint epistemology raises other questions. Do all women share a common standpoint? Why do Harding and Wood believe a feminist standpoint is more objective or less partial than other starting points for inquiry? Would grounding future research in the lives of women compel me to regard every report of feminine experience as equally true? Should we disregard what men have to say? The rest of this chapter will explore these issues and other questions raised by standpoint theory. The answers to these questions will make more sense if we understand the varied intellectual resources standpoint theorists have drawn upon to inform their analyses.

A FEMINIST STANDPOINT GROUNDED IN PHILOSOPHY AND LITERATURE

In 1807, German philosopher Georg Hegel analyzed the master-slave relationship to show that what people "know" about themselves, others, and society depends on which group they are in.[7] For example, those in captivity have a decidedly different perspective on the meaning of chains, laws, childbirth, and punishment than do their captors who observe the same "reality." But since masters are backed by the established structure of their society, it is they who have the power to make their knowledge claims stick.

Following Hegel's lead, Karl Marx and Friedrich Engels referred to the *proletarian standpoint.* They suggested that the impoverished poor who provide sweat equity are society's *ideal knowers,* as long as they understand the class struggle in which they are involved.[8] Harding notes that standpoint theory "was a project 'straining at the bit' to emerge from feminist social theorists who were familiar with marxian epistemology."[9] By substituting "women" for proletariat, and "gender discrimination" for class struggle, early feminist standpoint theorists had a ready-made framework for advocating women's way of knowing.

As opposed to the economic determinism of Marx, George Herbert Mead claims that culture "gets into individuals" through communication (see Chapter 4). Drawing on this key principle of symbolic interactionism, Wood maintains that gender is a cultural construction rather than a biological characteristic. "More than a variable, gender is a system of meanings that sculpts individuals' standpoints by positioning most males and females in disparate material, social and symbolic circumstances."[10]

Strains of postmodernism also weave throughout standpoint theory. When Jean-Francois Lyotard announced an "incredulity toward metanarratives," he included Enlightenment rationality and Western science.[11] Since many feminists regard these two enterprises as dominated by men who refuse to acknowledge their male-centered bias, they embrace a postmodern critique. In reciprocal fashion, postmodernists applaud the standpoint emphasis on knowledge as locally situated, though they push the idea to the point where there is no basis for favoring one perspective over another. As we shall see, Harding and Wood reject that kind of absolute relativism.

Harding and Wood have drawn upon these somewhat conflicting intellectual traditions without letting any one of them dictate the shape or substance of their standpoint approach. The resulting theory might seem a bewildering cross-hatch of ideas were it not for their repeated emphasis on starting all scholarly inquiry from the lives of women and others who are marginalized. In order to honor this central tenet of standpoint theory and to illustrate the way of knowing that Harding and Wood propose, I've excerpted events and dialogue from Toni Morrison's novel *Beloved.* Morrison won the Nobel Prize for Literature in 1993 and her book about Sethe, an African American woman who escaped from slavery, won the Pulitzer Prize for fiction.

Sethe was raised and married on a Kentucky farm belonging to a comparatively benign man who owned six slaves. When the owner died, an in-law known as "schoolteacher" arrived to "put things in order." Besides overseeing the farm, he worked on a book about the lives of slaves. In a grim caricature of ethnographic analysis, schoolteacher asked many questions and wrote down what they said in the notebook he always carried. He also tutored his two teenage nephews on the way to whip Sethe without breaking her spirit, instructed them to keep a detailed record of her animal characteristics, and referred to Sethe's value in terms of breeding potential—property that reproduces itself without cost.

The pivotal event in the novel occurs a month after Sethe and her children have escaped to her mother-in-law's home in Ohio. While working in the garden she sees four men in the distance riding toward the house—schoolteacher, a nephew, a slave catcher, and the sheriff. Sethe frantically scoops up her kids and runs to the woodshed behind the house. When schoolteacher opens the door a minute later, he sees a grizzly scene of death—two boys lying open-eyed in sawdust, a girl pumping the last of her blood from a throat slit by a cross-cut saw, and Sethe trying to bash in the head of her baby girl. Speaking for the four men, the nephew asks in bewilderment, "What she want to go and do that for?" Much of the book is an answer to that question as Toni Morrison describes the oppositional standpoints of a male slaveowner (schoolteacher) and a female slave (Sethe).

WOMEN AS A MARGINALIZED GROUP

Standpoint theorists see important differences between men and women. Wood uses the relational dialectic of autonomy-connectedness as a case in point (see Chapter 12): "While all humans seem to seek both autonomy and connectedness, the relative amount of each that is preferred appears to differ rather consistently between genders."[12] Men tend to want more autonomy; women tend to want more connectedness. This difference is evident in each group's communication. The masculine community uses speech to accomplish tasks, assert self, and gain power. The feminine community uses speech to build relationships, include others, and show responsiveness.[13]

Wood does not attribute gender differences to biology, maternal instinct, or women's intuition. To the extent that women are distinct from men, she sees the difference largely as a result of cultural expectations and the treatment that each group receives from the other. For example, Sethe would get "blood in her eye" whenever she heard a slur against any woman of color. When Paul D, the only living black male from her slave past, tells Sethe that he has a "bad feeling" about a homeless young woman she's taken in, Sethe retorts:

> "Well feel this, why don't you? Feel how it feels to have a bed to sleep in and somebody there not worrying you to death about what you got to do each day to deserve it. Feel how that feels. And if you don't get it, feel how it feels to be a coloredwoman roaming the roads with anything God made liable to jump on you. Feel that."[14]

Paul D protests that he never mistreated a woman in his whole life. Sethe snaps back, "That makes one in the world."

Sethe's words illustrate how otherness is engendered in women by the way men respond to them. The reality she describes also reflects the power discrepancies that Harding and Wood say are found in all societies: "A culture is not

"Actually, Lou, I think it was more than just my being in the right place at the right time. I think it was my being the right race, the right religion, the right sex, the right socioeconomic group, having the right accent, the right clothes, going to the right schools . . ."

experienced identically by all members. Cultures are hierarchically ordered so that different groups within them have positions that offer dissimilar power, opportunities, and experiences to members."[15] Along these lines, feminist standpoint theorists suggest that women are underadvantaged, thus men are overadvantaged—a gender difference that makes a huge difference.

Harding and Wood are quick to warn against thinking of women as a monolithic group. They point out that not all women share the same standpoint, nor for that matter do all men. Besides the issue of gender, Harding stresses economic condition, race, and sexuality as additional cultural identities that can either draw people to the center of society or push them out to the fringes. Thus, an intersection of minority positions creates a highly looked-down-upon location in the social hierarchy. Impoverished African American lesbian women are almost always marginalized. On the other hand, positions of high status and power are overwhelmingly "manned" by wealthy white heterosexual males.

Even more than Harding, Wood is troubled by the tendency of some feminists to talk as if there is an "essence of women," and then to "valorize" that quality. She believes that Carol Gilligan made this mistake by claiming that women, as opposed to men, speak in an ethical voice of care. (See the ethical reflection immediately following this chapter.) For Wood, biology is not destiny. She fears that "championing any singular model of womanhood creates a mold into which not all women may comfortably fit."[16] Yet as an unapologetic feminist committed to the equal value of all human life, Wood understands that a sense of solidarity is politically necessary if women are to effectively critique an androcentric world and work together for full emancipation and participation in public life.

Standpoint theorists emphasize the importance of social location because they are convinced that people at the top of the societal hierarchy are the ones privileged to define what it means to be female, male, or anything else in a given culture. We can see this power when Sethe recalls a time when schoolteacher accuses a slave named Sixo of stealing a young pig. When Sixo denies stealing the animal, schoolteacher takes on the role of Grand Interpreter:

> "You telling me you didn't steal it, and I'm looking right at you?"
>
> "No, sir."
>
> Schoolteacher smiled. "Did you kill it?"
>
> "Yes, sir."
>
> "Did you butcher it?"
>
> "Yes, sir."
>
> "Did you cook it?"
>
> "Yes, sir."
>
> "Well, then. Did you eat it?"
>
> "Yes, sir. I sure did."
>
> "And you telling me that's not stealing?"
>
> "No, sir. It ain't."
>
> "What is it then?"
>
> "Improving your property, sir."
>
> "What?"
>
> " . . . Sixo take and feed the soil, give you more crop. Sixo take and feed Sixo give you more work."
>
> Clever, but schoolteacher beat him anyway to show him that definitions belonged to the definers—not the defined.[17]

KNOWLEDGE FROM NOWHERE VS. SITUATED SCIENCE

Why is standpoint so important? Because, Harding argues, "the social group that gets the chance to define the important problematics, concepts, assumptions, and hypotheses in a field will end up leaving its social fingerprints on the picture of the world that emerges from the results of that field's research process."[18] Imagine how different a book by schoolteacher entitled *Slaves* would be from one of the same title written by Sethe (as told to Toni Morrison). The texts would surely differ in starting point, method, and conclusion.

Harding's insistence on local knowledge contrasts sharply with the claim of traditional Western science that it discovers "Truth" that is value-free and accessible to any objective observer. In her book *Whose Science? Whose Knowledge?* Harding refers to empiricism's claims of disembodied truths as "views from nowhere," or in the words of feminist writer Donna Haraway, "the God trick."[19] As for the notion of value-free science, Harding characterizes the claim as promoting "a fast gun for hire" and chides detached scientists that "it cannot be value-free to describe such social events as poverty, misery, torture, or cruelty in a value-free way."[20] Even Galileo's democratic ideal of interchangeable knowers is open to question. His famous statement, "Anyone can see through my telescope," has been interpreted by empirical scientists as dismissing concern for any relationship between the knower and the known.

Harding and other standpoint theorists insist that there is no possibility of an unbiased perspective that is disinterested, impartial, value-free, or detached from a particular historical situation. Both the physical and social sciences are always situated in time and place. She writes that "each person can achieve only a partial view of reality from the perspective of his or her own position in the social hierarchy."[21] Unlike postmodernists, however, she is unwilling to abandon the search for reality. She simply thinks that the search for it should begin from the lives of those in the underclass.

Suppose you were to do research on the topic of "family values." Rather than analyzing current political rhetoric or exploring the genesis of the growing home-school movement, Harding would suggest you frame your research questions and hypotheses starting with people like Baby Suggs, Sethe's mother-in-law. Morrison explains why this freed slave valued a son more than a man:

> It made sense for a lot of reasons because in all of Baby's life, as well as Sethe's own, men and women were moved around like checkers. Anybody Baby Suggs knew, let alone loved, who hadn't run off or been hanged, got rented out, loaned out, bought up, brought back, stored up, mortgaged, won, stolen or seized. So Baby's eight children had six fathers. What she called the nastiness of life was the shock she received upon learning that nobody stopped playing checkers just because the pieces included her children.[22]

Neither Harding nor Wood claim that the standpoint of women or any other minority gives them a clear view of "the way things are." Situated knowledge—the only kind there is—will always be partial. Standpoint theorists do maintain, however, that "the perspectives of subordinate groups are more complete and thus, better than those of privileged groups in a society."[23]

STRONG OBJECTIVITY: LESS PARTIAL VIEWS FROM THE STANDPOINT OF WOMEN

Why should the standpoints of women and other marginalized groups be less partial, less distorted, or less false than the perspectives of men who are in dominant positions? Wood offers two explanations: "First, people with subordinate status have greater motivation to understand the perspective of more powerful groups than vice versa."[24] Even if the meek don't inherit the earth, they have a special interest in figuring out what makes it turn, so taking the role of the other is a survival skill for those who have little control over their own lives. Lacking this motivation, those who wield power seem to have less reason to wonder how the "other half" views the world.

Wood's second reason for favoring the standpoint of groups that are constantly put down is that they have little reason to defend the status quo. Not so for those who have power. She asserts that "groups that are advantaged by the prevailing system have a vested interest in not perceiving social inequities that benefit them at the expense of others."[25] For the overprivileged, ignorance of the other's perspective is bliss, so it's folly to be wise. Certainly the men who came to take Sethe and her children back into slavery could be assigned to that clueless category. "What she want to go and do that for?" they asked in real bewilderment. If they or anyone else really wanted to know why a runaway slave would slit her daughter's throat, they'd need to begin their inquiry from the standpoint of slaves—women slaves, not from the perspective of masters, or even that of black men. They would discover Sethe's utter desperation:

> She saw them coming and recognized schoolteacher's hat. . . . And if she thought anything, it was No. No. Nonono. Simple. She just flew. Collected every bit of life she had made, all the parts of her that were precious and fine and beautiful and carried, pushed dragged them through the veil, out, away, over there where no one could hurt them. Over there. Outside this place, where they would be safe. . . .
>
> When she got back from the jail house, she was glad the fence was gone. That's where they had hitched their horses—where she saw, floating above the railing as she squatted in the garden, schoolteacher's hat. By the time she faced him, looked him dead in the eye, she had something in her arms that stopped him in his tracks. He took a backward step with each jump of the baby heart until finally there were none.
>
> "I stopped him," she said, staring at the place where the fence used to be. "I took and put my babies where they'd be safe."[26]

As gripping as these words are, Harding doesn't ask us to automatically accept Sethe's explanation or approve her drastic response just because they are the words and actions of a marginalized woman. After all, many of the free African American women in Morrison's novel condemn Sethe's drastic way of keeping her daughter Beloved safe from schoolteacher's hands. But Sethe's wrenching fear for her children's welfare is the stark reality of enslaved women everywhere (see the book/film *Sophie's Choice*). Harding emphasizes that it's the "objective perspective *from women's lives*" that provides a preferred standpoint from which to generate research projects, hypotheses, and interpretations.[27] Perhaps such research could seriously explore perceptions of "a fate worse than death."

Harding uses the term *strong objectivity* to refer to the strategy of starting research from the lives of women and other marginalized groups whose concerns and experience are usually ignored.[28] Her choice of label not only suggests the wisdom of taking all perspectives into account, but that knowledge generated from the standpoint of dominant groups offers, by contrast, only a *weak* objectivity. To illustrate this claim, she speaks directly of the oppositional standpoints of the kind described in Toni Morrison's *Beloved:* "It is absurd to imagine that U.S. slaveowners' views of Africans' and African Americans' lives could outweigh in impartiality, disinterestedness, impersonality, and objectivity their slaves' view of their own and slaveowners' lives."[29] The character of Sethe and millions of women situated in slavery would offer a heartfelt "Amen."

THEORY TO PRACTICE: COMMUNICATION RESEARCH FROM THE STANDPOINT OF WOMEN

If we want to see a model of communication research that starts from the lives of women, a good place to begin is Julia Wood's in-depth study of caregiving in the United States. Consistent with standpoint theory's insistence that all knowledge is situated in a time and place, the first chapter of Wood's *Who Cares? Women, Care, and Culture* describes her own situation as a white, heterosexual, professional woman who for nine years took on the consuming responsibility of caring for her infirm parents until they died. Her experience squared with her subsequent research findings:

> First, it seems that caring can be healthy and enriching when it is informed, freely chosen, and practiced within a context that recognizes and values caring and those who do it. On the other hand, existing studies also suggest that caring can be quite damaging to caregivers if they are unaware of dangers to their identities, if they have unrealistic expectations of themselves, and/or if caring occurs within contexts that fail to recognize its importance and value.[30]

Wood discovered that gendered communication practices reflect and reinforce our societal expectation that caregiving is women's work. After rejecting his daughter's proposal to hire a part-time nurse, her father mused, "It's funny, Julia. I used to wish I had sons, but now I'm glad I have daughters, because I couldn't ask a son to take this kind of time away from his own work just to take care of me."[31] She heard similar messages that devalued caregiving from male colleagues at her university. While praising Wood for her sacrifice, they reassured a fellow professor that he had taken the proper action by placing his mother in a nursing home: "Well, she surely understood that as busy as you are with your work you couldn't be expected to take on that responsibility."[32] Wood says these comments reveal the opposing gender-based privileges and restraints in our society. As illustrated in the book/film *One True Thing*, women are given the freedom to make caregiving a priority, but are denied the right to put their work first and still be a "good woman." Men are given the freedom to make their work a priority, but are deprived of the right to focus on caregiving and still be a "good man."

Wood suggests that a standpoint approach is practical to the extent that it generates an effective critique of unjust practices. She believes that "our culture itself must be reformed in ways that dissociate caring from its historical affiliations with women and private relationships and redefine it as a centrally important and integral part of our collective public life."[33] Perhaps a proposal in President Clinton's 1999 State-of-the-Union address is a first step. He endorsed a $1,000 tax write-off for families taking care of an incapacitated relative in their homes. A male network news commentator dismissed the idea as "more symbolic than significant." The female co-host chided that the symbolic recognition of worth was *quite* significant. She shared Wood's standpoint.

Another example of communication study that starts from the standpoint of women is the concept of *invitational rhetoric* proposed by Sonja Foss (University of Colorado at Denver) and Cindy Griffin (Colorado State University). They note that from Aristotle on down, the study and practice of rhetoric has been concerned with how to persuade others and thus gain control over them. Foss and Griffin regard this fascination with influence and power as a paternalistic bias, and propose the concept of "offering" as an alternative approach to rhetoric that more closely reflects the lives of women:

> Invitational rhetoric is an invitation to understanding as a means to create a relationship rooted in equality, immanent value, and self-determination. . . . In offering, rhetors tell what they currently know or understand; they present their vision of the world and show how it looks and works for them.[34]

Foss and Griffin suggest that we can take an invitation-to-understanding approach even when listeners want to argue. A my-way-is-Yahweh insistence tends to harden positions; a perspective offered as tentative can disarm a hostile audience. An attitude of offering may even transform the rhetorical situation into a safe setting where others feel valued and free to share their own perspectives. Of course, adversaries could pounce on our openness as a sign of weakness and move in for the verbal kill. If so, Julia Wood suggests we consider extending *grace* to the other, an option seldom raised in communication textbooks. Wood writes that "grace is granting forgiveness or putting aside our needs or helping another save face when no standard says we should or must do so."[35] Like invitational rhetoric, it's a response more easily seen from the standpoint of women.

CRITIQUE: DISCOVERING STANDPOINT(S) ON THE EDGE

While standpoint logic can be used to privilege the perspective of several marginalized social groups—African Americans, the poor, gays and lesbians—it has been most successfully employed by feminists to highlight and validate the standpoint of women. When used this way, advocates speak of "women's way of knowing," "how women think," and "the way women talk"—phrases that gloss over the differences among women and their commonality with men. Harding and Wood are careful not to essentialize women, and they even suggest that men can be feminists. In so doing, however, they are in danger of giving away any sense of feminine solidarity—a joint identity that provides the motive force to critique male-centered bias in the way that research questions are crafted and that knowledge is subsequently produced.

The tension between individual and collective identity doesn't disappear merely by insisting that women are different from men because of the way they've been treated. The approach that Harding and Wood adopt does avoid a simplistic biological determinism, but the contradiction between viewing women as a group and seeing individual differences still remains. Perhaps this is a dilemma we face any time we try to characterize a group of people, an ongoing tension akin to the separateness–connectedness dialectic that Baxter and Montgomery identify (see Chapter 12). If so, embracing each pole would appear to be a better strategy than denying the validity of either one. Midst much criticism from feminists and empiricists, this is the integrative strategy that Harding and Wood seem to adopt.

In many ways I find the logic of standpoint theory compelling. If all knowledge is tainted by the social location of the knower, then we would do well to start our search for truth from the perspective of people who are most sensitive to inequities of power and have the least to lose if findings challenge the status quo. Wood acknowledges that we may have trouble figuring out which social groups are more marginalized than others. As a white, professional woman, is she lower on the social hierarchy than her African American male colleague who has attained the same faculty rank at the university? Standpoint theory doesn't say, but it clearly suggests that we question much of the received wisdom that comes from an androcentric, Western European research establishment and replace it when a "strong objectivity" provides a more complete picture of the world. The idea energizes University of Wisconsin, Milwaukee sociologist Lynn Worsham and others who believe that minority standpoints can be a partial corrective to the biased knowledge that now passes for truth:

> In what I consider, in all sincerity, to be a heroic and marvelous conception, Harding turns the tables on philosophy and the sciences and constructs a sort of feminist alchemy in which the idea of standpoint, revamped by postmodern philosophy, becomes the philosophers' stone capable of transforming the West's base materials into resources for producing a more "generally useful account of the world."[36]

QUESTIONS TO SHARPEN YOUR FOCUS

1. What is common to the standpoints of *women, African Americans, the poor,* and *homosexuals* that may provide them with a *less false view* of the way society works?

2. How could we test the claim that *strong objectivity from women's lives* provides a more accurate view of the world than knowledge generated by a predominantly male research establishment?

3. Other feminists have criticized Harding and Wood for suggesting that men can learn to view the world from the *standpoint of women.* How might men do this? From your perspective, can a man be a *feminist?*

4. *Standpoint epistemology* draws on insights from *Marxism, symbolic interactionism,* and *postmodernism.* Based on what you've read in this chapter, which of these intellectual influences do you see as strongest? Why?

A SECOND LOOK

Recommended resource: Julia T. Wood, *Communication Theories in Action,* Wadsworth, Belmont, Calif., 1997, pp. 250–259.

Comprehensive statement: Sandra Harding, *Whose Science? Whose Knowledge? Thinking from Women's Lives,* Cornell University Press, Ithaca, N.Y., 1991.

Avoiding essentialism: Julia T. Wood, "Gender and Moral Voice: Moving from Woman's Nature to Standpoint Epistemology," *Women's Studies in Communication,* Vol. 15, 1993, pp. 1–24.

Women and care: Julia T. Wood, *Who Cares? Women, Care, and Culture,* Southern Illinois University Press, Carbondale, Ill., 1994.

Introduction of feminist standpoint: Nancy Hartsock, "The Feminist Standpoint: Developing the Ground for a Specifically Feminist Historical Materialism," in *Discovering Reality,* Sandra Harding and Merrill Hintikka (eds.), Reidel/Kluwer, Dondrecht, Holland/Boston, pp. 283–310.

Black feminist standpoint theory: Patricia Hill Collins, *Black Feminist Thought: Knowledge, Consciousness, and the Politics of Empowerment,* Routledge, New York, 1991.

Journalistic application: Meenakshi Gigi Durham, "On the Relevance of Standpoint Epistemology to the Practice of Journalism: The Case for 'Strong Objectivity,'" *Communication Theory,* Vol. 8, 1998, pp. 117–140.

Situated history of standpoint epistemology: Susan Hekman, "Truth and Method: Feminist Standpoint Theory Revisited," *Signs: Journal of Women in Culture and Society,* Vol. 22, 1997, pp. 341–365.

Feminist critique: Lynn Worsham, "Romancing the Stones: My Movie Date with Sandra Harding," *Journal of Advanced Composition,* Vol. 15, 1995, pp. 565–571.

CHAPTER 34

Muted Group Theory
of Cheris Kramarae

Cheris Kramarae maintains that language is literally a *man*-made construction.

> The language of a particular culture does not serve all its speakers equally, for not all speakers contribute in an equal fashion to its formulation. Women (and members of other subordinate groups) are not as free or as able as men are to say what they wish, when and where they wish, because the words and the norms for their use have been formulated by the dominant group, men.[1]

According to Kramarae and other feminist theorists, women's words are discounted in our society; their thoughts are devalued. When women try to overcome this inequity, the masculine control of communication places them at a tremendous disadvantage. Man-made language "aids in defining, depreciating and excluding women."[2] Women are thus a muted group.

Kramarae is professor of speech communication and sociology at the University of Illinois. She began her research career at that school in 1974 when she conducted a systematic study of the way women were portrayed in cartoons.[3] She found that women were notable mostly by their absence. A quick survey of the cartoon art I've used in this book will show that little has changed since Kramarae's study. Only eighteen of the fifty-seven cartoons contain female characters, and only ten of these women speak. All but two of the cartoonists are men.

Kramarae discovered that women in cartoons were usually depicted as emotional, apologetic, or just plain wishy-washy. Compared with the simple, forceful statements voiced by cartoon males, the words assigned to female characters were vague, flowery, and peppered with adjectives like *nice* and *pretty*. Kramarae noted at the time that women who don't appreciate this form of comic put-down are often accused by men of having no sense of humor or simply told to "lighten up." According to Kramarae, this type of male dominance is just one of the many ways that women are rendered inarticulate in our society. For the last twenty years Kramarae has been a leader in the effort to explain and alter the muted status of women and other minority groups.

MUTED GROUPS: BLACK HOLES IN SOMEONE ELSE'S UNIVERSE

The idea of women as a *muted group* was first proposed by Oxford University social anthropologist Edwin Ardener. In his monograph "Belief and the Problem of Women," Ardener noted the strange tendency of many ethnographers to claim to have "cracked the code" of a culture without ever making any direct reference to the half of society made up of women. Field researchers often justify this omission by reporting the difficulty of using women as cultural informants. Females "giggle when young, snort when old, reject the question, laugh at the topic," and generally make life difficult for scholars trained in the scientific (masculine) method of inquiry.[4] Ardener acknowledged the problem, but he also reminded his colleagues how suspicious they'd be of an anthropologist who wrote about the men of a tribe on the sole basis of talking only to the women.

Ardener initially assumed that inattention to women's experience was a problem of gender unique to social anthropology. But along with his Oxford co-worker Shirley Ardener, he began to realize that mutedness is due to the lack of power which besets any group that occupies the low end of the totem pole. People with little clout have trouble giving voice to their perceptions. Ardener says that their "muted structures are 'there' but cannot be 'realized' in the language of the dominant structure."[5] As a result, they are overlooked, muffled, and rendered invisible—"mere black holes in someone else's universe."[6]

Shirley Ardener cautions that a theory of mutedness doesn't necessarily imply that the muted group is always silent. The issue is whether people can say what they want to say when and where they want to say it, or must they "re-encode their thoughts to make them understood in the public domain?"[7] Cheris Kramarae is certain that men's dominant power position in society guarantees that the public mode of expression won't be directly available to women. Her extension of the Ardeners' initial concept offers insight as to why women are muted and what can be done to loosen men's lock on public modes of communication.

Kramarae argues that the ever-prevalent *public-private* distinction in language is a convenient way to exaggerate gender differences and pose separate sexual spheres of activity. This is, of course, a pitfall into which Deborah Tannen virtually leaps. Within this system the words of women are often considered bound to the home and the "small world" of interpersonal communication—of somehow lesser importance than the words of men, which resonate in the "large world" of significant political issues. She asks, "What if we had a word which pointed to the *connection* of public and private communication?"

Without such a word, I think of this textbook as a public mode of communication. I am a male. I realize that in the process of trying to present muted group theory with integrity, I may unconsciously put a masculine spin on Kramarae's ideas and the perceptions of women. In an effort to minimize this bias, I will quote extensively from Kramarae and other feminist scholars. Kramarae is just one of many communication professionals who seek to unmask the systematic silencing of a feminine "voice." I'll also draw freely on the words and experiences of other women to illustrate the communication double bind which Kramarae says is a feminine fact of life. This reliance on personal narrative is consistent with a feminist research agenda that takes women's experiences seriously.

THE MASCULINE POWER TO NAME EXPERIENCE

Kramarae starts with the assumption that "women perceive the world differently from men because of women's and men's different experience and activities rooted in the division of labor."[8] Kramarae rejects Freud's simplistic notion that "anatomy is destiny." She is certain, however, that power discrepancies between the sexes ensure that women will view the world in a way different from men. While women vary in many ways, in most cultures, if not all, women's talk is subject to male control and censorship. French existentialist Simone de Beauvoir underscored this common feminine experience when she declared "'I am woman': on this truth must be based all further discussion."[9]

The problem facing women, according to Kramarae, is that further discussions about how the world works never take place on a level playing field. "Because of their political dominance, the men's system of perception is dominant, impeding the free expression of the women's alternative models of the world."[10]

Note that my phrase *level playing field* is a metaphor drawn from competitive team sports—an experience more familiar to men than women. This is precisely Kramarae's point. As possessors of the public mode of expression, men frame the discussion. If a man wants to contest the point about a tilted playing field, he can argue in the familiar idiom of sports. But a woman who takes issue with the metaphor of competition has to contest it with stereotypical masculine linguistic terms.

Mead's symbolic interactionist perspective asserts that the extent of knowing is the extent of naming (see Chapter 4). If this is true, whoever has the ability to make names stick possesses an awesome power. Kramarae notes that men's control of the dominant mode of expression has produced a vast stock of derogatory, gender-specific terms to refer to women's talking—catty, bitchy, shrill, cackling, gossipy, chitchat, sharp-tongued, and so forth. There is no corresponding vocabulary to disparage men's conversation.

In case you think this lexical bias is limited to descriptions of speech, consider the variety of terms in the English language to describe sexually promiscuous individuals. By one count, there are twenty-two gender-related words to label men who are sexually loose—*playboy, stud, rake, gigolo, Don Juan, lothario, womanizer,* and so on. There are more than 200 words that label sexually loose women—*slut, whore, hooker, prostitute, trollop, mistress, harlot, Jezebel, hussy, concubine, streetwalker, strumpet, easy lay,* and the like.[11] Since most surveys of sexual activity show that more men than women have multiple sexual partners, there's no doubt that the inordinate number of terms describing women serves the interests of men.

In the socio-cultural section of Chapter 3, I introduced the Sapir-Whorf hypothesis which claims that language shapes our perception of reality. Kramarae suggests that women are silenced by not having a publicly recognized vocabulary through which to express their experience. She says that "words constantly ignored may eventually come to be unspoken and perhaps even unthought."[12] After a while, muted women may even come to doubt the validity of their experience and the legitimacy of their feelings.

MEN AS THE GATEKEEPERS OF COMMUNICATION

Even if the public mode of expression contained a rich vocabulary to describe feminine experience, women would still be muted if *their* modes of expression were ignored or ridiculed. Indeed, Kramarae describes a "good-ole-boys" cultural establishment that virtually excludes women's art, poetry, plays, film scripts, public address, and scholarly essays from society's mass media. For this reason, Kramarae sees mainstream communication as "malestream" expression.

Long before Edwin Ardener noted women's absence in anthropological research, Virginia Woolf protested woman's nonplace in recorded history. The British novelist detected an incongruity between the way men characterize women in fiction, and how they concurrently appear in history books. "Imaginatively she is of the highest importance; practically she is completely insignificant. She pervades poetry from cover to cover; she is all but absent from history."[13]

Feminist writer Dorothy Smith claims that women's absence in history is a result of closed-circuit masculine scholarship.

> Men attend to and treat as significant only what men say. The circle of men whose writing and talk was significant to each other extends backwards in time as far as our records reach. What men were doing was relevant to men, was written by men about men for men. Men listened and listen to what one another said.[14]

As an example of men's control of the public record, Cheris Kramarae cites the facts surrounding her change of name. When she was married in Ohio, the law required her to take the name of her husband. So at the direction of the state, she became *Cheris Rae Kramer.* Later when it became legal for her to be her own person, she reordered the sounds and spelling to Cheris Kramarae. Many people questioned Kramarae as to whether her name change was either loving or wise. Yet no one asked her husband why he kept *his* name. Kramarae points out that both the law and the conventions of proper etiquette have served men well.

We might assume that the advent of the Internet has put an end to men's gatekeeping role—at least as far as access to the World Wide Web is concerned. Kramarae's research shows that it isn't so.[15] Although electronic networks have provided women and other marginalized people a means to maintain quick and easy connections with kindred souls, male dominance is the rule rather than the exception. Indicators of race, age, physical ability, and appearance disappear in electronic chat rooms, but signatures on most networks reveal the sex of the writer. Men are the overwhelming users of the Net; they control the boards, and monopolize the talk. Even women-only boards are invaded by men—either overtly or covertly by their using pseudonyms to gain access.

WOMEN'S TRUTH INTO MEN'S TALK: THE PROBLEM OF TRANSLATION

Assuming masculine dominance of public communication to be a current reality, Kramarae concludes that "in order to participate in society women must transform their own models in terms of the received male system of expression."[16] Like speaking in a second language, this translation process requires constant effort and usually leaves a woman wondering whether she's said it "just right." One woman writer says men can "tell it straight." Women have to "tell it slant."[17]

Think back again to Mead's symbolic interactionism (see Chapter 4). His theory describes *minding* as an automatic momentary pause before we speak in order to mentally consider how those who are listening might respond. These periods of hesitation grow longer when we feel linguistically impoverished.

"That was a fine report, Barbara. But since the sexes speak different languages, I probably didn't understand a word of it."

According to Kramarae, women have to pick and choose their words carefully in a public forum. "What women want to say and can say best cannot be said easily because the language template is not of their own making."[18]

I have gained a new appreciation of the difficulty women face in translating their experiences into man-made language by discussing Kramarae's ideas with three women friends. Marsha, Kathy, and Susan have consciously sought and achieved positions of leadership in professions where women are rarely seen and almost never heard.

Marsha is a litigation attorney who was the first woman president of the Hillsborough County Bar association and is now running for president of the Florida Bar. A recent area magazine article spotlighted five "power players of Tampa Bay." General Norman Schwarzkopf was one; Marsha was another. Marsha attributes her success to a conscious shifting of gears when she addresses the law.

> I've learned to talk like a man. I consciously lower my voice, speak more slowly, think bigger, and use sports analogies. I care about my appearance, but a woman who is too attractive or too homely has a problem. A man can be drop-dead gorgeous or ugly as sin and get along OK. I've been told that I'm the most feared and respected attorney in the firm, but that's not the person I live with day by day. After work I go home and make reindeer pins out of dog biscuits with my daughters.

Kathy is an ordained minister who works with high school students. She is the most effective public speaker I have ever heard in a class. Working in an organization that traditionally excludes women from "up-front" speaking roles, Kathy is recognized as a star communicator. Like Marsha, she feels women have little margin for error when they speak in public.

> Women have to work both sides to pull it off. I let my appearance and delivery say feminine—jewelry, lipstick, warm soft voice. But I plan my content to appeal to men as well. I can't get away with just winging it. I prepare carefully, know my script, use lots of imagery from the world of guys. Girls learn to be interested in whatever men want to talk about, but men aren't used to listening to the things that interest women. I rarely refer to cooking or movies like *Thelma and Louise.*

Susan is the academic dean of a professional school within a university. When her former college closed, Susan orchestrated the transfer of her entire program and faculty to another university. She recently received the Professional of the Year award in her field. When she first attended her national deans' association, only eight out of fifty members were women.

> I was very silent. I hated being there. If you didn't communicate by the men's rules you were invisible. The star performers were male and they came on strong. But no one was listening; everyone was preparing their own response. The meeting oozed one-upmanship. At the reception it was all "Hail fellow well met." You wouldn't dare say, "Look, I'm having this rough situation I'm dealing with.

Have you ever faced this problem?" It was only when some of the women got together for coffee or went shopping that I could be open about my experiences.

Although their status and abilities clearly show that Marsha, Kathy, and Susan are remarkable individuals, their experience as women in male hierarchical structures supports muted group theory. Kramarae says that "men have structured a value system and a language that reflects that value system. Women have had to work through the system organized by men."[19] For women with less skill and self-confidence than Marsha, Kathy, or Susan, that prospect can be daunting.

SPEAKING OUT IN PRIVATE: NETWORKING WITH WOMEN

Susan's relief at the chance to talk freely with other women deans illustrates a central tenet of muted group theory. Kramarae states that "females are likely to find ways to express themselves outside the dominant public modes of expression used by males in both their verbal conventions and their nonverbal behavior."[20]

Kramarae lists a variety of back-channel routes that women use to discuss their experiences—diaries, journals, letters, oral histories, folklore, gossip, chants, art, graffiti, poetry, songs, nonverbal parodies, gynecological handbooks passed between women for centuries, and a "mass of 'noncanonized' writers whose richness and diversity we are only just beginning to comprehend."[21] She labels these outlets the female "sub-version" that runs beneath the surface of male orthodoxy.

These spaces created by women provide relief from and alternatives to the mainstream world. Kramarae uses the term *food groups* to capture the spirit of cooperation present in *women's world.* Her scenario highlights a group of women talking and drinking herbal tea around a "table laden with carob brownies and whole-wheat muffins."[22] Some of the qualities that she would use to characterize that world include interconnection, safety, holism, trust, mutuality, adaptability, and equal access to information.[23]

According to Kramarae, access to information is especially important for women:

> If the future of information is electronic, we need to ensure access for everyone, not just an elite. We imagine computer terminals connected to community systems in laundromats, homeless shelters, daycare centers, etc.—with sufficient support so that most people have access to the Internet.[24]

Although male-oriented Internet norms have already been established, she sees great potential for cyberspace to be a humane place for women because the technology is interactive. Kramarae envisions a world where no group creates policy for another, where everyone has equal input, even into the design of information systems.

Men are often oblivious to the shared meanings women communicate through alternative channels. In fact, Kramarae is convinced that "males have more difficulty than females in understanding what members of the other gender mean."[25] She doesn't ascribe men's bewilderment to biological differences between the sexes or to women's attempts to conceal their experience. Rather, she suggests that when men don't have a clue about what women want, think, or feel, it's because they haven't made the effort to find out. When British author Dale Spender was editor of *Woman's Studies International Quarterly*, she offered a further interpretation of men's ignorance. She proposed that many men realize that a commitment to listen to women would necessarily involve a renunciation of their privileged position. "The crucial issue here is that if women cease to be muted, men cease to be so dominant and to some males this may seem unfair because it represents a loss of rights."[26] A man can dodge that equalizing bullet by innocently declaring, "I'll never understand women."

SPEAKING OUT IN PUBLIC: A FEMINIST DICTIONARY

Like other types of critical theory, feminist theory is not content to merely point out asymmetries in power. The ultimate goal of muted group theory is to change the man-made linguistic system that keeps women "in their place." According to Kramarae, reform includes challenging dictionaries that "ignore the words and definitions created by women and include many sexist definitions and examples."[27] Traditional dictionaries pose as authoritative guides to proper language use, yet because of their reliance on male literary sources, lexicographers systematically exclude words coined by women.

In 1985, Kramarae and Paula Treichler compiled a feminist dictionary that offers definitions for women's words that don't appear in *Webster's New International* and also presents alternative feminine readings of words that do. Reissued in 1992, the dictionary "places *women* at the center and rethinks language from that crucially different perspective."[28] Kramarae and Treichler don't claim that all women use words the same way, but they include women's definitions of approximately 2,500 words in order to illustrate women's linguistic creativity and to help empower women to change their muted status. Figure 34.1 provides a sample of brief entries and acknowledges their origin.

SEXUAL HARASSMENT: COINING A TERM TO LABEL EXPERIENCE

Perhaps more than any other single entry in the Kramarae and Treichler dictionary, the inclusion of *sexual harassment* illustrates a major achievement of feminist communication scholarship—encoding women's experience into the received language of society. Although stories of unwanted sexual attention on the job are legion, until recently women haven't had a common term to label what has been an ongoing fact of feminine life.

In 1992, the *Journal of Applied Communication Research* published thirty stories of speech communication students and professionals who were sexually embarrassed, humiliated, or traumatized by a person who was in a position of academic power. All but two of the thirty accounts came from women. As Kra-

---

Appearance: A woman's appearance is her work uniform. . . . A woman's concern with her appearance is not a result of brainwashing; it is a reaction to necessity. (A Redstockings Sister)

Cuckold: The husband of an unfaithful wife. The wife of an unfaithful husband is just called a wife. (Cheris Kramarae)

Depression: A psychiatric label that . . . hides the social fact of the housewife's loneliness, low self-esteem, and work dissatisfaction. (Ann Oakley)

Doll: A toy playmate given to, or made by children. Some adult males continue their childhood by labeling adult female companions "dolls." (Cheris Kramarae)

Family man: Refers to a man who shows more concern with members of the family than is normal. There is no label *family woman,* since that would be heard as redundancy. (Cheris Kramarae)

Feminist: "I myself have never been able to find out precisely what feminism is: I only know that people call me a feminist whenever I express sentiments that differentiate me from a doormat." (Rebecca West)

Gossip: A way of talking between women in their roles as women, intimate in style, personal and domestic in topic and setting; a female cultural event which springs from and perpetuates the restrictions of the female role, but also gives the comfort of validation. (Deborah Jones)

Guilt: The emotion that stops women from doing what they may need to do to take care of themselves as opposed to everyone else. (Mary Ellen Shanesey)

Herstory: The human story as told by women and about women. . . . (Anne Forfreedom)

Ms.: A form of address being adopted by women who want to be recognized as individuals rather than being identified by their relationship with a man. (Midge Lennert and Norma Wilson)

One of the boys: Means NOT one of the girls. (Cheris Kramarae)

Parenthood: A condition which often brings dramatic changes to new mothers — "loss of job, income, and status; severing of networks and social contacts; and adjustments to being a 'housewife.' Most new fathers do not report similar social dislocations." (Lorna McKee and Margaret O'Brien)

Pornography: Pornography is the theory and rape is the practice. (Andrea Dworkin)

Sexual harassment: Refers to the unwanted imposition of sexual requirements in the context of a relationship of unequal power. (Catharine Mackinnon)

Silence: Is not golden. "There is no agony like bearing an untold story inside you." (Zora Neale Hurston). "In a world where language and naming are power, silence is oppressive, is violence." (Adrienne Rich).

FIGURE 34.1 Excerpts from Kramarae and Treichler's Feminist Dictionary
(Kramarae and Treichler, *Amazons, Blue-stockings, and Crones*)

marae notes, "sexual harassment is rampant but not random."[29] The anonymous story below is typical.

> He was fifty; I was twenty-one. He was the major professor in my area; I was a first year M.A. student. His position was secure; mine was nebulous and contingent on his support of me. He felt entitled; I felt dependent. He probably hasn't thought much about what happened; I've never forgotten.
>
> Like most beginning students, I was unsure of myself and my abilities, so I was hungry for praise and indicators of my intellectual merit. . . . Then, one November morning I found a note in my mailbox from Professor X, the senior faculty member in my area and, thus, a person very important to me. In the note Professor X asked me to come by his office late that afternoon to discuss a paper I'd written for him.

The conversation closed with his telling me that we should plan on getting to know each other and working together closely. I wanted to work with him and agreed. We stood and he embraced me and pressed a kiss on me. I recall backing up in surprise. I really didn't know what was happening. He smiled and told me that being "friends" could do nothing but enhance our working relationship. I said nothing, but felt badly confused. . . . This man was a respectable faculty member and surely he knew more about norms for student-faculty relationships than I did. So I figured I must be wrong to feel his behavior was inappropriate, must be misconstruing his motives, exaggerating the significance of "being friendly." . . . So I planned to have an "open talk" with him.

I was at a disadvantage in our "open talk," because I approached it as a chance to clarify feelings while he used it as an occasion to reinterpret and redefine what was happening in ways that suited his purposes. I told him I didn't feel right "being so friendly" with him. He replied that I was over-reacting and, further, that my small-town southern upbringing was showing. . . . I told him I was concerned that he wasn't being objective about my work, but was praising it because he wanted to be "friends" with me; he twisted this, explaining he was judging my work fairly, BUT that being "friends" did increase his interest in helping me professionally. No matter what I said, he had a response that defined my feelings as inappropriate.[30]

Muted group theory can explain this woman's sense of confusion and lack of power. Her story is as much about a struggle for language as it is a struggle over sexual conduct. As long as the professor can define his actions as "being friendly," the female student's feelings are discounted—even by herself. Had she been equipped with the linguistic tool of "sexual harassment," she could have validated her feelings and labeled the professor's advances as inappropriate and illegal.

According to Kramarae, when *sexual harassment* was first used in a court case in the late 1970s, it was the only legal term defined by women. Senatorial response to Anita Hill's testimony at the Clarence Thomas Supreme Court confirmation hearings showed that there is more work to be done before women can make their definition stick. For muted group theory, the struggle to contest man-made language continues.

CRITIQUE: IS A GOOD MAN HARD TO FIND (AND CHANGE)?

Feminist scholars insist that "the key communication activities of women's experiences—their rituals, vocabularies, metaphors, and stories—are an important part of the data for study."[31] In this chapter I've presented the words of thirty women who give voice to the mutedness they've experienced because they aren't men. I could have easily cited hundreds more. It strikes me that ignoring or discounting their testimony would be the ultimate confirmation of Kramarae's muted group thesis.

Unlike Deborah Tannen in her approach to gender differences presented in the previous chapter, Cheris Kramarae claims that questions of power are central to all human relationships. Both theories covered in the section on relationship maintenance support her contention (see Chapters 11 and 12). Watzlawick's interactional view states that all communication is either symmetrical or complementary, and Baxter and Montgomery's relational dialectics regards the willingness to relinquish a portion of personal power as central to the tug-of-war between separateness and connectedness. These theorists don't speak to Kramarae's assertion that we live in a patriarchal society, but their scholarship does validate her focus on control issues between men and women.

The question of men's motives is more problematic. Tannen criticizes feminist scholars like Kramarae for assuming that men are trying to control women. She acknowledges that differences in male and female communication styles sometimes lead to imbalances of power, but unlike Kramarae, she is willing to assume that the problems are caused primarily by men's and women's "different styles." Tannen cautions that "bad feelings and imputation of bad motives or bad character can come about when there was no intention to dominate, to wield power."[32]

Kramarae thinks that Tannen's apology for men's abuse of power is naive at best. She notes that men often ignore or ridicule women's statements about the problems of being heard in a male-dominated society. Rather than blaming "style differences," Kramarae points to the many ways that our political, educational, religious, legal, and media systems support gender, race, and class hierarchies. Your response to muted group theory may well depend on whether you are a beneficiary or a victim of these systems.

For men and women who are willing to hear what Kramarae has to say, the consciousness-raising fostered by muted group theory can prod them to quit using words in a way that preserves inequities of power. The term *sexual harassment* is just one example of how women's words can be levered into the public lexicon and give voice to women's collective experience. Phrases like *date rape, glass ceiling,* and *second shift* weren't even around when Kramarae and Treichler compiled their feminist dictionary in 1985, yet now these terms are available to label social and professional injustices that women face. Cheris Kramarae's insights and declarations of women as a group muted by men have helped shake up traditional patterns of communication between men and women.

QUESTIONS TO SHARPEN YOUR FOCUS

1. What words do you use with your same-sex friends that you don't use with members of the opposite sex? Does this usage support Kramarae's hypothesis of *male control of the public mode of expression*?

2. In a journal article about *dictionary bias,* Kramarae wrote the sentence, "I *vaginated* on that for a while."[33] Can you explain her word play in light of the principles of muted group theory? How does the meaning of the sentence change when you replace her provocative term with alternative verbs?

3. Given a definition of *sexual harassment* as "unwanted imposition of sexual requirements in the context of a relationship of unequal power," can you think of a time you harassed, or were harassed by, someone else?

4. Do you tend to agree more with Tannen's genderlect perspective or Kramarae's muted group theory? To what extent is your choice influenced by the fact that you are a *male* or a *female*?

A SECOND LOOK

Recommended resource: Cheris Kramarae, *Women and Men Speaking*, Newbury House, Rowley, Mass., 1981, pp. v–ix, 1–63.

Original concept of mutedness: Edwin Ardener, "Belief and the Problem of Women" and "The 'Problem' Revisited," in *Perceiving Women,* Shirley Ardener (ed.), Malaby, London, 1975, pp. 1–27.

Expanded treatment: Karen A. Foss, Sonja K. Foss, and Cindy L. Griffin, *Feminist Rhetorical Theories,* Sage, Thousand Oaks, Calif., 1999, pp. 38–68.

Annotated bibliography: Cheris Kramarae, Barrie Thorne, and Nancy Henley, "Sex Similarities and Differences in Language, Speech, and Nonverbal Communication: An Annotated Bibliography," in *Language, Gender and Society,* B. Thorne, C. Kramarae, and N. Henley (eds.), Newbury House, Rowley, Mass., 1983, pp. 151–342.

Feminist perspective in theory: Karen A. Foss and Sonja K. Foss, "Incorporating the Feminist Perspective in Communication Scholarship: A Research Commentary," in *Doing Research on Women's Communication: Perspectives on Theory and Method,* K. Carter and C. Spitzack (eds.), Ablex, Norwood, N.J., 1989, pp. 65–91.

Feminist critique of communication research: Sheryl Perlmutter Bowen and Nancy Wyatt (eds.), *Transforming Visions: Feminist Critiques in Communication Studies,* Hampton, Cresskill, N.J., 1992.

Feminist metacommunication: Julia T. Wood, "Dominant and Muted Discourses in Popular Representations of Feminism," *Quarterly Journal of Speech,* Vol. 82, 1996, pp. 171–205.

Women's ways of communicating: Karen A. Foss and Sonja K. Foss, *Women Speak: The Eloquence of Women's Lives,* Waveland, Prospect Heights, Ill., 1991.

Dictionary of women's words: Cheris Kramarae and Paula Treichler, *Amazons, Bluestockings, and Crones: A Feminist Dictionary,* 2d ed., Pandora, London, 1992.

Historical roots of feminist perspective: Lana Rakow and Cheris Kramarae (eds.), *The Revolution in Words: Righting Women,* 1868–1871, Routledge, New York, 1990.

Sexual harassment: Julia T. Wood (ed.), "Special Section—'Telling Our Stories': Sexual Harassment in the Communication Discipline," *Journal of Applied Communication Research,* Vol. 20, 1992, pp. 349–418.

Sexual harassment: Gary Kreps, *Sexual Harassment: Communication Implications,* Speech Communication Association, Falls Church, Va., 1993.

Ethical Reflections

CAROL GILLIGAN'S DIFFERENT VOICE

Carol Gilligan is professor of education in the Harvard Graduate School of Education. Her book, *In a Different Voice,* presents a theory of moral development claiming that women tend to think and speak in an ethical voice different from that of men.[1] Gilligan's view of gender differences parallels Deborah Tannen's analysis of men as wanting independence and women as desiring human connection. Gilligan is convinced that most men seek autonomy and think of moral maturity in terms of *justice.* She's equally certain that women desire to be linked with others and regard their ultimate ethical responsibility as one of *care.*

On the basis of the quantity and quality of feminine relationships, Gilligan contrasts women who care with men who are fair. Individual rights, equality before the law, fair play, a square deal—all these masculine ethical goals can be pursued without personal ties to others. Justice is impersonal. But women's moral judgment is more contextual, more immersed in the details of relationships and narratives.[2] Sensitivity to others, loyalty, self-sacrifice, and peacemaking all reflect interpersonal involvement. Gilligan's description of the feminine voice parallels Philipsen's analysis of the Nacirema speech code. In fact, most of his examples are drawn from women's conversation. Both authors observe care developing from a sense of connection.

Gilligan's work arose in response to the theory of moral development of her Harvard colleague Lawrence Kohlberg, who identified increasing levels of ethical maturity by analyzing responses to hypothetical moral dilemmas.[3] According to his justice-based scoring system, the average young adult female was a full stage behind her male counterpart. Women were rated as less morally mature than men because they were less concerned about abstract concepts like justice, truth, and freedom. Instead, they based their ethical decisions on considerations of compassion, loyalty, and a strong sense of responsibility to prevent pain and alleviate suffering. Their moral reasoning was more likely to reflect Buber's call for genuine I–Thou relationships than Kant's categorical imperative.

Gilligan is comfortable with the idea that men and women speak in different ethical voices. Yet when women don't follow the normative path laid out by men, "the conclusion has generally been that something is wrong with women."[4] She points out "the unfair paradox that the very traits that have traditionally defined the 'goodness' of women are those that mark them as deficient in moral development."[5]

Although Gilligan's theory is more descriptive than prescriptive, the underlying assumption is that the way things *are* reflects the way things *ought to be.* Most ethical theorists are disturbed at the idea of a double standard—justice

471

"The committee on women's rights will now come to order."

Reproduced by permission of Punch.

from some, care from others. Traditional moral philosophy has never suggested different ethics for different groups, yet readers of both sexes report that Gilligan's theory resonates with their personal experience.

SEYLA BENHABIB'S INTERACTIVE UNIVERSALISM

Seyla Benhabib has undertaken a formidable task. Recall that Enlightenment thinkers such as Kant, Locke, and Habermas have always believed "that reason is a natural disposition of the human mind, which when governed by proper education can discover certain truths."[6] Benhabib, who is a professor of government at Harvard University, wants to maintain that a universal ethical standard is a viable possibility. But she also feels the force of three major attacks on Enlightenment rationality in general, and Habermas' discourse ethics in particular (see pages 386–387). So she sets out to "defend the tradition of universalism in the face of this triple-pronged critique by engaging the claims of feminism, communitarianism, and postmodernism."[7] At the same time, she wants to learn from them and incorporate their insights into her interactive universalism.

Postmodern critique: In his widely discussed 1984 treatise, *The Postmodern Condition*, Jean-François Lyotard declares that there are no longer any "grand narratives" on which to base a universal version of truth.[8] Postmodernists dismiss any a priori assumptions or "givens" that attempt to legitimate the moral ideals of the Enlightenment and western liberal democracy. They are suspicious of consensus and Habermas' attempt to legislate rationality. Benhabib sums up the postmodern critique: "Transcendental guarantees of truth are dead; . . .

there is only the endless struggle of local narratives vying with one another for legitimization."[9] She appreciates the postmodern insistence that a moral point of view is an accomplishment rather than a discovery, but she is not "content with singing the swan-song of normative thinking in general."[10] Benhabib holds out the possibility that instead of reaching a consensus on how everyone should act, interacting individuals can align themselves with a common good.

Communitarian critique: If there is one commitment that draws communitarians and postmodernists together, it is the "critique of western rationality as seen from the perspective of the margins, from the standpoint of what and whom it excludes, suppresses, delegitimatizes, renders mad, imbecilic or childish."[11] Benhabib realizes the danger of pressing a global moral template onto a local situation. If we regard people as disembodied moral agents who are devoid of history, relationships, or obligations, we'll be unable to deal with the messiness of real-life contexts. To avoid this error, Benhabib insists that any panhuman ethic be achieved through interaction with collective concrete others—ordinary people who live in community—rather than imposed on them by a rational elite.

Feminist critique: Carol Gilligan, Deborah Tannen, Cheris Kramarae, Sandra Harding, and Julia Wood all agree that women's experiences and the way they talk about them are different from men's. Yet typical of rationalistic approaches, Habermas virtually ignores gender distinctions. His conception of discourse ethics speaks to issues of political and economic justice in the masculine-dominated public sphere. But he relegates the activities to which women have historically been confined—childrearing, housekeeping, satisfying the emotional and sexual needs of the male, tending to the sick and the elderly—to a private sphere where norms of freedom, equality, and reciprocity don't seem to apply.[12] Because of its emphasis on open dialogue in which no topics are regarded as trivial, interactive universalism would avoid privatizing women's experiences.

Despite the three critiques cited above, Benhabib believes that a new breed of universal ethic is still possible. "Such a universalism would be interactive not legislative, cognizant of gender differences, not gender blind, contextually sensitive and not situation indifferent."[13] It would be a moral framework that values the diversity of human beliefs without thinking that every difference is ethically significant.[14]

PART SIX

Integration

COMMUNICATION THEORY

Friends who know that I've written a book about communication theory often ask which theory is the best. Although I have my personal favorites, I find myself unable to come up with a satisfying answer. I take comfort in Karl Weick's assurance that there are inevitable trade-offs in any theoretical statement. I am also convinced that his idea of categorizing theories according to the compromises their authors make is a helpful way to keep us from becoming too impatient if we spot a flaw in their construction. Creating theory isn't easy.

Weick introduces the dilemma that empirically oriented theorists face by citing University of Alberta psychologist Warren Thorngate's Postulate of Commensurate Complexity: "It is impossible for a theory of social behavior to be simultaneously general, simple or parsimonious, and accurate."[1] The term *commensurate complexity* refers to the necessity of tacking on qualifications so that a theory can account for special circumstances. Thorngate expands on his postulate:

> The more general a simple theory, the less accurate it will be in predicting specifics. . . . The more accurate a simple theory . . . the less able it will be to account for something more than the most simple or contrived situation. . . . General and accurate theories cannot be [simple].[2]

The clock face in Figure CT.1 shows how Weick portrays the relationship of the three ideals. The hours of twelve, four, and eight align with Weick's three criteria—generaliz-

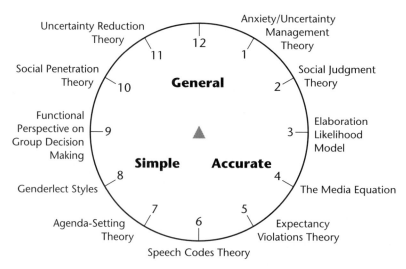

FIGURE CT.1 **Theoretical Trade-offs in Theory Construction**
(Based on Karl Weick's Clock-Face Model)

ability, accuracy, and simplicity, respectively. The remaining hour positions represent various combinations of the two criteria they fall between. As you can see, no one position can combine the three ideals, and to move closer to one is to move farther away from at least one other.

An hour hand pointing at two o'clock would indicate that a theory that holds true under most conditions will naturally be very complicated. Because of its intricate description of attitudes as multiple latitudes, Sherif's social judgment theory comes to mind (see Chapter 13).

Sherif could have chosen to advance or retreat the hour hand in order to reduce his theory's complexity, but only at the expense of generalizability or accuracy. He might have elected to limit social judgment theory's application to issues in which listeners are highly ego-involved, thus doing away with the messy problem of latitudes of noncommitment. That kind of four-o'clock treatment would be somewhat simpler and would have tremendous predictive power. But Sherif was unwilling to limit the theory's usefulness to situations where attitudes were firmly anchored.

Alternatively, Sherif could have moved counterclockwise, away from complexity, by describing attitudes as a single point on a line, as many persuasion theorists do. A simple ten-o'clock theory could still be applied in most situations; obviously Sherif believed its predictions would be wrong too much of the time. So, because accuracy and generalizability had high priority for Sherif, he opted for a complex theory.

In order to appreciate Weick's point about the trade-offs that confront a communication theorist, you have to be able to tell theoretical time. I'll make one circuit of the clock so that you can be clear about what the numbers represent. The placement of specific theories on the clock face reflects my evaluation of the

hard priority decisions their authors have made.

I stated in Chapter 2 that a good objective theory is useful. Since a theory placed at twelve o'clock could be applied in every situation, it would more than fulfill that requirement. But Weick suggests that there are no completely context-free approaches to social behavior. David Mortensen, a University of Wisconsin communication professor, agrees: "Communication never takes place in a vacuum; it is not a 'pure' process devoid of background or situational overtones."[3]

By giving up the fiction that their theories apply across the board, theorists at a two-o'clock position gain accuracy. A two-o'clock approach enlarges questions, adds conditions, and recognizes multiple causes for the same behavior. Whereas theories that cluster near the top of the dial feature high relevancy, a clockwise shift risks being obscure in order to more accurately reflect the complexity of human behavior.

The theorist at four o'clock is pure scientist—stating, testing, and rejecting null hypotheses. Chapter 2 claimed that a good objective theory is testable. The four-o'clock emphasis on accuracy looks for explanations that pass the test. The public often responds with "So what?"

Description at the bottom of the dial is "context specific." When asked to predict future trends, a six-o'clock theorist responds, "It depends. . . ." Quantitative research that originates here is usually run in the lab under highly contrived conditions. Qualitative research at the six-o'clock position is an interpretive collage of case study, grounded theory, participant observation, and ethnography. The data are rich, but application in other situations is limited.

Eight-o'clock theories collapse data into a single conclusion or a short list of principles that are easy to grasp. Deborah Tannen says that men inhabit a status culture, women live in a culture of connection. (see Chapter 32). Like other theorists who operate from this stance, Tannen is open to the charge of reductionism.

I find that students are often attracted to the ten-o'clock location on Weick's theoretical clock. It combines simplicity with relevance. Knowledge is distilled into easy-to-remember aphorisms or vivid metaphors. Intuitive hunches and inner feelings gain dignity when cast as speculative theory, which is portable across situations. Of course, ten-o'clock inquiry may elevate intriguing error to a position of truth, but Weick doesn't regard the danger as necessarily fatal:

> All explanations, no matter how bizarre, are likely to be valid part of the time. It's simply up to the originator of the idea to be smart enough or lucky enough to find those sites where the theory is accurately supported.[4]

Weick's clock-face representation of Thorngate's postulate explains why no approach in this book can avoid criticism. Each theory has at least one "soft spot" or Achilles' heel. The pursuit of two virtues is always at the expense of the third, but as Weick maintains, two out of three isn't bad. He says that theorists who try to do everything usually end up accomplishing nothing. The results are trivial, bland, and boring—easy targets for those who want to poke fun at academic pretention.

The Monty Python parody of theorizing is a case in point. The comedy troupe's brontosaurus sketch is a satire of theorists who are overly impressed with their ideas (see Figure CT.2). Appearing on a television talk show, Anne Elk proudly presents her theory, which tries to do it all:

> My theory that belongs to me . . . goes as follows and begins now. All brontosauruses

FIGURE CT.2   Anne Elk (John Cleese) Describes Her Brontosaurus Theory to Interviewer Graham Chapman on *Monty Python's Flying Circus*

are thin at one end, much thicker in the middle and then thin again at the far end. That is my theory, it is mine, and belongs to me and I own it.[5]

The theory is certainly accurate, undeniably simple, and general to the extent that it applies to every beast of that type. It is also trivial. To avoid this trap, Weick recommends that theorists intentionally select their preferred position on the face of the clock, and then "relax gracefully" with the problems that go with the territory.

Although Thorndike's postulate describes the compromises inherent in empirically oriented theories, it's not hard to imagine interpretive theorists facing similar trade-offs. Recall from Chapter 2 that I wrote that good interpretive theories (1) create understanding, (2) identify values, (3) stimulate agreement, (4) inspire aesthetic appreciation, and (5) change society. Perhaps no one theory can do it all. Consider two theories in this book that investigate gender and communication within a society. Neither Clifford Geertz' cultural approach to gender roles in Bali nor Cheris Kramarae's version of muted group theory are able to fulfill all of these functions.

Geertz' thick description of men's struggle for status at a Balinese cockfight strikes a responsive chord in males around the world. The imagery he uses as he tells the story of their risky wagers has great aesthetic appeal for readers of both sexes. But the inviting prose Geertz uses and the community of agreement that he generates preclude any attempt to change Indonesian society. A reformer he is not.

Geertz' weakness is Kramarae's strength. Feminist theory is meant to challenge the unequal distribution of power perpetuated by male control of the dominant modes of expression. Although Kramarae is high on intent to reform, she doesn't expect a broad spectrum of men who hold power to agree with her analysis. As for aesthetics, criticism of power abuse never looks elegant.

Along with Weick, I'm convinced that all theorists can't help but make trade-offs that inevitably prevent their constructions from being everything we might want. A certain forbearance on our part is appropriate. We should, however, try to understand the choices they've made.

As a way to help you pull together much of what you've learned, the final chapter examines which theorists have common commitments. I hope the objective/interpretive distinction I've used throughout the book has provided some insight, but now that you are familiar with a variety of theories, a more sophisticated integration is appropriate. If you should find this attempt at synthesis not entirely satisfying, I'll hope for the same tolerance you extend to the theorists. Confusion doesn't yield easily to clarity.

*"For heaven's sake, Harry! Can't you just relax and enjoy art, music,
religion, literature, drama and history, without trying to tie it all together?"*

Reproduced by permission of Punch.

CHAPTER 35

Order Out of Chaos

The one-chapter–one-theory organization I've adopted is a signature feature of this text. Students and instructors have been highly supportive of the format, but like most choices, there's a potential downside. The arrangement might have encouraged you to consider the thirty-two theories as thirty-two separate entities that stand alone with nothing but communication context to link them together. That would be unfortunate. In an effort to promote integrative thinking, I've inserted cross-references and made brief comments throughout the text. At this point, however, we need a more systematic way to compare and contrast the theories with each other. We need a meaningful way to bring order out of chaos.

In Chapters 1–3, I contrasted *objective* and *interpretive* scholarship. In this final chapter I return to that distinction as a way to integrate a variety of communication theories. Yet by this point in your study you probably realize that there's a problem with the dichotomy I set up. A number of theorists resist being pigeonholed in one camp or the other. They see their scholarship as drawing on both interpretive and objective insight, so an either/or assignment misses the eclectic nature of their work. For example, Ernest Bormann insists that symbolic convergence theory's fantasy theme analysis clarifies the values of a group—an interpretivist's endeavor. But he also contends that rhetorical visions have predictive power—an objectivist's goal. Bormann wants to occupy a middle ground.

The solution comes from James Anderson, professor of communication at the University of Utah. For three years, Anderson served as the editor of the *Communication Yearbook*, and for another three years he edited the journal *Communication Theory*—both official publications of the International Communication Association. In his book, *The Epistemology of Communication Theory*, Anderson recommends locating theories in relation to each other based on how their authors view the nature of the phenomenal world—the world that is accessible to the senses of sight, sound, taste, touch, and smell.[1] He pictures placing communication theories on a worldview continuum anchored by the terms *objective* and *hermeneutic*.

Hermeneutics is the study and practice of interpretation. Given that the term is not a household word, I'll use the more familiar synonym *interpretive* to designate the hermeneutical end of the scale:

OBJECTIVE _____ INTERPRETIVE

PLOTTING THEORIES ON AN OBJECTIVE-INTERPRETIVE SCALE

Anderson says that objective theorists believe in the unity of science. They see physics, biology, psychology, and communication as merely different windows through which to view a single physical reality. You may recall my description of a classroom demonstration in which I ask a student to immerse his or her hands into buckets filled with water at different temperatures (see Chapter 13). I use the exercise to illustrate social judgment theory's claim of consistent bias in psychophysical judgment. Anderson claims that no matter what the object of judgment—physical temperature or cognitive attitude—the objective theorist will assume that the same principles apply. All of the phenomenal world is a unified whole.

According to Anderson, interpretive theorists believe in multiple domains. They don't doubt the material reality of their office chairs or the lively presence of students who sit down to talk about course work. Yet neither physics nor biology contributes to their understanding of what people mean when they talk to each other. They say there is nothing objective about signs and significance. The social domain is separate from the material realm.

Anderson discusses a number of differences that set an objective world-view apart from the interpretive worldview. Objective theorists hold to a singular, independent, and autonomous social reality. The evidence speaks for itself. Conversely, interpretive scholars assume that reality is a conferred status. Interpretation is a human accomplishment that creates data. Texts never interpret themselves.

Objectivists assume that there is a timeless and far-flung quality to social reality. They see major theoretical principles as ahistorical and not dependent on local conditions. According to interpretivists, this isn't so. Knowledge is always viewed from a particular standpoint. A word, gesture, or act may have constancy within a given community, but it's dangerous to assume that interpretations can cross lines of time and space.

As for language, objective theorists tend to treat words as referential and representational. Words have specific meaning. The interpretive scholar, however, is more suspicious of the sign. For a thorough-going hermeneuticist such as Anderson, "the struggle for meaning is the work of everyday life and the placement of meaning is the successful expression of power."[2] In that sense, interpretive theorists are not detached observers of the human scene. They understand that they are part of the production process itself.

Figure 35.1 displays my evaluation of where each theory fits on the objective–interpretive continuum. While some of the assignments were easy to

	Objective				Interpretive
	1	2	3	4	5
Interpersonal Communication					
Symbolic Interactionism				●	
Coordinated Management of Meaning					●
Expectancy Violations Theory	●				
Interpersonal Deception Theory	●				
Constructivism		●			
Social Penetration Theory		●			
Uncertainty Reduction Theory	●				
The Interactional View				●	
Relational Dialectics				●	
Social Judgment Theory	●				
Elaboration Likelihood Model		●			
Group and Public Communication					
Functional Perspective on Group Decision Making		●			
Adaptive Structuration Theory				●	
Symbolic Convergence Theory			●		
Information Systems Approach				●	
Cultural Approach				●	
Critical Theory of Communication Approach					●
The Rhetoric		●			
Dramatism				●	
Narrative Paradigm				●	
Mass Communication					
Technological Determinism			●		
Semiotics				●	
Cultural Studies					●
Cultivation Theory	●				
Agenda-Setting Theory	●				
The Media Equation	●				
Cultural Context					
Anxiety/Uncertainty Management Theory	●				
Face-Negotiation Theory		●			
Speech Codes Theory			●		
Genderlect Styles				●	
Muted Group Theory				●	
Standpoint Theory				●	

FIGURE 35.1 Classification of Communication Theories According to Objective/Interpretive Worldview

make—theoretical "no brainers," as it were—others were close-call decisions. Fortunately the figure is printed on paper rather than etched in stone. I regard the chart as a work-in-progress rather than The Final Word.

In some respects, the entire text has been preparing you for this synthesis. Although I began with the either/or dichotomy of objectivist/interpretivist I have worked steadily to complicate the picture. Now that you have studied many—if not all—of the theories presented in this book, you are ready to take in the more complex theoretical scene Figure 35.1 suggests. I encourage you to work through the figure line by line. You may find that you need to jog your memory concerning a theory's main thrust or some of its key terms. If so, you might want to look in Appendix B—it offers a fifty-word summary of each theory that should help you recall what you learned earlier in the term.

I've consulted a number of scholars in the field to get their "read" on appropriate placements. Not surprisingly, they didn't always agree. In almost every case, however, the ensuing discussion sharpened my understanding of both the theory and the larger metatheoretical issues presented by Anderson. So that I'm not the only one to benefit, I'll briefly mention a few of the factors that complicated some of the decisions I made. For easier reference to positions along the continuum, I've numbered the five columns at the bottom of the figure.

"ON THE ONE HAND . . . ON THE OTHER"

The effort to capture the worldview of semiotics and relational dialectics is like trying to hit a moving target. In his lifetime, Barthes moved from a 1 to a 5. His early structuralist ideas saw the world in fixed categories. Before his death he had switched to talking of "floating signifiers" that could be employed by post-structuralists to support any point of view. Although Baxter and Montgomery's shift is not as dramatic, their increasing references to an unlimited number of relational contradictions, the dialogical views of Bakhtin, and the overall messiness of communication push their dialectical perspective in an interpretive direction.

Many feminist scholars may object that I haven't placed the work of Kramarae in the far right-hand column. Her theory has a strong reform agenda, and she sees the struggle over language as the crucial work of scholarship. Yet Kramarae also has a global worldview that often overrides individual interpretations and the importance of specific local contexts, so a placement in column 4 seems more appropriate.

A few theories are difficult to place because of the apparent disconnect between their stated philosophical commitments and their research methodologies. Delia has advocated an interpretive orientation that regards communication as "an emergent, creative activity through which human social reality is constantly being re-created, affirmed, repaired, and changed."[3] But the empirical research that Delia and his followers conduct and cite makes it clear that constructivism is more objective than interpretive. The situation is reversed for McLuhan. His objectivist claim of a deterministic relationship between technology and culture is at odds with the impressionistic nature of his "probes" and the anecdotal nature of the evidence that supposedly supports them. I've therefore assigned him to a schizophrenic 3, but wouldn't argue with a 2.

Finally, most rhetoricians see themselves involved in an interpretive enterprise, so the assignment of Aristotle's rhetoric to the objective side of the scale may seem a stretch. Yet the fact that Aristotle set out to *discover* and *categorize* all possible means of persuasion is evidence of a worldview more objective than interpretive. Many rhetoricians would object to my conclusion.

I hope you find this lack of theoretical consensus an encouragement rather than an embarrassment. It leaves an opening for you to be active in making your own informed decision about a theorist's commitments, rather than relegating you to the role of passive notetaker. Examine the list of theories in order to determine whether or not you want to switch some of them to different positions. Being able to articulate a rationale for shifting a given theory is a good sign that you understand both the theory and the differences between objective or interpretive endeavors.

One final note on the placement of theories on the objective/interpretive scale: If you ignore for the moment the midscale theories that have characteristics of both research communities, you'll find that roughly 60 percent of the theories reflect an objective orientation and the other 40 percent reflect an interpretive one. That sixty-forty ratio matches the mix of scholarship that Anderson sees in the field of communication.

FOUR OPTIONS FOR OBJECTIVE AND INTERPRETIVE SCHOLARS: REJECT, RESPECT, COOPERATE, MERGE

By now you may feel more comfortable with one type of communication theory than with another. I find my students almost equally divided in their preference for an interpretive or objective approach to the study of message meaning and behavior. What is the appropriate way to handle these differences? Is the field of communication best served by the two groups of scholars regarding each other as misguided adversaries, admired strangers, needed colleagues, or as partners in a mixed marriage? Without intentionally putting my thumb on the scale, I'll try to make a case for each position. Then you can decide.

1. Rejection of Inferior Scholarship

Anyone who has ever attended an academic conference knows that scholarship can be a rough-and-tumble affair. People on a search for truth mingle with teachers on a quest for tenure, and in both cases, tolerance for variant viewpoints is in short supply. Perhaps that's how it should be. In the debate between objective and interpretive researchers, University of Kentucky communication professors Robert Bostrom and Lewis Donohew claim that it's anti-intellectual to say that each side has something to offer. "We feel that self-deception is unhealthy, and that deception of others is even worse."[4]

Bostrom and Donohew are empiricists seeking objective truth, and they launch a blistering attack against theorists like Carl Rogers, Barnett Pearce and Vernon Cronen, Roland Barthes, Paul Watzlawick, and Stuart Hall for their interpretive approaches to communication study.

> Interpretivism . . . represents an intellectual nihilism in which the possibility of theory construction let alone reasoned action is impossible. . . . Theoretical anarchy and the substitution of pseudo-explanation for scientific explanation seems to us to be the inevitable results of the adoption of the interpretivist argument.[5]

Many critical scholars are equally disapproving of an objective empiricism that claims to be value-neutral and insists on staying ideologically naive about the way big business and big government use its findings to hang on to wealth and power. Stuart Hall admits to being "deeply suspicious of and hostile to empirical work that has no ideas because that just simply means that it does not know the ideas it has."[6] Hall is also disparaging about behavioral scientists' sole focus on outward behavior. He charges them with "consistently translating matters that have to do with signification, meaning, language, and symbolization into crude behavioral indicators, often justified in the name of a spurious scientificism."[7] Interpretive scholars often find scientists' conclusions trivial.

These "communication wars" between empiricists and rhetoricians are fought four times a year on the pages of the two leading journals published by the Speech Communication Association of America. The editorial policy of *Communication Monographs* clearly favors objective scholarship. Most contributors regard Carl Hovland, Kurt Lewin, Paul Lazarsfeld, and Harold Lasswell as the founding fathers of their research tradition. The *Quarterly Journal of Speech* usually prints only interpretive scholarship. Many writers in *QJS* consider Plato, Aristotle, Cicero, and Quintilian the founding fathers of their rhetorical tradition.

Which side is right? The answer is obviously a matter of divided opinion. But combative advocates of both groups would agree that integrity requires us to reject theory or research based on false assumptions. They insist that it would be wrong to compromise deeply held convictions to broker a peace based on theoretical weakness.

2. Respect and Celebration of Differences

Princeton University philosophical pragmatist Richard Rorty comes down equally hard on objective and interpretive theorists when either side claims an exclusive lock on truth. He agrees that there are irreconcilable differences between the two camps. Both groups are self-sealing language communities that don't—and really can't—talk to each other. The questions in one approach don't have answers in the other. For this reason, Rorty says, the debates between the sciences and the humanities about knowledge, methodology, and human nature are "not issue(s) to be resolved, only . . . differences to be lived with."[8]

Rorty's comments remind me of Deborah Tannen's thesis that male-female conversation is cross-cultural communication. Perhaps empirical and rhetorical communities are best understood as distinct cultures. Although members of one culture will never completely understand the shared meaning within the other culture, they can learn to accept and appreciate the diversity.

This respect and even celebration of differences takes place to a certain extent in the field of clinical psychology. The psychoanalytic, behavioristic, and humanistic schools of therapy differ in starting point, method, and conclusion. Yet most therapists ultimately applaud any approach that helps people.

The field of personality assessment offers another helpful analogy. Many of you have taken the Myers-Briggs Type Indicator, a personality test that measures individual preferences on four bipolar scales.[9] The sensing-intuition scale shows how people perceive or acquire information—how they go about finding out about things. As you read through the descriptions of sensing and intuition below, consider how close they are to the epistemological positions of objective and interpretive inquiry.

> *Sensing:* One way to "find out" is to use your sensing function. Your eyes, ears, and other senses tell you what is actually there and actually happening, both inside and outside of yourself. Sensing is especially useful for appreciating the realities of a situation.
>
> *Intuition:* The other way to find out is through intuition, which shows you the meanings, relationships, and possibilities that go beyond the information from your senses. Intuition looks at the big picture and tries to grasp the essential patterns.[10]

The descriptions above suggest that there may be separate personality profiles for students at your school who typically gravitate toward the sciences or the humanities. If there is a link between personality and worldview, it makes little sense to try to talk a person out of his or her way of acquiring knowledge. Perhaps it's best to recognize that the world would be a boring place if everyone were just like us, and to simply enjoy the differences.

3. Cooperation with Needed Colleagues

Even though the *reject* and *respect* options differ in emotional tone, both responses assume an insurmountable gap that separates the scientific objectivity from artistic interpretation. Cultivation theorist George Gerbner thinks that this assessment is too bleak. Gerbner pictures a symbiotic relationship between the two worldviews whereby scientists and artists help each other fulfill a promise that can't be reached by a single approach.

> Opposing science to art or humanistic scholarship presents a false dichotomy. . . . In communication terms, science is the human attempt to penetrate the realities of existence, and art is the effort to express them. Science thus works to make statements true while art struggles to make them compelling and believable. The two complement rather than contradict each other.[11]

Many who address the problem agree that scholars in the arts and sciences need each other, but they differ on the temporal order and the nature of the cooperative relationship. Some think that it takes an interpretive outlook to create theory, then a technical mind-set to test and refine it. Others believe that artists apply theory in practical situations, but only after scientists generate and prove it. A third view suggest that rhetorical scholars cast light on how messages are created, while objective researchers analyze the effect those messages have on others.

Perhaps the strong point of science is a rigorous comparison of multiple messages, while the forte of humanism is its imaginative, in-depth analysis of a single message. Anthropologist Gregory Bateson described rigor and imagination as the two great contraries of the mind. "Either . . . by itself is lethal. Rigor alone is paralytic death, but imagination alone is insanity."[12]

Rhetorician Marie Hochmuth Nichols echoed Bateson's call for the tempering effect that the sciences and humanities can have on each other. She claimed that "the humanities without science are blind, but science without the humanities may be vicious."[13] It would not be fair to claim that science has no concern for matters of ethics. Empirical researchers are trained to be scrupulously fair in the way they collect and handle data. Yet the question of value that interpretive scholars bring to communication studies can force objective scientists to deal with warm bodies who feel, rather than cold impersonal statistics. In like manner, scientists' requests for hard data can act as a reality check for the type of interpretive scholar who tends to take off on flights of fancy. If humanists can't offer evidence that allows others to reach similar conclusions, their analyses are suspect.

4. Legitimizing the Child of a Shotgun Marriage

University of Georgia speech communication professor Celeste Michelle Condit uses the analogy of a sexual liaison to describe the current relationship between social science and rhetoric in the communication discipline. She says that whether pure-blooded patriarchs of objective and interpretive scholarship like it or not, furtive contact between members of the two academic families has produced offspring that merge characteristics of both traditions. We should not be surprised or embarrassed if young scholars bear unmistakable resemblances to both parents.

> After all, rhetoric (the harlot of the arts) and the social science of communication (the sanctimoniously chaste youth) have been pressed up against each other for something around forty years now. Each has experienced a different torment, locked together in a tiny compartment of the university, scrapping for crumbs of academic prestige. . . . Each denies any hanky-panky, protesting respectively, that "the youth won't pay" and "she's no lady." There are signs, however, of offspring; there are increasing numbers of lines of study that borrow from the scholarly traditions of both rhetoric and social scientific communication research. Are these offspring legitimate?[14]

Condit's tentative answer is "yes." She notes that "after years of contact with Dame Rhetoric and the crowd with which she consorts (feminist theory, hermeneutics, critical theory, & co.), some communication scientists have dropped their idealistic pose."[15] They no longer insist on covering laws, universal truth, or value neutrality. Some rhetoricians have been equally tarnished through years of contact with pragmatic scientists. They now prize rhetorical theory-building above rhetorical criticism, write with technical precision rather than literary brilliance, and seem to downplay the consensus of the scholarly community as a validation of wisdom.

Instead of viewing this scientific-humanistic love child as an ugly embarrassment, Condit suggests that science and rhetoric be properly married (perhaps at an NCA convention), and that they baptize their child with the name "Understanding." She urges that Understanding receive training in research methodologies developed on both sides of the family tree—experimentation, survey research, textual analysis, and ethnography. This broad-based education in communication studies would stretch the child—and the child's teachers as well. Yet before long, the mixed-blood Understanding would outshine the pedigreed children of scientists or rhetoricians that lived in the academic neighborhood, and bring a new respectability to the family. Fact or fantasy? I encourage you to seek out your instructor's viewpoint.

A FINAL NOTE

In the Introduction I compared this book to a collection of charts—a scenic atlas of communication maps that professionals in the field consider worth viewing. I hope you've found your first look intriguing and now have a desire to explore some particular areas. I urge you not to be content with watching other people's travel slides; communication isn't an armchair activity. By all means, consider the perspectives of Burgoon, Baxter, Burke, and all the others. But also take a look for yourself. Unlike many academic disciplines, the study of communication is one in which we're all practitioners. Remember, however, that unexamined raw experience is not education. You need to ponder, probe, speculate, and follow your hunches if you wish to take advantage of the rich database that everyday talk provides. Two lists following this chapter could help you in your further study.

Appendix C catalogs academic journals that are particularly relevant to specific communication contexts. If you're really interested in communication theory, you need to read primary sources and understand the issues in the field. Appendix D offers my recommendation for quality movies that illustrate different aspects of the communication process. If you liked my extended references to *Nell, Children of a Lesser God, Roger & Me,* and *When Harry Met Sally,* you may want to check out a video and cull your own examples of theoretical principles at work. I recommend sampling an equal amount of material from each list.

The field is changing rapidly. There's no reason you have to stop with a first look at communication theory or settle for a secondhand glance. You've probably been mulling over an idea not suggested in these pages. Perhaps that notion could be developed and become the focus of a new chapter in a revised edition. Choose your theoretical perspective and the communication contexts that fascinate you, and switch from casual observation to an intensive gaze. Keep looking.

QUESTIONS TO SHARPEN YOUR FOCUS

1. Which five theories presented in this book are your personal favorites? According to Figure 35.1, are most of them *objective* or *interpretive* in nature? What does that tell you about your own *worldview*?

2. How do you view the relationship between objective and interpretive communication theory? Should scholars in opposing camps *reject, respect, cooperate,* or *merge* with each other?

3. What questions do you have about communication that were not addressed by any of the theories covered in this book? Under what *communication contexts* would theories that speak to these issues best fit?

4. Based on the theories you read about this term, what's the best piece of *practical advice* you have to offer someone who wants to be a more *effective communicator*?

A SECOND LOOK

Recommended resource: "Chautauqua: Are Rhetoric and Science Incompatible?" *Communication Monographs,* Vol. 57, 1990, pp. 309–332 (four articles).

Philosophy of communication: James A. Anderson, *Communication Theory: Epistemological Foundations,* Guilford, New York, 1996.

Defense of objective research: Robert Bostrom and Lewis Donohew, "The Case for Empiricism: Clarifying Fundamental Issues in Communication Theory," *Communication Monographs,* Vol. 59, 1992, pp. 109–129.

Defense of interpretive research: Robyn Penman, "Good Theory and Good Practice: An Argument in Progress," *Communication Theory,* Vol. 2, 1992, pp. 234–250.

Defense of pluralism: John Waite Bowers and James J. Bradac, "Contemporary Problems in Human Communication Theory," in *Handbook of Rhetorical and Communication Theory,* Carroll Arnold and John Waite Bowers (eds.), Allyn and Bacon, Boston, 1984, pp. 871–893.

Philosophical pragmatism and the scientific-humanistic dilemma: Richard Rorty, *Philosophy and the Mirror of Nature,* Princeton University, Princeton, N.J., 1979.

Interpretive research methodology: Arthur Bochner, "Perspectives on Inquiry: Representation, Conversation, and Reflection," in *Handbook of Interpersonal Communication,* 2d ed., Mark Knapp and Gerald Miller (eds.), Sage, Thousand Oaks, Calif., 1995, pp. 21–41.

New models of communication: Brenda Dervin, Lawrence Grossberg, Barbara J. O'Keefe, and Ellen Wartella (eds.), *Rethinking Communication, Vol. 1: Paradigm Issues,* Sage, Newbury Park, Calif., 1989.

Research programs: Brenda Dervin, Lawrence Grossberg, Barbara J. O'Keefe, and Ellen Wartella (eds.), *Rethinking Communication, Vol. 2: Paradigm Exemplars,* Sage, Newbury Park, Calif., 1989.

Mixed marriages in communication theory: William Purcell, "Are There So Few Communication Theories?" *Communication Monographs,* Vol. 59, 1992, pp. 94–97.

APPENDIX A
GLOSSARY

abstraction A component of cognitive complexity measured by the degree to which respondents to the RCQ see visible behavior in terms of internal traits, motives, and dispositions.

action plans According to uncertainty reduction theory, mental representations of anticipated behavioral sequences that may be used to achieve goals.

aha factor A subjective standard ascribing validity to an idea when it resonates with one's personal experience.

androgyny The quality of having a blend of both strong masculine and strong feminine characteristics.

anxiety According to AUM, an affective variable that includes the feeling of being uneasy, tense, worried, or apprehensive about what might happen.

appropriation According to adaptive structuration theory, the process of borrowing rules and resources from parent organizations or the larger culture.

assimilation A perceptual distortion that exaggerates similarities.

axiom A self-evident truth that requires no additional proof.

boomerang effect According to social judgment theory, persuasion in a direction that has the opposite impact from the desired effect.

canons of rhetoric The principal divisions of the art of persuasion established by ancient rhetoricians: invention, arrangement, style, delivery, and memory.

categorical imperative Duty without exception; for Immanuel Kant, the ethical rule to act only on that maxim which you can will to become universal law.

central route According to ELM, cognitive processing that involves scrutiny of message content; message elaboration.

CL (comparison level) According to social exchange theory, the threshold above which an outcome seems attractive; the minimal level for personal satisfaction.

CL$_{alt}$ (comparison level of alternatives) According to social exchange theory, the value of the best payoffs available outside the current relationship; the worst outcome a person will accept and still stay in a relationship.

codetermination According to critical theory of communication, corporate decision processes that invite open dialogue among all stakeholders.

cognitive complexity The degree of sophistication of the interpersonal constructs that we use to make sense of the world.

cognitive dissonance The distressing mental state caused by inconsistency between a person's beliefs or a belief and an action; an adverse motivation to change a belief.

cognitive heuristic A mental short cut used to bypass the clutter of verbal and nonverbal signals that bombard people throughout every conversation.

cognitive theory Systematic thought about mental structures and processes.

coherence According to CMM, the process of interpreting the world and assigning significance to our lives; persons-in-conversation who achieve coherence have created shared meaning.

collectivism An index of cultural variability; the extent to which people identify with a larger group that is responsible for taking care of them in exchange for group loyalty, as opposed to individualism.

collegial stories According to the cultural approach to organizations, unsanctioned anecdotes told about other people in the organization.

CALVIN AND HOBBES © 1986 Watterson. Reprinted with permission. All rights reserved.

commensurate complexity   The principle that a theory must become more complicated as its scope increases.

communication theory   An umbrella term for all careful, systematic, and self-conscious discussion and analysis of communication phenomena.

communicator reward valence   According to expectancy violations theory, the sum of the positive and negative attributes that a person brings to an encounter plus the potential he or she has to reward or punish in the future.

complementary communication   Interchange based on accepted differences in power.

concealment   A form of deception that tells only a portion of the truth.

congruence   According to Carl Rogers, the match between an individual's inner feelings and outer display.

consent   According to critical theory of communication, the process by which an employee actively, though unknowingly, accomplishes the interests of management in the faulty attempt to fulfill his or her own interests.

construct   The cognitive template or stencil we fit over reality, ordering our perceptions.

contrast   A perceptual distortion that exaggerates differences.

conventional design logic   According to constructivism, the implicit belief that communica-tion is a game played cooperatively, according to socially conventional rules and procedures.

cool media   According to McLuhan, low-definition channels of communication such as television and telephones that stimulate several different senses and require high audience participation.

coordination   According to CMM, joint action; the process by which persons collaborate in an attempt to bring into being their vision of what is necessary, noble, and good and to preclude the enactment of what they fear, hate, or despise.

corporate stories   According to the cultural approach to organizations, stories that reinforce management ideology and company policy.

cosmopolitan   According to CMM, communicators who intentionally converse in a socially eloquent way that promotes respectful dialogue and coordination.

counteractive communication   According to the functional perspective, interaction that members use to get the group back on track.

cross-cultural communication   The comparison of specific interpersonal variables such as conversational distance, self-disclosure, or styles of conflict resolution across two or more cultures, whereas intercultural communication refers to interaction between people of different cultures.

culture A socially constructed and historically transmitted pattern of symbols, meanings, premises, and rules; a code.

cybernetics The study of information processing, feedback, and control in communication systems.

cycles According to the information systems approach to organizations, double interacts best employed in situations of high equivocality.

deception A message knowingly transmitted by a sender to foster a false belief or conclusion by the receiver.

deliberative rhetoric Political speech centering on future policy.

dependent variable The way the effect is measured in a cause-and-effect hypothesis.

depenetration According to social penetration theory, the gradual process of withdrawing from closeness in a relationship.

determinism The assumption that behavior is caused by heredity and/or environment.

devil term According to dramatism, the word a speaker uses that sums up all that is regarded as bad, wrong, or evil.

dialogue According to Buber, a synonym for ethical communication; mutuality in conversation that creates the transaction through which we help each other to be more human.

differentiation A component of cognitive complexity measured by the number of separate personality constructs used to describe someone on the RCQ.

disassociation A strategy of distancing oneself from what he or she has done.

discourse According to Foucault, a group of statements that provide a way of representing knowledge about a particular topic at a historical moment; it produces and frames knowledge through language.

discursive closure According to critical theory of communication, systematically distorted communication in which those with power suppress potential dissent.

discursive formation According to cultural studies, the process by which unquestioned and seemingly natural ways of interpreting the world become ideologies.

disorientation According to relational dialectics, a nonfunctional response that arises from a feeling of overwhelming helplessness.

disruptive communication According to the functional perspective, interaction that diverts, retards, or frustrates group members' ability to achieve the task functions.

double bind A set of mutually exclusive expectations between parties that places the low-status person in a no-win situation.

double interact According to the information systems approach to organizations, a communication cycle that consists of act, response, and adjustment.

dramatic violence According to cultivation theory, depicting overt physical force against self or others, or compelling others to do something against their will through threats of pain, injury, or death.

dramatistic pentad According to dramatism, a tool to analyze how a speaker attempts to get an audience to accept his or her view of reality as true using five crucial elements of the human drama: act, scene, agent, agency, and purpose.

duality of structure According to adaptive structuration theory, rules and resources are both the medium and the outcome of interaction; they affect and are affected by what is done.

ego-involvement The centrality or importance of an issue to a person's life; according to social judgment theory, one indication is membership in a group with a known stand.

elaboration According to ELM, the extent to which a person carefully thinks about issue-relevant arguments contained in a persuasive communication.

empathic understanding The active process of laying aside personal views and entering into another's world without prejudice.

enactment According to the information systems approach to organizations, proactive communication in which members of an organization invent their environment rather than merely discover it; it is a precondition for sensemaking.

enthymeme An incomplete version of a formal deductive syllogism, leaving out a premise that is already accepted by the audience or omitting the obvious conclusion.

epideictic rhetoric Ceremonial speech centering on praise and blame.

episode In CMM, a recognized communication routine that has boundaries and rules—a recurrent language game.

epistemology The study of the origin, nature, method, and limits of knowledge.

equifinality A systems theory assumption that a given outcome could have been effectively caused by any or many interconnected factors.

equivocality The degree of ambiguity that is associated with information; too many possible meanings rather than not enough.

equivocation A form of deception that uses vague language to dodge an issue.

ethical imperative The premise that, in their constructions, theorists must grant the people they study the same autonomy that they grant themselves.

ethnography A method of participant observation designed to help a researcher experience a culture's complex web of meaning.

ethos Ethical proof, which comes from the speaker's intelligence, character, and goodwill toward the audience as they are revealed through the message.

excitation transfer According to Dolf Zillman, an effect of television viewing whereby the process of media-induced arousal carries over to unrelated real-life situations immediately following the program.

expectancy According to expectancy violations theory, what people predict will happen, rather than what they necessarily desire.

experiment A research method that manipulates an independent variable in order to judge its effect on a dependent variable and thus establish a cause-and-effect relationship.

expressive design logic According to constructivism, the implicit belief that language is a medium for openly and honestly expressing our thoughts and feelings.

face A metaphor for our public self-image.

face-giving The other-concerned facework strategy used to defend and support another person's need for inclusion.

face-restoration The self-concerned facework strategy used to preserve autonomy and defend against personal loss of freedom.

facework According to face-negotiation theory, the enactment of specific verbal and nonverbal messages that help to maintain and restore face loss, and to uphold and honor face gain.

falsifiability A feature of a good scientific theory—testability; a way to prove incorrect theories false.

falsification A form of deception that creates a fiction; a lie.

fantasy According to symbolic convergence theory, the creative and imaginative interpretation of events that fulfills a psychological or rhetorical need.

FOICS (function-oriented interaction coding system) Hirokawa's coding system for group discussion that classifies the function of specific statements.

forensic rhetoric Judicial speech centering on accusation and defense.

framing The process of calling attention to some aspects of reality while obscuring others, which might lead to different reactions; according to agenda-setting theory, the selection of a restricted number of thematically related attributions for inclusion in the media agenda when a particular object is discussed.

free will The assumption that behavior is predominantly voluntary.

functional utterance According to the functional perspective, an uninterrupted statement of a single member that appears to perform a specific function within the group interaction process.

GDSS (group decision support systems) Media technology used to promote idea creation and democratic decision making in computer assisted conferences.

gender A social construction of the characteristics of men and women that are often labeled as masculine and feminine; sex is a fact, while gender is an idea that has been learned and reinforced from others.

genderlect A term that suggests that masculine and feminine styles of communication are best viewed as two distinct cultural dialects and not inferior or superior ways of speaking.

generalized other According to symbolic interactionism, the sum total of responses and expectations that we pick up from our significant others; our "me".

global village McLuhan's concept of a new tribal world order in which everyone can be in touch with everyone else because of instantaneous electronic communication; closed human systems no longer exist.

god term According to dramatism, the word a speaker uses to which all other positive words are subservient.

golden mean Aristotle's approach that moderation is best; virtue develops habits that avoid extremes.

guilt-redemption cycle According to dramatism, the way we ultimately purge ourselves of an ever-present, all-inclusive sense of guilt in public discourse.

hegemony The preponderant influence or domination of one nation over another, or by extension, of the powerful over the weak.

hermeneutics The study and practice of interpretation.

hierarchy hypothesis According to uncertainty reduction theory, the prediction that when people are thwarted in their attempts to achieve goals, their first tendency is to make minor or low-level adjustments to their plans.

high-context culture A culture in which most of the information communicated is located either in the physical context or internalized in the person, but little is in the coded, explicit part of the message.

hot media According to McLuhan, high-definition channels of communication such as print and radio that focus on a single sense receptor and require low audience participation.

I According to symbolic interactionism, the spontaneous driving force that fosters all that is novel, unpredictable, and unorganized in the self.

ideal speech situation Habermas' optimal setting for determining right from wrong, where participants are free to listen to reason and speak their minds without fear of constraint or control.

identification According to dramatism, the common ground that exists between speaker and audience, such as physical characteristics, talents, occupation, background, experiences, personality, beliefs, and values.

I–It relationship According to Buber, an interpersonal relationship in which the other person is treated as a thing to be used, an object to be manipulated.

independent self According to face-negotiation theory, the degree to which people conceive of themselves as relatively autonomous from others; I-identity.

independent variable The way the cause is measured in a cause-and-effect hypothesis.

individualism An index of cultural variability; the extent to which people look out for themselves and their immediate family, as opposed to collectivism.

integration A component of cognitive complexity measured by the degree to which respondents recognize and reconcile conflicting impressions on the RCQ; according to relational dialectics, a way for parties to simultaneously respond to opposing forces without dilution or delusion; according to face-negotiation theory, a method of conflict management whereby an individual seeks to exchange information to find a collective solution.

interactive universalism The goal of an ethical consensus that would be interactive, not legislative, cognizant of gender differences, not gender blind, and contextually sensitive, not situation indifferent.

interdependent self According to face-negotiation theory, the degree to which people conceive of themselves as connected to others; *we*-identity.

interest aggregations According to agenda-setting theory, interest groups or clusters of people who demand center stage for their one overriding concern; single-issue advocates.

interpenetration of structures According to adaptive structuration theory, gradual change within a group due to the merging of discrepant rules and resources.

interpersonal communication The process of creating unique shared meaning.

interpretive scholarship The work of assigning meaning or value to communicative texts.

invitational rhetoric A request for mutual understanding as a means to create a relationship rooted in equality, immanent value, and self-determination, as opposed to traditional rhetoric, which emphasizes persuasion and control.

involvement According to critical theory of communication, organizational stakeholders' free expression of ideas that may or may not affect managerial decisions.

I–Thou relationship According to Buber, an interpersonal relationship in which we regard our partner as the very one we are, an end rather than a means to our end.

latitude of acceptance According to social judgment theory, the range of ideas and statements that strike a person as reasonable and worthy of consideration.

latitude of noncommitment According to social judgment theory, the range of ideas and statements that a person finds neither objectionable nor acceptable.

latitude of rejection According to social judgment theory, the range of ideas and statements that a person finds objectionable and unreasonable.

leakage Unconscious nonverbal cues that signal an internal state.

levelers Inclusive words that imply a shift of responsibility to others by downplaying individual choice.

limited effects model A mass communication model that characterizes society as a honeycomb of small groups bound by a rich web of personal ties and dependencies, and explains empirical findings of relatively small and scattered mass media impact.

logical force According to CMM, the moral obligation a person feels to act in a given way.

logos Logical proof, which comes from the line of argument in the speech.

looking-glass self According to symbolic interactionism, our mental self image that results from taking the role of the other.

loose coupling Weak connections within an organizational system whereby its different parts have a marginal effect on each other.

low-context culture A culture in which most of the information communicated is located in the explicit code of the message rather than in the physical context or internalized in the person.

mainstreaming According to cultivation theory, a process by which heavy viewers of television develop a common socially conservative outlook through constant exposure to the same images and labels.

managerial control According to critical theory of communication, corporate decision processes that systematically exclude the voices of people who are affected by the decisions.

managerialism According to critical theory of communication, discourse based on a systematic logic, a set of routine practices, and an ideology that privileges top-down control.

masculinity An index of cultural variability; clearly defined sex roles with male values of success, money, and material possessions dominant in society.

me   According to symbolic interactionism, the image of self seen in the looking glass of other people's reactions; the self's generalized other.

mechanistic approach   A functional approach that sees organizations as machines designed to accomplish specific goals, with workers as interchangeable parts.

message design logic   According to constructivism, three implicit theories—expressive, conventional, rhetorical—of the ways in which communication can be shaped to serve as means to ends.

meta-analysis   A statistical procedure that blends the results of independent research studies exploring the same relationship between two variables, such as the correlation between amount of television viewing and fear of violence.

metacommunication   Communication about communication; sometimes used to refer to communication about relationships.

metaperformance   According to speech codes theory, ritual actions that group members recognize as symbolic.

mindfulness   According to AUM, the process of thinking in new categories, being open to new information, and recognizing multiple perspectives; according to face-negotiation theory, an awareness of our own assumptions, viewpoints, and ethnocentric tendencies when entering any unfamiliar situation.

minding   According to symbolic interactionism, an inner dialogue used to test alternatives, rehearse actions, and anticipate reactions before responding.

minimal justification hypothesis   According to cognitive dissonance theory, the best way to achieve private attitudinal change is to offer just enough reward or punishment to elicit public compliance.

minimax principle   An economic approach to human behavior stating that people seek to minimize their costs and maximize their benefits as they interact with others.

mystery   According to CMM, the essence of a cosmopolitan attitude that views one's own life as a manifestation or part of something greater, characterized by rapt attention, open-mindedness, a sense of wonder, and perhaps even awe.

narration   Story; according to the narrative paradigm, symbolic actions (words and/or deeds) that have sequence and meaning for those who live, create, or interpret them.

narrative coherence   According to the narrative paradigm, one of two evaluative criteria for determining a good story; internal consistency with characters acting in a reliable fashion.

narrative fidelity   According to the narrative paradigm, one of two evaluative criteria for determining a good story; congruency between values embedded in a message and what listeners regard as truthful and humane.

narrow ridge   According to Buber, the path of dialogic living, distinguished by the tension between subjectivism and absolutism.

nonimmediacy   According to relational dialectics, a strategy for symbolically removing oneself from the situation.

objective scholarship   The scientific quest to understand, explain, and predict human behavior.

organizational culture   According to the cultural approach to organizations, a web of shared meaning; the residue of employee performances by which members constitute and reveal their culture to themselves and others.

organizing   According to the information systems approach, a way to make sense out of equivocal information.

outcome value   According to social exchange theory, the rewards minus the costs of a given course of action.

paradigm   A conceptual framework or worldview.

parsimony, rule of   Relative simplicity; given two plausible explanations for the same event, scientists favor the one less complicated.

participant observation   A method of adopting the stance of an interested yet ignorant visitor who carefully notes what people say and do in order to discover how they interpret their world.

participation   According to critical theory of communication, the process by which all stakeholders in an organization negotiate power and openly reach collaborative decisions.

pathos   Emotional proof, which comes from the feeling that the speech draws from the hearers.

penetration   According to social penetration theory, a metaphor for relational closeness that results from interpersonal vulnerability, especially self-disclosure.

peripheral route   According to ELM, cognitive processing that accepts or rejects a message based on nonrelevant cues as opposed to actively thinking about the issue.

personal space   The invisible, variable volume of space surrounding an individual that defines that individual's preferred distance from others.

personal stories   According to the cultural approach to organizations, stories that company personnel tell about themselves, often defining how they would like to be seen within the organization.

person-centered messages   Sophisticated communication that reflects an awareness of and adaptation to different relational contexts.

persons-in-conversation   According to CMM, the term used to designate interpersonal communication as seen from inside the process.

persuasion   Intentional influence that is more voluntary than coerced.

phenomenology   Intentional analysis of everyday experience from the standpoint of the person who is living it.

postmodernism   An epistemological stance that is suspicious of any truth claim; according to Lyotard, an incredulity toward grand narratives such as Marxism, Freudian psychology, or Christianity.

power distance   An index of cultural variability; the extent to which the less powerful members of society accept that power is distributed unequally.

powerful effects model   An early mass communication model that likened media messages to bullets fired from a machine gun into a crowd or to a hypodermic needle injecting a potent message directly into the audience.

pragmatism   An applied approach to knowledge; the philosophy that true understanding of an idea or situation has practical implications for action.

principle of veracity   Sissela Bok's ethical assumption that truthful statements are preferable to lies in the absence of special considerations.

production   According to adaptive structuration theory, the use of rules and resources in interaction.

promotive communication   According to the functional perspective, interaction that moves a group along the goal path by calling attention to decision-making functions.

proxemics   The study of people's systematic use of space as a special elaboration of culture.

punctuation   In spoken communication, the tone, emphasis, and cues that direct how a message is meant to be interpreted; alternatively, the way someone marks the beginning of an interpersonal interaction.

rational-world paradigm   A scientific approach to knowledge that assumes people are logical, making decisions on the basis of evidence and lines of argument.

RCQ (role category questionnaire)   A free-response instrument used by constructivists to measure a person's cognitive complexity.

reaffirmation   According to relational dialectics, an active recognition that dialectical tensions are ongoing and normal.

recalibration   According to relational dialectics, the process of temporarily reframing a situation so that the pulls on partners no longer seem oppositional.

reflective thinking   John Dewey's rationally based, systematic process of decision making that is the prototype of the functional perspective.

reframing   The process of stepping outside the current perspective and giving new meaning to the same situation.

relational dialectics   An approach to close relationships that emphasizes inherent ongoing tensions, struggles, and contradictions; e.g., a desire for connectedness and separateness.

reproduction   According to adaptive structuration theory, the reinforcement of system features already in place, maintaining the status quo.

requisite variety   According to the information systems approach to organizations, the degree of diversity and complexity an organization needs to match the level of ambiguity of the data it processes.

resonance   According to cultivation theory, the process by which congruence of symbolic violence on television and real-life experience of violence amplifies the fear of a mean and scary world.

resources   According to adaptive structuration theory, materials, possessions, or attributes that can be used to influence or control the actions of the group or its members.

rhetoric   According to Aristotle, the art of seeing all available means of persuasion; the intentional act of using words to have an effect.

rhetorical design logic   According to constructivism, the implicit belief that communication is the creation and negotiation of social selves and situation.

rhetorical vision   According to symbolic convergence theory, a collective view of social reality that develops when the same set of fantasy themes is voiced across many groups.

rituals   Repeated performances that articulate significant aspects of cultural life.

rules   According to adaptive structuration theory, propositions that make value judgments or indicate how something ought to be done.

segmentation   According to relational dialectics, the tactic of compartmentalization by which partners isolate different aspects of their relationship.

selection   According to the information systems approach to organizations, the interpretation of actions already taken; retrospective sensemaking.

selective exposure   The principle that people only pay attention to ideas they already believe because discrepant information would be mentally distressing.

self   According to symbolic interactionism, the ongoing process combining the "I" and the "me."

self-fulfilling prophecy   The tendency for our expectations to evoke responses that confirm what we originally anticipated.

self-referential imperative   The premise that theorists must include themselves as participants in their own constructions; they affect and are affected by their ideas.

semiotics (semiology)   The study of signs and their impact on society.

sexual harassment   Refers to the unwanted imposition of sexual requirements in the context of a relationship of unequal power.

sign   The combination of a signifier and a signified.

signified   The meaning ascribed to a sign.

signifier   The actual image of a sign.

sleeper effect   The tendency for the impact of source credibility to dissipate over time, often because the audience remembers the message but forgets the source.

social constructionism   The belief that persons-in-conversation co-construct their own social realities.

social learning theory   According to Albert Bandura, viewers imitate novel behavior they see on television; vicariously learned aggression can erupt in future antisocial behavior.

speech code   A system of socially constructed symbols, meanings, premises, and rules pertaining to communicative conduct.

spiraling alteration   According to relational dialectics, the practice of responding to dialectical forces by dealing with one pull at a time.

spiritual child   A metaphor for an interpersonal relationship; the relationship is a child born as the result of a couple's coming together and it requires continual nurture and care.

standpoint   Perspective; a place in time and space from which to view the world around us.

statistical significance   The quantifiable conclusion that the results of an empirical study cannot reasonably be explained by chance.

strategy   According to critical theory of communication, the overt practice of managerial control.

strong objectivity   According to standpoint theory, the intentional practice of starting research from the lives of women and other marginalized groups whose perspectives are less partial than those with power.

structuration The production and reproduction of social systems through members' use of rules and resources in interaction.

survey research A research method that employs questionnaires and face-to-face interviews to collect self-report data demonstrating what people think, feel, and intend to do.

suspicion A state of doubt or distrust that is held without sufficient evidence or proof.

symbolic convergence The process of sharing common fantasies, by which a collection of individuals is transformed into a cohesive group.

symmetrical communication Interchange based on equal power.

synergy A group product that is greater or better than all of its members could produce working on their own.

system A group of elements within a greater environment that affect each other and form a larger pattern that is different than the sum of its parts (e.g., weather system, central nervous system, delivery system).

tag question A short question at the end of a declarative statement, often used to soften the sting of potential disagreement and to invite participation in open, friendly dialogue.

test of publicity A method of determining ethical behavior; checking with a variety of fairminded people to see if they would endorse a proposed course of action.

text Any verbal or nonverbal intentional symbolic expression.

textual analysis A research method that describes and interprets the characteristics of any text.

thick description The process of tracing the many strands of a cultural web and tracking evolving meaning.

topoi According to Aristotle, the general and specific stock arguments marshaled by speakers to persuade an audience.

transcendent eloquence A characteristic of cosmopolitan communication that enhances coordination between disparate moral communities as it seeks human welfare as a worthy end in itself.

truth bias The persistent and pervasive expectation that people will tell the truth.

uncertainty According to uncertainty reduction theory and AUM, a cognitive variable that includes the doubts we have about our ability to predict the outcome of our encounters with strangers as well as to explain past behaviors.

uncertainty avoidance An index of cultural variability; the extent to which people feel threatened by ambiguity and create beliefs and institutions to try to avoid it.

unconditional positive regard An attitude of acceptance of another person that is not contingent on his or her performance.

uses and gratifications An approach to media effects suggesting that television viewers are selective, choosing programs that satisfy their need for information, personal identity, social interaction, or entertainment.

victimage Scapegoating; the process of designating an external enemy as the source of all personal ills.

violation valence According to expectancy violations theory, the perceived negative or positive value of a breach of expectations, regardless of who the violator is.

APPENDIX B
ABSTRACTS OF THEORIES

Listed below are brief summaries of the thirty-two theories covered in the book. I hope they will call to mind material you've read earlier. I've tried to remain faithful to key phrases that the theorists employ, but the summaries aren't substitutes for the fuller descriptions and extended examples that have gone before. With the exception of Bormann's symbolic convergence theory, which I've included under "Group and Public Communication," the abstracts are listed in the same order they appeared in the text.

There's a danger, of course, in trying to capture the gist of a theory in only a few lines. Each chapter is already a condensation and interpretation of the author's original work. By further collapsing the content into two or three sentences (a digest of a digest), I can't do justice to the complex ideas that each theorist has set forth. The capsule statements are designed merely to jog your memory.

At the end of each summary I've made an attempt to label the tradition of communication theory that undergirds that particular theorist's thinking (see Chapter 3). When a theory obviously has major roots in two traditions, I've named both, starting with the tradition I regard as most influential. Identifying the intellectual history of a theory can help you understand its key concepts; the knowledge can also help you appreciate what a theorist is trying to accomplish and why.

Interpersonal Communication

Mead's symbolic interactionism: Humans act toward people, things, and events on the basis of the meanings they assign to them. Once people define a situation as real, it's very real in its consequences. Without language there would be no thought, no sense of self, or no socializing presence of society within the individual. (Socio-cultural tradition)

Pearce and Cronen's coordinated management of meaning: Persons-in-conversation co-construct their own social realities by achieving coherence, coordinating actions, and experiencing mystery. Coherence is a unified context for stories told, coordination comes through stories lived, and mystery is a sense of wonder for stories unexpressed. (Socio-cultural and phenomenological traditions)

Burgoon's expectancy violations theory: Violating another person's interaction expectations can be a superior strategy to conformity. When the meaning of a violation is ambiguous, communicators with high reward valence can enhance their attractiveness, credibility, and persuasiveness by doing the unexpected. Communicators should act appropriately when the violation valence or their reward valence is negative. (Socio-psychological tradition)

Reproduced by permission of Punch.

Buller and Burgoon's interpersonal deception theory: Human beings are poor lie detectors in interactive situations. Although strategic deception often results in cognitive overload that leaks out through a deceiver's communication, respondents usually miss these telltale signs due to a strong truth bias. When respondents appear doubtful, deceivers can adjust their presentation to allay suspicion. (Socio-psychological tradition)

Delia's constructivism: People who are more cognitively complex in their perceptions of others have a greater ability to craft sophisticated communication that will achieve beneficial outcomes. They can employ rhetorical message design logic to create person-centered messages, which also seek to accomplish multiple goals. (Socio-psychological and rhetorical traditions)

Altman and Taylor's social penetration theory: Interpersonal closeness proceeds in a gradual and orderly fashion from superficial to intimate levels of exchange as a function of anticipated present and future outcomes. Lasting intimacy requires continual mutual vulnerability through breadth and depth of self-disclosure. (Socio-psychological tradition)

Berger's uncertainty reduction theory: When people meet, their primary concern is to reduce uncertainty about each other and their relationship. As verbal output, nonverbal warmth, self-disclosure, similarity, and shared communication networks increase, uncertainty decreases—and vice versa. Information seeking and reciprocity are positively correlated with uncertainty. (Socio-psychological tradition)

Watzlawick's interactional view: Relationships within a family system are interconnected and highly resistant to change. Communication among members has a content component, and a relationship component that centers on issues of control. The system can be transformed only when members receive outside help to reframe their metacommunication—communication about communication. (Cybernetic tradition)

Baxter and Montgomery's relational dialectics: Relationships are always in flux. Both parties experience conflicting pulls toward (1) connectedness-separateness, (2) openness-closedness, and (3) certainty-uncertainty—within their relationship and vis-à-vis their social networks. Couples cope with dialectical tension through strategies of denial, disorientation, spiraling alteration, segmentation, balance, integration, recalibration, and reaffirmation. (Phenomenological tradition)

Sherif's social judgment theory: The larger the discrepancy between a speaker's position and a listener's point of view, the greater the change in attitude—as long as the message is within the hearer's latitude of acceptance. High ego-involvement usually indicates a wide latitude of rejection. Messages that fall there may have a boomerang effect. (Socio-psychological tradition)

Petty and Cacioppo's elaboration likelihood model: Message elaboration is the central route of persuasion that produces major positive attitude change when unbiased listeners are motivated and able to scrutinize arguments that they consider strong. Message irrelevant factors hold sway on the peripheral path, a more common route that produces only minor shifts in attitude. (Socio-psychological tradition)

Group and Public Communication

Hirokawa and Gouran's functional perspective: Groups make high-quality decisions when members ignore gut feelings and rationally fulfill four requisite functions: (1) problem analysis, (2) goal setting, (3) identification of alternatives, and (4) evaluation of positive and negative consequences. Most group communication disrupts progress toward accomplishing these functional tasks, but counteractive communication can bring people back to rational inquiry. (Socio-psychological and cybernetic traditions)

Poole's adaptive structuration theory: Structuration is the production and reproduction of social systems by people's use of rules and resources in interaction. So when groups make decisions, communication matters. The duality of structures means that rules and resources members use will affect decisions, yet those structures will also be affected by those decisions. (Socio-cultural and cybernetic traditions)

Bormann's symbolic convergence theory: Sharing common fantasies transforms a collection of individuals into a cohesive group. Symbolic convergence occurs when group members spontaneously create fantasy chains that display an energized, unified response to common themes. A fantasy theme analysis across groups can reveal a rhetorical vision that contains motives to enact the joint fantasy. (Rhetorical and socio-psychological traditions)

Weick's information systems approach to organizations: Organizing is the process of making sense out of equivocal information through enactment, selection, and retention of information. Organizations survive in hostile environments when they succeed in reducing equivocality through retrospective sense-making. When faced with an ambiguous situation, managers should rely on double interacts rather than rules. Act first, plan later. (Cybernetic tradition)

Geertz and Pacanowsky's cultural approach to organizations: Humans are animals suspended in webs of significance that they themselves have spun. An organization doesn't have a culture, it is a culture—a unique system of shared meanings. A nonintrusive ethnographic approach interprets stories, rites, and other symbolism to make sense of corporate culture. (Socio-cultural tradition)

Deetz' critical theory of communication approach to organizations: The naive notion that communication is merely the transmission of information perpetuates managerialism, discursive closure, and the corporate colonization of everyday life. Language is the principal medium through which social reality is produced and reproduced. Managers can further a company's health and democratic values by coordinating stakeholder participation in corporate decisions. (Critical and phenomenological traditions)

Aristotle's rhetoric: Rhetoric is the art of discovering all available means of persuasion. A speaker supports the probability of a message by logical, ethical, and emotional proofs. Accurate audience analysis results in effective invention, arrangement, style, delivery, and presumably memory. (Rhetorical tradition)

Burke's dramatism: Life is drama. The dramatistic pentad of act, scene, agent, agency, and purpose is the critic's tool to discover a speaker's motives. The ultimate motive of rhetoric is the purging of guilt. Without identification, there is no persuasion. (Rhetorical and semiotic traditions)

Fisher's narrative paradigm: People are storytelling animals; all forms of human communication are fundamentally narrative. Listeners judge a story by whether or not it hangs together and rings true with the values of an ideal audience. Thus, narrative rationality is a matter of coherence and fidelity. (Rhetorical tradition)

Mass Communication

McLuhan's technological determinism: Pivotal changes in communication technology-the phonetic alphabet, the printing press, and the telegraph-have radically altered the way we process sensory experience. The medium is the message. We live in an early period of the electronic age, a revolutionary point in human history. (Socio-cultural and semiotic traditions)

Barthes' semiotics: The significant visual sign systems of a culture affirm the status quo by suggesting that the world as it is today is natural, inevitable, and eternal. Mythmakers do this by co-opting neutral denotative signs to become signifiers without historical grounding in second-order connotative semiotic systems. (Semiotic tradition)

Hall's cultural studies: The mass media function to maintain the ideology of those who already have power. Corporately controlled media provide the dominant discourse of the day that frames interpretation of events. The critic should not only seek to interpret culture, but to change it. Media audiences have the capacity to resist hegemonic influence. (Critical tradition)

Gerbner's cultivation theory: Television has become society's storyteller. Heavy television viewers see a vast quantity of dramatic violence, which cultivates an exaggerated belief in a mean and scary world. Mainstreaming and resonance are two of the processes that create a homogeneous and fearful populace. (Socio-cultural and socio-psychological traditions)

McCombs and Shaw's agenda-setting theory: The media tell us (1) what to think about, and (2) how to think about it. The first process (agenda setting) transfers the salience of items on their news agenda to our agenda. The second process (framing) transfers the salience of selected attributes to prominence among the pictures in our heads. (Socio-psychological tradition)

Reeves and Nass' media equation: People treat modern communication media as if they were human, so established principles of interpersonal communication also predict human responses to computers and television. The media equation (media = real life) is an unconscious, automatic response that occurs because our slow-to-evolve brains don't distinguish between mediated and real life experience. (Socio-psychological tradition)

Cultural Context

Gudykunst's anxiety/uncertainty management theory: Intergroup encounters are characterized by high levels of uncertainty and anxiety, especially when cultural variability is high. Effective communication is made possible by our ability to mindfully manage our anxiety and reduce our uncertainty about ourselves and the people with whom we are communicating. (Socio-psychological tradition)

Ting-Toomey's face negotiation theory: In conflict situations, mutual and other-face concerns of people in collectivistic cultures cause them to give face to others by avoiding, obliging, or compromising. Self-face concerns of people in individualistic cultures cause them to restore their own face by dominating, expressing emotion, or displaying passive aggression. Both cultures use integrating and third-party help, but in different ways. (Socio-cultural and socio-psychological traditions)

Philipsen's speech codes theory: Through ethnography of communication we know all cultures have a unique speech code that involves a distinctive psychology, sociology, and rhetoric. The meaning of a speech code is determined by speakers and listeners, and is woven into speech itself. Artful use of the code can explain, predict, and control talk about talk. (Socio-cultural tradition)

Tannen's genderlect styles: Male-female conversation is cross-cultural communication. Masculine and feminine styles of discourse are best viewed as two distinct cultural dialects rather than as inferior or superior ways of speaking. Men's report talk focuses on status and independence; women's rapport talk seeks human connection. (Semiotic and socio-cultural traditions)

Harding and Wood's standpoint theory: Different locations within the social hierarchy affect what is seen. The standpoints of marginalized people provide less false views of the world than do the privileged perspectives of the powerful. Strong objectivity requires that scientific research start from the lives of women, the poor, gays and lesbians, and racial minorities. (Critical tradition)

Kramarae's muted group theory: Man-made language aids in defining, depreciating, and excluding women. Women are less articulate in public because the words and the norms for their use have been devised by men. As women cease to be muted, men will no longer maintain their position of dominance in society. (Critical tradition)

APPENDIX C

ACADEMIC JOURNALS THAT FOCUS ON
COMMUNICATION THEORY

Overview
- Communication Abstracts
- Communication Monographs
- Communication Quarterly
- Communication Reports
- Communication Research
- Communication Studies
- Communication Theory
- Human Communication Research
- Southern Communication Journal
- Western Journal of Communication

Interpersonal Messages
- Et cetera
- Journal of Language and Social Psychology
- Journal of Nonverbal Behavior
- Research on Language and Social Interaction
- Symbolic Interaction

Cognitive Processing
- Cognitive Processing
- International Journal of Personal Construct Psychology
- Journal of Language and Social Psychology
- Journal of Social Cognition
- Psychological Review

Relationship Development
- Communication Monographs
- Human Communication Research
- Journal of Social and Personal Relationships
- Personal Relationships

Relationship Maintenance
- Human Communication Research
- Journal of Social and Personal Relationships
- Journal of the International Listening Association
- Mediation Quarterly
- Western Journal of Communication

Group Decision Making
- Group
- Group and Organizational Management
- Group and Organizational Studies
- Small Group Behavior
- Small Group Research

Organizational Communication
- Administrative Science Quarterly
- Group & Organization Management
- Management Communication Quarterly
- Organization

Public Rhetoric
- Philosophy & Rhetoric
- Quarterly Journal of Speech
- Rhetoric Review
- Rhetoric Society Quarterly
- Southern Communication Journal

Media and Culture
- Cultural Studies
- Critical Studies in Mass Communication
- Discourse & Society
- Discourse Studies
- European Journal of Cultural Studies
- International Journal of Cultural Studies
- Journal of Communication
- Journal of Communication Inquiry
- Journal of New Media: Technology, Society, Culture
- Media, Culture & Society
- Semiotica
- Social Semiotics
- The Communication Review

Media Effects
- Communication Research
- Journal of Broadcasting & Electronic Media
- Journal of Mass Media Ethics
- Journalism and Mass Communication Quarterly
- Mass Communication Review
- Media Psychology
- Political Communication
- Public Opinion Quarterly
- Written Communication

Intercultural Communication
- American Anthropologist
- Cross-Cultural Research
- Howard Journal of Communication
- International Journal of Conflict Management
- International Journal of Intercultural Relations
- Journal of Contemporary Ethnography
- Multilingua

Gender and Communication
- Gender & Society
- Discourse & Society
- Signs: Journal of Women in Culture and Society
- Women and Language
- Women's Studies in Communication

APPENDIX D

FEATURE FILMS THAT ILLUSTRATE
COMMUNICATION THEORY

Interpersonal Messages
- The Miracle Worker (General)
- Pygmalion / My Fair Lady (Symbolic interactionism)
- Nell (Symbolic interactionism)
- She's All That (Symbolic interactionism)
- Don Juan DeMarco (Coordinated management of meaning)
- Life Is Beautiful (Coordinated management of meaning)
- House of Games (Interpersonal deception theory)
- The Sting (Interpersonal deception theory)
- Secrets and Lies (Interpersonal deception theory)
- The African Queen (Expectancy violations theory)
- North by Northwest (Expectancy violations theory)

Cognitive Processing
- Oleanna (General)
- To Kill a Mockingbird (Constructivism)
- Anne of Green Gables (Constructivism)

Relationship Development
- Four Weddings and a Funeral (General)
- Brothers McMullen (Social penetration theory)
- Coming Home (Social penetration theory)
- Sleepless in Seattle (Social penetration theory)
- Driving Miss Daisy (Uncertainty reduction theory)
- Down in the Delta (Uncertainty reduction theory)
- Thousand Acres (Uncertainty reduction theory)

Relationship Maintenance
- Breaking Away (General)
- Ordinary People (Interactional view)
- Parenthood (Interactional view)
- What's Eating Gilbert Grape (Interactional view)
- When a Man Loves a Woman (Interactional view)
- A River Runs Through It (Interactional view)
- Beaches (Relational dialectics)
- Children of a Lesser God (Relational dialectics)

Influence
- The Color Purple (General)
- Stand and Deliver (General)
- Dead Man Walking (Social judgment theory)
- A Civil Action (Social judgment theory)
- Swing Kids (Social judgment theory)
- Norma Rae (Elaboration likelihood model)
- Twelve Angry Men (Elaboration likelihood model)
- My Cousin Vinny (Elaboration likelihood model)

Group Decision Making
- Crimson Tide (General)
- Stagecoach [1939] (General)
- Apollo 13 (Functional perspective)
- Flight of the Phoenix (Functional perspective)
- Dead Poets Society (Symbolic convergence theory)
- The Dream Team (Adaptive structuration theory)

Organizational Communication
- Das Boot / The Boat (Information systems approach)
- Good Morning, Vietnam (Cultural approach)
- Up the Down Staircase (Cultural approach)
- The Firm (Cultural approach)
- Roger & Me (Critical theory of communication approach)

Public Rhetoric
- Clarence Darrow (General)
- Inherit the Wind (General)
- Judgment at Nuremberg (General)
- Julius Caesar (The rhetoric)
- The Apostle (The rhetoric)
- Malcolm X (Dramatism)
- Smoke (Narrative paradigm)
- Forrest Gump (Narrative paradigm)

Media and Culture
- Network (General)
- Broadcast News (General)
- Medium Cool (Technological determinism)
- WarGames (Technological determinism)
- The Manchurian Candidate (Semiotics)
- The Year of Living Dangerously (Cultural studies)
- Wag the Dog (Cultural studies)

509

Media Effects
  Bob Roberts (General)
  The Candidate (General)
  Being There (Cultivation theory)
  All the President's Men (Agenda-setting
      theory)
  The Truman Show (The media equation)
  Avalon (The media equation)

Intercultural Communication
  A Passage to India (General)
  Witness (General)
  The Chosen (Anxiety/uncertainty
      management theory)
  Joy Luck Club (Face-negotiation theory)
  Iron and Silk (Face-negotiation theory)
  Dances with Wolves (Speech codes theory)
  Kramer vs. Kramer (Speech codes theory)
  Hoop Dreams (Speech codes theory)

Gender and Communication
  When Harry Met Sally (Genderlect styles)
  Sleepless in Seattle (Genderlect styles)
  Diner (Genderlect styles)

  Steel Magnolias (Genderlect styles)
  Beloved (Standpoint theory)
  Waiting to Exhale (Standpoint theory)
  White Man's Burden (Standpoint theory)
  The Little Mermaid (Muted group theory)
  Fried Green Tomatoes (Muted group theory)
  Tootsie (Muted group theory)
  Thelma and Louise (Muted group theory)

Ethical Reflections
  A Man for All Seasons (Interpersonal
      communication)
  Sophie's Choice (Interpersonal
      communication)
  Chariots of Fire (Group and public
      communication)
  Mr. Smith Goes to Washington (Group and
      public communication)
  Absence of Malice (Mass communication)
  Quiz Show (Mass communication)
  At Play in the Fields of the Lord (Intercultural
      communication)

PIDR). Requirements vary greatly around the ited States. Shailor's in-depth critique of mediation actices is based on three case studies, each co-ediated. By my reading of the text, at least five of the mediators were unsafe, only two showed compe-ncy, and none were artistic. Many of the problems ailor perceives as inherent to the mediation process uld alternatively be ascribed to poorly selected d/or poorly trained volunteers in a single program.

e Gerry Philipsen, "The Coordinated Management Meaning Theory of Pearce, Cronen and Associates," *Watershed Research Traditions in Human Communica-n Theory*, Donald Cushman and Branislav Kovačić ds.), State University of New York, 1995, pp. 13–43.

. Barnett Pearce, "A Sailing Guide for Social Con-ructionists," in *Social Approaches to Communication*, endy Leeds-Hurwitz (ed.), Guilford, New York, 95, p. 88.

rnon E. Cronen, "Coordinated Management of eaning Theory and Postenlightenment Ethics," in *nversation on Communication Ethics*, Karen Joy reenberg (ed.), Ablex, Norwood, N.J., 1991, p. 49.

erry Philipsen, "The Coordinated Management of eaning Theory of Pearce, Cronen and Associates," in *atershed Research Traditions in Human Communication eory*, Donald Cushman and Branislav Kovačić (eds.), ate University of New York—Albany, 1995, pp. 40–41.

'. Barnett Pearce and Stephen W. Littlejohn, *Moral nflict: When Social Worlds Collide*, Sage, Thousand aks, Calif., 1997, pp. 166–167.

ter 6: Expectancy Violations Theory

dee K. Burgoon, "A Communication Model of Per-nal Space Violations: Explication and an Initial Test," *uman Communication Research*, Vol. 4, 1978, p. 130.

dward T. Hall, *The Hidden Dimension*, Doubleday, arden City, N.Y., 1966, p. 1.

. H. Auden, "Prologue: The Birth of Architecture," in *bout the House*, Random House, New York, 1966, . 14.

dee K. Burgoon and Jerold Hale, "Nonverbal Ex-ectancy Violations: Model Elaboration and Applica-on to Immediacy Behaviors," *Communication Mono-aphs*, Vol. 55, 1988, p. 58.

andom House Webster's Electronic Dictionary and The-urus, College Edition, WordPerfect, Orem, Utah, 94.

dee K. Burgoon, "Cross-Cultural and Intercultural pplications of Expectancy Violations Theory," in *In-rcultural Communication Theory*, Richard Wiseman d.), Sage, Thousand Oaks, Calif., 1995, pp. 194–214.

dee K. Burgoon and Joseph Walther, "Nonverbal Ex-ectancies and the Evaluative Consequences of Viola-ons," *Human Communication Research*, Vol. 17, 1990, . 236.

dward Hall, "A System of Notation of Proxemic ehavior," *American Anthropologist*, Vol. 41, 1963, p. 1003–1026.

ited in Judee K. Burgoon, Valerie Manusov, Paul Mi-eo, and Jerold Hale, "Effects of Gaze on Hiring, Cred-

ibility, Attraction, and Relational Message Interpreta-tion," *Journal of Nonverbal Behavior*, Vol. 9, 1985, p. 133.

10 Douglas Kelley and Judee K. Burgoon, "Understand-ing Marital Satisfaction and Couple Type as Functions of Relational Expectations," *Human Communication Re-search*, Vol. 18, 1991, pp. 40–69.

11 Beth A. LePoire and Judee K. Burgoon, "Two Con-trasting Explanations of Involvement Violations: Ex-pectancy Violations Theory Versus Discrepancy Arousal Theory," *Human Communication Research*, Vol. 20, 1994, pp. 560–591.

12 Graham Chapman, John Cleese, Terry Gilliam, Eric Idle, Terry Jones, and Michael Palin, *The Complete Monty Python's Flying Circus: All the Words, Volume One*, Pantheon, New York, 1989, p. 40.

13 Judee K. Burgoon, "Nonverbal Violations of Expecta-tions," in *Nonverbal Interaction*, John Wiemann and Randall P. Harrison (eds.), Sage, Beverly Hills, Calif., 1983, p. 101.

14 Judee K. Burgoon, Joseph Walther, and E. James Baesler, "Interpretations, Evaluations, and Conse-quences of Interpersonal Touch," *Human Communica-tion Research*, Vol. 19, 1992, p. 256.

15 Burgoon, "Cross-Cultural and Intercultural Applica-tions," p. 209.

16 Burgoon is considering such a replacement. As yet un-published, her Interaction Adaptation Theory incorpo-rates some of EVT's principles, but it is definitely a new theory. Judee K. Burgoon, Lesa Stern, and Leesa Dillman, "Interaction Adaptation Theory: An Initial Explication," paper presented to the annual meeting of the International Communication Association, Sydney, Australia, July 11–15, 1994.

Chapter 7: Interpersonal Deception Theory

1 David Buller, Judee Burgoon, Aileen Buslig, and James Roiger, "Testing Interpersonal Deception Theory: The Language of Interpersonal Deception," *Communication Theory*, Vol. 6, 1996, p. 278.

2 Adapted from Steven McCornack, "Information Ma-nipulation Theory," *Communication Monographs*, Vol. 59, 1992, p. 8.

3 David Buller and Judee Burgoon, "Interpersonal De-ception Theory," *Communication Theory*, Vol. 6, 1996, p. 205.

4 Gerald Miller and James Stiff, *Deceptive Communica-tion*, Sage, Newbury Park, Calif., 1993, p. 69.

5 Miron Zuckermann and Robert Driver, "Telling Lies: Verbal and Nonverbal Correlates of Deception," *Mul-tichannel Integrations of Nonverbal Behavior*, Aron Sieg-man and Stanley Feldstein (eds.), Lawrence Erlbaum Associates, Hillsdale, N.J., 1985, pp. 129–148.

6 David Buller, Krystyna Strzyzewski, and Jamie Com-stock, "Interpersonal Deception: I. Deceivers' Reac-tions to Receivers' Suspicions and Probing," *Communi-cation Monographs*, Vol. 58, 1991, p. 1.

7 Ibid., p. 2.

8 The term *leakage* was first used by Paul Ekman and Wallace Friesen, "Nonverbal Leakage and Clues to De-ception," *Psychiatry*, Vol. 1, 1969, pp. 88–105.

ENDNOTES

Chapter 1: Talk about Theory

1 Ernest Bormann, *Communication Theory*, Sheffield Pub-lishing, Salem, Wis., 1989, p. 25.
2 Bob Garfield, "Diet Coke's refreshment packed in swimming trunks," *Advertising Age*, July 11, 1994, p. 3.
3 James A. Anderson, *Communication Theory: Epistemo-logical Foundations*, Guilford, New York, 1996, p. 27.
4 Ibid., p. 120.
5 Poet William Henley, "Invictus," in *The Home Book of Verse*, 9th ed., Burton E. Stevenson (ed.), Holt, Rinehart and Winston, N.Y., p. 3501.
6 Anderson, p. 133.
7 C. S. Lewis, *The Abolition of Man*, Macmillan, New York, 1944, p. 309.
8 George C. Homans, *The Nature of Social Science*, Har-court, New York, 1967, p. 4.
9 Robert Ivie, "The Social Relevance of Rhetorical Schol-arship," *Quarterly Journal of Speech*, Vol. 81, No. 2, 1995, p. 138a.
10 Lawrence Frey, Carl Botan, Paul Friedman, and Gary Kreps, *Investigating Communication: An Introduction to Research Methods*, Prentice-Hall, Englewood Cliffs, N.J., 1991.
11 Lana F. Rakow, "Don't Hate Me Because I'm Beautiful: Feminist Resistance to Advertising's Irresistible Mean-ing," *Southern Communication Journal*, Vol. 57, No. 2, 1992, p. 135.
12 *Dances with Wolves*, TIG Productions, 1990.
13 Clifford Geertz, "Thick Description: Toward an Inter-pretive Theory of History," *The Interpretation of Culture*, Basic Books, New York, 1973, p. 5.

Chapter 2: Weighing the Words

1 Richard Rodgers and Oscar Hammerstein II, "The Farmer and the Cowman," from *Oklahoma!*, Rodgers & Hammerstein Library, New York, 1943, pp. 140–142.
2 Ernest Bormann, *Small Group Communication: Theory and Practice*, 3d ed., Harper & Row, New York, 1990, p. 122.
3 Ernest Bormann, *The Force of Fantasy: Restoring the American Dream*, Southern Illinois University, Carbon-dale, Ill., p. x.
4 Karl R. Popper, *The Logic of Scientific Discovery*, Hutchinson, London, 1959, p. 59.
5 Abraham Kaplan, *The Conduct of Inquiry*, Chandler, San Francisco, 1964, p. 295.
6 Ernest Bormann, "Fantasy and Rhetorical Vision: The Rhetorical Criticism of Social Reality," *Quarterly Jour-nal of Speech*, Vol. 58, 1972, p. 399.
7 Bormann attributes this insight to Harvard psycholo-gist Robert Bales. I present Bales' interaction categories

for analyzing group discussion in the introduction to group decision making (see page 208). Bales changed his original category of "shows tension release" to "dramatizes" when he discovered that group mem-bers typically use verbal imagery to dispel discord.
8 Andrew Macdonald (William Pierce), *The Turner Di-aries*, 2d ed., National Vanguard, Washington, D.C., 1980.
9 Ernest Bormann, "Fantasy and Rhetorical Vision," p. 407.
10 Ernest Bormann, *Small Group Communication*, p. 122.
11 Karl Popper, *Conjectures and Refutations: The Growth of Scientific Knowledge*, Harper & Row, New York, 1965, pp. 36–37.
12 John Cragan and Donald Shields, *Symbolic Theories in Applied Communication Research*, Hampton, Cresskill, N.J., 1995, p. 42.
13 Ibid., pp. 40–47.
14 Ernest G. Bormann, *Communication Theory*, Sheffield Publishing Co., Salem, Wis., 1989, p. 214.
15 Klaus Krippendorff, "The Ethics of Constructing Com-munication," in *Rethinking Communication, Vol. 1: Para-digm Issues*, Brenda Dervin, Lawrence Grossberg, Bar-bara O'Keefe, and Ellen Wartella (eds.), Sage, Newbury Park, Calif., 1989, p. 83.
16 Ernest Bormann, *The Force of Fantasy*, p. ix.
17 Ibid., p. 88.
18 William H. Melody and Robert Mansell, "The Debate over Critical vs. Administrative Research: Circularity or Challenge," *Journal of Communication*, Vol. 33, No. 3, 1983, p. 103.
19 Ibid., pp. 223–242.
20 Barbara Warnick, "Left in Context: What Is the Critic's Role?" *Quarterly Journal of Speech*, Vol. 78, 1992, pp. 232–237.
21 Ernest Bormann, John Cragan, and Donald Shields, "In Defense of Symbolic Convergence Theory: A Look at The Theory and Its Criticisms After Two Decades," *Communication Theory*, Vol. 4, 1994, p. 274.
22 From Robert Frost, *A Masque of Reason*, cited in Ernest Bormann, "Symbolic Convergence Theory: A Commu-nication Formulation," *Journal of Communication*, Vol. 35, No. 4, 1985, p. 135.
23 Leigh Arden Ford, "Fetching Good out of Evil in AA: A Bormannean Fantasy Theme Analysis of *The Big Book* of Alcoholics Anonymous," *Communication Quarterly*, Vol. 37, 1989, pp. 1–15.
24 John Stewart, "A Postmodern Look at Traditional Communication Postulates," *Western Journal of Speech Communication*, Vol. 55, 1991, p. 374.
25 David Zarefsky, "Approaching Lincoln's Second Inau-gural Address," in *The Practice of Rhetorical Criticism*,

2d ed., James R. Andrews (ed.), Longman, New York, 1990, p. 69.

26 Bormann, Cragan, and Shields, "In Defense of Symbolic Convergence Theory, pp. 259–294.

27 See Burke's dramatism and Fisher's narrative paradigm, Chapters 21 and 22.

28 Kenneth Gergen, *Toward Transformation in Social Knowledge*, Springer-Verlag, New York, 1982, p. 109.

29 Ernest Bormann, "Fantasy Theme Analysis and Rhetorical Theory," in *The Rhetoric of Western Thought*, 5th ed., James Golden, Goodwin Berquist, and William Coleman (eds.), Kendall/Hunt, Dubuque, Iowa, 1992, p. 379.

Chapter 3: Mapping the Territory

1 10cc, Eric Stewart and Graham Gouldman, "The Things We Do For Love," from *Deceptive Bends*, St. Annes Music Ltd., 1977.

2 Robert T. Craig, "Communication as a Practical Discipline," in *Rethinking Communication*, Vol. 1, Brenda Dervin, et al. (eds.), Sage, Newbury Park, Calif., pp. 97–122.

3 Robert T. Craig, "Communication Theory as a Field," *Communication Theory*, Vol. 9, 1999, p. 120.

4 Ibid., p. 130.

5 The identification and titles of the seven traditions are taken from Craig (see Note 3). I have altered his order of presentation to match the conceptual plan of Figure 3.3. The boldface, minidefinitions of communication within each tradition are a paraphrase of and are consistent with Craig's conception. The selection of pioneer figures for each tradition was my decision and reflects the features of each tradition I chose to emphasize.

6 Wilbur Schramm, Director of the Stanford Institute for Communication Research, named four social scientists as "founding fathers" of communication research: Harold Lasswell, Kurt Lewin, Paul Lazarsfeld, and Carl Hovland. See Wilbur Schramm, "Communication Research in the United States," in *The Science of Human Communication*, Wilbur Schramm (ed.), Basic Books, New York, 1963, pp. 1–16.

7 Carl Hovland, Irving Janis, and Harold Kelley, *Communication and Persuasion*, Yale University, New Haven, Conn., 1953, p. 17.

8 Norbert Wiener, *The Human Use of Human Beings*, Avon, New York, 1967, p. 23.

9 This all-inclusive definition is attributed to Wilbur Schramm by former student Donald Roberts, now a professor at the Institute for Communication Research at Stanford University. See Note 6 above.

10 Claude Shannon and Warren Weaver, *The Mathematical Theory of Communication*, University of Illinois, Urbana, 1949, p. 66.

11 Cicero, *De oratore*, E. W. Sutton and H. Rackham (trans.), Harvard University, Cambridge, Mass., 1942, p. 25.

12 V. F. Ray, "Human Color Perception and Behavioral Response," *Transactions* of the New York Academy of Sciences, Vol. 16, No. 2, 1953; reproduced in Nancy

Hickerson, *Linguistic Anthropology*, Holt, Rinehart and Winston, New York, 1980, p. 122.

13 Paul Kay and Willet Kempton, "What is the Sapir–Whorf Hypothesis?" *American Anthropologist*, Vol. 86, 1984, pp. 65–79.

14 Edward Sapir, "The Status of Linguistics as a Science," in *Selected Writings*, David Mandelbaum (ed.), University of California, Berkeley, 1951 (1929), p. 160.

15 James Carey, *Communication as Culture*, Unwin Hyman, Boston, 1989, p. 23.

16 For an extended discussion of this socio-cultural concept, see Chapter 5: "The Coordinated Management of Meaning of W. Barnett Pearce & Vernon Cronen."

17 John Torpey, "Ethics and Critical Theory: From Horkheimer to Habermas," *Telos*, Vol. 19, No. 3, 1986, p. 73.

18 Herbert Marcuse, "Philosophy and Critical Theory," in *Negations: Essays in Critical Theory*, Free Association, London, 1988, p. 143.

19 Herbert Marcuse, "Repressive Tolerance," in *Critical Sociology*, Paul Connerton (ed.), pp. 310–311.

20 Theodor Adorno, "Sociology and Empirical Research," in *Critical Sociology: Selected Readings*, Paul Connerton (ed.), Graham Batram (trans.), p. 245.

21 Herbert Marcuse, cited in Tom Bottomore, *The Frankfurt School*, Routledge, London, 1989, p. 38.

22 Max Horkheimer, *Critical Theory: Selected Essays*, Herder & Herder, New York, 1972 (1937), p. 183.

23 Theodor Adorno, "Sociology and Empirical Research," in *Critical Sociology*, Paul Connerton (ed.), Graham Bartram (trans.), Penguin, Middlesex, England, 1978, p. 256.

24 Theodor Adorno, "Cultural Criticism and Society," in *Critical Sociology*, p. 276.

25 Craig, "Communication Theory as a Field," p. 148.

26 Carl Rogers, "This Is Me," in *On Becoming a Person*, Houghton Mifflin, Boston, 1961, p. 24.

27 Carl Rogers, "The Necessary and Sufficient Conditions of Therapeutic Personality Change," *Journal of Consulting Psychology*, Vol. 21, 1957, pp. 95–103.

28 Rogers, "This Is Me," p. 16.

29 Carl Rogers, "The Characteristics of a Helping Relationship," in *On Becoming a Person*, p. 52.

30 Craig, "Communication Theory as a Field," pp. 151–152.

Interpersonal Messages

1 I. A. Richards, *The Philosophy of Rhetoric*, Oxford University, London, 1936, p. 30.

2 An earlier version of these game metaphors appeared in my book, *Making Friends*, InterVarsity Press, Downers Grove, Ill., 1987, pp. 12–18.

Chapter 4: Symbolic Interactionism

1 *Nell*, 1994, Egg Pictures, Twentieth-Century Fox.

2 The three premises are found in Herbert Blumer, *Symbolic Interactionism*, Prentice-Hall, Englewood Cliffs, N.J., 1969, p. 2. I have paraphrased the principles for stylistic consistency and to avoid gender-specific language.

3 See W. I. Thomas and Dorothy Thomas, *The Child in America*, Knopf, New York, 1928.

4 June Wagner, *The Search for Signs of Intelligent Life in the Universe*, Harper Perennial, New York, 1990, pp. 15, 18.

5 For a fascinating account of a gorilla that developed these symbolic associations with the word *kitten*, see Francine Patterson, *Koko's Kitten*, Scholastic, New York, 1985. Mead wouldn't have been troubled by the existence of an animal that can communicate hundreds of symbols in American Sign Language (ASL). He regarded the symbol-using difference between humans and other primates as one of great magnitude— a quantitative rather than a qualitative distinction.

6 Peter M. Hall, "Structuring Symbolic Interaction: Communication and Power" in *Communication Yearbook 4*, Dan Nimmo (ed.), Transaction, New Brunswick, N.J., 1980, p. 50.

7 Douglas Hofstadter, "Changes in Default Words and Images Engendered by Rising Consciousness" in *The Production of Reality*, Peter Kollock and Jodi O'Brien (eds.), Pine Forge, Thousand Oaks, Calif., 1994, p. 112.

8 George Herbert Mead, *Mind, Self, and Society*, University of Chicago, Chicago, 1934, p. 43.

9 Kollock and O'Brien, p. 63.

10 Kingsley Davis, "Final Note on a Case of Extreme Isolation," in Kollock and O'Brien, pp. 78–84.

11 Harper Lee, *To Kill a Mockingbird*, Warner, New York, 1982, p. 282.

12 Ralph Waldo Emerson, "Astraea," *The Works of Ralph Waldo Emerson*, Vol. III, The Nottingham Society, Philadelphia, (no date), p. 121.

13 Mead, *Mind, Self, and Society*, p. 162.

14 George Herbert Mead, "The Social Self," *Journal of Philosophy, Psychology and Scientific Methods*, Vol. 10, 1913, p. 375.

15 Mead, *Mind, Self, and Society*, p. 174.

16 Their interpretation is open to question. As we learn later in the film, Nell's phonetic "may" is also the way she refers to her dead sister. When Nell reached toward the mirror, she might have seen her reflection as an image of her twin rather than of herself. If so, the psychologists' interpretation is added support for Blumer's first premise. They responded to Nell's communication on the basis of the meaning it had for *them*.

17 William Shakespeare, *As You Like It*, Act II, Scene VII, line 139, in *The Riverside Shakespeare*, G. Blakemore Evans (ed.), Houghton Mifflin Co., Boston, 1974, p. 381.

18 Erving Goffman, *The Presentation of Self in Everyday Life*, Doubleday Anchor, Garden City, N.Y., 1959.

19 Ibid., p. 56.

20 Joan P. Emerson, "Behavior in Private Places: Sustaining Definitions of Reality in Gynecological Examinations," in Kollock and O'Brien, pp. 189–202.

21 Jean Mizer, "Cipher in the Snow," *Today's Education*, Vol. 53, November 1964, pp. 8–10.

22 George Bernard Shaw, "Pygmalion," *Selected Plays*, Dodd, Mead, New York, 1948, p. 270.

23 Saul Alinsky, *Reveille for Radicals*, Vintage, New York, 1969 (1946), pp. 77–78.

24 Randall Collins, "Toward a Neo-M Mind," *Symbolic Interaction*, Vol. 1

Chapter 5: Coordinated Managemen

1 W. Barnett Pearce, "A Sailing Gu structionists," in *Social Approache* Wendy Leeds-Hurwitz (ed.), G 1995, p. 92–106.

2 W. Barnett Pearce, *Communication* dition, Southern Illinois Universit p. 114.

3 W. Barnett Pearce, *Interpersonal Co Social Worlds*, HarperCollins, New

4 Ibid., p. 198.

5 See Rom Harré, *Personal Being,* Press, Cambridge, Mass., 1984.

6 W. Barnett Pearce, "'Listening fo Public's Whining' or 'Working to C Public Communication.'" in press

7 Jonathan Shailor, *Empowerment in Critical Analysis of Communication* Conn., 1994, p. 127.

8 W. Barnett Pearce and Kimberly A dent Storytelling: Abilities for Sys and Their Clients," *Human System*

9 Pearce, *Interpersonal Communicatio*

10 The classic work on negotiation Fisher and William Ury, *Getting t* York, 1983.

11 Pearce, *Interpersonal Communicatio*

12 John Dewey, *Experience and Natur* 1925/1958, p.

13 Wittgenstein calls them "frames o ical Investigations,* (paras. 9, 23, 24

14 Shailor, p. 2.

15 Pearce, *Interpersonal Communicatio*

16 Ibid., p. 123. Pearce credits com John Shotter for this strategy.

17 W. Barnett Pearce, *Communication* dition, Southern Illinois Universi 1989, pp. 32–33.

18 Stephen Littlejohn, Jonathan Sha "The Deep Structure of Reality *New Directions in Mediation*, Josep Jones (eds.), Sage, Thousand Oa 67–83.

19 Pearce, *Communication and the* p. 77.

20 Ibid., p. 23.

21 Ibid., p. 84.

22 Ibid., p. 81.

23 Vernon Cronen, "Coordinated Ma ing: The Consequentiality of Com Recapturing of Experience," p. 38.

24 Pearce and Pearce, "Transcendent

25 Shailor, p. 34.

26 Pearce and Pearce, in press.

27 Certification of mediators is a ho the Society of Professionals in

9 Sir Walter Scott, "Marmion, Canto Sixth, XVII" in *The Poetical Works of Sir Walter Scott, Bart.,* Leavitt and Allen, New York, 1830, p. 427.

10 David Buller and Judee Burgoon, "Emotional Expression in the Deception Process," in *Handbook of Communication and Emotion: Research, Theory, Applications, and Contexts,* Peter Andersen and Laura Guerrero (eds.) Academic Press, San Diego, 1998, p. 389.

11 Sigmund Freud, "Fragments of an Analysis of a Case of Hysteria," *Collected Papers,* Vol. 3, Basic Books, New York, 1959 (1905), p. 94.

12 Miron Zuckerman, Bella DePaulo, and Robert Rosenthal, "Verbal and Nonverbal Communication of Deception," in *Advances in Experimental Social Psychology,* Vol. 14, 1981, Academic Press, New York, pp. 1–59.

13 Zuckerman and Driver, p. 137.

14 Bella DePaulo, Julie Stone, and G. Daniel Lassiter, "Deceiving and Detecting Deceit," in *The Self and Social Life,* Barry Schlenker (ed.), McGraw-Hill, New York, 1985, p. 331.

15 Steven McCornack and Malcolm Parks, "Deception Detection and Relationship Development: The Other Side of Trust," in *Communication Yearbook 9,* Margaret McLaughlin (ed.), Sage, Beverly Hills, Calif., 1986, p. 380.

16 Judee Burgoon, David Buller, Kory Floyd, and Joseph Grandpre, "Deceptive Realities: Sender, Receiver, and Observer Perspectives in Deceptive Conversations," *Communication Research,* Vol. 23, 1996, pp. 724–748.

17 McCornack, "Information Manipulation Theory," pp. 4–5. McCornack bases his position on the work of Paul Grice, *Studies in the Way of Words,* Harvard University, Cambridge, Mass., 1969. See also my discussion of Immanuel Kant's Categorical Imperative, p. 103.

18 Judee Burgoon, David Buller, Amy Ebesu, and Patricia Rockwell, "Interpersonal Deception: V. Accuracy in Deception Detection," *Communication Monographs,* Vol. 61, 1994, p. 320.

19 Judee Burgoon, David Buller, Leesa Dillman, and Joseph Walther, "Interpersonal Deception: IV. Effects of Suspicion on Perceived Communication and Nonverbal Behavior Dynamics," *Human Communication Research,* Vol. 22, 1995, p. 164.

20 Ibid.

21 Judee Burgoon, David Buller, Amy Ebesu, Cindy White, and Patricia Rockwell, "Testing Interpersonal Deception Theory: Effects of Suspicion on Communication Behaviors and Perceptions," *Communication Theory,* Vol. 6, 1996, p. 260.

22 Judee Burgoon, David Buller, Kory Floyd, and Joseph Grandpre, p. 736.

23 Judee Burgoon, "Toward a Processual View of Interpersonal Deception." Paper presented to the annual meeting of the International Communication Association, San Francisco, May 1989, p. 2.

24 Judee Burgoon, David Buller, Amy Ebesu, Cindy White, and Patricia Rothwell, p. 263.

25 Buller and Burgoon, "Interpersonal Deception Theory," p. 233.

26 McCornack and Parks, p. 380.

27 David Buller, Judee Burgoon, Cindy White, and Amy Ebesu, "Interpersonal Deception: VII. Behavioral Profiles of Falsification, Equivocation, and Concealment," *Journal of Language and Social Psychology,* Vol. 13, 1994, p. 392.

Ethical Reflections: Interpersonal Messages

1 Immanuel Kant, "On a Supposed Right to Lie from Altruistic Motives," in *Critique of Practical Reason and Other Writings in Moral Philosophy,* Lewis White Beck (trans. and ed.), University of Chicago, Chicago, 1964, p. 346.

2 Immanuel Kant, "Introduction to the Metaphysic of Morals," *The Doctrine of Virtue: Part II of The Metaphysic of Morals,* Mary Gregor (trans.), Harper & Row, New York, 1964, p. 23.

3 Immanuel Kant, *Groundwork of the Metaphysic of Morals,* H. J. Paton (trans.), Harper Torchbooks, New York, 1964, p. 88.

4 "Enarrationes in Psalmos LXIV.2," cited in *An Augustine Synthesis,* Erik Przywara (ed.), Sheed and Ward, London, 1936, p. 267.

5 Richard of Chichester (c. 1200), in *The Hymnbook,* The United Presbyterian Church in the U.S.A., New York, 1955, p. 445.

6 Augustine, *Enchiridion, on Faith, Hope and Love,* Henry Paolucci (trans.), Henry Regnery, Chicago, 1961.

7 Augustine, "On Lying," in *Treatises on Various Subjects,* Vol. 14, R. J. Deferrari (ed.), Catholic University, New York, 1952, Chapter 14.

8 Sissela Bok, *Lying: Moral Choice in Public and Private Life,* Vintage, New York, 1979.

9 Ibid., p. 48.

10 Ibid., p. 32.

11 Ibid., p. 263.

12 Ibid., pp. 95–108.

Chapter 8: Constructivism

1 Walter H. Crockett, "Cognitive Complexity and Impression Formation," in *Progress in Experimental Personality Research,* Vol. 2, B. A. Maher (ed.), Academic Press, New York, 1965, pp. 47–90.

2 Ann Mayden Nicotera, "The Constructivist Theory of Delia, Clark, and Associates," in *Watershed Research Traditions in Human Communication Theory,* Donald Cushman and Branislav Kovačić (eds.), State University of New York, Albany, 1995, p. 52.

3 Brant R. Burleson and Michael S. Waltman, "Cognitive Complexity: Using the Role Category Questionnaire Measure," in *A Handbook for the Study of Human Communication,* Charles Tardy (ed.), Ablex, Norwood, N.J., 1988, p. 15.

4 Ruth Ann Clark and Jesse Delia, "Cognitive Complexity, Social Perspective-Taking, and Functional Persuasive Skills in Second-to-Ninth-Grade Students," *Human Communication Research,* Vol. 3, 1977, pp. 128–134.

5 Roderick Hart and Don Burks, "Rhetorical Sensitivity and Social Interaction," *Speech Monographs,* Vol. 39, 1972, pp. 75–91.

6 Jesse Delia, Barbara O'Keefe, and Daniel O'Keefe, "The Constructivist Approach to Communication," in

Human Communication Theory, Frank E. X. Dance (ed.), Harper & Row, New York, 1982, p. 163.

7 See Shereen Bingham and Brant Burleson, "Multiple Effects of Messages with Multiple Goals: Some Perceived Outcomes of Responses to Sexual Harassment," *Human Communication Research*, Vol. 16, 1989, p. 192.

8 Barbara O'Keefe, "The Logic of Message Design: Individual Differences in Reasoning about Communication," *Communication Monographs*, Vol. 55, 1988, pp. 80–103.

9 Ibid., p. 84.

10 Dr. Seuss, *Horton Hatches the Egg*, Random House, New York, 1940, p. 165.

11 An "expressive minimal" message that reflects the speaker's internal state, but has no specific aim. See Bingham and Burleson, p. 192.

12 O'Keefe, p. 86.

13 A "conventional unifunctional message" aimed at stopping the sexual harassment once and for all. See Bingham and Burleson, p. 192.

14 O'Keefe, p. 87. For a comparison between rhetorical design logic and the concept of rhetorical sensitivity, see Glen McClish, "Humanist and Empiricist Rhetorics: Some Reflections on Rhetorical Sensitivity, Message Design Logics, and Multiple Goal Structures," *Rhetoric Society Quarterly*, Vol. 23, 1994, Summer/Fall, pp. 27–45.

15 A "rhetorical multifunctional" message designed to achieve multiple goals in a sexual harassment situation. See Bingham and Burleson, p. 193.

16 These three examples of comforting communication are from Brant Burleson, "Comforting Messages: Significance, Approaches, and Effects," in *Communication of Social Support*, Brant Burleson, Terrance Albrecht, and Irwin Sarason (eds.), Sage, Thousand Oaks, Calif., 1994, p. 12.

17 Ibid., p. 22.

18 Brant Burleson and Wendy Samter, "A Social Skills Approach to Relationship Maintenance," in *Communication and Relationship Maintenance*, Daniel Canary and Laura Stafford (eds.), Academic Press, San Diego, 1994, pp. 61–90.

19 Comments expressed in a student's journal.

20 Beverly Davenport Sypher and Theodore Zorn, "Communication-related Abilities and Upward Mobility: A Longitudinal Investigation," *Human Communication Research*, Vol. 12, 1986, pp. 420–431.

21 Brant Burleson, Jesse Delia, and James Applegate, "The Socialization of Person-Centered Communication: Parental Contributions to the Social-Cognitive and Communication Skills of Their Children," in *Perspectives in Family Communication*, Mary Anne Fitzpatrick and Anita Vangelisti (eds.), Sage, Thousand Oaks, Calif., 1995, pp. 34–76.

22 Delia, O'Keefe, and O'Keefe, "The Constructivist Approach to Communication," p. 167.

Relationship Development

1 Harold H. Kelley, Ellen Berscheid, Andrew Christensen, John Harvey, Ted Huston, George Levinger, Evie McClintock, Letitia Anne Peplau, and Donald Peterson, *Close Relationships*, W. H. Freeman, New York, 1983, p. 38.

2 See Jacqueline Wiseman, "Friendship: Bonds and Binds in a Voluntary Relationship," *Journal of Social and Personal Relationships*, Vol. 3, 1986, pp. 191–211, and Robert Hays, "Friendship," in *Handbook of Personal Relationships*, Steve Duck (ed.), John Wiley & Sons, New York, 1988, pp. 391–408.

3 Robert Sternberg, "A Triangular Theory of Love," *Psychological Review*, Vol. 9, 1986, pp. 119–135.

4 Robert Frost, "The Death of the Hired Man," in *The Poetry of Robert Frost*, Edward Lathem (ed.), Holt, Rinehart, and Winston, New York, 1969, pp. 34–36.

5 Lillian Rubin, *Just Friends*, Harper & Row, New York, 1985, p. 16.

6 Keith Davis and Michael Todd, "Friendship and Love Relationships" in *Advances in Descriptive Psychology*, Vol. 2, Keith Davis (ed.), JAI, Greenwich, Conn., 1982, pp. 79–122.

7 See Ron Adler and Neal Towne, *Looking Out/Looking In*, 8th ed., Harcourt Brace Jovanovich, Fort Worth, 1995, and John Stewart, *Bridges Not Walls*, 6th ed., McGraw-Hill, New York, 1995.

8 Erich Fromm, *The Art of Loving*, Harper & Row, New York, 1974, p. 3.

Chapter 9: Social Penetration Theory

1 Dalmas Taylor and Irwin Altman, "Communication in Interpersonal Relationships: Social Penetration Processes," in *Interpersonal Processes: New Directions in Communications Research*, Michael Roloff and Gerald Miller (eds.), Sage, Newbury Park, Calif., 1987, p. 259.

2 Harold H. Kelley and John W. Thibaut, *Interpersonal Relationships*, John Wiley & Sons, New York, 1978.

3 John Stuart Mill, *A System of Logic*, J. W. Parker, London, 1843, Book VI, Chapter XII.

4 C. Arthur VanLear, "The Formation of Social Relationships: A Longitudinal Study of Social Penetration," *Human Communication Research*, Vol. 13, 1987, pp. 299–322.

5 John Berg, "Development of Friendship between Roommates," *Journal of Personality and Social Psychology*, Vol. 46, 1984, pp. 346–356.

6 Betsy Tolstedt and Joseph Stokes, "Self-Disclosure, Intimacy, and the Depenetration Process," *Journal of Personality and Social Psychology*, Vol. 46, 1984, pp. 84–90.

7 Irwin Altman, Anne Vinsel, and Barbara Brown, "Dialectic Conceptions in Social Psychology: An Application to Social Penetration and Privacy Regulation," in *Advances in Experimental Social Psychology*, Vol. 14, Leonard Berkowitz (ed.), Academic Press, New York, 1981, p. 139.

8 VanLear, "The Formation of Social Relationships," and C. Arthur VanLear, "Testing a Cyclical Model of Communication Openness in Relationship Development: Two Longitudinal Studies," *Communication Monographs*, Vol. 58, 1991, pp. 337–361.

9 Paul H. Wright, "Self-Referent Motivation and the Intrinsic Quality of Friendship," *Journal of Social and Personal Relationships*, Vol. 1, 1984, pp. 115–130.

10 Richard Conville, *Relational Transitions: The Evolution of Personal Relationships*, Praeger, New York, 1991, pp. 19–40.

11 From John 15:13, *The New American Bible*, J. P. Kennedy & Sons, New York, 1970.

Chapter 10: Uncertainty Reduction Theory

1 Charles Berger, "Uncertainty and Information Exchange in Developing Relationships," in *Handbook of Personal Relationships*, Steve Duck (ed.), Wiley, New York, 1988, p. 244.

2 Charles Berger and Richard Calabrese, "Some Explorations in Initial Interaction and Beyond: Toward a Developmental Theory of Interpersonal Communication," *Human Communication Research*, Vol. 1, 1975, p. 100.

3 Charles Berger, "Beyond Initial Interaction: Uncertainty, Understanding, and the Development of Interpersonal Relationships," in *Language and Social Psychology*, H. Giles and R. St. Clair (eds.), Basil Blackwell, Oxford, Eng., 1979, pp. 122–144.

4 Charles Berger and William Gudykunst, "Uncertainty and Communication," in *Progress in Communication Sciences*, Vol. X, Brenda Dervin and Melvin Voigt (eds.), Ablex, Norwood, N.J., 1991, p. 23.

5 For an excellent introduction to attribution theory, see Kelly Shaver, *An Introduction to Attribution Processes*, Lawrence Erlbaum Associates, Hillsdale, N.J., 1983. Heider's theory is also described in the first two editions of this text (1991, 1994); see *www.afirstlook.com*.

6 Berger and Calabrese, pp. 99–112.

7 Joseph Cappella, "Mutual Influence in Expressive Behavior: Adult-Adult and Infant-Adult Dyadic Interaction," *Psychological Bulletin*, Vol. 89, 1981, pp. 101–132.

8 Berger and Gudykunst, p. 25.

9 Malcolm Parks and Mara Adelman, "Communication Networks and the Development of Romantic Relationships: An Extension of Uncertainty Reduction Theory," *Human Communication Research*, Vol. 10, 1983, pp. 55–79.

10 Ellen Berscheid and Elaine Walster, *Interpersonal Attraction*, 2d ed., Addison-Wesley, Reading, Mass., 1978, pp. 61–89.

11 Charles R. Berger, *Planning Strategic Interaction*, Lawrence Erlbaum Associates, Mahwah, N.J., 1997, p. 17.

12 Charles R. Berger, "Goals, Plans, and Mutual Understanding in Relationships," in *Individuals in Relationships*, Steve Duck (ed.), Sage, Newbury Park, Calif., 1993, p. 34.

13 Charles R. Berger, "Message Production Under Uncertainty," in *Developing Communication Theories*, Gerry Philipsen and Terrance Albrecht (eds.), State University of New York, Albany, 1997, p. 39.

14 Charles R. Berger, "Producing Messages Under Uncertainty," in *Message Production: Advances in Communication Theory*, John O. Green (ed.), Lawrence Erlbaum Associates, Mahwah, N.J., 1997, p. 222.

15 Personal correspondence from Charles Berger.

16 Berger, "Message Production Under Uncertainty," p. 39.

17 Charles R. Berger, "Inscrutable Goals, Uncertain Plans, and the Production of Communicative Action," in *Communication and Social Influence Processes*, Charles R. Berger and Michael Burgoon (eds.), Michigan State University, East Lansing, 1995, p. 17.

18 Berger, *Planning Strategic Interaction*, pp. 132–135.

19 Proverbs 15:22, New Revised Standard Version of the Bible.

20 Charles Berger, "Communicating Under Uncertainty," in *Interpersonal Processes: New Directions in Communication Research*, Michael Roloff and Gerald Miller (eds.), Sage, Newbury Park, Calif., 1987, p. 40.

21 Kathy Kellermann and Rodney Reynolds, "When Ignorance Is Bliss: The Role of Motivation to Reduce Uncertainty in Uncertainty Reduction Theory," *Human Communication Research*, Vol. 17, 1990, p. 7.

22 Ibid., p. 71.

23 Michael Sunnafrank, "Predicted Outcome Value During Initial Interaction: A Reformulation of Uncertainty Reduction Theory," *Human Communication Research*, Vol. 13, 1986, pp. 3–33.

24 Charles Berger, "Communication Theories and Other Curios," *Communication Monographs*, Vol. 58, 1991, p. 102.

25 Berger, "Communicating Under Uncertainty," p. 58.

Relationship Maintenance

1 John Stewart, "Interpersonal Communication: Contact Between Persons," *Bridges Not Walls*, 5th ed., John Stewart (ed.), McGraw-Hill, New York, 1990, pp. 13–30.

Chapter 11: The Interactional View

1 Alan Watts, *The Book*, Pantheon, New York, 1966, p. 65. For other examples of Watts' use of the life-as-a-game metaphor, see Alan Watts, "The Game of Black-and-White," *The Book*, Pantheon, New York, 1966, pp. 22–46; and Alan Watts, "The Counter Game" *Psychology East & West*, Ballantine, New York, 1969, pp. 144–185.

2 Paul Watzlawick, "The Construction of Clinical 'Realities'," in *The Evolution of Psychotherapy: The Second Conference*, Jeffrey Zeig (ed.), Brunner/Mazel, New York, 1992, p. 64.

3 Watzlawick, Beavin, and Jackson list five axioms rather than four. I have omitted one stating that human beings communicate both digitally and analogically because the distinction has proved to be meaningless for most readers and I have been unable to explain why it is important.

4 Paul Watzlawick, *The Language of Change*, W. W. Norton, New York, 1978, p. 11.

5 Paul Watzlawick, Janet Beavin, and Don Jackson, *Pragmatics of Human Communication*, W. W. Norton, New York, 1967, p. 54.

6 R. D. Laing, *Knots*, Pantheon, New York, 1970, p. 27.

7 Watzlawick, Beavin, and Jackson, p. 99.

8 L. Edna Rogers-Millar and Frank E. Millar III, "Domineeringness and Dominance: A Transactional View," *Human Communication Research*, Vol. 5, 1979, pp. 238–245.

9 Paul Watzlawick, John H. Weaklund, and Richard Fisch, *Change,* W. W. Norton, New York, 1974, p. 95.
10 Watzlawick, *Language of Change*, p. 122.
11 Watzlawick, "The Construction of Clinical 'Realities'," p. 61.
12 "Helping," Families Anonymous, Inc., Van Nuys, Calif., no date.
13 Janet Beavin Bavelas, "Research into the Pragmatics of Human Communication," *Journal of Strategic and Systemic Therapies*, Vol. 11, No. 2, 1992, pp. 15–29.

Chapter 12: Relational Dialectics

1 Leslie Baxter, "Interpersonal Communication as Dialogue: A Response to the 'Social Approaches' Forum," *Communication Theory*, Vol. 2, 1992, p. 330.
2 Leslie Baxter and Barbara Montgomery, *Relating: Dialogues and Dialectics*, Guilford, New York, 1996, p. 6.
3 Leslie A. Baxter, "Interpersonal Communication as Dialogue: A Response to the 'Social Approaches' Forum," *Communication Theory*, Vol. 2, 1992, p. 330.
4 Baxter and Montgomery, p. 8.
5 Leslie A. Baxter, "A Dialectical Perspective on Communication Strategies in Relationship Development," in *A Handbook of Personal Relationships*, Steve Duck (ed.), John Wiley & Sons, New York, 1988, p. 258.
6 Baxter and Montgomery, p. 43.
7 Hugh Lofting, *The Story of Dr. Doolittle*, J. B. Lippincott, Philadelphia, 1920, pp. 81–89.
8 Baxter, "Dialectical Perspective," p. 259.
9 Irwin Altman, Anne Vinsel, and Barbara Brown, "Dialectic Conceptions in Social Psychology: An Application to Social Penetration and Privacy Regulation," in *Advances in Experimental Social Psychology*, Vol. 14, Leonard Berkowitz (ed.), Academic Press, New York, 1981, pp. 107–160.
10 Baxter and Montgomery, pp. 185–206.
11 All the statements in the strategy section about relational satisfaction are based on Leslie A. Baxter, "Dialectical Contradictions in Relationship Development," *Journal of Social and Personal Relationships*, Vol. 7, 1990, pp. 69–88. Baxter now uses the label "denial" to describe the tactic that she used to call "selection."
12 For further information on this approach, see Leslie Baxter and William Wilmot, "Taboo Topics in Romantic Relationships," *Journal of Social and Personal Relationships*, Vol. 2, 1985, pp. 253–269.
13 Barbara Montgomery, "Relationship Maintenance Versus Relationship Change: A Dialectical Dilemma," *Journal of Social and Personal Relationships*, Vol. 10, 1993, p. 211.
14 Ibid., p. 221.

Influence

1 Kathy Kellermann and Tim Cole, "Classifying Compliance Gaining Messages: Taxonomic Disorder and Strategic Confusion," *Communication Theory*, Vol. 4, 1994, pp. 3–60.
2 John Cacioppo, "Attitudes and Evaluative Space: Beyond Bipolar Conceptualizations and Measures," Presidential Address, Society for Personality and Social Psychology, New York, Aug. 11–15, 1995.
3 Richard Petty and John Cacioppo, *Attitudes and Persuasion: Classic and Contemporary Approaches*, Wm. C. Brown, Dubuque, Iowa, 1981.
4 Leon Festinger, *A Theory of Cognitive Dissonance*, Stanford University, Stanford, Calif., 1957, p. 95. The 3rd edition of this text included a chapter on cognitive dissonance theory—see pp. 206–215. It is also available in the "Archives" section at *www.afirstlook.com*.

Chapter 13: Social Judgment Theory

1 Muzafer Sherif and Carolyn Sherif, *Social Psychology*, Harper, New York, 1969.
2 Muzafer Sherif, "Experiments in Group Conflict," *Scientific American*, Vol. 195, 1956, pp. 54–58.
3 Carolyn Sherif, Muzafer Sherif, and Roger Nebergall, *Attitude and Attitude Change: The Social Judgment-Involvement Approach*, W. B. Saunders, Philadelphia, 1965, p. 222.
4 Ibid., p. 225.
5 Ibid., p. 214.
6 Gian Sarup, Robert Suchner, and Gitanjali Gaylord, "Contrast Effects and Attitude Change: A Test of the Two-Stage Hypothesis of Social Judgment Theory," *Social Psychology Quarterly*, Vol. 54, 1991, pp. 364–372.
7 Kathryn Greene, Roxanne Parrott, and Julianne M. Serovich, "Privacy, HIV Testing, and AIDS: College Students' Versus Parents' Perspectives," *Health Communication*, Vol. 5, 1993, pp. 59–74.
8 S. Bochner and C. Insko, "Communicator Discrepancy, Source Credibility and Opinion Change," *Journal of Personality and Social Psychology*, Vol. 4, 1966, pp. 614–621.
9 Interview on *Morning Edition*, National Public Radio, May 31, 1995.

Chapter 14: Elaboration Likelihood Model

1 Richard E. Petty and John T. Cacioppo, *Communication and Persuasion: Central and Peripheral Routes to Attitude Change*, Springer-Verlag, New York, 1986, p. 7.
2 Richard E. Petty and John T. Cacioppo, *Attitudes and Persuasion: Classic and Contemporary Approaches*, Wm. C. Brown, Dubuque, Iowa, 1981, p. 256.
3 Robert B. Cialdini, *Influence: Science and Practice*, 2d ed., Scott, Foresman, Glenview, Ill., 1988.
4 Richard Petty and Duane Wegener, "The Elaboration Likelihood Model: Current Status and Controversies," in *Dual Process Theories in Social Psychology*, Shelly Chaiken and Yaacov Trope (eds.), Guilford, New York, 1999, pp. 44–48.
5 John Cacioppo, et al., "Dispositional Differences in Cognitive Motivation: The Life and Times of Individuals Varying in Need for Cognition," *Psychological Bulletin*, Vol. 119, 1996, pp. 197–253.
6 Richard Petty and John Cacioppo, "The Elaboration Likelihood Model of Persuasion," in *Advances in Experimental Social Psychology*, Vol. 19, Leonard Berkowitz (ed.), Academic Press, Orlando 1986, p. 129.
7 Shortly after I created this example in 1996, a backup musician for Smashing Pumpkins died from an overdose of heroin taken with the rock group's drummer, Jimmy Chamberlin. Corgan has now become a leading

ENDNOTES

Chapter 1: Talk about Theory

1 Ernest Bormann, *Communication Theory,* Sheffield Publishing, Salem, Wis., 1989, p. 25.
2 Bob Garfield, "Diet Coke's refreshment packed in swimming trunks," *Advertising Age,* July 11, 1994, p. 3.
3 James A. Anderson, *Communication Theory: Epistemological Foundations,* Guilford, New York, 1996, p. 27.
4 Ibid., p. 120.
5 Poet William Henley, "Invictus," in *The Home Book of Verse,* 9th ed., Burton E. Stevenson (ed.), Holt, Rinehart and Winston, N.Y., p. 3501.
6 Anderson, p. 133.
7 C. S. Lewis, *The Abolition of Man,* Macmillan, New York, 1944, p. 309.
8 George C. Homans, *The Nature of Social Science,* Harcourt, New York, 1967, p. 4.
9 Robert Ivie, "The Social Relevance of Rhetorical Scholarship," *Quarterly Journal of Speech,* Vol. 81, No. 2, 1995, p. 138a.
10 Lawrence Frey, Carl Botan, Paul Friedman, and Gary Kreps, *Investigating Communication: An Introduction to Research Methods,* Prentice-Hall, Englewood Cliffs, N.J., 1991.
11 Lana F. Rakow, "Don't Hate Me Because I'm Beautiful: Feminist Resistance to Advertising's Irresistible Meaning," *Southern Communication Journal,* Vol. 57, No. 2, 1992, p. 135.
12 *Dances with Wolves,* TIG Productions, 1990.
13 Clifford Geertz, "Thick Description: Toward an Interpretive Theory of History," *The Interpretation of Culture,* Basic Books, New York, 1973, p. 5.

Chapter 2: Weighing the Words

1 Richard Rodgers and Oscar Hammerstein II, "The Farmer and the Cowman," from *Oklahoma!,* Rodgers & Hammerstein Library, New York, 1943, pp. 140–142.
2 Ernest Bormann, *Small Group Communication: Theory and Practice,* 3d ed., Harper & Row, New York, 1990, p. 122.
3 Ernest Bormann, *The Force of Fantasy: Restoring the American Dream,* Southern Illinois University, Carbondale, Ill., p. 5.
4 Karl R. Popper, *The Logic of Scientific Discovery,* Hutchinson, London, 1959, p. 59.
5 Abraham Kaplan, *The Conduct of Inquiry,* Chandler, San Francisco, 1964, p. 295.
6 Ernest Bormann, "Fantasy and Rhetorical Vision: The Rhetorical Criticism of Social Reality," *Quarterly Journal of Speech,* Vol. 58, 1972, p. 399.
7 Bormann attributes this insight to Harvard psychologist Robert Bales. I present Bales' interaction categories for analyzing group discussion in the introduction to group decision making (see page 208). Bales changed his original category of "shows tension release" to "dramatizes" when he discovered that group members typically use verbal imagery to dispel discord.
8 Andrew Macdonald (William Pierce), *The Turner Diaries,* 2d ed., National Vanguard, Washington, D.C., 1980.
9 Ernest Bormann, "Fantasy and Rhetorical Vision," p. 407.
10 Ernest Bormann, *Small Group Communication,* p. 122.
11 Karl Popper, *Conjectures and Refutations: The Growth of Scientific Knowledge,* Harper & Row, New York, 1965, pp. 36–37.
12 John Cragan and Donald Shields, *Symbolic Theories in Applied Communication Research,* Hampton, Cresskill, N.J., 1995, p. 42.
13 Ibid., pp. 40–47.
14 Ernest G. Bormann, *Communication Theory,* Sheffield Publishing Co., Salem, Wis., 1989, p. 214.
15 Klaus Krippendorff, "The Ethics of Constructing Communication," in *Rethinking Communication, Vol. 1: Paradigm Issues,* Brenda Dervin, Lawrence Grossberg, Barbara O'Keefe, and Ellen Wartella (eds.), Sage, Newbury Park, Calif., 1989, p. 83.
16 Ernest Bormann, *The Force of Fantasy,* p. ix.
17 Ibid., p. 88.
18 William H. Melody and Robert Mansell, "The Debate over Critical vs. Administrative Research: Circularity or Challenge," *Journal of Communication,* Vol. 33, No. 3, 1983, p. 103.
19 Ibid., pp. 223–242.
20 Barbara Warnick, "Left in Context: What Is the Critic's Role?" *Quarterly Journal of Speech,* Vol. 78, 1992, pp. 232–237.
21 Ernest Bormann, John Cragan, and Donald Shields, "In Defense of Symbolic Convergence Theory: A Look at The Theory and Its Criticisms After Two Decades," *Communication Theory,* Vol. 4, 1994, p. 274.
22 From Robert Frost, *A Masque of Reason,* cited in Ernest Bormann, "Symbolic Convergence Theory: A Communication Formulation," *Journal of Communication,* Vol. 35, No. 4, 1985, p. 135.
23 Leigh Arden Ford, "Fetching Good out of Evil in AA: A Bormannean Fantasy Theme Analysis of *The Big Book* of Alcoholics Anonymous," *Communication Quarterly,* Vol. 37, 1989, pp. 1–15.
24 John Stewart, "A Postmodern Look at Traditional Communication Postulates," *Western Journal of Speech Communication,* Vol. 55, 1991, p. 374.
25 David Zarefsky, "Approaching Lincoln's Second Inaugural Address," in *The Practice of Rhetorical Criticism,*

2d ed., James R. Andrews (ed.), Longman, New York, 1990, p. 69.

26 Bormann, Cragan, and Shields, "In Defense of Symbolic Convergence Theory, pp. 259–294.

27 See Burke's dramatism and Fisher's narrative paradigm, Chapters 21 and 22.

28 Kenneth Gergen, *Toward Transformation in Social Knowledge,* Springer-Verlag, New York, 1982, p. 109.

29 Ernest Bormann, "Fantasy Theme Analysis and Rhetorical Theory," in *The Rhetoric of Western Thought,* 5th ed., James Golden, Goodwin Berquist, and William Coleman (eds.), Kendall/Hunt, Dubuque, Iowa, 1992, p. 379.

Chapter 3: Mapping the Territory

1 10cc, Eric Stewart and Graham Gouldman, "The Things We Do For Love," from *Deceptive Bends,* St. Annes Music Ltd., 1977.

2 Robert T. Craig, "Communication as a Practical Discipline," in *Rethinking Communication,* Vol. 1, Brenda Dervin, et al. (eds.), Sage, Newbury Park, Calif., pp. 97–122.

3 Robert T. Craig, "Communication Theory as a Field," *Communication Theory,* Vol. 9, 1999, p. 120.

4 Ibid., p. 130.

5 The identification and titles of the seven traditions are taken from Craig (see Note 3). I have altered his order of presentation to match the conceptual plan of Figure 3.3. The boldface, minidefinitions of communication within each tradition are a paraphrase of and are consistent with Craig's conception. The selection of pioneer figures for each tradition was my decision and reflects the features of each tradition I chose to emphasize.

6 Wilbur Schramm, Director of the Stanford Institute for Communication Research, named four social scientists as "founding fathers" of communication research: Harold Lasswell, Kurt Lewin, Paul Lazarsfeld, and Carl Hovland. See Wilbur Schramm, "Communication Research in the United States," in *The Science of Human Communication,* Wilbur Schramm (ed.), Basic Books, New York, 1963, pp. 1–16.

7 Carl Hovland, Irving Janis, and Harold Kelley, *Communication and Persuasion,* Yale University, New Haven, Conn., 1953, p. 17.

8 Norbert Wiener, *The Human Use of Human Beings,* Avon, New York, 1967, p. 23.

9 This all-inclusive definition is attributed to Wilbur Schramm by former student Donald Roberts, now a professor at the Institute for Communication Research at Stanford University. See Note 6 above.

10 Claude Shannon and Warren Weaver, *The Mathematical Theory of Communication,* University of Illinois, Urbana, 1949, p. 66.

11 Cicero, *De oratore,* E. W. Sutton and H. Rackham (trans.), Harvard University, Cambridge, Mass., 1942, p. 25.

12 V. F. Ray, "Human Color Perception and Behavioral Response," *Transactions* of the New York Academy of Sciences, Vol. 16, No. 2, 1953; reproduced in Nancy

Hickerson, *Linguistic Anthropology,* Holt, Rinehart and Winston, New York, 1980, p. 122.

13 Paul Kay and Willet Kempton, "What is the Sapir–Whorf Hypothesis?" *American Anthropologist,* Vol. 86, 1984, pp. 65–79.

14 Edward Sapir, "The Status of Linguistics as a Science," in *Selected Writings,* David Mandelbaum (ed.), University of California, Berkeley, 1951 (1929), p. 160.

15 James Carey, *Communication as Culture,* Unwin Hyman, Boston, 1989, p. 23.

16 For an extended discussion of this socio-cultural concept, see Chapter 5: "The Coordinated Management of Meaning of W. Barnett Pearce & Vernon Cronen."

17 John Torpey, "Ethics and Critical Theory: From Horkheimer to Habermas," *Telos,* Vol. 19, No. 3, 1986, p. 73.

18 Herbert Marcuse, "Philosophy and Critical Theory," in *Negations: Essays in Critical Theory,* Free Association, London, 1988, p. 143.

19 Herbert Marcuse, "Repressive Tolerance," in *Critical Sociology,* Paul Connerton (ed.), pp. 310–311.

20 Theodor Adorno, "Sociology and Empirical Research," in *Critical Sociology: Selected Readings,* Paul Connerton (ed.), Graham Batram (trans.), p. 245.

21 Herbert Marcuse, cited in Tom Bottomore, *The Frankfurt School,* Routledge, London, 1989, p. 38.

22 Max Horkheimer, *Critical Theory: Selected Essays,* Herder & Herder, New York, 1972 (1937), p. 183.

23 Theodor Adorno, "Sociology and Empirical Research," in *Critical Sociology,* Paul Connerton (ed.), Graham Bartram (trans.), Penguin, Middlesex, England, 1978, p. 256.

24 Theodor Adorno, "Cultural Criticism and Society," in *Critical Sociology,* p. 276.

25 Craig, "Communication Theory as a Field," p. 148.

26 Carl Rogers, "This Is Me," in *On Becoming a Person,* Houghton Mifflin, Boston, 1961, p. 24.

27 Carl Rogers, "The Necessary and Sufficient Conditions of Therapeutic Personality Change," *Journal of Consulting Psychology,* Vol. 21, 1957, pp. 95–103.

28 Rogers, "This Is Me," p. 16.

29 Carl Rogers, "The Characteristics of a Helping Relationship," in *On Becoming a Person,* p. 52.

30 Craig, "Communication Theory as a Field," pp. 151–152.

Interpersonal Messages

1 I. A. Richards, *The Philosophy of Rhetoric,* Oxford University, London, 1936, p. 30.

2 An earlier version of these game metaphors appeared in my book, *Making Friends,* InterVarsity Press, Downers Grove, Ill., 1987, pp. 12–18.

Chapter 4: Symbolic Interactionism

1 *Nell,* 1994, Egg Pictures, Twentieth-Century Fox.

2 The three premises are found in Herbert Blumer, *Symbolic Interactionism,* Prentice-Hall, Englewood Cliffs, N.J., 1969, p. 2. I have paraphrased the principles for stylistic consistency and to avoid gender-specific language.

3 See W. I. Thomas and Dorothy Thomas, *The Child in America,* Knopf, New York, 1928.

4 June Wagner, *The Search for Signs of Intelligent Life in the Universe,* Harper Perennial, New York, 1990, pp. 15, 18.

5 For a fascinating account of a gorilla that developed these symbolic associations with the word *kitten,* see Francine Patterson, *Koko's Kitten,* Scholastic, New York, 1985. Mead wouldn't have been troubled by the existence of an animal that can communicate hundreds of symbols in American Sign Language (ASL). He regarded the symbol-using difference between humans and other primates as one of great magnitude— a quantitative rather than a qualitative distinction.

6 Peter M. Hall, "Structuring Symbolic Interaction: Communication and Power" in *Communication Yearbook 4,* Dan Nimmo (ed.), Transaction, New Brunswick, N.J., 1980, p. 50.

7 Douglas Hofstadter, "Changes in Default Words and Images Engendered by Rising Consciousness" in *The Production of Reality,* Peter Kollock and Jodi O'Brien (eds.), Pine Forge, Thousand Oaks, Calif., 1994, p. 112.

8 George Herbert Mead, *Mind, Self, and Society,* University of Chicago, Chicago, 1934, p. 43.

9 Kollock and O'Brien, p. 63.

10 Kingsley Davis, "Final Note on a Case of Extreme Isolation," in Kollock and O'Brien, pp. 78–84.

11 Harper Lee, *To Kill a Mockingbird,* Warner, New York, 1982, p. 282.

12 Ralph Waldo Emerson, "Astraea," *The Works of Ralph Waldo Emerson,* Vol. III, The Nottingham Society, Philadelphia, (no date), p. 121.

13 Mead, *Mind, Self, and Society,* p. 162.

14 George Herbert Mead, "The Social Self," *Journal of Philosophy, Psychology and Scientific Methods,* Vol. 10, 1913, p. 375.

15 Mead, *Mind, Self, and Society,* p. 174.

16 Their interpretation is open to question. As we learn later in the film, Nell's phonetic "may" is also the way she refers to her dead sister. When Nell reached toward the mirror, she might have seen her reflection as an image of her twin rather than of herself. If so, the psychologists' interpretation is added support for Blumer's first premise. They responded to Nell's communication on the basis of the meaning it had for *them.*

17 William Shakespeare, *As You Like It,* Act II, Scene VII, line 139, in *The Riverside Shakespeare,* G. Blakemore Evans (ed.), Houghton Mifflin Co., Boston, 1974, p. 381.

18 Erving Goffman, *The Presentation of Self in Everyday Life,* Doubleday Anchor, Garden City, N.Y., 1959.

19 Ibid., p. 56.

20 Joan P. Emerson, "Behavior in Private Places: Sustaining Definitions of Reality in Gynecological Examinations," in Kollock and O'Brien, pp. 189–202.

21 Jean Mizer, "Cipher in the Snow," *Today's Education,* Vol. 53, November 1964, pp. 8–10.

22 George Bernard Shaw, "Pygmalion," *Selected Plays,* Dodd, Mead, New York, 1948, p. 270.

23 Saul Alinsky, *Reveille for Radicals,* Vintage, New York, 1969 (1946), pp. 77–78.

24 Randall Collins, "Toward a Neo-Meadian Sociology of Mind," *Symbolic Interaction,* Vol. 12, 1989, p. 1.

Chapter 5: Coordinated Management of Meaning

1 W. Barnett Pearce, "A Sailing Guide for Social Constructionists," in *Social Approaches to Communication,* Wendy Leeds-Hurwitz (ed.), Guilford, New York, 1995, p. 92–106.

2 W. Barnett Pearce, *Communication and the Human Condition,* Southern Illinois University, Carbondale, 1989, p. 114.

3 W. Barnett Pearce, *Interpersonal Communication: Making Social Worlds,* HarperCollins, New York, 1994, p. 366.

4 Ibid., p. 198.

5 See Rom Harré, *Personal Being,* Harvard University Press, Cambridge, Mass., 1984.

6 W. Barnett Pearce, " 'Listening for the Wisdom in the Public's Whining' or 'Working to Construct Patterns of Public Communication.' " in press.

7 Jonathan Shailor, *Empowerment in Dispute Mediation: A Critical Analysis of Communication,* Praeger, Westport, Conn., 1994, p. 127.

8 W. Barnett Pearce and Kimberly A. Pearce, "Transcendent Storytelling: Abilities for Systematic Practitioners and Their Clients," *Human Systems,* in press.

9 Pearce, *Interpersonal Communication,* p. 71.

10 The classic work on negotiation strategy is Roger Fisher and William Ury, *Getting to Yes,* Penguin, New York, 1983.

11 Pearce, *Interpersonal Communication,* p. 75.

12 John Dewey, *Experience and Nature,* Dover, New York, 1925/1958, p. 179.

13 Wittgenstein calls them "frames of life." See *Philosophical Investigations,* (paras. 9, 23, 241), pp. 5–6, 11, 88.

14 Shailor, p. 2.

15 Pearce, *Interpersonal Communication,* p. 31.

16 Ibid., p. 123. Pearce credits communication theorist John Shotter for this strategy.

17 W. Barnett Pearce, *Communication and the Human Condition,* Southern Illinois University, Carbondale, Ill., 1989, pp. 32–33.

18 Stephen Littlejohn, Jonathan Shailor, Barnett Pearce, "The Deep Structure of Reality in Mediation," in *New Directions in Mediation,* Joseph Folger and Tricia Jones (eds.), Sage, Thousand Oaks, Calif., 1994, pp. 67–83.

19 Pearce, *Communication and the Human Condition,* p. 77.

20 Ibid., p. 23.

21 Ibid., p. 84.

22 Ibid., p. 81.

23 Vernon Cronen, "Coordinated Management of Meaning: The Consequentiality of Communication and the Recapturing of Experience," p. 38.

24 Pearce and Pearce, "Transcendent Storytelling."

25 Shailor, p. 34.

26 Pearce and Pearce, in press.

27 Certification of mediators is a hotly debated issue in the Society of Professionals in Dispute Resolution

(SPIDR). Requirements vary greatly around the United States. Shailor's in-depth critique of mediation practices is based on three case studies, each co-mediated. By my reading of the text, at least five of the six mediators were unsafe, only two showed competency, and none were artistic. Many of the problems Shailor perceives as inherent to the mediation process could alternatively be ascribed to poorly selected and/or poorly trained volunteers in a single program.

28 See Gerry Philipsen, "The Coordinated Management of Meaning Theory of Pearce, Cronen and Associates," in *Watershed Research Traditions in Human Communication Theory,* Donald Cushman and Branislav Kovačić (eds.), State University of New York, 1995, pp. 13–43.

29 W. Barnett Pearce, "A Sailing Guide for Social Constructionists," in *Social Approaches to Communication,* Wendy Leeds-Hurwitz (ed.), Guilford, New York, 1995, p. 88.

30 Vernon E. Cronen, "Coordinated Management of Meaning Theory and Postenlightenment Ethics," in *Conversation on Communication Ethics,* Karen Joy Greenberg (ed.), Ablex, Norwood, N.J., 1991, p. 49.

31 Gerry Philipsen, "The Coordinated Management of Meaning Theory of Pearce, Cronen and Associates," in *Watershed Research Traditions in Human Communication Theory,* Donald Cushman and Branislav Kovačić (eds.), State University of New York—Albany, 1995, pp. 40–41.

32 W. Barnett Pearce and Stephen W. Littlejohn, *Moral Conflict: When Social Worlds Collide,* Sage, Thousand Oaks, Calif., 1997, pp. 166–167.

Chapter 6: Expectancy Violations Theory

1 Judee K. Burgoon, "A Communication Model of Personal Space Violations: Explication and an Initial Test," *Human Communication Research,* Vol. 4, 1978, p. 130.

2 Edward T. Hall, *The Hidden Dimension,* Doubleday, Garden City, N.Y., 1966, p. 1.

3 W. H. Auden, "Prologue: The Birth of Architecture," in *About the House,* Random House, New York, 1966, p. 14.

4 Judee K. Burgoon and Jerold Hale, "Nonverbal Expectancy Violations: Model Elaboration and Application to Immediacy Behaviors," *Communication Monographs,* Vol. 55, 1988, p. 58.

5 *Random House Webster's Electronic Dictionary and Thesaurus,* College Edition, WordPerfect, Orem, Utah, 1994.

6 Judee K. Burgoon, "Cross-Cultural and Intercultural Applications of Expectancy Violations Theory," in *Intercultural Communication Theory,* Richard Wiseman (ed.), Sage, Thousand Oaks, Calif., 1995, pp. 194–214.

7 Judee K. Burgoon and Joseph Walther, "Nonverbal Expectancies and the Evaluative Consequences of Violations," *Human Communication Research,* Vol. 17, 1990, p. 236.

8 Edward Hall, "A System of Notation of Proxemic Behavior," *American Anthropologist,* Vol. 41, 1963, pp. 1003–1026.

9 Cited in Judee K. Burgoon, Valerie Manusov, Paul Mineo, and Jerold Hale, "Effects of Gaze on Hiring, Credibility, Attraction, and Relational Message Interpretation," *Journal of Nonverbal Behavior,* Vol. 9, 1985, p. 133.

10 Douglas Kelley and Judee K. Burgoon, "Understanding Marital Satisfaction and Couple Type as Functions of Relational Expectations," *Human Communication Research,* Vol. 18, 1991, pp. 40–69.

11 Beth A. LePoire and Judee K. Burgoon, "Two Contrasting Explanations of Involvement Violations: Expectancy Violations Theory Versus Discrepancy Arousal Theory," *Human Communication Research,* Vol. 20, 1994, pp. 560–591.

12 Graham Chapman, John Cleese, Terry Gilliam, Eric Idle, Terry Jones, and Michael Palin, *The Complete Monty Python's Flying Circus: All the Words, Volume One,* Pantheon, New York, 1989, p. 40.

13 Judee K. Burgoon, "Nonverbal Violations of Expectations," in *Nonverbal Interaction,* John Wiemann and Randall P. Harrison (eds.), Sage, Beverly Hills, Calif., 1983, p. 101.

14 Judee K. Burgoon, Joseph Walther, and E. James Baesler, "Interpretations, Evaluations, and Consequences of Interpersonal Touch," *Human Communication Research,* Vol. 19, 1992, p. 256.

15 Burgoon, "Cross-Cultural and Intercultural Applications," p. 209.

16 Burgoon is considering such a replacement. As yet unpublished, her Interaction Adaptation Theory incorporates some of EVT's principles, but it is definitely a new theory. Judee K. Burgoon, Lesa Stern, and Leesa Dillman, "Interaction Adaptation Theory: An Initial Explication," paper presented to the annual meeting of the International Communication Association, Sydney, Australia, July 11–15, 1994.

Chapter 7: Interpersonal Deception Theory

1 David Buller, Judee Burgoon, Aileen Buslig, and James Roiger, "Testing Interpersonal Deception Theory: The Language of Interpersonal Deception," *Communication Theory,* Vol. 6, 1996, p. 278.

2 Adapted from Steven McCornack, "Information Manipulation Theory," *Communication Monographs,* Vol. 59, 1992, p. 8.

3 David Buller and Judee Burgoon, "Interpersonal Deception Theory," *Communication Theory,* Vol. 6, 1996, p. 205.

4 Gerald Miller and James Stiff, *Deceptive Communication,* Sage, Newbury Park, Calif., 1993, p. 69.

5 Miron Zuckermann and Robert Driver, "Telling Lies: Verbal and Nonverbal Correlates of Deception," *Multichannel Integrations of Nonverbal Behavior,* Aron Siegman and Stanley Feldstein (eds.), Lawrence Erlbaum Associates, Hillsdale, N.J., 1985, pp. 129–148.

6 David Buller, Krystyna Strzyewski, and Jamie Comstock, "Interpersonal Deception: I. Deceivers' Reactions to Receivers' Suspicions and Probing," *Communication Monographs,* Vol. 58, 1991, p. 1.

7 Ibid., p. 2.

8 The term *leakage* was first used by Paul Ekman and Wallace Friesen, "Nonverbal Leakage and Clues to Deception," *Psychiatry,* Vol. 1, 1969, pp. 88–105.

9 Sir Walter Scott, "Marmion, Canto Sixth, XVII" in *The Poetical Works of Sir Walter Scott, Bart.,* Leavitt and Allen, New York, 1830, p. 427.

10 David Buller and Judee Burgoon, "Emotional Expression in the Deception Process," in *Handbook of Communication and Emotion: Research, Theory, Applications, and Contexts,* Peter Andersen and Laura Guerrero (eds.) Academic Press, San Diego, 1998, p. 389.

11 Sigmund Freud, "Fragments of an Analysis of a Case of Hysteria," *Collected Papers,* Vol. 3, Basic Books, New York, 1959 (1905), p. 94.

12 Miron Zuckerman, Bella DePaulo, and Robert Rosenthal, "Verbal and Nonverbal Communication of Deception," in *Advances in Experimental Social Psychology,* Vol. 14, 1981, Academic Press, New York, pp. 1–59.

13 Zuckerman and Driver, p. 137.

14 Bella DePaulo, Julie Stone, and G. Daniel Lassiter, "Deceiving and Detecting Deceit," in *The Self and Social Life,* Barry Schlenker (ed.), McGraw-Hill, New York, 1985, p. 331.

15 Steven McCornack and Malcolm Parks, "Deception Detection and Relationship Development: The Other Side of Trust," in *Communication Yearbook 9,* Margaret McLaughlin (ed.), Sage, Beverly Hills, Calif., 1986, p. 380.

16 Judee Burgoon, David Buller, Kory Floyd, and Joseph Grandpre, "Deceptive Realities: Sender, Receiver, and Observer Perspectives in Deceptive Conversations," *Communication Research,* Vol. 23, 1996, pp. 724–748.

17 McCornack, "Information Manipulation Theory," pp. 4–5. McCornack bases his position on the work of Paul Grice, *Studies in the Way of Words,* Harvard University, Cambridge, Mass., 1969. See also my discussion of Immanuel Kant's Categorical Imperative, p. 103.

18 Judee Burgoon, David Buller, Amy Ebesu, and Patricia Rockwell, "Interpersonal Deception: V. Accuracy in Deception Detection," *Communication Monographs,* Vol. 61, 1994, p. 320.

19 Judee Burgoon, David Buller, Leesa Dillman, and Joseph Walther, "Interpersonal Deception: IV. Effects of Suspicion on Perceived Communication and Nonverbal Behavior Dynamics," *Human Communication Research,* Vol. 22, 1995, p. 164.

20 Ibid.

21 Judee Burgoon, David Buller, Amy Ebesu, Cindy White, and Patricia Rockwell, "Testing Interpersonal Deception Theory: Effects of Suspicion on Communication Behaviors and Perceptions," *Communication Theory,* Vol. 6, 1996, p. 260.

22 Judee Burgoon, David Buller, Kory Floyd, and Joseph Grandpre, p. 736.

23 Judee Burgoon, "Toward a Processual View of Interpersonal Deception." Paper presented to the annual meeting of the International Communication Association, San Francisco, May 1989, p. 2.

24 Judee Burgoon, David Buller, Amy Ebesu, Cindy White, and Patricia Rothwell, p. 263.

25 Buller and Burgoon, "Interpersonal Deception Theory," p. 233.

26 McCornack and Parks, p. 380.

27 David Buller, Judee Burgoon, Cindy White, and Amy Ebesu, "Interpersonal Deception: VII. Behavioral Profiles of Falsification, Equivocation, and Concealment," *Journal of Language and Social Psychology,* Vol. 13, 1994, p. 392.

Ethical Reflections: Interpersonal Messages

1 Immanuel Kant, "On a Supposed Right to Lie from Altruistic Motives," in *Critique of Practical Reason and Other Writings in Moral Philosophy,* Lewis White Beck (trans. and ed.), University of Chicago, Chicago, 1964, p. 346.

2 Immanuel Kant, "Introduction to the Metaphysic of Morals," *The Doctrine of Virtue: Part II of The Metaphysic of Morals,* Mary Gregor (trans.), Harper & Row, New York, 1964, p. 23.

3 Immanuel Kant, *Groundwork of the Metaphysic of Morals,* H. J. Paton (trans.), Harper Torchbooks, New York, 1964, p. 88.

4 "Enarrationes in Psalmos LXIV.2," cited in *An Augustine Synthesis,* Erik Przywara (ed.), Sheed and Ward, London, 1936, p. 267.

5 Richard of Chichester (c. 1200), in *The Hymnbook,* The United Presbyterian Church in the U.S.A., New York, 1955, p. 445.

6 Augustine, *Enchiridion, on Faith, Hope and Love,* Henry Paolucci (trans.), Henry Regnery, Chicago, 1961.

7 Augustine, "On Lying," in *Treatises on Various Subjects,* Vol. 14, R. J. Deferrari (ed.), Catholic University, New York, 1952, Chapter 14.

8 Sissela Bok, *Lying: Moral Choice in Public and Private Life,* Vintage, New York, 1979.

9 Ibid., p. 48.

10 Ibid., p. 32.

11 Ibid., p. 263.

12 Ibid., pp. 95–108.

Chapter 8: Constructivism

1 Walter H. Crockett, "Cognitive Complexity and Impression Formation," in *Progress in Experimental Personality Research,* Vol. 2, B. A. Maher (ed.), Academic Press, New York, 1965, pp. 47–90.

2 Ann Mayden Nicotera, "The Constructivist Theory of Delia, Clark, and Associates," in *Watershed Research Traditions in Human Communication Theory,* Donald Cushman and Branislav Kovačić (eds.), State University of New York, Albany, 1995, p. 52.

3 Brant R. Burleson and Michael S. Waltman, "Cognitive Complexity: Using the Role Category Questionnaire Measure," in *A Handbook for the Study of Human Communication,* Charles Tardy (ed.), Ablex, Norwood, N.J., 1988, p. 15.

4 Ruth Ann Clark and Jesse Delia, "Cognitive Complexity, Social Perspective-Taking, and Functional Persuasive Skills in Second-to-Ninth-Grade Students," *Human Communication Research,* Vol. 3, 1977, pp. 128–134.

5 Roderick Hart and Don Burks, "Rhetorical Sensitivity and Social Interaction," *Speech Monographs,* Vol. 39, 1972, pp. 75–91.

6 Jesse Delia, Barbara O'Keefe, and Daniel O'Keefe, "The Constructivist Approach to Communication," in

Human Communication Theory, Frank E. X. Dance (ed.), Harper & Row, New York, 1982, p. 163.

7 See Shereen Bingham and Brant Burleson, "Multiple Effects of Messages with Multiple Goals: Some Perceived Outcomes of Responses to Sexual Harassment," *Human Communication Research*, Vol. 16, 1989, p. 192.

8 Barbara O'Keefe, "The Logic of Message Design: Individual Differences in Reasoning about Communication," *Communication Monographs*, Vol. 55, 1988, pp. 80–103.

9 Ibid., p. 84.

10 Dr. Seuss, *Horton Hatches the Egg*, Random House, New York, 1940, p. 165.

11 An "expressive minimal" message that reflects the speaker's internal state, but has no specific aim. See Bingham and Burleson, p. 192.

12 O'Keefe, p. 86.

13 A "conventional unifunctional message" aimed at stopping the sexual harassment once and for all. See Bingham and Burleson, p. 192.

14 O'Keefe, p. 87. For a comparison between rhetorical design logic and the concept of rhetorical sensitivity, see Glen McClish, "Humanist and Empiricist Rhetorics: Some Reflections on Rhetorical Sensitivity, Message Design Logics, and Multiple Goal Structures," *Rhetoric Society Quarterly*, Vol. 23, 1994, Summer/Fall, pp. 27–45.

15 A "rhetorical multifunctional" message designed to achieve multiple goals in a sexual harassment situation. See Bingham and Burleson, p. 193.

16 These three examples of comforting communication are from Brant Burleson, "Comforting Messages: Significance, Approaches, and Effects," in *Communication of Social Support*, Brant Burleson, Terrance Albrecht, and Irwin Sarason (eds.), Sage, Thousand Oaks, Calif., 1994, p. 12.

17 Ibid., p. 22.

18 Brant Burleson and Wendy Samter, "A Social Skills Approach to Relationship Maintenance," in *Communication and Relationship Maintenance*, Daniel Canary and Laura Stafford (eds.), Academic Press, San Diego, 1994, pp. 61–90.

19 Comments expressed in a student's journal.

20 Beverly Davenport Sypher and Theodore Zorn, "Communication-related Abilities and Upward Mobility: A Longitudinal Investigation," *Human Communication Research*, Vol. 12, 1986, pp. 420–431.

21 Brant Burleson, Jesse Delia, and James Applegate, "The Socialization of Person-Centered Communication: Parental Contributions to the Social-Cognitive and Communication Skills of Their Children," in *Perspectives in Family Communication*, Mary Anne Fitzpatrick and Anita Vangelisti (eds.), Sage, Thousand Oaks, Calif., 1995, pp. 34–76.

22 Delia, O'Keefe, and O'Keefe, "The Constructivist Approach to Communication," p. 167.

Relationship Development

1 Harold H. Kelley, Ellen Berscheid, Andrew Christensen, John Harvey, Ted Huston, George Levinger, Evie McClintock, Letitia Anne Peplau, and Donald Peterson, *Close Relationships*, W. H. Freeman, New York, 1983, p. 38.

2 See Jacqueline Wiseman, "Friendship: Bonds and Binds in a Voluntary Relationship," *Journal of Social and Personal Relationships*, Vol. 3, 1986, pp. 191–211, and Robert Hays, "Friendship," in *Handbook of Personal Relationships*, Steve Duck (ed.), John Wiley & Sons, New York, 1988, pp. 391–408.

3 Robert Sternberg, "A Triangular Theory of Love," *Psychological Review*, Vol. 9, 1986, pp. 119–135.

4 Robert Frost, "The Death of the Hired Man," in *The Poetry of Robert Frost*, Edward Lathem (ed.), Holt, Rinehart, and Winston, New York, 1969, pp. 34–36.

5 Lillian Rubin, *Just Friends*, Harper & Row, New York, 1985, p. 16.

6 Keith Davis and Michael Todd, "Friendship and Love Relationships" in *Advances in Descriptive Psychology*, Vol. 2, Keith Davis (ed.), JAI, Greenwich, Conn., 1982, pp. 79–122.

7 See Ron Adler and Neal Towne, *Looking Out/Looking In*, 8th ed., Harcourt Brace Jovanovich, Fort Worth, 1995, and John Stewart, *Bridges Not Walls*, 6th ed., McGraw-Hill, New York, 1995.

8 Erich Fromm, *The Art of Loving*, Harper & Row, New York, 1974, p. 3.

Chapter 9: Social Penetration Theory

1 Dalmas Taylor and Irwin Altman, "Communication in Interpersonal Relationships: Social Penetration Processes," in *Interpersonal Processes: New Directions in Communications Research*, Michael Roloff and Gerald Miller (eds.), Sage, Newbury Park, Calif., 1987, p. 259.

2 Harold H. Kelley and John W. Thibaut, *Interpersonal Relationships*, John Wiley & Sons, New York, 1978.

3 John Stuart Mill, *A System of Logic*, J. W. Parker, London, 1843, Book VI, Chapter XII.

4 C. Arthur VanLear, "The Formation of Social Relationships: A Longitudinal Study of Social Penetration," *Human Communication Research*, Vol. 13, 1987, pp. 299–322.

5 John Berg, "Development of Friendship between Roommates," *Journal of Personality and Social Psychology*, Vol. 46, 1984, pp. 346–356.

6 Betsy Tolstedt and Joseph Stokes, "Self-Disclosure, Intimacy, and the Depenetration Process," *Journal of Personality and Social Psychology*, Vol. 46, 1984, pp. 84–90.

7 Irwin Altman, Anne Vinsel, and Barbara Brown, "Dialectic Conceptions in Social Psychology: An Application to Social Penetration and Privacy Regulation," in *Advances in Experimental Social Psychology*, Vol. 14, Leonard Berkowitz (ed.), Academic Press, New York, 1981, p. 139.

8 VanLear, "The Formation of Social Relationships," and C. Arthur VanLear, "Testing a Cyclical Model of Communication Openness in Relationship Development: Two Longitudinal Studies," *Communication Monographs*, Vol. 58, 1991, pp. 337–361.

9 Paul H. Wright, "Self-Referent Motivation and the Intrinsic Quality of Friendship," *Journal of Social and Personal Relationships*, Vol. 1, 1984, pp. 115–130.

10 Richard Conville, *Relational Transitions: The Evolution of Personal Relationships*, Praeger, New York, 1991, pp. 19–40.

11 From John 15:13, *The New American Bible*, J. P. Kennedy & Sons, New York, 1970.

Chapter 10: Uncertainty Reduction Theory

1 Charles Berger, "Uncertainty and Information Exchange in Developing Relationships," in *Handbook of Personal Relationships*, Steve Duck (ed.), Wiley, New York, 1988, p. 244.

2 Charles Berger and Richard Calabrese, "Some Explorations in Initial Interaction and Beyond: Toward a Developmental Theory of Interpersonal Communication," *Human Communication Research*, Vol. 1, 1975, p. 100.

3 Charles Berger, "Beyond Initial Interaction: Uncertainty, Understanding, and the Development of Interpersonal Relationships," in *Language and Social Psychology*, H. Giles and R. St. Clair (eds.), Basil Blackwell, Oxford, Eng., 1979, pp. 122–144.

4 Charles Berger and William Gudykunst, "Uncertainty and Communication," in *Progress in Communication Sciences*, Vol. X, Brenda Dervin and Melvin Voigt (eds.), Ablex, Norwood, N.J., 1991, p. 23.

5 For an excellent introduction to attribution theory, see Kelly Shaver, *An Introduction to Attribution Processes*, Lawrence Erlbaum Associates, Hillsdale, N.J., 1983. Heider's theory is also described in the first two editions of this text (1991, 1994); see *www.afirstlook.com*.

6 Berger and Calabrese, pp. 99–112.

7 Joseph Cappella, "Mutual Influence in Expressive Behavior: Adult-Adult and Infant-Adult Dyadic Interaction," *Psychological Bulletin*, Vol. 89, 1981, pp. 101–132.

8 Berger and Gudykunst, p. 25.

9 Malcolm Parks and Mara Adelman, "Communication Networks and the Development of Romantic Relationships: An Extension of Uncertainty Reduction Theory," *Human Communication Research*, Vol. 10, 1983, pp. 55–79.

10 Ellen Berscheid and Elaine Walster, *Interpersonal Attraction*, 2d ed., Addison-Wesley, Reading, Mass., 1978, pp. 61–89.

11 Charles R. Berger, *Planning Strategic Interaction*, Lawrence Erlbaum Associates, Mahwah, N.J., 1997, p. 17.

12 Charles R. Berger, "Goals, Plans, and Mutual Understanding in Relationships," in *Individuals in Relationships*, Steve Duck (ed.), Sage, Newbury Park, Calif., 1993, p. 34.

13 Charles R. Berger, "Message Production Under Uncertainty," in *Developing Communication Theories*, Gerry Philipsen and Terrance Albrecht (eds.), State University of New York, Albany, 1997, p. 39.

14 Charles R. Berger, "Producing Messages Under Uncertainty," in *Message Production: Advances in Communication Theory*, John O. Green (ed.), Lawrence Erlbaum Associates, Mahwah, N.J., 1997, p. 222.

15 Personal correspondence from Charles Berger.

16 Berger, "Message Production Under Uncertainty," p. 39.

17 Charles R. Berger, "Inscrutable Goals, Uncertain Plans, and the Production of Communicative Action," in *Communication and Social Influence Processes*, Charles R. Berger and Michael Burgoon (eds.), Michigan State University, East Lansing, 1995, p. 17.

18 Berger, *Planning Strategic Interaction*, pp. 132–135.

19 Proverbs 15:22, New Revised Standard Version of the Bible.

20 Charles Berger, "Communicating Under Uncertainty," in *Interpersonal Processes: New Directions in Communication Research*, Michael Roloff and Gerald Miller (eds.), Sage, Newbury Park, Calif., 1987, p. 40.

21 Kathy Kellermann and Rodney Reynolds, "When Ignorance Is Bliss: The Role of Motivation to Reduce Uncertainty in Uncertainty Reduction Theory," *Human Communication Research*, Vol. 17, 1990, p. 7.

22 Ibid., p. 71.

23 Michael Sunnafrank, "Predicted Outcome Value During Initial Interaction: A Reformulation of Uncertainty Reduction Theory," *Human Communication Research*, Vol. 13, 1986, pp. 3–33.

24 Charles Berger, "Communication Theories and Other Curios," *Communication Monographs*, Vol. 58, 1991, p. 102.

25 Berger, "Communicating Under Uncertainty," p. 58.

Relationship Maintenance

1 John Stewart, "Interpersonal Communication: Contact Between Persons," *Bridges Not Walls*, 5th ed., John Stewart (ed.), McGraw-Hill, New York, 1990, pp. 13–30.

Chapter 11: The Interactional View

1 Alan Watts, *The Book*, Pantheon, New York, 1966, p. 65. For other examples of Watts' use of the life-as-a-game metaphor, see Alan Watts, "The Game of Black-and-White," *The Book*, Pantheon, New York, 1966, pp. 22–46; and Alan Watts, "The Counter Game" *Psychology East & West*, Ballantine, New York, 1969, pp. 144–185.

2 Paul Watzlawick, "The Construction of Clinical 'Realities'," in *The Evolution of Psychotherapy: The Second Conference*, Jeffrey Zeig (ed.), Brunner/Mazel, New York, 1992, p. 64.

3 Watzlawick, Beavin, and Jackson list five axioms rather than four. I have omitted one stating that human beings communicate both digitally and analogically because the distinction has proved to be meaningless for most readers and I have been unable to explain why it is important.

4 Paul Watzlawick, *The Language of Change*, W. W. Norton, New York, 1978, p. 11.

5 Paul Watzlawick, Janet Beavin, and Don Jackson, *Pragmatics of Human Communication*, W. W. Norton, New York, 1967, p. 54.

6 R. D. Laing, *Knots*, Pantheon, New York, 1970, p. 27.

7 Watzlawick, Beavin, and Jackson, p. 99.

8 L. Edna Rogers-Millar and Frank E. Millar III, "Domineeringness and Dominance: A Transactional View," *Human Communication Research*, Vol. 5, 1979, pp. 238–245.

9 Paul Watzlawick, John H. Weaklund, and Richard Fisch, *Change,* W. W. Norton, New York, 1974, p. 95.

10 Watzlawick, *Language of Change,* p. 122.

11 Watzlawick, "The Construction of Clinical 'Realities',"
p. 61.

12 "Helping," Families Anonymous, Inc., Van Nuys, Calif., no date.

13 Janet Beavin Bavelas, "Research into the Pragmatics of Human Communication," *Journal of Strategic and Systemic Therapies,* Vol. 11, No. 2, 1992, pp. 15–29.

Chapter 12: Relational Dialectics

1 Leslie Baxter, "Interpersonal Communication as Dialogue: A Response to the 'Social Approaches' Forum," *Communication Theory,* Vol. 2, 1992, p. 330.

2 Leslie Baxter and Barbara Montgomery, *Relating: Dialogues and Dialectics,* Guilford, New York, 1996, p. 6.

3 Leslie A. Baxter, "Interpersonal Communication as Dialogue: A Response to the 'Social Approaches' Forum," *Communication Theory,* Vol. 2, 1992, p. 330.

4 Baxter and Montgomery, p. 8.

5 Leslie A. Baxter, "A Dialectical Perspective on Communication Strategies in Relationship Development," in *A Handbook of Personal Relationships,* Steve Duck (ed.), John Wiley & Sons, New York, 1988, p. 258.

6 Baxter and Montgomery, p. 43.

7 Hugh Lofting, *The Story of Dr. Doolittle,* J. B. Lippincott, Philadelphia, 1920, pp. 81–89.

8 Baxter, "Dialectical Perspective," p. 259.

9 Irwin Altman, Anne Vinsel, and Barbara Brown, "Dialectic Conceptions in Social Psychology: An Application to Social Penetration and Privacy Regulation," in *Advances in Experimental Social Psychology,* Vol. 14, Leonard Berkowitz (ed.), Academic Press, New York, 1981, pp. 107–160.

10 Baxter and Montgomery, pp. 185–206.

11 All the statements in the strategy section about relational satisfaction are based on Leslie A. Baxter, "Dialectical Contradictions in Relationship Development," *Journal of Social and Personal Relationships,* Vol. 7, 1990, pp. 69–88. Baxter now uses the label "denial" to describe the tactic that she used to call "selection."

12 For further information on this approach, see Leslie Baxter and William Wilmot, "Taboo Topics in Romantic Relationships," *Journal of Social and Personal Relationships,* Vol. 2, 1985, pp. 253–269.

13 Barbara Montgomery, "Relationship Maintenance Versus Relationship Change: A Dialectical Dilemma," *Journal of Social and Personal Relationships,* Vol. 10, 1993, p. 211.

14 Ibid., p. 221.

Influence

1 Kathy Kellermann and Tim Cole, "Classifying Compliance Gaining Messages: Taxonomic Disorder and Strategic Confusion," *Communication Theory,* Vol. 4, 1994, pp. 3–60.

2 John Cacioppo, "Attitudes and Evaluative Space: Beyond Bipolar Conceptualizations and Measures," Presidential Address, Society for Personality and Social Psychology, New York, Aug. 11–15, 1995.

3 Richard Petty and John Cacioppo, *Attitudes and Persuasion: Classic and Contemporary Approaches,* Wm. C. Brown, Dubuque, Iowa, 1981.

4 Leon Festinger, *A Theory of Cognitive Dissonance,* Stanford University, Stanford, Calif., 1957, p. 95. The 3rd edition of this text included a chapter on cognitive dissonance theory—see pp. 206–215. It is also available in the "Archives" section at *www.afirstlook.com.*

Chapter 13: Social Judgment Theory

1 Muzafer Sherif and Carolyn Sherif, *Social Psychology,* Harper, New York, 1969.

2 Muzafer Sherif, "Experiments in Group Conflict," *Scientific American,* Vol. 195, 1956, pp. 54–58.

3 Carolyn Sherif, Muzafer Sherif, and Roger Nebergall, *Attitude and Attitude Change: The Social Judgment-Involvement Approach,* W. B. Saunders, Philadelphia, 1965, p. 222.

4 Ibid., p. 225.

5 Ibid., p. 214.

6 Gian Sarup, Robert Suchner, and Gitanjali Gaylord, "Contrast Effects and Attitude Change: A Test of the Two-Stage Hypothesis of Social Judgment Theory," *Social Psychology Quarterly,* Vol. 54, 1991, pp. 364–372.

7 Kathryn Greene, Roxanne Parrott, and Julianne M. Serovich, "Privacy, HIV Testing, and AIDS: College Students' Versus Parents' Perspectives," *Health Communication,* Vol. 5, 1993, pp. 59–74.

8 S. Bochner and C. Insko, "Communicator Discrepancy, Source Credibility and Opinion Change," *Journal of Personality and Social Psychology,* Vol. 4, 1966, pp. 614–621.

9 Interview on *Morning Edition,* National Public Radio, May 31, 1995.

Chapter 14: Elaboration Likelihood Model

1 Richard E. Petty and John T. Cacioppo, *Communication and Persuasion: Central and Peripheral Routes to Attitude Change,* Springer-Verlag, New York, 1986, p. 7.

2 Richard E. Petty and John T. Cacioppo, *Attitudes and Persuasion: Classic and Contemporary Approaches,* Wm. C. Brown, Dubuque, Iowa, 1981, p. 256.

3 Robert B. Cialdini, *Influence: Science and Practice,* 2d ed., Scott, Foresman, Glenview, Ill., 1988.

4 Richard Petty and Duane Wegener, "The Elaboration Likelihood Model: Current Status and Controversies," in *Dual Process Theories in Social Psychology,* Shelly Chaiken and Yaacov Trope (eds.), Guilford, New York, 1999, pp. 44–48.

5 John Cacioppo, et al., "Dispositional Differences in Cognitive Motivation: The Life and Times of Individuals Varying in Need for Cognition," *Psychological Bulletin,* Vol. 119, 1996, pp. 197–253.

6 Richard Petty and John Cacioppo, "The Elaboration Likelihood Model of Persuasion," in *Advances in Experimental Social Psychology,* Vol. 19, Leonard Berkowitz (ed.), Academic Press, Orlando 1986, p. 129.

7 Shortly after I created this example in 1996, a backup musician for Smashing Pumpkins died from an overdose of heroin taken with the rock group's drummer, Jimmy Chamberlin. Corgan has now become a leading

figure in the "Just Say No" campaign against substance abuse.

8 Louis Penner and Barbara Fritzsche, "Magic Johnson and Reactions to People with AIDS: A Natural Experiment," *Journal of Applied Social Psychology,* Vol. 23, 1993, pp. 1035–1050.

9 Ibid., p. 1048.

10 Petty and Wegener, pp. 51–52.

11 Ibid., p. 42.

12 Paul Mongeau and James Stiff, "Specifying Causal Relationships in the Elaboration Likelihood Model," *Communication Theory,* Vol. 3, 1993, pp. 67–68.

13 Petty and Cacioppo, *Communication and Persuasion,* p. 32.

Ethical Reflections: Influence

1 Martin Buber, *I and Thou,* 2d ed., R. G. Smith (trans.), Scribner's, New York, 1958, pp. 60, 69.

2 Martin Buber, *Between Man and Man,* Macmillan, New York, 1965, p. 204.

3 Ronald Arnett, *Communication and Community,* Southern Illinois University, Carbondale, 1986, p. 37.

4 Kenneth Cissna and Rob Anderson, "The 1957 Martin Buber–Carl Rogers Dialogue, As Dialogue," *Journal of Humanistic Psychology,* Vol. 34, 1995, pp. 11–45.

5 Thomas R. Nilsen, *Ethics of Speech Communication,* Bobbs-Merrill, Indianapolis, 1966, p. 38.

6 Ibid., p. 35.

7 John Milton, *Aeropagitica,* John Hales (ed.), with introduction and notes, 3d ed., revised, Clarendon, Oxford, England, 1882.

8 John Stuart Mill, *On Liberty,* Gateway, Chicago, 1955.

9 Søren Kierkegaard, *Philosophical Fragments,* Princeton University, Princeton, N.J., pp. 17–28.

10 Em Griffin, *The Mind Changers,* Tyndale, Carol Stream, Ill., 1976, pp. 27–41; Em Griffin, *Getting Together,* InterVarsity, Downers Grove, Ill., 1982, pp. 159–167.

Group Decision Making

1 Robert Bales, *Interaction Process Analysis,* Addison-Wesley, Reading, Mass., 1950.

2 Irving Janis, *Groupthink,* 2nd ed., Houghton Mifflin, Boston, 1982. See also Em Griffin, *A First Look At Communication Theory,* 3rd ed., McGraw-Hill, New York, 1997, pp. 235–246.

3 Randy Hirokawa and Abran J. Salazar, "An Integrated Approach to Communication and Group Decision Making," in *Managing Group Life: Communicating in Decision-Making Groups,* Lawrence Frey and J. Kevin Barge (eds.), Houghton Mifflin, Boston, 1996, pp. 156–181.

Chapter 15: Functional Perspective on Group Decision Making

1 Some scholars also question the efficacy of communication in group decision making. See Dean Hewes, "A Socio-Egocentric Model of Group Decision-Making" in *Communication and Group Decision-Making,* Randy Hirokawa and M. Scott Poole (eds.), Sage, Beverly Hills, Calif., 1986, pp. 265–291.

2 Randy Hirokawa, "Avoiding Camels: Lessons Learned in the Facilitation of High-Quality Group Decision Making through Effective Discussion," The Van Zelst Lecture in Communication, Northwestern University School of Speech, May 24, 1993.

3 Dennis Gouran, "Group Decision Making: An Approach to Integrative Research" in *A Handbook for the Study of Human Communication,* Charles Tardy (ed.), Ablex, Norwood, N.J., 1988, pp. 247–267.

4 Proverbs 15:22, Revised Standard Version of the Bible.

5 Dennis Gouran, Randy Hirokawa, Kelly Julian, and Geoff Leatham, "The Evolution and Current Status of the Functional Perspective on Communication in Decision-Making and Problem-Solving Groups," in *Communication Yearbook 16,* Stanley Deetz (ed.), Sage, Newbury Park, Calif., 1993, p. 591.

6 Randy Hirokawa and Dirk Scheerhorn, "Communication in Faulty Group Decision-Making" in *Communication and Group Decision-Making,* Randy Hirokawa and M. Scott Poole (eds.), Sage, Beverly Hills, Calif., 1986, p. 69.

7 Hirokawa bases the distinction between rational and political logics on the work of Peter Senge, *The Fifth Discipline,* Doubleday, New York, 1990, p. 60.

8 Dennis Gouran and Randy Hirokawa, "The Role of Communication in Decision-Making Groups: A Functional Perspective" in Mary Mander (ed.), *Communications in Transition,* Praeger, New York, 1983, p. 174.

9 Randy Hirokawa, "Understanding the Relationship between Group Communication and Group Decision-Making Effectiveness from a Functional Perspective: Why 'It's Not All Bad' Isn't Quite 'Good Enough'," Thomas M. Scheidel Lecture, University of Washington, Seattle, April 24, 1998.

10 Randy Hirokawa, "Functional Approaches to the Study of Group Discussion," *Small Group Research,* Vol. 25, 1994, p. 546.

11 Randy Hirokawa and Poppy McLeod, "Communication, Decision Development, and Decision Quality in Small Groups: An Integration of Two Approaches." Paper presented at the annual meeting of the Speech Communication Association, Miami, November 18–21, 1993.

12 See, for example, J. Richard Hackman, "Work Teams in Organizations: An Orienting Framework," in *Groups That Work (and Those That Don't),* J. Richard Hackman (ed.), Jossey-Bass, San Francisco, 1990, pp. 1–14.

13 Ivan Steiner, *Group Process and Productivity,* Academic Press, New York, 1972, p. 9.

14 Randy Hirokawa, "Avoiding Camels," p. 8.

15 Dennis Gouran and Randy Hirokawa, "Counteractive Functions of Communication in Effective Group Decision-Making," p. 82.

16 Randy Hirokawa, "Group Communication and Problem-Solving Effectiveness I: A Critical Review of Inconsistent Findings," *Communication Quarterly,* Vol. 30, 1982, p. 139.

17 Randy Hirokawa, "Group Communication and Decision-Making Performance: A Continued Test of the Functional Perspective," *Human Communication Research,* Vol. 14, 1988, p. 512.

18 Hirokawa, "Understanding the Relationship."

19 Cited in Randy Hirokawa, "Researching the Role of Communication in Group Decision-Making: A

Functional Theory Perspective." Paper presented at the annual meeting of the Central States Communication Association, Chicago, April 11–14, 1991, p. 19.

20 Dennis Gouran, Randy Hirokawa, Kelly Julian, and Geoff Leatham, "The Evolution and Current Status of the Functional Perspective on Communication in Decision-Making and Problem-Solving Groups" in *Communication Yearbook 16,* Stanley Deetz (ed.), Sage, Newbury Park, Calif., 1993, pp. 574–579.

21 Robert Craig, "Treatments of Reflective Thought in John Dewey and Hans-Georg Gadamer." Paper presented at the 1994 Convention of the International Communication Association, Sydney, Australia, July 11–15, 1994.

22 John Dewey, *How We Think,* Heath, New York, 1910.

23 John Cragan and David Wright, "Small Group Communication Research of the 1980s: A Synthesis and Critique," *Communication Studies,* Vol. 41, 1990, pp. 212–236.

24 Cynthia Stohl and Michael Holmes, "A Functional Perspective for Bona Fide Groups" in *Communication Yearbook 16,* Stanley Deetz (ed.), Sage, Newbury Park, Calif., 1993, p. 601.

25 See John Cragan and David Wright, "The Functional Theory of Small Group Decision-Making: A Replication," *Journal of Social Behavior and Personality,* Vol. 7, 1992 (Special Issue). Reprinted in John Cragan and David Wright (eds.), *Theory and Research in Small Group Communication,* Burgess, 1993, pp. 87–95.

26 B. Aubrey Fisher, "Decision Emergence: Phases in Group Decision Making," *Speech Monographs,* Vol. 37, 1970, pp. 53–66.

27 B. Aubrey Fisher, *Small Group Decision Making,* 2d ed., McGraw-Hill, New York, 1980, p. 149.

28 Marc Orlitzky and Randy Hirokawa, "To Err Is Human, to Correct for It Divine: A Meta-analysis of the Functional Theory of Group Decision-Making Effectiveness." Paper presented at the annual meeting of the National Communication Association, Chicago, November 19–23, 1997.

Chapter 16: Adaptive Structuration Theory

1 Marshall Scott Poole, "Decision Development in Small Groups I: A Comparison of Two Models," *Communication Monographs,* Vol. 48, 1981, p. 4.

2 Marshall Scott Poole and Jonelle Roth, "Decision Development in Small Groups IV: A Typology of Group Decision Paths," *Human Communication Research,* Vol. 15, 1989, pp. 323–356.

3 Poole, "Decision Development in Small Groups I, p. 4.

4 Anthony Giddens, *The Constitution of Society: Outline of the Theory of Structuration,* University of California, Berkeley, 1984, p. 14.

5 Robert Boynton, "The Two Tonys: Why Is the Prime Minister So Interested in What Anthony Giddens Thinks?" *The New Yorker,* October 6, 1997, p. 67.

6 Giddens, *Constitution of Society,* p. xvi.

7 Marshall Scott Poole, "Group Communication and the Structuring Process," in *Small Group Communication,* 7th ed., Robert Cathcart, Larry Samovar, and Linda Henman (eds.), Brown & Benchmark, Madison, Wis.,

1996, p. 87. Definition based on Anthony Giddens, *Central Problems in Social Theory: Action, Structure and Contradiction in Social Analysis,* University of California, Berkeley, 1979, pp. 64–76.

8 Giddens, *Central Problems,* p. 5; *Constitution of Society,* p. 6.

9 Giddens, *Constitution of Society,* pp. 19–22.

10 Marshall Scott Poole, David Seibold, and Robert McPhee, "The Structuration of Group Decisions," in *Communication and Group Decision Making,* 2nd ed., Sage, Thousand Oaks, Calif., 1996, p. 115.

11 For an example of an ethnographic study of structuration, see Lisa A. Howard and Patricia Geist, "Ideological Positioning in Organizational Change: The Dialectic of Control in a Merging Organization," *Communication Monographs,* Vol. 62, 1995, pp. 110–131.

12 For further information, consult Opportunity International's website at *www.opportunity.org.*

13 Marshall Scott Poole, David Seibold, and Robert McPhee, "Group Decision-Making as a Structurational Process," *Quarterly Journal of Speech,* Vol. 71, 1985, p. 79.

14 Poole, Seibold, and McPhee, "Structuration of Group Decisions," p. 119.

15 Poole, "Group Communication," p. 90.

16 Poole, Seibold, and McPhee, "Structuration of Group Decisions," p. 141.

17 Poole, "Group Communication," p. 87.

18 Ibid.

19 Poole, Seibold, and McPhee, "Structuration of Group Decisions," p. 122.

20 Marshall Scott Poole and Gerardine DeSanctis, "Understanding the Use of Group Decision Support Systems: The Theory of Adaptive Structuration," in *Organization and Communication Technology,* Sage, Newbury Park, Calif., 1990, p. 179.

21 Gerardine DeSanctis, Marshall Scott Poole, George Desharnais, and Howard Lewis, "Using Computing to Facilitate the Quality Improvement Process: The IRS-Minnesota Project," *Interfaces,* Vol. 21, No. 6, 1991, p. 33.

22 Giddens, *Central Problems,* p. 71.

23 Marshall Scott Poole and Gerardine DeSanctis, "Microlevel Structuration in Computer-Supported Group Decision Making," *Human Communication Research,* Vol. 19, 1992, p. 7.

24 Marshall Scott Poole, "Do We Have Any Theories of Group Communication?" *Communication Studies,* Vol. 41, 1990, p. 243.

25 Poole, Seibold, and McPhee, "Structuration of Group Decisions," p. 120.

26 Poole, "Group Communication," p. 94.

27 John Cragan and David Wright, "Small Group Communication Research of the 1980s: A Synthesis and Critique," *Communication Studies,* Vol. 41, 1990, pp. 212–236.

28 Poole, "Do We Have Any Theories of Group Communication?" p. 240.

29 Ibid., p. 246.

30 Kenneth Chase, "A Spiritual and Critical Revision of Structuration Theory," *Journal of Communication and Religion,* Vol. 16, No. 1, 1993, p. 8.

Chapter 17: Information Systems Approach to Organizations

1 Karl Weick, *The Social Psychology of Organizing,* Addison-Wesley, Reading, Mass., 1969, p. 40.

2 Karl Weick, *Sensemaking in Organizations,* Sage, Thousand Oaks, Calif., 1995, pp. 17–62.

3 G. P. Huber and R. L. Daft, "The Information Environments of Organizations," in F. M. Jablin, L. L. Putnam, K. H. Roberts, and L. W. Portor (eds.), *Handbook of Organizational Communication,* Sage, Newbury Park, Calif., 1987, p. 151.

4 Weick, *The Social Psychology of Organizing,* 2d ed., 1979, p. 11, referring to M. D. Cohen and J. G. March, *Leadership and Ambiguity,* McGraw-Hill, New York, 1974.

5 1 Corinthians 12:12–21, Revised Standard Version of the Bible.

6 Charles Darwin, *The Origin of Species,* Dent, New York, 1967 (1859).

7 Weick, *Sensemaking,* pp. 54–55, 174.

8 Ibid., p. 12. Weick attributes the story to Graham Wallas, *The Art of Thought,* Harcourt Brace, New York, 1926, p. 106, and repeatedly refers to it as the core idea of retrospective sensemaking.

9 Linda Putnam and Ritch Sorenson, "Equivocal Messages in Organizations," *Human Communication Research,* Vol. 8, 1982, pp. 114–132.

10 Gary Kreps, "A Field Experimental Test and Re-evaluation of Weick's Model of Organizing," in *Communication Yearbook 4,* Dan Nimmo (ed.), Transaction Books, New Brunswick, N.J., 1980, pp. 389–398.

11 Weick, *The Social Psychology of Organizing,* 2d ed., p. 51.

12 Weick, *Sensemaking,* p. 54.

Chapter 18: Cultural Approach to Organizations

1 Clifford Geertz, "Thick Description: Toward an Interpretive Theory of Culture," in *The Interpretation of Cultures,* Basic Books, New York, 1973, p. 5.

2 Michael Pacanowsky and Nick O'Donnell-Trujillo, "Organizational Communication as Cultural Performance," *Communication Monographs,* Vol. 50, 1983, p. 129. (Pacanowsky's early work was co-authored with Nick O'Donnell-Trujillo from the communication department at Southern Methodist University. Because Pacanowsky was the lead author in these articles and Nick Trujillo's scholarship has taken a critical turn, I refer in the text of this chapter only to Pacanowsky. For critical ethnography, see Nick Trujillo, "Interpreting November 22: A Critical Ethnography of an Assassination Site," *Quarterly Journal of Speech,* Vol. 79, 1993, pp. 447–466.)

3 Michael Pacanowsky and Nick O'Donnell-Trujillo, "Communication and Organizational Cultures," *Western Journal of Speech Communication,* Vol. 46, 1982, p. 121.

4 Pacanowsky and O'Donnell-Trujillo, "Organizational Communication," p. 146.

5 Ibid., p. 131.

6 Pacanowsky and O'Donnell-Trujillo, "Communication and Organizational Cultures," p. 116.

7 Clifford Geertz, "Deep Play: Notes on the Balinese Cockfight," in *Myth, Symbol, and Culture,* Norton, New York, 1971, p. 29.

8 Geertz, "Thick Description," p. 5.

9 Gareth Morgan, *Images of Organization,* Sage, Newbury Park, Calif., 1986, pp. 130–131.

10 Pacanowsky and O'Donnell-Trujillo, "Communication and Organizational Cultures," p. 127.

11 Michael Pacanowsky, "Communication in the Empowering Organization," in *Communication Yearbook 11,* James Anderson (ed.), Sage, Newbury Park, Calif., 1988, pp. 357, 362–364.

12 Ibid., p. 357.

13 Ibid., p. 358.

14 Ibid., pp. 366–368.

15 Ibid., p. 123.

16 Michael Pacanowsky, "Slouching Towards Chicago," *Quarterly Journal of Speech,* Vol. 74, 1988, p. 454.

17 Geertz, "Deep Play," pp. 5, 26.

18 Pacanowsky and O'Donnell-Trujillo, "Organizational Communication," p. 137.

19 Linda Smircich, "Concepts of Culture and Organizational Analysis," *Administrative Science Quarterly,* Vol. 28, 1983, pp. 339–358.

Chapter 19: Critical Theory of Communication Approach to Organizations

1 *Roger & Me,* produced and directed by Michael Moore, Dog Eat Dog Films, 1989, distributed by Warner Bros.

2 *Time,* February 12, 1990, p. 58.

3 Stanley Deetz, *Transforming Communication, Transforming Business: Building Responsive and Responsible Workplaces,* Hampton, Cresskill, N.J., 1995, p. 33.

4 *Time,* January 29, 1996, p. 24.

5 Stanley Deetz, *Democracy in an Age of Corporate Colonization: Developments in Communication and the Politics of Everyday Life,* State University of New York, Albany, 1992, p. 349 and p. 15.

6 *Time,* February 5, 1996, p. 45.

7 Deetz, *Democracy,* p. 43.

8 Deetz, *Transforming Communication,* p. 68.

9 Deetz, *Democracy,* p. 129.

10 Deetz, *Transforming Communication,* p. 4.

11 Stanley Deetz, "Future of the Discipline: The Challenges, the Research, and the Social Contribution," in *Communication Yearbook 17,* Stanley Deetz (ed.), Sage, Newbury Park, Calif., 1994, p. 577.

12 Deetz, *Democracy,* p. 222.

13 Ibid., p. 217.

14 Ibid., p. 235.

15 Ibid., p. 310.

16 Deetz, *Transforming Communication,* p. 114.

17 Ibid., p. xv.

18 Used with permission. As with other references to students, I've changed her name to protect confidentiality. To read student application logs for other theories, see *www.afirstlook.com* (Click on Resources for Teachers).

19 Ibid., p. 85.

20 Deetz, *Democracy,* p. 47.

21 Deetz, "Future of the Discipline," p. 587.

22 Deetz, *Transforming Communication*, p. 3.
23 Ibid., pp. 50–51.
24 Ibid., p. 2.
25 Deetz, *Democracy*, p. 169.
26 Deetz, *Transforming Communication*, pp. 170, 175–184.
27 Ibid., p. 182.
28 Robert McPhee, "Comments on Stanley Deetz' *Democracy in an Age of Corporate Colonization*," paper presented at the 1995 Annual Convention of the Speech Communication Association, San Antonio, November 15–18, 1995.
29 George Cheney, et al., "Democracy, Participation, and Communication at Work: A Multidisciplinary Review," in *Communication Yearbook 21*, Michael Roloff (ed.), Sage, Thousand Oaks, Calif., 1998, p. 79.
30 Deetz, "Future of the Discipline," p. 581.
31 Deetz, *Transforming Communication*, pp. 173–174.

Public Rhetoric

1 Henri Marrou, *A History of Education in Antiquity*, George Lamb (trans.), University of Wisconsin, Madison, 1982, p. 194.
2 Aristotle, *On Rhetoric: A Theory of Civil Discourse*, George A. Kennedy (ed. and trans.), Oxford University, New York, 1991, p. 36.
3 Plato, *Gorgias*, Lane Cooper (trans.), Oxford University, New York, 1948, p. 122.
4 Plato, *Phaedrus*, 277, W. C. Helmbold and W. B. Rabinowitz (trans.), Bobbs-Merrill, Indianapolis, 1956, p. 72.
5 1 Corinthians 2:4, New Revised Standard Version of the Bible.
6 1 Corinthians 9:22, New Revised Standard Version of the Bible.
7 Hugh C. Dick (ed.), *Selected Writings of Francis Bacon*, Modern Library, New York, 1955, p. x.

Chapter 20: The Rhetoric

1 Clarke Rountree, "Sophist," in *Encyclopedia of Rhetoric and Composition: Communication from Ancient Times to the Information Age*, Theresa Enos (ed.), Garland, New York, 1996, p. 681.
2 Aristotle, *On Rhetoric: A Theory of Civil Discourse*, George A. Kennedy (ed. and trans.), Oxford University Press, New York, 1991, p. 35.
3 David J. Garrow, *Bearing the Cross*, William Morrow, New York, 1986, p. 284.
4 Aristotle, *On Rhetoric: A Theory of Civil Discourse*, George A. Kennedy (ed. and trans.), Oxford University, New York, 1991, p. 33.
5 Lloyd Bitzer, "Aristotle's Enthymeme Revisited," *Quarterly Journal of Speech*, Vol. 45, 1959, p. 409.
6 Attributed to Ralph Waldo Emerson by Dale Carnegie, *How to Win Friends and Influence People*, Pocket Books, New York, 1982, p. 29.
7 Aristotle, p. 122.
8 Lane Cooper, *The Rhetoric of Aristotle*, Appleton-Century-Crofts, New York, 1932, Introduction.
9 Aristotle, p. 258.
10 Ibid., p. 244.
11 Ibid., p. 223.

12 Amos 5:24, Revised Standard Version of the Bible.
13 Aristotle, p. 30.
14 Voltaire, *Dictionnaire Philosophique*, "Aristotle," in Oeuvres Complètes de Voltaire, Vol. 17, Librairie Garnier, Paris, p. 372.

Chapter 21: Dramatism

1 Marie Hochmuth Nichols, "Kenneth Burke and the New Rhetoric," *Quarterly Journal of Speech*, Vol. 38, 1952, pp. 133–144.
2 Kenneth Burke, "Rhetoric—Old and New," *The Journal of General Education*, Vol. 5, 1951, p. 203.
3 See, for example, Marshall Prisbell and Janis Anderson, "The Importance of Perceived Homophily, Levels of Uncertainty, Feeling Good, Safety, and Self-Disclosure in Interpersonal Relationships," *Communication Quarterly*, Vol. 28, 1980, No. 3, pp. 22–33.
4 Ruth 1:16, Revised Standard Version of the Bible.
5 Kenneth Burke, *A Grammar of Motives*, Prentice-Hall, Englewood Cliffs, N.J., 1945, p. xv.
6 Kenneth Burke, *Language as Symbolic Action: Essays on Life, Literature, and Method*, University of California, Berkeley, 1966, pp. 44–52.
7 Kenneth Burke, "Definition of Man," in *Language as Symbolic Action*, University of California, Berkeley, 1966, p. 16.
8 Paul Dickson, *The Official Rules*, Dell, New York, 1978, p. 165.
9 Kenneth Burke, *Permanence and Change: An Anatomy of Purpose*, Bobbs-Merrill, Indianapolis, 1965, pp. 69–70, also entire Part II; Burke, *Attitudes Toward History*, Hermes, Los Altos, Calif., 1959, pp. 308–314.
10 Burke, *Permanence and Change*, p. 283.
11 Nichols, p. 144.

Chapter 22: Narrative Paradigm

1 Walter R. Fisher, *Human Communication as Narration: Toward a Philosophy of Reason, Value, and Action*, University of South Carolina, Columbia, 1987, p. 24.
2 Ibid., p. xi.
3 Walter R. Fisher, "Toward a Logic of Good Reasons," *Quarterly Journal of Speech*, Vol. 64, 1978, pp. 376–384.
4 See Hosea 1–3, 11 in the Old Testament.
5 Fredrick Buechner, *Peculiar Treasures*, Harper & Row, New York, 1979, pp. 45–46.
6 Fisher, *Human Communication as Narration*, p. 58.
7 Walter R. Fisher, "Clarifying the Narrative Paradigm," *Communication Monographs*, Vol. 56, 1989, pp. 55–58.
8 See Chapter 2, "The Hunt for a Universal Model (1970–1980)," pp. 27–28.
9 Fisher, *Human Communication as Narration*, p. 194.
10 Ibid., p. 20.
11 Ibid., p. 109.
12 Ibid., pp. 187–188.
13 Ibid., p. 188.
14 William G. Kirkwood, "Narrative and the Rhetoric of Possibility," *Communication Monographs*, Vol. 59, 1992, pp. 30–47.
15 Fisher, *Human Communication as Narration*, p. 67.
16 Ibid., p. 194.

Ethical Reflections: Group and Public Communication

1 Aristotle, *On Rhetoric: A Theory of Civil Discourse*, George A. Kennedy (ed. and trans.), Oxford University, New York, 1991, p. 36.
2 Theodore White, *The Making of the President*, 1964, Atheneum, New York, 1965, p. 228.
3 Aristotle, *Nicomachean Ethics*, H. Rackham (trans.), Harvard University, Cambridge, Mass., 1934, Bk. 4, Chap. 7.
4 Cornel West, *The American Evasion of Philosophy: A Geneology of Pragmatism*, University of Wisconsin, Madison, 1989, p. 86.
5 Ibid., p. 239.
6 Reinhold Niebuhr, *Christian Realism and Political Problems*, Charles Scribner's Sons, New York, 1953, pp. 1–14. See also Niebuhr's *Moral Man and Immoral Society*.
7 See Cornel West, *Prophecy Deliverance*, Westminster Press, Philadelphia, 1982, pp. 95–127.
8 West, *American Evasion*, p. 233.
9 Good Samaritan, Luke 10:25–37; Prodigal Son, Luke 15:11–32.
10 Cornel West, "Why I'm Marching in Washington," *New York Times*, October 14, 1995, p. 19.

Media and Culture

1 Elihu Katz and Paul Lazarsfeld, *Personal Influence*, The Free Press, Glencoe, Ill., 1955.
2 See J. G. Blumler and Elihu Katz, *The Uses of Mass Communication: Current Perspectives on Gratifications Research*, Sage, Beverly Hills, Calif., 1974; and Elihu Katz, "The Uses of Becker, Blumler, and Swanson," *Communication Research*, Vol. 6, 1979, pp. 74–83.
3 See "New Perspectives on Media and Culture," William Biernatzki and Robert White (eds.), *Communication Research Trends*, Vol. 8, No. 2, 1987, pp. 1–13; and Robert White, "Mass Communication and Culture: Transition to a New Paradigm," *Journal of Communication*, Vol. 33, No. 3, 1983, pp. 279–301.

Chapter 23: Technological Determinism

1 "Playboy Interview: Marshall McLuhan," *Playboy*, March 1969, p. 54.
2 Tom Wolfe, "Suppose He Is What He Sounds Like . . . ," in *McLuhan: Hot & Cool*, Gerald Stearn (ed.), Dial, New York, 1967, p. 19.
3 "Playboy Interview: Marshall McLuhan," p. 59.
4 Marshall McLuhan and Quentin Fiore, *The Medium Is the Massage*, Random House, New York, 1967, p. 50.
5 Jesus, John 8:32, New International Version of the Bible.
6 "Playboy Interview: Marshall McLuhan," p. 70.
7 Ibid., p. 62.
8 Ibid., p. 158.
9 Douglas Ehninger, "Marshall McLuhan: His Significance for the Field of Speech Communication," *Speech Journal*, Vol. 6, 1969, p. 19.
10 Alice Cooper, "School's Out Forever," Warner Bros., 1972.
11 Marshall McLuhan, *The Mechanical Bride*, Vanguard, New York, 1951. See *Journal of Communication*, Vol. 42,

No. 4, 1992. The entire issue is devoted to state-of-the-art technology and applications of virtual reality.
12 "Playboy Interview: Marshall McLuhan," p. 66.
13 Donna J. Haraway, *Simians, Cyborgs, and Women: The Reinvention of Nature*, Routledge, London, 1991.
14 Dan M. Davin in *McLuhan: Hot & Cool*, p. 183.
15 Dwight Macdonald in *McLuhan: Hot & Cool*, p. 203.
16 Christopher Ricks in *McLuhan: Hot & Cool*, p. 25.
17 George N. Gordon, "An End to McLuhanacy," *Educational Technology*, January 1982, p. 42.
18 Tom Wolfe in *McLuhan: Hot & Cool*, p. 15.
19 Malcolm Muggeridge, *Christ and the Media*, Eerdmans, Grand Rapids, Mich., 1977.
20 Kenneth Boulding in *McLuhan: Hot & Cool*, p. 57.
21 Robert Putnam, "Bowling Alone: America's Declining Social Capital," *Journal of Democracy*, Vol. 6, No. 1, 1995.

Chapter 24: Semiotics

1 James R. Beniger, "Who Are the Most Important Theorists of Communication?" *Communication Research*, Vol. 17, 1990, pp. 698–715.
2 Ferdinand de Saussure, *Course in General Linguistics*, Wade Baskin (trans.), McGraw-Hill, New York, 1966, p. 16.
3 Roland Barthes, "The World of Wrestling," in *Mythologies*, p. 17.
4 Ibid., pp. 19, 24.
5 See Barthes' use of this phrase in *The Semiotic Challenge*, p. 85. Barthes used these words to describe rhetoricians' efforts to categorize figures of speech—alliteration, hyperbole, irony, etc. The phrase is even more appropriate to characterize Elements of Semiology.
6 Donald Fry and Virginia Fry, "Continuing the Conversation Regarding Myth and Culture: An Alternative Reading of Barthes," *The American Journal of Semiotics*, Vol. 6, No. 2/3, 1989, pp. 183–197.
7 Irwin Levine and L. Russell Brown, "Tie a Yellow Ribbon Round the Ole Oak Tree," Levine and Brown Music, Inc., copyright 1973.
8 Barthes, "Myth Today," in *Mythologies*, p. 118.
9 W. Thomas Duncanson, "Issues of Transcendence and Value in a Semiotic Frame," a paper presented to a joint session of the Religious Speech Communication Association and the Speech Communication Association Convention, San Francisco, Nov. 19, 1989, p. 29.
10 Barthes, "The World of Wrestling," in *Mythologies*, p. 25.
11 Kyong Kim, *Caged in Our Own Signs: A Book About Semiotics*, Ablex, Norwood, N.J., 1996, p. 189.
12 Anne Norton, *Republic of Signs: Liberal Theory and American Popular Culture*, University of Chicago Press, Chicago, 1993, p. 60.
13 Douglas Kellner, "Cultural Studies, Multiculturalism, and Media Culture," in *Gender, Race and Class in Media: A Text-Reader*, Gail Dines and Jan M. Humez (eds.), Sage, Thousand Oaks, Calif., 1996, p. 15.
14 Dick Hebdige, *Subculture: The Meaning of Style*, Methuen, London, 1979, p. 130.

15 Stuart Hall, "The Work of Representation," in *Representation: Cultural Representations and Signifying Practices,* Stuart Hall (ed.), Sage, London, pp. 13–74.

Chapter 25: Cultural Studies

1 Stuart Hall, "Ideology and Communication Theory," in *Rethinking Communication Theory,* Vol. 1, Paradigm Issues, Brenda Dervin, Lawrence Grossberg, Barbara O'Keefe, and Ellen Wartella (eds.), Sage, Newbury Park, Calif., 1989, p. 52.

2 Ibid., p. 48.

3 Theodor W. Adorno, "The Culture Industry: Enlightenment as Mass Deception," in *The Dialectic of the Enlightenment,* Max Horkheimer and Theodor W. Adorno (eds.), Continuum, New York, 1995, pp. 120–167.

4 Antonio Gramsci, *Selections from the Prison Notebooks of Antonio Gramsci,* edited and translated by Quintin Hoare and Geoffrey Nowell Smith, International Publishers, New York, 1971.

5 Michel Foucault, *The Archaeology of Knowledge,* Tavistock, London, 1982, p. 80.

6 Stuart Hall, *Representations: Cultural Representations and Signifying Practices:* Sage, London, 1997, p. 6.

7 Ibid., p. 2.

8 Michel Foucault, *Madness and Civilization: A History of Insanity in the Age of Reason,* Random House, New York, 1965.

9 Foucault, *The Archaelogy of Knowledge,* p. 46.

10 Douglas Kellner, *Media Culture: Cultural Studies, Identity and Politics Between the Modern and the Postmodern,* Routledge, New York, 1995, pp. 198–228.

11 Ibid., p. 210.

12 Ibid., p. 218.

13 Stuart Hall, "The Whites of Their Eyes: Racist Ideologies and the Media," in *Silver Linings,* George Bridges and Rosalind Brunt (eds.), Lawrence and Wishart, London, 1981, pp. 31–33.

14 Robert Frost, "Stopping by Woods on a Snowy Evening," *Poetry of Robert Frost,* Holt, Rinehart and Winston, New York, 1969, p. 224.

15 Clifford Christians, "Normativity as Catalyst," in *Rethinking Communication Theory,* Vol. 1, *Paradigm Issues,* Brenda Dervin, Lawrence Grossberg, Barbara O'Keefe, and Ellen Wartella (eds.), Sage, Newbury Park, Calif., 1989, p. 148.

16 Samuel Becker, "Communication Studies: Visions of the Future," Wartella, p. 126.

Media Effects

1 Paul Lazarsfeld, Bernard Berelson, and Hazel Gaudet, *The People's Choice,* Duell, Sloan and Pearce, New York, 1944.

2 A. W. van den Ban, "A Review of the Two-Step Flow of Communication Hypothesis," in *Speech Communication Behavior,* Larry L. Barker and Robert Kiebler (eds.), Prentice-Hall, Englewood Cliffs, N.J., 1971, pp. 193–205.

3 Fredric Wertham, *Seduction of the Innocent,* Rinehart, New York, 1954.

4 Dolf Zillmann, "Excitation Transfer in Communication-Mediated Aggressive Behavior," *Journal of Experimental Social Psychology,* Vol. 7, 1971, pp. 419–434.

5 Albert Bandura, *Social Learning Theory,* Prentice-Hall, Englewood Cliffs, N.J., 1977.

6 Tony Schwartz, *The Responsive Chord,* Doubleday, New York, 1973.

Chapter 26: Cultivation Theory

1 George Gerbner and Larry Gross, "Living with Television: The Violence Profile," *Journal of Communication,* Vol. 26, 1976, No. 2, p. 76.

2 Ibid., p. 77.

3 Jerome H. Skolnick, *The Politics of Protest,* Simon and Schuster, New York, 1969, pp. 3–24.

4 George Gerbner, Larry Gross, Nancy Signorielli, Michael Morgan, and Marilyn Jackson-Beeck, "The Demonstration of Power: Violence Profile No. 10," *Journal of Communication,* Vol. 29, No. 3, 1979, p. 180.

5 Albert Bandura, *Social Learning Theory,* Prentice-Hall, Englewood Cliffs, N.J., 1977. Earlier editions of this text included a chapter on social learning theory. It is available at *www.afirstlook.com* in the archives section.

6 George Gerbner, Larry Gross, Michael Morgan, and Nancy Signorielli, "The 'Mainstreaming' of America: Violence Profile No. 11," *Journal of Communication,* Vol. 30, No. 3, 1980, p. 11.

7 George Gerbner, Larry Gross, Michael Morgan, and Nancy Signorielli, "Charting the Mainstream: Television's Contributions to Political Orientations," *Journal of Communication,* Vol. 32, No. 2, 1982, p. 103.

8 Ibid., p. 117.

9 Gerbner, Gross, Morgan, and Signorielli, "The 'Mainstreaming' of America," p. 15.

10 George Gerbner, Larry Gross, Nancy Signorielli, Michael Morgan, and Marilyn Jackson-Beeck, "The Demonstration of Power: Violence Profile No. 10," *Journal of Communication,* Vol. 29, No. 2, 1979, p. 196.

11 Michael Morgan and James Shanahan, "Two Decades of Cultivation Research: An Appraisal and a Meta–analysis," in *Communication Yearbook 20,* Brant Burleson (ed.), Sage, Thousand Oaks, Calif., 1997, pp. 1–45.

12 Ibid., p. 20.

13 Ibid., pp. 27–28.

14 I'm grateful to Purdue University media effects researcher Glenn Sparks for this analogy.

15 Morgan and Shanahan, p. 5.

Chapter 27: Agenda-Setting Theory

1 Maxwell McCombs, "News Influence on Our Pictures of the World," in *Media Effects: Advances in Theory and Research,* Jennings Bryant and Dolf Zillmann (eds.), Lawrence Erlbaum Associates, Hillsdale, N.J., 1994, p. 4.

2 Maxwell McCombs and Donald Shaw, "A Progress Report on Agenda-Setting Research." Paper presented to the Association for Education in Journalism, Theory and Methodology Division, San Diego, Calif., April 18–27, 1974, p. 28.

3 Walter Lippmann, *Public Opinion,* Macmillan, New York, 1922, p. 3.

4 Bernard C. Cohen, *The Press and Foreign Policy,* Princeton University, Princeton, N.J., 1963, p. 13.

5 Theodore White, *The Making of the President 1972,* Bantam, New York, 1973, p. 245.

6 Paul Lazarsfeld, Bernard Berelson, and Hazel Gaudet, *The People's Choice,* Duell, Sloan and Pearce, New York, 1944.

7 G. Ray Funkhouser, "The Issues of the 60's: An Exploratory Study in the Dynamics of Public Opinion," *Public Opinion Quarterly,* Vol. 37, 1973, p. 69.

8 Shanto Iyengar, Mark Peters, and Donald Kinder, "Experimental Demonstrations of the 'Not-So-Minimal' Consequences of Television News Programs," *American Political Science Review,* Vol. 76, 1982, pp. 848–858. The experiment reported is only one of a series of studies conducted by Iyengar and Kinder at Yale and the University of Michigan. See their book cited in "A Second Look" for further work.

9 Maxwell McCombs and Tamara Bell, "The Agenda-Setting Role of Mass Communication," in *An Integrated Approach to Communication Theory and Research,* Michael Salwen and Donald Stacks (eds.), Lawrence Erlbaum Associates, Hillsdale, N.J., 1996, p. 100.

10 C. J. Bosso, "Setting the Agenda: Mass Media and the discovery of famine in Ethiopia," in *Manipulating Public Opinion,* M. Margolis and G. A. Mauser (eds.), Brooks/Cole, Pacific Grove, Calif., 1989, pp. 153–174.

11 J. H. Zhu, "Issue Competition and Attention Distraction: A Zero-Sum Theory of Agenda-Setting," *Journalism Quarterly,* Vol. 69, 1992, pp. 825–836.

12 Ken Auletta, "On and Off the Bus: Lessons from Campaign '92," *1-800-President,* Twentieth Century Fund, New York, 1993, p. 69.

13 John Carey, "How Media Shape Campaigns," *Journal of Communication,* Vol. 26, No. 2, 1976, pp. 52–53.

14 James Tankard, et al., "Media Frames: Approaches to Conceptualization and Measurement," Annual Meeting of the Association for Education in Journalism and Mass Communication, Boston, August, 1991.

15 Maxwell McCombs, New Frontiers in Agenda Setting: Agendas of Attributes and Frames," *Mass Comm Review,* Vol. 24, 1997, in press.

16 Robert Entman, "Framing: Toward Clarification of a Fractured Paradigm," *Journal of Communication,* Vol. 43, No. 3, 1993, p. 52.

17 Toshiro Takeshita and Shunji Mikami, "How Did Mass Media Influence the Voters' Choice in the 1993 General Election in Japan? A Study of Agenda Setting," *Communication Review,* Vol. 17, pp. 27–41.

18 Esteban Lopez Escobar, Juan Pablo Llamas, and Maxwell McCombs, "The Spanish General Election in 1996: A Further Inquiry into Second Level Agenda Setting Effects." Paper presented to the World Association for Public Opinion Research, Edinburgh, Scotland, September, 1997.

19 Salma Ghanem, "Media Coverage of Crime and Public Opinion: An Explanation of the Second Level of Agenda Setting." Unpublished doctoral dissertation, University of Texas at Austin, 1996. The study is also described in McCombs, "New Frontiers in Agenda Setting," pp. 11–12.

20 Maxwell McCombs, "New Frontiers in Agenda Setting."

21 McCombs, "News Influence," p. 11.

22 Ibid., p. 6.

23 Gerald Kosicki, "Problems and Opportunities in Agenda-Setting Research," *Journal of Communication,* Vol. 43, No. 2, 1993, p. 113.

24 Donald Shaw and Maxwell McCombs (eds.), *The Emergence of American Political Issues,* West, St. Paul, Minn., p. 12.

25 Maxwell McCombs, "New Frontiers in Agenda Setting."

Chapter 28: The Media Equation

1 Byron Reeves and Clifford Nass, *The Media Equation: How People Treat Computers, Television, and New Media Like Real People and Places,* Cambridge University Press, New York, 1996, p. 5.

2 Ibid.

3 B. J. Fogg and Clifford Nass, "Silicon Sycophants: Effects of Computers that Flatter," *International Journal of Human-Computer Studies,* Vol. 46, 1997, pp. 551–561.

4 Reeves and Nass, p. 7.

5 Philip Zimbardo, Ebbe Ebbesen, Christina Maslach, *Influencing Attitudes and Changing Behavior,* 2nd edition, Addison-Wesley, 1977, pp. 3–4.

6 Kathleen Hall Jamieson, *Packaging the Presidency,* 2nd edition, Oxford University Press, New York, 1992; James Check and Neil Malamuth, "Pornography and Social Aggression: A Social Learning Theory Analysis," in *Communication Yearbook 9,* Margaret McLaughlin (ed.), Sage, Beverly Hills, Calif., 1986, pp. 181–213; Glenn Sparks, "Paranormal Depictions in the Media: How Do They Affect What People Believe?" *Skeptical Inquirer,* July/August, 1998, pp. 35–39.

7 Reeves and Nass, p. 251.

8 Ibid., p. 12.

9 Benjamin Detenber and Byron Reeves, "A Bio-Informational Theory of Emotion: Motion and Image Size Effects on Viewers," *Journal of Communication,* Vol. 46, 1996, No. 3, p. 66.

10 Reeves and Nass, p. 13.

11 Clifford Nass and S. S. Sundar, "Are Computers Social Actors? Are Programmers Psychologically Relevant to Human-Computer Interaction?" Unpublished manuscript summarized in Reeves and Nass, pp. 184–186.

12 Youngme Moon and Clifford Nass, "How 'Real' are Computer Personalities? Psychological Responses to Personality Types in Human-Computer Interaction," *Communication Research,* Vol. 23, 1996, p. 670.

13 Ibid.

14 Reeves and Nass, p. 255.

15 Ibid., p. 38.

16 Byron Reeves, Matthew Lombard, Geetu Melwani, "Faces on the Screen: Pictures or Natural Experience?" Paper presented to the International Communication Association, Miami, 1992. The study is also summarized in Reeves and Nass, pp. 35–51.

17 Reeves and Nass, p. 51.

18 Donn Byrne, *The Attraction Paradigm,* Academic Press, Orlando, 1971.

19 Clifford Nass, Youngme Moon, B. J. Fogg, Byron Reeves, and D. Christopher Dryer, "Can Computer Personalities Be Human Personalities?" *International Journal of Human-Computer Studies,* Vol. 43, 1995, pp. 223–239. The study is also summarized in Reeves and Nass, pp. 89–99.

20 Reeves and Nass, p. 96.
21 Nass, Moon, et. al., p. 227.
22 Ibid., p. 234.
23 Reeves and Nass, p. 181. They cite W. J. Small, *To Kill A Messenger: Television News and the Real World,* Hastings House, New York, 1970.
24 Reeves and Nass, p. 145. For greater detail, see Clifford Nass, Byron Reeves, and Glenn Leshner, "Technology and Roles: A Tale of Two TVs," *Journal of Communication,* Vol. 46, No. 2, 1996, pp. 121–128.
25 Reeves and Nass, p. 149.
26 Clifford Nass and S. S. Sundar, "Are Computers Social Actors? Are Programmers Psychologically Relevant to Human-Computer Interaction?" Unpublished manuscript. The study is summarized in Reeves and Nass, pp. 181–189.
27 Clifford Nass, Youngme Moon, and Nancy Green, "Are Machines Gender Neutral? Gender-Stereotypic Responses to Computers with Voices," *Journal of Applied Social Psychology,* Vol. 27, 1997, pp. 864–876.
28 Clifford Nass, Youngme Moon, and Paul Carney, "Are Respondents Polite to Computers? Social Desirability and Direct Responses to Computers," *Journal of Applied Social Psychology,* in press; Clifford Nass, B. J. Fogg, and Youngme Moon, "Can Computers Be Teammates?" *International Journal of Human-Computer Studies,* Vol. 45, 1996, pp. 669–678; Youngme Moon and Clifford Nass, "Are Computers Scapegoats? Attributions of Responsibility in Human-Computer Interaction," *International Journal of Human-Computer Studies,* Vol. 49, 1998, pp. 79–94.
29 Leon Festinger, *A Theory of Cognitive Dissonance,* Stanford University, Stanford, Calif., 1957. Earlier editions of the *First Look* text included a chapter on cognitive dissonance theory. See the Archives section of *www.afirstlook.com.*
30 John Alderman, "Personality Problems," *HotWired, http://www.hotwired.com/books/96/42/index1a.html.*
31 Nass, Moon, Fogg, Reeves, and Dryer, p. 225.
32 Steve Duck, *Meaningful Relationships: Talking, Sense, and Relating,* Sage, Thousand Oaks, Calif., 1994, p. 107.
33 Ibid., pp. 123–124.

Ethical Reflections: Mass Communication

1 Sonja Foss, Karen Foss, and Robert Trapp, *Contemporary Perspectives on Rhetoric,* Waveland Press, Prospect Heights, Ill., 1991, pp. 241–272. (Like all interpreters of Habermas, Foss, Foss, and Trapp refer to his dense writing style. For that reason, all citations in this ethical reflection are from secondary sources. For an overview of Habermas' thinking, see Jane Braaten, *Habermas's Critical Theory of Society,* SUNY, Albany, N.Y., 1991. For a primary source, see Jürgen Habermas, "Discourse Ethics: Notes on a Program of Philosophical Justification," Trans. Shierry Weber Nicholsen and Christian Lenhardt, in *Communicative Ethics Controversy,* Seyla Benhabib and Fred Dallmayr (eds.), M.I.T. Press, Cambridge, Mass., 1990, pp. 60–110.
2 Theodore Glasser, "Communicative Ethics and the Aim of Accountability in Journalism," *Social Responsibility: Business, Journalism, Law, Medicine,* Louis Hodges

(ed.), Vol. 21, Washington & Lee University, Lexington, Va., 1995, pp. 41–42.
3 Ibid., p. 49.
4 Ibid., pp. 34–35.
5 Ibid., p. 47.
6 Ibid., p. 47.
7 Robert McChesney, "Off Limits: An Inquiry into the Lack of Debate over Ownership, Structure and Control of the Mass Media in U.S. Political Life," *Communication,* Vol. 13, 1992, pp. 1–19.
8 Clifford Christians, John Ferré, and Mark Fackler, *Good News: Social Ethics and the Press,* Oxford University, New York, 1993.
9 Richard Rorty, *Philosophy and the Mirror of Nature,* Princeton University, Princeton, N.J., 1979, p. 373.
10 Christians, et al., p. 192.
11 Martin Buber, *I and Thou,* 2d ed., R. G. Smith (trans.), Scribner's, New York, 1958, pp. 60, 69.
12 Christians, et al., pp. 69, 73.
13 Ibid., p. 89.
14 Ibid., pp. 78, 111–113.
15 Ibid., p. 92.

Intercultural Communication

1 Gerry Philipsen, *Speaking Culturally: Exploration in Social Communication,* State University of New York, Albany, 1992, p. 7.
2 Gerry Philipsen, "Speaking 'Like a Man' in Teamsterville: Cultural Patterns of Role Enactment in an Urban Neighborhood," *Quarterly Journal of Speech,* Vol. 61, 1975, pp. 13–22.
3 Donal Carbaugh, "Communication Rules in Donahue Discourse," in *Cultural Communication and Intercultural Contact,* Donal Carbaugh (ed.), Lawrence Erlbaum Associates, Hillsdale, N.J., 1990, pp. 119–149.
4 See chapter on cultural variability in William B. Gudykunst and Stella Ting-Toomey, *Culture and Interpersonal Communication,* Sage, Newbury Park, Calif., 1988, pp. 39–59.
5 Edward T. Hall, *Beyond Culture,* Anchor, New York, 1977, p. 91.

Chapter 29: Anxiety/Uncertainty Management Theory

1 Matthew 28:20, King James Version of the Bible.
2 William B. Gudykunst, "Uncertainty and Anxiety," in *Theories in Intercultural Communication,* Young Yun Kim and William B. Gudykunst (eds.), Sage, Newbury Park, Calif., 1988, pp. 125–128.
3 William B. Gudykunst, "Toward a Theory of Effective Interpersonal and Intergroup Communication: An Anxiety/Uncertainty Management (AUM) Perspective," in *Intercultural Communication Competence,* R. L. Wiseman and J. Koester (eds.), Sage, Newbury Park, Calif., 1993, p. 70 (note 4).
4 Figure 29.1 is taken from the 1993 version of AUM. Because the chapter was to appear in an edited book on intercultural communication competence, Gudykunst organized the "superficial causes" of anxiety and uncertainty into the three traditional components of competence—motivational factors, knowledge factors, and skill factors. The 1995 revision of the theory clusters

these causes into six categories: (1) self and self-concept, (2) motivation, (3) reactions to strangers, (4) social categorizations, (5) situational processes, and (6) connections to strangers. I have retained the 1993 diagram and its organization because the 1995 version contains no schematic representation of the theory.

5 William S. Howell, *The Empathic Communicator,* Wadsworth, Belmont, Calif., 1982, pp. 29–33.

6 Ellen Langer, *The Power of Mindful Learning,* Addison-Wesley, Reading, Mass., 1997.

7 William B. Gudykunst, *Bridging Differences: Effective Intergroup Communication,* Sage, Newbury Park, Calif., 1991, p. 13.

8 William B. Gudykunst and Stella Ting-Toomey, *Culture and Interpersonal Communication,* Sage, Newbury Park, Calif., 1988, pp. 58–59.

9 The numbering and wording of the axioms is taken from Gudykunst's 1995 update of AUM. William Gudykunst, "Anxiety/Uncertainty Management (AUM) Theory: Current Status," in *Intercultural Communication Theory,* R. L. Wiseman (ed.), Sage, Thousand Oaks, Calif., 1995, pp. 8–58.

10 I. A. Richards, *Basic English and Its Uses,* W. W. Norton, New York, 1943.

11 Michael Sunnafrank, "Uncertainty in Interpersonal Relationships: A Predicted Outcome Value Interpretation of Gudykunst's Research Program," in *Communication Yearbook 12,* James A. Anderson (ed.), Sage, Newbury Park, Calif., 1989, p. 355.

12 William Gudykunst, "Anxiety/Uncertainty Management (AUM) Theory: Current Status," in *Intercultural Communication Theory,* R. L. Wiseman (ed.), Sage, Thousand Oaks, Calif., 1995, p. 42.

13 Stella Ting-Toomey, "Cultural and Interpersonal Relationship Development: Some Conceptual Issues," in *Communication Yearbook 12,* James A. Anderson (ed.), Sage, Newbury Park, Calif., 1989, p. 379.

14 Brenda Dervin, "Comparative Theory Reconceptualized: From Entities and States to Processes and Dynamics," *Communication Theory,* Vol. 1, 1991, pp. 59–69

Chapter 30: Face-Negotiation Theory

1 Stella Ting-Toomey and Atsuko Kurogi, "Facework Competence in Intercultural Conflict: An Updated Face-Negotiation Theory," in *International Journal of Intercultural Relations,* Vol. 22, 1998, p. 190.

2 Harry C. Triandis, *Individualism & Collectivism,* Westview, Boulder, Colo., 1995, pp. 10–11.

3 Ting-Toomey and Kurogi, p. 190.

4 Ibid., p. 187.

5 Penelope Brown and Stephen Levinson, "Universals in Language Usage: Politeness Phenomenon," in *Questions and Politeness: Strategies in Social Interaction,* Esther N. Goody (ed.), Cambridge University, Cambridge, Eng., 1978, p. 66.

6 L. Yutang, *My Country and My People,* John Day, Taipai, Republic of China, 1968, p. 199.

7 Stella Ting-Toomey, "Intercultural Conflict Styles: A Face-Negotiation Theory," in *Theories in Intercultural Communication,* Young Yun Kim and William

Gudykunst (eds.), Sage, Newbury Park, Calif., 1988, p. 215.

8 Ting-Toomey and Kurogi, p. 192.

9 M. A. Rahim, "A Measure of Styles of Handling Interpersonal Conflict," *Academy of Management Journal,* Vol. 26, 1983, pp. 368–376.

10 Stella Ting-Toomey, Ge Gao, Paula Trubisky, Zhizhong Yang, Hak Soo Kim, Sung-Ling Lin, and Tsukasa Nishida, "Culture, Face Maintenance, and Styles of Handling Interpersonal Conflict: A Study in Five Cultures," in *International Journal of Conflict Management,* Vol. 2, 1991, pp. 275–296.

11 Stella Ting-Toomey, John G. Oetzel, and Kimberlie Yee-Jung, "Self-Construal Types and Conflict Management Styles." Paper presented at the Western States Communication Association Convention, Denver, Colo., February 1998, p. 5. The authors use "neglect" interchangeably with "passive aggression." I use the latter term because it seems to best capture the meaning of the survey items they used to define the construct.

12 Ting-Toomey and Kurogi, p. 194.

13 Ibid., p. 199, see Proposition 14.

14 Stella Ting-Toomey, *Communicating Across Cultures,* Guilford, New York, 1999, p. vii.

15 Ting-Toomey and Kurogi, p. 196.

16 Hazel Markus and Shinobu Kitayama, "Culture and the Self: Implications for Cognition, Emotion, and Motivation," *Psychological Review,* Vol. 2, pp. 224–253.

17 John Oetzel, "The Effects of Self-Construals and Ethnicity on Self-Reported Conflict Styles," *Communication Reports,* Vol. 11, 1998, p. 140, and Ting-Toomey, Oetzel, and Yee-Jung. See also William Gudykunst, Yuko Matsumoto, Stella Ting-Toomey, et al., "The Influence of Cultural Individualism–Collectivism, Self Construals, and Individual Values on Communication Styles Across Cultures," *Human Communication Research,* Vol. 22, 1996, pp. 510–540.

18 Ting-Toomey and Kurogi, p. 218.

Chapter 31: Speech Codes Theory

1 Gerry Philipsen, "Speaking 'Like a Man' in Teamsterville: Culture Patterns of Role Enactment in an Urban Neighborhood," *Quarterly Journal of Speech,* Vol. 61, 1975, pp. 13–22; Gerry Philipsen, "Places for Speaking in Teamsterville," *Quarterly Journal of Speech,* Vol. 62, 1976, pp. 15–25.

2 Clifford Geertz, "Thick Description: Toward an Interpretive Theory of History," *The Interpretation of Culture,* Basic Books, New York, 1973, p. 5.

3 Dell Hymes, "The Ethnography of Speaking," in T. Gladwin and W. C. Sturtevant (eds.), *Anthropology and Human Behavior,* Anthropological Society of Washington, Washington, D.C., 1962, pp. 13–53.

4 Gerry Philipsen, "A Theory of Speech Codes," in *Developing Communication Theory,* Gerry Philipsen and Terrance Albrecht (eds.), State University of New York, Albany, 1996, p. 126.

5 Donal Carbaugh, "Deep Agony: 'Self' vs. 'Society' in a Donahue Discourse," *Research on Language and Social Interaction,* Vol. 22, 1988/89, pp. 179–212.

6 Tamar Katriel and Gerry Philipsen, "'What We Need Is Communication': Communication as a Cultural Category in Some American Speech," *Communication Monographs,* Vol. 48, 1981, pp. 302–317.

7 Gerry Philipsen, *Speaking Culturally: Explorations in Social Communication,* State University of New York, Albany, 1992, p. 7.

8 Ibid., p. 4.

9 Ibid., p. 6.

10 Philipsen, "A Theory of Speech Codes," p. 139.

11 Philipsen, *Speaking Culturally,* p. 110.

12 Ibid., p. 113, citing P. Berger, B. Berger, and H. Kellner, *The Homeless Mind: Modernization and Consciousness,* Vintage, New York, 1973, p. 89.

13 Ibid., p. 76. Also see Katriel and Philipsen, "'What We Need Is Communication,'" p. 308.

14 Philipsen, "A Theory of Speech Codes," p. 140.

15 Tamar Katriel, *Talking Straight: Dugri Speech in Israeli Sabra Culture,* Cambridge University, Cambridge, Eng., 1986.

16 Philipsen, "Mayor Daley's Council Speech," in *Speaking Culturally,* pp. 43–61.

17 Philipsen, *Speaking Culturally,* pp. 77–80.

18 Philipsen, "A Theory of Speech Codes," p. 148.

19 Dwight Conquergood, "Poetics, Play, Process, and Power: The Performance Turn in Anthropology," *Text and Performance Quarterly,* Vol. 1, 1989, pp. 82–95.

20 James Clifford, *Predicament of Culture,* Harvard University Press, Cambridge, Mass., p. 49.

21 Conquergood, "Poetics, Play, Process, and Power," p. 87.

22 Dwight Conquergood, "Ethnography, rhetoric, and performance," *Quarterly Journal of Speech,* Vol. 78, 1992, p. 90.

23 Robin Wilson, "A Professor's Commitment to 'Shattered Cultures,'" *The Chronicle of Higher Education,* Vol. 40, No. 20, 1994, p. A6.

Gender and Communication

1 Robin Lakoff, *Language and Women's Place,* Harper & Row, New York, 1975.

2 Kathryn Dindia, "Men are from North Dakota, Women are from South Dakota." Paper presented at the National Communication Association convention, November 19–23, 1997.

3 Carol Tavris and Carole Wade, *The Longest War: Sex Differences in Perspective,* 2d ed., Harcourt Brace Jovanovich, San Diego, 1984, pp. 37–78; see also Mary Steward Van Leeuwen, *Gender & Grace,* Inter-Varsity, Downers Grove, Ill., 1990, pp. 53–71.

4 Sandra L. Bem, "Androgyny vs. the Tight Little Lives of Fluffy Women and Chesty Men," *Psychology Today,* Vol. 9, 1975, pp. 58–62.

5 Cheris Kramarae, "Gender and Dominance," in *Communication Yearbook 15,* Stanley A. Deetz (ed.), Sage, Newbury Park, Calif., 1992, pp. 469–474.

Chapter 32: Genderlect Styles

1 Deborah Tannen, *You Just Don't Understand,* Balantine, New York, 1990, p. 42.

2 Deborah Tannen, *Conversational Style: Analyzing Talk Among Friends,* Ablex, Norwood, N.J., 1984.

3 Ibid., p. vii.

4 Tannen, *You Just Don't Understand,* p. 259.

5 Ibid., p. 279.

6 Ibid., p. 16.

7 Ibid., p. 108.

8 Tannen, *You Just Don't Understand,* p. 48.

9 Ibid., p. 212.

10 Ibid., p. 62.

11 Ibid., p. 72.

12 Ibid., p. 150.

13 Ibid., pp. 120–121, 298.

14 Tannen, *Conversational Style,* p. 38.

15 Ken Burke, Nancy Burroughs-Denhart, and Glen McClish, "Androgeny and Identity in Gender Communication," *Quarterly Journal of Speech,* Vol. 80, 1984, pp. 482–497.

16 Julia Wood and Christopher Inman, "In a Different Mode: Masculine Styles of Communicating Closeness," *Journal of Applied Communication Research,* Vol. 21, 1993, pp. 279–295.

17 Senta Troemel-Ploetz, "Review Essay: Selling the Apolitical," *Discourse & Society,* Vol. 2, 1991, p. 497.

18 Ibid., p. 491.

19 Ibid., p. 495.

Chapter 33: Standpoint Theory

1 Julia T. Wood, *Communication Theories in Action,* Wadsworth, Belmont, Calif., 1997, p. 250.

2 Sandra Harding, "Comment on Hekman's 'Truth and Method: Feminist Standpoint Theory Revisited': Whose Standpoint Needs the Regimes of Truth and Reality?" *Signs: Journal of Women in Culture and Society,* Vol. 22, 1997, p. 384.

3 Sandra Harding, *Whose Science? Whose Knowledge? Thinking from Women's Lives,* Cornell University Press, Ithaca, N.Y., 1991, pp. 269–270.

4 Meenakshi Gigi Durham, "On the Relevance of Standpoint Epistemology to the Practice of Journalism: The Case for 'Strong Objectivity,'" *Communication Theory,* Vol. 8, 1998, p. 117.

5 Julia T. Wood, "Gender and Moral Voice: Moving from Woman's Nature to Standpoint Epistemology," *Women's Studies in Communication,* Vol. 15, 1993, p. 13.

6 Julia T. Wood, "Feminist Scholarship and the Study of Relationships," *Journal of Social and Personal Relationships,* Vol. 12, 1995, p. 110.

7 Georg Wilhelm Friedrich Hegel, *The Phenomenology of Mind,* Macmillan, New York, 1910, pp. 182–188.

8 Friedrich Engels, "Socialism: Utopian and Scientific," and "The Origin of the Family, Private Property, and the State," in *The Marx-Engels Reader,* Robert Tuckeer (ed.), W. W. Norton, New York, 1978, pp. 701–702, 734–736. See also Sandra Harding, "The Instability of the Analytical Categories of Feminist Theory," in *Sex and Scientific Inquiry,* Sandra Harding and Jean O'Barr (eds.), University of Chicago Press, Chicago, 1987, p. 292.

9 Harding, "Comment on Hekman's 'Truth and Method'," p. 389.

10 Julia T. Wood, "Feminist Scholarship," p. 111.

11 Jean-Francois Lyotard, *The Postmodern Condition: A Report on Knowledge,* University of Minnesota Press, Minneapolis, 1984, p. xxiv.

12 Julia T. Wood, "Engendered Relations: Interaction, Caring, Power and Responsibility in Intimacy," in *Social Context and Relationships*, Steve Duck (ed.), Sage, Newbury Park, Calif., 1993, p. 37.
13 Wood, "Feminist Scholarship," p. 112.
14 Toni Morrison, *Beloved*, Alfred Knopf, New York, 1987, pp. 67–68.
15 Wood, *Communication Theories*, p. 251. See also Harding, *Whose Science?* p. 59.
16 Wood, "Gender and Moral Voice," p. 8.
17 Morrison, p. 190.
18 Harding, *Whose Science? Whose Knowledge?* p. 192.
19 Ibid., p. 269; Donna Haraway, "Situated Knowledges: The Science Question in Feminism and the Privilege of Partial Perspective," *Feminist Studies* 14:3, 1988.
20 Harding, *Whose Science? Whose Knowledge?* pp. 159, 58.
21 Ibid., p. 59.
22 Morrison, p. 23.
23 Wood, *Communication Theories*, p. 257.
24 Ibid., p. 254.
25 Ibid.
26 Morrison, pp. 163–164.
27 Harding, *Whose Science? Whose Knowledge?* p. 167.
28 Ibid., pp. 149–152.
29 Ibid., p. 270.
30 Julia T. Wood, *Who Cares? Women, Care, and Culture*, Southern Illinois University Press, Carbondale, Ill., 1994, p. 4.
31 Ibid., p. 6.
32 Ibid., pp. 8-9.
33 Ibid., p. 163.
34 Sonja K. Foss and Cindy L. Griffin, "Beyond Persuasion: A Proposal for an Invitational Rhetoric," *Communication Monographs*, Vol. 62, 1995, pp. 5, 7.
35 Julia T. Wood, *Communication Mosaics: A New Introduction to the Field of Communication*, Wadsworth, Belmont, Calif., 1998, p. 187. I include a chapter on "Accountability and Forgiveness" in my book, *Making Friends* (InterVarsity, 1987).
36 Lynn Worsham, "Romancing the Stones: My Movie Date with Sandra Harding," *Journal of Advanced Composition*, Vol. 15, 1995, p. 568.

Chapter 34: Muted Group Theory

1 Cheris Kramarae, *Women and Men Speaking*, Newbury House Publishers, Rowley, Mass., 1981, p. 1.
2 Barrie Thorne, Cheris Kramarae, and Nancy Henley (eds.), *Language, Gender and Society*, Newbury House Publishers, Rowley, Mass., 1983, p. 9.
3 Cheris Kramarae, "Folklinguistics," *Psychology Today*, Vol. 8, June 1974, pp. 82–85.
4 Edwin Ardener, "Belief and the Problem of Women," in *Perceiving Women*, Shirley Ardener (ed.), Malaby, London, 1975, p. 2.
5 Edwin Ardener, "The 'Problem' Revisited," in *Perceiving Women*, Shirley Ardener (ed.), Malaby, London, 1975, p. 22.
6 Ibid., p. 25.
7 Shirley Ardener, "The Nature of Women in Society," in *Defining Females*, Halsted, New York, 1978, p. 21.
8 Kramarae, *Women and Men Speaking*, p. 3.

9 Simone de Beauvoir, *The Second Sex*, H. M. Parshley (ed. and trans.), Bantam, New York, 1964, p. xv.
10 Kramarae, *Women and Men Speaking*, p. 3.
11 Julia P. Stanley, "Paradigmatic Women: The Prostitute," in *Papers in Language Variation*, David L. Shores and Carole P. Hines (eds.), University of Alabama, Tuscaloosa, 1977, p. 7.
12 Kramarae, *Women and Men Speaking*, p. 1.
13 Virginia Woolf, *A Room of One's Own*, Hogarth (Penguin edition), 1928, p. 45.
14 Dorothy Smith, "A Peculiar Eclipsing: Women's Exclusion from Man's Culture," *Women's Studies International Quarterly*, Vol. 1, 281–295.
15 Cheris Kramarae and H. Jeanie Taylor, "Women and Men of Electronic Networks: A Conversation or a Monologue?" in *Women, Information Technology, and Scholarship*, H. Jeanie Taylor, Cheris Kramarae, and Maureen Ebben (eds.), Women, Information Technology, and Scholarship Colloquium, Center for Advanced Study, Urbana, Ill., 1993, pp. 52–61.
16 Kramarae, *Women and Men Speaking*, p. 3.
17 Tillie Olsen, *Silences*, Delacorte/Seymour Lawrence, New York, 1978, p. 23.
18 Kramarae, *Women and Men Speaking*, p. 19.
19 Ibid., p. 12.
20 Ibid., p. 4.
21 Cheris Kramarae and Paula Treichler, *Amazons, Bluestockings, and Crones: A Feminist Dictionary*, 2d ed., Pandora, London, 1992, p. 17.
22 Brinlee Kramer, "Brinlee Kramer," in *Women Who Do and Women Who Don't Join the Women's Movement*, Robyn Rowland (ed.), Routledge & Kegan Paul, Boston, 1994, p. 170.
23 Karen A. Foss, Sonja K. Foss, and Cindy L. Griffin, *Feminist Rhetorical Theories*, Sage, Thousand Oaks, Calif., 1999, p. 48.
24 H. Jeanie Taylor and Cheris Kramarae, "Creating Cybertrust from the Margins," *Renaissance in Social Science Computing*, Orville Vernon Burton (ed.), University of Illinois Press, Urbana, in press.
25 Kramarae and Treichler, p. 4.
26 Dale Spender, *Man Made Language*, Routledge & Kegan, London, 1980, p. 87.
27 Cheris Kramarae, "Punctuating the Dictionary," *International Journal of the Sociology of Language*, Vol. 94, 1992, p. 135.
28 Kramarae and Treichler, p. 4.
29 Cheris Kramarae, "Harassment and Everyday Life," in *Women Making Meaning: New Feminist Directions in Communication*, Lana Rakow (ed.), Routledge, New York, 1992, p. 102.
30 Julia T. Wood (ed.), "Special Section—'Telling Our Stories': Sexual Harassment in the Communication Discipline," *Journal of Applied Communication Research*, Vol. 20, 1992, pp. 383–384.
31 Karen A. Foss and Sonja K. Foss, "Incorporating the Feminist Perspective in Communication Scholarship: A Research Commentary," in *Doing Research on Women's Communication: Perspectives on Theory and Method*, K. Carter and C. Spitzack (eds.), Ablex, Norwood, N.J., 1989, p. 72.

32 Deborah Tannen, *Conversational Style: Analyzing Talk Among Friends,* Ablex, Norwood, N.J., 1984, p. 43.

33 Kramarae, "Punctuating the Dictionary," p. 146.

Ethical Reflections: Cultural Context

1 Carol Gilligan, *In a Different Voice: Psychological Theory and Women's Development,* Harvard University, Cambridge, Mass., 1982.

2 Summary statement of Seyla Benhabib, "The Generalized and the Concrete Other: The Kohlberg–Gilligan Controversy and Feminist Theory," in Seyla Benhabib and Drucilla Cornell (eds.), *Feminism as Critique,* University of Minnesota, Minneapolis, 1987, p. 78.

3 Lawrence Kohlberg, *Essays on Moral Development, Volume One: The Philosophy of Moral Development, Moral Stages and the Idea of Justice,* Harper & Row, San Francisco, 1981, p. 12.

4 Gilligan, p. 18.

5 Carol Gilligan, "In a Different Voice: Women's Conceptions of Self and Morality," *Harvard Educational Review,* Vol. 47, 1977, p. 484.

6 Seyla Benhabib, *Situating the Self: Gender, Community and Postmodernism in Contemporary Ethics,* Routledge, New York, 1992, p. 4.

7 Ibid., p. 2.

8 Jean-Francois Lyotard, *The Postmodern Condition: A Report on Knowledge,* Geoff Bennington and Brian Massumi (trans.), University of Minnesota, Minneapolis, 1984.

9 *Situating the Self,* p. 209.

10 Ibid., p. 229.

11 Ibid., p. 14.

12 Benhabib's critique of Habermas draws on Nancy Fraser, "Rethinking the Public Sphere," *Justice Interruptus,* Routledge, New York, 1997, pp. 69–98.

13 *Situating the Self,* p. 3.

14 Seyla Benhabib, "The Generalized and the Concrete Other," in *Feminism as Critique: Essays in the Politics of Gender in Late-Capitalist Societies,* Seyla Benhabib and Drucilla Cornell (eds.), University of Minnesota Press, 1987, pp. 77–95.

Communication Theory

1 Warren Thorngate, "'In General' vs. 'It Depends': Some Comments on the Gergen-Schlenker Debate," *Personality and Social Psychology Bulletin,* Vol. 2, 1976, p. 406.

2 Ibid.

3 C. David Mortensen, "Communication Postulates," in *Contexts,* Jean N. Civikly (ed.), Holt, Rinehart and Winston, New York, 1975, p. 21.

4 Karl Weick, *The Social Psychology of Organizing,* 2d ed., Addison-Wesley, Reading, Mass, 1979, p. 39.

5 Graham Chapman, John Cleese, Terry Gilliam, Eric Idle, Terry Jones, and Michael Palin, *The Complete Monty Python's Flying Circus: All the Words, Volume Two,* Pantheon, New York, 1989, p. 119.

Chapter 35: Order out of Chaos

1 James A. Anderson, *Communication Theory: Epistemological Foundations,* Guilford, New York, 1996, pp. 13–46. Specifically, Anderson asks of each theorist, "What is the nature of the phenomenal world?"—a question of ontology.

2 Ibid., p. 58.

3 Jesse Delia and Lawrence Grossberg, "Interpretation and Evidence," *Western Journal of Speech Communication,* Vol. 41, 1977, p. 36; reiterated in Jesse Delia, Barbara O'Keefe, and Daniel O'Keefe, "The Constructivist Approach to Communication," in *Human Communication Theory,* 2d ed., Frank E. X. Dance (ed.), New York, Harper & Row, 1982, p. 147.

4 Robert Bostrom and Lewis Donohew, "The Case for Empiricism: Clarifying Fundamental Issues in Communication Theory," *Communication Monographs,* Vol. 59, 1992, pp. 126–127.

5 Ibid., pp. 109 and 127.

6 Stuart Hall, "Ideology and Communication Theory," in *Rethinking Communication,* Vol. 1, Brenda Dervin, Lawrence Grossberg, Barbara O'Keefe, and Ellen Wartella (eds.), Sage, Newbury Park, Calif., 1989, p. 52.

7 Ibid., p. 42.

8 Richard Rorty, *Consequences of Pragmatism,* University of Minnesota, Minneapolis, 1982, p. 197.

9 Isabel Briggs Myers, *Introduction to Type,* Consulting Psychologists, Palo Alto, Calif., 1987.

10 Ibid., p. 5.

11 George Gerbner, "The Importance of Being Critical—In One's Own Fashion," *Journal of Communication,* Vol. 33, No. 3, 1983, p. 361.

12 Gregory Bateson, *Mind and Nature: A Necessary Unity,* Bantam, New York, 1979, p. 242.

13 Marie Hochmuth Nichols, *Rhetoric and Criticism,* Louisiana State University, Baton Rouge, 1963, p. 18.

14 Celeste Michelle Condit, "The Birth of Understanding: Chaste Science and the Harlot of the Arts," *Communication Monographs,* Vol. 57, 1990, p. 323.

15 Ibid., p. 324. The term *hermeneutics* refers to principles of interpreting a text. In this context, the label designates a postmodern approach that has been influenced by European philosophers like Foucault, Heidegger, and Derrida. For an introductory discussion to postmodernism, see John Stewart, "A Post-modern Look at Traditional Communication Postulates," *Western Journal of Speech Communication,* Vol. 55, 1991, 354–379.

CREDITS AND ACKNOWLEDGMENTS

Part One: Overview

Page 7: Bob Garfield column reprinted from the July 11, 1994 issue of *Advertising Age.*

Page 15 (Fig. 1.1): Twenty Questions to Guide Evaluation of Four Research Methods excerpted from Lawrence R. Frey, Carl H. Botan, Paul G. Friedman, and Gary L. Kreps, *Interpreting Communication Research: A Case Study Approach.* Prentice Hall, Englewood Cliffs, NJ, 1992, pp. 30–31, 89, 96, 130, 164, 171–172, 260–262, 292.

Page 20: Lyric excerpts of "The Farmer and The Cowman" by Richard Rodgers and Oscar Hammerstein II. Copyright (C) 1943 by WILLIAMSON MUSIC. Copyright Renewed. International Copyright Secured. Reprinted by Permission. All Rights Reserved.

Page 34: "The Things We Do For Love" written by Graham Gouldman and Eric Stewart and published by Man-Ken Music, Ltd. (BMI) © 1977. Reprinted by permission.

Page 37 (Fig. 3.1): Shannon and Weaver's Model of Communication from *The Mathematical Theory of Communication.* Copyright 1977 by the Board of Trustees of the University of Illinois. Used with the permission of the University of Illinois Press and the author.

Page 40 (Fig. 3.2): Richards' Semantic Triangle based on C. K. Ogden and I. A. Richards, *The Meaning of Meaning.* Harcourt Brace & World, New York, 1946, pp. 1–23.

Part Two: Interpersonal Communication

Pages 50–52: "Game Metaphors" taken from MAKING FRIENDS (& MAKING THEM COUNT) by Em Griffin. © 1987 by Em Griffin. Used by permission of InterVarsity Press, P.O. Box 1400, Downers Grove, IL 60515.

Pages 54–55: Quotes from THE SEARCH FOR SIGNS OF INTELLIGENT LIFE IN THE UNIVERSE by Jane Wagner. Copyright © 1986 by Jane Wagner Inc. Reprinted by permission of HarperCollins Publishers, Inc.

Page 67 (Fig. 5.2): M.C. Escher's *Bond of Union* © 1999 Cordon Art B.V. - Baarn - Holland. All rights reserved.

Page 71 (Fig. 5.3): Atomic-Serpentine Model from INTERPERSONAL COMMUNICATION: MAKING SOCIAL WORLDS by W. Barnett Pearce. Copyright © 1994 HarperCollins College Publishers Inc. Reprinted by permission of Addison-Wesley Educational Publishers Inc.

Page 81: "Prologue: The Birth of Architecture," from COLLECTED POEMS by W.H. Auden. Copyright © 1976 by Edward Mendelson, William Meredith and Monroe K. Spears, Executors of the Estate of W.H. Auden. Reprinted by permission of Random House Inc.

Pages 92–93 (Fig. 7.1): Propositions of Interpersonal Deception Theory, Buller and Burgoon, "Interpersonal Deception Theory," *Communication Theory,* Vol. 6, 1996, pp. 210–235, abridged and paraphrased.

Page 122: "The Death of the Hired Man" from THE POETRY OF ROBERT FROST, edited by Edward Connery Lathem, Copyright 1930, Copyright 1939, © 1969 by Henry Holt and Company, Inc. Reprinted by permission of Henry Holt and Company, Inc.

Page 141 (Fig. 10.1): Theorems of Uncertainty Reduction Theory based on Charles Berger and Richard Calabrese, "Some Explorations in Initial Interaction and Beyond: Toward a Developmental Theory of Interpersonal Communication," *Human Communication Research,* Vol. 1, 1975, p. 100.

Pages 148–149 (Fig. RM.1): Fifty Strategies for Relationship Maintenance in Marriage reprinted with permission from Leslie A. Baxter and Kathryn Dindia, "Marital Partners' Perceptions of Marital Maintenance Strategies," *Journal of Social and Personal Relationships,* Vol. 7, No. 2, Copyright 1990, by permission of Sage Publications Ltd.

Page 155: Excerpt from KNOTS by R. D. Laing. Copyright © 1970 by R. D. Laing. Reprinted by permission of Pantheon Books, a division of Random House, Inc. and Routledge.

Page 157 (Fig. 11.2): Matrix of Transactional Types from Rogers-Millar, Edna and Farace, Richard, "Analysis of Relational Communication in Dyads: New Measurement Procedures" in HUMAN COMMUNICATION RESEARCH, Volume 1, Number 3, p. 233. Copyright © 1975. Reprinted by Permission of Sage Publications, Inc.

Pages 167–168, 172: Quotes from CHILDREN OF A LESSER GOD by Mark Medoff. Copyright © 1980, 1987 by Westmark Productions, Inc. Reprinted by permission of William Morris Agency, Inc. on behalf of the Author. Copyright © 1995 by Paramount Pictures. All Rights Reserved. Script Excerpts used with permission.

Page 181 (Fig. 13.1): Ned's Cognitive Map Regarding Air Safety based on Carolyn Sherif, Muzafer Sherif, and Roger Nebergall, *Attitude and Attitude Change: The Social Judgment-Involvement Approach,* W. B. Saunders, Philadelphia, 1965.

Page 186 (Fig. 13.2): Sleep Study Results adapted from S. Bochner and C. Insko, "Communicator Discrepancy, Source Credibility and Opinion Change," *Journal of Personality and Social Psychology,* Vol. 4, 1966, pp. 614–622.

531

INDEX